Christian Spirituality

Christian
Spirituality

The Essential Guide to the
Most Influential Spiritual Writings
of the Christian Tradition

Edited by
Frank N. Magill and Ian P. McGreal

1817

Harper & Row, Publishers, San Francisco
Cambridge, Hagerstown, New York, Philadelphia, Washington
London, Mexico City, São Paulo, Singapore, Sydney

FIRST EDITION

Library of Congress Cataloging-in-Publication Data

Christian spirituality.

    1. Christian literature—History and criticism.
I. Magill, Frank Northen, 1907–   . II. McGreal,
Ian Philip, 1919–
BR117.C48   1988   200   87-45713
ISBN 0-06-065373-6

88 89 90 91 92 RRD 10 9 8 7 6 5 4 3 2 1

CONTENTS

Preface   xi

Acknowledgements   xv

Contributors   xvii

Clement of Alexandria: *The Instructor* and
    Miscellanies, (c. 190–200)   1

Origen: *Commentary on the Song of Songs*, (c. 240)   7

Saint Cyprian: *The Dress of Virgins*, (c. 249)   13

Saint Athanasius: *The Life of Saint Anthony*, (c. 357)   19

Saint Basil the Great: *The Long Rules*, (c. 358)   24

Saint Gregory of Nyssa: *The Life of Moses*, (c. 390)   29

Evagrius Ponticus: *The Praktikos* and *Chapters on Prayer*,
    (late 4th C.)   34

Saint Jerome: *The Letters of Saint Jerome*, (370–419)   39

Saint Augustine: *The Confessions of Saint Augustine*, (c. 400)   45

John Cassian: *The Conferences of John Cassian*, (c. 420)   51

Dionysius: *Mystical Theology*, (c. 500)   57

Benedict of Nursia: *Rule for Monasteries*, (c. 525) 60

Saint Gregory the Great: *Pastoral Care*, (c. 590) 65

John Climacus: *The Ladder of Divine Ascent*, (c. 640) 71

Saint Maximus the Confessor: *The Four Hundred*
Chapters on Love, (c. 640) 76

Saint Symeon the New Theologian:
The Practical and Theological Chapters, (11th C.) 82

Saint Anselm of Canterbury: *The Prayers and Meditations*
of Saint Anselm, (c. 1099) 87

Hugh of Saint Victor: *Noah's Ark*, (1125–1130) 93

William of Saint Thierry: *The Meditations of William of*
Saint Thierry, (c. 1128–1136) 100

Bernard of Clairvaux: *On Loving God*, (c. 1126–1141) 105

Aelred of Rievaulx: *The Mirror of Charity*, (c. 1143) 110

Richard of Saint Victor: *Benjamin Minor* and
Benjamin Major, (c. 1160) 116

Saint Bonaventura: *The Mind's Road to God*, (c. 1259) 122

Mechthild of Magdeburg: *The Flowing Light*
of the Godhead, (1265) 128

Johannes Eckhart: *The Sermons and Treatises of*
Meister Eckhart, (c. 1300–1327) 133

Henry Suso: *The Little Book of Eternal Wisdom*, (c. 1328) 139

Unknown: *The Little Flowers of St. Francis*, (c. 1330) 144

Richard Rolle: *The Fire of Love*, (c. 1343) 149

Jan van Ruysbroeck: *The Sparkling Stone*, (c. 1350) 153

Unknown: *Theologia Germanica*, (c. 1350) 159

John Tauler: *The Sermons of John Tauler*, (c. 1330–1361) 165

Saint Catherine of Siena: *The Dialogue of Saint Catherine*
of Siena, (c. 1370) 171

Walter Hilton: *The Ladder of Perfection*, (c. 1390) — 176

Julian of Norwich: *Revelations of Divine Love*, (c. 1393) — 181

Unknown: *The Cloud of Unknowing*, (late 14th C.) — 186

Saint Thomas à Kempis: *The Imitation of Christ*, (c. 1418) — 192

Margery Kempe: *The Book of Margery Kempe*, (c. 1432–1436) — 198

Nicholas of Cusa: *The Vision of God*, (1453) — 203

Desiderius Erasmus: *Enchiridion Militis Christiani*, (1503) — 209

Martin Luther: *The Freedom of a Christian*, (1520) — 215

Francisco de Osuna: *The Third Spiritual Alphabet*, (1527) — 221

Saint Thomas More: *A Dialogue of Comfort Against Tribulation*, (1534–1535) — 226

Saint Ignatius Loyola: *The Spiritual Exercises of St. Ignatius Loyola*, (1548) — 232

Fray Luis Ponce de León: *The Names of Christ*, (1583–1585) — 238

Saint John of the Cross: *Ascent of Mount Carmel* and *Dark Night of the Soul*, (c. 1587) — 242

Saint Teresa of Ávila: *Interior Castle*, (1588) — 249

Benedict Canfield: *The Rule of Perfection*, (1608) — 254

Johann Arndt: *Four Books on True Christianity*, (1605–1610) — 261

Saint Francis of Sales: *Introduction to the Devout Life* and *On the Love of God*, (1609, 1616) — 267

Jacob Boehme: *The Way to Christ*, (1624) — 273

John Donne: *Devotions Upon Emergent Occasions*, (1624) — 279

George Herbert: *The Temple*, (1633) — 286

Sir Thomas Browne: *Religio Medici*, (1642–1643) — 290

Lancelot Andrewes: *Private Devotions*, (1648) — 297

Richard Baxter: *The Saints' Everlasting Rest*, (1650) — 303

Jeremy Taylor: *The Rule and Exercises of Holy Living and Holy Dying*, (1650, 1651) — 309

Blaise Pascal: *Pensées*, (1670)   315

Philipp Jacob Spener: *Pia Disideria*, (1675)   320

John Bunyan: *The Pilgrim's Progress* and *Grace Abounding
    to the Chief of Sinners*, (1678, 1667)   326

Madame Guyon: *A Short and Very Easy
    Method of Prayer*, (1685)   332

Brother Lawrence: *The Practice of the Presence of God*, (1692)   336

George Fox: *The Journal of George Fox*, (1694)   340

François Fénelon: *Christian Perfection*, (1704–1717)   346

William Law: *A Serious Call to a Devout and Holy Life*, (1728)   353

Jonathan Edwards: *A Treatise Concerning Religious
    Affections*, (1746)   359

Nicholaus Ludwig Count von Zinzendorf: *Nine Public
    Lectures*, (1748)   366

Jonathan Edwards: *The Life of David Brainerd*, (1749)   372

John Wesley: *A Plain Account of Christian Perfection*, (1766)   378

John Woolman: *The Journal of John Woolman*, (1774)   385

William Blake: *Songs of Innocence and of Experience*,
    (1789, 1794)   391

William Wilberforce: *Real Christianity*, (1797)   397

Hannah More: *Practical Piety*, (1811)   401

Charles Grandison Finney: *Lectures on Revivals of
    Religion*, (1835)   405

Ralph Waldo Emerson: *The Divinity School Address*, (1838)   410

Phoebe Palmer: *The Way of Holiness*, (1843)   416

Søren Kierkegaard: *Purity of Heart Is to Will One Thing*, (1847)   421

Horace Bushnell: *Christian Nurture*, (1860)   428

Jean-Pierre de Caussade: *Self-Abandonment to Divine
    Providence*, (1861)   434

Hannah Whitall Smith: *The Christian's Secret of a
Happy Life*, (1870) 438

Unknown: *The Way of a Pilgrim*, (1884) 442

Saint Thérèse of Lisieux: *The Story of a Soul*, (1899) 446

R. P. Augustine Poulain: *The Graces of Interior Prayer*, (1901) 452

William James: *The Varieties of Religious Experience*, (1902) 459

Rufus Jones: *The Double Search: Studies in Atonement
and Prayer*, (1906) 466

Baron Friedrich von Hügel: *The Mystical Element
of Religion*, (1908) 472

Evelyn Underhill: *Mysticism*, (1911) 479

Gerard Manley Hopkins: *The Poems of
Gerard Manley Hopkins*, (1918) 484

G. K. Chesterton: *St. Francis of Assisi*, (1924) 491

Albert Schweitzer: *Out of My Life and Thought*, (1931) 496

D. Elton Trueblood: *The Essence of Spiritual Religion*, (1936) 501

Dietrich Bonhoeffer: *The Cost of Discipleship* and
Letters and Papers from Prison, (1937, 1951) 509

Frank C. Laubach: *Letters by a Modern Mystic*, (1937) 516

Amy Wilson Carmichael: *If*, (1938) 521

Charles Williams: *The Descent of the Dove*, (1939) 524

Thomas R. Kelly: *A Testament of Devotion*, (1941) 530

Olive Wyon: *The School of Prayer*, (1943) 536

Donald M. Baillie: *God Was in Christ*, (1948) 541

A. W. Tozer: *The Pursuit of God*, (1948) 547

Howard Thurman: *Jesus and the Disinherited*, (1949) 551

Simone Weil: *Waiting for God*, (1950) 556

Louis Lavelle: *The Meaning of Holiness*, (1951) 563

Nels F. S. Ferré: *The Sun and the Umbrella*, (1953) 569

Douglas V. Steere: *On Listening to Another,* (1955)   576

Alfred Delp: *The Prison Meditations of Father Alfred Delp,* (1956)   582

Pierre Teilhard de Chardin: *The Divine Milieu,* (1957)   586

Elisabeth Elliot: *Shadow of the Almighty: The Life and*

     Testament of Jim Elliot, (1958)   592

Thomas Merton: *New Seeds of Contemplation,* (1962)   598

Dag Hammarskjöld: *Markings,* (1964)   603

Martin Luther King, Jr.: *Strength to Love,* (1964)   609

C. S. Lewis: *Letters to Malcolm: Chiefly on Prayer,* (1964)   615

Agnes White Sanford: *The Healing Gifts of the Spirit,* (1966)   622

Anthony Bloom: *Beginning to Pray,* (1970)   627

Jacques Ellul: *Prayer and Modern Man,* (1970)   632

E. Glenn Hinson: *A Serious Call*

     to a Contemplative Life-Style, (1974)   637

Henri J. M. Nouwen: *Reaching Out,* (1975)   643

Morton T. Kelsey: *The Other Side of Silence:*

     A Guide to Christian Meditation, (1976)   649

Richard J. Foster: *Celebration of Discipline,* (1978)   655

Raimundo Panikkar: *Myth, Faith and Hermeneutics,* (1979)   661

M. Basil Pennington: *Centering Prayer,* (1980)   668

Gustavo Gutiérrez: *We Drink from Our Own Wells,* (1983)   673

Index of Titles   679

Index of Contributors   683

Index of Major Themes   687

Index of Authors   693

PREFACE

Among the 125 selected works represented in this volume of essay-reviews are many of the most thoughtful and revealing interpretations of the elusive tenets of Christian spirituality available. Actually, to define Christian spirituality in finite terms would be impossible because of the broad range of responses the experience evokes in individuals. This work brings the reader to a wide variety of insights as revealed to Christian commentators. For example, Origen's (185–254) *Commentary on the Song of Songs*, known as an allegorical interpretation of the Bible, teaches that Scripture has a spiritual message that mystically unites the soul with the divine Word. Saint Bonaventura (1221–1274) offers the reader six stages of the soul's powers to ascend to God through a special unity of the spirit. Other Christians have searched and found the way to God through spiritual union with the divine, as did the unknown author of *The Cloud of Unknowing* of the late fourteenth century, who through contemplation and meditation reached the plateau of human unity with God.

Those searching for the Way through Christian spirituality receive admirable encouragement from Ralph Waldo Emerson in his *Divinity School Address* delivered at Harvard University in 1838, in which he urged graduating divinity students to go out and "... acquaint men at first hand with Deity." This was a vision perhaps ahead of its time in nineteenth century New England.

E. Glenn Hinson, in his *A Serious Call to a Contemplative Life-Style* (1974), recommends a full commitment to God despite the overwhelming distractions of a secularized society. As he points out, never before has there been such a need to turn away from daily distractions and seek a contemplative relationship with a personal God. Only then can human spiritual needs have the opportunity to grow toward sacralization.

Another important work published in the 1970s is *The Other Side of Silence: A Guide to Christian Meditation* by Morton J. Kelsey, in which the author urges readers to develop Christian meditation so that they may achieve spiritual reality within a society not attuned to religious contemplation.

Those interested in Christian spirituality generally agree that union with God comes about through prayer. The need for communication with a Supreme Being and the yearning for a signal in response have been part of human society since its beginnings, and few known societies have failed to seek this connection in one way or another.

One of the striking examples of the thought behind the Oneness sought through Christian spirituality is John Donne's familiar passage from *Devotions upon Emergent Occasions*, "any man's death diminishes me, . . . therefore never send to know for whom the bell tolls; it tolls for thee." This vision points directly to the need of all humans for God's spiritual acceptance.

"Prayer is the state of the heart in which it is united to God in faith and love," said Madame Guyon in *A Short and Very Easy Method of Prayer* (1685), for which she was imprisoned in 1688, suspected of heresy. Undeterred in her determination to spread the blessings of communion with God, she was again imprisoned and spent four years in the Bastille for her beliefs. According to Johann Arndt, a devotee of Thomas à Kempis's *The Imitation of Christ*, true Christians carry the Kingdom of God within themselves. Nurtured by Christian spirituality the Kingdom heralds eternal life. Beliefs such as this enabled Madame Guyon and other early Christians to endure persecution.

Among the early Christians of influence was Evagrius Ponticus (345–399), who believed a life of prayer moves the seeker toward the final goal of Christian spirituality: the contemplation of God himself. A superb theologian, Evagrius admired the works of Origen and was friendly with Saint Gregory of Nyssa.

Some twelve hundred years after Evagrius, *The Practice of the Presence of God* appeared, the work of a simple man (Brother Lawrence, 1611–1691), whose loving and reverential letters were published posthumously. For Brother Lawrence, prayer was a sense of the presence of God. By his earnest, unlettered approach Brother Lawrence showed that God is accessible to all who seek him in faith.

In *The Pursuit of God* (1948), A.W. Tozer points out that the practice of Christian spirituality is a natural human response to the Creator. In his simple and straightforward approach, Tozer has been likened to Brother Lawrence. Tozer's insistence that God can be known only through personal experience places him in good company with many great Christians throughout the ages, among them George Herbert, who in *The Temple* (1633), stresses the spiritual needs of the soul and holds that union with God comes about through prayer and trust.

Conventionally, space is limited in prefaces. For this reason many of the fine works included in this volume are not commented upon here, but readers will readily recognize those with special personal appeal.

Frank N. Magill

ACKNOWLEDGEMENTS

The editors wish to acknowledge the conscientious and creative assistance of the following consultants on the great works of Christian spirituality: Richard J. Foster, Paul Ramsey, M. Basil Pennington, John K. Roth, Jean Faurot, Glenn Hinson, Nancy A. Hardesty, and Frederick Ferré.

We also want to thank the contributors in general, who throughout the book's preparation continued to think about what we were doing and to make suggestions that strengthened the book. Their articles reflect the enthusiasm and careful thought that they brought to their work.

F. N. M. and I. P. M.

CONTRIBUTORS

William Loyd Allen (Ph.D., Southern Baptist Theological Seminary), now teaching at Brewton-Parker College, Mt. Vernon, Georgia, has written a number of articles for religious journals on monastic spirituality and personal piety.

Harry James Cargas (Ph.D., St. Louis University), professor of literature and religion at Webster University, St. Louis, Missouri, is the editor of *Holocaust and Genocide Studies*, an international journal, and the author of twenty-three books, including *A Christian Response to the Holocaust* and *In Conversation With Elie Wiesel*.

Bowman L. Clarke (Ph.D., Emory University), professor of philosophy at the University of Georgia, is the editor of the *International Journal for Philosophy of Religion*, author of *Language and Natural Theology*, and coauthor with Eugene T. Long of *God and Temporality*.

Luke E. Dysinger (O.S.B., M.D.), Novicemaster at St. Andrew's Priory in Valyermo, California, was awarded a Certificate in Theology from Oxford University and the M.D. from the University of Southern California School of Medicine.

Jean H. Faurot (Ph.D., University of Toronto), emeritus professor of philosophy, California State University, Sacramento, is the author of *Problems of Political Philosophy* and *The Philosopher and the State*.

Frederick Ferré (Ph.D., University of St. Andrews, Scotland), professor of philosophy at the University of Georgia, is the author of a number of influential books, including *Language, Logic and God, Basic Modern Philosophy of Religion*, and *Shaping the Future*. He is coeditor (with John E. Smith and Joseph Kockelmans) of *The Challenge of Religion*.

Paul F. Ford (Ph.D., Fuller Theological Seminary) lectures in theology at Loyola Marymount University, Fuller Seminary, and Mount St. Mary's College in Los Angeles. He is the author of *Companion to Narnia*.

Mary E. Giles (Ph.D., University of California, Berkeley), professor of humanities and religious studies at California State University, Sacramento, is the author of *The Feminist Mystic, When Each Leaf Shines*, and *The Poetics of Love: Meditations With John of the Cross*. She translated Francisco de Osuna's *The Third Spiritual Alphabet* and is editor of the journal *Studia Mystica*.

Douglas H. Gregg (Ph.D., University of Southern California), chaplain and associate professor of religious studies at Occidental College, has written numerous articles on social ethics as well as case studies in Christianity and Christian ethics.

Nancy A. Hardesty (Ph.D., University of Chicago) is an independent scholar, freelance writer, and editor. She is the author of *All We're Meant to Be, Women Called to Witness, Great Women of Faith*, and *Inclusive Language in the Church*.

Thomas E. Helm (Ph.D., University of Chicago), professor of religion at Western Illinois University, has written articles for the *Journal of Religion, Religion in Life*, and other religious journals.

E. Glenn Hinson (D. Phil., Oxford University; Th.D., Southern Seminary, Louisville), professor of church history, Southern Baptist Theological Seminary, has written extensively. His books include *A Serious Call to a Contemplative Life Style, The Reaffirmation of Prayer*, and *The Early Church Fathers*.

David M. Holley (Ph.D., University of Texas, Austin), professor of philosophy and religion at Grand Canyon College in Phoenix, Arizona, has published a number of articles in *The American Philosophical Quarterly*, the *International Journal of Applied Philosophy*, and other philosophical and religious journals.

James M. Houston (D. Phil., Oxford University), professor of spiritual theology, Regent College, Vancouver, British Columbia, and former founding principal and chancellor of Regent College, is the author of *I Believe in the Creator* and *Prayer as a Transforming Friendship*.

William J. Leonard (Ph.D., Boston University), professor of church history at the Southern Baptist Theological Seminary, is the author of *Word of God Across the Ages* and *Early American Christianity*.

Ian P. McGreal (Ph.D., Brown University), professor of philosophy, California State University, Sacramento, is the author of *The Art of Making Choices, Problems of Ethics*, and *Analyzing Philosophical Arguments* and coeditor of *Christian Spirituality* as well as of the earlier *Masterpieces of World Philosophy* and *Masterpieces of Christian Literature*.

Robert James Meindl (Ph.D., Tulane University), professor of English, California State University, Sacramento, is the translator of *Studies in John Gower* by Maria Wickert.

M. Basil Pennington, O.C.S.O. (S.T.L., Pontifical University of Saint Thomas Aquinas; J.C.L., Pontifical University of Gregoriana, Rome), Assumption Abbey, Ava, Missouri, is the author of a number of books, including *Centering Prayer, Daily We Touch Him, Centered Living,* and *Thomas Merton Brother Monk.*

Amanda Porterfield (Ph.D., Stanford University), associate professor of religion, Syracuse University, is the author of *Feminine Spirituality in America: From Sarah Edwards to Martha Graham.*

John K. Roth (Ph.D., Yale University), Russell K. Pitzer Professor of Philosophy, Claremont McKenna College, Claremont, California. The most recent of his fifteen published books are: *Approaches to Auschwitz: The Holocaust and Its Legacy* (with Richard L. Rubenstein), *The Questions of Philosophy* (with Frederick Sontag), and *American Ground: Vistas, Visions, and Revisions* (with Robert H. Fossum).

Gary R. Sattler (Dr. Theol., University of Marburg, West Germany), assistant professor of Christian formation and discipleship, Fuller Theological Seminary, is the author of *God's Glory, Neighbor's Good: A Brief Introduction to the Life and Writings of August Hermann Francke.*

Rowland A. Sherrill (Ph.D., University of Chicago), professor and chair in the department of religious studies, Indiana University, is the author of *The Prophetic Melville: Experience, Transcendence, and Tragedy.*

Brent Waters (D. Min., School of Theology, Claremont) is Omer E. Robbins Chaplain to the University of Redlands. He has written articles for religious journals on Christianity and evolution, moral issues in the university, and other subjects relating to his profession.

Dallas Willard (Ph.D., University of Wisconsin), professor in the School of Philosophy, University of Southern California, is the author of *In Search of Guidance, Logic and the Objectivity of Knowledge: Studies In Husserl's Early Philosophy* and *The Spirit of the Disciplines.*

THE INSTRUCTOR *AND* MISCELLANIES

Author: Clement of Alexandria (c. 150–c. 211/16)

Born and reared in Athens, Clement came to Alexandria around 180. He served as a teacher and then, from 190 to 202 , as head of the "school" of Alexandria founded by Pantaenus, accommodating Christian faith to the burgeoning number of cultured and well-educated folk who were then making inquiry. A Platonist, he drew heavily from Alexandrian Gnostics, but distinguished himself from them at critical points. His three major extant works—*Address to the Greeks, The Instructor,* and *Miscellanies*—were directed to three different audiences—the unconverted, the cultured faithful, and those who sought a higher level of *gnosis* or spiritual knowledge.

Type and subject of work: The *Instructor* is a practical treatise on Christian living; *Miscellanies,* a somewhat more diffuse treatise chiefly on Christian Gnosticism.

First transcribed: c. 190–200

MAJOR THEMES

Our chief instructor is the Work of God, the risen Christ, who spoke in ancient times through both the Greek philosophers and the Hebrew prophets, became incarnate and taught in the flesh, and still continues to teach through the Spirit.

*We can learn from the Work in many ways but especially through his own
instruction in the Gospels.*

*In behavior Christians should adhere to the principle of moderation in food,
drink, dress, speech, and other aspects of life.*

*Philosophy is not, as some argue, useless for Christians; on the contrary, it
may contribute to the cultivation of piety, preparing the Hellenic mind for reception of Christ, the Word of God.*

*Faith is an essential prerequisite for spiritual understanding (gnosis) whose
aim is the vision of God. It is a "voluntary preconception, an assent of piety"
given as a gift which entails obedience to the Word of God.*

*Human beings possess free will, and thus must do good works, but since the
soul was weakened as a result of the Fall, they must have the Instructor to guide
them in doing good.*

*Grace alone can equip the soul to rise above the divine light, attaining the
perfection of love which the "gnostic" should achieve in learning from the
Instructor.*

Clement divided *The Instructor (Paedagogos)* into two major parts.
In book one he urged his pupils to strive to imitate the Word, who is
without sin and who can heal unnatural human passions. God loves
humankind. Humankind should reciprocate by fulfilling God's commandments, turning away from evil and doing what is good. The un-
erring guide is the Instructor, Christ, who in the flesh demonstrated
not only the theory but the practice of virtue. Christians must come to
him like children who are gentle and teachable. In baptism they are
cleansed and enlightened and begin a journey toward perfection in
knowledge (*gnosis*) and, ultimately the vision of God. Enlightenment
leads to withdrawal from material things and a quest for spiritual
nourishment by the Word, who feeds us as a mother feeds her children. He also chastises us so that we will keep striving toward the
blessed life. He models the true life, both human and divine, and if
we conform to him, we will truly live.

In books two and three Clement sets forth from Scriptures the practical rules for conducting the Christian life, emphasizing Stoic suppres-
sion of desire (*apatheia*) and moderation as the way to distinguish
Christians from pagans in the use of food, drink, home furnishings, conduct at banquets and parties, wearing of adornments and perfumes,
sleep, sexual intercourse (for procreation only), clothing and footwear,
jewelry, toiletry, reliance on slaves, bathing, wealth, exercise, and even
walk. All of these things, Clement insisted, should agree with the teachings of the Instructor as found in the Scriptures.

The *Miscellanies (Stromateis)*, as the title suggests, contains a variety
of materials, but each of its seven books stresses a dominant theme. Book

one discusses the relationship between philosophy and Christian truth; book two, faith and *gnosis* vis-à-vis the purpose of humankind; book three, marriage (against certain heretical sects); book four, martyrdom and gnostic perfection; book five, the knowledge of God and symbolism; book six, philosophy and revelation and human sciences as they prepare the true gnostic; and book seven, the true gnostic. Clement was the first Christian writer to grapple seriously with the question of the relationship of Christian faith to philosophy and culture. With him began a true Christian Platonism and humanism.

In book one Clement expressed his vigorous opposition to those who wanted to restrict Christian investigation to "what is most necessary and which contains the faith" or who thought philosophy was introduced by "an evil influence, for the ruin of humankind." His main aim in the *Miscellanies* was to prove that philosophy was "in a sense a work of Divine Providence." God is the source of all knowledge, including secular science and art. It served the Greeks as a Pedagogue to Christ, just as the Old Testament prophets served the Jews. Against those who contended for faith alone, Clement insisted that even interpretation of Scriptures required preparation in Hellenic philosophy. For him the ideal gnostic was one who could bring everything—geometry, music, grammar, and philosophy—to bear on truth, culling what is useful from what must be discarded. The Christian should avoid some elements, such as Epicurean rejection of providence and deification of pleasure or Stoic pantheism, not philosophy itself. If one were to bring together the fragments of eternal truth found in Hebrew and Greek philosophy, one would find the perfect Word, the truth.

Clement here confused his basis thesis when he outlined the history of Greek philosophy, for he argued that the Greeks borrowed from the "barbarians," the Jews—a viewpoint he inherited from predecessors. If the divine Work taught the great philosophers directly, they would not have had to rely on the writings of Moses or Old Testament prophets. (Evidently Clement was stretching his argument to make philosophy as acceptable as he could to those who said, "Bible alone!"). Unlike other Fathers, Clement disallowed connections between heresies and philosophy. Philosophy might espouse errors, but they would not be as bad as heresies. Its purpose was to lead to truth, even if imperfectly.

In book two Clement defined faith as essentially a religious attitude based on Scriptures and adherence to the Word. The Christian, however, should not remain content with faith. It is really a point of departure of *gnosis* (spiritual or mystical understanding) and an essential prerequisite to it. As adherence to the Word, faith is the basis of the whole spiritual life. From the Word it draws the impetus for growth in such virtues as Stoics like Chrysippus admired—endurance, patience, continence, temperance, obedience, and preeminently *apatheia*. By practicing these the "gnostic" comes to resemble God as nearly as possible, the goal of humankind.

Like Augustine two centuries later, Clement insisted that faith must precede understanding. Not established by logical proofs, indeed incapable of demonstration, understanding depends on free assent to the Word, the Instructor. The Greek philosophers themselves said as much. The "gnostic," therefore, is "fixed by faith." The aim of faith is "assimilation to God" so that a person may become righteous and holy and endowed with wisdom.

In book three Clement repudiated the wife-sharing practiced by the Carpocratians and Epiphanians and the rejection of marriage by Marcionites and other dualists. He himself argued in favor of continence. The purpose of marriage is strictly procreation and not pleasure.

After a brief review of the way in which he used Scriptures to evaluate philosophy and a capsule on the nature of the Stromateis in book four, Clement presented a case of Christian martyrdom. The "gnostic," he insisted, will readily accept martyrdom because of being already prepared for it by cultivation of virtue. He condemned both the cowardice of heretics who fled persecution and the impulsiveness of the faithful who rushed out to be martyred. He praised Stoic *apatheia*, insisting it entailed something positive, namely, desire for "treasure in heaven." Those who "gnostically" devote themselves to contemplation enter into a state of identity in which they despise death. Women as well as men, seeking the same end, share this call to martyrdom and may exhibit the supreme example of love of God and of neighbor from which all other virtues derive.

Discussion of martyrdom led Clement to his recurrent theme of the character of the true "gnostic." Paul provided the preeminent example in Ephesians 4:11-13. The objective of the "gnostic" is perfect harmony with the will of God so as to restore "truly perfect nobleness" and attain to the fullness of Christ.

Christians have varied gifts, but the apostles, who model the perfection of "gnostics," achieved perfection in all. "Gnostics" do not seek simply to avoid evil or do good out of fear, but do good in all things out of love "for the sake of its own excellence," thus living "after the image and likeness of the Lord." The perfect person will always pay careful heed to cultivation of good habits and putting off of bad, especially inordinate affection for material things. "Gnostics" gradually withdraw from sensual things and concentrate on spiritual, thus moving imperceptibly toward God as God draws closer to them. True perfection, in the last analysis, consists in the knowledge and love of God, who is not subject to proof. Clement repudiated those who negated the physical. True "gnostics" occupy themselves with God "morally, physically, and logically" and combine knowledge, righteousness, and holiness perfectly.

In book five Clement reiterated his belief in the integral connection between faith and *gnosis*. Rejecting Marcion's predestinarian theory, he insisted that human beings must exercise freedom of choice. Because human capacities for apprehending spiritual realities have been weakened by sin, however, we needed a divine Teacher, the Saviour, whom God sent as "the secret and sacred token of the great Providence." The truth, the Word of God, must be pursued by the intellect, particularly because God spoke many things that are symbolic.

Indeed almost all Scripture is symbolic and thus will only yield its treasures to those who approach often. Paul, "the divine apostle," confirms this approach in his writings. Since God cannot be comprehended in words, we must understand the Unknown "by divine grace and by the Word alone that proceeds from God." Knowledge of God thus comes as a divine gift. It must be learned through Christ, the test of all truth.

In book six Clement returned again to philosophy as a preparation for the true "gnostic." To undergird his case, he elaborated the conventional Christian theory of Greek "theft" of "barbarian" (especially Hebrew) philosophy. Although prepared to admit that the Greeks had some independent knowledge of God, he insisted that Christians surpassed both Greeks and Jews in their worship and understanding. The Greeks knew God "in a Gentile way," the Jews "Jewishly," but Christians "in a new and spiritual way." Though philosophy prepared the Greeks and the law the Jews, both lacked faith taught by the Instructor. Among Christians the true philosophers are those who love wisdom, the Creator and Teacher of all things; among the Greeks, only those who argue about virtue. Inasmuch as Christ is himself Wisdom, the knowledge of things present, past, and future conserved in the tradition which comes from him is wisdom. Once again, at this point Clement observed that the apostles were perfect "gnostics." They possessed the same quality of *apatheia* Jesus did, as was fitting for perfect persons. "Gnostics" also master all knowledge that contributes to the truth and do not fear Hellenic philosophy, which aids in securing truth. The first human being was neither perfect nor imperfect, but capable of receiving virtue such as the "gnostic" alone attains in this life, namely, *apatheia*. Those who have "exercised themselves in the Lord's commandments and live perfectly and gnostically according to the gospel" belong to the ranks of the apostles and are the true presbyters and deacons of the Church and will achieve the highest places in heaven. "Gnostics" distinguish themselves by their likeness to the mind of the Master, whereas heretics depart from Christ's teaching most in that they do not walk "according to the ecclesiastical rule."

In book seven Clement continued his sketch of the character of the "gnostic." "Gnostics" spend their whole lives in that service of God which leads to the salvation of humankind, a true sacrifice. Having a firm grip on themselves and a knowledge of God, they subject themselves completely to God's will. Because God is impassible (*apathe*), he requires no sacrifice but rather wishes holiness of lives. "Gnostics" offer this not just at times of worship but in whatever they do. They avoid theaters, luxuries, and banquets and strive for purity of thought, praying for what is really good. Prayer, therefore, is very proper to them and they never neglect any occasion for prayer. Above all, "gnostics" are truly pious, examples of virtue in all things, striving toward perfection, the face-to-face meeting with God. One must begin with faith, "a compendious knowledge of essentials," but one must proceed to gnosis, "a sure and firm demonstration of the things received through faith."

Here Clement established again the distinction between the Church and the sects in response to Jewish and Gentile criticisms. Christians observe essential articles of faith that heretics disregard and thus hold firmly to the truth. More important still, they live truly pious lives. If some still doubt the distinction, however, they may learn from study of the Scriptures how heretics depart from truth. To "gnostics" Scriptures are "pregnant," to heretics they are "barren," for they spurn the Lord's own voice, not using Scriptures at all or using only parts and perverting the natural sense of the words. Whereas Christians are characterized by knowledge and pagans by ignorance, heretics are characterized by conceit.

E. Glenn Hinson

Recommended Reading

Edition used: Clement of Alexandria. *Christ the Educator*. Translated by Simon P. Wood. New York: Fathers of the Church, Inc., 1954. *The Stromata, or Miscellanies*. Translated by A. Cleveland Coxe. The Ante-Nicene Fathers, vol. 2. Grand Rapids, Mich.: Eerdmans, 1956. Reprint. Translations modernized to avoid sexist language.

———. *The Exhortation to the Greeks, The Rich Man's Salvation,* and *The Fragment of an Address Entitled, To the Newly Baptized*. Translated by G. W. Butterworth. London: W. Heinemann; New York: Putnam, 1919. A useful annotated translation of other writings of Clement.

Ferguson, John. *Clement of Alexandria*. New York: Twayne, 1974. A popular biography by an accomplished scholar.

Lilla, Savatore R. C. *Clement of Alexandria: A Study in Christian Platonism and Gnosticism*. London: Oxford University Press, 1971. A basic critical interpretation of Clement.

Tollinton, R. B. *Clement of Alexandria: A Study in Christian Liberalism*. 2 vols. London: Williams & Norgate, 1914. A still indispensable classic.

COMMENTARY ON THE SONG OF SONGS

Author: Origen (185–254)

Origen ("the Adamant," as his contemporaries called him) was the most important Christian thinker prior to Augustine of Hippo. After the official formulation of Church doctrine by the great councils, his teachings were regarded as at some points heretical, but this did not diminish his great authority in the field of biblical scholarship, though it partly accounts for the fact that many of his writings have been lost and others preserved only in part, as is true of the present work. Educated in Alexandria in the same milieu that produced Clement of Alexandria and the philosopher Plotinus, Origen spent his last twenty-four years in Caesarea, which remained the center of his influence. He wrote entirely in Greek, though some of his works have survived only in Latin translations. This is true of his *Commentary on the Song of Songs.*

Type and subject of work: Allegorical interpretation of the Bible

First transcribed: c. 240

MAJOR THEMES

All Scripture has one or more spiritual meanings besides its literal meaning.

The Song of Songs is a wedding poem representing the love of a rustic bride and a royal bridegroom.

On the moral level it represents the love of Christ and his Church.

On the mystical level it represents the union of the soul with the divine Word.

In a lengthy prologue to his *Commentary,* Origen points out that, like his counterparts, the Greek philosophers, Solomon divides all knowledge into three parts—ethics, physics, and contemplation—for in the book of Proverbs Solomon teaches moral science by means of short maxims; in Ecclesiastes he teaches natural philosophy, showing at the same time the vanity of corporeal things; and in the Song of Songs he teaches that love is the way by which the soul attains communion with God. Origen also notes that these three books mark out the three stages through which one must pass on the way to perfection: purification, illumination, and divinization. "If, then, a man has completed his course in the first subject, as taught in Proverbs, by amending his behaviour and keeping the commandments, and thereafter, having seen how empty is the world and realized the brittleness of transitory things, has come to renounce the world and all that is therein, he will follow on from that point to contemplate and desire the things that are not seen and that are eternal."

That the Song of Songs has a spiritual meaning was maintained by Jewish scribes, who took it as a celebration of God's faithfulness to Israel. This interpretation is presupposed in such New Testament passages as speak of Christ as the bridegroom and of the Church as the bride. An older contemporary of Origen, Hippolytus of Rome, had already written a commentary developing this point of view. But Origen went further and was the first to extend the spiritual interpretation of the Song to include the unitive experience of the individual soul, so much prized in the religious and philosophical circles of his day. According to Origen, all Scripture may be read on three levels, corresponding to the three parts of the human constitution—material, psychical, and spiritual. There is a material meaning for beginners, whose understanding is restricted to sense-knowledge; a moral meaning for those who live on the level of affections and the will; and a mystical meaning for the perfect, who have attained to the plane of spiritual insight. Thus, according to Origen, if we read Solomon's Song on the first level it is an epithalamium in the form of a dramatic poem; on the second level it is a dialogue between Christ and his Church—Origen's interpretation on this level is the basis for the chapter headings in the King James version of the Bible; on the third level it is the sweet exhalation of the individual soul whose only desire is to be made one with God's Word.

In his verse by verse commentary, Origen tries to do justice to each of the three levels of meaning. The first verse reads, "Let him kiss me with the kisses of his mouth." No background is given, but Origen imagines the bride pining at home for her beloved, whose coming she waits with impatience. She is wearing the ornaments that he has presented to her together with a rich dowry; but she regards these as of but little consolation in the absence of his person. Such, says Origen, is the content of the "actual story." And, if to the reader, it seems remarkable that he knows these details, we may remind ourselves that he regards the literal story as no more than a watery reflection of spiritual truths, and that persons who read with the eye of the spirit are quite warranted in reading what they know about the heavenly marriage back into the earthly story. How far this holds true of Origen's *Commentary* is immediately apparent when we turn from the actual story to the "inner meaning" that it has for the Church, regarded as "a corporate personality," longing for union with Christ and saying, with reference to the divine go-betweens—the inspired men of old who have described the beauty of her betrothed and presented her with a heavenly dowry—that she is sated with gifts and wants him to come himself and "pour the words of his mouth into mine." The story yields a comparable meaning to the questing individual. Just as the Church strains to go beyond the Law and the Prophets, so the soul, whose betrothal gifts are her rational endowments and whose instructors are the philosophers, is impatient of these treasures and prays "that her pure and virginal mind may be enlightened by the illumination and visitation of the Word of God Himself."

As he proceeds with his commentary, Origen develops the actual story along the lines of a drama with two speakers and with choruses of attendants. One speaker is the bride, a peasant maiden; the other is the bridegroom, who is a king but who sometimes appears in the guise of a shepherd. The reconstruction is somewhat arbitrary, as Origen seems to recognize, comparing himself to a hunter who, hot on a trail, often finds himself forsaken by the track-marks and is forced to retrace his steps in order to learn where he went astray. In the opening scenes, he says, the bride stands at a crossing of two ways, looking in each direction, for she does not know from which way her betrothed will be coming. He arrives at last and she exults in his beauty. Next, he takes her to his royal chamber with all its treasures, and she speaks to him in the presence of their attendants. It seems, says Origen, that as a husband the bridegroom comes and goes, for "all through this little book we must expect to find the Bridegroom sometimes being sought as one who is away, and sometimes speaking to the Bride as being present with her." In one scene we have the bride asking to be shown more of the palace. In another she is at her cottage in the country, when, looking out of a window, she sees her beloved approaching; and, it being springtime, he invites her to join him in the cleft of a great rock: "Arise, come, my neighbor, my fair one, my dove."

Origen finds the spiritual interpretations less difficult than the literal, no doubt because they do not form a connected exposition but are so many separate meditations.

Some passages yield their clearest meaning when understood as referring to the Church. One such passage, which Origen develops at length, is the verse, "I am dark and beautiful, O ye daughters of Jerusalem" (1:5). The bride knows that the fine ladies of the court complain about her complexion, but she says that she lacks neither natural beauty nor refined manners. This means, says Origen, that the Jews were mistaken in their attitude toward the Church, which in the third century was composed wholly of Gentiles. Although it cannot claim to be descended from Abraham nor to have received the training of Moses's law, it can say, "I have my own beauty, all the same. For in me too there is that primal thing, the image of God wherein I was created; and, coming now to the Word of God, I have received my beauty." Origen takes this occasion to introduce the story of the queen of Sheba, and underlines the similarity between this Ethiopian woman, who came from afar to hear the wisdom of Solomon, and the Church, which comes to Christ out of the Gentile nations.

A passage that lends itself best to a mystical interpretation is one in which the bride exclaims, "Strengthen me with ointments, encompass me with apples, because I am wounded with love (*caritas*)" (2:5). Connecting the last phrase with the reference in Isaiah (49:2) to a chosen arrow, and contrasting the whole image with the pagan myth of Eros or Cupid, Origen speaks of the soul as "wounded by the darts of love." "If there is anyone anywhere who has at some time burned with this faithful love of the Word of God; ... if there is anyone who has been pierced with the loveworthy spear of his knowledge, so that he yearns and longs for Him by day and night ... , that soul then says in truth: 'I have been wounded by love.'"

In the speech that the bridegroom delivers to the bride through the window of her cottage, addressing her as his dove and bidding her come, he goes on to speak of winter having passed and the flowers having appeared, and he remarks, "The voice of the turtle-dove is heard in the land." This change of season, when thought of in relation to the individual soul, means that until the storms of desire and passion have ceased, the soul does not achieve union with the Word, but that when the rains are over she will hear the voice of wisdom represented by the dove, which spends its time far from the crowd but "speaks among the perfect, the deep wisdom of God which is hidden in mystery." Thought of in relation to the Church, the voice of the turtle stands for the coming of Christ and the outpouring of the Holy Spirit, after which God no longer speaks through his servants the prophets but reveals himself directly through his Son.

Origen's pace is leisurely, permitting him to turn aside from the romance as occasion demands and enlarge on the more didactic expressions. For example, after the bride asks to be brought into the house of gladness where a banquet is to be held, she says, "Set ye in order love (*caritas*) in me" (2:4). These words provide Origen an occasion, not to distinguish between fleshly love (*amor*) and spiritual love (*caritas*)—which he has done already in the prologue—but to alert Christians to the special claims that some persons have on their love. People are to love God without any measure; but love for one's neighbor needs to be ordered so that there is a right proportion going to each one. It is wrong to think that we should have the same love for everyone: the same kind, yes, but not the same degree. Origen's rule is that the more godly a person is, the more worthy that person is of love, and he mentions especially spiritual guides and persons who live holy lives. Even within one's own household there should be degrees of love; and, though we are commanded to love our enemies, some enemies ought to be loved more than others according to how well they fulfill the commandments of God.

Sometimes the "actual story" is rather beyond belief. When the bridegroom begins his first speech (1:8) he exhibits what Origen calls "a certain sternness." What he says is, "Unless thou know thyself ... go and feed thy goats." However improbable this speech may sound on the story level, it does make good sense on the moral and spiritual levels, being, as Origen observes, identical with the advice given to the Greeks by one of the seven wise men. There are two kinds of self- knowledge, Origen explains. The first kind calls for self-examination. A soul needs to ask about her disposition and her intentions, whether she is upright and whether she has the same zeal for each of the virtues; whether, moreover, she is making progress toward perfection, and, if so, whether others share in the benefits. Bad temper, gloominess, love for glory, resentment—these are some of the things one should look for. The second kind of self-knowledge is more difficult. It is theology in the highest sense; and, though not everyone is obliged to pursue it, pastors and teachers ought to do so unless they want to be demoted. It includes knowledge of the Father through the Son, as promised in the gospels, but it also includes knowledge of the origin and destiny of humanity. To know oneself, one must ask about the human constitution, its elements, how it was formed, what brought it to its present state, what happens to it at death, and so on. The main thing is to understand that before the creation of the material world human beings and angels were united to the eternal Word and that humanity's present condition is due to a fall, from which God in his providence is laboring to redeem our race. Two points need to be remembered: that human beings are completely free; and that God in his providence does everything that he can to reunite them to himself, short of infringing on their freedom. Origen does not go into these matters here, because his readers can find them discussed in his other books. What he does is of more practical importance, namely, to remind the soul that she "has indeed been set in the path of progress, but as not yet attained the summit of perfection. She is called beautiful because she is advancing." And as long as she is making progress she will not have to go back and feed the goats.

Jean H. Faurot

RECOMMENDED READING

Edition used: Origen. *The Song of Songs: Commentary and Homilies.* Translated and annotated by R. P. Lawson. Ancient Christian Writers, no. 26. Westminster, Md.: Newman Press, 1957. Views Origen not merely as a scholar but as "a master mystic, one who has exerted tremendous influence on Christian spirituality and piety, and to whom monasticism through the ages is greatly indebted for inspiration." The *Homilies* make a good introduction to the *Commentary.*

Chadwick, Henry. *Early Christian Thought and the Classical Tradition: Studies in Justin, Clement, and Origen.* New York: Oxford University Press, 1966. Leading church historian submits the conventional biographical material to critical examination. Excellent survey of Origen's system.

Daniélou, Jean. *Origen.* Translated from the French by Walter Mitchell. New York: Sheed & Ward, 1955. Book-length study of life and teaching from Roman Catholic viewpoint.

Louth, Andrew. *The Origins of the Christian Mystical Tradition from Plato to Denys.* Oxford: Clarendon Press, 1981. Worth reading as a whole. Chapter 4, "Origen," draws largely on the *Commentary.*

THE DRESS OF VIRGINS

Author: Saint Cyprian, Caecilius Cyprianus (c. 200–258)
No details of the author's life prior to his conversion have been preserved. Thascius, as he was then called, was a Carthaginian of patrician stock, a teacher of rhetoric, and a public figure. He renounced paganism and became a Christian, A.D. 246, and barely three years later—having distributed his considerable wealth to the needy— he was chosen by the Christians of Carthage to be their bishop. During the Decian persecution (250–251) Cyprian took cover; but during the Valerian persecution (257–258) he was executed by the sword—the first African bishop to die as a martyr to the faith. As bishop, Cyprian was active in trying to heal divisions brought about by the persecutions, and he is remembered especially for his address, *The Unity of the Church,* in which he lays down his doctrine of a united episcopate in which the authority of each bishop is independent, forming a joint-tenure with that of every other. His discourse *The Dress of Virgins* must have been written when there was peace between the Empire and the Church.

Type and subject of work: Address on ascetic theology

First transcribed: c. 249

MAJOR THEMES

Great rewards are in store for those who dedicate their bodies as well as their souls to God.

It is inconsistent for those who have renounced marriage to take pains to adorn their bodies.

A woman of wealth should devote her patrimony to caring for the poor.

The Church's virgins should avoid every possible occasion of reproach.

Saint Cyprian's *de habitu virginum* is directed to virgins, whom the author exalts as "the flower of the tree that is the Church." It is concerned with dress, or more generally with adornment, because self-adornment epitomizes the temptations that the true virgin has to overcome. While he writes as their bishop, Cyprian speaks "rather through affection than authority," not as claiming a right to censure but as expressing deep concerns.

Before taking up his subject, Cyprian speaks in general terms of the Christian life as one of discipline. "Embrace discipline," David said (Ps. 2:12). "He that rejecteth discipline is unhappy," said Sirach (Wisd. of Sol. 3:11). "Condemn not the discipline of God," said Solomon (Prov. 3:11). "I will give you pastors according to my own heart, and they shall nourish you feeding you with my discipline," said Jeremiah (Jer. 3:15). The Latin *disciplina*, like the Greek *paideia*, which it is used to translate, means instruction or teaching, and, by extension, discipline or administration. The whole of religion, says Cyprian, proceeds from reverence and obedience; and anyone who wishes to withstand the winds and storms of the world must bring his life under the discipline of God.

A second preliminary topic is God's command not to defile the body, which has as its basis the doctrine that the body of the Christian is a temple of the Holy Spirit. Applying to the convert Christ's words to the infirm man, "Behold, thou art made whole; sin no more lest some worse thing happen to thee" (John 5:15), Cyprian remarks that if there is any excuse for those who commit sin before they have knowledge of God's discipline, there is none for those who have become members of the Church.

The larger question concerning the grace of continence and its place in the lives of Christians is nowhere dealt with at any length. Cyprian takes it for granted that persons who have renounced the lust of the flesh and have dedicated their bodies as well as their souls to God are destined to a great reward, and he is at pains to explain that our Lord's saying about men making themselves eunuchs for the kingdom of heaven (Matt. 19:11, 12) applies to both sexes, since "almost universally in the Scriptures God addresses the first formed because they are two in one flesh, and in the man is signified likewise the woman." Later in the address he says that God's initial pronouncement, commanding man to increase and multiply, applied only to the age when the world was underpopulated and that from the time of Christ he counsels continence, but that he only counsels it: "God does not order this but encourages it; nor does He impose the yoke of necessity, since the choice of the will remains free." Cyprian adds that in a special sense "the greater sanctity and trust of the second birth" belong to those "who no longer have the desires of the flesh and of the body."

We should like to have more information on the place that virgins occupied in the Church of that period. There were as yet no monastic establishments either for men or for women, and any woman who renounced marriage and dedicated her body to Christ did so privately. It seems, however, that the Church recognized their vows and ranked them as a distinct body, so that any scandal arising among them brought reproach on the Christian community as a whole. That there were scandals, Cyprian admits. "The Church frequently bewails her virgins ... and detestable gossip about them." The source of the problem seems to have been that the only women who could afford to renounce marriage belonged to the leisure class and were women who found it easier to renounce the responsibilities of marriage than to give up the social life that their wealth and standing made available to them. In brief—and this is the sum of Cyprian's address—they wanted no husband as master, least of all God's Son.

Cyprian marshals his argument under the concept of adornment. Women who have not renounced marriage can say that they adorn their bodies in order to please their husbands. "But a virgin in the Church glories in the appearance of her flesh and in the beauty of her body!" To what end? "You are discovered, O virgin, you are exposed; you boast of being one thing and you are striving to be another. You defile yourself with the stains of carnal concupiscence, although you are a candidate for innocence and modesty." Paul, says Cyprian, gloried only in the cross of Christ. If a virgin takes any account of her flesh let her glory in her sufferings. "Let her glory when she suffers in the confession of the Name, when a woman is found stronger than the men who are inflicting the torture, when she endures fire, or the cross, or the sword, or beasts, that she may be crowned. These are the precious jewels of the flesh; these are the better ornaments of the body."

Cyprian now voices the virgins' response: We are wealthy and rich! Can we be blamed for living in our accustomed style? But this, Cyprian argues, is no excuse for a follower of Christ. Those are rich who are rich in the promises of God, whose blessings are spiritual and an everlasting possession; and he quotes Paul and Peter who wrote that women should array themselves not in costly attire and with outward ornaments but with modesty and sobriety and the ornamentation of the heart. You say that you are rich, he resumes; but not all things that can be done ought to be done. In making yourselves a public show you kindle the fire of hope in young men. Can you be numbered among the virgins of Christ while yielding yourselves the object of men's lusts? You say you are rich; but remember Peter, who, possessing neither silver nor gold, worked miracles because he was rich in faith. And why lavish wealth on your bodies? "Let the poor feel that you are rich! Feed Christ!" A large patrimony, says Cyprian—who knew—is a temptation and should be used to atone for one's faults rather than to increase them. "That you may preserve to the end the glory of virginity, that you may succeed in attaining the rewards of God, pray with the prayers of many!"

In nothing that he says does Cyprian suggest that those who are the objects of the Church's concern are wantons, either in thought or in deed—simply that they have not considered to what their behavior may lead. Immodest dress leads to shameful conduct. The fashions of the day are becoming only to prostitutes. "Who would not detest and shun what has caused another's ruin? ... What madness to think that you yourself will not perish from the same causes from which you know that others have perished."

Here the orator interrupts himself. He wants to mention other dangers to the blessings of continence besides those that go with adornment, but he cannot leave the subject of adornment without saying something about cosmetics. "At this point in my address, because of the fear of God which faith excites in me, and the affection which brotherhood demands, I think that not only virgins and widows but married women also, and all women in general should be warned that the work of God and His creature and image should in no way be falsified by employing ... any cosmetic at all that spoils the natural features." Suppose that a painter succeeded in rivaling nature's composition: Would he not be indignant if a less skillful person meddled with his work? "And you—do you think that you will perpetrate such wicked and rash insolence, an offence against the Artist, God, without being punished?" This is no superficial sin. Cyprian reminds his readers that Christ's sacrifice must be celebrated with "the unleavened bread of sincerity and truth" (1 Cor. 5:7). Do "sincerity and truth" comport with painted eyes and colored hair? No one, he says, can partake of Christ while trying to pretend that she is somebody she is not.

But there are other dangers to continence besides those arising from self-adornment; from the subject of immodest dress Cyprian turns to that of immodest behavior. Two things he mentions as accepted in Carthaginian social life that were clearly detrimental to "modest and sober manners." Pagan wedding parties, with their drunkenness and disgraceful talk, where "the bride is incited to tolerate and the bridegroom to become emboldened in lust," are hardly the place for a Christian virgin, he writes; "She may remain a virgin in body and mind, but by her eyes, ears, and tongue she has diminished the purity that she possessed." And how can the virgin's liberty be stretched to include mixed

bathing where "the honor and modesty of the body are laid aside together with the clothing"? "You gaze upon no one immodestly, but you
yourself are gazed upon immodestly." "Consider," he says, "whether,
when she is clothed, such a one is modest among men who has grown in
immodesty by the boldness of her nakedness."

In his peroration, Cyprian contrasts the broad and the narrow ways
mentioned in the gospels. When they adorn their bodies and insist on
exercising their liberty, Christian virgins are taking the broad and easy
way that leads to destruction, though when they dedicated their bodies
to God they chose the narrow and difficult way. This latter is the path of
martyrs, he points out, but it is also the path of virgins and of all the just.
The fruit of martyrdom is said to be one hundredfold, but that of virgins
is sixtyfold. And as the martyrs are engaged in no easy struggle, no more
are virgins; coming second in order of grace, they must come next in
power of endurance. The ascent is not easy. If climbing hills is exhaust-
ing, what of the ascent to heaven! "Persevere, virgins, persevere in what
you have begun to be." When virgins need encouragement, let them remember what Christ said of the glory of the resurrection, where there is
neither marriage nor giving in marriage, but men shall be as the angels.
"What we shall be you have begun to be. The glory of the resurrection
you already have in this world." As a final word, Cyprian recommends
that the Church's virgins confer with one another from time to time, so
that the younger may learn from the experience of the older, and the
older be refreshed by the others' zeal.

Cyprian was not the first, nor was he the last, of the Church fathers
to write on the subject of women's dress, nor is his treatment of the subject particularly original. But his book was widely used because of the
clarity of its reasoning and the smoothness of its style.

Jean H. Faurot

RECOMMENDED READING

Edition used: Cyprian, Saint. *Treatises*. Edited by Roy J. Deferrari, New York:
  Fathers of the Church, Inc., 1958. General introduction by the editor, with
  further introduction to *The Dress of Virgins*, by Sister Angela E. Keenan,
  translator of the treatise.

Benson, E. W. *Cyprian: His Life, His Times, His Work*. London: Macmillan, 1897.
  Monumental work of a great Anglican archbishop. Long out of print; remains the leading monograph on Cyprian.

Bévenot, M. "Cyprian, Saint," In *New Catholic Encyclopedia*, 4:564–566. New
  York: McGraw-Hill, 1967. All that is known about the life and work of Cyprian, by the leading modern authority.

Tertullian, Quintus. "On the Apparel of Women," translated by S. Thelwall, In

The Library of the Ante-Nicean Fathers, vol. 4, pp. 14–25. Grand Rapids, Mich.: Eerdmans, 1956. Reprint of 1885 publication. Written about 202 A.D. Cyprian calls Tertullian his master, and draws on this and others of his works.

THE LIFE OF SAINT ANTHONY

Author: Saint Athanasius, Bishop of Alexandria (c. 298–373)

The Life of Saint Anthony is an encomium composed perhaps as early as a year after the so-called father of Egyptian monasticism died in 356. In it the bishop of Alexandria, who played a major role in the formation of the Nicene Creed in 325, enlisted the celebrated hermit to set forth his own theory of asceticism, views of Neoplatonic philosophy, and opposition to Arianism. Uncertainty thus exists about the authenticity of the account, but one can assume it represents the voice of Athanasius as much as that of Anthony while retaining fairly accurate depictions of fourth-century hermitism in Egypt. Athanasius introduced monasticism to the West in 338 during one of this five exiles as a result of the Arian controversy. He composed numerous treatises of a polemical nature, the best known of which was *On the Incarnation of the Word* (c. 320).

Type and subject of work: Biography emphasizing Saint Anthony's spiritual life

First transcribed: c. 357

MAJOR THEMES

The ideal Christian is not the hero of the battlefield or the affairs of state but the saint characterized by simplicity and self-denial and by great love of the Faith, the Church, and God.

The central human battle, bringing the self under control (viewed by Anthony as a battle against demons), must be fought with discipline, prayer and Bible

reading, fasting, vigils, and virtues such as graciousness, kindness, meekness or humility, forbearance, and love.

In Christ's death on the cross, God has provided the wherewithal to overcome the forces of evil, and we may share in his victory.

Solitude is as essential to the perfecting of the saint as water is to the survival of a fish.

Athanasius wrote *The Life of Saint Anthony* at the request of other Egyptian monks who wanted to model their lives after his. Athanasius confessed that he, too, admired the saint and saw in his life "an ideal pattern of the ascetical life."

Anthony, according to the bishop, was the son of affluent Christian parents. He "did not take to schooling," however, shunning companionship of other children and preferring "to lead a simple life at home." Even as a child, he lived an exemplary life, attending church, paying attention to Scriptures read, and avoiding rich and fancy foods his parents' wealth afforded him.

Orphaned at about eighteen or twenty, he cared for his very young sister for about six months. One day as he walked along reflecting on how the apostles had left all to follow Jesus, how the Jerusalem community in Acts sold all and laid it at the apostles' feet for the needy, and how such persons can find treasures in heaven (Eph. 1:18; Col. 1:5), he entered a church where Jesus' words to the rich young man were being read (Matt. 19:21). Interpreting these words as spoken directly to him, he gave the property he had inherited to the townspeople, sold all other possessions and distributed the proceeds (except for a little kept back for his sister) among the poor, placed his sister in the care of nuns, and devoted himself to the ascetic life.

For a time Anthony sought out every hermit he heard about. To support himself, he did manual labor, using some of his earnings for food and giving the rest to the poor. He prayed "without ceasing" (1 Thess. 5:17) and read Scriptures so attentively that nothing escaped him, retaining everything in memory. From different ascetics Anthony acquired the ingredients for the devout life: graciousness, earnestness in prayer, forbearance and kindness, patient endurance, meekness, and, above all, devotion to Christ and love for one another in addition to undertaking such disciplines as vigils, fasting, and sleeping on the ground. Villagers became so fond of the youth who never quarreled with anyone that they called him "God's Friend."

Following the psychology of the day, Athanasius depicted the *askesis* of Anthony as a battle with the Devil and his hordes of demons. The Devil tried to lure him away from the ascetic life by reminding him of his former property, the care of his sister, love of family or money or

fame, the pleasures of food and other amenities of life, and by representing the austerities of the way Anthony had chosen. Anthony's determination, nevertheless, prevailed over these and other temptations such as
lust, for the grace of God gave him the victory. Not even when disguised
as the spirit of fornication could the Devil best him, as the saint constantly invoked God as his helper (Ps. 117:7). The success, of course, was
not Anthony's but the Savior's as Anthony practiced his discipline with
increased earnestness. He spent entire nights without sleep in order to
pray without ceasing. He ate only once a day, after sunset, and sometimes every other day. He touched no food except bread and salt and
drank only water. He slept on a rush mat or bare ground. He avoided
anything that would enervate the body, mindful of the trust of Paul's
word, "When I am weak, then I am strong" (2 Cor. 12:10).

Anthony, at about age thirty-five, pursued his battle in the tombs
near his village. "Demons" nearly killed him one night. Fortunately a
friend discovered him as he lay on the ground unconscious and carried
him to the village church. Before he recovered, however, Anthony demanded that he be carried back to the tomb where he could finish the
fight, convinced that nothing could separate him from the love of Christ
(Rom. 8:35). A horrifying struggle took place that night as the Devil and
his host used every power or ruse they had to defeat Anthony. In the
end God heard the saint's urgent pleas, driving away the demons and
restoring him immediately to health. When asked why he did not do
that at the beginning, God responded that he was waiting to see how the
saint himself would fight.

Inspired with still greater zeal for the service of God, Anthony
sought greater solitude on the mountain of Pispir. The Enemy pursued
him, tempting him with silver and gold strewed along his path. But
nothing could halt Anthony. He secured himself in an abandoned fort;
demons fought him fiercely, but he vanquished all of them. After nearly
twenty years of solitude he ventured forth and ministered to many by
miraculous healings. Monasteries sprang up all over the mountains and
deserts. Once Anthony led an entourage across the crocodile-infested
Arsinoe canal by simply praying. In ceaseless conferences he taught
many to love the ascetic way.

When Anthony addressed fellow monks concerning their calling,
he exhorted them to persist, for the reward of heaven would far exceed
the effort on earth. Monks should forsake earth's riches to possess what
they can take with them—wisdom, justice, temperance, fortitude, understanding, charity, love of the poor, faith in Christ, meekness, and
hospitality. The Lord will not forgive those who relax their discipline. If
any person persists in spiritual effort, the Lord will help, cooperating to
do good (Rom. 8:28). No one should look back as Lot's wife did, Anthony
warned. Because the kingdom is within (Luke 17:21), monks can ad-

vance in virtue just where they are. Neither anger nor concupiscence should enslave monks, but they must be vigilant, for the demons lurk nearby. Demons are fallen creatures but not created so, for God does not create evil. Thus they do not want human beings to go to heaven whence they fell. They want especially to trip monks by inciting evil thoughts, but the sign of the cross fortifies against them. The demons use many ruses to get control of those who love God, yet by the grace of Christ their tactics fail. Sometimes they quote Psalms or other Scriptures, don the guise of monks, and simulate pious talk. They should be ignored, Anthony advises. The Lord silenced them so that monks should not listen but simply attend to their discipline. Since monks live their lives in defiance of the Devil, demons have no power over them; if they had any power, they would not come in droves and use all sorts of deceptions. Job shows that the Devil can exercise only whatever power the Lord grants. Monks should fear God alone, therefore, and use an upright life and faith in God as weapons against demons, for "they dread ascetics for their fasting, their vigils, their prayers; their meekness, calmness, contempt of money, lack of conceit, humility, love of the poor, almsgiving, freedom from anger, and, most of all, their loyalty to Christ." Pay no heed to them if they pretend to foretell the future, counsels the saint, for God alone knows this. This is how demons led people astray by Greek oracles. Sometimes they may guess what is right, Anthony concedes, but they cannot know what Providence holds in store. Monks should pray for partnership with the Lord and for a pure mind rather than for knowledge of the future. A vision of God is vastly different from one contrived by demons, which causes terror and confusion. A vision of holy ones will produce ineffable joy and contentment and courage and calmness of thought. If fear reigns, the enemies are present. Monks must not put on airs about casting out demons for, after all, it is the Savior who does this. Anthony knows from experience, he tells the monks, that Christ can overcome the fiercest demons.

Anthony had such a profound effect on the monks that "their solitary cells in the hills were like tents filled with divine choirs." And the whole land "was like seeing a land apart, a land of piety and justice." Anthony sighed constantly for the heavenly mansions, begrudging the time he spent feeding his body rather than his soul. He yearned for martyrdom in 311 during the persecution under Maximin Daja. The encouragement he offered other monks led a judge to forbid the presence of monks in his court. Yet his martyrdom stood revealed in the daily life of the ascetic and his piety in victories over demons.

Besieged by the sick and infirm, Anthony again sought greater solitude, this time in the Inner Mountain. When Saracens burdened themselves to supply him bread, he went into farming for himself. Although alone and now old, he still had to battle the menace of demons. Occasionally he exchanged visits with the monks along the Nile who regarded him "as a father." He witnessed the flight of the soul of Amoun of Nitria when the old ascetic died, and he experienced numerous visions, confirming himself to be a "God taught" person.

Anthony was respectful of the clergy, Athanasius reports. He stood firmly against Meletians, Arians, and pagans. He possessed "a very high degree of practical wisdom," despite lack of formal education. He shamed many pagans who presumed they were wise. Faith depends not on rational proofs, he argued, but on disposition of soul. Christianity's "proof" lies in its success in winning converts and overcoming evil. True to his vocation, Anthony was not awed when the emperor Constantine wrote to him and Anthony replied only to urge the emperor to be humane and just on behalf of the poor. He foresaw the ravaging of the churches by Arians two years before it happened. He healed "not by giving out commands, but by praying and by calling upon Christ's name." Only reluctantly did he leave his mountain solitude, for monks cannot live apart from it lest they "lose sight of the inner life." Yet, Athanasius recounts, Anthony did defend the Orthodox against Arians, and he was God's physician to Egypt.

Still urging monks to maintain the faith against Meletians and Arians, Anthony anticipated his death on a visit to the Outer Mountain. He hurried back to the Inner Mountain where he died a few months later at 105 years of age. He asked two followers to bury him in a secret place.

E. Glenn Hinson

RECOMMENDED READING

Edition used: Athanasius, Saint. *The Life of Saint Anthony*. Translated and annotated by Robert T. Meyer. Ancient Christian Writers, no. 10. Westminster, Md.: Newman Press, 1950.

———. *The Incarnation of the Word of God*. Translated by a religious of C.S.M.V., S.Th. Introduction by C. S. Lewis. New York: Macmillan, 1946. The most important of Athanasius's theological writings.

Chadwick, Owen. *John Cassian*. 2d ed. Cambridge: Cambridge University Press, 1968. Cassian systematized the wisdom of the desert fathers in his *Conferences* and *Institutions* composed between 415 and 435.

Merton, Thomas. *The Wisdom of the Desert*. New York: New Directions, 1960. Selections from the desert monks by a noted contemplative.

THE LONG RULES

Author: Saint Basil the Great (c. 330–379)

Basil was born into a strong family of saints in Annesi in Cappodocia (Asia Minor). He received his earliest spiritual training from his saintly grandmother, Macrina; then he went to the schools in Caesarea, Constantinople, and Athens. During his studies he became a close friend of Gregory of Nazianzen, who later was also called "the Great." They left school in search of true wisdom. After traveling through Egypt and Syria they started the first truly cenobitic monastery for which Basil wrote the well-moderated *Long Rules*. When he was forty he was elected bishop of Caesarea. He suffered a great deal from the doctrinal controversies of the time and played an important role in their solution. Besides the *Rules*, we have some of Basil's letters and sermons and doctrinal works, most notably one on the Holy Spirit.

Type and subject of work: A monastic rule with theological foundations and practical norms

First transcribed: c. 358

MAJOR THEMES

Monastic life is a life of retirement and freedom from worldly distractions.

The Lord is merciful but he is also just; let us not, therefore, make his loving kindness an excuse for indolence.

There are three kinds of dispositions: that of the slave who obeys out of fear of punishment, that of the hireling who obeys in hope of a reward, and that of the son who obeys out of love.

It is impossible to gain proficiency in meditation and prayer while a multitude of distractions is dragging the soul about and introducing into it anxieties about the affairs of this life.

The goal of Christianity is the imitation of Christ, insofar as is conformable with the vocation of each individual.

Saint Basil's *Long Rules* have had an immense influence for they became and remained the basic text after the Gospels for monastic life in the Christian East and inspired Benedict of Nursia when he wrote his *Rule for Monasteries*, which prevailed in the West. It is a specifically monastic text, yet it contains the principles of the spiritual life with rich theological insight, making it valuable reading for all who seek to lead a devout life.

The *Long Rules* is made up of a proportionately long preface and fifty-five questions and answers. The questions, which supposedly come from his disciples, do not follow any clear order and there is a lot of repetition in the responses. The responses vary in length from less than a page to six or seven pages.

Basil describes the monastic life as "the life of retirement and freedom from worldly distractions as an aid to the observance of evangelical doctrine." He calls his disciples to a careful and complete obedience: "Let us make it our common concern and resolve not to allow any precept whatsoever to elude our vigilance." He evokes the example of the great men of old, Job, David, and Daniel and of all the saints whose companionship and reward we hope to share. The Lord is merciful but he is also just: "Let us not, therefore, know God by halves nor make his loving kindness an excuse for our indolence."

The saint notes that there are three kinds of dispositions: that of the slave who obeys out of fear of punishment, that of the hireling who obeys in hope of a reward, and that of the son who obeys out of love. All three are legitimate attitudes toward God and impel one toward complete obedience. The important thing is to know the will of God and do it. As a strong cenobite, Basil relies on the community to help discern that will when it is not evident: "That which is obscure can be more easily discerned by the earnest scrutiny of several persons."

The first question rightly is on order—the order of the Lord's commands to be fulfilled. As is very frequently the case, Saint Basil draws his response directly from the Sacred Scriptures, from the mouth of the Lord himself. Here he uses Christ's words to the scribe: "You shall love the Lord your God with your whole heart, your whole soul, your whole strength and your whole mind. This is the greatest and the first commandment. And the second is like it: You shall love your neighbor as yourself." The instinct to love God is implanted in us naturally and from God comes the power to live holily and virtuously.

Saint Basil likes to define things, hence he defines vice ("the wrong use, in violation to the Lord's command, of what has been given us by God for a good purpose") and virtue ("the use with a good conscience of these same gifts in accordance with the Lord's command"). He likes clear thinking, so he argues by using sharply drawn syllogisms: "Men are, by nature, desirous of the beautiful. But that which is truly beautiful and desirable is the good. Now, the good is God. Since all creatures desire the good, therefore, all creatures desire God."

He wastes no time before soaring to the heights. Even in his second response he speaks of the effect of the Divine Beauty, the impulses of love stirred up by the touch of Divine Love. This is perhaps the richest of the responses. The emphasis of the saint is on the good. He runs through sacred history, enumerating the greatest of the benefits we have received from the Lord: "He is so good that he does not exact a recompense, but is content merely to be loved in return for his gifts."

At the same time his realism depicts the opposite with concrete imagery: "Separation and estrangement from God are more unbearable than the punishment reserved for hell and more oppressive to the sufferer than the being deprived of light is to the eye, even if there is no pain in addition, or than the loss of his life is to an animal." The worst part of evil for Basil is that "we provide the Enemy of Christ with the matter for boasting and with cause for exalting over him who died for us and rose again."

Basil's realism continues to be evident in the third response where he speaks of the necessary corollary to love of God, namely, love of neighbor. The fulfillment of these two great commands depends on the fear of God (4—the numbers in parentheses refer to the questions and responses in the *Long Rules*), vigilance coming from "the holy thought of God stamped upon our souls as an ineffaceable seal by continuous and pure recollection" (5), and detachment (6). Our aim must always be "the keeping of the commandments in a manner pleasing to God." Human respect should never hold us back.

Saint Basil is writing for monks, so he takes up in the sixth response what is the distinctive characteristic of the monastic way: "A secluded and remote habitation also contributes to the removal of distractions from the soul." It is impossible to gain proficiency in meditation and prayer while a multitude of distractions is dragging the soul about and introducing into it anxieties about the affairs of this life.

It is not good for man to be alone. Basil sees many advantages to living in common with like-minded brothers: It is easier to supply corporal necessities, we are given opportunities to practice charity, common life helps us discern our defects, all the corporal works of mercy can be practiced by the group as a group, the members share each others gifts, and so forth. Community life offers more blessings than can be fully and easily enumerated. It is an area for combat, a good path of progress, continual discipline, and a practicing of the Lord's commandments, when brethren dwell in community (7).

To enter into the community one must renounce oneself and all one possesses. This includes carnal affections, relatives and friends, one's own way of life, external goods, vainglory, life in society, and useless desires. Such renunciation—and this is the main point—is the first step toward the likeness of Christ, who, being rich, became poor for our sake (8). Basil urges his disciples to use prudent care in distributing their goods to the poor (9). In the following questions (10-12, 14) the legislator moves on to more practical considerations in regard to the admission into the community of sinners, slaves, married persons, apostates, and children. There is a lot of excellent pedagogy in his program for training the children (15).

The value of many elements of life are set forth by the saint with depth of insight: silence (13), moderation in dining (16-21) and clothing (22), communal living (25), and spiritual direction (26).

Obedience has a preeminent importance for Basil; many questions explore the various facets relative to it and the interactions between superiors and subjects (25-30, 43-45, 47-48). In addition, there is a sort of penal code (50-53). A particularly interesting response is the one that instructs the subject to accept humbly the corporal ministrations of the superior (31). Basil comes out in favor of some kind of federation of monasteries to support superiors in their difficult ministry (35, 54).

The holy legislator treats extensively of work, not allowing monks to use their pious profession as an excuse not to earn their bread with the sweat of their brow. He offers a real theology of labor. At the same time his many practical provisions offer safeguards against worldly attitudes creeping into the monks' marketing and other contacts with secular negotiations (37-42).

The final response in the Rules is a long defense of the use of medical arts by monks, with a caution: "We must take great care to employ this medical art, if it should be necessary, not as making it wholly accountable for our state of health or illness, but as redounding to the glory of God and as a parallel to the care given the soul." Because some abuse the art, that does not mean monks have to repudiate it. Rather, moving to a more general position, Basil argues that others' abusive use of any of the arts or crafts ought to be reprimanded by the monks' good use of them.

In summary, for Basil, "the goal of Christianity is the imitation of Christ according to the measure of his Incarnation, insofar as is conformable with the vocation of each individual." He enjoins: "We should hold to our objective of pleasing God and see to it that the soul's benefit is assured, fulfilling thus the Apostle's precept: 'Whether you eat or drink or whatsoever you do, do all to the glory of God.'"

M. Basil Pennington

RECOMMENDED READING

Edition used: Basil, Saint. *Ascetical Works*. Translated by Sister M. Monica Wagner, C.S.C. The Fathers of the Church, vol. 9. New York: Fathers of the Church, Inc., 1950.

―――. *Exegetic Homilies*. Translated by Sister Agnes Clare Way, C.D.P. The Fathers of the Church, vol. 46. Washington, D.C.: Catholic University Press, 1963. These homilies help us to understand more fully the scriptural sources used by Saint Basil and his way of interpreting them.

―――. *The Letters*. Translated by Roy J. Deferrari. 4 vols. The Loeb Classical Library. New York: Putnam, 1926–1934. Though edited, these letters, as most, give a candid insight into the author and his general approach to life as a context for his *Rules* and his theological outlook.

Fedwick, Paul Jonathan. *The Church and the Charisma of Leadership in Basil of Caesarea*. Toronto: Pontifical Institute of Mediaeval Studies, 1979. An exhaustive study of a key concept in the *Rules* of Saint Basil and in his general ecclesiology, with an extensive bibliography.

Pennington, M. Basil, O.C.S.O. *A Place Apart: Monastic Prayer and Practice for Everyone*. New York: Doubleday, 1983. The volume contains a presentation of Saint Basil's theology of work with a practical application of it to lay life today.

Word and Spirit: A Monastic Review. Vol. 1: *In Honor of Saint Basil the Great*. Mass.: St. Bede's Publications, 1979. A collection of essays on Saint Basil by the most competent scholars of our times, commemorating the sixteenth centenary of the saint's death.

THE LIFE OF MOSES

Author: Saint Gregory of Nyssa (c. 335–c. 395)
Gregory of Nyssa, one of the three great Cappadocian hierarchs and theologians, was born into a family of saints. At first he pursued a career as a rhetorician, but later entered the monastery founded by his brother, Basil the Great. Before he was forty he was named bishop of Nyssa and as such took a leading part in the Council of Constantinople. In his later years he wrote more on the moral and mystical development of the individual Christian.

Type and subject of work: A formal treatise taking the form of a scriptural commentary, dealing with Christian perfection

First transcribed: c. 390

MAJOR THEMES

Anything in Sacred Scripture that in its literal sense would be unworthy of God must have some hidden inner meaning.

The command to wash one's garments before ascending Sinai calls for the removal of those stains the inner person has contracted from worldly pursuits before ascending to God.

It is only when the passions are destroyed that one is free to pursue the spiritual path through the desert.

Knowledge of God is important, right conduct even more so.

The true servant of God is the one who waits upon the divine and prays that he might follow.

Growth in virtue always opens the way to still greater virtue.

Ultimately, God is unknowable; he transcends all sense perception and all rational concepts; to see God is to know him as unknowable.

The appetitive part of the soul is filled with desires for the things of this world and is never satisfied; nonetheless, it does support and impel the rational part, which must ever remain in charge and unite the appetites to the spirit.

Gregory of Nyssa's *The Life of Moses* has been published in two books. The first, entitled "The Life of Moses or Concerning Perfection in Virtue," contains a relatively short prologue or covering letter and then the "history" or paraphrase of the biblical story of Moses as found in Exodus and Numbers. The second, "Contemplation on the Life of Moses," is about four times as long and develops the spiritual meaning of the text. The life of Moses becomes a symbol of the spiritual journey of the Christian to God. At the end of this second book there is a short conclusion.

In his text Gregory indicates some of the criteria to be used in finding the spiritual sense of the Bible. Since "the Law does not instruct us how to eat'"—"Nature ... is a sufficient Lawgiver" in this regard—there must be an allegorical meaning to the Passover meal. Whatever Gregory thought was unnecessary or out of place in Scripture he judged to be there for some deeper meaning. Where something evil was commanded in the sacred text an allegorical meaning must be present. The "spoiling of the Egyptians" was not morally justified; therefore a "loftier meaning is more fitting than the obvious one." Anything that in its literal sense would be unworthy of God must have some hidden inner meaning. Since to describe God as having a back or a face is not congruous with the divine nature, these references have spiritual meanings.

Gregory is always on the lookout for interpretations that instruct in virtue, even where these are multiple. Anything that is edifying or provides a useful lesson or profitable advice is brought out. Since a pilgrim's soiled clothes would hardly be an impediment to approaching God, the command to wash one's garments before ascending Sinai must be calling for the removal of those stains the inner person has contracted from worldly pursuits. For his interpretations, Gregory looks to the Old and New Testaments and to the living tradition of the Alexandrian school. However, along with this there is much that is new. His overall synthesis is quite original, and he encourages the readers to seek on their own to find yet richer spiritual meanings.

Gregory calls special attention to those features of Moses' life that may be considered a withdrawal from active involvement in the affairs of this world. In Midian "he lived alone in the mountains away from the turmoil of the marketplace." On Sinai, he left the people behind and "boldly approached the very darkness itself." Gregory encourages the solitary life. If this is not possible, then at least one should seek those of "like disposition and mind." However, the Moses who had known the discipline of the desert was called forth to lead the people and he whom God instructed in the cloud was sent down to instruct others, sharing what he had received. Contemplation must flow over into action.

Asceticism is emphasized in Gregory's treatise. It is more powerful than the wisdom of the Egyptians. The coverings of the tabernacle are interpreted as the mortification of the flesh. Such asceticism is the adornment of the Church. Passions must be controlled. It is only when these "firstborn" of evil are destroyed that one is free to pursue the spiritual path through the desert. Just as animals had to be kept away from Sinai, so must the senses be controlled. Basic enemies of the Christian life—pride, envy, and pleasure seeking—are given extensive treatment by Gregory.

The positive side is not neglected. The theological virtues are carefully considered. The rod of Moses is the word of faith whereby he prevails, while each pilgrim has a staff of hope. Knowledge of God is important, right conduct even more so. Meditation sends up a melodious voice to God.

The central theme of Gregory's spiritual way is "to follow God." The true servant of God is the one who "waits upon the divine voice and prays that he might follow behind." This basic obedience is emphasized rather than specifics of prayer, meditation, and sacred reading. We are made in the image of God. This image was tarnished by the fall. Christ took on our human nature in order to restore us to our original likeness. Conversion to Christ, receiving his redemption, enables us once again to manifest God. This is an unending process as we reach into the infinity of God and enter into an ever greater participation in his divinity.

The most distinctive idea in Gregory's teaching is the idea of eternal progress. Perfection is not something achieved, it is progress. "How then would one arrive at the sought-for boundary when he can find no boundary?" "The perfection of human nature consists perhaps in its very growth in goodness." Moses' attainments throughout the journey emphasize that from each summit attained new horizons open out. Moses "always found a step higher than the one he had attained." Growth in virtue always opens the way to still greater virtue.

However, this perpetual growth does not imply a lack of satisfaction, Gregory writes. The more one enjoys God, the more one desires such enjoyment, but there is a stability in the good. There is a joy in going on and on. "The continual development of life to what is better is the soul's way to perfection."

Gregory does sometimes make much of the particular sequence of events as he finds them in the sacred text. Nonetheless, life is not compressed into some preconceived way. Some things do logically follow others in life, but Moses' life is a pattern more in its constant going forward than in its actual inner ordering.

The treatise does have a rich doctrinal content. Gregory uses the three great events of Moses' life: the revelation at the burning bush, the reception of the Law on Sinai, and Moses' experience of God in passing, to develop his teaching on God. God is being, a self-subsisting nature —the only One. All else depends on him for subsistence. By participating in his existence, we all exist. Ultimately, Gregory claims, God is unknowable; he transcends all sense perception and all rational concepts; to see God, is to know him as unknowable; he is all-sufficient to himself; he is boundless; it is by following him that we get to know him; insofar as we see him, we desire to see him yet more.

So that we can "see" God, he became man in Christ, born of a virgin. The two natures of Christ are clearly affirmed. The burning bush, Moses' rod, the leper's hand, the manna, the tabernacle, and the stone tablets are all figures of the incarnation. Christ did indeed exist always, yet in a moment of time he was created as man. He came to redeem. The cross has its figures in the Moses story: the outstretched arms of efficacious prayer, the wood that sweetened the waters of Marah, the bunch of grapes suspended on wood coming from the Promised Land, and the brazen serpent. If the skins of the tabernacle were dyed red, it was because redemption comes through the blood of Christ.

The Holy Spirit receives surprisingly little treatment in this treatise, in spite of the earlier doctrinal struggles in which Gregory was involved. Nonetheless the Spirit was the means of the incarnation and grace lives within us through the Spirit. The cloud that led the Chosen People was a figure of the Spirit; the lamps in the tabernacle, its inner light.

Gregory has a particular anthropology. There are three dimensions to the human soul: the appetitive, the rational, and the spirit. The appetitive is filled with desires for the things of this world and is never satisfied. Nonetheless it does support and impel the rational part, which must ever remain in charge and unite the appetites to the spirit. Much of Gregory's moral direction is geared toward this domination of the rational. "All the movements of our soul are shepherded ... by the will of guiding reason." Gregory struggles with the question of the freedom of this will of reason and the role of the divine. Freedom is important. We, as it were, give birth to ourselves by our own free choice in accordance with whatever we wish. Each of us finds ourself between an angel appointed by God's providence and a demon who seeks to drag us down. Which way we will go is our decision. "We have in ourselves, in our own nature and by our own choice, the causes of light or of darkness, since we place ourselves in whichever sphere we wish to be." Gregory tends to see the divine activity as a sort of cooperation with this, with our movement toward the good, toward virtue.

Gregory saw Moses as a very great saint, a friend of God, powerful before his Lord. In this life, Caesarius, for whom he wrote this treatise, and all readers can find the pattern of a virtuous way of life that leads to divine friendship.

M. Basil Pennington

RECOMMENDED READING

Edition used: Gregory of Nyssa. *The Life of Moses.* Translation, Introduction, and Notes by Abraham J. Malherbe and Everett Ferguson. Preface by John Meyendorff. Classics of Western Spirituality. New York: Paulist Press, 1978.

Daniliou, Jean. *From Glory to Glory: Texts from Gregory of Nyssa's Mystical Works.* Edited and translated by H. Musurillo. New York: Scribner, 1961. A good introductory selection of Gregory's writings with a competent introduction; the most available and popular edition in English.

Goggin, T. A. *The Times of Saint Gregory of Nyssa as Reflected in the Letters and the Contra Eunomium.* Washington, D.C.: Catholic University Press, 1947. This doctoral dissertation helps to place Gregory and his writings fully in context and to give a sense of those for whom he was writing.

Gregory of Nyssa. *The Lord's Prayer and the Beatitudes.* Ancient Christian Writers, vol. 18. Westminster, Md.: Newman Press, 1954. Two comparable treatises that complement the teaching in the *Life of Moses,* with a good introduction.

———. *Selected Works.* Translated by William Moore and Henry Wilson. Writings of the Nicene and Post-Nicene Fathers, ser. 2, vol. 5. Grand Rapids, Mich.: Eerdmans, 1955. The most complete selection of the writings of Gregory of Nyssa available in English.

Harvanek, R. F. "Saint Gregory of Nyssa." In *New Catholic Encyclopedia,* vol. 6:794–796. New York: McGraw-Hill, 1967. A concise presentation of the monk and his writings.

THE PRAKTIKOS *AND* CHAPTERS ON PRAYER

Author: Evagrius Ponticus (345–399)

The son of a bishop, Evagrius was ordained lector by Saint Basil, who probably introduced him to "Christianized" classical philosophy, especially the writings of Origen. In 379 he was ordained deacon by Basil's friend, Saint Gregory Nazienzen; and at the Second Ecumenical Council in 381 he distinguished himself as a superb theologian and defender of orthodoxy. He also became friends and shared ideas with Saint Gregory of Nyssa. Evagrius's promising ecclesiastical career was cut short when he fled Constantinople, possibly to avoid an impending illicit romance. He eventually became a monk in Egypt, a disciple of Saint Macarius the Great at Nitria. He came to live the austere life of a hermit, supporting himself by copying manuscripts. His synthesis of monastic spirituality with "Origenism" was a subject of controversy even during his lifetime; and his writings were officially condemned in 553 (Origen's had been condemned in 543), chiefly for speculation concerning the preexistence of souls and the eventual restoration of all things to unity with God (*apokatastasis*).

Type and subject of works: Both the *Praktikos* and the *Chapters on Prayer* are collections of aphorisms and relatively brief paragraphs (called "chapters") detailing the spiritual struggles of the monk and offering advice to those seeking to deepen their life of prayer and experience of God.

First transcribed: Late fourth century

MAJOR THEMES

The spiritual life of the Christian may be divided into two parts: first, the moral (ascetical) struggle against temptation and the quest of the virtues; second, the life of prayer, or growth in contemplation of God.

The moral-ascetical journey (praktike) begins in faith and the fear of God, progresses through obedience to the commandments in the rejection of sin and the cultivation of virtue, and culminates in apatheia, *a state of abiding peace and freedom and overwhelming compulsions, which in turn gives birth to spiritual love* (agape).

The final goal of Christian prayer, indeed of Christian existence, is the contemplation of God. Growth in this true knowledge of God begins with the contemplation of God through nature and progresses to the contemplation of God himself.

Evagrius's writings represent a fusion of the wisdom of early Christian monasticism with the goals and speculations of classical philosophy. He was concerned to find a common answer to both the monk's desire to "pray without ceasing" and the philosopher's yearning for endless contemplation of "The One." Evagrius's spirituality is based on a "therapeutic" model: The purpose of creation is the ultimate restoration of all created beings to union with God. The goal of human existence is to draw as near to God as possible. The human being who truly lives "according to nature" is thus one in whom all the desires and powers of the soul are directed toward their natural end—namely, the contemplation of God.

In his writings Evagrius takes on the role of physician to the human soul, diagnosing the ills to which the human heart is subject, prescribing spiritual remedies, and foretelling both the inner battles that must be waged on the way to God and the joy and peace that will ultimately be won. He describes a twofold process by which human beings draw near to God. First is the path of ethical-moral purification, with which the *Praktikos* is chiefly concerned. Second is the journey of deeping prayer—the path of contemplation, discussed to some extent in the *Chapters on Prayer.*

Neither the *Praktikos* nor the *Chapters on Prayer* appears at first glance to contain on orderly exposition: They seem, rather, to resemble the Wisdom Literature of the Old Testament, containing as they do pithy aphorisms and relatively brief (and occasionally unrelated) discussions of complex spiritual subjects. This appearance is deceptive, however: Evagrius adopted the style of his masters and confreres, the

desert monks, who were often asked to condense their experience of
God into a brief sentence or phrase. The 100 "chapters" of the *Praktikos*
and 153 *Chapters on Prayer* represent the distilled essence of an exceedingly sophisticated spiritual system, part of which Evagrius inherited
from Origen, and to which he added his own surprisingly modern psychological insights. The result is a set of writings that must be read more
than once and savored slowly.

The *Praktikos* is the first book of a spiritual trilogy. In it Evagrius describes the journey of spiritual purification that must be undertaken by
the soul that yearns for union with God. The second and third books of
the trilogy, the *Gnostikos* and the *Kephalia Gnostika*, describe in detail Evagrius's theories of divine contemplation; they are not yet available in
English translation.

The *Praktikos* begins with an explanation of the symbolic meaning of
the monastic habit worn in Egypt: The parts of the habit correspond to
different aspects of Christian renunciation and asceticism. This introduces the traditional Christian virtues that must be cultivated by all
those who undertake the *praktike*, the way of spiritual purgation and
preparation for deeper prayer and contemplation.

The moral-ascetical journey of the Christian begins in faith and the
fear of God: This is manifested through obedience to God's commandments and through faithfulness during the inevitable (and purifying)
interior battles that are the result of demonic temptation. Vivid descriptions of the moral struggles through which Christians must pass are
found in chapters six to fourteen of the *Praktikos*, where Evagrius discusses the eight "evil thoughts," precursors to the medieval "seven
deadly sins." Chapters fifteen to thirty-four contain advice on avoiding
and overcoming these "evil thoughts." For Evagrius no natural human
desire or power of the soul is evil in itself: All of creation exists in order
to bring us back to God. Anger, for example, is a useful weapon that
should be directed against the demons responsible for temptation.

The soul that struggles faithfully against sin and temptation is
strengthened even further through the exercise of the virtues, through
which it learns hope. Finally it is given the gift of *apatheia*, a term borrowed from Stoic philosophy for which no modern English equivalent
exists. To translate *apatheia* as "freedom from the passions" would be
misleading, since most Christians today would interpret this (as did
some of Evagrius's unsympathetic contemporaries) as implying the absence of emotion. On the contrary, *apatheia* gives birth to *agape*, spiritual
love: The soul gifted with *apatheia* sheds tears of both repentance and
joy, and is filled with love for God to whom it speaks "as to a loving
father." *Apatheia* is a state of calm, of freedom from overwhelming compulsions, in which the Christian can live more truly for God and enter

more deeply into his presence. The state bordering on *apatheia* is described in chapters fifty-seven to ninety; and the *Praktikos* concludes with vignettes from the lives of the desert fathers that illustrate Evagrius's teaching.

In the *Chapters on Prayer* spiritual growth is described as a progression through different forms of prayer. Prayer is "an ascent of the Spirit to God" in which the Christian passes from the prayer of repentance and reconciliation with God to prayer that unites all rational beings and effects the sanctification of the world. There is, first, a movement from the sanctification of self to the sanctification of others. This in turn leads from prayer that sees God shining through the multiplicity of created things to prayer that seeks only the simple unity of God himself. This is a progression from seeing God through the forms of creation to a vision of God who is formless—a passing from thoughts and concepts about God to the God who is "beyond every thought and perception."

This prayer "of the most intense love" which is beyond images and words is another name for *apatheia*. It is the goal for which the spiritual battles of the *praktike* are a preparation. In it the virtues that have been slowly and painfully nurtured in the soul reach their flower by enabling the Christian to turn to God through his creation. Ultimately this "pure prayer" ("contemplation," "theology") leads the soul to the simple unity of God himself. Thus in Evagrius's teaching on prayer a continuity is described between the struggles of the *praktike* and the life of contemplation: Each activity nourishes and strengthens the other.

Luke E. Dysinger

RECOMMENDED READING

Edition used: Evagrius Ponticus. *The Praktikos and Chapters on Prayer.* Translated with an Introduction and Notes by John Eudes Bamberger, O.C.S.C. Cistercian Studies Series, no. 4. Kalamazoo: Mich.: Cistercian Publications, 1978.

Bamberger, Abbot John Eudes. Introduction to *The Praktikos and Chapters on Prayer.* Cistercian Studies Series, no. 4. Kalamazoo, Mich.: Cistercian Publications, 1978. Monk and psychiatrist Bamberger presents Evagrius's teachings in a concise and lucid manner in his Introduction.

Bouyer, Louis. "Erudite Monasticism." In *A History of Christian Spirituality*, vol. 1: *The Spirituality of the New Testament and the Fathers.* New York: Seabury Press, 1982. A useful discussion of Evagrius's writings may be found in chapter 15.

Kline, Francis. "The Christology of Evagrius and the Parent System of Origen." *Cistercian Studies* 20 (1985):155–183. A sympathetic analysis of Evagrius's (and Origen's) more controversial teachings, including portions of Evagrian texts previously unpublished in English.

Tugwell, Simon. "Evagrius Ponticus." In *Ways of Perfection*. Springfield, Ill.:
    Templegate, 1985. In chapter 3, Tugwell provides a discussion of Evagrius's
    writings.

THE LETTERS OF SAINT JEROME

Author: Saint Jerome (c. 340–420)
A native of Dalmatia who went to Rome to complete his studies, Jerome in more equable times would probably have become a professor of literature. As things turned out, his ready pen was employed translating the Bible into Latin—the so-called Vulgate version. Jerome had traveled widely, had lived as a hermit in the desert near Antioch, had improved his command of Greek and learned some Hebrew, and had been ordained a presbyter when, in 382, he was called to Rome as an assistant to Pope Damasus. Circles dedicated to ascetic living welcomed him in Rome and when he left Rome in 385 some of his disciples went with him to Bethlehem, where he spent the remainder of his long life. Although he lived in a monastery he kept in touch with the world by writing letters of which a representative collection has survived.

Type and subject of work: Letters on Christian living

First transcribed: 370–419

MAJOR THEMES

The Christian life is a battle, whether one chooses to fight it in the wilderness or in the city.
The highest prize awaits those who turn their backs on the world and take up a monastic life.

Men wishing to become priests should submit to monastic discipline before receiving ordination.

Marriage makes it difficult for a person to renounce the world and attain to perfect love of God; hence, the young are advised to remain virgins, and widows and widowers not to remarry.

Those of Jerome's letters that have enduring interest are of a formal nature, written with the expectation that they would be copied and passed from hand to hand. We often find him referring readers to other letters just as he refers them to his books. Many of the letters have to do with the monastic life, concerning which there was increasing interest as well as much need for guidance. But monasticism was only one aspect of Jerome's message for his generation, which was simply a serious call to a devout and holy life. The Roman world, less than a century after the conversion of Constantine the Great, was nominally Christian but still largely pagan. Hitherto persecution had kept the Church fairly honest. Now not to be a Christian was considered bad form. Never had the Roman world been so corrupted—and confused. Jerome was a picturesque individual in whom learning was combined with experience of the desert. People wrote to him from every quarter seeking his counsel. What they got was strong medicine: Repent and be converted; separate yourselves from corrupt society; discipline your bodies; renounce wealth and social position; read the Bible and the writings of the saints; minister to the sick and the poor; and pray constantly.

The times were turbulent. Between the death of Constantius (A.D. 361) and the accession of Theodosius the Great (A.D. 379), five emperors and three usurpers had met their deaths. With the Goths ravaging Europe and Huns at large in Asia Minor, no one felt safe. In a letter to a young man from Marseilles (A.D. 411), Jerome writes, "May our renunciation of the world be a matter of free will and not of necessity! However, in our present miseries, with swords raging fiercely all around us, he is rich enough who is not in actual want of bread, he is more powerful than he needs be who is not reduced to slavery."

Jerome distinguished between being a Christian in the world and turning one's back on the world in order to pursue perfection. In his own case renouncing the world meant not merely leaving family and friends to go and live in the desert—he was prepared for this; it also meant disposing of his library of Greek and Latin authors, which he could not make up his mind to do even though he knew that clinging to pagan authors was all one with drinking the cup of Christ and the cup of the Devil at the same time. While he was in Antioch, ready to depart for the Syrian desert, the matter resolved itself. Jerome fell seriously ill and in a delirium he believed he stood before the judgment seat. When he represented himself as a Christian, the Judge said, "Thou liest; thou are a Ciceronian, not a Christian. 'For where thy treasure is there will thy heart be also.'" When he cried for mercy, the sound of his voice was drowned out by the noise of the lash; and he was pardoned only when he swore never again to read the works of pagan authors.

Jerome stayed in the desert for five years, slowly inuring himself to its torments. "I remember that often I joined night to day with my wailings and ceased not from beating my breast till tranquility returned to me at the Lord's behest." He was not a member of a community, but there were other monks in the vicinity, and, when he could not by fasting overcome "the promptings of sin and the ardent heat of my nature," he put himself in the hands of a converted Jew and learned Hebrew. "How often I despaired, how often I gave up and then in my eagerness to learn began again ... those can testify who were then living with me. I thank the Lord that from a bitter seed of learning I am now plucking sweet fruits." He also wrote letters, including one to his close friend, Heliodorus, who had accompanied him to the desert but after a while had returned to civilization. "Why are you such a timid Christian?" Jerome writes. "Are you looking for an inheritance in this world, you who are a joint-heir with Christ? Consider the meaning of the word monk [*monachos*. solitary], your proper designation. What are you, a solitary, doing in a crowd?" Heliodorus was ordained a presbyter and later was made a bishop, and his friendship with Jerome continued. Jerome was himself ordained when he left the desert, and he came to look upon organized monastic life as a kind of seminary for the secular clergy.

Reconciled, it seems, to the fact that he was temperamentally unsuited to the solitary life, Jerome, as a counselor, concerned himself largely with the question how one can be in the world and not of the world, how, in Paul's words, he can "use the world as not abusing it" (1 Cor. 7:31). Writing in the satiric vein common in the classical world, he often approaches this question by portraying false Christians. There are priests, he says, who at home never had anything to eat but millet and coarse bread but who now dine so well that they know the names of every kind of fish, can tell on what coast an oyster was gathered, and have learned to prize a dish solely on its rarity and cost. Other priests he portrays as paying court to old men and women without heirs, sitting by their bedsides, fetching the basin, impatient of the doctor's calls, hardly able to conceal their chagrin when the patient shows signs of getting well. "With what labor they seek an empty inheritance! At less trouble they could have bought for themselves the pearl of Christ." He is just as hard on Christian ladies, "putting on a fresh frock every day, and even so unable to get the better of the moth." Some, in pursuit of piety, wear one dress until it falls to pieces even though their trunks bulge with clothes. They spend their money on costly scrolls, lettered in gold and ornamented with jewels, while Christ lies naked at their doorsteps in the persons of the poor. When they give alms they "sound a trumpet" like the woman lately observed with her band of eunuchs handing out coins at the door of Saint Peter's. When a ragged woman ran in front to get a second coin, the grand lady clenched her fist and bloodied her nose.

Satire, however, is not of much help to a person seeking spiritual direction, and because of this Jerome frequently uses the form of a funeral panegyric. One such is his portrait of the ideal theological candidate, Nepotion, a nephew of Heliodorus. He had been a soldier, and when he laid aside his military belt, "he gave all his army savings to the poor. For he had read the words: 'If thou wilt be perfect, sell that thou hast, and give to the poor and follow me.' He kept nothing for himself except a coarse tunic and cloak to protect him from the cold." Although he burned with a desire to enter a monastery, he saw that his duty was to stay with his uncle, "in whom he saw a pattern of every virtue and from whose lessons he could profit at home." Passing through the usual stages he was at last ordained a presbyter. "Good Jesus! how he sobbed and groaned! how he forbade himself food and fled from the eyes of all!" For he looked on the priesthood not as a glory but as a burden. So, he busied himself with acts of charity and mercy and encouraged others to do the same. First in industry among his fellow priests he was last in honor. Widows and virgins he honored as mothers and sisters. In private he forgot the clergyman and submitted to the severities of the monk, only tasting his uncle's dishes, "thus both avoiding superstition and yet keeping to his rule of self- restraint." When he conversed it was to bring forward some biblical text and to listen modestly to what others had to say, offering no opinion of his own but modestly citing what Cyprian and Tertullian, and Hilary had written. "Let others add shilling to shilling, fastening their claws on married ladies' purses and hunting wealth by flattering attention; ... let them possess wealth in the service of a poor Christ such as they never had in the service of a rich devil.... Our dear Nepotion tramples gold underfoot, books are the only thing he desires. But while he despises himself in the flesh and walks abroad in splendid poverty, he yet seeks out everything that may adorn his church."

Had Jerome lived a hundred years earlier, he would no doubt have left us a Book of Martyrs. As it is, the *Letters* take the place of a Lives of the Saints. One such life, in the form of a funeral panegyric, is that of Fabiola, whom Jerome with typical exaggeration speaks of as another Magdalene, her fault being that, contrary to the rules of the Church, she had divorced a worthless husband and married a second time. After the death of her second husband, she did public penance—unusual for a woman of wealth—and devoted the rest of her life to works of charity. "When she was restored to communion, what did she do? Did she forget her sorrows in the midst of happiness? Nay, she preferred to break up and sell all that she could lay hands on of her property and when she had turned it into money she disposed of everything for the benefit of the poor." She founded an infirmary and personally gathered up the sick and helped to care for them. Many people, says Jerome, show mercy with the purse, overlooking the fact that the sufferer is made of the same clay as ourselves. Not so Fabiola. "She was, indeed, such a comforter that many poor people who were well fell to envying the sick." This is not to say that her concerns were limited to the sick: she also supplied clothes and food to the poor, aided monasteries, and traveled the seas to disperse her bounty. When she visited Jerome in Bethlehem she especially endeared herself by asking endless questions about biblical passages. Her desires to put her charities in other hands and flee from Rome were only partly realized. The last that we hear, she was at Ostia—Rome's port city—where she established and helped maintain a hospice for travelers in distress.

In Jerome's eyes the most formidable obstacles in the way of Christian perfection are marriage and the family. Under the Old Covenant, where the rule was, Be fruitful and multiply, marriage was praised and obedience to parents was second only to obedience to God. Not so under the New Covenant, which sets sons against fathers and daughters against mothers, and which commands virginity to all who can receive it. Jerome has the usual things to say against sexual indulgence, and he regards marriage as no more than a concession to fleshly weakness; but his chief objection to it is that it puts a husband or a wife, together with a mountain of worldly cares, between the soul and God. Virginity is nonattachment: as such it is essential for those who are determined in their desire to achieve perfection in the present life. But, with other Fathers of the Church, Jerome also perceived in virginity a mystical dimension. In a set piece, "The Virgin's Profession," addressed to Eustochium, he argues that the virgin Christ is a jealous Bridegroom and demands virginity in the soul that wants to receive his favors. In Jerome's view, marriage belongs to the order brought on by the Fall. "Death came through Eve: life has come through Mary.... As soon as the Son of God set foot on earth, He formed for himself a new household, that as He was adored by Angels in heaven He might have angels also on earth." Everyone worships the thing he loves," says Jerome. "Wherefore we must take all care that abstinence may bring back to Paradise those whom repletion once drove out."

Jerome's letters are not all concerned with personal piety and with clerical ideals. An important group has to do with doctrinal disputes, in which Jerome appears as a formidable and not always kindly defender of Catholic tradition. But everywhere he reveals himself as a deeply spiritual man waging a war against the world, the flesh, and the Devil.

Jean H. Faurot

RECOMMENDED READING

Edition used: Hieronymous, Saint. *Select Letters of St. Jerome.* English translation by F. A. Wright. Cambridge: Harvard University Press, 1933. Eighteen letters, Latin and English, with a brief "Life of Jerome."

Burke, Eugene P. "St. Jerome as Spiritual Director." *In A Monument to Saint Jerome,* pp. 143–170. Edited by Francis X. Murphy. New York: Sheed & Ward, 1952. Develops Jerome's teaching on such topics as renunciation, virginity, prayer, study, and mortification.

Kelly, J. N. D. *Jerome: His Life, Writings, and Controversies.* New York: Harper & Row, 1975. For the general reader by an authority in patristic Christianity.

Murphy, Francis X. "Jerome, Saint." In *New Catholic Encyclopedia,* 7:872–874. New York: McGraw-Hill, 1967. Handy overall account of the man and his work.

THE CONFESSIONS OF SAINT AUGUSTINE

Author: Saint Augustine (354–430)

One of the doctors of the Catholic church, Saint Augustine was raised a Christian but resisted participation in life from that perspective for many years. His mother, Saint Monica, nurtured him in the faith as best she could in spite of his mistresses (one of whom bore him a son), his attraction to generally pagan learning, and later his immersion in heretical (Manichaean) religions. A professor and author in his early thirties, Augustine encountered Saint Ambrose in Milan, converted to orthodoxy, and was baptized in 387. He later became a priest, then bishop of Hippo. His best-known works, written in the period 397–416, include *The Confessions, The City of God,* and *On the Trinity.*

Type and subject of work: Spiritual autobiography

First transcribed: c. 400

MAJOR THEMES

God cannot be the cause of evil; evil is the absence of the good.
Time is nothing except in relation to temporal events.
Faith is wisdom; all values stem from God.

This first, and some will consider the greatest, of autobiographies as we know them in the modern sense, has a very imbalanced structure.

Books one through nine are a kind of backward reflection, covering the period from the author's birth to his religious conversion to Christianity. In books ten through twelve, Augustine no longer tells us about his past life but exercises a theological inquiry into memory, time, and creation. The final chapter, book thirteen, is also on the creation theme but as a confession to God, in rather direct style, of his faith.

Augustine begins by wondering whether one should first pray to God for help or to praise him and whether or not a person (Augustine always uses "man" for what clearly is meant for humanity, generally) must first know God before calling on him for aid. In humility the author asks if there is something in himself that is fit to contain the infinite God. And, he asks, why does God show such concern for this finite man? We learn that Augustine came from a household of believers (with the exception of his father) and learning was an important aspect of his early life. But we read of what Augustine considers the sins he committed as a baby: crying too much over insignificant things, being selfish, and experiencing jealousy. Later he sinned by disobeying his parents. Even when his learning went well, he was guilty of more concern over the fate of characters in classic literature than in the state of his own soul. In games he cheated to win and asks, ironically, if this is the innocence of childhood. His sin, he concludes, was in looking for pleasure, beauty, and truth not in God but in himself.

In the second book Augustine confesses two failings, lust and thievery. He admits to having run wild, sexually, because he could not distinguish between true love and mere casual sexuality. He thinks that he should have listened more carefully to the scriptural admonition that he who is married will be more concerned with pleasing a wife than with God's claim. His lust gripped him in his sixteenth year and was to trouble him for some time to come. The youth apparently had it too easy, partly because his father provided for too many of his wants, caring more for his son's earthly success than for his spiritual growth. As for stealing, Augustine tells of robbing from a pear tree near his family's property, glorying not in the eating of the fruit but in doing that which was forbidden.

In book three we learn that the narrator moved to Carthage and found himself "in the midst of a hissing cauldron of lust." Friendship became perverted by lewdness and then, caught in "a snare of my own choosing," he fell in love. This led to jealousy, fear, anger, and quarreling. At the same time the theater, looked upon with great suspicion by the Church, attracted him. Yet in the midst of this, Augustine recognizes that God watched over him faithfully. While pursuing his ambition to be a good speaker, Augustine was introduced to the work of Cicero, and this encounter with the pagan writer had an enormous impact on the future saint. It altered his prayers and his search turned from empty dreams to the "passion for the wisdom of eternal truth." And with the financial support of his mother, his father having died two years previously, when Augustine was seventeen, he pursued the study of Scripture with something beyond the understanding of the proud. The youth kept to many of his bad habits, however, but his mother, Monica (later to be canonized as a saint), prayed for him unceasingly, particularly after a dream that consoled her about her son and after a bishop told her to persevere in her prayers and they would be answered.

The years from age nineteen to twenty-eight are the time span covered in book four. During this period, Augustine taught the art of public speaking. It was a time, he writes, when he was led astray and when he led others astray as well. He also had a mistress then, whom he does not name, and she was his only lover at the time—he remained faithful to her. As a writer his skills developed and he won a poetry competition while flirting with astrology, which he later dropped. The severe illness of a friend was the cause of much reflection for Augustine. What baptism meant to the ill young man impressed the author deeply and when the friend died, Augustine became frightened in contemplating his own end. This did not keep him from writing a multivolume work he called *Beauty and Proportion*, the manuscript of which was lost and never recovered. Some thoughts on those topics, however, are shared with the reader of *The Confessions*. Among the conclusions is Augustine's notion that in goodness there is unity, but in evil some kind of disunion.

The next segment of *The Confessions* represents the autobiographer's twenty-ninth year, a time when he was drawn ever closer to God. Initially his interest was in Manichaean theology. (Mani, the founder of this heretical sect, advocated a dualistic doctrine that regarded matter as evil, the spirit as good.) For nearly nine years Augustine had hoped to hear Faustus, the Manichaean bishop of great reputation, develop the theory of Mani. When at last the opportunity came, great disappointment accompanied the event. "He was a great decoy of the devil," Augustine decided, one who was able to win disciples through charm rather than reason, his scholarship being very weak.

After this experience Augustine decided to teach in Rome and he left Carthage. Upon arrival in his new home he became very ill but still had no desire to be baptized. Upon recovery, he began teaching literature and public speaking but later applied for work in Milan where he met Bishop Ambrose who was to have a profoundly positive impact on him. Augustine's interest in the Church grew and he became a catechumen but chose not to go beyond that preparatory step at that time.

The faith and faithfulness of Augustine's mother is told in book six. Her remarkable devotion to her son is indicated, as is the influence of Bishop Ambrose which was hinted at in the previous chapter. Augustine went to hear the great preacher every Sunday and he came to realize that the web of deception woven around him by others could be broken. "From now on I began to prefer the Catholic teaching." But there was no instantaneous change in Augustine's habits. He calls himself eager for fame, wealth, and marriage. An obstacle to this last was his mistress, who left him, with their son, vowing to accept the affections of no other man as she returned to Africa. Now thirty, Augustine was increasingly attracted to the Church, "But not so fast! This life is too Sweet." So Augustine prepared to marry; his proposal was accepted, but the nuptials were put off for two years. Returning at least in part to his old ways, he took another mistress.

The author recognizes in the next book that his adolescence was gone and he was approaching mature manhood, yet his behavior grew more disgraceful and his self-delusion greater. From such introductory remarks, Augustine makes the transition to a discussion of the nature of evil. His conclusion is that for God, "evil does not exist." Evil is a lack, an absence of good. Anything that has substance is good, therefore evil can have no substance. Furthermore, anyone who finds fault with any portion of God's creation is bereft of reason. They fail to comprehend that wickedness is not a substance but a perversion. As this segment ends, Augustine tells how he was slowly being drawn into Christ's orbit, particularly through intensive reading of the Scriptures.

The story of the episode that finally led to Augustine's total embracing of Christianity comes in book eight. He writes of the influence that he felt from talking with Ambrose's spiritual father, Simplicianus. Augustine was moved, too, in reading the story of Saint Anthony, the Egyptian monk who struggled so long and successfully to remain chaste, a condition the narrator admits to having approached this way in prayer: "Give me chastity and continence, but not yet." A terrific struggle, sometimes manifesting itself physically, took place in Augustine as he seemed to undergo a spiritual tug-of-war for his soul's commitment. He got to the point where he tore his hair, hammered his forehead with his fists, and the like. The future saint was at once both attracted to heaven and resisting the call. The final push came when he randomly opened up a book containing the epistles of Saint Paul and read the first lines his eyes fell on, lines counseling against reveling and drunkenness. Needing no further sign, Augustine rushed to tell his mother of his newfound strength in faith, much to Monica's great joy.

Book nine may be considered the last chapter of the first—and considerably longest—section of *The Confessions*. Here we read of Augustine's surrender to God: through Ambrose, through the Scriptures, and through like-minded companions who were baptized into the faith as Augustine was. This proved an emotionally overwhelming experience for him. He also tells of particular miracles: of Ambrose's vision telling him where the uncorrupted bodies of two holy martyrs were to be located and how these "relics" were the occasion of cures of various physical maladies for a number of persons. While once again praising the virtues of his mother—who, like other good women of that era, understood her subservient role to her husband (master, according to the author)—Augustine renders a quite unflattering description of his father. But the writer believes that through the efforts of the former, who died at age fifty-six, the latter was "won" for Christ.

There appears to be quite a break in the Augustinian technique beginning with book ten. The emphasis now is not so much on what happened but on examining what certain experiences might mean. What is God? he asks, having searched among all the things of the earth, the sea, the chasms of the deep, even into himself. The conclusion is that "He is the Life of the life of my soul." Then comes a relatively long reflection on memory, where Augustine sees all as being preserved separately, according to category. He marvels at this ability to store up enormous treasures of knowledge and the senses, even suggesting that certain things must have been in his mind even before he had learned them. But God lies beyond memory, in himself, above us, because "You are Truth." God's existence is not established by logic but must be accepted as a premise. Augustine asks the question why it is that when he preaches truth it sometimes engenders hostility, "although men love happiness which is simply the enjoyment of truth"? He decides that we love what is not true by pretending that it is.

One of the best-known sections of *The Confessions* is next, containing the author's attempt to come to grips with the idea of time. The problem arises for him out of the Bible because there the concept of creation out of nothing is revealed. This, some had said, raised the issue of an absolute beginning, something that human experience simply could not conceive. (What happened *before* the creation always comes to mind.) Augustine responded by explaining that time does not have the same kind of being as events that occur in time. It is appropriate to ask particular questions about a sequence of events but not what happened before all events. Time, he observed, has no substantiality outside of its relation to temporal events.

Books twelve and thirteen both contain analyses of creation with a look also, into the validity of the Scriptures. Most of Augustine's efforts here are concentrated on the opening of Genesis. Yet the two chapters are quite different in approach. In the first part of this volume (one-nine), we have an author who tells us about a life as if he were an objective viewer, almost another person looking in on himself and telling us about what he sees. In the next part (ten-twelve), the narrator and the person whose life is being retold are one. The final section (thirteen) still finds the "two Augustines," but the tone here is considerably altered. As critics have observed, the writer is no longer presented as one in pursuit of a heavenly goal but rather as one who communicates and who confesses to God directly his own understanding that faith is wisdom. The entire volume leads to this final point. Some have suggested that the last book, perhaps even the final four, was appended to Augustine's work in later editions. But when we see that there is a unity of approach leading up to the final confession of faith, we are no longer concerned about unity of tone and voice.

Harry James Cargas

RECOMMENDED READING

Edition used: Augustine, Saint. *Confessions*. Translated by R. S. Pine-Coffin. New York: Penguin Books, 1961.

——. *City of God*. Translated by Marcus Dods. New York: Modern Library, 1950. An initial Christian philosophy of history.

——. *On the Psalms*. Translated by Scholastica Hebgin and Felicitas Corrigan. 2 vols. New York: Newman Press, 1960. Augustine's theological reflections on thirty-seven psalms are here rendered with excellent notes by the translators.

——. *The Trinity*. Translated by Stephen McKenna. Washington, D.C.: Catholic University Press, 1963. The epic treatment, influential and comprehensive.

Pope, Hugh. *St. Augustine of Hippo*. Garden City, N.Y.: Doubleday, Image Books, 1961. A study of the saint's life, his thought, and his influence on Western civilization.

THE CONFERENCES OF JOHN CASSIAN

Author: John Cassian (c. 365–c. 435)

Authors argue inconclusively concerning John Cassian's origins, birthplace, and early life, though these were clearly in the West and probably in Gaul. He was drawn while still young to the monastic way of life and entered a monastery in Bethlehem. With his community's blessing he spent, first, seven years and then returned for an indefinite period to Egypt in search of deeper monastic wisdom. Toward the end of the fourth century he went to Constantinople where he was ordained a deacon by John Chrysostom. His connection with this confessor of the faith required his leaving the city in 404. He went first to Rome, then to Marseille where he founded two monasteries, one for women and one for men. Besides the *Conferences* he wrote (c. 420) *The Twelve books of the Institutes of the Coenobia* and *The Seven Books on the Incarnation of the Lord Against Nestorius*.

Type and subject of work: Practical spiritual treatises on basic questions concerning the monastic life

First transcribed: c. 420

MAJOR THEMES

The goal of life is the kingdom of God; the aim is charity, which consists in purity of heart.

The monastic life is clearly a contemplative life.

No virtue can come to full term or endure without the grace of discernment.

There are three causes of spiritual dryness: carelessness, the Devil, and God, who permits it so that we can better know ourselves and know that all is gift.

We are tried for three different reasons: for our probation, for our improvement, and sometimes because we deserve it.

To attain to continual prayer we must clear away our vices, lay a foundation of humility, build up the virtues, quiet the mind and heart, and rise to contemplation of God.

Friendships are constant because the friends are detached from possessions, prefer the desires of the other, seek first the blessing of love and peace, forsake all anger and help each other in this, and realize that death will come and this friendship will pass into an eternal love.

The twenty-four conferences, reportedly coming from fifteen abbots or spiritual fathers who flourished in the deserts of northern Egypt in the last decades of the fourth century, are divided into three groups. Each group or part has its own proper preface. The first ten conferences, dedicated to Bishop Leontius and the monk Helladius, seem to be the more basic. The next seven are reported as coming from John's first sojourn of seven years in Egypt. They are dedicated to two abbots, Honoratus and Eucherius, who became bishops. The final seven are dedicated to four fellow monks. In his preface to the third section Cassian points out that the purpose of the conferences is not to proclaim the miracles of the Fathers but to set forth what is necessary for a perfect life.

The *Institutes* which John had written just prior to the *Conferences* were concerned primarily with the externals of the monastic life as it was lived in the coenobium. The *Conferences* are more concerned with the interior life and the anchoritic life or the life of the hermit. There does not seem to be any perceptible order in which the conferences are arranged, apart from a chronological order that may well be part of a literary fiction. The subject matter is very variant. Some of the conferences are rich in teaching that is still relevant, for example, the two conferences of Abbot Isaac on prayer, and Abbot Joseph's conference on friendship. Others are more esoteric, for example, Abbot Theonas's conference on nocturnal illusions. Some are concerned with a mythology that interests us less today, such as Abbot Serenus's discourse on angels and devils. The teaching on grace and free will, most notably in Abbot Chaeremon's third conference, has proved the most controversial part of Cassian's writings and in the West has won for him the label of semi-Pelagian.

The opening conference, the first of Abbot Moses, treats of what is indeed the most basic question: the goal and aim of the monastic life. The goal is the kingdom of God; the aim is charity "which consists in purity of heart." If purity of heart remains whole and unharmed in us, then nothing can injure us even if we are forced to omit some of the other subordinate virtues. "To cling always to God and to the things of God—this must be our major effort, this must be the road that the heart follows unswervingly."

For Cassian, the monastic life is clearly a contemplative life. But "contemplation of God can be understood in more than one fashion. For God is not solely known by way of that astonished gaze at his ungraspable nature, something hidden thus far in that hope that comes with what has been promised us. He can also be sensed in the magnificence of his creation, in the spectacle of his justice, and in the help he extends each day to the running of the world."

Cassian finds the signs of God both in persons and in nature: "He can be sensed too when with well-purified minds we consider what he has achieved in each generation by means of his saints. He can be sensed when we gaze with trembling hearts at that power of his which controls, guides, and rules everything, when we contemplate his immense knowledge and his knowing look which the secrets of the heart cannot evade. His presence is known when we meditate on the fact that the sands of the sea are numbered by him, that he keeps a count of the waves. Astounded, we reflect that every drop of rain, every day and every hour of all the centuries, everything past and everything to come are all facts of which he is aware. Overwhelmed with wonder we think of that unspeakable mercy of his which allows him to endure with unfailing patience the numberless crimes committed at every moment while he watches."

In a later conference (nineteen) John distinguishes the aim of the cenobitic life, which is "to mortify and crucify all desires and, according to the salutary command of evangelical perfection, to take no thought for the morrow" and the eremitical life, which seeks "to set the mind free from all earthly things and to unite it, as far as human frailty allows, with Christ." The cenobite, while he is cared for by the monastery, is involved in its affairs. The anchorite is to have attained that degree of detachment, that he can take care of himself and yet remain fully free. "He is truly and not partially perfect who with equal imperturbability can put us with the squalor of the wilderness in the desert, as well as the infirmities of the brethren in the coenobium."

Obviously there is need of discernment, in choosing the way in which one should walk. The second conference is about this. "No virtue can come to full term or endure without the grace of discernment." It is discernment that leads the enduring monk to God and that keeps all the virtues intact. The first evidence of humility is when everything done and thought of is submitted to the scrutiny of one's spiritual father. "It is clear that the road to perfection is revealed by the Lord to no man who is in a position to have teachers, who in fact has small regard for the ideas and the practices of older men."

Monastic formation was summed up in the formula "follow whatever you see our elders do or teach ... because if men have good and simple ideas on all things and are anxious faithfully to copy whatever they see taught or done by their elders, instead of discussing it, then the knowledge of all things will follow through experience." Some things can be learned only by experience. This has been the monastic tradition, which has suffered much in our times, Cassian writes, when candidates want to discuss things and understand them before doing them.

The third conference is on renunciation. Cassian likes to set things forth in threes (in this conference he speaks first of the three kinds of vocations or ways in which we are called): The first renunciation has to do with the body, riches, the goods of this world; the second, our past with all its vices and passions; and the third, which withdraws the spirit from the visible to contemplate the invisible: "Our passion is for the unseen."

The next conference tells us that there are three causes of spiritual dryness: carelessness, the Devil, and God, who permits it so that we can better know ourselves and know that all is gift. This helps us to grow. In this conference we also hear of the carnal, the natural, and the spiritual (taken from Pauline inspiration), which equal the cold, the lukewarm, and the hot.

The fifth conference, that of Abbot Serapion, treats of what is one of the better-known themes of Cassian, the eight principal faults: gluttony, fornication, pride, vainglory, covetousness, anger, spiritual sloth (accidie), and dejection. Both experience and Scripture assure us that they can be overcome and eradicated only with the help of God, no matter how great our own exertions, energy, and freewill.

Abbot Theodore's conference (six) about the death of the saints again comes up in threes: There are three things in this world, the good, bad, and indifferent. A deed, though, must be judged not by the result but by the purpose of the doer. The abbot also tells us that we are tried for three different reasons: for our probation, for our improvement, and sometimes because we deserve it.

The conferences of Abbot Isaac on prayer (nine and ten) are important. Our aim—indeed, we are so commanded, writes Cassian—is continual prayer. To attain to this we must clear away our vices, lay a foundation of humility, build up the virtues, quiet the mind and heart (the father warns against excessive work), and rise to contemplation of God. There are four kinds of prayer, exemplified by Jesus and Saint Paul: *supplication*, crying out from our sinfulness; *prayer*, committing ourselves to God; *intercession*, seeking the good for ourselves and others—we should never ask anything not found in the Lord's Prayer, of which Cassian gives an insightful commentary; and *thanksgiving*, acknowledging the good received in all. From here we enter into nonconceptual prayer, the perfect prayer wherein the one who prays no longer knows he prays.

Prayer is difficult because it calls for steadfastness, persistence, and self-gift. It will call forth from us all the works of mercy; not my will, but yours be done. We must enter our chamber (turn within), close the door (leave the noises of the world behind), and pray in secret (without any display).

It is in conference ten that we have Cassian's most precious contribution, a concrete practical method for entering into deep prayer. A word, received from a father or from the Scriptures (he proposes the first verse of Psalm 69), is interiorized until it comes down to "the poverty of a single word" that centers our whole being on God in love. "This prayer centers on no contemplation of some image or other. It is masked by no attendant sounds or words. It is ... an insatiable thrust of the soul. Free from what is sensed and, ... the soul pours itself out to God." There is no doubt that for Cassian this is the summit of human activity. As he says in the third conference of Abbot Thomas (twenty-three): "Contemplation, i.e., meditation on God, is the one thing, the value of which all the merits of our righteous acts, all our aims at virtue, come short of."

But Cassian is not inhuman or totally otherworldly. Besides all the very down-to-earth, practical teaching on the human struggle with vice and for virtue, he also emphasizes the role of human friendship. Of course, it is not those transient kinds of friendship that depend on "different kinds of connexions either of gain or desires, or kinship, or business, so when any occasion for separation intervenes they are broken." It is rather friendship that is based on virtue or genuine goodness. Such friendships are constant because the friends are detached from possessions, prefer the desires of the other, seek first the blessing of love and peace, forsake all anger and help each other in this, and realize that death will come and this friendship will pass into an eternal love.

There are many other riches to be found within these conferences that bring to us one of the oldest spiritual traditions in the Christian community, such as wise instruction on fasting (twenty-one) and mortification (twenty-four) and Abbot Nesteros's teaching on spiritual knowledge, exploring the different senses of Scripture (fourteen).

M. Basil Pennington

RECOMMENDED READING

Edition used: Cassian, John. The Conferences. Writings of the Nicene and Post-Nicene Fathers, ser. 2, vol. 11. Grand Rapids, Mich.: Eerdmans, 1955. This edition omits two of the conferences: 12 and 22.

———. *Conferences*. Translation and Preface of Colm Luibheid. Introduction by Owen Chadwick. Classics of Western Spirituality. New York: Paulist Press, 1985. This is the most available English text, with a good introduction. However, it contains only nine of the conferences: 1–3, 9–11, 14–15 and 18.

Chadwick, Owen. *John Cassian*. Cambridge: Cambridge University Press, 1950. The authoritative study on Cassian.

Chitty, Derwas. *The Desert a City: An Introduction to the Study of Egyptian and Palestinian Monasticism Under the Christian Empire*. Oxford: Basil Blackwell, 1966. This study places Cassian and his conferences fully in context.

Maximovitch, John. "St. John Cassian and the Foundation of Orthodox Monasticism in the West." In *The Orthodox Word*, vol. 5, no. 2, pp. 57–71. San Francisco: Orthodox Books & Icons, 1969.

MYSTICAL THEOLOGY

Author: Dionysius, the Pseudo-Areopagite (fl. c. 500)
Little in fact is known of the author apart from what can be adduced
from his writings. This alleged disciple of Saint Paul and first bishop of
Athens is commonly identified today as a late fifth- early sixth-century
Syrian monk. We have three other significant treatises ascribed to him:
The Heavenly Hierarchy, The Ecclesiastical Hierarchy, and *The Divine Names.*
He has had immense influence on Christian spirituality through the
commentaries written on his works by Maximus the Confessor in the
seventh century. In the ninth century he was translated into Latin by
John Scotus Erigena. Thomas Aquinas often cited him as an authority.

Type and subject of work: A strongly Neoplatonic treatise on mystical
theology

First transcribed: c. 500

MAJOR THEMES

*The Deity possesses all the positive attributes of the universe, yet more
strictly it does not, for it transcends them all.*
The Deity is beyond all distinctions of good and evil.
*By rejecting all knowledge we can possess a knowledge that exceeds under-
standing, the Darkness of Unknowing.*
*This negative method must be wholly distinguished from the use of positive
statements.*

The higher we ascend, the more we are reduced to silence.

The universal Cause, transcending all, is neither impersonal nor lifeless nor irrational nor without understanding, but is beyond all qualities, faculties, categories of rational thought.

The Deity is not Spirit, Sonship, or Fatherhood.

This very short treatise of five chapters is, as Dionysius himself shows, the pinnacle of his teaching.

The *Mystical Theology*, which begins with a prayer to the Trinity, is addressed to Timothy—perhaps Saint Paul's disciple by that name. In regard to his own teaching, Dionysius claims the authority of Saint Bartholomew the Apostle.

The chapters are geared toward motivating the reader to seek union with God in mystical contemplation rather than being content with some rational understanding of him. For this purpose the author insists that we not only purify ourselves morally but even leave behind rational thought and sense experience. Like many writers of this genre, he issues a warning against sharing this treatise with the uninitiated. The work falls very clearly on the side of the theology of negation or apophaticism.

We truly get to know God not by apprehending him with our understanding. The reasoning powers must enter into a passive stillness, allowing the highest faculty in the human person to possess God with a knowledge that exceeds understanding. This knowledge is a darkness that is beyond light. At this level we praise God by a transcendent hymnody; namely, by letting go of all thoughts and images and simply giving our naked self to God to be united with him.

The affirmative way begins with what is most like the Deity and then surpasses it. The negative way begins by denying what is most different from the Deity and arises to the negation of all categories of thought. Dionysius illustrates this assertion by tracing his own path through his previous writings. In *Symbolic Divinity* (no longer extant) the search for the Deity began with metaphorical titles drawn from the world of sense and applied to the nature of God, such as his functions, instruments of activity, places, passions, and emotions. In *The Divine Names* the author begins from the titles of God formed by the intellect. Finally, in the *Outlines of Divinity* (no longer extant) it is the revelations that come through the Sacred Scriptures that are his source. Dionysius notes that the higher one ascends, the greater is the brevity of speech. And this, his highest treatise, is the briefest of all.

He sums up his teaching in his last sentence: "The Deity transcends all affirmation by being the perfect and unique Cause of all things, and transcends all negation by the pre-eminence of Its simple and absolute nature—free from every limitation and beyond them all"—in a word, incomprehensible.

An earlier age of faith more in tune with mystical experience held Dionysius in higher regard than does our present age, which is more rationalistic in its theological approach. Orthodox Christian theologians are a bit uncomfortable with him because of what they see as an excessive emphasis on the Godhead and unity, to the detriment of the substantiality of the Trinity of Persons. There is some fear that the Neoplatonic philosopher eclipses the theologian. Dionysius's writings do suffer from an obscurity of style that makes translation uncertain. This obscurity does not arise from a lack of skill on the part of the author but out of a desire to conceal the lofty truths he is dealing with from the ridicule of the profane. He is very concise, especially in this last treatise, uses Platonic expressions, invents new words and striking new expressions. Some see him as having an important role in Christian dialogue with Eastern religions.

M. Basil Pennington

RECOMMENDED READING

Edition used: Dionysius the Pseudo-Areopagite. *The Divine Names and Mystical Theology.* Translated by James Jones. Milwaukee: University of Milwaukee Press, 1980.

———. *The Divine Names.* Translated by the Editors of the Shrine of Wisdom. Brook, Surrey, England: Shrine of Wisdom, 1957. God is first considered in his undifferentiated aspect; then his differentiated aspect is examined in terms of his attributes represented by the divine names.

Dionysius Areopagita. *The Works of Dionysius the Areopagite.* Translated by the Reverend John Parker. London and Oxford: J. Parker & Co. 1897–1899. Includes the *Divine Names,* the *Mystic Theology,* the *Heavenly Hierarchy,* and the *Ecclesiastical Hierarchy.*

Maximus Confessor. *The Ascetic Life, The Four Centuries on Charity.* Translated and annotated by Polycarp Sherwood. Westminster, Md.: Newman Press, 1955. The writings of Maximus helped to restore the balance between Neoplatonism and Christian orthodoxy; his commentaries on Dionysius enabled the work of Dionysius to have a profound effect on Christian spirituality.

Sparrow-Simpson, W. J. "The Influence of Dionysius in Religious History." In *The Divine Names and the Mystical Theology.* Translated by C. E. Rolt. London: Society for Promoting Christian Knowledge, 1940. The best study available in English concerning Dionysius's overall place in Christian tradition.

RULE FOR MONASTERIES

Author: Benedict of Nursia (c. 480–550)

Benedict was born in the region of Nursia, northeast of Rome; the traditional date of 480 cannot be far from the truth. He went to Rome to study and underwent a religious conversion that led him to renounce the world. He first joined some ascetics at Enfide, east of Rome, and then, for three years, lived in complete solitude at Subiaco. He was later joined by many disciples for whom he established twelve monasteries. Persecution led him to withdraw to Monte Cassino, eighty miles south of Rome, where he established what became a large, flourishing cenobium. He gained a widespread reputation as a holy man, endowed with special charisms. He died around the middle of the century.

Type and subject of work: A monastic rule with spiritual teaching and practical norms

First transcribed: c. 525

MAJOR THEMES

The Rule *is for those who wish to return to God by the way of obedience.*

It is through patience that we share in the passion of Christ and merit to share in his kingdom.

There are four kinds of monks: hermits or anchorites, who live alone; sarabites, detestable men who live in small groups and do their own will; gyrovagues, who spend their lives going from one monastery to another; and cenobites, who live in community under a rule and an abbot.

Obedience is the first step of humility, which comes naturally to those who cherish Christ above all.

In the twelve steps of humility the whole of Benedictine mysticism is summed up, from conversion, through interior purification and exterior expression, to the perfect love of God where all is now done no longer out of fear but out of love of Christ, good habits, and delight in virtue.

Benedict of Nursia's *Rule for Monasteries* has had an immense influence on the shaping of Western Christianity. Its influence grew slowly as popes sent forth Benedictine monks to evangelize the nations. Then under the influence of Benedict of Aniane, with imperial assistance, it became normative for all monasteries in the West and has remained the dominant monastic rule ever since.

The *Rule* is made up of a rather extensive prologue and seventy-three chapters, the last few of which seem to have been added to a completed text and show a somewhat different influence from that of the *Rule of the Master*, which seems to have been the main influence on the *Rule*. The influences of Basil the Great and John Cassian are evident, and they are referred to in the *Rule*, the latter implicitly.

The prologue is a paternal admonition, rich in spiritual teaching. Benedict writes the *Rule* for the one who wishes to return to God by the way of obedience. This calls for repentance and good works. Saint Benedict seeks to establish a school of the Lord's service that is moderate in its demands but that will lead to the heights: "As we progress in this way of life and in faith, we shall run in the path of God's commandments, our hearts overflowing with the inexpressible delight of love." It is through patience that we share in the passion of Christ and merit to share in his kingdom.

In the first chapter the holy legislator speaks of the different kinds of monks: hermits or anchorites, who live alone; sarabites, detestable men who live in small groups and do their own will; gyrovagues, who spend their lives going from one monastery to another; and cenobites, who live in community under a rule and an abbot. These latter are the strongest, and for them Benedict writes his *Rule*.

Therefore, in chapter two Benedict immediately speaks about the abbot, the spiritual father who is believed to hold the place of Christ in the monastery and has supreme authority. He is, however, always to remember that he must answer to the Lord, and he is to seek constantly the advice of the brethren: "Everything is to be done with counsel." The abbot is to be elected by the brethren. He, in turn, names his prior—his second in command—and a cellarer, who administers all the temporalities under the direction of the abbot.

Benedict next devotes four chapters to basic monastic spirituality. Chapter four is a concise catalogue of the "instruments of good work," going from the decalogue to the ultimate piece of advice: If you fail in everything else "never despair of the mercy of God."

Humility is the Benedictine way; and obedience, which is the "first step of humility, which comes naturally to those who cherish Christ above all," is treated extensively in chapter five and frequently comes up in the rest of the *Rule*. Silence, also, merits a chapter, as an expression and safeguard of humility, before Benedict begins his central chapter on the steps of humility. In these twelve steps the whole of Benedictine mysticism is summed up, from conversion, through interior purification and exterior expression, to the perfect love of God where all is now done no longer out of fear but out of love of Christ, good habits, and delight in virtue.

"Nothing is to be preferred to the work of God"—that is, the community prayer, which is drawn from the Church of Rome and unites the monk with the Church. The next eleven chapters (eight–eighteen) lay down its order and then chapter nineteen speaks of inner dispositions, giving a simple, all-embracing rule: "Let the mind be in harmony with the voice." A brief but powerful chapter follows on personal prayer: "We must know that God regards our purity of heart and tears of compunction, not our many words." He will return to this when he speaks of the oratory. Provision is made for reading to nourish this prayer, during the work of God, during meals, before the final service of the day, and in private during the day.

Before launching into a penal code, Benedict has a chapter on deans who will assist the abbot in a large monastery, and another on a very important element in the monk's life that profoundly affects all others: his sleep. Eight chapters (twenty-three–thirty) lay down not only the penalties but the great pastoral care the abbot must exert in regard to the erring: "The abbot must exercise the utmost care and concern for the wayward brothers."

After offering a chapter on the cellarer, who is to be like a father to the whole community, Benedict considers the temporalities and temporal services, always bringing in theological principles to ground his very practical provisions: "Regard all utensils and goods of the monastery as sacred vessels of the altar." "Whoever needs less should thank God ... whoever needs more should feel humble." "To each according to his need." "The brothers should serve one another ... for such service increases reward and fosters love." "Care of the sick must rank above and before all else, so that they may truly be served as Christ, for he said: 'I was sick and you visited me.' "

As Benedict says in concluding his summary list of monastic works: "The workshop where we are to toil faithfully at all these tasks is the enclosure of the monastery and stability in the community." Benedict has a sense of the monastery as the monks' place; therefore travel is carefully regulated, as is the reception of guests. Christ comes in these latter, especially when they are poor; therefore, they are due great honor and all humane care.

There is a detailed code concerning the admission of new members: "Do not grant newcomers to the monastic life an easy entry ... test the spirits to see if they are from God." Priests are esteemed, but as monks they are to find their place in the ranks of the brethren: "The monks keep their rank in the monastery according to the date of their entry."

Chapter seventy-two is one of the most beautiful chapters in the *Rule:* On Good Zeal: "To their fellow monks they show the pure love of brothers; to God, loving fear; to their abbot, unfeigned and humble love. Let them prefer nothing whatever to Christ, and may he bring us all together to everlasting life."

In a final chapter, Benedict humbly protests that his *Rule* is but for beginners. For those who want to go further, he points to the Scriptures —"What page, what passage of the inspired books of the Old and New Testament is not the truest guides for human life?"—and to John Cassian and Basil the Great.

M. Basil Pennington

RECOMMENDED READING

Edition used: Benedict of Nursia. *1980: The Rule of St. Benedict in Latin and English with Notes.* Edited by Timothy Fry, O.S.B. Collegeville, Minn.: Liturgical Press, 1981.

———. *The Rule of the Master.* Translated by Luke Eberle. Cistercian Studies Series, vol. 6. Kalamazoo, Mich.: Cistercian Publications, 1977. This more extensive and less balanced rule is considered to be Benedict's most proximate source. A study of it brings out Benedict's moderating wisdom.

De Vogue, Adalbert. *The Rule of Saint Benedict: A Doctrinal and Spiritual Commentary.* Cistercian Studies Series, vol. 54. Kalamazoo, Mich.: Cistercian Publications, 1983. This concise commentary, written by the foremost scholar in Benedictine studies in our times, bases contemporary interpretations on the most solid scholarship and shares a depth of spiritual wisdom that can come only from a prolonged, serious living of the *Rule.*

McCann, Justin. *Saint Benedict.* New York: Doubleday, 1958. A widely accepted, objective study of the life of Saint Benedict.

Rees, Daniel et al. *Consider Your Call: A Theology of Monastic Life Today.* Cistercian Studies Series, vol. 18. Kalamazoo, Mich.: Cistercian Publications, 1983. A large group of qualified scholars from the English Benedictine Congregation have collaborated to explore the living of the *Rule* today.

Wathen, Ambrose G. *Silence: The Meaning in the Rule of Saint Benedict*. Cistercian Studies Series, vol. 22. Kalamazoo, Mich.: Cistercian Publications, 1983. Beyond its value as a thorough study of a basic element of Benedictine spirituality, Wathen's volume has a special utility in that it gives a comparative introduction for all the Western monastic rules that preceded Benedict's.

Pastoral Care

Author: Saint Gregory the Great (c. 540–604)

A civil administrator who became a monk and used his family inheritance to found seven monasteries, Gregory accepted the office of bishop of Rome with reluctance. He did much to revive spirituality in his day and through his vigor and executive ability set the course of the Church for the next one thousand years. Missions, charity, worship, and education all received his attention. Besides attending to his administrative duties, he preached and wrote extensively, and he is considered, with Saints Ambrose, Augustine, and Jerome, one of the teachers (*doctores ecclesiae*) whose writings convey most purely the Catholic tradition.

Type and subject of work: Exhortations to the secular clergy

First transcribed: c. 590

Major Themes

So great are the dangers that accompany the office of bishop, no one should accept it who can in good conscience refuse it.

A bishop worthy of his calling combines an active with a contemplative life.

Those who rule in Christ's stead should combine discipline with compassion.

In preaching, a bishop should make every effort to suit his admonition to the conditions of his hearers.

This is a book about the active life. The writings of Saint Augustine of Hippo had familiarized the Western Church with the distinction between the claims of "the two lives," and although Augustine had praised the life of contemplation above that of action, he had also said that it would not be right for a person worthy of being entrusted with the active ministry of the Church to hold back from the troubles that go with a life in the world in order to engage in study and contemplation. Gregory the Great followed Augustine in this as in most of his teachings. He wrote his *Book of Morals* for the benefit of contemplatives; but he wrote *Pastoral Care* for the secular priesthood, being, as Dom Butler says, "the first to lay down the master principles that should regulate the lives of the pastoral clergy."

Pastoral Care is a book of moderate length. The first two parts, which make up less than a third of the whole, are directly concerned with the requirements of the office of bishop. The third and longest part is a guide to preaching and counseling. The fourth is a brief conclusion on the dangers of pride to those in high office.

Part one has to do with who should and who should not be made bishop. Saint Paul said that those who desire that office desire a good thing, but he added by way of warning that a bishop must be blameless in his life. What he meant, says Gregory, was: "I praise what you seek, but acquaint yourselves first with what you are seeking, lest by neglecting to take the measure of your fitness, you become the more blameworthy and detestable, in that you hasten to be seen by all on the pinnacle of honor." Gregory mentions the example of Isaiah, who said, "Lo, here am I, send me"; but he counterbalances this example with the case of Jeremiah, who protested, "Ah, Lord God, behold, I cannot speak for I am a child." Both men, says Gregory, responded out of love: Jeremiah, zealous for the contemplative life, out of love for God; Isaiah, desiring the active life, out of love for his neighbor. "The one feared that by preaching he should forfeit the benefits of quiet contemplation; the other that by not preaching he suffer harm from lack of arduous work." But Jeremiah did not long resist, and Isaiah did not venture upon the ministry until he had been purged. Gregory, who had himself tried to hide when he learned that he was about to be made bishop of Rome, here reflects not merely on the dangers that beset the man who is raised to high office —he may forget all his good intentions and not merely stumble but cause others to stumble— but also on the sin that a man commits who, devoted to contemplation and thinking only of his own advantage, disregards the needs of his neighbors.

Gregory is particularly concerned that the candidate for bishop be a person of genuine religious experience. It is not enough for him to have mastered spiritual precepts through study; he must also have carried them into practice. Not only must his outer life be beyond reproach; he must be preeminently a man of prayer, for nothing is more futile than having as an intercessor a person who is out of favor with the incensed person. Gregory wrote, as he must have lived, under a calm dread of "the Judge within," who "first sees invisibly" what is in the heart and "afterward reprehends by open punishment." "Wherefore, let the man who is still fettered with worldly desires take heed lest, by arousing the anger of the strict Judge for taking complacency in his position of glory, he become the author of ruin to his subjects."

Part two, headed "The Life of the Pastor," reminds the prelate that, in addition to performing the functions of his office, he must maintain a life of rectitude. As is characteristic of his method, Gregory deals with his subject in terms of contraries. The bishop must be pure in thought and exemplary in conduct; know how to keep silent and how to speak to advantage; be aloof in contemplation and sociable in sympathy; be meek toward the godly and bold toward sinners.

We do not find in *Pastoral Care* any emphasis on ceremonial holiness such as characterizes the notion of priesthood in the Old Testament. Instead Gregory places the emphasis on purity of heart, calling to mind the dread of the Judge within, which purifies the mind from being tainted either by spiritual presumption or by unclean thoughts—not that any man can keep these from entering his mind, but that he must repulse and overcome them. So also, in his outward behavior, the priest is obliged not merely to do what is righteous in the midst of a corrupt world but also to take a lead in doing good and in showing mercy.

On the subject of speech, Gregory is mainly concerned to have the bishop speak out. "For just as incautious speech leads men into error, so, too, unseasonable silence leaves in error those who might have been instructed." Moreover, he must speak not merely to his flock but in defense of his flock before worldly potentates. But always the important thing is that his speech be "not a mere torrent of words" but words suited to "produce a progeny of righteous thoughts in the heart of his hearers."

An ever-recurring problem for the Christian who is living in the world is to harmonize a spirit of meekness with the force necessary to resist evil. When a bishop corrects his subjects he must keep in mind that while he punishes a fault in virtue of his authority, in his own person he is nothing above the brother whom he corrects. Both humility and discipline must be preserved; and the ruler must take care lest he mistake sloth for humility and by relaxing discipline lose his authority and harm the Church.

Gregory never loses sight of the claims of the life of the spirit and of the need for pastors to remember that Christians are strangers and pilgrims in the world, their citizenship being in heaven. He uses as his example the apostle Paul, who was transported into paradise and saw things that cannot be spoken, but who let no detail of the life of his churches go unattended; for example, the marital problems in the church at Corinth. Allegorically, Gregory points to Moses going in and out of the Tabernacle: "While within he is caught up in contemplation, outside he devotes himself to the affairs of the weak." Many pastors, he says, rejoice in the business of the outside world and never regard the interior matters that they should teach others, with the result that those who want to make spiritual progress are discouraged and turn away. But some, he says, err in the opposite direction, not giving enough care to external matters, so that their flock, not finding in their pastor a compassionate heart, are unsympathetic to his words of exhortation.

How far should the bishop pay attention to his critics? Presumably he is less desirous of being well thought of by men and women than of being approved by the Judge within. At the same time it is part of humility to accept criticism, as when Peter suffered rebuke from Paul. Thus, good rulers humbly accept "the free and sincere words of their subjects"; but moderation must prevail lest in exercising freedom of expression subjects be permitted to fall into pride.

The title of part three, which may or may not have come from the author, is "How the Ruler Should Teach and Admonish His Subjects by His Holy Life." That is completely misleading. Gregory gives here a series of short homilies meant to serve as examples of how to preach. His approach, once again, is to take pairs of opposites and to show that whatever the subject of admonition, it will mean one thing to part of the audience and something else to another part. There will be women and men, young and old, rich and poor, hale and sick, and so on—thirty-six pairs in all. Of the pairs some are conventional, so that Gregory finds little to say about them that is not part of proverbial wisdom. Such are the chapters on slaves and masters, the wise and the dull, the slothful and the hasty. Some, on the other hand, rise out of special situations, as when in admonishing the ministry he contrasts preachers who are ignorant of Scripture with those who know the Bible but are not humble. The wisdom here is not proverbial but is obvious once the situation is so described.

Gregory makes a good deal of these antitheses. First, if we want to be heard sympathetically, says Gregory, we must put ourselves in the position of those whom we are trying to influence. For example, in "How to admonish the insolent and the fainthearted," he notes that the former, while they disdain reproof, esteem what they do as being especially excellent. When we reprove them we ought not to mention their insolence but rather show that what they take to be well done is in fact done badly, "so that a wholesome confusion may ensue from what they believe won glory for them." The fainthearted, on the other hand, are best corrected if we refer to some of their good points, touching on their faults not by way of reproving them for what they have done but as a prohibition of what should not be done. "Thus the favor shown them will encourage their zeal for the things which we approve."

Second, there are numerous faults that are best brought to the fore when paired with an opposite fault. Gluttony, for example, is a well-known vice. Gregory brings against it the usual charge that the Enemy uses it to incite other lusts, thereby binding the soul in a net of sins. Its opposite, abstemiousness, would by contrast seem to be a virtue. But, as a matter of fact, says Gregory, because gluttony is so disgusting, the abstemious person is peculiarly liable to the sin of pride. To counteract his pride, he recommends that the abstemious person "bestow on the poor what they subtract from their own nourishment." Another pair of opposites, which take on additional meaning when considered in conjunction, are kindliness and envy. By defining "kindly" as the opposite of "envious" Gregory unveils an imperfection in the former that might go unnoticed. What the envious has but the other lacks is a burning desire to make excellence his own. "The kindly-disposed are to be told that when they behold the deeds of neighbors they should examine their own heart, and not presume on the actions of others, nor praise what is good, while declining to do it likewise." The envious, on the other hand, are to learn the old axiom, "Become what you are"; and, if they cannot imitate what they admire in others, let them "consider how efficacious is charity, which renders the works of another's labor our own, without any labor on our part."

That the sick should be admonished in a different way from the healthy is clear enough, and even the great pope is not able to overcome the embarrassment that those who are in good health experience at the bedside of those who are seriously ill. Gregory had, indeed, the advantage that he was much of the time a sick man; but this did not save him from resorting to platitude. The healthy are to be warned that if they will not serve God when they enjoy the favor of good health, that favor may at any time be withdrawn and they will have lost their chance; whereas, the sick are to be told that ill health is a sign of God's favor, seeing that whom God loves he chastises. Already in Gregory we find developed the view that bodily affliction is a twofold blessing: "It both cleanses sins committed and restrains such as could be committed." Pain cleanses of wickedness when the mind assimilates it and takes it as penitence. It restrains from sin when, like Balaam's ass, the body is held back from dangers that the mind fails to see. Gregory mentions impatience as the sin that especially besets the sick, and provides his fellow bishops with an example of how meditating on the Redeemer's passion helps the sufferer to endure evil without complaining.

Gregory reminds himself, in conclusion, that preachers are but heralds of the Giver and must never allow themselves to think of the message as their own. They are like the rooster of whom Job asked, "Who gave the cock understanding?" And they do well to imitate him, for, before he crows, he first shakes his wings and beats himself with them until he is himself fully awake. In this way he can make himself heard by his deeds as well as by his words.

Jean H. Faurot

RECOMMENDED READING

Edition used: Gregory the Great, Saint. *Pastoral Care*. Translated and annotated by Henry Davis, S.J. Westminster, Md.: Newman Press, 1955. Useful introduction.

Butler, Dom Cuthbert. *Western Mysticism: The Teachings of Saints Augustine, Gregory, and Bernard on Contemplation and the Contemplative Life*. London: Arrow Books, 1922. Notes that while Gregory's activities and influences in other spheres have been fully recognized, his role as a mystic and as a teacher of mystical theology has been neglected by modern students of the subject. Excellent collection of texts and a running commentary.

Dudden, Frederick H. *Gregory the Great: His Place in History and Thought*. 2 vols. London: Longmans, Green & Co., 1905. Reissued New York: Russell & Russell, 1967. Standard work; excellent. *Pastoral Care* is discussed in vol. 1, pp. 230–238.

———. "Gregory, Saint (surnamed the Great)." In *Encyclopaedia Britannica*, 11th ed., vol. 12, pp. 566–568. Cambridge: Cambridge University Press, 1910. Best short account.

THE LADDER OF DIVINE ASCENT

Author: John Climacus (c. 579–c. 649)
John's dates are much debated, nor is the place of his birth known. John
was sixteen when he arrived at Sinai to become a monk. For the first few
years he lived with a spiritual father, Abba Martyrius, then he retired to
a solitary life at Tholas, some five miles from the fortress monastery of
Saint Catherine. Forty years later he was elected abbot of the monastery.
It was while he was superior that he wrote *The Ladder of Divine Ascent* at
the request of the abbot of Raithu. As a supplement to *The Ladder* he
wrote a short treatise entitled *To the Shepherd*, describing the task of the
abbot or spiritual father. Shortly before his death he resigned, appoint-
ing his brother George as his successor, and regained the solitary life.

Type and subject of work: A directory of monastic spirituality

First transcribed: c. 640

MAJOR THEMES

*Withdrawal from the world is a willing rejection of all that is materially
prized.*

*All monastic life takes one of three forms: There is the road of withdrawal
and solitude, the life of stillness shared with one or two brothers, and the practice
of living patiently in community.*

Fear is the starting point of love, and purity is the foundation of theology.

*The beginning of prayer is to rid oneself of distractions; the middle stage is
concentration on what is being thought; its conclusion is rapture in the Lord.*

He who loves the Lord has first loved his brother.

The Ladder of Divine Ascent was written for monks. The form of John's text, with its thirty sections or steps, was suggested by the biblical image of the ladder that Patriarch Jacob saw reaching up to heaven, with angels ascending and descending. The text has had immense influence on the formation of Eastern Christian monasticism. It is read in the monasteries during Lent and it is frequently depicted in icons, frescoes, and manuscripts. The spiritual father (oftentimes Climacus himself) ushers the monks to the foot of the ladder. As they ascend, good angels assist them and evil angels try to pull them off and drop them into the gaping jaws of hell. (Abba John's proper name, Climacus, comes from the Greek word for ladder.)

The Ladder is composed with great subtlety and art, a rhythmic prose approaching poetry, yet there is an apparent abruptness about the text. John uses short, sharp sentences, pithy definitions, and paradoxical aphorisms: "The growth of fear is the starting point of love, and total purity is the founding of theology.... The Word of the Lord, being from the Lord, remains eternally pure.... Purity makes of a disciple someone who can speak of God, and he can move on to a knowledge of the Trinity.... He who loves the Lord has first loved his brother, for the latter is proof of the former."

John enters upon his climb without any introduction. The first three steps concern themselves with the break from the world: renunciation, detachment, and exile. This may seem very negative, but there is a strong positive element in John's understanding of it. "All this is done by those who willingly turn from the things of this life, either for the sake of the coming kingdom, or because of the number of their sins, or on account of their love of God." The body retains its role in the monastic life: "The monk has a body made holy, a tongue purified, a mind enlightened. Asleep or awake, the monk is a soul pained by the constant remembrance of death. Withdrawal from the world is a willing hatred of all that is materially prized, a denial of nature for the sake of what is above nature."

When the monk has reached this third step he is well on the way; he "should look neither to right nor left." The next twenty-three steps devote themselves to the cultivation of the virtues and the extirpation of the vices, what the Fathers called the active life.

The most fundamental of the virtues for John is that of obedience. He found in the desert three forms of monastic life: "All monastic life may be said to take one of three forms. There is the road of withdrawal and solitude for the spiritual athlete, there is the life of stillness [*hesychia—contemplation*] shared with one or two brothers; and there is the practice of living patiently in community." John favored the middle way, where one would not have all the distractions and cares of the large cenobitic community nor the risks of being totally alone, lacking the good of obedience.

John's treatment of obedience is followed by the steps of penitence, remembrance of death, and sorrow. Then he begins upon a long consideration of the passions—sixteen steps: anger, malice, slander, talkativeness, falsehood, despondency, gluttony, lust, avarice (two steps), insensitivity (three steps), fear, vainglory, and pride. The number of steps devoted to the struggle with the passions should not be misunderstood. By and large, these considerations are shorter than those given to the virtues, and within each step there is consideration of the virtues that help the monk overcome the particular passion.

Indeed, the second step concerning avarice (step sixteen) is on poverty (step seventeen), and this is one of the more beautiful and rich chapters in *The Ladder*. Its approach is deeply spiritual and even mystical, as is *The Ladder* as a whole—John's concern is more with the spiritual than with the material and legislative aspects of monastic life. "The poverty of a monk is resignation from care.... The poor monk is lord of the world. He has handed all his cares over to God, and by his faith has obtained all men as his servants. If he lacks something, he does not complain to his fellows and he accepts what comes his way as if from the hand of the Lord. In his poverty he turns into a son of detachment." The monk who has had a taste of heaven easily thinks nothing of what is below. John concludes the step: "This is the seventeenth step. He who has climbed it is traveling to heaven unburdened by material things."

The second step concerning insensitivity (step eighteen) turns to prayer: "The man who considers with sensitivity of heart that he is standing before God will be an immovable pillar of prayer.... The truly obedient monk often becomes suddenly radiant and exultant during his prayers.... Prayer tests the zeal of a monk and his love for God." The next chapter is on alertness.

After considering the passions, John returns to the "higher virtues" of the active life, those that lead into the contemplative life: simplicity, humility, and discernment. "Among beginners, discernment is real self-knowledge; among those midway along the road to perfection, it is a spiritual capacity to distinguish unfailingly between what is truly good and what in nature is opposed to the good; among the perfect, it is a knowledge resulting from divine illumination, which with its lamp can light up what is dark in others."

In his discussion of discernment, John offers programs of study for beginners, for the intermediate, and for teachers. He warns about spending too long in the beginner's stage. He offers a couple of spiritual alphabets. In general, discernment is "a solid understanding of the will of God in all times, in all places, in all things, and it is found only among those who are pure in heart, in body, and in speech."

Before entering into the third stage of his ladder (the last four steps), John offers a "Brief Summary of All the Preceding Steps" in the form of five pages of epigrams, rich in his usual concrete earthiness: "Eggs warmed in dung hatch out. Unconfessed evil thoughts hatch evil actions.... Galloping horses vie with each other. A zealous community encourages individual zeal.... A man in a fever ought not commit suicide. Right up to the moment of death we should never despair."

The chapter on stillness (step twenty-seven) is one of the most practical for monks. The following chapter outlines the way of prayer: "The beginning of prayer is the expulsion of distractions from the very start by a single thought [*monologistos*]; the middle stage is concentration on what is being said or thought; its conclusion is rapture in the Lord." John concludes the rich teaching in this chapter: "You cannot discover from the teaching of others the beauty of prayer. Prayer has its own special teacher in God." It is in the course of these chapters that John passes on the traditional teaching on the "Jesus Prayer"; he is the first to use this expression.

A short step on dispassion—"Dispassion is an uncompleted perfection of the perfect ... a dispassionate soul is immersed in virtues as a passionate being is in pleasure"—leads to the summit of the ladder: faith, hope, and love (step thirty). "And now at last, after all that has been said, there remains that triad, faith, hope, and love, binding and securing the union of all. 'But the greatest of these is love,' since that is the very name of God himself." In the end, the "empress" (love) speaks to John's soul: "My love, you will never be able to know how beautiful I am unless you get away from the grossness of the flesh. So let this ladder teach you the spiritual union of the virtues. And I am there on the summit."

Climacus concludes his work with "A Brief Summary and Exhortation": "Ascend, my brothers, ascend eagerly. Let your hearts resolve to the climb.... Run, I beg you, run with him.... Baptized in the thirtieth year of his earthly age, Christ attained the thirtieth step on the spiritual ladder, for God indeed is love, and to him be praise, dominion, power. In him is the cause, past, present, and future, of all that is good forever and ever. Amen."

M. Basil Pennington

RECOMMENDED READING

Edition used: John Climacus. *The Ladder of Divine Ascent*. Translated by Colm Luibheid and Norman Russell. Introduction by Kallistos Ware. Classics of Western Spirituality. New York: Paulist Press, 1982.

Hausherr, Irenee. *The Name of Jesus.* Translated by Charles Cummings. Cistercian Studies Series, vol. 44. Kalamazoo, Mich.: Cistercian Publications, 1978. This study, while it does tend to play down a bit the contribution of Saint John Climacus, does place his teaching on the Jesus Prayer fully in context.

John Climacus. *The Ladder of Divine Ascent*. Translated by Archimandrite Lazarus.

Moore. Introduction by Muriel Heppell. London: Faber & Faber, 1959. Reprinted Willits, Calif.: Eastern Orthodox Books, 1973. This edition, besides the helpful introduction of Muriel Heppell, contains the ancient "Life of Abba John" by Daniel, monk of Raithu, and other relatively ancient documents.

— — —. *The Ladder of Divine Ascent*. Translated by Archimandrite Lazarus Moore. Boston: Holy Transfiguration Monastery, 1978. This updated edition of Moore's translation (which has been compared with additional manuscripts) includes a translation of Climacus's *To the Shepherd*.

The Sayings of the Desert Father: The Alphabetical Collection. Translated by Benedicta Ward. Foreword by Metropolitan Anthony. Cistercian Studies Series, vol. 59. Kalamazoo, Mich.: Cistercian Publications, 1975. These sayings give us the flavor as well as the actual source from which John Climacus drew much of his wisdom.

The Four Hundred Chapters on Love

Author: Saint Maximus the Confessor (c. 580–662)
Born in Constantinople to an aristocratic Christian family, Maximus left the position of secretary to the emperor Heraclius around 613 to enter the monastery at Chrysopolis. Leaving the monastery during the Persian invasion of 626, he traveled through North Africa and to Rome. A rigorous opponent of the Monothelite heresy (the doctrine that Christ had only one, divine, will), he, along with the pope, was arrested by the emperor in 653 and was exiled. In 661 he was tried for treason and was sentenced to have his tongue cut out and his right hand cut off for refusing to stop preaching against Monothelitism. He died shortly thereafter and received the name "Confessor" because of his boldness. Other significant writings are *Commentary on the "Our Father"* (c. 640) and *The Church's Mystagogy* (c. 625).

Type and subject of work: Theological, speculative essay combining Neoplatonism and orthodox Christianity on the nature of God and how persons are to achieve unity with God

First transcribed: c. 640

Major Themes

True love seeks only the knowledge of God, this knowledge requiring total detachment from earthly things.

As the soul is better than the body, and God better than the world, anyone who prefers the body to the soul or the world to God is like an idolater.

Pure prayer, better even than the virtues, assists the mind in pursuit of divine love.

Whoever loves God loves all persons without regard for whether they are just or unjust.

Utter detachment from desire for things and from passionate thoughts of things, and harmony with others are required for knowledge of God.

A person's intentions are what God judges, since actions derive their value from motives.

The substance of beings is not coexistent with God, but created by God, and thus beings receive their eternal being or nonbeing from God.

There can be knowledge about God, but he is unknowable "in himself."

In his prologue to *The Four Hundred Chapters on Love,* Maximus writes to Father Elpidius, probably another monk and perhaps a superior, that he went through the "holy Fathers" as background for his thoughts.

Maximus's opening statement in the "First Century" sets the basic theme that the rest of the chapters (actually brief paragraphs) develop in detail—albeit not at all systematically, several specific topics appearing here and there throughout. Most crucial of all is love for the knowledge of God; not knowledge *about* God, but *of* God. Maximus warns us, however, that "It is impossible to reach the habit of this love if one has any attachment to earthly things."

Thus love of God is the motivation, and detachment is the means. Since all things have been made by God, God is better than anything, and since the soul is better than the body and God is better than the world, anyone who prefers body to soul or world to God is like an idolater.

There appears in Maximus a sort of reciprocal relationship: As detachment gives rise to love, so deepest love for God causes the mind to become totally detached. This pure prayer brings one to God and renders the mind insensible to all things.

Love for others is a key element in the contemplative life; it acts as a sort of measure of one's purity. We are to love all people equally—with money, the word of God, and service—regardless of whether they are just or unjust, just as God loves all equally.

The pure mind is no longer ignorant, but is illumined by divine light. The pure soul is free of passions and rejoices in divine love. That is, the pure person is free of attachment to ideas and objects of desire, detachment being "a peaceful state of the soul in which it becomes resistant to vice."

To this end, a person seeking detachment must afflict the flesh with fasting and vigils, sleeping on the ground, chanting, prayer, and chastity. However, a sure sign of attachment is that the person makes a great deal of the ascetic exercises.

Pride and anger are two great dangers. They lead to slander and enmity of others and reflect attachment and a lack of love when others
slander us.

Also dangerous are the images we carry about that cause passions to
arise in us. Without these images and the passions they cause, objects
themselves would hold little sway over us, Maximus writes.

Love and self-control (both significant elements in Evagrian spirituality) cut away the passions that are manifest in body and soul. To elimi-
nate the passions is necessary, since anyone who does not disdain
absolutely everything temporal, not only pleasures, but pain as well,
does not possess pure love.

To this end God sends or allows humility and stress, since humility
cuts out the passions of the soul, while distress does so for bodily
passions.

Fear of God in the fear of punishment brings about ascetic practices
and detachment, while the fear of God as one who loves brings reverence to the soul.

If one does not learn detachment and self-control, when memory
brings a thought to mind passions are aroused which then take hold of
the mind, leading to actual sinning.

The liberated mind, however, writes Maximus, can contemplate
creatures and then move on to the knowledge of the Holy Trinity.

Detachment from things per se is good, but detachment from
thoughts of them is even better. Thus, demons attack us through our
thoughts more powerfully than through our deeds.

In the "Second Century" Maximus begins with the reciprocal relationship between detachment, or undistracted prayer, and love for God.
There are two types of pure prayer: The first arises from fear of God and
hope, the second from "divine desire and total purification." In the first,
the one who prays is lost in prayer; in the second, the one who prays is
seized by God.

As with most things, Maximus comments, people love others for all
sorts of reasons: A good reason is for God's sake; a neutral reason is for
nature's sake (as a parent loves a child); bad or passionate reasons are
vainglory, greed, and love of pleasure.

The believer who is making progress on the road to detachment will
surely be beset by demons of pride, blasphemy, confusion, pain, and the
like. If we follow Christ, our model, however, these onslaughts, advises
Maximus, will only strengthen us and hasten our pilgrimage.

Things in and of themselves are good; it is our passionate attachment to images or things and our misuse of objects or ideas that is evil.
Asceticism will help in our struggle against this evil, Maximus assures
us.

There are definitely stages on the journey. Maximus uses figures in the ecclesiastical hierarchy: Whoever anoints the mind and drives away passions has the character of a deacon; whoever illumines the mind and is free of false knowledge has that of a priest; whoever perfects it with knowledge of the Holy Trinity has that of a bishop. At the end one receives "the grace of the theology," or communion with God.

Maximus makes much of the Trinity, for he argued with those who would separate Christ and the Father: "... it is necessary both to preserve the one God and to confess the three persons, each one in his individuality." For God is united, yet without distinction. Whoever is perfect in love, then, also knows no distinction in love between slave and free or male and female.

War is waged in the soul: We are moved to the good by natural tendencies such as pity and hope for kindness from others, by angels and a good will (discerning good and evil, we choose the good), while we are moved to the evil by passion (desires), demons, and a bad will (discerning good and evil, we still choose the evil).

Most important are our intentions and our love. Demons will trip up the monk with pride in either the monk's good deeds or the monk's spiritual superiority over another. Suffering will help, however, for it returns one to humility and eliminates pride.

Bodily virtues such as ascetic practices are important, but not crucial, since infirmity can rule them out. Virtues of the soul, however, such as love, patience, and the like, must be present, since they are not subject to infirmity and old age.

God allows demons to war upon persons so that they will learn to distinguish virtue from vice, hold fast to the virtue they have acquired in struggle, remain humble, hate vice all the more for the experience of it, remember their weaknesses and God's power.

In good Greek fashion, Maximus states that our natural rational element must be subjected to God's word in order to control our irrational nature.

Common sense tells us that four things affect us, Maximus writes, namely, angels, demons, the weather, and our life-style.

Finally, with reference to Psalm 23, Maximus writes that because human life itself is a "shadow of death," the believer can walk through it and death itself without fear.

Maximus emphasizes again in the "Third Century" that the vices are caused by our misuse of the faculties of the soul, since God's creation is not evil. Thus, not even demons are evil by nature, but rather by the misuse of their natural faculties. Thus the one who loves God struggles not against things or images of things, but against passions related to these images.

In creating a rational and intelligent nature, God has granted it temporal being, and eternal being in its essence, and goodness and wisdom in its will. Thus while everyone is in God's image, only the good and wise are in God's likeness.

The human will is absolutely crucial, for God can cause people to exist forever or not at all, but sharing in God's goodness and wisdom depends upon the will of a rational being.

Impurity of mind consists of false knowledge, ignorance of "universals," passionate thoughts, and consenting to sin. Impurity of soul means not acting according to nature (that is, being subject to the Divine Logos). Impurity of body is a "sin in deed."

Maximus goes on to repeat and rephrase concerns found in the first two "Centuries."

In the "Fourth Century" Maximus begins by stating that no one can know *why* God created *when* God did, for God's wisdom is not subject to human knowledge. As one saint said, "Unbridled speculation can push you over the precipice."

Against the Greeks, Maximus refutes the idea that created things exist eternally with God, for God alone is infinite.

With most mystics, Maximus affirms that God is knowable and unknowable: "Knowable in ideas about him, unknowable in himself." Thus experience of and participation in God, not ideas or fancies, is the way to know God.

Maximus goes on to repeat warnings about strife between believers, the importance of humility and ascetic practices, the need for detachment, the acceptability of thought so long as it is thought without passions, and the importance of love as the only way of living among Christ's disciples and, in detachment, of coming to God.

Gary R. Sattler

RECOMMENDED READING

Edition used: Maximus Confessor. *Selected Writings*. Translation and Notes by George C. Berthold. Classics of Western Spirituality. Mahwah, N.J.: Paulist Press, 1985. Also includes "The Trial," "Commentary on the Our Father," and several other works by Maximus.

Maximus the Confessor. *The Church, the Liturgy and the Soul of Man*. Translated, with Historical Note and Commentaries by Dom Julian Stead, O.S.B. Still River, Mass.: St. Bede's Publications, 1982. Essays on Maximus's *Mystagogia*, an explanation of the meaning of the liturgy, and a translation of the *Mystagogia* itself.

Thunberg, Lars. *Microcosm and Mediator: The Theological Anthropology of Maximus the Confessor*. Acta Seminarii Neotestamentici Upsaliensis 25. Lund:

Gleerup; Copenhagen: Munksgaard, 1965. An excellent introduction to Maximus's anthropology, especially in understanding his concept of the deification of the person.

THE PRACTICAL AND
THEOLOGICAL CHAPTERS

Author: Saint Symeon the New Theologian (949–1032)
Born to parents of the lesser provincial nobility in Asia Minor, George
("Symeon" was his monastic name) was sent at the age of eleven to the
imperial capital of Constantinople, where he was reared by an uncle
who prepared him for a political career. His uncle died when George
was fourteen and he became attracted to the monastery of Studios,
where the monk Symeon (known as "the Pious" or simply as "the Stud-
dite") became his spiritual father. This monk, it should be noted, was
neither a priest nor the superior of Studios.

George continued his political career under the spiritual direction of
Symeon the Pious, and at the age of twenty-one had an experience of
divine light one evening while praying. He became an imperial senator,
but decided at the age of twenty-seven to enter the monastery of
Studios.

He took the same monastic name as his spiritual father and placed
himself completely under the elder Symeon's direction. The relationship between the two Symeons became a source of concern of the monks
and superior of Studios, and the young Symeon was offered the choice
of either joining another monastery or ceasing to have Symeon the Pious as his spiritual father. He chose to join the monastery of Saint Mammas in 977, where he was ordained priest three years later, and soon
elected superior. He revitalized the prayer life of his monastery and
soon transformed Saint Mammas into a model community.

In 987, the elder Symeon died, and his spiritual son immediately instituted at Saint Mammas the cult (veneration as a saint) of his spiritual father. This act, unauthorized as it was by higher ecclesiastical authorities, provided the pretext for conflicts between Symeon and Stephen, chancellor of the Patriarch of Constantinople; the real basis for the controversy, however, seems to have been official concern that Symeon's spiritual doctrine (described below) undermined ecclesiastical authority. Symeon resigned as superior of Saint Mammas in 1005 and was tried and condemned to exile in 1009, although he was not required to recant either his teaching or his conviction that his spiritual father was a saint. In exile Symeon transformed the ruined church of Saint Marina into a thriving monastery. Although rehabilitated and offered a bishopric by the Patriarch, Symeon preferred to remain at Saint Marina, where he died in 1032.

Type and subject of work: Brief paragraphs addressed to monks, describing the Christian's spiritual journey to God and the experience of divine contemplation

First transcribed: Eleventh century

MAJOR THEMES

Contemplation of God, both the vision of God and the experience of his indwelling as "light and fire," is the goal of Christian life and is a state to which all Christians are called.

Growth in Christian life involves fervent prayer "with tears," which purifies the believer and prepares him for the indwelling of the Holy Spirit.

The experience of God's indwelling is an essential prerequisite for anyone who serves as spiritual father (spiritual director) to another Christian and is charged with the sacramental remission of sins.

Symeon's spiritual doctrine is rooted in the rich tradition of the Eastern Fathers who preceded him, especially Evagrius Ponticus, Maximum Confessor, and John Climacus. According to their teaching, Christian spiritual growth begins with the "active" (ascetical) struggle to obey God's commandments and resist temptation. This leads to *apatheia*, freedom from overwhelming compulsions, which in turn gives birth to love, *agape*. This renders possible a deepening in contemplative prayer, that is, the ability to see God in all of creation (the contemplation of nature—*theoria physike*) and ultimately to behold God in himself ("theology"—*theoria*). In the development of this tradition prior to Symeon's time there had been a tendency to see growth in true contemplation as something possible only for monks. Isaac of Ninevah, for example, whose writings were widely read in the Byzantine world, had stressed the necessity of withdrawal from the world and of solitude for growth in contemplation.

Symeon, however, modified and added significantly to this tradition. He believed that the vision of God, contemplation, is something to which all Christians, married or celibate, hermits or city dwellers, are called. The life of asceticism and growth in contemplative prayer is possible for any Christian in any walk of life. The solitude of the desert is not absolutely required for inner stillness before God (*hesychia*), although it is a great help.

In Symeon's writings the ascetical life that must precede and accompany the experience of contemplation is viewed in a more positive way than in the writings of certain of his predecessors. *Apatheia*, the result of the ascetical struggle, is not merely freedom from overwhelming compulsions and desires: It is a purification that requires the grace of God in order to take place and that prepares the heart of the believer for the indwelling of the Holy Spirit.

The transition from the life of ascetical struggle to the life of contemplation is less abrupt in Symeon's writings than in those of his predecessors. These two aspects of Christian growth intertwine and become a continuum through Symeon's emphasis on the tears that accompany the sincere Christian's prayer. Symeon described two kinds of tears: first, the bitter tears of repentance and fear; second, the sweet tears of joy. This distinction, however, is not overly stressed; and the tears that Symeon described seem at times to represent a mingling of sorrow and joy as well as a progression from sorrow to joy. For Symeon these tears accompanying prayer are like a second baptism, wiping away postbaptismal sin. But they are not merely a remedy for sin: They are more positively viewed as the necessary preparation for the experience of contemplation, the indwelling of the Holy Spirit in the heart of the believer.

In Symeon's writings, as in those of the Fathers who preceded him, the climax and goal of Christian life is union with God. Such union is not deferred until heaven: It can and should be anticipated and experienced through contemplative prayer by the Christian living on earth. Christian contemplation is thus for Symeon not only the vision of God who is light and fire; it is also an experience of the indwelling of this divine light in the heart of the believer. Symeon agreed with his predecessors in distinguishing between the contemplation of God through creation and the contemplation of God in himself. However he described the latter not as a lofty and nearly unattainable goal, but rather as the normative experience for all Christians who take their faith seriously. He regarded this experience of God's indwelling as an essential prerequisite for those who serve as spiritual fathers or who are charged by the Church to sacramentally remit the sins of believers.

Growth in Christian life, according to Symeon, never involves a dichotomy between the contemplative experience of God and service to one's neighbor. Obedience to the commandments and a special concern for the poor and neglected are the characteristics of those who have been purified by tears and have "received the flame." Thus Symeon's spirituality does not focus exclusively on the vertical relationship between man and God, but rather views the experience of God's indwelling as the source of genuine compassion and service to one's neighbor.

Although *The Practical and Theological Chapters* were written for monks, the teachings of Symeon described above can be applied without reserve to all Christians. In Symeon's teaching on spiritual fatherhood, however, a more specifically monastic frame of reference appears through his emphasis on monastic obedience. In the Eastern monastic tradition represented by Symeon, a very special type of obedience is rendered to the spiritual father, who may or may not be the superior of the monastery. In obeying the spiritual father in all things, down to the least details of ascetical observance, the monk learns to put aside his own will and literally to see Christ in another human being. Thus the extravagant language of obedience that Symeon employed in describing the relationship between spiritual father and son is best understood within the context of monastic community life, and is perhaps the area of his teaching least easily applicable to the situation of Christians living in the world.

Luke E. Dysinger

RECOMMENDED READING

Edition used: *Symeon the New Theologian: The Practical and Theological Chapters and the Three Theological Discourses.* Translation and Introduction by Paul McGuckin, C.P. Cistercian Studies Series, no. 41. Kalamazoo, Mich.: Cistercian Publications, 1982.

Bouyer, Louis. "St. Symeon the New Theologian." In *A History of Christian Spirituality.* Vol. 2: *The Spirituality of the Middle Ages,* Appendix "Byzantine Spirituality." Edited by J. Leclercq, F. Vandenbroucke, and L. Bouyer. New York: Seabury Press, 1982. Fr. Bouyer's concise summary of the origins of Orthodox spirituality contains an excellent twelve-page condensation of Symeon's life and teaching.

Maloney, George, S.J. *The Mystic of Fire and Light: St. Symeon the New Theologian.* Denville, N.J.: Dimension Books, 1975. A detailed and readable account of Symeon's life and spiritual doctrine.

Symeon the New Theologian, Saint. *Hymns of Divine Love: Songs of Praise by One of the Great Mystics of All Church History*. Translated by George A. Maloney, S.J. Denville, N.J.: Dimension Books, 1975. Symeon wrote his hymns both as abbot of Saint Mammas and during his exile. In them are to be found all the different aspects of his spirituality, expressed as joyful songs of praise to the God with whom he enjoyed spiritual intimacy.

THE PRAYERS AND MEDITATIONS OF SAINT ANSELM

Author: Saint Anselm of Canterbury (c. 1033–1109)

Anselm was born at Aosta in northern Italy. In 1059, he entered the Norman abbey of Bec in Normandy, where he lived for thirty years. The prior of the monastery was Lanfranc, who became Anselm's teacher and was later to become archbishop of Canterbury, to be succeeded by Anselm. Anselm became prior at Bec at the age of thirty, and in 1078 he was elected abbot. In 1093, King William II (William Rufus) nominated Anselm archbishop of Canterbury. Anselm was involved in dissension with the king (and later with Henry I) over the investiture of bishops, and in 1097 he went into exile in Rome for three years; he was again in exile from 1103 to 1107. While at Bec (between 1070 and 1080) Anselm wrote the *Prayers and Meditations* and also the *Proslogion*; his *Cur Deus Homo* was written during his first period of exile, while he was at the monastery at Liberi in southern Italy. He died April 21, 1109.

Type and subject of work: Prayers and meditations in rhymed prose (Latin)

First transcribed: 1070–1080, except for "Meditation on Human Redemption," c. 1099

Major Themes

*Prayers are confessions of sin and appeals to God to have mercy, to strength-
en the petitioner's faith, and to help the petitioner to love God by living in conformity to his will.*

*Sin is a sickness, a wound, a torpor; through the intercession of Mary, God's
grace may free the sinner from the burdens of sin.*

Sinners must believe if they are to understand.

*Saint Paul and Jesus are mothers by their affection, kindness, and mercy;
Christ as mother consoles and comforts the sinner and gives life to the dead.*

*If the sinner acknowledges sin and petitions God, then through the interces-
sion and forgiveness of Christ, the Savior, sin will be forgiven and one will be
drawn into union with God.*

Anselm's work *Prayers and Meditations* was written to provide spiritual guidance. Although the contents are powerful, moving, and effective as expressions of devotion and as appeals to repentance by prayer,
their primary value resides in their spirituality, not in their manifest literary virtues. These prayers and meditations were offered by Saint Anselm to those who sought expression for their consciousness of sin and
wished to appeal to God in all due humility and with effective faith. The
"poems" (perhaps deserving of this description by virtue of their
rhymed prose and their striking imagery) are personal, not public, prayers; they suit the soul in solitude; they speak of what might otherwise be
unsaid.

Anselm wrote his prayers—or, rather, the prayers of his composition, intended for the use of any other—to stir the reader from the "torpor" of sin, to arouse in the reader the love of God, and to encourage the
reader to use the prayers—in whole or in part—as petitions to God.

The "Prayer to God" begins with a call for mercy on the petitioner, a
sinner. There is an early declaration of the intention to follow God's
commands: to do what God wills, and to shun what he forbids. "Let me
believe and hope, love and live, / according to your purpose and your
will," the prayer reads.

In Anselm's "Prayer to Christ," the petitioner thanks Christ for his
gifts "which deserve a better return of love"; and he or she declares that
"my soul will pay its debt / by some sort of praise and thanks, / not as I
know I ought, but as I can." (There is something of a paradox here: Western thought traditionally has assumed that "If I ought, I can," and, indeed morality requires this implication, but Anselm expresses humility
in this way, the idea being that the sinner must struggle even to approach what, were the sinner not a sinner, it would be entirely reasonable to require of the soul.

In this prayer, the "Prayer to Christ," Anselm expresses regret that he did not know Christ, that he was not able to see him and to suffer with him: "Alas for me, that I was not able to see / the Lord of Angels humbled to converse with men, / when God, the one insulted, / willed to die that the sinner might live," and he continues his lament by saying, "Alas that I did not deserve to be amazed / in the presence of a love marvellous and beyond our grasp. / Why, O my soul, were you not there / to be pierced by a sword of bitter sorrow / when you could not bear / the piercing of the side of your Saviour with a lance?"

Then, at the extremity of regret and longing for the Christ not known and not sufficiently loved, the petitioner calls out: "What shall I say? What shall I do? Whither shall I go? / Where shall I seek him? Where and when shall I find him? / Whom shall I ask / Who will tell me of my beloved?"

The poem closes with the poignant words, "Lord, meanwhile, let my tears be my meat day and night, / until they say to me, 'Behold your God,' / until I hear, 'Soul, behold your bridegroom.' / Meanwhile, let me be fed with griefs, / and let my tears be my drink; / comfort me with sorrows ..."

The "Prayer to St. Mary," to be offered "when the mind is weighed down with heaviness," calls upon Mary to heal the penitent who is "sick with the sickness of vice, / in pain from the wounds of crimes, / putrid with the ulcers of sin." The one who prays acknowledges that "a huge dullness is between you and me," and that the petitioner is "so filthy and stinking / that I am afraid you will turn your merciful face from me." The sinner asks Mary for mercy and pleads that "by a glance from your mercy" she cure him. The sinner is in a quandary: Unless the sins be confessed, they cannot be cured; but if they are confessed, they are seen to be detestable. The only hope is that Mary, "by virtue of the blessed fruit of your womb," will enable the sinner's soul to be made whole. (Two other poems to Mary follow; each bears a unique message.)

Again, in the "Prayer to St. Peter," the petitioner confesses, "I am not able to break out of the shadows / of the torpor that holds me / because of the filth of my sins." Peter is asked to have mercy, to be a kind shepherd, to "gather up the lamb of Christ." "Do not make demands according to his wickedness," the penitent says, referring to himself as sinner, "but make allowance according to his prayer." The suppliant acknowledges that he (or she) deserves to suffer "because I have sinned of my own free will," but the appeal is to mercy, not to justice (since what is just is that the sinner be denied hope).

The "Prayer to St. Paul" is stirring in its appeal to Paul and to Christ as mothers: "Dear mother, recognize your son / by the voice of his confession; / he recognizes his mother by her loving compassion." (Paul is addressed as "Mother.") Then: "And you, Jesus, are you not also a mother? Are you not the mother who, like a hen, / gathers her chickens under her wings." Anselm writes of Christ as one who "longing to bear sons into life, / you tasted of death, / and by dying you begot them." Hence, "... you, Lord God, are the great mother."

And the image continues: "Then both of you are mothers. / Even if you are fathers, you are also mothers. / For you have brought it about that those born to death / should be reborn to life ..."

Anselm (here showing himself as philosopher) explains and justifies his attribution: "Therefore you are fathers by your effect / and mothers by your affection. / Fathers by your authority, mothers by your kindness. / Fathers by your teaching, mothers by your mercy. / Then you, Lord, are a mother, / and you, Paul, are a mother too."

The final petition is to Christ as mother; the sinner, as one who is dead, appeals to the Savior: "Mother, know again your dead son, / both by the sign of your cross and the voice of his confession. / Warm your chicken, give life to this dead man, / justify your sinner."

Anselm's prayers to the saints—among them John the Baptist, John the Evangelist, Stephen, Nicholas, Benedict, and Mary Magdalene—all follow the basic pattern: Anselm (as the sinner and suppliant) confesses and deplores his sin; he calls upon the saint for mercy and asks for intercession; finally, the appeal, as an expression of faith, hope, and the desire for understanding and hence knowledge, is directed to God himself.

The appeal to Saint Mary Magdalene is especially poignant, for Anselm calls upon her to remember how much the sinner longs for forgiveness and reconciliation, but he is careful to remark that he recalls her sins not as a reproach but as a device for calling upon "the boundless mercy by which they were blotted out." The petition is finally directed to Christ directly: "Hear me, for your love, / and for the dear merits of your beloved Mary, / and your blessed Mother, the greater Mary."

Anselm offers a "Prayer for Friends" (in which, as sinner, he confesses that he is hardly worthy to petition God, even if what he asks is love for those he loves), and he follows it with a "Prayer for Enemies" (in which he says he prays "as I can" but wishes he could do more; he asks that the punishment for those who hate him and for himself be that they all love one another, that they obey God "with one heart in love").

Anselm's "Meditation 1" is subtitled "A meditation to stir up fear," while his "Meditation 2" is "A lament for virginity unhappily lost."

The first meditation expresses at great length and by means of striking imagery how detestable the soul of the sinner is to God, who nonetheless nourishes and waits for that soul. The sinner is a barren tree but even worse: "useless creeping thing ... foul smelling sinner.... The rotting corpse of a dog smells more tolerable than the soul of a sinful man to God ... not a man, but ... more vile than a beast, worse than a corpse." Anselm reflects in fear on the wrath of the Almighty and quakes before "the horrible chaos of Hell ... the wrath of the judge." In despair he calls out, "Who will deliver me out of the hands of God?" But then he remembers Jesus, the Savior, and enjoins, "Take heart, sinner, and do not despair." He calls upon Jesus to have mercy upon him, so that he may enjoy, praise, and glorify Father, Son, and Holy Spirit.

In the second meditation, the "lament for virginity unhappily lost," Anselm chastises himself as fornicator, as a soul "unfaithful to God, false to God, an adulterer from Christ." The penitent addresses his own soul: "You were once the spouse of the king of heaven but with alacrity you have made yourself the whore of the tormentor of hell." It is clear that Anselm is writing of all sin as a staining of the soul, a "loss of virginity," and his primary concern as sinner is with the distance that sin creates between the soul and God. But he calls upon God in his mercy to spare the sinful soul; God's power and mercy are such that the punishment "of the fornicator who is penitent" can be avoided.

The "Meditation on Human Redemption," was written about twenty years after the other prayers and meditations, while Anselm was at the monastery in Liberi in southern Italy. The meditation includes a summary of the heart of the first book of Anselm's *Cur Deus Homo*, a work in which he meditated on the question of why God became man (completed shortly before the writing of the "Meditation on Human Redemption"), but it is an independent work of prayerful reflection itself, designed to arouse human compunction in the full realization of the agonizing cost of the redemptive act of Christ's dying on the cross.

"God was not obliged to save mankind in this way," writes Anselm, "but human nature needed to make amends to God like this. God had no need to suffer so laboriously, but man needed to be reconciled thus." The soul is called upon to realize how much its whole being owes to Christ, and God is asked to admit the petitioner "into the inner room of your love."

The *Proslogion* (written in 1078) concludes the volume of the writings appearing under the title *The Prayers and Meditations of Saint Anselm*. The *Proslogion* contains Anselm's famous "ontological" argument (to the effect that since God is the being than whom none greater can be conceived, he must exist, for if one conceives of God as having ultimate greatness but lacking existence, then a being greater than that can be conceived, namely, a being with all the greatness and perfections of the previously conceived being but necessarily existing as well). But considered in company with the *Prayers and Meditations*, the *Proslogion* can be appreciated as itself a prayer and meditation, even though it contains accidentally (by virtue of Anselm's intellectual genius, brought into service of his spirituality) one of the most amazing (although, many critics would say, logically faulty) deductive arguments in the history of theological thought. Hence, what seems most in accord in the *Proslogion* with what is to be found in the *Prayers and Meditations* is Anselm's disclaimer and confession that prefaces his famous proof: "Lord, I am not trying to make my way to your height, / for my understanding is in no way equal to that, / but I do desire to understand a little of your truth / which my heart already believes and loves. / I do not seek to understand so that I may believe, / but I believe so that I may understand; / and what is more, / I believe that unless I do believe I shall not understand."

Ian P. McGreal

RECOMMENDED READING

Edition used: Anselm, Saint. *The Prayers and Meditations of Saint Anselm.* Translation and Introduction by Sister Benedicta Ward, S.L.G. Foreword by R. W. Southern. Harmondsworth, Middlesex, England: Penguin Books, 1973. Reprinted 1979, 1984. This edition also includes the *Proslogion.* The translation and introduction by Sister Benedicta Ward are excellent; the translation is accurate and suggests the poetic character of Anselm's writings; the introduction is thorough, illuminating, and indispensable as a guide. R. W. Southern's foreword is also helpful and is especially effective in its account of Anselm's poetic style in Latin; Southern quotes fourteen lines form Anselm's third prayer to Saint Mary to illustrate Anselm's use of rhymes and assonances.

———. *Anselm of Canterbury.* Edited and translated by Jasper Hopkins and Herbert Richardson. 4 vols. Toronto and New York: Edwin Mellen Press, 1974–1976. Hopkins (of the Department of Philosophy, University of Minnesota) and Richardson (University of Toronto) have produced a careful, clear collection of Anselm's works. Volume 3 contains the translation of *Cur Deus Homo,* Anselm's brilliant attempt to explain why God became man. Volume 4 is a discussion by Hopkins of hermeneutical and textual problems in Anselm's treatises; it addresses itself to the advanced scholar.

Evans, G. R. *Anselm and Talking About God.* Oxford: Clarendon Press, 1978. These Birkbeck Lectures of 1959 deal in a very interesting and helpful way with Anselm's uses of language in talking about God; the principal treatises are discussed in turn.

Hopkins, Jasper. *A Companion to the Study of St. Anselm.* Minneapolis: University of Minnesota Press, 1972. An intelligent and perceptive guide to the reading of Anselm, particularly for those interested in the understanding and criticism of Anselm's proofs for the existence of God and his ideas concerning the relation of faith to reason.

NOAH'S ARK

Author: Hugh of Saint Victor (1096–1141)

Little is known about Hugh's life; it is not even clear whether he was French or German. The Augustinian Canons, the order to which he belonged, were not monks but secular priests living together under a rule for study and contemplation. Their abbey outside Paris was new when Hugh arrived there as a student. He was soon lecturing and writing; and within his short lifetime he had made Saint Victor famous and had defined his character for the rest of the century. Study and contemplation were, indeed, the fabric of Hugh's life. An early work, the *Didascalion*, was a program of study. His *De Sacramentis* was a doctrinal treatise, the prototype of the summas of the next century. His commentary on the *Celestial Hierarchy* did much to enhance the reputation of Dionysius the Areopagite in the West. A highly esteemed commentary on *Ecclesiastes* was left unfinished.

Type and subject of work: Spiritual treatises involving biblical exposition

First transcribed: 1125–1130

MAJOR THEMES

Having lost their original power of knowing the Creator, human beings love instead the world that they can know.

The restlessness of the human spirit is the result of the instability of the objects of human love.

Noah's ark is a symbol of the work whereby God restores to the believer the knowledge of God that is necessary if the believer is to love God.

Noah's Ark is a collection of spiritual writings, mostly of a devotional nature, centered about the figure of the ark. The three meanings (literal, allegorical, tropological) of the ark provide the frame into which the author fits an informal talk on a passage from Saint Augustine, a sermon on God's House, and a series of meditations on the Tree of Wisdom. All these pieces are imbued with Hugh's zeal for Christian education. Living in a time of intellectual ferment, when serious thinkers were asking what direction the Church should take, Hugh maintained that the task of the Church is to teach humankind the way to heaven and argued that if this task is to be accomplished, it needs a clergy both learned in Scripture and practiced in prayer, after the model of Saints Jerome, Augustine, and Gregory the Great.

The theme of Hugh's book is set forth in an informal talk, parts of which appear in book one and parts in book four. Hugh tells, at the outset, of a chapter-meeting when he was in the chair. Discussion turned to Augustine's comment about the restlessness and instability of the human heart until it cleaves to God; and someone asked him to say a few words about the cause of these unstable movements and about ways in which stability can best be achieved. Hugh's remarks proved so gratifying to the brethren that he felt impelled to commit them to writing. Humanity's instability is a result of its attachment to the multiplicity and mutability of the creature. In their original condition, human beings lived always with a sense of God's presence within them, and did nothing outwardly that did not originate in their love of God. When they tried to divide their love between Creator and creature they were cut off from God's presence and henceforth could know nothing but the outer world. God set about humanity's rehabilitation immediately, but he made no provision for restoring its inner sight. Instead he chose to lead men and women by faith back along the way of the creatures, using the route that they had taken when they fell. Because "a mind accustomed to things that can be seen cannot so soon rise to unseen things" God chose a place and a people, and prepared a Savior, working partly through angels, partly through human beings, and partly by himself, "so that just as the human soul makes progress by climbing in its thoughts from the deeds of men to the deeds of angels, and from the deeds of angels to the acts of God, so also it may gradually grow accustomed to unifying itself, and to approaching nearer to the true simplicity, in proportion as it gets further off from multiplicity."

It goes with Hugh's way of thinking that the whole of creation is a sacrament—a visible form of an invisible grace. In a sermon on God's

House, Hugh makes this clear. God's house is the world, but it is also the Church, and it is in the faithful soul. "God is everything for you, and God has made everything for you," he says; and he lists various biblical images that symbolize God's activity in the world—the heavens, the morning star, a trumpet, a vine, a tower, a wedding-chamber, a flock, a dove, a rose, a river. "Make Him a temple, make Him a house, make Him ... an ark of the covenant, make Him an ark of the flood. No matter what you call it, it is all one house of God."

Noah's ark seems to have been the subject of a seminar or lecture course. To illustrate the object of his reflections, Hugh brought with him to class two pictures, one of the ark, and one of Christ portrayed as Isaiah saw him enthroned in the temple. "This your eyes shall see outwardly so that your soul may be fashioned to its likeness inwardly. You will see there certain colours, shapes, and figures which will be pleasant to behold. But you must understand that these are put there, that from them you may learn wisdom, instruction, and virtue, to adorn your soul." Hugh's use of paintings agrees well with his sacramental understanding of the world, and, more particularly, with medieval views about the way to read the Bible, expounding first the literal or historical meaning of a text, then its spiritual or allegorical meaning, then its figurative or tropological meaning.

The two pictures belong together, says Hugh, because the ark is the Church and the Church is the body of Christ. Still, Hugh's reason for bringing them together must strike us as curious. By means of the ark he could show that the Church, three hundred cubits in length, extends from the beginning of time to the end of time; but he wanted also to show that the Church is not confined to time, that its beginning and its ending are in eternity; and to do this he needed the picture from Isaiah, in which Christ is represented with his head and feet hidden by the wings of two seraphim. Only the part of Christ's body that belongs to time is exposed to view: The head and the feet belong to eternity. "For," says Hugh, in one of his rare references to the mystical experience, "whenever we are caught up into ecstasy of soul and ponder His eternity, we find in Him no beginning and no end. For we reach His head, when we reflect that He was before all things ... [and] to His feet, when we consider that ... He is after all things."

Hugh's description and explanation of the ark, though of slight interest in our day, were remarkable at the time for the emphasis that he placed on historical investigation. Hugh complained that biblical expositors were often at fault for neglecting the literal sense of Scriptures in their eagerness to get on with its deeper meaning. True to his belief that it is precisely on the historical plane that God manifests his purpose, Hugh encouraged scholars to get the broadest education possible; and in his own study he did not hesitate to revise the Latin Bible in the light of

such Hebrew as he could learn from local rabbis and to correct traditional interpretations in the light of what he understood of natural science.

That Hugh's allegorical interpretation is not at all satisfactory to us
may be because we expect too much. By its very nature, allegorical interpretation is piecemeal, in contrast to tropological interpretation, which
considers the passage as a whole. Hugh picks out a few significant details. The three hundred cubits of the ark's length signify the duration of
the Church through three ages—the period of natural law, the period of
written law, and the period of grace; the fifty cubits of its breadth stand
for its membership (forty-nine is perfection, the total of all believers)
plus one, Christ, the head; the thirty cubits of its height denote the thirty books of Scripture; the three decks (in some passages Hugh reckons
the number of decks at five) point to the three ranks of believers—those
in the world, those fleeing from the world, and those who have left the
world and are near to God. The door and the window stand for the active
and the contemplative lives.

But Hugh himself may have had no great enthusiasm for these traditional interpretations. At least, he cuts them short, saying that the special subject that he means to discuss is the Ark of Wisdom. This was a
new concept. For Hugh, the Church as the visible ark has its counterpart
not in the invisible Church as we might have supposed, but in the Truth
of the Ages embodied in Scripture. This is the subject of book two,
where we are asked to distinguish between the kind of existence that
things have in nature and history and the kind of being they have in
thought. For, says Hugh, the rational soul resembles the mind of God in
that past, present, and future there transcend the limits of time and exist
together. "If we have begun to live persistently in our own heart
through the practice of meditation, we have already in a manner ceased
to belong to time; and, having become dead as it were to the world, we
are living inwardly with God." For Hugh, meditation is a process of
thinking whereby one seeks to unravel something complex or to penetrate something obscure, in contrast to contemplation, which finds everything plain, and spontaneously grasps it in its entirety. Any attempt
to investigate the hidden meaning of Scripture is meditation. For example, the pitch used to seal the ark both outside and in means that the
believer must be gentle in his actions and loving in his thoughts. "Pitch
is of a fiery nature, and is born of earth that has been struck by lightning; and charity is generated in the soul stricken with fear of divine
judgment." In this example, meditation makes use of secular learning.
More typically, when we meditate, we avail ourselves of scriptural
knowledge, glossing one text by reference to another, as we see when
we turn to Hugh's meditations on the Tree of Wisdom. For example,
"The fear of the Lord is the beginning of wisdom" is glossed in the light
of the saying "Taste and see how gracious the Lord is." When the soul

considers the torments of the damned, it looks for a way of escape, and when it finds safety in God it embraces him with loving desire.

All this is very remote from modern interests, as remote as the sculpture and stained glass and manuscript illumination that have come down to us from those times. But there are passages in Hugh's discussion of wisdom that would be hard to improve on. One such is his exposition of the three storeys of this ark, which denote three kinds of thought: right, profitable, and necessary. "A treasure hid, and knowledge hid, what profit is either?" asks Ecclesiasticus. Right thoughts are profitable only when they lead to virtuous conduct; but virtues themselves are unprofitable if they are outward only. One thing is supremely necessary, and that is charity, which is necessary because it is not knowledge but charity that unites the soul to God. In another passage of some subtlety, Hugh develops the thought that spiritual pride is a danger accompanying the contemplative life. Among contemplatives, he says, the tree of wisdom often shoots up to such a height as to imperil mental health. Conscious of having chosen the better way, a person may look down on those who are satisfied with the active life, become scornful and censorious, and get to the point where he cannot abide them. The only cure is to lop off the top of the tree and make the branches spread. "It is good for him to be compelled for a time to turn outwards, making a break with the contemplative life and taking up the charge of external responsibilities, so that he may learn by experience how difficult it is to be bound by one's duty to look after external affairs, without giving up the desire for the inner life." Book three consists wholly of these fifteen meditations.

Book four is made up of loose ends. The sermon on God's House had as its third point the house that human beings build for God within their souls. Hugh returns to this point at the beginning of book four. The notion of God abiding in the heart of the believer is fundamental to Christian teaching. But Hugh gives it a new turn when he puts the emphasis on humanity's part in building a place for God. In our inexperience and weakness we cannot build it without God's help; nevertheless, we must do the heavy work, which consists in bringing order and discipline into the chaos of our interior life. Think of God above in his unshakable stability; think of the infinite confusion of the world below. Think in between of "the human soul rising out of this world towards God and, as it rises, gathering itself ever more into a unity." The soul has three possibilities, says Hugh: It can divide itself and attend to several things; it can concentrate itself solely on one thing; or it can narrow the range of its attention. The first possibility we ought not to submit to; the second we ought but cannot in this life; the third, with God's help, is possible here below—we can and should recollect our hearts from unrestrained distraction, and, by striving, gain some semblance of stability.

To explain how the soul can become more stable, Hugh goes back to his talk about how human beings forsook their Maker and can recover a place in God's presence only by following the path marked out in Scripture. Humanity fell by exercising its capacity for choice. "The divine economy of our restoration is, therefore, supremely well ordered in that he who fell of his own choice should rise ... of his own choice too." Here lies the explanation, not merely why God lets us struggle against great difficulties, but also why he shows himself only partly to us in this life. It is only as we learn to walk by hope and trust that we arrive at the appreciation of God's love and faithfulness that makes it certain we will not fall again.

The figurative or tropological explanation of Noah's ark, which we look for in book four, is reserved for the very end, where we are shown that, besides representing the Church afloat in the stormy world, the ark also represents a secure place in the hearts of believers surrounding which the floods of concupiscence continues to rage. There are people who have no ark and who know no world except that of the flesh. There are others who have an ark but do not abide in it: Hugh takes a jab at scholars who attend Church and receive the sacrament but do so insincerely because they love pagan authors more than they love the Holy Book. Finally, there are those who have an ark and abide in it; for, says Hugh, every man so long as he lives in this corruptible world has to struggle against fleshly desires: "In the good, the waters of this flood do indeed begin to lessen ... according to the difference of their graces. But the earth of the heart of man can never be entirely dried out while this life lasts."

Among spiritual seekers in every age there are some who claim to have achieved perfection, who say, "What do I want with this ark? The flood of concupiscence has dried up in me." Hugh was, if we may say so, an imperfectionist. In his *Soliloquy on the Earnest Money of the Soul*, he represents Man reminding his Soul that it was loved by the Bridegroom when it was completely loathsome and that now, when it has put aside its former vileness, there are still qualities in it which He does not like, although He considers not so much what the soul is but what it wishes to be and what progress it is making. When Soul points to certain mystical transports granted to it, it is cautioned: "He comes to touch you, not to be seen by you; to admonish you, not to be beheld.... He offers the first and certain signs of His love, not the plenitude of its perfect fulfillment! In this especially is there evidence of the pledge of your espousal, for He who in the future will permit Himself to be contemplated and possessed by you forever now presents Himself to you that you may know how well-disposed He is. Meanwhile you are consoled in His absence, since by His visits you are continually refreshed lest you grow weak."

Jean H. Faurot

RECOMMENDED READING

Edition used: Hugh of Saint-Victor. *Selected Spiritual Writings*. Translated by a Religious of C.S.M.V. Introduction by Aelred Squire, O.P. London: Faber & Faber, 1962. *Noah's Ark* and other selections, with an excellent introduction.

Copleston, F. C. *A History of Medieval Philosophy*. New York: Harper & Row, 1972. Not to be confused with the author's full-length *A History of Philosophy*. Chapter 7, "Twelfth Century Schools," devotes a section to Saint Victor and its leading representatives.

Hugh of Saint Victor. *Soliloquy on the Earnest Money of the Soul*. Translation and Introduction by Kevin Herbert. Milwaukee: Marquette University Press, 1956. Brief and readable. Shows Hugh's use of symbols in meditation.

Smalley, Beryl. *The Study of the Bible in the Middle Ages*. London: Basil Blackwell & Mott, 1952. Paperback, Notre Dame, Ind.: University of Notre Dame Press, 1964. Indispensable for the study of Hugh and his school.

THE MEDITATIONS OF WILLIAM OF SAINT THIERRY

Author: William of Saint Thierry (c. 1085–1148/9)
The place and date of William of Saint Thierry's birth is unknown. He and his brother Simon went in search first of a good education and then of a good monastic life. They entered the reformed monastery of Saint Nicaise whence William was chosen abbot of Saint Thierry. The turning point in William's life came when he met Bernard of Clairvaux and was deeply drawn to the great Cistercian. In obedience to Bernard he continued as abbot of Saint Thierry, working for reform among the Benedictines, for fifteen or more years. But finally he yielded to his longings and joined the Cistercians at Signy, where he spent the last twelve or thirteen years of his life. Besides his important spiritual treatises, such as the *Meditations,* and *Exposition on the Song of Songs,* and the *Golden Epistle,* he wrote some important theological works, especially to counteract the errors of Peter Abelard. He died on the Feast of the Nativity of the Blessed Virgin Mary, September 8, in 1148 or 1149.

Type and subject of work: A collection of didactic meditations

First transcribed: 1128–1136

MAJOR THEMES

The human person is truly free and responsible, yet God in his eternal wisdom foreknew all and by his grace is the first cause of all the good in the created person.

*There is always a certain tension between two extremes: the human person
and his misery and God and his infinite perfections.*
The mediation of the Redeeming Christ gives hope.
Ultimately, all human reasoning has to be left behind.
"When and how and as far as the Holy Spirit wills" the seeker is brought
into the experience of God.

William tells us himself that he compiled this collection of meditations from among his writings with a view of helping novices to learn
how to pray. In publishing his *Meditations* William followed in the foot-
steps of a father of the Church to whom he looked as a master, Augustine
of Hippo, and used a form that was held in honor during his own time;
witness the meditations of Anselm of Bec, John of Fecamp, Hugh of
Saint Victor, and others. William had put together a collection of twelve
meditations. In the course of this century, Dom Jean-Marie Dechanet
found an additional meditation among the works of William that have
come down to us and this "thirteenth" meditation is now often published with the original twelve.

William's first meditation leaps right into the midst of things, treating of a most profound and most difficult question that is bound to arise
for any person who begins to ponder seriously on his or her relationship
with the divine: the knotty problem of the foreknowledge of God and
the freedom and responsibility of the individual, or the mystery of predestination. William had explored this in his *Exposition on the Epistle to
the Romans* and had called forth from his friend and master, Bernard of
Clairvaux, his treatise *On Grace and Free Will*. Those who have approached the question more rationally have often fallen on one side or
the other: limiting God's foreknowledge and causality or limiting the
human person's freedom or responsibility. William holds the completely orthodox position that the human person is truly free and responsible, yet God in his eternal wisdom foreknew all and by his grace is the
first cause of all the good in the created person. Speaking to God, as he
does throughout these meditations, William says: "And as you by fore-
knowing do not constrain the future to be such as you foreknow, so can
you not yourself be forced to foreknow anything by the mere fact of its
futurity." How it all comes together and why God's grace is efficacious
in some and not in others remains a mystery. Almost quoting Augustine,
William concludes: "Why one should be taken into grace and another
rejected, is a question you had best not ask, unless you wish to go
astray."

Each meditation opens with a verse from Scripture, and after this
first key meditation, we can see a certain line of progression. At the
opening of the second meditation the psalmist invites William to come

close to God in order to be illumined. But a formidable objection appears, for the Lord said to Moses: "No man shall see me and live"—the opening verse of the third meditation. The fourth responds with the reminder that God is merciful, and the fifth carries this through with its reflections on the Passion of Christ, the supreme expression of the Divine Mercy. Then ensues a dialogue. First we have the Lord calling to William: "Come up here." William replies: "My face has sought your face." And the Lord replies: "Show me your face." But William still holds back, recalling the words of Isaiah the Prophet: "Let the wicked be taken away, that he see not the glory of God." Yet he turns to his Savior: "God forbid that I should glory save in the cross of our Lord Jesus Christ." And so, in spite of his sinfulness and misery he continues his prayerful pursuit with verses from the Psalms, which he as a monk would have constantly prayed in the monastic choir: "Turn us again, O God of Hosts: Show your face, and we shall be saved." "Hear my prayer, O Lord, give ear to my supplication in your truth; hear me in your righteousness."

While there seems then to be some order in the meditations, actually within each meditation William is very free in moving from one topic to another. Basically it is concern about contemplation and union with God through love, expressed with a personal warmth as well as with deep theological insight. The *Meditations* draws us into William's labor of love and understanding. There is always a certain tension between two extremes: William and his misery and God and his infinite perfections—at least this is the way William sees it. Yet the meditator cries: "I am wearisome and hateful to myself whenever I perceive that I am not with you." The mediation of the Redeeming Christ gives hope, and the author dares even to consider with a certain boldness the inner life of the Trinity. He is fascinated by and constantly drawn by the Face of God. And the traditional Cistercian doctrine of the restoration of the "image" in fallen man is present.

Ultimately though, all human reasoning has to be left behind: "How does perception come into all this? Of what avail are mental images? Can reason, or rational understanding, effect anything? No. For although reason sends us to you, O God, it cannot of itself attain to you. Neither does that understanding which, as a product of reason, has lower matters for its sphere of exercise, go any further than does reason itself; it is powerless to attain to you. But the understanding which is from above carries the fragrance of its place of origin; there is nothing human in its operation, it is all divine. And, where it is inpoured, it carries along with itself its own reasons which function independently of the inferior reason."

But "when and how and as far as the Holy Spirit wills," the seeker is brought into the experience of God. He comes to "see God as the Father sees the Son, or the Son the Father ... but not in every way the same." In the face of such realization, the meditator can only exclaim: "O Charity, Charity, you have brought us to this that, because we love God and the Son of God, we are called and we are gods and the sons of God!"

The meditations are certainly filled with very lofty teaching that can encourage the beginner because the teaching is set forth so forthrightly and honestly by a man who acknowledges readily his own weakness and sin. The texts also contain much simple and practical knowledge.

One of the meditations that might prove most useful to the novice in a practical way is the eleventh. Here William is struggling with the question of whether he should or can lay down the abbatial charge at Saint Thierry and retire to the Cistercians. But his struggle is presented in the bare lines of a vocational choice such as the novice might face in trying to decide whether he should go on to make vows as a monk. And the struggle is presented in a delightfully lively way, through a dialogue cast into the "mouths" of the inner components of the person: the spirit, the soul, the intentions, the marrow, and the joints. It is a graphic experience of inner turmoil and struggle, ending in the accord: "Let us cry with our whole heart and mind: 'Jesus, Son of David, have mercy on me.'" (There is indication here and elsewhere in the writings of William of Saint Thierry, who had an unusual familiarity with the Greek fathers, that the practice of the Jesus Prayer was not unknown to the author.)

The thirteenth meditation seems to come from a later period of William's life, when the vocational question had been resolved and he had transferred to the Cistercians. He had sought this for over fifteen years, since first catching sight of Bernard of Clairvaux. But as so often happens, when a long sought-for goal is attained, there is a backwash. "Lord you have led me astray," cries the much-tried meditator. He pours out his miseries, but in the end: "The end of the law is charity, and that is the end of my prayer. O you who have willed to be called charity, give me charity, that I may love you more than I love myself, not caring at all what I do with myself, so long as I am doing what is pleasing in your sight."

M. Basil Pennington

RECOMMENDED READING

Edition used: William of Saint Thierry. *The Works of William of Saint Thierry. Volume One: On Contemplating God. Prayer. Meditations.* Translated by Sister Penelope, C.S.M.V. Cistercian Fathers Series, vol. 3. Spencer, Mass.: Cistercian Publications, 1971.

Brooke, Odo. *Studies in Monastic Theology.* Cistercian Studies Series, vol. 37. Kalamazoo, Mich.: Cistercian Publications, 1980. The volume contains seven significant studies on William of Saint Thierry by the foremost English-language student of William. It concludes with an extensive bibliography.

Dechanet, Jean-Marie. *William of Saint Thierry: The Man and His Work.* Translated by Richard Strachan. Cistercian Studies Series, vol. 10. Spencer, Mass.: Cistercian Publications, 1972. The best available biography of William of Saint Thierry, which places all his writings in the context of his life.

McGinn, Bernard, ed. *Three Treatises on Man: A Cistercian Anthropology.* Cistercian Studies Series, vol. 24. Kalamazoo, Mich.: Cistercian Publications, 1977. The volume includes William's treatise, "The Nature of the Body and Soul," with a most helpful introductory study by Dr. McGinn that clarifies William's anthropological outlook.

William of Saint Thierry. *Exposition on the Epistle to the Romans.* Translated by John Baptist Hasbrouck. Edited with an introduction by John D. Anderson. Cistercian Fathers Series, vol. 27. Kalamazoo, Mich.: Cistercian Publications, 1980. This treatise of William's, along with Dr. Anderson's introduction, will place William's first meditation fully in context.

———. *The Golden Epistle: A Letter to the Brethren at Mont Dieu.* Translated by Theodore Berkeley, O.C.S.O. Introduction by Jean-Marie Dechanet, O.S.B. Cistercian Fathers Series, vol. 12. Spencer, Mass.: Cistercian Publications, 1971. This is a synthetic treatment of his spirituality written by William toward the end of his life, completing his teaching in the *Meditations.*

ON LOVING GOD

Author: Bernard of Clairvaux (1090–1153)

Bernard was born of a noble family, one of seven sons and a daughter, but he was prepared more for the clerical life than for the martial arts. When he decided to enter the cloister he spent a year in preparation and recruited some thirty relatives and friends. He entered Citeaux in 1112 and three years later was sent to start the abbey of Clairvaux where he served as abbot until his death. He founded some sixty monasteries and assisted in the founding of over three hundred others. Though his desire was for a secluded life, his great abilities involved him in the politics of church and state. He ruined his health with excessive asceticism when young, but found a freedom to live a life of complete love for God and for his fellows. He has left us many rich writings including a commentary on the Song of Songs.

Type and subject of work: A short spiritual treatise on the essence of Christian living

First transcribed: c. 1126–1141

MAJOR THEMES

The reason for loving God is God himself.

The measure for such love is to love without measure.

We should love God because of his gifts to us: first of all himself, then all the gifts of nature, and finally the gift of ourselves.

The whole of the spiritual life is a response to God's gratuitous love.

If we know ourselves, we are already on the way to God, because God created us in his own image.

No one can seek God unless one has first been found by God and is led to find God in order that one might seek him more.

We love ourselves for our own sake; we love God for our own sake; we love God for his sake; we love ourselves for God's sake.

On Loving God was written in response to some questions addressed to Bernard by Haimeric, cardinal deacon and chancellor of the See of Rome. It incorporates a letter earlier addressed to the monks of the Grande Chartruse, epistle eleven in Bernard's corpus.

Immediately Bernard sets forth his basic response and the basic principles of his whole treatment of love: The reason for loving God is God himself. The measure for such love is to love without measure. These principles contain everything, yet they are not enough; it is necessary to know what they contain.

What Bernard says is very simple. He starts with three elementary chapters about the reasons for loving God, which he sets forth in a very logical yet very suggestive way. (Books of meditation as such did not come into being among the Cistercians until the thirteenth century, but this book is in fact a method of meditation. In other words, it is not broken up into points of meditation, but if we follow the steps of Bernard we will see a clear logical order.)

We should love God because of his gifts to us: first of all himself, then all the gifts of nature, and finally the gift of ourselves.

God gave himself to us in a wholly gratuitous love. To quote Saint John, "He first loved us." Almost in the style of a newspaper report Bernard asks: Who, to whom, how much? Who loves? He who has not need of his creatures loves with the love of majesty that does not seek its own. The whole of the spiritual life is a response to this gratuitous love. Whom does he love? His extreme opposite, the nefarious sinner, who has disobeyed him. How has he loved? To the fullest extent possible: He has given his very Son to be crucified for us.

When Bernard comes to speak about the gifts of God in nature in general he is eloquent, but this section lacks the strength and insight of the preceding and following. Bernard has a rich existential understanding of humanity.

God deserves to be loved even by infidels who do not know God but know themselves. Bernard's view of human nature is very optimistic to the glory of God the creator. If we know ourselves, we are already on the way to God, because God created us in his own image. He has endowed us with supreme dignity of freedom and the ability to know our own dignity.

Our dignity lies in our freedom to love God, Bernard writes. If we are aware we can love God, then what keeps us from loving him? We do not use our freedom precisely because we are not aware of it. Our understanding has been obscured by sin and passion. We cannot see on our own; we need the grace of Christ, which has been given to us. So we are twice the beneficiaries: in creation and in re-creation. We need to look at the mysteries of Christ, the author of life, who submitted himself to death on the cross. The whole of creation comes back to life in the resurrection of Christ. Surrounded now by the fruits of the tree of the cross we can be nourished. We pick them and eat them by meditating on the mysteries of faith that make Christ present in our hearts. This develops into contemplation. His love prepares our love and then rewards it.

No one can seek God unless that person has first been found by God, Benedict states, and the seeker is led to find God in order that he or she might seek God more.

Love is natural and it is good. It is one of the four basic instincts in us: love, joy, fear, and sorrow (Bernard is following Boethius here), the roots of all our activities. Love is central. These instincts are given to us by God so that we can serve him with the help of his grace.

The most basic form of love is carnal and social love. Carnal love is that natural love we have to care for our own bodies, keeping them within the limits willed by God, which gives glory to him. But we cannot just care for ourselves. We have to restrain our love of self in order to love others so that we can find our place among them and share all that God has given to us in common. To see and do this we need both self-denial and God's grace. The first degree of love, the love of self, has to be understood in this fuller sense—loving self as a social person, disciplining oneself to be socially integrated.

Bernard sets forth four degrees of love. His division is not so much psychological as philosophical or theological, coming from the nature of the human person. Yet Bernard constantly brings in our experience of these and this is psychological.

Bernard's four degrees of love are: We love ourselves for our own sake. We love God for our own sake. We love God for his sake. We love ourselves for God's sake.

This clear ordering of things is typical of Bernard, the order of his mind perceiving the order in things. What is most interesting is the way in which Bernard moves from one to the other in developing these degrees of love. What is basic throughout is an obedience to the will or plan of God.

That God wants us to love ourselves is expressed in the needs of our nature. Fundamental to all spiritual life is this: that we start with what is. We ourselves are a gift of God. But we ourselves share a common human nature with our neighbor; therefore our neighbor is our other self, equally to be cared for. If there is a conflict between our needs and those of our neighbor, nature calls upon us to provide first for our fellow creature. This is Bernard's high sense of human nature. His argument is cogent—we all expect a parent to sacrifice for a child; we honor one who lays down life for another.

Bernard moves on. When we sacrifice ourselves for our brother or sister, reaching out to the other, God will reach out to us, and we will move to the second degree of love. We will know God's help and care and love him for it. As we experience God's help we are able to help others more with his help. In this experience we come to know God's loving care for all. God himself is perceived as good and we love him for his goodness, for himself. As we come to love God in himself, we love because we love. Our love grows constantly. We are now free from any why. Our love, like God's, becomes wholly gratuitous, and in this we begin to love ourselves as God does. Bernard declares that this degree of love is not possible on earth. We still have to care for ourselves. But if we do this for God's sake, we are approximating the divine love.

In the included letter to the Carthusians, Bernard makes an important contribution to one of the theological controversies of the time. Some argued that charity in us is but the indwelling of the Holy Spirit. Bernard comes out for what became the commonly accepted doctrine. Charity is God; it is the divine substance, but it is also the gift of God. Where charity signifies the Giver, it is of the substance; where it is gift, it is a quality.

M. Basil Pennington

RECOMMENDED READING

Edition used: Bernard of Clairvaux. *On Loving God.* Cistercian Fathers Series, vol. 13: *The Works of Bernard of Clairvaux;* vol. 5: *Treatises II.* Washington, D.C.: Cistercian Publications, 1974.

Butler, Cuthbert. *Western Mysticism.* London: Constable, 1922. Reprinted New York: Harper & Row, 1966. This classic excellently places Bernard of Clairvaux and his contribution in its historical context in the development of spiritual theology.

Gilson, Étienne. *The Mystical Theology of Saint Bernard.* Translated by A. H. C. Downers. New York: Sheed & Ward, 1939. The most insightful study of Bernard of Clairvaux available in English, written by an eminent medieval scholar. Gilson also includes a masterful study of Bernard's sources.

Leclercq, Jean. *Bernard of Clairvaux and the Cistercian Spirit.* Translated by Claire Lavoie. Cistercian Studies Series, vol. 16. Kalamazoo, Mich.: Cistercian Publications, 1976. Leclercq, who did the critical edition of Bernard's writings and one of the more important biographical studies, here offers an updated and somewhat popularized presentation of the monk and his milieu.

Pennington, M. Basil. "Two Treatises on Love." In *The Last of the Fathers*. Still River, Mass.: St. Bede's Publications, 1983. A comparative study of Bernard's *On Loving God* and the study on love of his friend, William of Saint Thierry, who was both disciple and mentor.

THE MIRROR OF CHARITY

Author: Aelred of Rievaulx (c. 1110–1167)

Aelred was born in Northumberland, the son of a priest. After serving at the court of King David of Scotland, he entered Rievaulx Abbey in 1134. In 1142 he became novice master and wrote his first treatise, *The Mirror of Charity*. The following year he was elected abbot of Revesby, and four years later, abbot of Rievaulx. During the twenty years he served as abbot he wrote historical works, the lives of saints, sermons, and treatises, the longest and best known being *Spiritual Friendship*, filling out the teaching of *The Mirror of Charity*.

Type and subject of work: A spiritual treatise summing up the basics of monastic spirituality

First transcribed: c. 1143

MAJOR THEMES

There are three ways of life: the basic order of nature, the order of necessity and the monastic order.

The inner attitude is the important thing; this is what gives monastic observances their meaning and desirability.

The monastic observances are good and useful for those who want to be free in Christ's yoke and to be freed from the yokes of the lust of the flesh, the lust of the eyes, and the pride of life.

A cosmic vision is the only context within which the life of a contemplative monk can have its true meaning.

Those who love God bear patiently all that God does to them and are zealous in carrying out God' precepts.

Perfect charity is perfect unity of being and action in him who is One and One Love.

We do not find in Aelred's *Mirror of Charity* an altogether orderly treatise. There is a basic order, given to him by Bernard of Clairvaux, who commanded him to write the work. Aelred does adopt certain paradigms, notably Saint John's lust of the flesh, lust of the eyes, and pride of life, and Leviticus's three Sabbaths. Yet he comes at the magnificent many-faceted gem of charity from many directions and uses many modes of approach: the rich typology of the Old Testament, exegesis of the New, the wisdom of the Fathers, the tight precise definitions and distinctions of the scholastics, and open and oftentimes very humble personal sharing. All of this adds up to an immensely rich and varied treatise, a teacher's manual of the novice master and novice mistress that can provide a lasting basis for a most solid, stimulating, and inspiring formation program and course of instruction.

Aelred sees three ways of life: the basic order of nature, the order of necessity, and the monastic order. It is to the last that he addresses his treatise, but it is important that the candidate be fully cognizant of the first two so that he can embrace the third with true freedom. This is important for Aelred.

There were those in Aelred's days—as in our own—who, out of false humanism, were attacking the austere ways of traditional Benedictine monasticism. Bernard, in his prefatory letter, called upon Aelred to show "how false it is to think that charity is lessened by a life of austerity." In the course of his defense of the monastic life, and at other points in the treatise, Aelred lists what he considers the basic austerities or observances of the life: vigils—the best corrective to a light and wandering temperament; daily manual labor; poor food; rough clothes; fasts—the best weapon to fight lust; silence—the sword against anger; recollection; patience; bearing temptations; turning from the world and the things of the world; and walking in the way of obedience.

Aelred does not develop his teaching on these for the most part. He directs his readers to Benedict's *Rule for Monasteries*, Cassian's *Institutes*, and the Fathers in general. He gives very balanced instruction on the importance of maintaining the observance and the due use of dispensations. Aelred presupposes in the persons with whom he is concerned that basic attitude called for by Saint Benedict: that they truly seek God.

For Aelred, the inner attitude is the important thing. This is what gives the monastic observances their meaning and desirability. The observances are good and useful for those who want to be free in Christ's yoke and to be freed from the yokes of the lust of the flesh, the lust of the eyes, and the pride of life. Herein lies Aelred's true humanism. A large segment of the treatise is given to showing practically how this freedom can be achieved.

The treatise seeks to put all this and the person in a large context, the one that proclaims the person's true dignity and meaning. The *Mirror* opens with a cosmic vision and it is important that this be conveyed to the novice, for it is the only context within which the life of a contemplative monk can have its true meaning.

In presenting this Aelred does not hesitate to employ a profound and well-developed theology that is not only cosmic but trinitarian and anthropological. He presupposes in his reader an extensive familiarity with Sacred Scripture, with the Old Testament and the New. His references are many, his exegesis at times incisive.

While Aelred's approach is primarily patristic and his dependence on the Fathers extensive, he is not afraid of the clarity of the scholastics. He defines and distinguishes, and distinguishes his distinctions. For example, as he tries to establish a clear norm for helping the novice distinguish between true charity and natural feelings, he goes through a whole series of such distinctions.

In the course of his very rich treatise, Aelred touches upon an amazingly large number of concerns and meets each with some very practical instruction and pastoral advice.

Considering the extensive amount of attention he gives to it, Aelred considered the question of feelings, consolation, and emotions a very important one for the novice. To a great extent, the beginner's faith rests on feelings and the intensity of love is judged by them. If Aelred's *Mirror* was to reflect the true image of charity, which must be guided by faith, it was absolutely essential to give the novice the means of sorting things out. He sums up his teaching:

> The visitations of God's grace that come to us in the form of feelings and emotions are for God to bestow when and where and to whom he wills. It is not for us to seek them, or even to ask for them, and if God should suddenly remove them from us, our wills must be in agreement with his. For the man who loves God is the man who bears patiently with all that God does to him, and who is zealous in carrying out God's precepts.

Aelred is very frank and concrete in speaking about the temptations novices have to face. At times novices will be burdened by the weight of natural desires for earthly things. When life is hard and wearisome they will be tempted to lose themselves in a world of wishful thinking, looking forward to the time when they will be in a position to command rather than to obey, and presuming liberties that are not theirs to take. They might even be beset with the "blasphemous thought" that the service of God is all in vain and that there is no reward for those who keep his commandments.

Aelred sees, then, the importance of encouragement, of helping novices to see their present life in contrast to their past, of giving them a true norm to judge this spiritual growth. For this last, Aelred draws extensively from Scripture, and later sums it up in these words: "The quality of our will can be judged by two things, namely by the way we bear with whatever God sends us in the way of suffering and by the way we fulfill his commands."

In the light of his later writings it is not surprising to find that Aelred gives relatively extensive teaching on friendship in this treatise on love. Aelred's approach is realistic: "I take it for granted that we cannot all enjoy each other." His cautions are many, summed up in this strong statement: "Friendship is the most dangerous of all our affections."

Related with this theme of friendship, but in some ways going beyond it, is the consideration of fraternal correction. Aelred gives very practical and concise instruction on this, considering not only the need of brothers to help each other in this and the role of superiors, but also the need sometimes for the brethren to correct the superior.

Aelred in his instruction of the novices does not forget that they will someday, please God, be responsible leaders in the community. So we find him considering matters such as the kind of music monks should employ—along with considerations on the role of song in prayer by which the novice immediately profits, monastic architecture and furnishings, and even finances, "since even the management of money comes within the scope of charity."

Aelred does not believe that the problems and abuses that exist in monastic communities should be hidden from the new men. He accepts the idealism, the enthusiasm that is proper to the beginner, but warns them, "Be careful to remember that there is no perfection in this life that may not be closely aped by people who are insincere. And I don't want you to be put off by them, when you discover frauds in religious life, as you certainly will." He repeatedly points out monastic failings and even makes this rather caustic statement: "In fact it happens only too often that those most ill-suited to govern are put in positions of power simply to keep them quiet, and to stop their getting completely out of hand—a lamentable state of affairs."

Aelred does not give any specific instruction on the sacramental life. Concern for the liturgy of the hours, the work of God, is prevalent. Confession was probably seen very much in the context of the novice's relationship with and openness to his novice master. The frequent allusions to the Eucharist gives strong witness to the very significant place this had in the monk's life. Certainly there can be no doubt about the importance Aelred placed on devotion to Jesus in his human life and passion.

For Aelred, all is ordered to a contemplative union with God. To bring this out, in his third part he employs the typology drawn from the book of Leviticus: the three Sabbaths. The Sabbath was for Aelred tranquility of mind, peace and rest in the heart. There is the Sabbath day, found when one is at peace with oneself; the Sabbath year, when one is at peace with one's neighbor—one's own family and house, friends, all Christians, all Jews, all nonbelievers, and all enemies; and the Sabbath of Sabbaths, the Jubilee Year, when one enters into the rest of God, in "the greatest of all joys, which is found only in the contemplation of God."

Aelred's concern here is with unity, and with the monk's being what he is supposed to be: monos—one. This is the ultimate meaning, the perfect imaging or mirroring of charity; perfect unity of being and action in him who is One and One Love. To conclude in Aelred's own words:

> And since there is no division in true unity, we must take care not to let our minds and hearts be distracted by this or that, but simply to be at one with God, who is One. Let all be in him, and all about him, and through him, and with him. Let us know him alone, and enjoy him alone, and being always one with him, we shall always be at rest in him, celebrating our perpetual Sabbath.

M. Basil Pennington

RECOMMENDED READING

Edition used: Aelred of Rievaulx. *The Mirror of Charity*. Translated by Geoffrey Webb and Adrian Walker. London: Mowbray, 1962.

———. *On Spiritual Friendship*. Translated by Mary Eugenia Laker, S.S.N.D. Cistercian Fathers Series, vol. 5. Washington, D.C.: Cistercian Publications, 1974. This much more extensive work, written in dialogue form, is Aelred's most popular work and completes in some ways the *Mirror of Charity*, but it must be read in the context of the *Mirror* to be properly understood.

Daniel, Walter. *Life Aelred of Rievaulx*. Edited and translated by F. M. Powicke. Oxford Medieval Texts. Oxford: Clarendon Press, 1950. This life by Aelred's own infirmarian is well presented by Powicke and gives the flavor of Aelred's own times.

Hallier, Amedee. *The Monastic Theology of Aelred of Rievaulx*. Translated by Columban Heaney. Cistercian Studies Series, vol. 2. Spencer, Mass.: Cistercian Publications, 1969. Based on a doctoral thesis, this is the most authoritative study of the doctrine of Aelred. The volume contains a special introduction by Thomas Merton.

Squire, Aelred. *Aelred of Rievaulx*. Cistercian Studies Series, vol. 50. Kalamazoo, Mich.: Cistercian Publications, 1981. Squire, in writing his biography, places each work written by Aelred in the context of his life and briefly summarizes its content.

BENJAMIN MINOR *AND* BENJAMIN MAJOR

Author: Richard of Saint Victor (died 1173)

Whether Richard, a Scotsman, arrived at the Abbey of Saint Victor before the death of the renowned Hugh is not certain. In any case he is to be thought of as one of Hugh's several able disciples. That he left a more indelible mark on history than other members of the community results from the special attention that he gave in his writings to the subject of contemplation, or, as we know it, mysticism. All Victorines were to some degree contemplatives even as all were biblical scholars; and Richard, though a busy man, who served as prior of the abbey for more than a decade, is mainly remembered for his contributions to mystical theory. Dante found him ensconced in the circle of the sun along with Isadore of Seville and the Venerable Bede, and remarked of him that in contemplation he was more than a man (*Paradiso X*).

Type and subject of work: Treatises on the life of contemplation

First transcribed: c. 1160

MAJOR THEMES

The right ordering of person's emotional life is a prerequisite to contemplation.

So also is such self-knowledge as the mind's powers of imagination, reason, and intellect make possible.

There are six kinds of contemplation differing according to the use that the mind makes of its different powers.

Although ecstasy can occur in any of these kinds, it usually occurs on the level of pure intellection.

Richard of Saint Victor left several writings meant to explain and encourage the practice of contemplation for the use of young men entering the abbey. Contemplation, along with study, was one of the two declared ends of the Augustinian Canons of which Saint Victor was a chapter. Of these writings the best known are two books, commonly designated by the mysterious titles *Benjamin Minor* and *Benjamin Major*. The mystery is easily dispelled. In the first book Richard uses Benjamin to personify contemplation. He was the last of Jacob's twelve sons (besides a daughter), each of which Richard uses to personify one of the virtues. In the second book Benjamin does not appear but, because the book deals with contemplation, students attached his name to this book as well, giving the mistaken impression that the two books are parts of one work. In the Middle Ages neither book bore Benjamin's name. The first was referred to as "The Twelve Patriarchs"; the second, which makes use of the figure of the ark of the sanctuary, was referred to as "The Mystical Ark."

Richard begins *Benjamin Minor* as if he were giving a chapel talk. "Let young men hear a sermon about youth," he says, announcing as his text a verse from the Psalms: "let them wake up the words of the prophet: 'There is Benjamin, a youth, in ecstasy of mind'" (Ps. 67:28 Vulgate; 68:27 AV). Then, after saying that it is impossible to speak profitably about the ecstatic experience, he turns to his subject, which is not about Benjamin but about Leah and Rachel, the two wives of Jacob, who, in the hands of biblical commentators had long been used (like Martha and Mary in the Gospel story) to symbolize the active and the contemplative lives. In the Old Testament saga, Jacob, a trickster who had been forced to leave home because he had cheated his twin brother Esau out of the birthright, was tricked by his uncle Laban, who after promising him Rachel, his second daughter, arranged that his first daughter, Leah, take her place in the marriage bed. Jacob had agreed to work seven years for Rachel, and it was quickly arranged that he should work fourteen years and have the twain. The moral of the tale, according to Richard, is that he who wants to wed the fair Rachel (wisdom) must first be wed to the unprepossessing Leah (righteousness). For, although anyone who desires righteousness can achieve it, wisdom is something that all desire but that few can attain.

As the allegory develops, Jacob, representing the human soul, is said to possess two main faculties: Leah is volition, Rachel is reason. But, as if two wives are not enough, each wife has a handmaid: Zilpah (Leah's) is sensation; Bilhah (Rachel's) is imagination. Jacob has children by all four women. A large part of what follows is what was once called moral and mental philosophy: Through the fanciful meanings that he gives to the names of their offspring, Richard develops a speculative account of humanity's active and intellectual powers. And it must be said that, like a good clinician, Richard devotes to each child the proper attention, irrespective of the favoritism of the father and the jealousies of his wives.

Leah's first four children are the religious affections: Reuben is the fear of God; Simeon is contrition; Levi is hope of forgiveness; Judah is love of God. Richard gives special attention to Judah, remarking not merely on Leah's thankfulness for such a fine boy but also on Rachel's envy; for, it was after Judah's birth that Rachel went begging to Jacob saying, "Give me children or I die." Why, Richard asks, did Rachel's desire for children grow stronger after the birth of Judah? Because Judah represents the love of unseen things; and this love it is that moves Rachel to press her husband to take Bilhah. The lesson is clear. Everyone knows, says Richard, how hard it is for the untaught mind to attend to unseen things. It can desire the incorporeal but it cannot grasp it, for it is hard to attend to what is unseen except under the image of something corporeal. That is where Bilhah comes in. Her children, Dan (factual imagination) and Naphtali (fictitious imagination), are means to knowing. Meanwhile Zilpah (sensation) has two sons, Gad (abstinence) and Asher (patience); and Leah herself has two more sons, Issachar (humility) and Zebulon (hatred of sin). All of these virtues are treated by Richard at the length that they deserve; for, the author's intention in *Benjamin Minor* was not to exalt contemplation by itself but to show that it is the crown of a virtuous life.

Still, as in the Bible, a wholly new story begins when Rachel at last has a son of her own, Joseph, whom his father loves more than the others because he signifies discretion, without which no good thing can be acquired. We see, moreover, why Joseph could only be born of Rachel (reason), and why he is born so late—because discretion comes only with much learning and experience. Long afterwards Benjamin is born, signifying contemplation, proving that the soul that has not long practiced knowing its own invisible nature cannot know the invincible things of God. Indeed, the rational soul is a mirror in which God can be seen, and the true Joseph will spend much time polishing the mirror and gazing into it. Or, to use as a figure the Mount of Transfiguration, the soul that examines its own spiritual nature may be viewed as ascending the peak of perfect knowledge, of which Peter witnessed, "It is good for us to be here!" Many fail in the attempt to climb this mountain, and of those who succeed many come down too soon. Perhaps you have climbed there, Richard says to his reader. "Learn to live there. . . . Truly with much practice it will, in the end, become a delight to you, so much so that, without any difficult effort, you will often be able to be there; you will even find it painful to rest anywhere else but there."

Wonderful things happened on this mountain: Moses and Elijah appeared; Christ's garments were transfigured. But greater still were to follow. The voice of God the Father was heard, and with that the hearers, who had been standing, fell to the ground. This means that the power of the human mind fails in the presence of God. Three disciples accompanied Jesus as he climbed the mountain, symbolizing the bodily senses, memory, and reason. It is only when these are prostrate that the depth of intellect expands to take in the secrets of divine inspiration—a truth that is also symbolized by the fact that Rachel dies in giving birth to Benjamin.

Rachel's death is one thing and Benjamin's birth another, signifying two kinds of contemplation. Both kinds transcend reason, but the former is not contrary to it whereas the latter is. Both belong to the third heaven witnessed to by the apostle Paul, who beheld there things not lawful to utter. To the first heaven belongs faith, to the second, reason —exemplified by Joseph, who also stands for meditation. When Joseph was viceroy of Egypt he sent for Benjamin, and when the two embraced, we see divine revelation and human reason agreeing in witnessing to the same truth. Does the reader object to having Scripture give different meanings to one and the same thing? "But everywhere it adds something by which it prevents the sense from being altogether hidden. In Rachel's death contemplation rises above reason; Benjamin's going down to Egypt is contemplation condescending to the imagination; by the embrace of Benjamin and Joseph human reason gives support to the divine revelation."

Benjamin Major is more than twice the length of *Benjamin Minor* but it is more limited in scope, being simply an expansion of the Rachel-parts of the latter, that is, the parts that have to do with knowledge. Imagination, reason, and intellect, which were personified in *Benjamin Minor*, are here made the basis for a system for classifying the various modes of contemplation. Six modes are possible. Imagination can function by itself or in combination with reason; and there are two ways in which reason can serve, besides the ways in which it combines with intellectual insight. For example, imagination alone enables us to contemplate God in a flower, but in combination with reason it enables us to contemplate him in the development of a plant in which the blossom has a place. Similarly, imagination can aid reason to comprehend the circuits of heavenly bodies; and, having learned how to abstract from sensible contents, reason can contemplate God in the unimaginable activities of humanity's heart and mind. Rising to divine things, reason can contemplate certain attributes of God; but, on the highest level, it must yield place to the light of pure intellection.

One who knows the story of Rachel and her two sons feels quite at home with these explanations and hardly feels the need for a further allegory. But Richard is more comfortable with pictures than with concepts, and he likes to support his opinions with scriptural authority. Happily, the six ways of contemplating God are clearly set forth in the book of Exodus, where we read that Moses was called up Mount Sinai and given the pattern of the ark of the covenant, which was then built by Bezaleel, and was served by the high priest Aaron. Each of these men represents a different way in which it is possible for the mind to attain to ecstasy: Moses by grace, Bezaleel by effort, and Aaron by teaching. But, more to the point at hand, the six salient features of the ark of the covenant represent the six ways of contemplating God: The wood of which the ark was built represents pure imagination; the overlay of gold and the golden crown represent the two combinations of imagination and reason; the golden mercy seat represents pure reason; and the two golden cherubim, with their wings extended over the mercy seat, represent the two stages of intellectual insight.

In outline this sounds very scholastic and ill-adept. Distinctions can be invented at will, but humankind's thoughts and experience will not be bound thereby. We sense this from the beginning when, seeking a definition of contemplation, Richard lays it down that, unlike meditation, which he defines as motivated thinking, contemplation is free and spontaneous thinking. Thus, he distinguishes three kinds of mental activity: random thinking, meditation, and contemplation. But although Richard loves his distinctions (almost as much as he loves his allegories) he never uses them as more than helps. "It often happens," he writes, "that in the wanderings of our thinking, the soul meets with something which it passionately desires to know and presses on strongly towards it. But if the mind satisfying its desire applies itself with zeal to this king of investigation it already exceeds the bounds of thinking by thinking, and thought passes over into meditation. The same thing happens in the case of mediation. For when a truth has been long sought, and is at last discovered, the mind usually receives it greedily, wonders at it with exultation and for a long time rests therein in wonder. And this already shows meditation exceeding its bounds and passing over into contemplation." Moreover, Richard allows that the same thing is true of the levels of contemplation: Ordinarily, he says, ecstasy takes place when the soul has ascended to the point where it has left behind not merely imagination but reason as well; yet there is no rule, for ecstasy may occur on the level of simple imagination as well as on the highest level of abstraction. Moses, in order to see the ark, had to climb the mountain and pass through the cloud of darkness; but Bezaleel, the craftsman, did not go near the mountain, which shows that "some of these works may be and are generally known in contemplation, without any ecstasy."

The mystical way is sometimes represented as an ascent, but at other times it is described as a withdrawal of the person within himself. Aaron, the high priest, is a symbol of the latter, because for him the ark is within the veil of the tabernacle. There is no reason to be bothered by this difference, Richard assures us. "As we understand the top of the mountain to signify the apex of the mind, so by the Holy of Holies we understand the innermost part of the human mind. But undoubtedly in the human soul, the apex is the same as the inmost point, and the deepest place is one with the highest. And we mean the same thing by the top of the mountain as by the mercy seat in the tabernacle of the covenant."

Richard's books are carefully composed and his analysis of the kinds of contemplation was undoubtedly helpful to the great numbers in religious orders who needed a conceptual framework within which to orient their spiritual search. In the main, Richard follows the way of ascending knowledge that characterizes the Augustinian tradition. But, as the last quotation shows, he believed that it is possible to combine this affirmative way with the negative way advocated by Dionysius the Areopagite, according to which one enters God's throne room only by withdrawing within oneself. Richard's books were widely read and their influence can be traced not only in France, but in England, Germany, and Spain as well.

Jean H. Faurot

RECOMMENDED READING

Edition used: Richard of Saint Victor. *Selected Writings on Contemplation*. Translation, Introduction, and Notes by Clare Kirchberger. London: Faber & Faber, 1972. Ample selection from the Benjamin books, with excellent introduction, including a useful account of the influence of these works.

Copleston, Frederick, S.J. *A History of Philosophy*. 6 vols. Vol. 2: *Medieval Philosophy*. London: Burns Oates & Washburne, 1950. Full treatment of Richard's philosophy, pp. 178–182.

Richard of Saint Victor. *The Twelve Patriarchs; the Mystical Ark; Book Three of the Trinity*. Translation and Introduction by Grover A. Zinn. New York: Paulist Press, 1979. Complete text of both Benjamins. A forty-nine-page introduction carefully outlines each work. Essential reading.

THE MIND'S ROAD TO GOD

Author: Saint Bonaventura (Giovanni di Fidanza, 1221–1274)
Giovanni di Fidanza was born in central Italy near Viterbo in 1221. He studied under Alexander of Hales at the University of Paris, where Bonaventura later became a professor of theology. He entered the Franciscan order in 1242, was made general of the Franciscans in 1257, and bishop of Albano in 1273. Gregory X made him a cardinal shortly before Bonaventura's death in 1274. He was canonized by Sixtus IV in 1482 and made a doctor of the church by Sixtus V in the sixteenth century. Bonaventura's other notable works include *Retracing the Arts to Theology (Reductio artium in theologiam,* c. 1250) and *The Three Ways (De triplici via,* c. 1250).

Type and subject of work: Spiritual instruction through mystical theology

First transcribed: c. 1259

MAJOR THEMES

The six wings of the Seraph correspond to the six stages of illumination by which the soul ascends to God.

Six stages of the soul's powers enable us to ascend by six stages to God: sense, imagination, reason, intellect, intelligence, and conscience.

We may ascend to God by reflecting on his traces in the sensible world, by considering our natural powers as reflecting God, and by achieving illumination through Christ as mediator.

Each of these three modes of understanding is twofold: We see God through them and in them.

The six stages, then, are these: We understand God through sensible things as bearing the traces of his creative power; we see God in sensible things as essence, potency, and presence; we enter our own minds and see God's image stamped upon our natural powers; by grace we see the First Principle in ourselves; by reflecting on pure being, we know God as unity; by reflecting on the goodness of pure being, we know God as trinity.

In the prologue to the *Itinerarium,* Saint Bonaventura tells of ascending Mount Alverna thirty-three years after the death of Saint Francis and shortly after having become minister general of the Franciscans to meditate and seek spiritual peace in the very place where Saint Francis had experienced the miraculous vision of the crucified Seraph. While in that place Bonaventura had the same vision, and he reports, "While looking upon this vision, I immediately saw that it signified the suspension of our father himself in contemplation and the way by which he came to it."

The six wings of the Seraph, he writes, are to be understood as signifying the six stages of spiritual illumination by which the soul ascends to God. The way is only by the blood of the Lamb, Bonaventura adds, for the six stages of illumination begin with God's creatures and lead up to God only "through the Crucified."

(The recounting of the miraculous vision illuminates Bonaventura's subtitle, "The Mendicant's Vision in the Wilderness," and makes understandable Bonaventura's honorific designation as "The Seraphic Doctor.")

The basic image of Bonaventura's spiritual allegory is that of a six-winged angel, seen as bearing three pairs of wings, each pair symbolizing one of the three major phases in the ascent to God. The first pair of stages involves reflecting on the sensible, corporeal world; the second pair consists in the contemplation of the mind's own powers; the third is contemplation of God's essence. The ascent to God, then, calls for seeing God through and in the body, then through and in the mind, and, finally, through and in the features of pure being.

Bonaventura accordingly divides his treatise into seven chapters, the first six having to do with the six stages of illumination, and the seventh with the mystical experience of the union with God by which peace comes to the spirit.

Throughout his account of the stages in the ascent to God Bonaventura emphasizes that the securing of beatitude, the "fruition of the highest good," requires divine help. None can be blessed, the saint writes, "unless he ascend above himself, not by the ascent of his body but by that of his heart," and then he adds, "But we cannot be raised above ourselves except by a higher power raising us up."

Prayer is vitally important also, Bonaventura writes. Divine help comes to those who seek it by means of prayer "from their hearts humbly and devoutly." Just as Bonaventura himself was illuminated about the stages in the ascent to God only after having humbly and devoutly prayed on Mount Alverna, so others can find through prayer the kind of knowledge needed for the ascent.

The world is a ladder for ascending to God because just as a work of art reveals much about the artist, so the world bears traces of God's hand. Accordingly, Bonaventura advises, "we ought to proceed through the traces which are corporeal and temporal and outside us; and this is to be led into the way of God." To seek God through recognizing and appreciating the signs of his creative power in the world we sense is the first mode of understanding and ascent.

The second mode of understanding is by taking our own minds as the objects of reflection, for our minds "are the eternal image of God, spiritual and internal." Having learned the *way* of God by examining the world, we proceed to awareness of the *truth* of God through and in our minds.

The third and final mode of ascent is by turning our minds to what is "eternal, most spiritual, and above us," the First Principle of being, God himself.

Bonaventura summarizes his preliminary account of the three modes of understanding and ascent by calling attention to the three aspects or, one might say, prospects of the mind. In the first mode, the mind refers to body, "whereby it is called animality or sensuality"; the mind then looks into itself, and in that aspect it is spirit; finally, the mind looks above itself, and here it is properly called "mind." Body, spirit, and mind, then, are aspects of the soul realized in the contemplative ascent to God.

These three modes are twofold, he next comments, "in so far as we happen to see God in one of the aforesaid modes as *through* a mirror and *in* a mirror." Thus, just as God made the world in six days and rested on the seventh, so the "microcosm," the soul, "by six successive stages of illumination is led in the most orderly fashion to the repose of contemplation."

Corresponding to the six stages of ascent are the six stages of the soul's powers by which that ascent is made; namely, sense, imagination, reason, intellect, intelligence, and "the illumination of conscience (*Synteresis*)." These powers of the soul must be exercised through prayer, holy living, and striving for truth by way of the sixfold ascent.

The soul can become aware of God's power, wisdom, and benevolence by contemplating, believing, and reasoning: By the contemplation of created things one may come to understand the significance of their actual existence; by believing one can become aware of the significance of the habitual course of things; and by reasoning one can grasp the principles of things and their potential excellence.

Having explained in chapter one how the soul by the use of its powers can begin the ascent to God by reflecting on the traces of God to be found in the created, corporeal things outside us, Bonaventura proceeds in chapter two to explain how one can move from seeing God *through* the objects of our senses to seeing God *in* the sensible world.

We know the world through our senses, Bonaventura declares: we *apprehend* the world through the five senses. We then *delight* in the natural form, power, and operations of things. Finally, we *judge* insofar as we use our intellectual powers of abstraction to appreciate the principles of things. It is the "number" in things, their rhythmical proportion, that is the primary trace of God. Through apprehension, responsive delight, and intellectual judgment, then, we realize the power, wisdom, and goodness of God.

In the third chapter Bonaventura calls upon us to enter into ourselves, to examine our own minds as the mirror through which God can be seen, for in our minds "the divine image shines."

To see the reflection of God in our minds requires use of the powers of memory, intellect, and choice. Memory enables us to retain and represent all things present, past, future, simple, and eternal. (According to Bonaventura, memory "retains the past by recalling it, the present by receiving it, the future by foreseeing it.") Memory, intelligence, and will reflect the Blessed Trinity, "Father, Word, and Love," Bonaventura concludes; memory leads to eternity, intelligence to truth, the power of choice to goodness. Thus, the soul in the "trinity of its powers" is "the image of God."

Bonaventure turns now to "The Reflection of God in His Image Reformed by the Gifts of Grace." He begins chapter four with the remark that "since not only by passing through ourselves but also within ourselves is it given to us to contemplate the First Principle, and this is greater than the preceding, therefore this mode of thought reaches to the fourth level of contemplation." The emphasis here is on the word *in*; on the third level of contemplation the soul recognized the powers of God *through* contemplation on the mind's own powers, but now one is called upon to see God *in* the mind.

But no one can be illuminated and find the First Principle in the finite, created mind who does not receive the gift of grace. The soul cannot intuit the divine in itself unless "the Truth, having assumed human power in Christ, should make itself into a ladder, repairing the first ladder which was broken in Adam." We are called upon, therefore, to "believe in Him, hope in Him, and love Him"; Christ will then be the

Mediator by whom the soul can so enter into itself as to find and accordingly take delight in the Lord *in* itself.

The third mode of contemplation, the fifth and sixth stages of the ascent to God, may now be undertaken. Bonaventura reminds us that we may contemplate God not only *outside* ourselves through his traces and *inside* ourselves through his reflected image in the mind, but also *above* ourselves "through His light, which has signed upon our minds the light of eternal Truth."

By reflection on God as *Being*, one realizes God's essential attributes (this would be the fifth stage); and then by knowing God as *Goodness*, one would know the three Persons of God (the sixth stage).

Bonaventura advises (in chapter five, "Of the Reflection of the Divine Unity in Its Primary Name Which Is Being"), "If you wish then to contemplate the invisible traits of God in so far as they belong to the unity of His essence, fix your gaze upon Being itself." God is pure Being in that there is nothing of nonbeing in God and there is absolute actuality. Pure Being is divine.

We are accustomed to thinking of particular beings and of potentialities and possibilities, and often we are absorbed with what is not actual; hence, it is difficult to fasten our minds on being, pure being that is Being, the divine unity that is God. Bonaventura writes of the "blindness of the intellect" and of the "mind's eye, intent upon particular and universal beings" that accordingly does not contemplate Being itself.

But if one can concentrate on pure Being, Bonaventura writes, "If you see this in the pure simplicity of your mind, you will somehow be infused with the illumination of eternal light."

In chapter six, "Of the Reflection of the Most Blessed Trinity in Its Name, Which Is Good," Bonaventura begins by developing a point introduced at the close of the previous chapter; namely, that pure Being is goodness, the Good. The Good is the foundation of the contemplation of the "divine emanations," the Trinity. Since the Good is better than nonbeing, "it cannot rightly be thought of unless conceived as both three and one." The Good must be "self-diffusive"; that is, the Good must be productive of good, pouring forth love and receiving love; it must be Word and Gift in virtue of being Good; it must be Father, Son, and Holy Ghost. Hence, as pure Being, God is unity and the Good, but since the Good is necessarily a Trinity, God is necessarily both Unity and Trinity.

Bonaventura's effort to reconcile polarities and resolve paradoxes is more a celebration of God's essence and emanations than it is a clarification. The emphasis is on the blessedness of God and the wonders of discovery at the heights of contemplation. Bonaventura's principal theme remains clear even in the midst of his most intellectual, theological efforts: by reflecting on the world outside, the soul inside, and the God above, one is brought to the elevated condition of repose in the presence of God.

In the closing chapter of his work, Bonaventura emphasizes the proposition of faith that the passage up the six steps of contemplation to the seventh stage of repose and illumination by supreme wisdom is made possible by Christ: "In this passage Christ is the way and the door, Christ is the stairway and the vehicle, like the propitiary over the ark of God and the mystery which has been hidden from eternity."

The seventh and final stage of mental and mystical elevation (of the kind granted to both Saint Francis and to Bonaventura on the heights of Mount Alverna by the vision of the seraph with six wings nailed to the cross) is one in which all intellectual operations cease "and the whole height of our affection should be transferred and transformed into God." This ultimate stage of elevation, Bonaventura adds, is "mystical and most secret, which no man knoweth but he that hath received it."

Despite his effort to describe the mind's six stages in the passage that culminates in the unifying experience of divine illumination, Bonaventura exultantly concedes that "If you should ask how these things come about, question grace, not instruction; desire, not intellect; the cry of prayer, not pursuit of study; the spouse, not the teacher; God, not man; darkness, not clarity; not light, but the wholly flaming fire which will bear you aloft to God with fullest unction and burning affection."

Ian P. McGreal

RECOMMENDED READING

Edition used: Bonaventura, Saint. *The Mind's Road to God*. The Library of Liberal Arts. New York: Liberal Arts Press, 1953.
———. *Bonaventure: The Soul's Journey into God, the Tree of Life, the Life of St. Francis*. Translated and introduced by Ewert Cousins. Classics of Western Spirituality. New York: Paulist Press, 1978. This is a useful and clear presentation of three of Saint Bonaventura's most important writings.
Bougerol, Jacques Guy. *Introduction to the Works of Bonaventure*. Translated by José de Vinck. Paterson, N.J.: St. Anthony Guild Press, 1964. A helpful guide to Bonaventura's principal works.
Gilson, Étienne. *The Philosophy of St. Bonaventure*. Translated by Dom Illtyd Trethowan and F. J. Sheed. New York: Sheed & Ward, 1938. Gilson's scholarly analysis enhances his careful presentation of the historical context of Bonaventura's life and works.

THE FLOWING LIGHT
OF THE GODHEAD

Author: Mechthild of Magdeburg (1210–1297)
Mechthild was born in the archbishopric of Magdeburg, and it seems
likely from her language, references to court life, and apparent culture
that she was of noble or at least well-born parents. She had a brother
Baldwin; we know nothing of any other family. When she was twelve,
she received her first revelation of the Holy Spirit. Afterward she says
that she "could no longer have given way to serious daily sins." In 1233,
when she was twenty-three, she moved into the city of Magdeburg and
lived as a Beguine, a laywoman who lived in community and cared for
the sick and needy. She later became a Dominican Tertiary, popularly
known as the *Domini cane*—the dogs of the Lord. She may have lived in
the Convent of Saint Agnes and may even have been its abbess from
1273. However, persecution led her to seek refuge in the Cistercian convent in Helfde in Saxony, where Gertrud was abbess, about 1285. She
became seriously ill and went totally blind toward the end of her life.

Type and subject of work: An account, often poetic, of Mechthild's
mystical revelations

First transcribed: 1265

MAJOR THEMES

God created the soul because divine love made it necessary.
God is love.
The soul is created for loving communion with God, as a bride with her bridegroom.
That relationship is one of total mutuality.
"God has enough of all good things save of intercourse with the soul; of that He can never have enough."

We know little of Mechthild's life apart from her book of revelations. In part four, chapter two, she gives us some details. As a child she knew nothing of God, she says, except the usual Christian beliefs. Although she tried to follow them diligently with all her heart, she did not ask God for the special revelations she was given. Yet she notes that when she was alone, in her twelfth year, she was so overpoweringly greeted by the Holy Spirit that she "could no longer have given way to any serious daily sin." That loving greeting continued every day until her present writing: thirty-one years later.

In order to bring her body into subjection to her spirit, she "aimed heavy blows" at it for twenty years: sighing, weeping, confession, fasting, watching, recollection, discipline, prayer. She felt herself such a poor, miserable sinner. But finally God called her to follow and to trust God in all things. When she shared this with her confessor, he suggested that she begin to write of her experiences. Though she felt shame at her unworthiness that "a poor despised little woman, should write this book out of God's heart and mouth," she began the task.

Readers were surprised "at the masculine way in which this book is written," which grieved her "to the heart" that she, "a sinful woman, had so to write." She could only attribute the strength of her writing to the same God who made the apostles strong and fearless, who gave Moses such courage before Pharaoh, and who gave Daniel wisdom to speak in his youth.

She wrote on loose sheets of paper that were later collected, edited, copied, and eventually translated from Low German into Latin by Heinrich of Halle, lector of Neu-Ruppin and a pupil of Albertus Magnus. She wrote for fifteen years in this way; Heinrich copied and circulated the first six parts of her book during her lifetime. It may well have been read by Dante. The seventh part was written later, for the nuns at Helfde.

Her primary theme is God's love toward the soul and the soul's response to that love. She writes of God as saying to the soul:

> That I love thee continuously is My Nature
> For I Myself am Love;
> That I love thee fervently is My Desire
> For I long to be greatly loved.
> That I love thee long comes form My Eternity,
> For I am everlasting and without end.

And the soul, in return, praises God:

> O God! so generous in the outpouring of Thy gifts!
> So flowing in Thy Love!
> So burning in Thy desire!
> So fervent in union!
> O Thou who dost rest on my heart
>   Without whom I could no longer live!

Mechthild's revelations are often framed as dialogues, love poems between God and soul. She is clearly influenced by Bernard of Clairvaux's homily on the Song of Songs. She was also quite familiar with the works of Richard of Saint Victor and Joachim of Fiore. The mystical love of God and the soul is often described in terms of courtly love, using the cadences of worldly love songs as well as biblical, numerical, and symbolic imagery.

> In one playlet, for example, the senses say to the soul:
> We have heard a whisper.
> The Prince comes to greet thee,
> In the dew and the song of the birds!
> Tarry not, Lady!

The soul responds by putting on "a shift of humility" and over that a "white robe of chastity" and "a mantle of Holy Desire which she has woven out of all the virtues." She goes forth to meet the Youth and they begin a Dance of Praise, a mystical image dating back to Plotinus. Wearied at the end of the dance, she still resists the senses' efforts to stop short of union with God, to be content with various consolations. She knows she must go beyond the senses into the fiery glory of the Godhead, yet she is reassured:

> Fish cannot drown in the water
> Birds cannot sink in the air,
> Gold cannot perish
> In the Refiner's fire.

This has God given to all creatures
To foster and seek their own nature,
How then can I withstand mine?
　　I must to God—
My Father through nature
My Brother through humanity.
My Bridegroom through love,
His I am for ever!

She is aware that in union the "SELF must go!" yet in the end she also realizes the paradox that

Where two lovers come secretly together
They must often part, without parting.

The self must go and yet the soul remains itself, united with God, one and still two.

In another piece, an allegory on justification by faith, she finds herself in a great church where John the Baptist was to sing the mass, assisted by John the evangelist and Peter. Our Lady stood in the highest place in the choir, with Saint Catherine, Saint Cecilia, bishops, martyrs, and a great company of maidens. She felt unworthy among the crowd of saints, but when she looked down she found herself clothed in a reddish- brown cloak, which was "fashioned of love and signified her longing for God and all holy things." Embroidered on the cloak were the words "Gladly would I die of love!" The white wafer became the slain Lamb on the altar and, at her request, the Lamb "laid itself on its own image in the stall of her body."

Her spiritual advice rings true across the ages with such aphorisms as this one on perfection: "To be gladly unhonoured, gladly disregarded, gladly alone, gladly still, gladly to be lowly, gladly to be esteemed, gladly to be one of many." In the sixth part of the book, presumably written when she was superior of her convent, she gives advice on administration. It was not easy. She begins: "In my community there is a spiritual person through whom I suffer much owing to her bad habits, and because she will follow me in nothing." Yet her advice was "thou shalt have an eagle eye to mark the conduct of those under thee, lovingly, not in irritation. If you find any secretly tempted, stand by them with all thy love, then God will lead them to be open with thee."

One of the charms of this book, written over a period of twenty or thirty years, even though the parts are not necessarily in the order originally written, is that one can glimpse how the stages in Mechthild's spiritual journey corresponded to her physical and emotional life. This is particularly true in reading part seven, which was written later and in which she reflects back on her life. Earlier she had spoken briefly of her childhood. The core of the book was written in her physical and sexual prime. Part seven reflects her illnesses in old age. She laments the weaknesses of her life, and yet God reassures her: "Thy childhood was a companion of My Holy Spirit; thy youth was a bride of My humanity, in thine old age thou art a humble house-wife of My Godhead." Her meditations offer comfort to searching Christians at all stages of life.

Although she often speaks of the Devil and records dialogues with beings that would tempt her to sin and to stray from her goal of spiritual union, she maintains her confidence in God's love, in God's power to save one from all sin, and in God's help in resisting all temptation. She knew that no matter how forsaken she might feel, that she was never alone. God was always near and she was always surrounded by saints and angels offering her strength, courage, and comfort.

Nancy A. Hardesty

RECOMMENDED READING

Edition used: Mechthild of Magdeburg. *The Revelations of Mechthild of Magdeburg (1210–1297) or The Flowing Light of the Godhead.* Translated and edited by Lucy Menzies. London: Longmans, Green & Co., 1953. Only modern edition.

Kemp-Welch, A. *Six Mediaeval Women.* London, 1913. Includes an essay on Mechthild.

Underhill, Evelyn. *Mysticism.* New York: Dutton, 1911, 1961. The classic treatment of the mystical tradition. Quotes Mechthild often.

———. *Mystics of the Church.* London: Methuen & Co., 1925. Has material on Mechthild.

THE SERMONS AND TREATISES OF MEISTER ECKHART

Author: Johannes Eckhart (c. 1260–1327/8)
Born in Thuringia of noble parents, Johannes Eckhart entered the Dominican order in Erfurt. He moved up in the order after attaining his master's degree (hence receiving the title "Meister") in Paris. Concerning himself mainly with union with the Godhead, which already is within the person, he became a popular and famous preacher at Strassburg and Cologne. His preaching finally led him to be tried as a heretic, and after his death some of his teachings were declared heretical. However, in 1980 the Dominican order formally requested that all censures be lifted.

Type and subject of work: A collection of sermons and treatises that speculate on the nature of God and how one may attain unity with the Godhead

First transcribed: c. 1300–1327

MAJOR THEMES

The ground of God and the ground of the soul are the same ground; therefore, it behooves the person to enter his or her soul through ascetic practices in order to facilitate union with God.

Union with God or "the birth of God in the soul" requires utter disinterest, or detachment from things temporal. Thus the highest goal of humanity is total stillness and silence, for God is utterly still and silent, and like attracts like.

The way to utter disinterest through stillness and silence is the ascetic way: embracing suffering, keeping vigils, fasting, and the like; yet these practices must always be seen as helps to detachment and never as ends in themselves, lest they become mere "externals" that interfere with the quest for detachment as much as the very things they are intended to help the seeker overcome.

Beneath literal statements Scripture contains a hidden message, which is to be interpreted in light of the superiority of spirit over matter and the interior life over the exterior life.

The experience of God cannot last and must be sought again and again until one is finally united eternally with God in the hereafter.

Eckhart is concerned in his preaching, as are his followers Henry Suso (1295–1366) and John Tauler (c. 1300–1361), to emphasize the unfathomable depth and greatness of God, which can be "known" experientially but not rationally, and to encourage his listeners to seek this experiential knowledge. Another primary concern is "the birth of God in the soul." This occurs through detachment from all creatures (this detachment aided by the usual ascetic practices), and is the union of the soul with God, both soul and God sharing the same ground. Eckhart is speculative and dualistic, even in his sermons, and frequently weaves his speculations into his preaching. His Neoplatonism is evident throughout his works. Here, rather than "proof text" from a number of sermons, we will examine a few of his sermons that illustrate major themes, and finish with a brief look at one of his treatises, "About Disinterest."

In a Christmas sermon Eckhart emphasizes the importance of the eternal birth of Christ in the soul. Christ was indeed born in Bethlehem, "Yet if it does not occur in me, how could it help me? Everything depends on that." This birth can occur only in a pure soul, pure because God is pure and in the soul because only the soul is, at its core, like God; that is, without thought or action.

The senses serve the soul, providing it with information and possibility, but the core of the soul is without information about itself, since, being like God, it cannot be apprehended by the senses.

Because the soul is free of senses and ideas, because it simply is, God can unite with it. Like unites with like. Thus God begets God's Son in the soul because it is there that Creator and creature (soul) are already one. Thus it is an event in and of itself, rather than an idea, or knowledge of an event. The soul may receive God when it ceases to rely on its agents (the senses), hoping to receive some idea about God.

In silence and withdrawal, in forgetting the ideas and concepts gained through thought and perceptions, the soul receives not the right idea of God, but God. The birth of the Son in the person is at the same time the birth of the person in God. Eckhart tends to interpret Scripture in an extremely dualistic manner. He interprets, for example, Christ's admonition to forsake self and even father and mother to mean, " 'Whosoever will not depart from the externality of creatures cannot be born or received in this divine birth.' By robbing yourself of all externalities you are admitted to the truth."

In another Christmas sermon Eckhart again points out that the birth of Christ occurs in the essence of the soul, "For creatures are only God's footprints, but by nature, the soul is patterned after God." Thus the soul alone is designed to receive the birth of God, which brings all joy and peace. In the cores of their beings sinners and saints are alike, but the birth of God in the soul brings "new light," which radiates out through the believer. To receive the birth of God in the soul, then, one must rid it of ideas and the effects of creatures. If the agents of the soul (the senses) are not to clutter the person's being, then they must be recollected by the soul and used for the soul's purposes.

Eckhart claims that the sinful person's core is filled with darkness and thus cannot comprehend the new light, and yet it is to this very core that the person must go if one is to find light and truth in the first place. On the one hand we are to remain uncluttered by our faculties and on the other we are to "focus all our faculties on the contemplation, the knowing of the unique ... eternal truth." Typical of contemplative mystics, Eckhart advises the seeker to forget all ideas and remain in un-self-consciousness, in stillness and silence. "Our blessedness does not depend on the deeds we do, but rather on our passiveness to God." Elsewhere, however, he also says that even if one is caught up in contemplation, it is better to go help the needy person.

Even in a sermon on Luke 2:49 ("I must be about my father's business"), Eckhart finds occasion to preach about the eternal birth, for "To know this birth at the core of the soul it is necessary above all that one should be about his Father's business." In this sermon Eckhart's anthropology comes out: "Man has an active intellect, a passive intellect, and a potential intellect." Active intellect is the thinking mind, passive intellect is the mind that remains inactive and lets God work in it, and potential intellect is the mind that has "a prevision of what is to be done."

If one is to be detached from temporal things, is one to give up acts of love as well? Hardly, for contemplation and the acts of love that flow from it are one in God. Even Paul's admonition to Timothy to "preach the word!" is spiritualized; Eckhart states expressly that this refers not to the spoken word, but to the "inborn, secret word that lies hidden in the soul. This is what he preached, so that it might instruct the faculties of people and nourish them."

This must occur in stillness and in solitude, for in silence God does for the contemplative what the active intellect does for the natural person. The stilled mind is God's workshop, as it were, because it can experience God "the bedrock": "The object and existence of the mind are essential and not contingent. The mind has a pure, unadulterated being of its own." Again Eckhart sets up an apparently contradictory situation. We are to be still, yet "There is Truth at the core of the soul but it is covered up and hidden from the mind," and thus the mind cannot come to rest.

Nonetheless, we are urged to stillness. "Above all, claim nothing for yourself. Relax and let God operate you and do what he will with you." At the same time we are urged to "external acts of virtue": praying, reading, singing, watching, fasting, doing penance—all meant to keep us from ungodly things. These are contingent, however, and may be boldly dropped when one has a "true spiritual experience." Vows and practices that are no longer necessary or that turn out to be hindrances rather than helps are to be dropped, for unity with God takes precedence over everything.

In a sermon on Matthew 15:4, "Honor thy Father," Eckhart covers several areas integral to his thought. First he points out that while no one is so simple that he or she cannot find help in Scripture and no one is so clever as to discover all the mysteries of Scripture, there is always "a second or hidden meaning, for [the literal] reading of the Scriptures differs from what they really intend."

Second, he speculates on the meaning of the birth of God's Son as "the idea of [God's] own nature." God cannot be demonstrated by analogy, but must be encountered within the core of the soul, for God remains withdrawn within the core of God's own being. Thus as "each takes what it can identify in itself," so our soul can receive God because "the idea of the soul and the idea of God are identical."

This leads to a third important element, ascetic practices. Because our sense perceptions, and our dependence upon them, cloud the soul, and because it is the unclouded soul that receives God, nature's "symbols" must be destroyed and its essence, where God dwells, must be sought. Here a key sentence for Eckhart is, "If you want the kernel, you must break the shell."

Suffering, fourthly, plays a key role, for "when a man suffers and knows discomfort, he is nearest to the light." In the darkness in which we know nothing the light of God will shine. But Eckhart then hastens to warn against attaching ourselves to this darkness, lest we miss the light.

In the treatise "About Disinterest" (translated elsewhere as "On Detachment") Eckhart begins by interpreting "the one thing necessary" (Luke 10:42) as disinterest. Disinterest is that state of being in which one is again similar to God as the soul and God were one before creation. Eckhart even argues with Saint Paul (1 Cor. 13), putting disinterest higher than love.

Since "Everything likes its own habitat best," and God dwells in purity and unity (which are due to disinterest), the disinterested heart naturally draws God to itself. This identification of God and the person, then, means salvation for the person.

Second, Eckhart puts disinterest ahead of love because love compels one to suffer for others or for God and suffering causes one to be at least aware of the source of suffering, whereas disinterest (which draws God) is aware of nothing and is therefore sensitive only to God. Experience must be of something, but disinterest "comes so close to zero [nothingness] that nothing but God is rarefied enough to get into it."

He also puts disinterest above humility, for humility requires self-denial while disinterest goes beyond that (and thus can attract God). As one abases oneself before creatures in humility, one at least is aware of them, and awareness, of course, precludes the disinterest necessary to draw God.

Disinterest is also superior to mercy, for mercy is a response to human need and troubles the heart.

What, then, is disinterest? A disinterested mind is "unmoved by any contingent affection or sorrow, or honor, or slander, or vice.... Unmoveable disinterest brings man into his closest resemblance to God." Here Eckhart is speaking of God in God's essence. The incarnation, according to Eckhart, made not the slightest ripple in the disinterest of God. Thus disinterest does not preclude activity, per se, but it does preclude any sort of investment in the activity, or outer person. Eckhart uses the example of a door—the swinging door is the outer person while the hinge is the inner person, unmoved and unchanged despite the movement of the door it supports. "Pure disinterest is empty nothingness."

If God is to do God's will, God must find a disinterested heart, and can enter and work only "according to the preparation and sensitivity he finds in each." In fact, a disinterested person has no prayer but one, that he or she may be uniform with God.

At its height, disinterest is not even aware of its knowledge, or loves its own love, and is even "in the dark about its own light." Eckhart even interprets the sending of the Holy Spirit in this manner; it is as if Christ was saying, "You take too much pleasure in my visible form and therefore the perfect pleasure of the Holy Spirit cannot be yours." Thus disinterest brings God and, therefore, life. Eckhart's basic dualistic understanding of the world is clearly reflected in his statement, "There is no physical or fleshly pleasure without some spiritual harm, for the desires of the flesh are contrary to those of the spirit and the desires of the spirit are contrary to those of the flesh." Eckhart goes so far as to say that "the pleasure we take in the physical form of Christ diminishes our sensitivity to the Holy Spirit."

Thus we must flee all contact with things temporal—ideas, people, creatures, and preconceptions—and remain empty and still so that God, who is beyond creatureliness and is void may be united with the void of our soul. Any experience of God will only be temporary, and our loss of it will bring great pain, but we are immediately to set about inwardness of contemplation.

Gary R. Sattler

RECOMMENDED READING

Edition used: *Meister Eckhart: A Modern Translation.* Translated by Raymond B. Blakney. New York: Harper & Row, 1941.

Clark, James M. *The Great German Mystics.* New York: Russell & Russell, 1949, 1970. A basic introduction to the lives and thought of Eckhart, Tauler, and Suso.

Eckhart, Meister. *The Essential Sermons, Commentaries, Treatises and Defense.* Translation and Introduction by Edmund Colledge, O.S.A. and Bernard McGinn. Ramsey, N.J.: Paulist Press, 1981. An excellent, if brief, collection and translation of a wide variety of Eckhart's Latin and German works, with a very good introduction.

The Little Book
of Eternal Wisdom

Author: Henry Suso (Heinrich Seuse, c. 1295–1366)
Born near Lake Constance, on the border between Switzerland and Germany, Heinrich Seuse at the age of thirteen entered the Dominican friary. He found the monastic life somewhat difficult until experiencing conversion. A devoted follower of Eckhart, he was a severe ascetic, popular preacher, venerated spiritual director, and leader of the "Friends of God" movement. His first work, *The Little Book of Truth* (c. 1327), extols the value of true religious, mystical submission.

Type and subject of work: A practical devotional work in dialogue form; meditation on Christ's humanity as the way to know God

First transcribed: c. 1328

Major Themes

God attracts the elect, even though they may not know it.

To know God one must know and love him in his suffering humanity; this is the speediest way to salvation.

God, who is love, confounds the believer as Judge, as One who is silent, and as One who lets friends suffer; yet we know that God always does what is best.

Mary is worthy of great praise and blessing both for her glory and her grief.

We must learn to die in this life by dying to self.

God asks not perfection, but our best.

In his foreword, Suso explains that "a Preacher" (himself) received a number of meditations from God, "and wrote them in German, because he had so received them from God." The visions that he received "took place solely by meditation in the light of Holy Writ whose answers can deceive in nothing." His intent is to be helpful to the reader, expounding everything "with reference to our interior." The visions that the preacher records are of conversations between two parties: the Servant and Eternal Wisdom, or the Servant and the Virgin Mary (whose responses follow the word Answer). It is Suso's anticipation that the reader will be moved to love, light, yearning, or some other vehicle for renewing the reader in grace.

The first part of *The Little Book of Eternal Wisdom* begins with an account of a servant who is disgusted and dejected in his spiritual pilgrimage. The Servant is in despair because in his quest he seems to have fallen ever farther away from what he truly has sought. At this point, in the very beginning of the book, Eternal Wisdom assures the Servant of his election: "But now, open thy interior eyes and see who I am. It is I, the Eternal Wisdom, who, with the embrace of My eternal providence, have chosen thee in eternity for Myself alone." God's faithfulness, despite the seeker's unfaithfulness, gives hope. The Servant need only know and love God in God's "suffering humanity" if he is to behold God in God's "uncreated Divinity."

At this point God reveals the horror and suffering of Christ's passion, confounding the Servant, who says, "I would needs seek Thy divinity, and Thou showest me Thy humanity." The believer's path is clearly laid out: "No one can attain divine exaltation ... except by passing through the image of My human abasement and bitterness.... My humanity is the way one must go, My Passion the gate." Eternal Wisdom invites the Servant to join in "knightly resolve," and mentions later that, "For him who has a good second the fight is half won." (This sort of military dueling language is not uncommon to the German medieval mystics, many of whom came out of the upper classes whose stock-in-trade was warfare of all sorts.) It is in God's self-revelation in God's "assumed Humanity" and in the struggles of the believer that one may even begin to comprehend the "bottomless abyss of My hidden mysteries" that no one can fathom.

The way into this abyss, then, is to participate in the good works of Christ through asceticism. Eternal Wisdom then goes on to describe the horror and pain of crucifixion, endured solely out of love for humankind.

The Servant's response is one of utter humiliation and sorrow at having rejected Christ for the offerings of a world that then turned its back on him. Nothing is left but despair. The answer? The totally forgiving grace of God and the ascetic self-denial of the believer.

Suso is concerned to stress that on the seeker's part only total renunciation of self and world will do. On God's part there is already grace and sweet concern; indeed, this is manifested in the very desire of the believer to seek after God in the first place. Nonetheless, temporal love and worldly values must be eliminated if the seeker is to fit into the divine order, for "it is as impossible as to compress the heavens together and enclose them in a nutshell" as it is for a person to love God and still indulge in temporal love. Why do we work so hard for what does not satisfy? In the end we will have to give a reckoning of wasted words, works, and time. But the Servant becomes aware that such hard words move only some to repentance and asks Eternal Wisdom to tell, for those of tender heart, how "Thou art a Mother of beautiful love, and how sweet Thy love is."

It is the love of God that allows God's "incomprehensible good" which is unutterable to be seen by humanity in spiritual perceptions. In language reminiscent of the courtly songs of the *Minnesaenger*, Wisdom describes herself as so faithful, lovely, and tender for "poor languishing souls to kiss, that all hearts ought to break for My possession." So pure and good is Wisdom that one "drop" of her makes all the things of this world bitter. To give oneself wholly to her (that is, to practice the ascetic disciplines) is to assure oneself of joy here and heaven hereafter. Suso takes great pains to point out both the need for the believer to accept the grace of God and yet participate wholeheartedly in the disciplined life.

The Servant raises three problems. The seeker, knowing God's kindness, is confounded when God appears as Judge, but Wisdom points out that God does not change, rather God's appearance depends on whether the seeker is with or without sin.

A second problem is that God seems to withdraw from God's friends, remaining silent, but Wisdom asserts that it is not to enjoy God's presence but to do God's will, which should be one's highest joy. Besides this, adversity (in this case, God's silence) serves to preserve our virtue. Furthermore, God is to be found most purely in silence.

The third problem has to do with God's friends undergoing so much temporal suffering. Wisdom dismisses this as the complaint of a person of "a sick faith and of small works, of a lukewarm life, and undisciplined spirit." We should know by now that God always does and allows what is best for us.

The reader is then warned of the many who chose temporal joys over discipline and love and now endure the everlasting agonies of hell, whereas those who know themselves to be simply pilgrims in this hostile land will receive immeasurable joy as their reward. There is an "accidental reward," which is the delight souls receive for conquering "here below," and there is the "essential reward," which is "the contemplative union of the soul with pure Divinity," in which the soul enters "the vast wilderness and unfathomable abyss of the unknown Godhead, wherein they are immersed, overflowed, and blended up." Here Suso sounds most like the more speculative Eckhart. Suso has a more profound respect, however, for the integrity of the individual in mystical union.

Suso presents suffering, a favorite topic of the mystics, as a gift of God intended to keep people from indulging the "pernicious lusts" to which they are inclined by nature. Rather than complain, let us submit to God in all things, for "Suffering kills suffering." Suffer now so that you will not have to suffer eternally. Suffering makes one like Christ and awakens the slumbering sinner. Indeed, Patience in suffering is superior to raising the dead, or the performing of other miracles."

To meditate on the Passion of Christ is the highest wisdom, for in it everything is to be found. If one cannot weep for Christ's sufferings, then one should rejoice for the salvation Christ has gained for us. This meditation can spare one "any purgatory at all."

One dies to self when one strives to do one's best and is scorned for it, keeps oneself pure and innocent, renounces the love of all humankind, abandons even friends when they come between one and Christ, and detaches oneself from temporal things.

The Queen of Heaven is our protectress and intercessor, "the immediate mediatrix of all sinners." When in sin one despairs of God, one can still cling to the Queen of Heaven, "the door of compassion," and again attain to grace. Suso then offers a moving portrayal of Mary's agony over her Son's crucifixion, and again over her anguish at receiving her Son from the cross.

In the second part Suso teaches that we should learn to die by dying to self and all the world. Until we learn this, we are wasting our time fretting about doctrine. Those who are unprepared die like cattle, ignorant and blind, lamenting, "Why did I not learn to die all the time?" Like a little bird caught in the claws of a falcon, "I am unconscious of everything except that I would gladly escape and cannot." We are advised to confess, abstain, remember purgatory, and meditate on death. Then Suso gives a vivid portrayal of an unprepared man in the throes of death.

This can be escaped, of course, if one lives an interior and godly life. Remain secluded, he advises, be free of external influences, "disenthrall thyself" of things of chance, remain in "divine contemplation," practice asceticism—but in moderation—and remember the presence of God continually. No one on earth can live in divine vision at all times, but one should strive for it.

As Eternal Wisdom is most precious, we are to receive her in the mystery of the sacrament. As a large house can shape itself in a fragment of a mirror or the vast heavens compress themselves into one's eye, so Eternal Wisdom can come to us "under the little shape of the bread." Suso counters coarse materialism by reminding the reader that there is more to reality than meets the eye. We are to receive God with "spiritual hunger and actual devotion," cleansed of sin, adorned with virtue, love, submission, and purity.

In response to the Servant's concern with what the partaker receives, Wisdom seems offended, "Is that a fitting question for a lover? What have I better than Myself?" Any other benefits seem precious to us simply because they are visible. Again Suso point out that God does not change, but the person's condition determines how God is perceived and received: "To the well prepared I am the bread of eternal life, to the little prepared the bread of dryness, but to the unprepared I am a deadly blow, an eternal curse." It is not one's emotions, however, that determine one's preparedness, but rather one's intent and life: "A man, provided he only does his part, should not withdraw himself because of spiritual dryness."

God is praiseworthy because of God's unsurpassable beauty. The glories of nature draw us to God and yet these cannot compare to the glories of God. All praise disappears in its own littleness "in the deep abyss of Thy goodness." Praise is most fitting and, indeed, at the resurrection body and soul shall be united in God's praise. Praise and contemplation lift the soul to heaven, finding their reason to praise in the divine abyss, in "the first origin of all good, and then in its outflowing springs."

Suso closes part two with a prayer of praise and hope for eternal salvation.

Part three consists of "One Hundred Meditations and Prayers, comprised of a few words," such as "Tender Lord! 1. At that hour Thou wast forsaken for my sake of all men; 2. Thy friends had renounced Thee; 3. Thou stoodst naked and robbed of all honour and raiment." Suso then goes on to conclude the work by explaining that in a final vision he knew that he was to complete this task, and so he did.

Gary R. Sattler

RECOMMENDED READING

Edition used: Suso, Blessed Henry. *Little Book of Eternal Wisdom.* 2d ed. London: R. & T. Washbourne, 1910.

Clark, James M. *The Great German Mystics.* New York: Russell & Russell, 1949, 1970. A basic introduction to the lives and thought of Eckhart, Tauler, and Suso.

Suso, Henry. *The Exemplar: Life and Writings of Blessed Henry Suso,* O.P. Edited by Nicholas Heller, Translated by Sister M. Ann Edward, O.P. 2 vols. Dubuque, Iowa: Priory Press, 1962. A collection of Suso's writings with a solid introduction.

THE LITTLE FLOWERS OF ST. FRANCIS

Author: Unknown
Stories originally written down from the oral tradition by Brother Ugolino di Monte Santa Maria (1270–1340) and later condensed and translated into Italian by a gifted anonymous author.

Type and subject of work: Tales and legends of Saint Francis (1182–1226)—"El Poverello" or the little poor man of Assisi—and his companions in thirteenth-century Italy

First transcribed: c. 1330

MAJOR THEME

True joy, peace, and happiness are found only in loving, knowing, and serving God and the neighbor with true humility, simplicity, compassion, meekness, patience, and obedience to Christ.

The spirit of simplicity, humility, and joyful obedience of Saint Francis and his jubilant followers, who tramped the thirteenth-century plains and hills of Italy, winning the hearts and minds of countless citizens of their day, is wonderfully captured in *The Little Flowers of St. Francis*. Not a biography, or even a historical chronology of Francis or his movement, *The Little Flowers* is a collection of incidents drawn together more than one hundred years after Francis's death. In a straightforward

and moving style, the stories capture the buoyancy and childlike innocence of the early medieval spirit and bring one into the Christlike presence of the saint.

Born in 1182 to a wealthy cloth merchant, Francis was an attractive
and fun-loving youth given to revelry and worldly excitement. He
dreamed of being a soldier and fighting in the crusades but was captured following a local battle and spent a discouraging year in prison.
There followed a long period of illness that led to his awakening to
more serious questions about life and to a search for God.

About age twenty-five, following a trip to Rome and attempts to care
for lepers, Francis heard God speak to him from the wooden crucifix of
an abandoned church at San Damiano: "Francis, go repair my house,
which is falling into ruins." Three times the voice spoke, and when
Francis came to himself, he obeyed in the most literal way, by beginning
the physical rebuilding of the church at San Damiano. Soon, the whole
church was to feel the effects of his obedience as thousands followed
after him in the most widespread spiritual awakening in the Catholic
church of the Middle Ages.

Francis understood his vocation in simple gospel terms. *The Little
Flowers* recounts how one day, after mass at the church of San Nicolo,
Francis and Brother Bernard prayed to the Lord Christ that he reveal to
them through the Scripture his path of obedience for them. Opening the
text, their eyes fell on the words: "If you wish to be perfect, go, sell all
you have, and give to the poor, and come, follow Me." They opened the
Scripture a second time and read: "Take nothing for your journey, neither staff, nor wallet, nor bread, nor money." And then a third time: "If
anyone wishes to come after Me, let him deny himself, and take up his
cross, and follow Me." Closing the Bible, Francis exclaimed to Bernard
that this was the counsel of Christ and that they should go and do perfectly what Christ commanded them. For Francis, Christ was enough.
The renewal movement he founded was a return to the gospel teachings
of Jesus with such force that it shook the entire world.

Francis exerted a strange attraction on the people of his time. Brother Masseo asked him one day, "Why after you? Why after you? . . . Why
does all the world seem to be running after you? . . . You are not a handsome man. You do not have great learning or wisdom. You are not a no-
bleman. So why is all the world running after you?" Francis, rejoicing in
the Spirit, answered that it was perhaps because of all men he had the
least to boast of in himself. No one was more vile or insufficient and
thus he had been chosen because God chooses what is foolish to shame
the wise so that all excellence and goodness may be seen to come from
God and not from his creatures.

Such humility was evident in the way Francis sought guidance
through the prayers of friends, in his willing acceptance of ridicule and

public insult, and in his gentle and forgiving spirit toward all people. In one incident, some robbers came begging food from the brothers, and the one in charge drove them away. When Francis heard what had happened, he scolded the brother in charge, saying that sinners are led back to Christ by holy meekness rather than cruel scolding. Reminding him that Jesus came as a physician to be with the sick, he sent the brother to find the robbers and give them food and seek their pardon. All three robbers were in this way brought back to God.

This same quality of gentleness provides the secret of Francis's legendary influence over animals. He preached to the birds who remained quiet and attentive before flying away in the pattern of a cross to the four corners of the earth; he calmed the fierce wolf of Gubbio and helped the people of that community to overcome their fears. He was an instrument of God's peace, both in the human world and in nature.

Francis's pure vision of gospel life was rooted in poverty and the joy of simple living close to the earth. On one occasion "Francis and Brother Masseo went begging bread in a small village. Masseo, a tall, handsome, imposing figure, was more successful in his begging than the small and insignificant-looking Francis. The two brought their begged pieces of bread to a nearby spring with a flat rock that served as their table. When Francis saw the larger pieces of bread that Masseo had begged, he was filled with intense joy, and exclaimed over and over, louder each time, "Oh, Brother Masseo, we do not deserve such a great treasure as this!" Finally, Masseo protested that such poverty and lack of things could hardly be considered a treasure. They had no cloth, no knife, no dish, no bowl, no table, no house. Francis replied that what made it a great treasure was that nothing had been prepared by human labor, but everything had been given by God—the begged bread, the fine stone table, and the clear spring. "Therefore, I want us to pray to God that He may make us love with all our hearts the very noble treasure of holy poverty."

Poverty, for Francis, was not a romantic ideal. He wanted to be poor because Jesus was poor and the biblical promises were made to the poor. He thought the gospel could be preached only to the poor because they alone had the freedom to hear it without distorting it for their own purposes. One could only see rightly from a place of weakness and poverty: "For poverty is that heavenly virtue by which all earthly things are trodden under foot . . . by which every obstacle is removed from the soul so that it may freely enter into union with the eternal Lord God." In contrast to the rest of the human race, Francis hurried in the direction of poverty, certain that he was following in the steps of Christ.

A joyous trust also characterized the simplicity of the early Franciscans. When the movement was only a few years old, Francis called all of the friars together, nearly five thousand brothers, to an open camp meeting on the plain at Saint Mary of the Angels. Several prominent people, including Saint Dominic, were present as observers. When everyone had assembled, Francis rose to preach, encouraging the brothers in love, prayer, praise to God, service to others, and patience in adversity. He concluded with the command that the brothers not have "any care or anxiety concerning anything to eat or drink or the other things necessary for the body, but to concentrate only on praying and praising God ... because He takes special care of you." Saint Dominic was greatly surprised at Francis's command and thought he was proceeding in a impudent way. What would the friars eat? Who would care for them? But soon, from all the surrounding countryside, people arrived bringing food and drink. A great celebration followed as the friars praised God for his provision. Saint Dominic reproached himself and knelt before Francis, saying, "God is truly taking care of these holy little poor men, and I did not realize it. Therefore I promise henceforth to observe the holy poverty of the Gospel."

The dominant keynote in Francis's life was joy—joy in God, in poverty, in the wonders of creation, in the cross of Christ. One of the most delightful stories in *The Little Flowers* concerns how Francis taught Brother Leo the meaning of perfect joy. Walking together in the rain and bitter cold, Francis spoke to Leo of all the things that people believed would bring joy, such as having all knowledge, or healing the sick, or converting prominent people to the Franciscan order. After each recounting, Francis added: "Perfect joy is not in that." Brother Leo finally begged Francis to tell him where to find perfect joy. Francis then began an imagined account of how the two of them would be shabbily treated at the friary they were approaching, and how they would be humiliated, beaten, and left hungry in the cold and rain, and how that was the context of perfect joy. He concluded: "Above all the graces and gifts of the Holy Spirit which Christ gives to His friends is that of conquering oneself and willingly enduring sufferings, insults, humiliations, and hardships for the love of Christ."

To read *The Little Flowers* is to discover a man in love with God, lost in the joy of relationship to Christ, the greatest of all lovers. Francis's life reveals what is happening in the heart of God: not omnipotence but humility; not cold omniscience but endless self-revelation; not detached judgment but relentless welcoming and giving. There seems no bottom to Francis's grateful happiness, no matter the amount of his suffering. Eyewitnesses tell us that he was so filled with gladness he would pick up a stick and place it across his arm like a bow on a violin and play, dance, and sing to the Lord in an ecstasy of joy. Bonaventura recounts that even on his deathbed, two years after mystically receiving the stigmata of Christ in his own body, Francis wanted to go forward again because he had still done so little to heed and obey the call of Christ. Such joyful obedience and humility, love and simplicity, shine through *The Little Flowers of St. Francis* so that to read it today is to be carried across time into the presence of Francis and his followers and to want to join them in a more faithful, less selfish, more joyful following after Christ.

Douglas H. Gregg

RECOMMENDED READING

Edition used: *The Little Flowers of St. Francis.* Translated and edited by Raphael Brown. Garden City, N.Y.: Doubleday, Image Books, 1958.

Fortini, Arnaldo. *Nova Vita di San Francisco* (1959). Translated into English as *Francis of Assisi* by Helen Monk. New York: Crossroad, 1981. Fortini, one of the foremost Franciscan historians, moves beyond the spiritual portraits of the early biographies to give a critical reconstruction of the social, economic, political, and religious milieux during the time of Saint Francis.

Green, Julien. *God's Fool: The Life and Times of Francis of Assisi.* Translated by Peter Heinegg. San Francisco: Harper & Row, 1985. A lively, sensitive, and authoritative biography.

Habig, Marion A., ed. *St. Francis of Assisi, Writings and Early Biographies: English Omnibus of the Sources for the Life of St. Francis.* Chicago: Franciscan Herald Press, 1973. The complete sourcebook, including authentic writings of Saint Francis, the earliest biographies by Thomas Celano (1228) and Bonaventura (1263), and other material, along with extensive introductions, historical notes, and bibliography.

THE FIRE OF LOVE

Author: Richard Rolle (1300?–1349)

Desiring to be a hermit, Richard Rolle left Oxford University at age nineteen and returned to his native Yorkshire. At first supported by a family friend, he later became attached to a Cistercian community at Hampole, where he died, probably from plague, on September 29, 1349. Despite efforts to have him beatified—miracles occurred at his tomb and a local cult arose—the formal process was never completed. Writing in English as well as Latin, he left a substantial body of work, including lyrics, scriptural commentaries, epistles, and treatises. His other major works are *The Mending of Life* (probably written after *The Fire of Love*) and *The Melody of Love* (date unknown).

Type and subject of work: Religious treatise on the contemplation of God

First transcribed: c. 1343

MAJOR THEMES

Solitary contemplation creates the essential precondition for the soul's journey to God.

Engaged in solitary meditation of the Lord, the most intense contemplatives will burn with the heat of God's presence, rejoice in spiritual song, and taste honeyed sweetness.

The prologue to *The Fire of Love* presents in encapsulated form the content of the work, the method of which will comprise patterned repetitions and intensifications of the previously expressed. Sitting in chapel (as we find out in chapter fifteen), Richard was astonished beyond words when he experienced a burning that was not imagined, but real, "as if it were being done by a physical fire." Burning heat boiled up in his soul, bringing with it, however, "unprecedented comfort." When he recognized that this heat was not earthly in origin, he "melted, rejoicing" in the intensity of what he now knew to be spiritual heat.

This heat that penetrated his spirit and comforted his devotions with sweetness was Richard's introduction into the rapture of the contemplative life at its best. "I had not thought," he exclaims, "such ardor could come interiorly to anyone in this exile, for its inflamed my soul in such a way that it was just as if elemental fire burned there." Yet this was not the same fire that is sometimes said to inflame others who burn in love of Christ, even though occupied diligently in divine service and scornful of the world. It is a physical fire, "just as when a finger is placed in the fire." It sets the soul aflame with an actual burning desire for the love of Christ, and is in proportion to what the flesh can bear. Moreover, this fire at its most intense would be too powerful for mere human beings. It would make life unendurable for those who had known its pure power, for they would without a doubt embrace it totally and, "breathing forth the soul in this honey-sweet fire itself," delay there, departing from the world and joining the community of the angelic choir.

The great obstacle to the attainment of such a rapture is, of course, the flesh, which interrupts contemplative tranquillity with the needs of the body, human love, and the concerns of the worldly exile. Spiritual love, when attained, will burn away mortal concerns; and therefore, Richard tells us, he has called this love "fire" as a metaphor, because it burns and illumines. Elsewhere he will insist upon the literal fact of his fire, but here he allows that it can be considered metaphorically (the same will be so of sweetness and song). Eternal love will, for instance, warm the soul made dark by cold, dispel its torpor, and set it on fire with desire for God. It will thaw the soul, burn away sleep,and invigorate the human spirit weighed down by worldly fatigue and ease alike.

The Fire of God is offered at prologue's end to the unsophisticated and untaught of the world, not to the great theologians "ensnared in infinite questionings" or the worldly wise. It is a book for those trying to love God, who cannot be known in arguing but "in doing and in loving." The very first condition Richard sets his readers, therefore, is that they flee all earthly rank, hate all "the ostentation and empty glory of learning," and, living strictly in poverty, "place themselves in the love of God by praying and meditating." In this way a "small interior flame of uncreated love" will appear, focus effort on itself, and lift men and women up "in loveable and most pleasant burning ardor" for God.

The forty-two chapters that make up the work circle about the themes stated in the prologue, restating and developing them in a loose series of spirals. For the most part it is fair to say that Richard's method is nonlinear. He rejects the way of those learned theologians whose knowledge he considers everywhere inadequate to the search for God. Realigned, straightened out, as it were, Richard's commentary includes much that is familiar.

Rejection of the world is the point of departure for the spiritual search. Carnal desire, love of self, all love that does not aim toward God must be overcome. Laboring long and patiently, the seeker will surmount the world's temptations and begin to approach God's incomprehensibility. Seekers will be aided by the fire of love, which will begin to burn from them worldly impurities. Fasting and abstaining—although not to the extent that their meditative powers are diminished—they will experience God as heat, sweetness, and song.

Having abandoned the vanity of the world and having become dedicated to spiritual exercise—because all who love God are moved to work—the seeker must also become a contemplative. While there are active men and prelates who have been made justly famous by their virtue and knowledge, they must not judge themselves capable of the abandonment necessary to the purest search for God. Granted that some worldly ecclesiastics are better than some contemplatives, nevertheless the best contemplatives surpass the best actives. The soul that has not abandoned totally all worldly vanity will not feel the fire of eternal love as Richard has felt it.

In particular Richard speaks against the idea that God can be studied, revealed through the efforts of the human mind, known in the usual intellectual sense. He insists everywhere on the vastness of God, his mystery, his ineffability. We are presumptuous when we think the human mind an adequate instrument for the discovery of the infinite spirit. The results of such human presumption are vainglory, pride of self, and confusion. Theologians are doomed in their efforts from the start, for "he knows God perfectly who understands him to be incomprehensible."

Richard's three metaphors—burning, song, sweetness—require some commentary. To begin with, the burning that he insists upon is the ardor of the soul for God the beloved. The imagery is pervasively sexual and is substantiated by relevant biblical quotations and allusions. Christ is the lover and the soul is his beloved, burning with desire and with expectations of the supreme joys to come. While Richard is not so daring in his spiritual sexuality as, for instance, Donne will be later when he calls upon God to ravish him that he might be chaste, neither does he try to overlook or disguise the core of his metaphor. Indeed, so important is the love of God that its chief rival on earth, love of women, becomes again and again the topic of discussion. There is no sin more damnable than lust, no sinner more damned than the lustful man, no creature more dangerous to spiritual attainment than woman. While Richard admits that friendship with women is possible, he considers it greatly hazardous to the contemplative's goals and best avoided to the extent possible.

The song that accompanies burning and evolves such great joy in the spirit is angelic song and the choir of the heavenly host its source. Human music is by no means a similar phenomenon, for its is one of the distracting pleasures of the world. The soul inflamed by God finds itself in communication with the angels, enraptured by the glory of eternal song praising the beloved object of the contemplative's ardent spiritual search.

The sweetness that often follows the burning and accompanies the song is generally "honeyed" and attended by heavenly intoxication. With the rapture of love and divine song comes now the blissful joy of divine drunkenness. These three famous metaphors—fire, song, sweetness—are Richard's spiritual intensifications of three of the world's most ecstatic experiences: passion, music, transport.

Robert J. Meindl

RECOMMENDED READING

Edition used: Rolle, Richard. *The Fire of Love and The Mending of Life.* Translated by M. L. del Mastro. Garden Ctiy, N.Y.: Doubleday, Image Books, 1981.

———. *The Mending of Life.* (See *Edition used* above.) Date unknown, but probably written late in Richard's life. An account of how to cleanse the soul in preparation for the contemplative life.

Arnould, E. J. "Richard Rolle of Hampole." In *Pre-Reformation English Spirituality*, pp. 132–144. Edited by James Walsh, S.J. New York: Fordham, [c. 1965]. An excellent and concise account of the present state of Rolle scholarship.

Comper, Frances M. M. *The Life of Richard Rolle Together with an Edition of His English Lyrics.* London: Dent, 1929. Reprinted. New York: Barnes & Noble, 1969. Still the standard life.

Rolle, Richard. *Melos Amoris.* Edited by E. J. F. Arnould. Oxford: Blackwell, 1957. Emphasizes the melody that comes from union with god. Noted for its atypical Latin style, lyrical and alliterative, which has been a bar to translation.

THE SPARKLING STONE

Author: Jan van Ruysbroeck (1293–1381)
Ruysbroeck was trained for the priesthood by his uncle, a canon at the collegial church of Saint Gudule, at Brussels. Ordained in 1317, he served at this church until 1343, when, with his uncle and another canon, he withdrew to a nearby hermitage. As the group grew in numbers, a priory was formed under the rules of the Augustinian Canons. Although Ruysbroeck is remembered for his writings, he exercised less influence on his own generation by his writings than by his saintly life. Of his books the most systematic is *The Adornment of the Spiritual Marriage* (c. 1346). However, the reader is advised to start with one of the shorter works, either *The Book of Supreme Truth* or *The Sparkling Stone*, the latter of which, according to Evelyn Underhill, reaches "the high water mark of mystical literature."

Type and subject of work: Treatise concerning the way to perfection

First transcribed: c. 1350

MAJOR THEMES

God calls all men to union with himself and bestows gifts as an aid to virtuous living.

Those who disobey the call are cut off from God's grace, but if anyone repents, this grace will be restored to him.

Those who obey the call must prove themselves as faithful servants of God and learn the joys of God's secret friends before they experience the ecstasy that is reserved for the sons of God.

The mystical union is symbolized by the sparkling stone, which is also a symbol of Christ's humanity.

The Sparkling Stone takes its title from Revelation 2:17, "To him that overcometh I will give a sparkling stone, and in the stone a new name written which no man knoweth save he that receiveth it." According to Jan van Ruysbroeck, the stone is Jesus Christ. It is but a pebble, round and smooth, which we tread on without noticing what we are doing; but to those able to receive it, the stone is white and shining, an irradiation of the glory of God, a flawless mirror in which all things are alive. Allegorically, its roundness signifies that truth has no beginning and no end; its smoothness, that truth is equitable; its slightness that, though immaterial, divine truth bears up heaven and earth by its strength. The new name written in it attests to the individual's life-achievement. When the person was baptized with water and received his earthly name, he was innocent; when he is baptized by the Holy Spirit and receives his heavenly name, he is an overcomer. The book, in fact, has but little to say about the stone, being concerned instead with what one must do to be worthy of receiving it. And this is indicated by its second title, *The Treatise of Perfection of the Sons of God.*

Everyone "who would live in the most perfect state of holy church" must, according to Ruysbroeck, fulfill three conditions: He must be "a good and zealous man; an inward and ghostly man; and an uplifted and God-seeing man." The first of these conditions has to do with obedience to God's commandments; the second, with entering on the narrow way marked out by the evangelical counsels; the third, with losing oneself in the abyss of God's love. In ascetical literature these are often spoken of as the three stages on the way to perfection: the beginner, the proficient, and the perfect. In *The Sparkling Stone* they are further designated as the faithful servant, the secret friend, and the hidden son.

Before he enlarges on the characteristics of those who have set foot on the way of perfection, Ruysbroeck has some words for persons who disobey the divine call; for, he notes, just as there are stages on the way toward union with God, there are also stages leading in the opposite direction—five in number.

First are the slothful, who live for pleasure and for worldly gain. Because their hearts are drawn in many directions they are not prepared to receive God's grace, nor would they be able to keep it if it were given them.

Next below these are the irresolute. Though they live in mortal sin, these souls are not at ease. Fearing God, they do good works, and they honor godly persons and seek their prayers. But as long as they cannot resolve to turn from their sin they remain unworthy of God's grace.

A third class in this rake's progress are heretics and infidels. No matter what kind of lives they lead, they cannot attain to holiness and to the enjoyment of God's presence because they lack faith.

The fourth are the overtly godless who hold all spiritual life as fraudulent and who live only for material gains. They sin against the Holy Ghost, and, although there is nothing to keep them from being converted, this rarely happens.

Farthest from God are the hypocrites. They perform good works but not for God's glory nor even as helps toward their own salvation, but to gain a reputation for holiness and to win the emoluments that go with such a reputation. People take them to be good men and women, but at heart they are false, being turned away from God and from every virtue. Ruysbroeck calls them hirelings. All of these, he points out, enjoy many gifts intended by God as aids to virtue, such as health, beauty, wisdom, riches, and worldly dignity—gifts that God bestows, as he does the sunshine and the rain, on the just and the unjust alike; but whereas the just use these gifts to serve God and his friends, the unjust use them to serve the world, the flesh, and the Devil.

Ruysbroeck makes theology simple. Every person determines his or her own destiny. Each sinner has been inwardly called to union with God, and whenever a sinner enters into himself and is displeased with his sinful life, he is free to change directions: "how wicked soever he may have been before, in that very instant he becomes good, and is susceptible of God, and filled with the grace of God." If he renounces himself and makes it his goal to do what God demands of him, grace will flow forth and give him discernment and strength in whatever measure his soul desires. The desire may be weak or strong. There are impulsive individuals who want, or think they want, to be rapt immediately into God's presence. Ruysbroeck would not discourage any; but he insists that progress toward this goal must be measured and orderly. One cannot experience the privileges of the secret friend of God until he has proved himself a faithful servant, and much less a hidden son until he knows what it is to be a secret friend.

Ruysbroeck's account of the faithful servant is a development of traditional teachings about the active, as over against the contemplative life. The life of the faithful servant is directed outward into the world and consists mainly of obeying God's law and performing good works. It is characteristic of Ruysbroeck, however, to stress the intentional element, which determines whether obedience may be adjudged faithful. Many there are who serve God not out of love but out of fear; and fear translates into self-love, which, according to Ruysbroeck, is the root of all evil. These, therefore, are hirelings and false servants. The "fear of the Lord" is rightly called "the beginning of wisdom," but only because it keeps the sinner within hailing distance of the path of true righteousness. When, with God's grace, the hireling detaches himself from himself and feels true love, he becomes a faithful servant; for "perfect love casts out fear" and fills a person with hope and trust. The faithful servant, Ruysbroeck calls "a good and zealous man." It is important that he have a clear conscience, which comes with examining himself and with using the means provided by the Church for purging sins. On the positive side, he must be meticulous in obeying God and the Church, and above all else, he must learn to perform every action solely because God has willed it and with a view to increasing God's glory. So far, but only so far, the faithful servant is an inward man. Like God's secret friends and his hidden sons, the faithful servant lives by the love of God, desires to do God's will, and has the satisfaction of knowing that he is no hypocrite; but because he has as yet no inkling of what it is to serve God with inward love, he remains an outward man and may, in his ignorance, fall into the way of finding fault with inward and contemplative men and women who seem to him to be lazy and good for nothing.

If, as Ruysbroeck suggests, Martha in the Gospel story typifies the faithful servant, her sister Mary, who, Jesus said, had chosen the better part, typifies the secret friend. "All such friends God calls and invites inward and he teaches them the distinctions of inward exercises and many a hidden way of ghostly life." The archaic term *ghostly* is well-suited to inward-turning souls, who "must forsake all fleshly lusts and loves and must cleave with longing and love to God alone, and thus possess him." Ruysbroeck distinguishes three levels of achievement. First, the inward-turning man must free his heart of images, because images are tokens of attachment to the material world, and every such attachment must be given up. It is only by sinking into an "imageless nudity" that one disencumbers one's mind and is able in thought and will to begin one's upward striving. When one is stripped of every relic of worldly attachment one achieves the second level, called inward freedom. Henceforth one can perform with love and zeal those exercises of devotion that were hitherto beyond one's power. And one's reward is union with God—the third level of the life of secret or inward friendship. Whoever in inward exercises achieves a purity of will so that one "means nought else but the glory of God" will "feel from within a true union with God" that renews itself perpetually, each act of spirit rising toward new union; and "this perpetual renewal in activity and in union is a ghostly life." This is a worthy achievement. Good things fall to God's friends because they please him. Still, they have not entirely overcome selfhood. They possess God by their own act of loving adherence, and, although they feel themselves to be one with God, they also feel "a difference and an otherness between God and themselves." True sons and daughters of God are those who have been rapt out of themselves and been burned up in the flame of love.

Ruysbroeck's attempts to describe the so-called mystical union have been greatly admired and much studied by people interested in mysticism. They have a certain literary splendor; and perhaps one does the author an injustice in describing the style. There is the usual talk about finding (or losing) oneself in an immeasurable and directionless abyss as a result of rising above reason and above all virtue, above even the intentional exercises of love. The self is said to be melted into Unity and to die back into God, and to achieve fruition as it is drawn into the fathomless abyss and enfolded in love. One way of describing the trance experience reduces the self to an eye; and Ruysbroeck's alternative name for the hidden son of God is the God-seeing man. The powers of the spirit are idled, and in its idleness the spirit is flooded with Light. "And this Light is nothing else than a fathomless staring and seeing. What we are that we behold; and what we behold, that we are; for our thought, our life, and our being are uplifted into simplicity, and made one with the Truth which is God." The vision ends as abruptly as it begins: For, our powers do not pass away; and when we engage them again and try to comprehend what has happened to us, we "fall back into reason" and into ordinariness.

Something like this is what we have come to expect in mystical writings, whether sacred or profane. There are passages, however, in which Ruysbroeck gives quite a different account of union with God, making it seem quite a passionate affair. When the soul learns that it is loved there arises "a gaping and eager craving" so that "all that we taste, against all that we lack, is but like a single drop of water against the whole sea." And this, he says, stirs the human soul with a storm of fury of which the heat is so great that love flashes between the soul and God like lightning in the sky. This whole storm of love is, he says, "above reason and way-less"—that is, beyond logical distinctions. But at least what Ruysbroeck writes about the experience is not above reason, and if it means anything at all it means that sometimes the mystic feels that he is one with God and sometimes he feels that he is not. Ruysbroeck seems to acknowledge that this is the case. There is, he says, an "indrawing touch" of God that invites us to be "melted and noughted into the Unity," in response to which we can only relax and let God work his blessedness in us. But there is also an "outpouring touch," that leaves us to ourselves and teaches us to use our freedom. It is the latter touch that opens the powers of the soul, "especially the desirous power," and makes us feel the incomprehensibility and unfathomability of God's sweetness so that the more we taste the more we want.

Ruysbroeck wrote with practical ends in view. The book is mainly intended for "those who live in the spirit," partly to encourage them when they grow weary in their spiritual labors, but also to warn them against presuming that they have attained to union while they are as yet unable to relinquish selfhood. The book also has a special word for those who are able to slip in and out of the trance condition at will. It is, that even though in the loving embrace "each one is himself a fruition of love, and he cannot and dare not seek for anything beyond his own," nevertheless, when he slips out of the trance and back into the ordinary world, he is supposed to share the blessings that he has received with brothers and sisters of the community. In Ruysbroeck's formula, the son of God becomes "an outflowing man to all in common." Just as Christ was sent down from heaven, so his disciple is "sent down by God from these heights" and "must always spend himself on those who have need of him." He becomes a willing instrument of God, and the works that he does, he reckons not as his own but gives all glory to God. "And by this he possesses a universal life, for he is ready alike for contemplation and for action, and is perfect in both of them."

Jean H. Faurot

RECOMMENDED READING

Edition used: Petry, Ray C., ed. *Late Medieval Mysticism.* Library of Christian Classics, vol. 13. Philadelphia: Westminister Press, 1957.

John of Ruysbroeck. *The Adornment of the Spiritual Marriage. The Sparkling Stone. The Book of Supreme Truth.* Translated by Dom C. A. Wynschenk. Edited by Evelyn Underhill. London: John M. Watkins, 1916, 1951. The best commentary on Ruysbroeck is more Ruysbroeck.

Maeterlinck, Maurice. *Ruysbroeck and the Mystics.* Translated by Jane T. Stoddart. London: Hodder & Stoughton, 1894. A long preface prepared by the eminent symbolist poet and dramatist for his translation of the *Spiritual Marriage.* Contains long excerpts from most of Ruysbroeck's writings. A beautiful work but hard to find.

Stace, Walter T. *The Teachings of the Mystics.* Mentor Books. New York: New American Library of World Literature, 1960. A book of readings, including four chapters from *The Adornment of the Spiritual Marriage* and three chapters from *The Book of Supreme Truth.* Important introductory chapter, "What Is Mysticism?" in which Stace compares Ruysbroeck's teachings with those of the Upanishads.

Underhill, Evelyn. *Ruysbroeck.* London: G. Bell & Sons, 1916. Underhill's favorite of all the mystics. His theory of transcendence viewed not as a passing from one life to another but as a perpetual deepening, widening, heightening, and enriching of human existence.

THEOLOGIA GERMANICA

Author: Unknown

The work apparently originated about 1350 within an informal group called Friends of God, which owed its inspiration to Meister Eckhart. The unknown author is today referred to as "the Frankfurter" because of a tradition attributing the manuscript to a priest of the order of Teutonic Knights stationed at Frankfurt-am-Main. *Eyn Deutsch Theologia* is the title that Martin Luther gave to the work when he published the manuscript as a contribution to the rising protest against what German nationalists such as Ulrich von Hutten regarded as the arrogance and intolerance of the Italians. Luther paid tribute to the book: "Next to the Bible and Saint Augustine no other book has come to my attention from which I have learned more concerning God, Christ, man, and what all things are." This judgment, he later qualified. Certainly there is little in the book that points in a distinctively Protestant direction.

Type and subject of work: Chapters toward a theology of Christian living

First transcribed: c. 1350

MAJOR THEMES

God, whose Being is the foundation of all creation, is the only unchangeable Good.

When creatures turn away from the unchangeable Good and attach themselves to the changeable, they greatly offend the Creator.

Unwilling to tolerate disobedience in his creation, God took to himself human nature in order that thereby obedience might overthrow disobedience.

The perfect union between God and human beings that took place in Christ also partly takes place in the Godlike disciple.

Renunciation, resignation, disinterested love, and simple obedience are marks of humankind's union with God.

Martin Luther was not wrong in calling this work a theology—theology on a small scale, of course, and practical rather than speculative in outlook; but theology nonetheless, in that the author is at great pains to ground the counsels that he offers in a doctrine of God, of the world, of humanity's fall, and of Christ's work of redemption. The counsels, moreover, have a unifying theme arising out of a specific problem that the author faced. He stood in the middle of a revivalist movement that was much in need of direction. Expressions such as "living a godlike life" and "participating in the divine nature" were in the air—expressions as likely to bring out the worst in some hearers as to bring out the best in others. Meister Eckhart, John Tauler, and Henry Suso provided noble leadership; but there was need for a handbook that would pull things together. At least, such was the objective that our unknown Frankfurter took upon himself.

The doctrine of God that we find here owes more to pseudo-Dionysius and his Greek forebears than it does to Holy Scripture. Like the ancient Greeks, our author had been overpowered by the concept of pure Being—indivisible, unchangeable, immovable—in contrast to which the natural world, including humanity, seemed unsubstantial. Like Eckhart, he distinguished between Godhead, which is without will or knowledge or any determinate properties, and God proper, who expresses himself and knows himself and loves himself in the persons of the Trinity. And he thought of creation as a further manifestation of Eternal Being. "Without the creature, this would lie in His own Self as a Substance or well-spring, but would not be manifested or wrought into deeds. Now God will have it to be exercised and clothed in a form, for it is there only to be wrought out and executed. What else is it for?" Thus the world flows out of God's own Substance, and as such can only be called good. "All that is, is good, in so far as it hath Being. The Devil is good in so far as he hath Being." What is not good is the creature's claiming for itself what belongs to the Creator alone. This comes about, if not naturally at least understandably; for, as the author observes, each creature in virtue of its creature-nature pursues particular ends—innocently enough until these ends are perceived as goods; for, this is what happens when, instead of looking to God for what they need in due season, they fence off fields and fill their barns, as if they were lord of creation and had no need for God. "Sin," says the Frankfurter, "is nought else, but that the creature turneth away from the unchangeable Good and be taketh itself to the changeable." This the Devil did when he set up his claim to be somewhat and to have something. "This setting up of a claim and his I and Me and Mine, these were his going astray, and his fall." And so with Adam. He could have eaten seven apples and been none the worse for it: If he had never claimed anything as his own, he would not have fallen. And that was just the beginning. "I have fallen a hundred times more often than Adam," exclaims the author; "how shall my fall be amended?"

The problem posed by disobedience must appear to self-centered human beings, if they think of it at all, as their problem. That is not the way God sees it. No one hates disobedience the way God does. He can never be reconciled to it. He would, says the Frankfurter, die a hundred deaths "all for one disobedient man, that he might slay disobedience in him, and that obedience might be born again." And it was to this end that God "took human nature or manhood upon Himself and was made man, and man was made divine." There are several points here that could be elaborated. First, we are not dealing with the usual theory of salvation according to which individuals are saved from the consequences of sin: It is not the consequences of sin but sin itself that had to be dealt with. Second, although God is the workman, the work is wrought in humanity. "Man could not without God, and God should not without man," says our author; "God must ... take to Himself all that is in me, within and without, so that there may be nothing in me which striveth against God or hindereth His work." Third, the way is Christ, whose human nature was so emptied of self and all creaturely will and purpose as to be no more than a "house and habitation of God." Finally, though on one can ever be as perfect in obedience as Christ was, still it is possible for one to come near enough "to be rightly called Godlike, and 'a partaker of the divine nature.'"

The Frankfurter is not a mystic in the usual sense of the word. Only in passing does he mention the three stages (purification, enlightenment, union) whereby, according to the followers of pseudo-Dionysius, the soul climbs to the heavenly presence. Union for him is not a feeling nor is it a vision: It is obedience, a matter of disciplining the appetites and eliminating self-will, of becoming "wholly at one with the One Eternal Will of God, or altogether without will, so that the created will should flow out into the Eternal Will, and be swallowed up and lost therein, so that the Eternal Will alone should do and leave undone in us." Our author offers no exercises or rules, for union is not the creature's achievement. Make yourself ready! is good advice, but only with the understanding that none but God can make a person ready, and that "God giveth as much care and earnestness and love to the preparing of a man as to the pouring in of his Spirit when the man is prepared." For the rest, let things be as they are and let events transpire as they must. When union has been achieved, the outward creature moves here and there with no other concern than that what it does is "necessary and right." To live or die, to do or to endure, to go or to stay are all indifferent to it. Purposes and goals cease to have meaning, and though the body moves among the creatures, the inward person remains unmoved with the Creator. "If the inward man have any Wherefore in the actions of the outward man, he saith only that such things must be and ought to be, as are ordained by the Eternal Will." An illustration from Eckhart shows how this can be. That author speaks of the soul of Christ as having two eyes: The right eye, fixed on the Godhead, remained "in the full intuition and enjoyment of the Divine Essence and Eternal Perfection"; the left eye, directed toward creation, took note of the different creatures, which were better and which worse, and ordered the outward person to act accordingly. The difference between Christ and the godlike man, says our author, is that in Christ the vision of neither eye interferes with that of the other, whereas in the godlike man the two hinder each other, and the left eye must be closed if the right eye is to see into eternity.

The Frankfurter does not disguise the difficulty of following in the way that Christ walked. In contrast to the Brothers of the Free Spirit, a libertarian group that held themselves beyond good and evil, subject to no law, and free to enjoy nature to the fullest, our author represents the godlike life as at once the bitterest and the noblest of lives. It is the bitterest because it goes against nature and the self; but to those with inward sight it is the best and noblest, because "when the Good is known it cannot but be longed for and loved so greatly that all other love ... fadeth away." That followers of Christ are not exempt from distress and anguish should not surprise us when we recall that Christ's soul had to descend into hell before it could ascend to heaven. Just so, before entering the kingdom of heaven, true penitents must perceive who and what they are and consider that they are unworthy that this earth should bear them up. "Let me perish! ... I live without hope!" they cry. But God has laid his hand on them so that they may learn the peace that comes with forsaking worldly goals and seeking one's happiness in God. "This hell and this heaven are two good safe ways for a man in this present time, and happy is he who truly findeth them." It is the one who is in neither of these states that should be concerned, the one who is so busy with the world as never to have beheld what manner of person he or she is.

The Christ of the fourteenth century was very much "a man of sorrows and acquainted with grief." Quite properly the godlike person must be portrayed in sombre hues.

The godlike person's first characteristic is renunciation. The ideal is "for a man to renounce himself in all things, and to live as wholly and purely in true obedience as Christ did." None can achieve this to perfection, but everyone must try. "It all lieth in the matter of obedience.... The more the Self, the I, the Mine abate in man, the more doth God's I, that is, God Himself, increase in him." This must be learned at the start. We must not suppose that one comes to knowledge of God through reading and study, as those are likely to do who are gifted with good understanding. We do not attain to godliness by clinging to such elements of the world but by denying ourselves and taking up his cross and following him.

Second comes resignation. "We must lie still under God's hand, and be obedient and resigned and submit to him." This includes submission to what we receive at the hands of his creatures. We are not to resist evil, for in fighting against affliction we are fighting against God. Such peace as this world affords comes only to the inward person, that we may be joyful and patient while bearing our cross.

Third, when we pray we must never ask for anything that is to our own advantage. People say that, since God wills the best for each person, he ought to help them achieve their desires. Now, it is true that God is eager to help us achieve what is truly best for us, but that is not the same as helping one to become a bishop or a magistrate. "Be assured, he who helpeth a man to his own will, helpeth him to the worst that he can."

Fourth, we are to take up the life of Christ, not with any thought of reward, but because God loves and esteems it so greatly. More prosaically put, to the virtuous man "virtue is its own reward and he is content therewith, and would take no riches in exchange for it."

Fifth, in the truly godlike, love includes all creatures, whose welfare will be to them as their own. Even to those who afflict the godlike and wish them harm they will show kindness, "as though God in human nature were to say, 'I am pure and simple Goodness, and therefore I cannot will, or desire, or rejoice in, or do or give anything but goodness. If I am to reward thee for thy evil and wickedness, I must do it with goodness, for I am and have nothing else.'"

Finally, in the obedient or godlike person, there is no willing, no fixing of goals and choosing of means. Suppose some devil or Adam were to say that Christ was not bereft of self because he often spoke of himself and glorified himself, the answer must be that "when a man in whom truth worketh, hath and ought to have a will towards anything, ... it must be that the truth may be seen and manifested." But to conclude from this that "there was a Wherefore in Christ" would be like saying to the sun, Wherefore do you shine? The sun must reply, "I cannot do otherwise, for it is my nature, ... and the light I give is not of myself and I do not call it mine." So with the godly man and woman. "In them is no willing, nor working nor desiring but has for its end goodness as goodness, for the sake of goodness, and they have no other Wherefore than this."

Jean H. Faurot

Recommended Reading

Edition used: *Theologia Germanica*. Translated from the German by Susanna Winkworth. London: Macmillan, 1901. Originally published in 1854 shortly after the discovery at Würzburg of a different manuscript from the one used by Luther. Includes a historical introduction by the translator.

Jones, Rufus M. *Studies in Mystical Religion*. London: Macmillan, 1909. Chapter 13, "The Friends of God," includes a discussion of the *Theologia Germanica*, pp. 291–297. Jones points out that "to hide one's life, to be anonymous" was part of the ideal of the Friends of God.

The Theologia Germanica of Martin Luther. Translation, Introduction, and Commentary by Bengt Hoffman. New York: Paulist Press, 1980. Useful account of the different manuscript traditions. The translator, a Lutheran, evaluates the work in the light of contemporary Christian ethics.

THE SERMONS OF JOHN TAULER

Author: John Tauler (c. 1300–1361)

Born in Strassburg and buried in the same city, John Tauler spent his entire life in towns along the Rhine. As a member of the Order of Preachers (Dominicans) he received a thorough education; and, though details are difficult to establish, Tauler was quite possibly a fellow student with Henry Suso under Meister Eckhart at Cologne. He was certainly influenced by Eckhart's writings, and the papal bull condemning certain of Eckhart's doctrines must have been a blow to the younger man. Another trial was the struggle between John XXII and Louis of Bavaria, which forced him to choose whether to continue his pastoral duties in spite of the papal ban. Of the numerous writings attributed to Tauler in former times, none are today accepted as genuine except about half of the sermons and one or two letters. The sermons, delivered extemporaneously in churches of Dominican nuns, were written from memory by the nuns, who seem to have done a good job, although the manuscripts have suffered at the hand of copyists. Mention should be made of the so-called "History of Master John Tauler," sometimes published in earlier editions of the sermons, which professes to tell of Tauler's conversion through the ministry of a lay member of the Friends of God but which has been shown to have little or no basis in fact.

Type and subject of work: Sermons on the Christian vocation

First transcribed: c. 1330–1361

Major Themes

Although the human soul contains an eternal element that draws it toward God, the disorder brought about by the Fall has made the temporal element predominant.

Souls must be purged of love of self and love of other creatures before they can be united with God.

Persons who obey Christ and the Church are assured of salvation even though most of their purging remains to be done after death.

Those who, following the counsels of perfection, enter a religious order and undertake an ascetic life make faster progress.

Ascetics who achieve a high degree of purification experience mystical union in the present life.

Not everyone thirsts after eternal life, and of those who do some thirst more feverishly than others. That is the message that John Tauler finds in Christ's words, "If any man thirst, let him come to me and drink" (John 7:37). "Three kinds of men experience this thirst, and each kind differently, one kind being beginners, the second those who are making some progress, and the third are perfect, as far as may be in this life." The distinction must have appeared obvious to Christian mystics in the Middle Ages, and is mentioned by Tauler in several connections. We find it, for example, in a sermon on vocations. "Walk worthy of the vocation in which you are called" (Eph. 4:1), where those who are making progress are called proficients, and where everyone is enjoined not to "repine on account of the place he is given, for God is the Lord and allots to every one his right degree." The distinction was, for Tauler, a practical one, concerned as he was that his sermons should reach all his hearers. For, although he was preaching in convents, his congregation always included lay members of the community and often, on special days, a cross section of the local populace.

First, then, come devout laymen and -women. They are only beginners, but the important thing is that they have made a start and are walking in the way that leads to God. God's grace is at work in them. They are "placed in a worldly state of life," but they are not "worldly hearted men." The latter, unfortunately, are found everywhere, both in the secular and the religious estates. They are not among those who thirst after God. But there are all sorts and conditions of men and women who desire to know God and to obey his will; and Tauler never loses sight of their needs. Or, to put the matter in a larger perspective, he never allows his hearers, whatever their pretensions, to forget the basics without which no spiritual progress is possible. Thus, we hear him commending craftsmen "having only God in mind and heart and decent support of their family," and peasants engaged in hard toil "thinking only of God," in order to remark that "these souls, following their humble calling in all simplicity of heart, shall fare better at the last day than many members of orders, who are not true to their vocation."

The visible Church, with its means of grace and its twofold law —love God and love one's neighbor—exists for beginners. It speaks to them in terms of commandments (in contrast to the evangelical counsels, which are for those of higher vocations). They are to believe its teaching and obey its ordinances. The way is sure and the humblest who accept their vocation and follow it are certain to reach God after their souls have been cleansed in purgatory. But there are dangers: not merely occasional temptation to mortal sin—in its presence one must "run to the cross"—but also habitual servitude to venial sins, which Tauler is adept at uncovering. Prayer, for the beginner, will be mostly verbal, but it must not on that account be merely external. The Christian walk is a walk with God, who is never absent from the souls of those whom he has chosen for his friends. What he wants is our love, and to get this he must win our affection away from the world, which he does partly by giving us joy and partly by giving us sorrow. The problem with joy is that we tend to bask in the pleasure it gives and make no further advance, whereas suffering is a medicine that lessens our desire for the creature and increases our desire for the Creator. This is true even in little things—a sore finger, cold feet, a spiteful neighbor. "We know how carefully the painter calculates the strokes of his brush.... God is a thousand times more intent upon making a man the masterpiece of His Divine art; and He does this by His strokes of suffering and His colors of pain." More severe adversity has the further use of putting our sincerity to test: Often human beings cannot tell whether they are seeking God's will or their own. Grievous suffering reveals the hand of God. "When trouble comes, then God's true friends fly to the feet of Jesus, and there they suffer in all patience, lost in his love, accepting every pain from His hand."

This is good Catholic teaching, but with a decidedly mystical slant. No attempt whatever is made to fit God into the framework of claims and counterclaims that gives rise to our notions of merit and demerit and of reward and punishment. Nothing is to be gained by attending mass or by reciting prayers apart from the improvement that they bring about in one's inner disposition. Christ is not thought of as making satisfaction for humanity's sins but as leading souls out of captivity to sin. Purgatory is not punishment but precisely a purge—an "indulgence" would do no good. Hell is the unfortunate destiny of souls who know that they lack the grace necessary to repent and find their way back to God, whom nevertheless they secretly desire above all else. Tauler gives the following overview: "The inner man has come from God, and he is a noble being, made after God's image and likeness. And as he comes from God, so he is invited and urgently called back to God, so that, being drawn into the Divine life, he may become partaker of all good. The blessedness that belongs to God by nature the soul may hereby obtain by grace."

The proficient are further advanced than the beginner mainly because, having freed themselves from temporal wants, they can be full-time Christians. This means that, in addition to obeying the commandments, they can take seriously the counsels of perfection that we read in the gospels but for the most part ignore. "That we may follow this vocation rightly and perfectly," says Tauler, "holy Church, guided by the Spirit of God, has formed various orders and communities, well adapted to aid us to this end, and they are provided with appropriate rules." The explicit vows of poverty, chastity, and obedience are, however, scarcely more than a token of the radical turning from the world and from the lower to the higher self which must take place in the soul of anyone who wants to use the present life to make progress toward eternal life. This is bitter medicine; but, in Tauler's view, if we do not take it in this life we must take it in the life to come.

In Tauler's view the human predicament is too complicated to be treated in traditional dualistic terms. He has no use for long vigils and for hair shirts as means of taming the flesh. Humankind's problem is not that of a soul imprisoned in a body but that of a disordered soul. According to Tauler's diagnosis, all our woes can be traced to what has been called (C. B. Macpherson) possessive individualism—the claim of everyone to be "the proprietor of his own person and capacities" and of whatever in the world he can lay his hands on. We are held back from God by self-love, by love of external things, by self-will. If we are to be delivered from this bondage we must make a complete turnabout. "If God is to come into the soul, creatures must first go out—all that is not God must go out.... A man must surrender himself captive, empty, detached, and ready—in total self-annihilation." Nothing is more characteristic of Tauler's ascetic preaching than his exhortation to abandonment, detachment, resignation, and renunciation. But another word for this is love. "Dear children, you know not what love is. You feel great sensible devotion and spiritual sweetness, and that you call love. No, by no means; love is the burning and destroying of self, real self-denial, steadfast yearning for God in a spirit of abandonment to Him, the soul melted into God in a persevering state of resignation to Him; such is love."

The "dear children" whom Tauler addresses are not equally lovable. Some have been truly converted, he says, but others superficially if at all. The former, fully persuaded of their nothingness, are poor in spirit and want the lowest offices. They are gentle and affectionate, ready to help, "even rejoicing in poverty and humiliations, for which they return unfeigned thanks to God." The falsely converted have the faults opposite to these virtues. Some of the audience must have blushed—or turned white with anger—when he mentioned the tendency of some to "volunteer instructing others with a flood of talk, discoursing boastfully of high spirituality ... with a great show of humility lest their real condition be suspected."

For Tauler, Christianity was, as people say, a life, not a doctrine. Still, it was a thought-out life; and though Tauler's office was that of a preacher and not that of a professor of theology, he was an unusually well instructed man, conscious of his debt to a long tradition. This comes out in his doctrine of the soul, which must be kept in mind if his ascetic teachings are to be understood. In a sermon on the text, "Be renewed in the spirit of your mind" (Eph. 4:23), Tauler distinguishes between the highest part of the soul, called spirit—the part that is akin to God—and the lower part—the sensible and intellectual faculties. In between these lies mind (*Gemüt*), which is a stable inclination either toward spirit and God or toward the faculties and the external world. According to Tauler, human beings stand "on the boundary between time and eternity," having been made for action in the world of creatures, but also for contemplation of God's truth and love. There is no reason that these two functions should be in conflict, nor were they in conflict in Christ's human nature, whose soul "was ever turned towards the Godhead, as far as His higher faculties were concerned," while "as to His lower powers, these were constantly moving in His life of work and suffering." In humankind after the Fall, the parts of the soul remain, but the eternal element and the temporal element are horribly confused, and the monstrous fiction of a self, supposedly standing over against both God and the world, has taken possession of our minds. It is this fraud that must be rooted out by ascetic exercises if we are to be restored to a proper relation with God. Human beings cannot do it: Their part is merely to yield themselves up to what God has in store for them.

With this bit of doctrine in mind we are ready to consider the third level of achievement—perfection as far as it may be achieved in this life. Presumably the term *perfect* was in common use in convents to designate persons notable for their rigorous observances—"many prayers and kneelings, and much fasting, and other such devout practices." No doubt also it was sometimes used to designate ecstatics. Tauler does not use it in either of these ways. The former he says would do well to reduce their outward observances and concentrate on the interior life. The latter he treats with compassion, advising the priors to excuse them from their usual obligations while they are incapacitated, warning at the same time that those who indulge themselves in "devotional sweetness" are falling behind in their proper vocation: It is, after all, only the lower faculties that are here engaged.

What Tauler calls for is a transformation of the person "into a God-like form, uniting the created spirit with the uncreated deity." This is no mere exercise. When one truly yields the self, allowing God to do his work in the soul, a person's "whole interior life is thrown into confusion ... all his pious practices seem set at nought, and the spiritual lights heretofore granted him seem to have gone quite out." There will be a rush of heavenly joy: "How long has the Holy Trinity waited for us that we might share the divine joy eternally!" But this will be followed by great suffering as God begins the "terrible process of stripping and deprivation" that must take place before a man can behold the truth, after which "every sorrow vanishes away—he seems to himself to be a man risen from the dead." Using the language of Saint Augustine, Tauler speaks of God as an abyss in which the things of time and this world have no place. However, he seems to correct the father when he goes on to say that the divine life embraces the whole creation, reminding us that though God is contemplation he is also act, and that when a soul is at one with God it too "with a kind of wide-sweeping and yet most simple prayer," upholds the necessities of all Christians. "Nothing is to be discovered in them but a Divine existence."

Thus, the passage back and forth between eternity and time is the key to understanding the life of the perfect. However much he rejoices in contemplation, the God-formed man "goes forth in his outward activity ... and again returns into the same divine center and source." As a master workman has many under him although he himself does not work, so the interior life is set over the exterior. "In the depths of his soul he is immersed in God, ... and every external work down to the least and smallest is in the service of the interior."

Jean H. Faurot

RECOMMENDED READING

Edition used: Tauler, John. *The Sermons and Conferences.* English translation with Introduction by Walter Elliott. Washington, D.C.: Apostolic Mission House, 1910. Includes 130 sermons and the spurious "History of the Reverend John Tauler." A translation of Julius Hamberger's German edition (Frankfurt am Main, 1864).

Clark, James M. *The Great German Mystics: Eckhart, Tauler and Suso.* Oxford: Basil Blackwell, 1949. A literary and historical study. Most convenient account in English of scholarly opinion concerning the authenticity of the writings attributed to Tauler. Ferdinand Vetter's 1910 edition containing eighty-one rmons is taken as a starting point.

Ozment, Steven E. *Homo Spiritualis: A Comparative Study of the Anthropology of John Tauler, John Gerson, and Martin Luther in the Context of Their Theological Thought.* Leiden: E. J. Brill, 1969. Attempt by a leading scholar of Reformation theology to reconstruct Tauler's doctrine of the soul and his interpretation of the mystical union.

THE DIALOGUE OF
SAINT CATHERINE OF SIENA

Author: Saint Catherine of Siena (1347–1380)
Born the twenty-fourth of twenty-five children in her family in the district of Siena, Caterina di Giacomo di Benincasa was to become the patron saint of Italy and a doctor of the Catholic church. A lay member of the Order of Saint Dominic, who had vowed her virginity to God at the age of seven, she was an ascetic, mystic, and activist. She worked for peace within the Church when Florence was placed under an interdict by the pope. She visited Pope Gregory XI in Avignon to mediate in the political dispute where she also promoted a crusade against the Muslims. When the papacy returned to Rome she participated in the reorganization of the Church under Urban VI. She died apparently worn out by her efforts in the life of sacrifice that she had led.

Type and subject of work: Report of mystical experience

First transcribed: c. 1370

MAJOR THEMES

Love is the way to perfection.
Christ is the bridge between heaven and earth.
Five kinds of tears correspond to the conditions of the soul.
Love involves grief for one's own sin and that of others.
Obedience to the Word is the remedy to the sin of Adam.

Much of this book was dictated by Catherine while she was in a state of ecstasy and was recorded by members of her religious community. She begins by discussing the intimate relationship of truth and love. Catherine next discusses the beauty and dignity of each person who becomes perfect in proportion to union with the Creator. Then follow four petitions that she makes to God: for herself (to be permitted to suffer so as to atone for her sins); for reformation of the Holy Church; for peace in the world, and for the entire world in general; for the effects of Providence in everything, but particularly for a special intention. She indicates that she is relying on God's promise to Saint John and others that God will show himself to those who love him.

There is a brief reply from God to the first petition. She is told of the need for infinite desire in relation to works even though they are finite, because sin done against God is sin done against the Infinite Good. So God wishes infinite grief in his creature concerning her own sins and through the sorrow she feels for sins that she sees committed by her neighbors. But she is promised that the pain she feels through love will nourish rather than dry up the soul.

God then explains in some detail what the role of the neighbor is in regard to a person's spiritual development. Pride destroys charity and affection toward the neighbor and is the main source of every evil. When we deprive a neighbor of that which he or she ought to be given, a secret sin is committed. God gives each person a special virtue that draws to the soul all others bound by love. But unless we make our act of love through God, it is meaningless. The virtues such as faith, patience, benignity, kindness, fortitude, and perseverance are then extolled. It is discernment or holy discretion that is the light of all the other virtues, Catherine is told.

Thus end what some call the prologue and the section titled (not by Catherine herself but by later editors) "The Way of Perfection." The next series of chapters—and here the lead of those editors is followed—is called "Dialogue." Here the future saint lists three petitions to which God gives a short reply. These petitions correspond roughly to the second and fourth petitions of the prologue (Church reform and the role of Providence in all things). Catherine seeks mercy for God's people and for all aspects of the life of the Church, to its very core. She is concerned with all grace that is manifested through material things and temporal experiences. To this God answers by reminding Catherine that the world has already received the great gift it needs for redemption and that is Christ, the Redeemer, himself. But this gift brings with it a tremendous responsibility that we must be aware of.

Catherine implores God to be merciful to the entire world. He says, in return, that selfish love is a poison that can undermine all and he recalls to her that he is the God of all, of the evildoer as well as of the good. Then the fourteenth-century mystic asks specifically for grace for her spiritual director, Raymond of Capua (later her biographer), and God tells her of the way of truth, using the metaphor of Christ as bridge. He also speaks of the twofold vineyard, which is composed of the individual's soul and the Church. For spiritual growth this vineyard must be nurtured by all who wish to serve God. This "dialogue" section closes with praise rendered divine love and Catherine's expressed desire to learn more about Christ as the necessary bridge. "I remember that you wanted to show me who are those who cross over the bridge and those who do not. So, if it would please your goodness to show me, I would gladly see and hear this from you."

The heart of the book follows and has been signified as "The Bridge." Christ, the only begotten Son, is the bridge that spans heaven and earth. This, God says, is one result of the union that he has made with man, the creature fashioned out of clay. The approach is in three steps: Two were made with the wood of Jesus' cross. The third—which still retains its bitter taste—is the gall and vinegar he was given to drink. These three steps symbolize the states of the soul and they are likened to the Crucifixion experience in this account. In the first step, when the soul lifts her feet from the affections of the earth, she strips herself of worldly vice. As a result of step two, the soul is filled with love and with virtue. In the final step she tastes the peace of God.

The Bridge is built of the stones of true and sincere virtues. On the Bridge is an inn where food is given the travelers. Those who go over the Bridge go to eternal life while those who travel beneath the Bridge go to everlasting death. These latter suffer four pains: the deprivation of seeing God, the worm of Conscience, the vision of the Devil, and the torment of a fire that burns but does not consume. Those who make spiritual progress pass from a state of imperfection (acting in servile fear) to arrival in the state of perfection (filial love).

This section may be regarded as God's response to Catherine's plea for his mercy to be extended to the entire world. Nor does this response end here but continues at some length. At this point, however, Catherine observes that she has seen several kinds of tears, and she asks for instructions about each of these types. God tells her that there are those of the wicked as well as of those who fear God; there are the tears of those who imperfectly love him, and of those whose weeping is perfect because they love God in total abandon. Finally, there are the sweet tears of great peace that are joined to the fourth.

Catherine then thanks God, praising him for the gift of love. From this she feels she has the permission to ask for grace and mercy while searching for his truth. She requests further guidance from God, at this point, concerning how she should advise others who come to her for counsel and how she can tell whether a spiritual visitation truly comes from God or is a deception of which she should be wary. (Regarding this last, Catherine recalls that she has been told if the visitation left her spirit glad and encouraged her toward virtue, then this was indeed a divine intervention but she wishes assurance on this point.)

Truth is what the seeker in this book yearns for and the next pages are devoted to such an inquiry. She learns that there are three kinds of lights by which we may see reality. These are called the imperfect, the perfect, and finally the most perfect lights. First is ordinary light which all human beings need, regardless of their earthly situation. Those who walk in perfect light do so in two separate ways: Some men and women rise above this world and practice the mortification of their bodies; some kill their own self-wills and "find their nourishment at the table of holy desire." Others should be reproved only gently. When they are clearly living sinfully, that is another matter, but in general God counsels that neighbors' apparent vices must not be harshly judged nor are their degrees of perfection to be judged. Furthermore, not all are expected to live their spiritual lives in the same manner or to follow the same path to holiness.

There is some repetition here of previous advice and admonitions; then Catherine is urged to ask for more and is given a new promise of mercy. She then again praises God, particularly for his truth and beseeches God anew. The ecstatic requests the grace necessary to remain totally faithful to God's truth. She asks this not only for herself but for her companions as well, particularly for two priests who were her confessors, "those two pillars, the fathers you have appointed for me on earth to guide and teach me, who am so wretchedly weak, from the beginning of my conversion until now." One of these men is Raymond of Capua who was to become the mystic's first biographer. The other is probably Tommaso della Fonte, an earlier confessor and a man who was a companion to her throughout her relatively brief life.

She then asks for some indication of the extent of the sins of evil clergymen so that she may increase her sorrow and desire for mercy. This recalls her earlier petition on behalf of the entire sacramental life at the heart of the Church. God promises an answer and tells Catherine that her "two pillars" will receive the grace they need from God through her. But, he warns her, "never fail to trust Me for my providence will never fail you."

The next section begins with God's praise for his ministers, the priests through whom the sacraments are administered, particularly the Eucharist. Something of the nature of the Eucharist is also discussed. The host given in holy communion loses none of its glory upon being divided, just as fire divided remains fire. When Catherine receives this sacrament she lives in God and God in her, she is told. Then God tells her of the sins of the clerics, but not until he first notes that those who persecute the clergy are working against God himself. Nevertheless, in some priests, "selfish love is alive in them." Some do not correct people in order to curry favor with them; others exemplify great pride. Certain clerics are ruled by their senses, some by an acquisitiveness of material things. Drunkenness, too, is a sin for many of them and some are lustful in word and deed. Catherine reacts to all that she has heard with a prayer of praise for God. She portrays him as light and fire, as the supreme charity, and as the great fulfiller of all that is honestly desired. Again she begs God for mercy for the world in general and for the Church in particular.

God's providence is the subject of the next several segments of *The Dialogue*. He speaks of his general providence in creation, in redemption, and in the sacraments, as well as in his gift of the virtue of hope and in the Law. He then relates his special providence in particular events in history and in the lives of people. God indicates that he allows the world to bring forth many troubles to prove the virtue of people and "that I may have reason to reward them for their suffering and the violence they do themselves." Subsequently, Catherine says that she wishes to be instructed concerning obedience. She wants to know how perfect it is, where she can find it, what might cause her to lose it, who gives it to her, and by what sign she might know whether or not she has it.

The woman is told that the sign that one has the virtue of obedience is patience; the impatient have it not. The fullness of obedience, God says, is found in the gentle, loving Word, his only begotten Son, for Jesus' obedience was even to a shameful death on the cross. Pride causes us to lose that virtue. This caused Adam's sin and it was not only he who fell here but the whole human race as well. Jesus left this key of obedience to the gate of heaven and whoever fails to avail himself of it risks living in damnation. Perfect obedience is found in those who bind themselves to the obedience of a religious order or in those, outside such orders, who submit their wills to a spiritual teacher who will help them to advance more speedily to unlock the gate of heaven.

The work ends with a recapitulation by God of all that has gone before, followed by Catherine's final hymn of praise to the Trinity and a prayer that she may be clothed in God's truth.

Harry James Cargas

RECOMMENDED READING

Edition used: Catherine of Siena, *The Dialogue*. Translated by Suzanne Noffke, O.P. New York: Paulist Press, 1980.

Gardner, Edmund, G. *Saint Catherine of Siena*. London: Dent, 1907. Gives the background as well as the life of Catherine through a study of the religion, literature, and history of fourteenth-century Italy.

Raymond of Capua. *The Life of St. Catherine of Siena*. Translated by George Lamb. New York: Kennedy, 1960. The first biography of the saint, written by her confessor who shared many of her experiences.

THE LADDER OF PERFECTION

Author: Walter Hilton (1340–1396)
Practically nothing is known of the life of Hilton. It is clear from his writings that he was a learned man, and references to him as Magister indicate that he may have been a doctor of theology. His early life was perhaps spent as a hermit, his middle years as a scholar, and his last as an Augustinian canon at the priory of Thurgarten in Nottinghamshire. A number of manuscripts note that his death occurred on the Vigil of the Annunciation, 1395 (March 24, 1396 by the present calendar). Although Hilton wrote widely in English and Latin, his fame rests almost exclusively upon *The Ladder of Perfection*. *Mixed Life* (date unknown), perhaps his best-known work after *The Ladder*, teaches holiness to those who live in the world.

Type and subject of work: Religious treatise on the contemplative stages whereby God is reached

First transcribed: c. 1390

MAJOR THEMES

Only contemplatives can ever know God mystically.
Mystical union with God can be achieved by progress upward along a scale of contemplative experiences that will lead to ineffable oneness with the Lord.
Perfect union with God is not possible in this world.

Book One of *The Ladder of Perfection* is directed to an anchoress who has apparently requested spiritual guidance from Hilton. It concerns the contemplative life in general, but focuses on its prefatory reaches.

The first degree of contemplation concerns knowing God and such spiritual matters as can be attained by reason. It is simply the application of natural intelligence to the study of teachings and the Scriptures. This knowledge is used improperly by some, who consequently fall into the sin of pride. The second degree concerns love and is generally expressed in unlearned people who think on God and are inspired by the Holy Ghost to great devotion. It concerns not the intellect but the feelings, and has two stages. The lower may be known by actives, whose style of life will inevitably, however, make its presence fleeting. The higher stage is achieved only by contemplatives, who may then proceed to the third level, which involves both knowledge and love. It occurs when a person leaves all earthly and carnal love, all worldly thoughts and imaginings, and departs the bodily senses. One's intellect is able to see God and one's emotions burn with love. In this state of knowing and feeling the ecstatic soul is joined with God.

The foundation for contemplation requires humility, firm faith, and a right intention, Hilton writes. Those who seek it must have a deep conviction of their own unworthiness and the extent to which they depend upon God's mercy. The need to chastise the faults of others presupposes an abiding conviction of one's own unworthiness. Wholehearted belief in the articles of faith and the sacraments comprises a second prerequisite. One must love and respect all the laws and ordinances that rule the Church in matters of faith, the sacraments, and Christian conduct. Right intention, a determination and desire to please God, is the third prerequisite. In all that they do, the contemplatives will turn to the thought of Christ, because the world is trivial and irksome.

Prayer and meditation are the means the contemplative employs. Prayer, the rising of the heart to God that leaves behind all earthly thought, destroys sin and aids the acquisition of virtue. Prayer has three degrees. Vocal prayer cleanses the soul of all that is worldly and carnal and is best to begin with, especially such prayers as the Pater Noster, the Hail Mary, and the Psalter, until the contemplative is able to think of spiritual matters. The second degree of prayer is also vocal, but inspired by spontaneous devotion and without set formulae. The contemplative simply speaks to God, as though he were present, out of his or her concerns. God is especially pleased by this form of direct, unpremeditated communication. The third degree is not vocal at all, but in the heart only. Great purity of heart is therefore its precondition, and it is possible only to those especially adept and practiced in spiritual exercise.

Meditation generally begins with the contemplation of one's sins and leads to great sorrow, weeping, and asking of pardon. This is a necessary cleansing of the soul. The cleansed sinner then progresses to a meditation on God's incarnation or on the compassion of Mary. The mind is detached from the world and the seeker sees Jesus seized, bound, beaten, scourged, and condemned, sees his humility and cruel death. Such a contemplation of God's humanity is necessary before any contemplation of Christ's divinity is possible.

The power to meditate will be withdrawn at times, and at others the Devil will interfere. Thus one must know one's own soul and the way in which sin reduces its powers and stains it. The root of sin, which has caused the soul all its wretchedness and misery, must be eradicated. Knowledge of the Passion reminds people of God's love and leads them to restore the dignity of their souls. Desiring Jesus we find him within ourselves, break from sin and vanity, and reform ourselves to his likeness through humility and charity. Constant reflection upon one's sinfulness leads the sinner to the knowledge of sin necessary to oppose it and to the ability to hate sin in others while still loving them. Desiring humility and charity, a person learns to close the window of the senses as well as of the imagination. In this way one will recognize the dark image of sin, its clothing, and its members, and be able to contrast it with the image of Jesus, learn to crucify sin, conform to the image of Jesus, and form Jesus within oneself.

Book two of *The Ladder*, perhaps written several years after Book one and addressed to no one person, is distinctly more Christ-oriented and deals more with the advanced stages of contemplation.

Because the soul of the human being is an image of God fallen through sin, all who believe in Christ and love him will seek forgiveness. The passion and death of Christ will lead all but heretics, Jews, and pagans to reform their souls and restore in them the image of God. That image will be restored fully only in heaven, where the soul will attain the state it might have had but for the Fall. The partial reform of the soul may be in faith or in feeling. The first is easily had, sufficient for salvation, and suitable for beginners and actives. The second can be had only through great spiritual labor, frees the soul from desire of worldly pleasures, makes the soul aware of the workings of grace, and is only for the perfect and for contemplatives.

The image of God is lost through original and actual sin, and may be restored through baptism and penance. The reformed soul will still show the mark of sin and be both beautiful and ugly at the same time, like the speaker in Canticles 1:6: "Do not consider me because I am black, because the sun has discolored me." Some people will never be reformed to the likeness of God, some are reformed in faith, and some are reformed in faith and feeling. Those who allow the feminine senses to overcome the masculine reason will wallow like beasts in the world. Those who fear God, reject the senses, and conduct their lives to please him will be reformed to his likeness in faith. The soul that avoids the senses and has no inclination to sin is reformed in feeling.

Reform in faith is easily attained, Hilton writes, but reform in both faith and feeling requires much labor and perseverance. It is only for those who reach the state of perfection and requires great grace and long spiritual exercise. Reform in feeling is the highest state that a soul can come to in this life and can only be attained by wisely regulated spiritual exercises. Grace and one's own efforts are alike required to achieve the perfect love that marks reform in feeling, and humility is the prerequisite for grace. Only a person of great humility, charity and faith, prepared to suffer much in body and soul, may reach Jerusalem, the city of Peace which is Contemplation.

One who seeks reform in both faith and feeling must, like a pilgrim to Jerusalem, leave all behind, Hilton avers. Steadfast and resolute, one must overcome all obstacles that the world, the flesh, and the Devil can erect, and push on, stopping only for necessary food and rest. The desire for reform in feeling comes from Jesus, who is our guide. Loving Jesus and desiring oneness with him, the soul will enter the luminous darkness of that good night that forces out false love of the world and brings nearer the true day and the blessed light of Christ. In the unpeaceful —because unaccustomed—darkness the soul learns to deny the world and think of a fruitful nothing. Grace and the desire for Jesus destroy all tendency to sin and become in the luminous darkness a beacon that marks the heavenly Jerusalem.

Four stages mark the reform of the soul, as Saint Paul teaches: the call, justification, exaltation, and glorification. First the soul is called from the vanity of the world, begins to advance on the road of righteousness and to come through mortification into the darkness of worldly rejection, finds peace through a partial reform of feeling, and is then fully reformed in the happiness of heaven.

Hilton writes that knowledge of our soul is necessary to knowledge and love of God, which has three stages. The first is by faith alone without any knowledge of God by grace. The second is by faith alone with knowledge of Jesus' humanity through the imagination. The third extends to God himself insofar as possible on earth and can be experienced only by those who have been reformed in feeling, which is to be filled with knowledge of God's will, with understanding, and with spiritual wisdom. God opens the eyes of the soul to himself by three degrees of reform: in faith, in faith and feeling, and in complete feeling (known only by the soul in the presence of God).

The spiritual vision of God is caused by his love for the soul, Hilton claims. God is uncreated love and arouses created love in the soul. The gift of uncreated love is given us before we love God and leads us to love and desire him and to forsake the world. It makes light and easy the exercise of all virtue. The soul comforted with uncreated love feels no external trials and is reformed with a new consciousness of virtue.

Love destroys sin and instills virtue. It destroys pride and creates humility of two types: that arising from the consideration of one's own sins and misery and that arising when the intellect is illuminated to see God. It destroys anger and envy and reestablishes peace, patience, and perfect charity. It destroys accidie, covetousness, lust, gluttony, and all sensual pleasure, replacing them with sweetness.

The soul thus cleansed can rise to contemplate God in a state of rest characterized by great spiritual activity and silence. By grace the soul withdraws into a secret chamber where it sees God, hears his counsels, and is wonderfully consoled. Sometimes this grace is withdrawn when one sinks back into natural weakness. It will, however, return in time. When the special grace is lacking, one is dull and inept in performing spiritual exercises.

Sometimes the light of grace will lead to prayer, Hilton writes. The Pater Noster is probably best for the uneducated and the Psalter for the educated. The prayer of a contemplative is only of the soul, which will receive the gift of understanding Holy Scripture and see how God—concealed in the Bible—reveals himself to those who love him. His secret presence in the Scriptures is like his secret voice heard in the soul. Its spiritual eyes having been opened, the soul can see the Church Militant as it is—black and ugly in the sinner, beautiful and lovely in the elect—and the angels, both fallen and blessed. The blessed spirits will aid the soul, teach it as masters, free it from worldly illusions, and show it how to hear with spiritual joy the secret whisper of God.

Robert J. Meindl

RECOMMENDED READING

Edition used: Hilton, Walter. *The Scale of Perfection.* Translated by Dom Gerard Sitwell, O.S.B. London: Burns Oates, 1953.

———. *The Stairway of Perfection.* Translated by M. L. Del Mastro. Garden City, N.Y.: Doubleday, Image Books, 1979. An excellent and readily available translation with useful introduction.

Milosh, Joseph E. *The Scale of Perfection and the English Mystical Tradition.* Madison: University of Wisconsin Press, 1966. A sensitive reading of *The Ladder* that orients it to time and tradition.

REVELATIONS OF DIVINE LOVE

Author: Julian of Norwich (1342–c. 1423)
An anchoress who lived in solitude in Norwich, England, in the late fourteenth century, she is called "Julian" because her cell was attached to the parish church of Saint Julian in Conisford at Norwich. We do not know her given name. She received her revelations on May 13, 1373, when she was thirty and a half years old.

Type and subject of work: This classic of mystical theology is the record of and meditation on sixteen visions Julian had.

First transcribed: c. 1393

MAJOR THEMES

Creation "lasts and always will, because God loves it; and thus everything has being through the love of God."

The Devil is overcome; all Satan's power is locked in God's hands.

Sin is necessary but has no substance. We recognize it in the pain it causes us. That pain purges us, shows us ourselves, and leads us to seek God's mercy.

"Jesus is our true Mother in nature by our first creation, and he is our true Mother in grace by his taking our created nature"; Christ on the cross gave us birth and in Holy Communion nourishes us at her breast.

The Trinity can be understood in a rich multitude of ways.

This work has various titles and two versions. It is sometimes called *Revelations of Divine Love*, or *A Shewing of God's Love, Showings*, or simply *Revelations*. The "short text" has twenty-five chapters and simply tells about the sixteen visions or revelations that Julian was given. Although the first paragraph of the extant manuscript says she was "a devout woman, and her name is Julian, who is a recluse at Norwich and still alive, A.D. 1413," scholars agree that it was probably written shortly after the visions were received in 1373. The eighty-six chapters of the "long text" are the fruit of twenty years of meditation on the meaning of what she received, as she says in chapter two, on May 30, 1373.

Julian tells us that she desired three graces from God: to have a recollection of Christ's Passion, to have a bodily sickness when she was thirty, and to have, of God's gift, three wounds—contrition, compassion, and longing with her will for God. She wanted to see with her own eyes Christ's suffering on the cross, as did Mary his mother, Mary Magdalene, and "others who were Christ's lovers."

Chapter two of the short text thus begins, "And when I was thirty and a half years old, God sent me a bodily sickness in which I lay for three days and three nights." She was so sick that on the fourth night she was given last rites. On the seventh night she appeared to be at the point of death. Her mother stood by the bed, and a priest placed a crucifix before her face. The bottom half of her body already felt dead, and she felt the upper part of her body beginning to die. Suddenly all pain left—and the visions began.

She remembered her desire to witness the Passion, and suddenly as she gazed at the crucifix, she "saw the red blood trickling down from under the crown, all hot, flowing freely and copiously, a living stream, just as it seemed ... that it was at the time when the crown of thorns was thrust down upon his blessed head."

At the same time she had a spiritual vision of God's love. She saw that God "is to us everything which is good and comforting for our help." She realized that God "is our clothing, for he is that love which wraps and enfolds us, embraces us and guides us, surrounds us for his love, which is so tender that he may never desert us." She also saw something small, "no bigger than a hazelnut," round as a ball, lying in her hand. She was given to understand that it was everything that is made. She marveled because it seemed so little that it could "suddenly fall into nothing." But God showed her that "it lasts and always will, because God loves it; and thus everything has being through the love of God." Always intrigued by the Trinity, she learned from this vision that "God is the Creator and the lover and the protector."

She speaks of the first vision as corporeal and bodily, of others as spiritual. Other visions concerned Christ's scourging and the discoloration of his face. She saw Christ overcome the Devil, and she saw the Virgin Mary. Other visions brought spiritual understandings of sin, prayer, the Trinity, God's sovereignty, and death (Christ's and ours). Throughout, she is impressed with God's love.

In her visions and her meditations on them, she is fascinated with the Trinity. She works it over and over. In her first vision, she realized that God "always was and is and ever shall be, almighty, all wisdom and all love." In chapter twenty-two of the short text she speaks of "sovereign power, sovereign wisdom, sovereign goodness."

The long text contains one of the clearest expositions in spiritual literature of the fact that God is our Mother as well as our Father (for scriptural references, see Isa. 42:14, 46:3, 49:25, 66:13; Ps. 131:2). Julian notes in chapter fifty-two that "God rejoices that he is our Father, and God rejoices that he is our Mother, and God rejoices that he is our true spouse, and that our soul is his beloved wife." Again in chapter fifty-eight she says that "in our making, God almighty is our loving Father, and God all wisdom is our loving Mother, with the love and goodness of the Holy Spirit, which is all one God, one Lord."

She speaks particularly of Christ as "our Mother, brother and saviour," an image common in the earlier Middle Ages, particularly with Anselm. In chapter fifty-seven she had noted that "so our Lady is our mother, in whom we are all enclosed and born of her in Christ ...; and our saviour is our true Mother, in whom we are endlessly born and out of whom we shall never come." Julian talks of how we were born out of the travail of Christ's Passion. She goes on to say that as "the mother can give her child to suck of her milk," so "our precious Mother Jesus can feed us with himself, and does, most courteously and most tenderly, with the blessed sacrament."

Vitally aware of God's love, Julian was also aware of sin, which she described as "the greatest pain that the soul can have." Despite God's constant nurture, we fall into sin because of our own inconstancy and by the prompting of our enemy, the Devil. She tried to reconcile what she knew of God's loving acceptance and the Church's teaching on sin. In the long text, chapter forty-five, she says of God, "I saw him assign to us no kind of blame." Yet she knew herself to be a sinner.

In wrestling with this quandary, she was given a vision by God of a master and a servant. The lord was sitting in state, at rest and in peace. The servant stood in front of the lord, ready and eager to do the lord's bidding. The lord sends the servant out on an errand. The servant dashes off, and in his haste falls down and is injured. Though the lord is still nearby, the servant feels himself to be alone and in great pain and weakness. So, blinded by pain and perplexed, he even nearly forgets about the lord's love and confidence. Julian understood that in part this was the story of Adam and of Jesus. Adam came and fell; Jesus came to earth and took on the weakness of human flesh and died. "Dying, we are constantly protected by Christ, and by the touching of his grace we are raised to true trust in salvation," Julian writes; "We cannot in this life keep ourselves completely from sin, in the perfect purity that we shall have in heaven. But we can well by grace keep ourselves from the sins which would lead us to endless torment."

After fifteen visions had appeared, she tells us in chapter sixty-seven of the long text, she fell asleep, and in a dream she saw the Devil at her throat, but she "trusted to be saved and protected by the mercy of God" and she awoke. When she went to sleep again, it was with "great rest and peace, without sickness of body or fear of conscience." Thereafter God showed her spiritually her soul in the midst of her heart, "as wide as if it were an endless citadel." And she realized that "the place which Jesus takes in our soul he will nevermore vacate, for in us is his home of homes and his everlasting dwelling." This is Julian's description of her experience of mystical union.

In chapter eighty-six of the long text, Julian summarizes what she had learned in fifteen years of questioning the meaning of her visions: "What, do you wish to know your Lord's meaning in this thing? Know it well, love was his meaning. Who reveals it to you? Love. What did he reveal to you? Love. Why does he reveal it to you? For love."

In the short text she notes that she learned that we have two kinds of sickness of which God wishes to cure us: impatience and despair. The cure is to realize that not only is God "almighty and may do everything, and that he is all wisdom and can do everything," but also to know that God "is all love and wishes to do everything." Julian's ultimate faith is found in a recurring phrase: "All is well, and every kind of thing will be well."

In Julian's writings we find one of the clearest and yet most complex records of the soul of a mystic.

Nancy A. Hardesty

RECOMMENDED READING

Edition used: Julian of Norwich. *Showings*. Translation and Introduction by Edmund Colledge and James Walsh. New York: Paulist Press, 1978. This most recent edition contains both short and long texts, along with a very full and helpful introduction.

―――. *A Shewing of God's Love*. Edited by Anna Maria Reynolds. London: Sheed & Ward, 1958. This edition contains only the short text, yet the use of certain words such as "homely" and "courteous" in the translation captures Julian's tone more faithfully.

Underhill, Evelyn. *Mysticism.* New York: Dutton, 1961. The unparalleled classic in the field. Will help the reader understand the tradition exemplified by these works. Underhill uses examples often from Julian.

Wolters, Clifford. *Julian of Norwich: Revelations of Divine Love.* Hammondsworth, England: Penguin Books, 1966. Another edition available. Helpful introduction.

THE CLOUD OF UNKNOWING

Author: Unknown

The linguistic and manuscript evidence seems to indicate that *The Cloud of Unknowing* was written in the northeast midlands of England in the last half of the fourteenth century. Three other works are explicitly said to be the work of the author of *The Cloud of Unknowing*: the *Book of Privy Counselling*, the *Epistle of Prayer*, and *Denis' Hid Divinity*. The internal evidence of his writings indicates that the author was a priest, dedicated to the contemplative life, and recognized as a spiritual father. He was a competent theologian, with a great knowledge of patristic and monastic literature. He knew some elements of the teaching of Saint Thomas Aquinas.

Type and subject of work: A treatise of practical spiritual instruction

First transcribed: Late fourteenth century

MAJOR THEMES

If one strives to fix one's love on God while forgetting all else, which is the work of contemplation, God in his goodness will bring one to a deep experience of God.

Even Christians called primarily to a life of active service must at times lay aside their activity and give time to meditation and communion with God.

One must be a person of faith, sufficient faith to believe in the Divine Presence hidden beyond the cloud of unknowing.

One must have turned from sin toward God in love, a love strong enough to make one seek God in the darkness of his incomprehensibility, leaving behind other attractions and desires.

It is not what you are nor what you have been that God sees with his all-merciful eyes, but what you desire to be.

It is God, and he alone, who can fully satisfy the hunger and longing of our spirit which, transformed by his redeeming grace, is enabled to embrace him by love.

The Cloud of Unknowing is not an orderly treatise. It is repetitious. It has its share of digressions. It is primarily addressed to an enthusiastic young disciple, age twenty-four, who is prone to overdo things even while he struggles with some natural fickleness and laziness. It inserts basic human and Christian teaching at random points.

The treatise leaves us with a sense of helplessness in the face of our divine aspirations. But it also leaves us with a certain comfortableness with that sense of helplessness, for here the author, a wise spiritual father who clearly seems to have found his way, keeps reassuring us that this confusion is all right—quite to be expected. We really have to do only one thing, and that is to leave things in the hands of God, to turn ourselves over to him, to accept his gift of himself which is the union of contemplation. "But if you strive to fix your love on him, forgetting all else, which is the work of contemplation I have urged you to begin," this wise father assures us, "I am confident that God in his goodness will bring you to a deep experience of himself."

The father tells us for whom he has written *The Cloud of Unknowing*: "I have in mind a person who, over and above the good works of the active life, has resolved to follow Christ (as far as humanly possible with God's grace) unto the inmost depths of contemplation ... who has first been faithful for some time to the demands of the active life."

The father sees some Christians called primarily to a life of active service, but these must at times lay aside their activity and give time to meditation and communion with God. Others are called primarily to a Christian life centered on prayer and contemplation, but these too must lay aside their primary concern at times to attend to human and social affairs. Thus he speaks of two degrees in each life: a higher and a lower; and he sees the higher degree of the active life coalescing with the lower degree of the contemplative. It is here where most good Christians are situated but each with his or her proper call with its particular emphases.

One must be a person of faith, sufficient faith to believe in the Divine Presence hidden beyond in the cloud of unknowing. One must have turned from sin toward God in love, a love strong enough to make one seek God in the darkness of his incomprehensibility, leaving behind other attractions and desires. When the father comes to express concretely what this means, he is not as demanding as we might have expected: "If you ask me when a person should begin his contemplative work I would answer not until he has first purified his conscience of all particular sins in the Sacrament of Reconciliation as the Church prescribes ... Once having done what the Church requires, he should fearlessly begin the contemplative work." The past does not matter, the author insists: "Some who have been hardened habitual sinners arrive at the perfection of this work sooner than those who have never sinned grievously"—nor even present weakness: "In choosing your present way of life you made a radical commitment to God and this remains despite temporary lapse" (the father seems decidedly up-to-date in speaking here about a fundamental option)—but only one's true desire: "It is not what you are nor what you have been that God sees with his all-merciful eyes, but what you desire to be."

Going on to close the treatise with a passage from Saint Augustine that reads, "The entire life of a good Christian is nothing less than holy desire," the father seems clearly to indicate that this way of contemplative prayer is for all Christians. However, in prescribing the contemplative way, he respects diversity of ways within it, a position well developed with biblical imagery in the previous chapters where he says: "It is important to realize that in the interior life we must never take our own experiences (or lack of them) as the norm for everyone else." Earlier he has affirmed: "How often it happens that the grace of contemplation will awaken in people of every walk and station of life, both religious and lay alike."

Far from excluding anyone from seeking to develop the contemplative dimensions of life, the father seems to imply that its development is essential for the fulfillment of human life: "It is God, and he alone, who can fully satisfy the hunger and longing of our spirit which, transformed by his redeeming grace, is enabled to embrace him by love." The activities of the lower degree of the active life (the corporal works of mercy) in themselves leave much of our natural human potential untapped. At this stage one lives, as it were, outside oneself and beneath oneself. As one advances to the higher degree of the active life (which merges with the lower degree of the contemplative life) one becomes increasingly interior, living more from the depth of oneself and becoming, therefore, more fully human. For the fulfillment of the human spirit one must have a spiritual life; for fulfillment of the Christian spirit that has been given us at baptism, one must have a full Christian life, one of intimate communion of God.

One of the objections against this work of contemplation is its emptiness; it is an experience of nothingness, of being nowhere—it is idleness, a quietism. And the first to raise this objection is the contemplator:

"Who do you suppose derides it as an emptiness? Our superficial self, of course." Those closest to us quickly join in: "... family and friends descend upon them in a storm of fury and criticism, severely reproving them for idleness."

Right from the start the father assures his son of the preeminent fruitfulness of contemplation: "What I am describing here is the contemplative work of the spirit. It is this which gives God the greatest delight. For when you fix your love on him, forgetting all else, the saints and angels rejoice and hasten to assist you in every way—though the devils will rage and ceaselessly conspire to thwart you. Your fellow men are marvelously enriched by this work of yours, even if you may not fully understand how; the souls in purgatory are touched, for their suffering is eased by the effects of this work and, of course, your own spirit is purified and strengthened by this contemplative work more than by all others put together." The father continues: "For I tell you this, one loving blind desire for God alone is more valuable in itself, more pleasing to God and to the Saints, more beneficial to your own growth, and more helpful to your friends, both living and dead, than anything else you could do." But—"It cannot be explained, only experienced."

Our Master has said: "Judge a tree by its fruit." There should be some fruits that the objective observer should be able to experience. And the father speaks of these: "Moreover, in contemplation the second and subsidiary command of charity it also completely fulfilled. The fruits of contemplation bear witness to this even though during the actual time of prayer the skilled contemplative has no special regard for any person in particular, whether brother or stranger, friend or enemy ... when he speaks or prays with his fellow Christian at other times, the warmth of his love reaches out to them all, friend or enemy, stranger and kin alike."

"Genuine goodness is a matter of habitually acting and responding appropriately in each situation as it arises, moved always by the desire to please God," the father writes. Other norms he notes are the general good use of time and the regard for communal prayer: "The true contemplative has the highest esteem for the liturgy and is careful and exact in celebrating it, in continuity with the tradition of our Fathers." These fruits of contemplation can be readily perceived and might therefore reassure some, looking in from the outside, as to the value of contemplative prayer—but probably not many. And they do not touch the more significant meaning and value of contemplative practice for the human community. There is a bonding, transcending time and place, with Jesus, "creator and dispenser of time," which enables the contemplative to "share all Jesus has and enter the fellowship of those who love Him," including "the communion of the blessed." Each member "must do his share however slight to strengthen the fellowship as it strengthens him."

The father is not, in this work, offering a full systematic treatment of the spiritual life. His concern here is about a way of prayer but that is a part of a whole life and a whole attitude. This latter is important. Nonetheless, he does offer a very simple, traditional method of prayer that can be drawn out from his work.

Simply sit relaxed and quiet. Center all your attention and desire on God, and let this be the sole concern of your mind and heart. If you want to gather all your desire into one simple word that the mind can easily retain, choose a short word rather than a long one, but choose one that is meaningful to you (such as the world *God* or *love*). Fix the word in your mind so that it will remain there, come what may.

(The father's advice involves words of encouragement and the reminder that the darkness of the cloud of unknowing comes between the contemplator and the God one desires to reach; despite the darkness, one wills to reach out to God.)

Be careful in this work (the father continues); never strain your mind or imagination, for truly you will not succeed in this way; leave these faculties at peace. It is best when the word chosen for contemplation is wholly interior without a definite thought or actual sound. Let this little word (the father enjoins) represent to you God in all his fullness; let nothing except God hold sway in your mind and heart.

(One may be distracted by remembering some task undone or one may find that some disrupting thought is clouding one's attention, the father comments—but, he advises, if one answers with the word chosen, if one resists intellectualizing about its meaning and, instead, holds the word before oneself in all its simplicity, one may escape distractions.)

Put all thoughts of other creatures—past, present, and future—under a "cloud of forgetting."

If in this way you strive to fix your love on him (the father reassures us), forgetting all else, which is the work of contemplation I have urged you to begin, I am confident that God in his goodness will bring you to a deep experience of himself.

M. Basil Pennington

RECOMMENDED READING

Edition used: *The Cloud of Unknowing.* Edited by James Walsh, S.J. Classics of Western Spirituality. New York: Paulist Press, 1981.

The Cloud of Unknowing and Related Treatises. Edited by Phyllis Hodgson. Analecta Cartusiana, Vol. 3. Salzburg: University of Salzburg, 1982. This volume includes Phyllis Hodgson's new edition of *The Cloud of Unknowing* and the related texts on contemplative prayer that are argued to come from the same author: *The Book of Privy Counselling, The Epistle of Prayer, The Epistle of Discre-tion, Hid Divinity, Benjamin Minor, The Study of Wisdom,* and *Of Discerning of Spirits.* It also contains six pages of bibliography.

Johnston, William. *The Mysticism of the Cloud of Unknowing.* New York: Desclee, 1967. The author gives and extensive study of the mysticism of the period and also compares the teaching of *The Cloud of Unknowing* with that of Saint John of the Cross and other apophatic mystics. There is a good introduction by Thomas Merton.

Pennington, M. Basil. *Centering Prayer: Renewing an Ancient Christian Prayer Form.* New York: Doubleday, 1980. This study places *The Cloud of Unknowing* in its full historical context within the ever-renewing Christian tradition and gives a very practical modern presentation of its basic teaching.

Szarmach, Paul E., ed. *An Introduction to the Medieval Mystics of Europe.* Albany: State of University of New York Press, 1984. This collection of fourteen es-says contains a good study of *The Cloud of Unknowing* by John P. H. Clark.

THE IMITATION OF CHRIST

Author: Saint Thomas à Kempis (1380–1471)

Born Thomas Hemerken in the German city of Kempten, Thomas followed an elder brother to a religious center in the Netherlands, later entering a monastery where he lived for nearly seven decades. He entered the priesthood in 1413 and devoted much of his time to copying manuscripts and directing novices. In 1425 he was made sub-prior of his monastery. In addition to *The Imitation of Christ,* he wrote sermons, devotional works, and biographies of Saint Lydwine and Gerard Groote (1340–1384), who has sometimes been suggested as the author of this volume. He died after completing a chronicle of Mount Saint Agnes in his ninety-second year in the sixty-third year of his religious life and the fifty-eighth year of his priesthood.

Type and subject of work: Spiritual meditations on perfecting the life of a monk

First transcribed: c. 1418

MAJOR THEMES

The example of Christ should be followed in all things.
Secular learning may be spiritually dangerous.
Vanities of the world are to be despised.
The words of detractors should not pain us.
All trust is to be put in God alone.
The Eucharist is especially profitable for the spiritual life.

Perhaps the most widely read religious book in history, outside of the Bible itself, this fifteenth-century classic was written by a monk for monks. Nevertheless, countless others have read it for spiritual guidance. While there is some question of who the actual author of the text was, readers seem to have had little trouble accepting the authenticity of its message.

The first of four books is titled "Admonitions Useful for a Spiritual Life." The need to imitate or follow Christ is immediately established by Thomas. While in the rest of the volume he indicates a certain respect for learning, there is a clear caution in his opening remarks, especially in his famous sentence: "I would rather feel compunction of heart for my sins than merely know the definition of compunction." He also opens by advising the reader to despise the world with all its snares that obstruct spiritual perfection.

It is a good life that refreshes the mind, Thomas writes, and it is a clear conscience that allows for trust in God. The most profitable learning is in truthful knowledge and a full despising of the self. Nothing hinders growth in holiness more than our own regard for ourselves. On judgment day we will not be asked what we read but how we have lived. It is vanity to put trust in any person or crated thing. Overfamiliarity with others is to be avoided while the virtue of obedience is to be cultivated.

We must not easily judge others but we can judge ourselves with great spiritual profit, Thomas continues. God is the sole judge of others and does so not according to the greatness of an act but according to the intention of the doer. It is important to break one's own will if we would have peace and concord with others. The example of the holy fathers and saints is to be followed: They served the Lord through all adversities; they suffered willingly for Christ's sake; they refused all honors and bodily pleasures to gain everlasting life; they prayed constantly and renounced much to be faithful to God.

The purpose of good men depends not so much on themselves and their wisdom but on their Maker. "Man proposes, but God disposes," Thomas writes. Humility and charity must be cultivated and the key to controlling casual desire is found in the discipline against the tendency toward gluttony that many have. Each should develop, too, a love of solitude and of silence. Thomas warns against the perils to the spiritual life done by mingling with people. Security is not found with others but in God.

It is amazing, the author writes, how we can rejoice in this life if we merely consider how far we are in exile and what great danger our souls are constantly in. Meditation on death rather than on long life will cause us to work seriously to amend our lives. Each morning we should doubt that we will live until night; that will help us to order our lives. It is foolish to think our lives will last long. The world's business counts but little; we should regard ourselves as pilgrims and strangers on this earth.

A natural extension of contemplating death is in meditating on the last judgment and on the punishment to be meted out for sin. This will aid us to wish to change our lives and to concern ourselves with the state of our souls before all else. Two things explicitly, Thomas urges, are extremely helpful in the positive altering of one's life: a withdrawal of the self from the things toward which the body most generally tends, and a dedicated effort to develop the virtues one most needs.

The first section concludes with the advice that one who lives a religious life and tries to do so without discipline is unlikely to achieve any good but rather fall into great ruin.

"Admonitions Leading to the Inner Life" is the way book two is titled. Since Christ has told us that the kingdom of God is within each of us, it behooves us therefore to turn inward and reject the basically wretched world. Peace and joy are found through the Holy Spirit and not through wicked people. We must prepare our hearts for Christ, the true Spouse, allowing him unencumbered entrance. This implies trust in God, which should motivate all that we do. God should be both our love and our fear above all else.

Thomas assures the reader that if one once enters the sacred wounds of Jesus and there tastes his love, one would care nothing for this world. To be free from all inordinate affections should be one's great desire. This freedom will help one to acknowledge personal defects humbly. To be quiet and to suffer but awhile is the way to holiness. In time of such trials, God will defend the believer. "A peaceful and patient man is of more profit to himself and to others, too, than a learned man who has no peace." Such peace comes from a zealous regard for one's own soul, from the practice of charity which is to be extended to others, and from humility.

It is necessary for the monk to cultivate a pure mind and to be of simple intention, to develop a knowledge of himself, and to be able to be content in a pure conscience. He must recognize the familiar friendship of Jesus and learn to love Jesus above all else. He should remember, also, to show gratitude to God for his many blessings. The fourteenth-century writer then observes that while many persons love the kingdom of heaven, very few are willing to bear Jesus' cross. Many wish his consolation but they want it at very little cost to themselves. They should take up Christ's cross, Thomas urges, and learn how profitable patience is in the face of adversity.

Book three, the longest part of this volume, is called "The Inward Speaking of Christ to a Faithful Soul." The manner in which we are to hear God's word is with humility, according to Thomas. Many refuse to hear that word, however, preferring instead to listen to the world. Such, though, is not the way to that which is everlasting. God's word, written on the heart, will serve as well in times of temptation.

We must learn to be conversant with God in truth and, again, in humility. Love of God will produce incalculable effects. With yet another reference to humility, Thomas says that this is the virtue that keeps grace close to us. Through that same virtue we will see ourselves as the miserable creatures we are in God's eyes. We will then be able to realize how wonderful it is to serve him and turn our backs on the world.

Care needs to be taken that the desires of our heart are properly disciplined. Patience and striving against all sensual desires are important elements of this discipline. Obedience, the example of which was set by Christ, is also essential. We must be wary not to take inordinate pride in the good acts we do.

In seeking solace and comfort, we will find the truest forms in God, who is to be the goal of all study and every thought we have. Our sufferings are to be borne patiently, regardless of the source, according to Thomas, and are to be taken as from the hand of God. We should rest in God in all things, recalling always his great blessings. The four things that bring peace to the soul are obedience, poverty, humility, and conformity to the will of God.

A free mind is a blessing, while love of self is an obstacle to love of God, Thomas insists. We must call upon God in time of tribulation and trust completely that we will recover our former grace through devout devotion. The heart is unstable and one's full intention in everything that one does must be directed toward God.

Thomas reminds his monks that the conditions of this life offer no complete protection from temptation. He also warns against the vain judgments of persons—why should we dread the opinion of another, one who will be here today but not tomorrow, while God endures forever? Spiritual freedom is gained through a purified forsaking of ourselves and of our own will which is submerged in God's will. When you experience certain dangers, "You enter into your soul by prayer" in order to pursue perfection, since no person is good in and of oneself. This means that one cannot properly glorify oneself in anything, but may be glorified only through one's creator.

Since all earthly honor is to be despised, we must not put our trust in people who are worldly, and we should be very suspicious of secular learning, which may be based in vanity. As counseled earlier, we should not be concerned with outer things (as opposed to interior matters) and always disregard the judgments of others on us. We should be wary of what others say because they so often and easily offend with their words. Particularly when evil words are uttered are we to place our confidence in God. We must be prepared to suffer gladly for the life that is to come. "Labor busily and faithfully in My vineyard, and I will shortly be your reward." A great reward is promised those who persevere against sin.

At times when one does not feel like performing high works of devotion, it is good to do physical labor. One should abandon oneself and follow Jesus by taking up the Savior's cross. Nor should one despair though showing failings in the quest for perfection. All hope and faith are to be placed in God who is "the end of all good things."

The final book deals with what Thomas calls the sacrament of the altar. Thomas starts this segment by indicating how great the reverence must be in one who receives holy communion. He writes of a humble familiarity to be developed, and he reminds monks that there is no need to travel the world to see the relics of the saints when all that they need for spiritual growth is to be found in the sacrament of communion. The great goodness of God is offered in the blessed sacrament, which is so marvelous in that the Creator comes down to the lowest of creatures thus raising them to devout heights.

It is profitable to the soul to receive communion often (the general wisdom of Thomas's time urged against frequent communicating), and he says that there are many advantages given to those who properly receive the sacrament that is the life of the soul, the medicine for spiritual illness. Vices are cured by it, passions are held in check, temptations are overcome, and faith is increased. He next expounds on the value of the priesthood and follows this with admonitions as to how one ought to prepare oneself to receive communion properly.

One must search one's conscience and express true regret for one's sins, following this with a firm purpose of amendment. One must make a free and full offering of oneself to God, and of all one's possessions as well. One's duty is also to pray for the souls of others. Nor should holy communion be easily neglected. The dangers of excessive scrupulosity are also discussed by Thomas. Advice follows on how to say mass, not rapidly or in too overlong a fashion.

Christ's body in communion plus the Sacred Scriptures are most necessary to the spiritual help of all, Thomas claims. The devout person will greatly desire to be made one with Jesus in communion, Thomas advises, adding that the grace of devotion is gained through a humility of spirit and a forsaking of the self in favor of God. No one should try to hide anything from Christ while continually seeking his grace. Christ should be received with great affection and burning love, and communion is to be received not in curiosity but in a submission to the will to Christ. Faith, Thomas concludes, is to prevail over reason.

Harry James Cargas

Recommended Reading

Edition used: Thomas à Kempis. *The Imitation of Christ.* Garden City, N.Y.: Doubleday, Image Books, 1955.

Merton, Thomas. *The Seven Storey Mountain.* New York: Signet Books, 1952. Often called a modern *Imitation,* this is the autobiography of a twentieth-century restless soul that found peace in a monastery.

Thomas à Kempis. *Vera Sapientia or True Wisdom.* Translated by Frederick Byrne. New York: Benziger, 1904. May be regarded as a continuation of many of the thoughts begun in the *Imitation.*

THE BOOK OF MARGERY KEMPE

Author: Margery Kempe (c. 1373–c. 1440)

A religious mystic, Margery Kempe was the daughter of John Burnham, the mayor of Lynn, a leading English town of the day. In 1393 she married John Kempe and had fourteen children before vowing chastity and beginning in 1414 a series of pilgrimages to Jerusalem, Rome, Germany, and Spain. She was in Rome for the celebration of the confirmation of the canonization of Saint Bridget of Sweden in 1415. About 1417 she went to Santiago de Compostella in northwestern Spain. She was back in Lynn when the Guildhall burned in 1421. Her husband died about 1425 and a son died about 1432. Several years later she journeyed with her daughter-in-law to Germany. Apparently illiterate, she dictated her book to two clerks approximately between 1432 and 1436.

Type and subject of work: The first extant spiritual biography in English

First transcribed: c. 1432–1436

MAJOR THEMES

God loves, is revealed to, and uses quite ordinary people.

The religious life of an ordinary fourteenth-century person has many similarities with and some differences from that of a twentieth-century Christian.

Chastity was considered a premier virtue, even for married couples in the Middle Ages, though "lechery" or adultery was also widespread, even among clerics.

Pilgrimage to such places as Jerusalem, Rome, and Santiago de Compostella was a common form of religious devotion.

Margery Kempe, who usually refers to herself as "this creature," begins her book by noting that at age twenty she married a burgess of Lynn and "was with child within a short time, as nature would." The rigors of childbirth were such that she despaired of life. She called for a confessor but failed to confess one thing that she felt she should and was so troubled that she "went out of her mind and was wondrously vexed and laboured with spirits for half a year, eight weeks and odd days." In the end Christ appeared to her and reminded her that though she may have forsaken him, he had never forsaken her. She was restored to her senses and resumed her household duties.

Though she felt bound to God by this experience, she would not forsake her pride or pompous array. Her hoods, cloaks, and dresses were the envy of the neighborhood. She decided to become a brewer. She was the best in town for several years until things started to go wrong and her servants left her. Next she tried milling, but horses refused to turn her mill. She concluded that God was trying to tell her something. So she asked God's mercy, forsook her pride, covetousness, and desire for vainglory, and did penance. Thus began her religious life.

Shortly after her religious awakening, she began to feel that she should not "commune fleshly" with her husband. The "debt of matrimony" became abominable to her. She asked to live chastely with him, but he "would have his will and she obeyed" even though she wept copiously throughout. And even though she felt called to celibacy, she was tempted to adultery with another man who first importuned her and then declined when she consented.

Finally after several years and several children, Christ promised her that if she would fast every Friday, she would have her desire by Whitsunday. When her husband approached her on the Wednesday of Easter week, she prayed, "Jesus Christ, help me," and her husband "had no power to touch her at that time in that way, nor ever after with any fleshly knowledge."

Later on a trip to York together they got into another argument over the marriage bed. Her husband finally agreed that if she paid his debts before she set off for Jerusalem and if she resumed eating with him on Fridays, he would set her body "free to God." She and her husband eventually took vows of chastity before the bishop of Lincoln and she adopted white clothing as a sign of her purity.

For many years thereafter they lived apart to avoid any slander that they were not keeping their vows. However, when her husband suffered a serious fall down the steps in his house, she took him into her home and nursed him for several years until his death in 1431. In 1433 and 1434 she took a trip to Danzig and returned through Germany and Holland. The last reference historians have found to Margery is in 1439.

One of her revelations was that God did love wives "and specially those wives who would live chaste," though God considered the state of maidenhood more perfect and more holy than the state of widowhood and that more perfect than wedlock. Jesus promised her that despite her married state, she could dance with the maidens in heaven because she was a maiden in her soul.

Margery also experienced miracles. Once on a Friday before Whitsun Eve she was in church when she heard a loud noise. As she was kneeling, suddenly from the highest part of the church roof, a three-pound stone and a six-pound piece of beam fell down on her back. At first she felt great pain and thought she would die, but soon she cried "Jesus, mercy" and the pain was gone.

She seems to have had a number of visions, revelations, and gifts of wisdom. On a number of occasions she startled people by revealing their past sins or informing them of the eternal state of deceased loved ones or predicting future events. She records a number of times in which not only Jesus appeared to her, but also the Virgin Mary, the apostles, and various saints.

A chief characteristic of her piety was "full plenteous and abundant tears" and "boisterous sobbings." This seemed to annoy her neighbors and some of those dignitaries she visited in various lands. Some understood it as evidence of her great devotion; others called her a hypocrite. Her fasting and crying made her travel companions on her trip to the Holy Land so irate that in Constance they refused to travel any farther with her. She finally agreed not to testify to them at meals and they let her eat with them at Venice, but there she slipped and so she had to take to her chamber and eat alone for six weeks. She wanted to sail on the same boat with them, but they refused. She then had a vision in which God told her to take another boat anyway, so they decided they better take it too. In Jerusalem she experienced "great weeping and sobbing" at the tomb, "wept and sobbed wonderfully" at the cross, "wept with great compassion" at the stone of marble where Christ's body had lain, and "cried so loud that it was a wonder to hear it" at the Mount of Calvary. She prayed that her crying be stopped since it caused her so much trouble, but Christ refused her request.

For a time she was persecuted and threatened with burning as a Lollard, though she does not appear to have been one. She was jailed in Leicester, though her jailer put her in his own house, under care of his wife, and let her eat at his own table and go to church whenever she wanted. They even put two of her pilgrimage companions in jail. But God visited the town with such a thunderstorm that the people were frightened and demanded that the pilgrims all be let go. Eventually she was examined as to her views in the church of All Hallows, Leicester, by the abbot and dean, and was found to be orthodox. Yet her persecution continued and she was jailed in various places.

When she quoted from the Gospels, some accused her of preaching and noted that Saint Paul forbad women's preaching, but she refused to be silenced. She noted that she did not really preach because she did not come into a pulpit, but simply spoke what was on her mind and heart.

In her travels she met and talked with many important people. She and her husband made their vow of chastity before Philip Repington, bishop of Lincoln. Her visit to Dame Julian, an anchoress in Norwich (c. 1342–1420), is our major confirmation of that mystic's life. She confronted both the archbishops of Canterbury and York as well as various lesser church officials concerning their lack of sanctity.

Her usual procedure was to share with them her revelations and insights and to record their scorn or praise. Her narrative is interspersed with accounts of the spiritual lessons she learned, but its charm lies in its recounting of one Christian's life in the fifteenth century.

Margery's book reveals her as a very strong-willed and forthright woman who managed to have a life of her own despite marriage and fourteen children. She had a ready wit and refused to let any man put her down. She was very able in defending her faith under examination, and she could turn the tables on her accusers. She also appears as a very vain and self-centered woman, always glorying in the attention paid her, whether favorable or unfavorable. Her book is a remarkably revealing portrait both of Margery as a person and of the life of her times.

For many the discovery of the full text of *The Book of Margery Kempe* in 1934 was a disappointment. Before that time she was known through a series of extracts printed as a "short treatise" by Wynkyn of Worde in 1501. The extracts, carefully chosen for their devotional content (most were conversations between Margery and Christ or the Blessed Virgin), led most readers to think that the missing book was similar to Walter Hilton's *Ladder of Perfection* (c. 1390), Richard Rolle's *The Fire of Love* (*Incendium Amoris*) (c. 1343), or Dame Julian's *Revelations of Divine Love* (c. 1393), all of which Margery was familiar with. Her book in full revealed that it was not a treatise on contemplation, nor was she the spiritual equal of her mystical compatriots. Dom David Knowles describes her as "filling every role from that of saintly mystic to that of hysterical exhibitionist." She appears to be basically a sincere person, a woman of faith and goodwill, charitable in word and deed. Her account reveals that she had many supporters among church leaders whom other sources declare to be men of sound judgment and piety. She certainly displays courage and candor in her encounters with both friends and foes.

Nancy A. Hardesty

RECOMMENDED READING

Edition used: Kempe, Margery. *The Book of Margery Kempe*. Edited by W. Butler-Bowdon. New York: Devin-Adair, 1944.

Knowles, David. *The English Mystical Tradition*. New York: Harper & Row, Harper Torchbooks, 1961. A helpful and scholarly overview.

THE VISION OF GOD

Author: Nicholas of Cusa (1401–1464)

Nicholas of Cusa, commonly referred to as Cusanus, received his early schooling from the mystically oriented Brethren of the Common Life, after which he studied philosophy, science, and law at Heidelberg and then at Padua. An early work, *Universal Reconciliation* (1433), represents the active side of his career, devoted to bringing together conciliar and papal factions of the Church and to the reunion of the eastern and western branches of Christendom. But throughout his life, Nicholas kept abreast of philosophical and scientific developments, and undertook, in *The Learned Ignorance* (1440), a new synthesis of faith and reason. *The Vision of God* (1453) is a book of meditations, composed for the monks at the Benedictine abbey at Tegernsee, who, moved by their reading of his earlier work, had asked him to send them a method of contemplation.

Type and subject of work: Meditations on mystical theology

First transcribed: 1453

MAJOR THEMES

Because in God seeing comprises knowing, loving, and working, God's vision bestows existence.

Attempts to apprehend God as if he were an object plunge the mind into darkness from which it emerges only when it learns the limits of understanding.

To one who has reached the vantage point of this "learned ignorance," faith and love open the way into the mysteries of the Trinity and the Incarnation.

The full title of this book is *The Vision of God or the Icon*; for when Nicholas sent the book to the monks at Tegernsee, he also sent an icon of the kind known as omnivoyant, the face of which appeared to be looking in every direction. The brethren were asked to keep the picture before them when the book was being read, but it was suggested that first they make the experiment of viewing the icon from every angle, persuading themselves that the immovable gaze of the pictured face followed the movement of each individual. " 'Tis by means of this perceptible image that I propose to uplift you, my most loving brethren, by a certain devotional exercise unto mystical theology," he wrote. And in his words of address, having prayed for the power to utter marvels beyond our reason, he expresses his hope of leading them "into the divine darkness" wherein they may in one measure or another perceive "the light inaccessible" and have a foretaste of "the feast of everlasting bliss."

Nicholas does not offer his readers a technique of contemplation. Rather, he proposes a series of thought-experiments, following what we may call the method of comparisons; for, at the beginning, he explains that if he is to transport them in human fashion to things divine, he can do so only through comparisons. That he is offering them a devotional exercise and not a logical demonstration after the manner of the schools he begs them to remember. Mystical theology moves in a circle; and if they are to use the method of comparisons they must start with three assumptions: first, that each creature depends on God for its particular excellence; second, that God is "the summit of all perfection, and greater than can be conceived"; third, that in God the excellencies that exist separately in the creatures form an incomprehensible unity. For instance, since we have sight, we can be certain that absolute sight exists in God, yet in such a way that God's sight is one with his being, his knowing, and his working.

Each of the twenty-five chapters of Nicholas's book is a separate meditation, addressed directly to God. There are no milestones or boundary markers along the path. Still, when a reader reaches chapter sixteen and becomes aware of the familiar ground of creedal theology, the reader notes that the last ten meditations form a distinct set. Likewise, when one looks back, one can see that the first ten meditations, which focus directly on the icon, form a set. Finally, it dawns on the reader that the middle chapters—considerably more difficult than the earlier ones—are a review of Nicholas's major philosophical work, *The Learned Ignorance*. Following these cues, we may divide the book into three main parts; and, since according to the author all theology is necessarily figurative or symbolic, we may label the first set of meditations "The Face," the second set "The Door," and the third set "Paradise," or "The Tree of Life."

The all-seeing icon suggests numerous edifying applications, particularly when God's sight is taken to be identical with his being, his love, and his goodness. Though immutable, the divine vision follows the movements of each creature, beholding even the secrets of our hearts. And, with God, "to behold is to give life," so that through God's look we are "made to increase and endure," and are established with his Son in the heavenly kingdom. To the eye of faith, the icon speaks of God's enduring care and, indeed, of his sustaining power. "Thy Being, Lord, letteth not go of my being. I exist in that measure in which Thou are with me, and, since Thy look is Thy being, I am because Thou are with me, and if Thou didst turn Thy glance from me I should cease to be." In these and similar passages Nicholas affirms, with Augustine of Hippo and Anselm of Canterbury, that every intelligent creature has immediate knowledge of God. God's seeing and his being seen by humankind are one and the same. "What else, Lord, is Thy seeing, when Thou beholdest me with pitying eye, than that Thou art seen of me? In beholding me Thou givest Thyself to be seen of me, Thou who art a hidden God." This intimacy between the believer and the one whom he or she ventures to call "My God" and "My Father" constitutes a major strand in Nicholas's thinking. Today we might call it the I-Thou relation.

While Nicholas ponders how a creature can be said to draw near to God when it is God who upholds one's very being, God speaks within the heart: "Be thine own self and I too will be thine." Then, upon reflecting that humanity's will is the image of God's power, Nicholas responds: "O Lord, Thou Sweetness most delectable, Thou hast left me free to be mine own self, if I desire. Hence, if I be not mine own self, Thou art not mine ... I now perceive that, if I hearken unto Thy Word, which ceaseth not to speak within me ... I shall be mine own, and Thou wilt be mine, and wilt grant me to behold Thy face, and I shall be whole."

This Augustinian strand, however, is interwoven in this first part with a second strand deriving from Dionysius the Areopagite, and ultimately from Greek philosophy. Here the immediate experience of God recedes and critical judgment takes its place. The bugaboos of anthropomorphism and cultural relativism raise their heads; and, in order to defend the faith, the believer must abstract from the face of the icon to the notion of face per se. A face visible to the eye of the flesh must have colors and measurable features; but if we look on the icon with the eye of the understanding, we apprehend that these do not pertain to a face's essence, that "true face is free from any limitation, it hath neither quantity nor quality, nor is it of time or place." From such considerations it follows that God's face, since it is for a youth the face of a youth and for an old man the face of an old man—and why not for a lion the face of a lion?—must be the Absolute Face, "the pattern and true type of all faces," in short, the Face of faces, which of course is not really a face at all, any more than Aristotle's Form of forms (his designation for God) is a form, or than Plato's Idea of the Good (his designation for the Ultimate) is an idea—or a good! In Nicholas's language, God's Face enfolds all faces, or, what is the same thing, God's Face is unfolded in individual faces. But such thoughts bring us to the limits of understanding. If God's Face appears veiled in human faces, it can appear unveiled only in "a certain secret and mystic silence where there is no knowledge or concept of face." It is a "cloud, darkness, or ignorance" through which a seeker must pass. "But that very darkness revealeth Thy Face to be there beyond all veils."

Nicholas's second set of meditations takes us deep into mystical theology. They no longer center on God's vision and humankind's, but on the fertile ignorance into which the mind is plunged when it recognizes the total disproportion between the creature and the Creator—what Nicholas calls "wise," or "learned," ignorance. Nicholas's ruling metaphor through these meditations is a wall that excludes us from God's presence because of our having eaten from the Tree of Knowledge. "I have learnt," says the author in a typical passage, "that the place wherein Thou art found unveiled is girt around with the coincidence of contradictories, and this is the wall of Paradise wherein Thou dost abide." According to Nicholas, human understanding, based as it is on the law of noncontradiction (that a thing cannot both be and not be in the same way at the same time), does not hold true of ultimate reality, where what to our thinking are contradictories do exist together.

Nicholas does not have to look far for examples. The omnivoyant icon, which does not move, seems to move as it follows the movements of the beholder. Though this is an illusion, it poses the theological question how it is that God, being eternal, can engage himself with events in time. Nicholas offers as an acceptable comparison the ideal clock as it exists in the mind of the clockmaker. The actual clock strikes six an hour before it strikes seven; but in the craftsman's mind six and seven occur at the same instant. "Eternity, therefore, both enfoldeth and unfoldeth succession, since the concept of the clock, which is eternity, doth alike enfold and unfold all things." The example may have given the brethren food for thought, and Nicholas thanks God for the nourishment that "the milk of comparisons" furnishes him until he is ready for more solid fare. For genuine nourishment, however, one must chew on the thought that the opposition implied in pairs of concepts such as eternity and time, creator and creature, cause and effect, enfolding and unfolding exists only outside the wall of the coincidence of contradictions. In general terms, the opposition between same and other, which is fundamental to human thought processes, does not exist inside the wall beyond which

God dwells. In a chapter titled "How God Enfoldeth All Things Without Otherness," Nicholas tries another comparison. If the hand of a man is amputated, we say quite properly that it is other than the body; but this is not the case as long as the hand is attached to the arm and forms a part of the whole. Nor is it the case that the hand is other than the head or the foot, inasmuch as different members are included in the "pure, simple, incommunicable" being of a living person. God's being, which is infinite, includes all individuals, whether whole or maimed; it even includes severed hands—otherwise they would cease to exist. By this comparison, says Nicholas, we perceive how it is that "otherness in unity is without otherness" and how "the opposition of opposites is an opposition without opposition."

The door in the wall of coincidence symbolizes the point to which Nicholas has brought us. "I go in, passing from the creatures to Thee . . . ; I go out passing from Thee to the creatures . . . I go in and out simultaneously when I perceive how going out is one with going in." No figure, perhaps, better depicts the daily experience of the contemplative.

The third set of meditations is concerned with what lies inside the wall. From the door Nicholas has comprehended that God is incomprehensible and has found sweetness and nourishment in this truth. However, as he explains to the reader, he is not among those who, like the apostles Paul and John, have been "rapt beyond the wall of coincidence into Paradise" and have seen God face to face; hence, he can only give thanks for the revelation that these have received and accept it on faith as part of the teaching of the Church. Meanwhile, he believes that it is possible by means of comparisons to make somewhat more comprehensible to our minds what has been revealed by the saints, and, in this way, to convey some foretaste of God's "honey-sweet giving."

Nicholas began his book using sight as a figure to raise the mind from the creature to the Creator. Here he uses love in a similar way, and by means of this comparison he hopes to shed light on the teaching that God is one and three. If we are to speak of love at all we require a subject, an object, and a verb (the bond). If one loves oneself one is both lover and beloved as well as love, the bond; in other words, one loves an other than is not an other—a clear image of the Trinity; for, the Father is lover, the Son is beloved, and the Holy Spirit is love. From these considerations, Nicholas invites us to think of the union within the person of Christ between the Son of God and the Son of man; for, although human nature cannot be united to God as lover, "for in this aspect Thou art not its object," it can be united to God as beloved, "since the lovable is the lover's object." Nicholas pays particular attention to the doctrine that Christ is the Word of God, comparing the Father to a craftsman who makes all things according to a pattern, which is the Son, by the motive power of his hands, which is the Spirit. The tenor of these discussions, it must be said, is never speculative but always devotional and Christ-centered.

Christ is the mediator by whom the rational spirit attains to absolute truth. "For the Father is invisible to all, and visible only to Thee, His Son, and after Thee, to him who through Thee and Thy revelation shall be found worthy to behold Him." Christ is not, of course, visible to the wise of this world, who stand outside the wall where opposites are one. But inside the wall none can see the Father but those who are united to Christ. "O good Jesus, Thou art the Tree of life, in the Paradise of delights, and no one may feed upon that desirable life save from Thy fruit."

Historically, Nicholas of Cusa was a transitional figure, as the thoughtful reader of these meditations must perceive. The closed universe of the Middle Ages was being opened up. Cusa maintained that God is infinite and that only as such is he adequate to humanity's desire. Adam and Eve are symbols, but so is Christ. Old humanity has fallen short of God's expectations, but a new humanity rising out of Christ, the archetypal man, is taking its place. Viewed in this perspective Nicholas is an important forerunner of the humanism of the Renaissance.

Jean H. Faurot

RECOMMENDED READING

Edition used: Nicholas of Cusa. *The Vision of God.* Introduction by Evelyn Underhill. Translated with a biographical note by Emma Gurney Salter. New York: Dutton, 1928. Republished, New York: Frederick Ungar, 1960.

Cassirer, Ernst. *The Individual and the Cosmos in Renaissance Philosophy.* Translated by Mario Domandi. New York: Barnes & Noble, 1963. Chapter 1, "Nicholas Cusanus," pp. 7–45, contains a penetrating discussion of Nicholas's contribution to Western thought by a leading philosopher. Includes an extended comment on *The Vision of God.*

Jaspers, Karl. *The Great Philosophers.* Edited by Hannah Arndt. Translated by Ralph Manheim. New York: Harcourt, Brace & World, 1966. See volume 2, pp. 116–272 for a critical account of Nicholas's achievements as a churchman and thinker by a leading existentialist philosopher.

Maurer, Armand A. "Nicholas of Cusa." In *Encyclopedia of Philosophy,* 5:498–500. Edited by Paul Edwards. New York: Macmillan, 1967. A good general introduction.

Nicholas of Cusa. *On Learned Ignorance.* A Translation and Appraisal of *De Docta Ignorantia* by Jasper Hopkins. Minneapolis: Arthur J. Banning Press, 1981. An authoritative work. Situates Cusa firmly in the tradition of Christian Platonism, playing down modern attempts to read more modern ideas into his writings.

ENCHIRIDION MILITIS CHRISTIANI

Author: Desiderius Erasmus (1469–1536)
Sometimes called a prince of Christian humanists, Erasmus was educated among the Brethren of the Common Life, entered the Augustinian priory of Steyn (1486), and studied in Paris at the College of Montaigu. His devotion to the ideals of Christian humanism is evident in his editions of the early church fathers and above all in his monumental edition of the New Testament (1516). Among his other important works are *The Praise of Folly* (1511), the *Colloquies* (1519), and *On Free Will* (1524).

Type and subject of work: Christian ethics that provides a rule for Christian life in the world

First published: 1503

MAJOR THEMES

Life for the Christian is one of perpetual vigilance against ignoble passions and the seductive illusion that truth and happiness are possible in this world.

The best defense is prayer and knowledge: Prayer is at once the desire for things eternal and the love of virtue for Christ's sake alone; knowledge is the gift of spiritual discernment made possible by the study of Holy Scripture and prepared for by the reading of ancient literature.

The Christian, journeying through this worldly maze of error and illusion, needs to guard against trusting in either public opinion or propriety in the outward observance of religious forms.

Just as true religion is an inward, undogmatic piety, the Christian life is a renunciation of worldly wisdom for the wisdom of God.

During his second stay in England (1505–1506), Erasmus set in motion a plan to bring into modern critical editions Christianity's sacred literature. In March of 1516 the first issue of that labor—the Greek New Testament—was published, followed in the fall of that year by a nine-volume critical edition of Jerome. The years that followed indicate the magnitude of Erasmus's scholarship and the scope of his program to restore the religious wisdom of the Greek and Latin fathers. A total of thirty folio volumes of critically edited patristic texts appeared, and Erasmus was working on Origen at the time of his death. Yet three works, all apparent diversions from his scholarly labors, deserve to be remembered and read for what they reveal about the great Christian humanist's program for purifying Christianity of ceremonialism and the linguistic corruptions of its sacred literature, and returning Christ and his teachings to the center of religious life. *The Praise of Folly*, written while Erasmus was a houseguest of Thomas More, and the *Colloquies*, prepared as pedagogical exercises for his students in Paris, give us Erasmus as satirist, acutely sensitive to the incongruities of human behavior, intent on clearing the thicket of ritualism and superstition that obscured the pure, simple, clear, sound teachings of the gospel. The Erasmus of the *Enchiridion*, though very much the same man, is more the image of Hans Holbein's portrait, a gentle scholar and teacher, patient in elucidating his undogmatic ethical piety.

Undertaken at the request of a pious wife whose husband was a rakish soldier with little religion and no liking for priests, the *Enchiridion* seems an unlikely book for setting forth for the first time his theological program. Erasmus himself describes the book as an "offhanded little piece," hastily written lest this husband, probably one John of Trazegnies, come under the influence of those who would try "to steer him into monastic life." If John of Trazegnies in fact read a copy of the *Enchiridion* presented him by the author, he must surely have enjoyed the jest. He might also have liked the choice of title: The Greek word *enchiridion* was a witty double entendre, meaning at once "small handbook or manual" and "dagger or poinard." Though the first English translator called the work the *Manuel of a Christian Knyght*, it might just as well have been titled the "Dagger of the Christian Soldier."

Though a pacifist who pilloried war in *The Complaint of Peace*, Erasmus came naturally by the military metaphor of the *Enchiridion*. That metaphor is found in Paul; Origen used it of the whole Bible. Above all, Erasmus's view of the human condition required it. From the start, we are told that life is fraught with danger on all sides, that assault is imminent from every quarter, that life is perpetual warfare. But, attack comes not from without but within; it is to be expected not from a stranger but from "a foe more intimate, more domesticated." The war for which the Christian is being equipped is in short not one "between man and man, but between man and himself."

Given this state of affairs, knowledge of self and human nature is essential for the soldier who would not ineptly prepare to encounter the enemy. Drawing on the anthropological views of the philosopher Plato and the apostle Paul, Erasmus says that the human being is a creature divided, split between a lower, carnal, fleshly nature and a higher, rational, spiritual one. On the one hand, the body exercises influence on human allegiance, drawing it almost irresistibly toward the pleasure afforded by visible objects. On the other, the spirit struggles to break free of its earthly encumbrance. Yearning for things that are true and eternal. Between these two powerful impulses, the mind or heart is like a factious commonwealth, riddled by rival interest groups that banish even the thought of peace. This dualism is extended also to the discussion of religious meaning and practice. When speaking of a biblical text or a religious or cultic practice, Erasmus thinks in terms of an elemental opposition between external and internal and likes to quote Paul's verse: "The letter kills; it is the spirit that quickens." And so he warns against "sterile literality" in biblical exegesis and the sacerdotal, ritualistic, and dogmatic in religion.

In addition to this dualism, a tripartite division of human nature is presented. This view suggests that human nature consists of spirit, soul, and flesh, and is of special interest because it emphasizes the importance of human freedom for the theological program elaborated in the *Enchiridion*. In this framework, both spirit and flesh are natural motions, which unencumbered tend either toward celestial things or toward brutish ones. And what merit is there, Erasmus asks rhetorically, in doing things prompted by nature (the love of family or a friend) or abhorring their neglect? Christianity requires more. Though with nothing of Kierkegaard's passionate intensity, Erasmus believes nevertheless that Christianity's uniqueness lies in its denial of natural impulses in a sacrificial act of freedom. "But suppose you have arrived at this situation," he writes, "where either you must reject your feeling for father, suppress your love for your children, disregard your friend's goodwill—or offend God? Now what are you going to do?" The flesh pulls one way, the spirit another, and the soul must decide on a course of action. It must choose between the human impulse and the divine.

The Christian soldier, taking measure of the enemy, is also advised to consider the weapons most useful for defense against the enemy's assault. Of particular value in the Christian's armory are prayer and knowledge. Prayer is that almost Platonic desire that lifts the soul heav-

enward; knowledge is the gift of discrimination that presents prayer
ideas worthy of desire. In the wider cause of Christian letters, humanists
like Erasmus believed the new learning of the Renaissance itself instrumental in the study of Holy Scripture, the restoration of theology, and
the revivification of the religious life.

The spirit of the age's liberal Catholic reform is evident in the recommended course of study for the Christian soldier. Sacred Scripture
ought to be the point of departure, but it should not be approached "list-
lessly, hesitantly, as most Christians do." Next, the work of pagan poets
and philosophers should be read, though with moderation and careful
attention to moral content. Finally, the writings of the early church fathers are commended as guides to spiritual meaning. Origen, Ambrose,
Jerome, and Augustine receive special mention as authors skilled (as
Duns Scotus and other "moderns" are not) in penetrating the letter to
the inward, hidden sense of the sacred text. But at this point Erasmus is
reminded that his purpose is to "outline a way of life" and "not a course
of study," and so he turns again to the question of how the Christian
soldier is equipped for any eventuality with a weapon not too cumber-
some, yet serviceable against a sudden assault.

As a handbook for "the art of living happily," the *Enchiridion* offers
its reader a list of rules that, "like the thread of Daedalus," are to be followed in extricating the self from the labyrinthine errors of the world.
These precepts take Erasmus's Christocentric moral philosophy, his philosophy of Christ, as their touchstone. Christ, we are told, is the author
of wisdom, the true light, the only light that dispels the world's darkness. The Christian must keep the eye steadily on him. Apart from
Christ the soul is sensual, is driven by ambition and greed, seeks its own
pleasure, lives for itself. This is the sum of worldly wisdom that does not
know Christ. Neither the visible form of Christian life and worship or
the name of Christ makes the attending of masses, the "mumbling" of
psalms, the veneration of relics, buying of indulgences, or other such
practices genuinely Christlike. All together are barren and profitless
when done in the spirit of the world, that is, with regard to "public
opinion or profit." Unless external rites are restored to Christ, and the
material forms of religion are guided by a desire for things that are "truly lasting, immutable, and true," worship is carnal and even the sacraments have no saving value.

Apart from an inward devotion to Christ, the whole panoply of religious observance is without religious value. Yet allowance is made for
human weakness, spiritual infancy, and for a period of maturation as
"our weakness [is drawn] toward spirituality." In this, Erasmus proved
more patient of progressive spiritual transformation than Luther and
more tolerant of "fleshly ceremonies" than the Zurich reformer, Ulrich
Zwingli. Yet we mistake the fundamental religious character of his pro-

gram for reform if we see it as "ethical" in the ordinary sense of that word. The ethical impulse of the *Enchiridion* is best understood as an ethical piety, whose reference is Christ alone. The decision for or against a particular course of action is measured solely by this criterion. Is something deserving of praise or blame? That depends entirely on the degree to which Christ is intended. If public opinion, self-regard, or personal profit are the reason for celebrating a mass or making a confession or praying to a saint, the deed is barren, even injurious to the soul. It matters not that religious propriety is observed. On the other hand, things done for Christ *alone* bring about a change of heart and a transformed life. The rule, in short, is quite simple. Whatever diverts the heart from Christ is worldly, carnal, and of the Devil; whatever converts the heart to Christ is heavenly and spiritual.

The rules for the Christian soldier are then guides for living well in this world. Like the thread of Daedalus, they trace the way out of this worldly maze of error and illusion. And, between the world's wisdom and God's, there can be no accommodation. The Christian soldier must choose to follow either the spirit or the flesh, Christ or the Devil, divine folly or the wisdom of the world. The choice is quite simple: Should intelligibility in the eyes of the world be sacrificed for Christ's sake? If, for example, prudence dictates the course of action, it is a wise thing to acquire property, work to keep it, look to it for assurance of future happiness. Such behavior is by all calculations judicious and farsighted. Yet the gospel is never generous to those who are anxious about this life. Its counsel, though folly from any perspective but the eternal, is that "we should be foolish in material matters." On this Erasmus is bold to present us with an "either/or": "If you are in the world, you are not in Christ."

The Christian soldier true to Christ must put aside concern for profit or public approval and all that "smacks of the flesh, not the spirit." Erasmus gives the example of a husband's love for his wife. What are the ways a man may love his wife? Of course, he can love in the conventional sense, because the woman is a wife in name, or he can cater to "his own bent," loving in a carnal sense for the sake of sexual pleasure. These are wholly intelligible reasons as the world understands reasons. But, Erasmus says, there is another way. He can love his wife "most deeply because in her [he sees] the likeness of Christ, that is to say, goodness, modesty, sobriety, chastity." Here virtue exists without regard for the self or the world. Prudence or self-regard does not enter consideration. Love's motion is rather a free, spontaneous, natural motion of the spirit, a kind of "pure madness and folly."

Virtue that springs from regard solely for Christ is virtue of "heroic proportion" and beyond the reach of many. Yet persons who fall short of its attainment still benefit from Erasmus's advice. He tells them not to give up the attempt or even slack off their striving to come as near the goal as possible. He urges them in the closing pages of the *Enchiridion* to take their stand in "politic morality." Better prudential ethics than a headlong plummet into baseness. And, though this course means fore-going "ultimate felicity," it carries the soul a step nearer.

The recommendation for these lesser souls is to remember the original dignity of the human creature, the crown of creation in whose mind is found "at once the images and the secret dwelling places of divinity." They also would do well to think of God's love and of the price paid by Jesus Christ for the redemption of humankind. How incongruous that such a creature—the glory of creation and the subject of so great a love—should become "one body and one spirit with God—and one body with a tart." The satiric potential exploited in the *Colloquies* and *The Praise of Folly* is here, but the purpose of the *Enchiridion* is to put a dagger in the hand of the Christian soldier and not a scalpel at the service of its author. Finally, the weaker souls might attend to education and the cultivation of good habits. Beyond this more practical advice Erasmus does not venture, except to say that it is always to be hoped that God will bestow what the spirit desires.

Thomas E. Helm

RECOMMENDED READING

Edition used: *The Enchiridion of Erasmus*. Translated and edited by Raymond Himelick. Bloomington: Indiana University Press, 1963.

Bainton, Roland. *Erasmus of Rotterdam*. New York: Scribner, 1969. This biography emphasizes the importance of the Brethren of the Common Life in Erasmus's religious development and Erasmus's part in the liberal Catholic and Protestant reformations of the sixteenth century.

Harbison, E. Harris. "Erasmus." In *The Christian Scholar in the Age of the Reformation*, pp. 69–102. New York: Scribner, 1956. An excellent essay on the relation between Erasmus's scholarship, his faith, and his program for reform.

Huizinga, Johan. *Erasmus*. New York: Scriber, 1924. Huizinga is skilled at biographical portraiture, and in this classic biography he gives insight into the character of the great Christian humanist.

Spitz, Lewis. "Desiderius Erasmus." *In Reformers in Profile: Advocates of Reform 1300–1600*, pp. 60–83. Edited by B. A. Gerrish. Philadelphia: Fortress Press, 1967. This is an excellent overview of the religious thought and significance of Erasmus the reformer.

THE FREEDOM OF A CHRISTIAN

Author: Martin Luther (1483–1546)
A man of deep piety and immense courage and energy, Luther fueled the Protestant Reformation in Germany during the first half of the sixteenth century through his ardent experiential faith and prolific writings. In 1520 alone, he wrote *An Appeal to the German Nobility* and *The Pagan Servitude of the Church*, as well as *The Freedom of a Christian*.

Type and subject of work: An impassioned account of the nature of Christian faith and life

First published: 1520

MAJOR THEMES

The Christian, justified by grace through faith alone, is completely free of any necessity to establish worthiness before God through ceremonial, legal, and moral works.

The Christian, responding to what God has so freely given in Christ, disciplines the body and serves the neighbor in love, without any expectation of reward or thought of self-justification.

"Who then can comprehend the riches and the glory of the Christian life?" asks Luther, near the end of his treatise on *The Freedom of a Christian*. The Christian can do all things and has all things and is filled with "the love which makes us free, joyful, almighty workers and conquerors over all tribulation, servants of our neighbors, and yet lords of all." But who lives this Christian life in our day? It is neither preached about nor sought after so that Christians do not know why they bear the name of Christ. Surely, he says, it is because God dwells in us so that by faith in God we become Christs to one another and treat our neighbors as Christ has treated us, that "Christ may be the same in all . . . that we may be truly Christian."

These challenging words, written in 1520 during a time of extreme conflict with the papacy, express the heart and soul of Luther's treatise on Christian liberty in which he sets forth, with simplicity and clarity, the essence of Christian faith and life. The book is dedicated as a "token of peace and good hope" to Pope Leo X, whom Luther calls "a lamb in the midst of wolves" and "a Daniel among lions" because of the wickedness present in the Roman Curia surrounding the pope. Luther writes in a bold and straightforward style, confident that though he has written a small book in size, "it contains the whole of Christian life in a brief form, provided you grasp its meaning." Subsequent generations have confirmed it as one of Luther's most important and enduring writings, especially in its clear articulation of the central Reformation concept of justification by faith.

Born in 1483 in Eisleben, Germany, Luther was preparing for a vocation in law when, in the summer of 1505, he was caught in a violent thunderstorm and knocked to the ground by a bolt of lightning. This experience seemed to provide a culmination and partial answer to the religious questions that troubled him, and two weeks later he entered the Augustinian monastery at Erfurt. In 1508 he became professor of theology at the University of Wittenberg; and in 1517, to protest the corrupt sale of indulgences by the church, he nailed ninety-five theses challenging this practice to the door of the Castle Church in Wittenberg. This proved to be the spark that ignited the Protestant Reformation.

But the truly great event in Luther's life was his breakthrough into personal faith and freedom in Christ which came, in the years 1513–1519, through careful study and teaching of the Scriptures. Luther's major problem had been how to stand in holiness before a righteous, demanding God. And, in recovering the biblical meaning of the righteousness of God—as mercy, not judgment—Luther came to the belief that a person stands before God in the light of God's grace alone, not dependent on any good work or infusion of righteousness through the sacraments. The joy and freedom of a Christian was that in faith; one need not look to oneself, a broken sinner, but only to God's mercy and goodness. It was this wonderful liberation and joy that Luther speaks of so passionately to Pope Leo in *The Freedom of a Christian.*

Luther outlines the main argument of his treatise by setting down two propositions concerning the freedom and the bondage of the spirit:

"A Christian is a perfectly free lord of all, subject to none. A Christian is a perfectly dutiful servant of all, subject to all." These seemingly contradictory statements are held together in tension and provide an outline of the two main parts of the treatise that follow: the first part in which Luther shows how the inner spiritual person is justified and set free by faith alone; and the second part in which he shows that the outward carnal person, saved by faith, necessarily engages in good works and serves the neighbor in Christian love.

The inner person has nothing to gain from outward external acts such as fasting, going on pilgrimages, or performing "sacred" duties. "Such works produce nothing but hypocrites." Neither will secular dress or activities necessarily harm the spiritual person. Only one thing is absolutely necessary for Christian life, righteousness, and freedom. That one thing is the Word of God, the gospel of Christ. Jesus says, "'Man shall not live by bread alone, but by every word that proceeds from the mouth of God.'" The soul can do without anything except the Word of God, writes Luther. If it has the Word of God it is rich and lacks nothing because it has life, truth, light, peace, salvation, joy, wisdom, power, and every incalculable blessing of God. And what is this Word of God? The gospel concerning Jesus, who was made flesh, crucified, raised from the dead, and glorified through the Spirit. This gospel, preached, feeds the soul and makes it righteous, sets it free, and saves it by faith. And this Word of God cannot be received by any works of the flesh, but only by faith.

The Scripture is divided into two parts: commandments (law) and promises (gospel). The commandments teach what ought to be done, but they do not give the power to do it. The law thus convicts a person of wrongdoing and sin and leads to despair. But the promises of God set the person free, for what cannot be accomplished by works of the law is easily and quickly accomplished through faith. "The promises of God give what the commandments of God demand ... so that all things may be God's alone, both the commandments and the fulfilling of the commandments." It is then through faith alone without works that the soul is justified by the Word of God, made a free child of God, and filled with every blessing.

Faith derives such great power from God for three reasons: First, it lives and rules in the soul. A person is free from all external works or law when the soul, like iron exposed to fire, glows as the Word of God imparts its life-giving qualities.

Second, faith alone truly honors God. When trust is given, the soul consents to be obedient to God's will and allows itself to be treated according to God's good pleasure. Clinging to God's promises, "it does not doubt that he who is true, just, and wise will do, dispose, and provide all things well." And, to the contrary, what greater rebellion and contempt can there be against God than not believing his promises? For this makes God a liar and doubts that he is truthful, ascribing truthfulness to one's self but lying and vanity to God. It is to make an idol of one's self!

Third, faith "unites the soul with Christ as a bride is united with her bridegroom." As in a marriage covenant, everything is held in common, the good and the evil, so that the soul can take glory in the goodness of Christ as though it were its own, and Christ takes the sin, death, and evil of the soul upon himself.

Through faith, Christians also become like kings and priests to God, in the manner of Christ. As kings, Christians are exalted above all things in spiritual power and rule in the midst of enemies or oppression, because God works in all things for good to those who believe. As priests, Christians are worthy to come before God in intercession for others and to teach one another divine things. The priesthood is not for a select group of "ecclesiastics," but is for all believers, though not all are called to teach or preach publicly.

Those who are called to preach must do so boldly, proclaiming Christ in such a way that faith is established in the heart of the believer, so that Christ becomes "Christ for you and me." When Christian liberty is rightly preached, showing the ways in which Christians are all kings and priests and therefore lords of all, then nothing has power to harm or frighten. "'Thanks be to God who gives us the victory through our Lord Jesus Christ.'"

Luther, having dealt with the inner spiritual person, now turns to a discussion of the outward carnal human being and the proper place of good works in the Christian life. "If faith does all things," he asks, "why then are good works commanded?" Because a Christian, though by faith a free lord of all and subject to none, is also a servant of all and subject to all. Good works, though not determinative of one's relation to God, follow from faith as day follows night, as good fruit comes from a good tree. Good works serve especially to discipline the body and meet the neighbor's needs.

The body needs to be disciplined by good works because Christians still live in the world with its temptations and bodily enticements that hinder the spiritual person. Right actions reduce the body to subjection and purify it of its evil lusts so that all things may join with it in loving and praising God. The discipline of good works can be effective in conforming the outer bodily person to the inner spiritual person, as the Christian does such works out of spontaneous love in obedience to God.

Good works can also be effective in behalf of the neighbor. The Christian lives not for self, but for others, in the freest servitude. It is toward this end that the body is brought into subjection, that one may more sincerely and freely serve others. The Christian is to consider nothing except the need and the advantage of the neighbor, so that faith takes action through love, finding expression in cheerful and loving service done without expectation of reward. Just as the heavenly Father has in Christ freely come to our aid, says Luther, so "each one should become as it were a Christ to the other that we may be Christs to one another and Christ may be the same in all, that is, that we may be truly Christians."

Luther concludes that a Christian is not caught up in the self, but in Christ and the neighbor. The Christian lives in Christ through faith, in the neighbor through love. Faith catches one up beyond the self to God. Love moves beneath the self into the neighbor. Yet the Christian always remains in God's love. And the Christian's freedom will never be used as license to disregard works, ceremonies, or ritual, but will despise only that which expresses a lack of faith in God and a trust in one's own works.

Throughout *The Freedom of a Christian*, Luther's concern is to put the gospel into clear perspective. In faith a person stands before God in the light of grace. There is no other possibility. From the Christian who has understood this, good works flow forth as naturally as good fruit comes from a good tree. This is inevitable. Only where faith *and* works are present is the cost and joy of belonging to God understood and experienced. "Who then can comprehend the riches and glory of the Christian life? It can do all things and has all things and lack nothing." To read Luther's passionate vision of the Christian's faith and life is to see more clearly and understand more fully the depth and reality of Christian love and freedom.

Douglas H. Gregg

RECOMMENDED READING

Edition used: Dillenberger, John. *Martin Luther: Selections from His Writings.* Garden City, N.Y.: Doubleday, Anchor Books, 1961. Contains Luther's three Reformation treatises of 1520 along with carefully selected works that show the historical and theological development of Luther's thought.

Bainton, Roland H. *Here I Stand: A Life of Martin Luther.* New York: Abingdon Press, 1950. Popular history, superbly done, without sacrificing scholarship or precision.

Forell, George W. *Faith Active in Love.* Minneapolis: Augsburg, 1954. A thorough and balanced exploration of the principles underlying Luther's social ethics.

Rupp, Ernest Gordon. *Luther's Progress to the Diet of Worms, 1521.* New York: Harper & Row, Harper Torchbooks, 1951. A vivid account of Luther's development in the critical years leading to his break from the Catholic church.

Spitz, Lewis W. *The Protestant Reformation, 1517–1559.* New York: Harper & Row, 1985. An outstanding, well-written assessment of the Protestant Reformation and Luther's crucial role in its development.

THE THIRD SPIRITUAL ALPHABET

Author: Francisco de Osuna (1492–1541?)
Little is known of the author of a work that was to influence one of Spain's most famous mystics, Saint Teresa of Ávila, and through her, countless others. Osuna was ordained about 1519–1520 and three years later entered a Franciscan monastery where, as a guide for meditation, he formulated maxims and arranged them in alphabetical order. He composed three such alphabets, each with twenty-three distichs to correspond with the twenty-two letters and tilde of the Spanish alphabet, and later glossed them as treatises on the passion (1528), prayer and ascetic practices (1530), and recollection (1527). A total of six Alphabets appeared, though not all follow the alphabetical format: *Ley de amor* (Law of love), 1530), fifty-one rules of love; *Norte de los estados* (The North Star of ranks, 1531), advice to people in all social ranks on Christian ideals; and *Gracioso convite* (Gracious banquet, 1530), on the Eucharist. Osuna's life was devoted to preaching and writing in both Spanish and Latin during a time of religious renewal and ferment in Spain. His work in the Franciscan order took him to France, Belgium, and Italy.

Type and subject of work: Theological explanation of experiential description of mystical prayer under the rubric of "recollection"

First published: 1527

Major Themes

Recollection is a general term for prayer, including vocal prayer accompanied by thinking, mental prayer, and passive prayer.

Recollection is also the process of prayer wherein the soul becomes increasingly passive with respect to God.

Eventually recollection is an ongoing alertness to God intensified by moments of acute awareness of God when the soul is infused with wisdom beyond rational understanding.

The way of recollection is primarily affective, but recollection is not quietism.

Recollection is open to everyone, including women and married people.

Francisco de Osuna wrote during a fertile yet dangerous time in Spain. Mysticism was in the air in the sixteenth century, fostered by translations in Spanish of the writings of early and later mystics such as Dionysius the Areopagite, Meister Eckhart, Bernard of Clairvaux, and John Gerson; translations of the New Testament; the ideas of Erasmus and interiorized Christianity; and the practice and teaching of mental prayer in and out of monasteries. In the forefront of the push for a Christianity purified of extraneous external practices were laywomen who, with laymen and religious, especially Franciscan priests, inspired small gatherings for the purpose of prayer. Among the charismatic women leaders were Francisca Hernández and Isabel de la Cruz, both of whom were brought before the Inquisition on charges that included teaching quietist doctrines.

The practice that was sure to rouse the suspicion of the Inquisition was mental prayer which, defined briefly, is to think about the meaning of words that are said, whether aloud or silently. On the basis of this definition mental prayer sounds innocent, but when some advocates professed their utter inability to do anything whatsoever in prayer except abandon themselves to divine grace, the ranks of the prayerful split and the stage was set for the Inquisition to attack. On one side were the advocates of *dejamiento* (abandonment) who went so far in the abandon to God's grace that they denied the efficacy of virtuous deeds, vocal prayer, external devotion, penitence, and even the Eucharist, claiming, in the last instance, that the Eucharist was more effectively present in the heart than in a bit of bread. Opposing them were the defenders of *recogimiento*, or recollection, who accepted the sacramental and devotional life of the Church while nourishing an inner prayer that at least in the beginning stages required mental effort.

Osuna clearly was in the camp of the second group; his *Third Spiritual Alphabet* is not only a personal statement of belief in the prayer of recollection but also its most eloquent description and bold defense. To ap-

preciate the vigor of the treatise and its author's courage, we need to remember that only two years before its publication, the Inquisition had
made its first public statement against the *alumbrados* (enlightened
ones), condemning their practice of *dejamiento*.

The twenty-three treatises of *The Third Spiritual Alphabet* trace the
journey inward in terms of recollection. The initial five treatises are a
preparation for the journey, which is to be made primarily through the
heart. Osuna first clarifies that the goal of union with God is proper to
all Christians; he then counsels as appropriate to understanding our relationship with God the response of gratitude for the general work of
creation, particular blessings we receive, and favors bestowed by God
that we do not discern. Our general response is to be affective with the
understanding become blind, the will deaf to all but love for God, and
the memory dumb. The fifth treatise is an exhortation to a careful examination of conscience—counsel the pilgrim is to heed not only at this
point of beginning recollection but all along the journey.

The sixth treatise is among the most important of the Alphabet.
Osuna emphasizes first that, although each must find an individual path
to God, all should practice recollection in imitation of our Lord Jesus
Christ who went into the desert to pray alone. He states that recollection
is the term for mystical theology or wisdom infused into the soul and
offers several other names for it: the art of love, union, profundity, con-
cealment, abstinence, drawing near, enkindling, welcome, consent, the
marrow and fat of sacrifice, attraction, adoption, arrival, height, spiritual
ascension, and the third heaven. In general, recollection gathers together the senses, sensuality and reason, bodily members and virtues, the
soul's three powers with its highest faculty, and God and the soul.

Treatises seven through twelve develop recollection as the art of
emptying the heart from within. Osuna recommends first purgation of
thought (seven), actions and speech (nine), memory and will (eleven),
and understanding (twelve). In the order of purgations, Osuna's meth-
odology is similar to that of Saint John of the Cross, reflective perhaps of
the Scholastic training they had in common.

Osuna also details reasons for learning and teaching recollection; offers practical advice on the choice of a spiritual director (eight); and advises how to respond when the intensity of love erupts in outcries and
gestures (nine). His discussion of sighing, groaning, and bodily movements during prayer suggests that these phenomena may be a mark of
progress in prayer; his commonsensical advice, however, is to control
the outbursts unless in doing so interior devotion wanes. Anticipating
the teaching of later Carmelite mystics, Osuna refused to measure spirituality by extraordinary phenomena that affect the senses and emotions.

The tenth treatise is a beautiful exposition of the favors God bestows
along the journey, including the gifts of tears, teaching, and healing. In
distinguishing the tears of beginners, proficients, and perfects, Osuna

once again honors the tripartite division of the mystical way and the movement from active to passive consciousness.

The inward journey intensifies in subtlety as in the eleventh and twelfth treatises Osuna describes the purgation of the higher faculties of memory, will, and understanding. Memories of worldly pleasures are to be erased, leaving only images of the Sacred Humanity and of God on a general, universal level. Purgation of the will is accomplished both actively, as the soul strives to desire only God, and passively, when the heart inexplicably is moved to desire God. The twelfth treatise in its entirety is a culminating point in *The Third Spiritual Alphabet* as the soul is taught to rely not on natural knowledge or even understandings that come in a supernatural way—as when one hears voices from the outside—but on knowledge received in the darkness of unknowing.

Having described the process whereby the senses and higher faculties are recollected, Osuna explains in following treatises experiences that come to the soul well along the mystical way. His topics include vocal prayer, prayer of the heart, and mental or spiritual prayer (thirteen); the need for gentle discipline in the practice of prayer and the purgation of passions, especially joy and sadness (fourteen); and general and special recollection (fifteen). His descriptions of prayer are perceptive, as when he distinguishes between general recollection as a state of alertness to God and special recollection as moments of retiring into the heart (he recommends at least two hours each day of special recollection). In regarding recollection as a process of prayer, Osuna differs from Teresa, for whom recollection was one kind of prayer.

Treatise sixteen on love is a second culminating point in the Alphabet. Osuna's advice is that we learn to draw love from everything in creation and refer it to God.

The remaining treatises are unified by a pattern of alternating themes; Osuna treats now prayer, now problems and obstacles: love and infused prayer (sixteen); suffering and imitating Jesus Christ in hardship as well as glory (seventeen); spiritual prayer (eighteen); humility and temptations (nineteen and twenty); the heights of prayer wherein the soul understands in darkness (twenty-one); zeal and perseverance (twenty-two and twenty-three).

Just as treatises twelve and sixteen are climactic points, so also is treatise twenty-one. Culminating all the preceding material in the treatise, Osuna expounds the role of understanding in the *vía negativa* of recollection, elaborating the doctrine of the negative way and clarifying misunderstandings about the practice of *no pensar nada*. Osuna supports the belief of affective mystics that it is the will rather than the understanding that enables wisdom to be received into the soul. In the third degree of silence the soul is transformed in God, its understanding quieted so that it understands nothing happening about it. In the highest part of the soul, God's image is imprinted and there are received divine understandings which the understanding cannot understand. Although the understanding is asleep and the will at rest in this union of soul with God, the perfection is not the no pensar nada condition of the quietists. Osuna maintains that not only must one learn to quiet oneself by mental discipline during the purgative and illuminative stages of the journey, but even the most advanced souls must always exercise their understanding. Recollection is a process that requires unceasing vigilance.

Francisco de Osuna's *Third Spiritual Alphabet* is important in its own right as a detailed description of the interior journey as well as a source of inspiration for both Saint Teresa of Ávila and Saint John of the Cross. The fusing of the affective and intellectual that is a hallmark of later Carmelite spirituality informs the *Alphabet*. The structure of the *Alphabet* is not as rigorous as that of Saint John's treatises, but the ascent away from the known to the unknown that Osuna traces through increasingly subtle forms of recollection is similar to Saint John's. If Saint Teresa is a favorite with spiritual pilgrims today, it is in large part because her appealing style is enlivened by images she met in Osuna's work. A traveler on the mystical way and spiritual director for many others, Francisco de Osuna, like Saint Teresa and Saint John, drew on rich experiential resources to create a treasure house of practical advice, wisdom, and love of God.

Mary E. Giles

RECOMMENDED READING

Edition used: Osuna, Francisco de. *The Third Spiritual Alphabet.* Translation and introduction by Mary E. Giles. New York: Paulist Press, 1981.

Calvert, Laura. *Francisco de Osuna and the Spirit of the Letter.* Chapel Hill: North Carolina Studies in the Romance Languages and Literatures, 1973. A careful and illuminating study.

A DIALOGUE OF COMFORT AGAINST TRIBULATION

Author: Saint Thomas More (1478–1535)

The son of a prosperous London lawyer, Thomas More studied briefly at Oxford University before studying law at Lincoln's Inn. Although he had seriously considered joining a religious order, he decided upon a career in the world, becoming a member of Parliament for London and later a counselor to Henry VIII. More was active in the humanistic revival, in the spirit of which he wrote *Utopia* (1516). But the spread of religious liberalism taught him caution; and the bulk of his later writings are in defense of the Catholic church against the reformers. During Henry VIII's divorce proceedings, More held the office of Lord Chancellor, but was ineffectual. His refusal to recognize Henry as the head of the English church led to his imprisonment for fourteen months in the Tower awaiting execution on the charge of treason. The *Dialogue of Comfort* was written during this time. More was knighted in 1521 and was canonized in 1935.

Type and subject of work: Dialogue on the uses of adversity

First transcribed: 1534–1535

MAJOR THEMES

Tribulation is a gracious gift of God to those who believe his promises, because it draws them near to him, and because it diminishes the pains of purgatory.

Many temptations arise from fleshly appetites, from pride, and from covetousness, and catch people unawares.

The special danger connected with persecution is that the threat of persecution forces one to make a deliberate choice whether to hold onto worldly things and so lose hope of heaven.

Thomas More's *A Dialogue of Comforts Against Tribulation* is a big book, only a fraction of which is directly devoted to tribulation and its comfort. The leisurely pace of the dialogue, its cheerful tone, and its amusing tales suggest that More was less concerned with winning an argument than in spending his last days in an agreeable and useful manner. This was no small achievement. More's great fear was that he might not conduct himself well in the hands of his persecutors. In the activity of writing this calm discourse he was acting the part of a superior man, like Socrates in Plato's dialogue *Phaedo.* Undoubtedly More's motivation included other elements, such as justifying his self-sacrifice to his uncomprehending family and friends, and leaving a monument to succeeding generations. Even so, the arguments set forth in the book are less impressive than the writing of it.

More chose Catholic Hungary, overrun at the time by Turks, as the setting for the dialogue. A young man, Vincent, visits an older and ailing uncle, Antony, seeking words of wisdom. He gets them, along with a stream of anecdote. The old man apologizes for dominating the conversation, but carries on for hours, wearying the reader more than himself. There are three books, representing three visits by Vincent to his uncle. Book one expounds the Christian view that tribulation is meritorious. Book two takes up temptation as a special form of tribulation. Book three is concerned with the temptation for Hungarian Christians to embrace Islam in the face of persecution, and, by analogy, for English Christians to give up their connection with Rome as Henry VIII was demanding of them.

In part one, Antony explains and defends what he holds to be the teaching of the Bible and of the doctors of the Church; namely, that tribulation is "a gracious gift of God." Tribulation, he understands in a broad sense that includes "every such thing as troubleth and grieveth the man, either in body or mind." Comfort, he takes not to be some present pleasure but "the consolation of good hope ... of some good growing toward him." There is, he says, no real comfort to be found in natural reason because it is ignorant of our final end. Only those find comfort who suffer and die in the faith that God rewards their patience.

Anthony uses the term *medicinable* (possessed of healing properties) to assess the value of tribulations. Directly medicinable are sufferings brought on by a person's sin, such as ill consequences to one's health resulting from intemperance, or being jailed for committing a crime.

When the guilty repent and accept their punishment, the suffering that they have to endure on earth is subtracted from what they must otherwise endure in purgatory. In another sense, suffering that is not clearly the result of past sins may be medicinable in preventing future sins, as when loss of health or wealth or beauty protects a person against temptations that he or she might not have strength to resist. A third kind of suffering, quite unrelated to sin, Antony calls "more than medicinable," because it provides those who bear it patiently with an opportunity to earn great merit. For example, says Antony, if I were consoling a man who was known for his great virtue and who was threatened with torture at the hands of the Turk, it would be only right to tell him that if he held fast to his faith he would upon his death pass immediately to glory. Even if he were not virtuous but refused to give up his faith, his suffering and death would, through the merit of Christ's passion, earn for him a martyr's crown. No part of his suffering need be counted against purgatory, but the whole will be accepted as an offering to Christ and will increase his final reward in heaven.

When Antony goes on to say that it augurs ill for a person's final state if he enjoys continued prosperity on earth, Vincent objects. How is it that we pray in church for health and prosperity for our rulers; and how is it that great and good men, such as Abraham, enjoyed their wealth undiminished throughout their lives? In reply, Antony points out that mental pains are as distressing as bodily pains and that no one can tell what tribulations others may be going through. An outwardly prosperous man such as King David may secretly live "in a contrite heart and a life penitential." (We know that More, although prosperous, scourged himself and wore a hair shirt.) In sum, tribulation is "the far better thing in this world toward getting of the very good that God giveth in the world to come," because of the merit attached to patient acceptance of God's will.

In part two the ruling metaphor changes. More is no longer thinking of the scales of divine justice in which suffering is weighed against glory, but of the Devil and his stratagems for gaining possession of each person's soul. Here tribulation is taken in the sense of trial rather than in the sense of suffering; and the trials are distinguished according to whether the Devil uses deception (temptations) or fights in the open (persecutions).

More's text for this long sermon—for that is what it comes to—is Psalm 90 as it stands in the Latin Bible. (In the Hebrew Bible, used by Protestant translators, it is numbered Psalm 91.) More translates: "The truth of God shall compass thee about with a pavis: thou shalt not be afeard of the night's fear, nor of the arrow flying in the day, nor of the business (*negotium*) walking about in the darknesses, nor of the incursion or invasion of the devil in the midday." A pavis was a full-length shield used in the Middle Ages. The truth of God's promise is not, says Antony, "a little round buckler that scant can cover the head," but "a long large pavis that covereth all along the body." The remainder of the text points to four kinds of temptation from which God promises to defend those who seek protection from him. The first three kinds are dealt with in book two, and the fourth in book three.

The first kind of temptation, "the fear of the night," concerns morbid obsessions such as may attack a man in solitary confinement, especially during sleepless nights such as More himself experienced after his fall from the king's favor. More gives fifty pages to these nocturnal fears, extending them to include various mental aberrations such as pusillanimity, scrupulosity, and suicidal mania. The best comfort he has to offer is to point out that since the fears are irrational, they had best be met by appeal to reason. Since the devils have no power to directly harm people, they excite their imaginations, which has the same effect as when people call up to a man who is walking on a high bridge telling him that he will surely fall.

The second kind of temptation is that which comes to persons when they are suddenly raised to wealth and power. Like an arrow shot by a boy into the air, they rise to heady heights and are subjected to temptations of pride and ambition for which they are not prepared. Antony saw this happening among favorites of a prince (the party that rose to power when Anne Boleyn was made queen) and not least of all among members of the clergy (Thomas Cromwell and Thomas Cranmer). His advice was, Stand in fear, but temper your fear with hope that, since God raised you to this place, he will assist you to use it well. (There is also the clear reminder that what goes up must come down.)

The third kind of temptation has to do with the ordinary person's round of life. There are, besides night and day, dusk and dawn; and in these twilights "the devil that is called business" is busy walking about. "He setteth some to seek the pleasures of the flesh ... and some he setteth about incessant seeking for these worldly goods." More has in mind here the traditional distinction between the active and the contemplative lives, and the perils that attend the former. "For is not the going about the serving of the flesh a business that hath none end, but evermore from the end cometh to the beginning again? Go they never so full to bed, yet evermore on the morrow as new be they to be fed again as they were the day before." The active life, Antony says, is a busy maze, with hell at the center. Nevertheless, it is indispensable to this world. In spite of Jesus' words, "He that forsake not all that ever he hath cannot be my disciple," it is plain that we can no more do without men of business than we can without craftsmen and farmers; and Antony ventures that a propertied man who keeps a good household and remembers his duty to the poor may "in merit match another man's forsaking of all." The latter is meritorious, says Antony, only if the forsaking be undertaken with the end of devoting one's life to contemplation. When Jesus excused Mary from helping in the kitchen he did it because she had chosen this better part.

This is the end of book two. Dinner is served and Antony takes a nap while Vincent goes out on an errand. When Vincent returns he brings a fresh rumor from Constantinople that the Turks are embarking on a new invasion. Antony, an old trooper, is not much impressed, though he acknowledges that a showdown is inevitable. Meanwhile, the report serves to animate the discussion and to give substance to the otherwise somewhat tenuous notion of "the assault of the noonday devil." A noonday temptation is one that is open and aboveboard. Whereas the danger of the previously mentioned temptations is that they take a person unawares, the danger of the fourth lies in the fact that one is painfully aware of it; for, the trial presented by the Turkish conquest lay not so much in the ruthlessness of the conquerors as in their custom of giving Christians a chance to abandon their faith and become Moslems. They had a choice, just as Thomas More had a choice. Would they hold fast to life, liberty, and possessions at the cost of spending eternity in hell, or would they give up all of these in the faith that, suffering with Christ, they would also reign with him?

Antony urges the importance of thinking through the options well in advance of the time of decision, and sets himself the project of taking up one by one the various "griefs and pains" with which Christians are threatened and rehearsing such comforts and consolations as come to his mind. The main part of this discussion, conducted with surprising levity, is the revaluation of values that we might expect from a person awaiting execution for treason who is constantly being reminded that he does not have to go through with it. More's strategy is to take the reader backstage and so disabuse him of the effects gained by means of scenery and costume and memorized speeches. What is fame, Antony asks, "but a blast of another man's mouth, as soon passed as spoken, whereupon he that setteth his delight, feedeth himself but with wind"? There follows a long and humorous section on flattery, including a story about Cardinal Wolsey who, it seems, once had his doubts about what his courtiers were saying, and asked More to tell him the truth, which More did, only to hear himself called a fool. From showing the vanity of a good estate in the world, Antony goes on to consider imprisonment, slavery, and a shameful death. Not forgetting the pavis—God's promise not to allow his faithful to be tempted above what they are able to withstand—Antony argues at length that there is no real difference between being a slave and being free or between being in prison and being at large. The world, he says, is a prison; God is the jailer; kings no less than beggars are in keep; and everyone is under sentence of death and liable to tortures along the way.

The argument takes a somewhat different turn when Vincent doubts his ability to stand up to physical torture. Antony admits that there is no way in which reason can lessen the pain; but he points out that many people do in fact endure great torment for things they hold especially dear. So it can be with the Turk's tortures. The only question is whether heaven is worth it, keeping in mind also the greater suffering that awaits those who are turned away from heaven.

The book concludes with a meditation on Christ's passion.

Jean H. Faurot

Recommended Reading

Edition used: More, Thomas, Saint. *A Dialogue of Comfort Against Tribulation*. Edited with an Introduction and Notes by Frank Manley. New Haven: Yale University Press, 1977. A popular version of volume 12 of the new Yale edition of *The Complete Works of St. Thomas More*. Manley's introduction is helpful.

Marius, Richard. *Thomas More: A Biography*. New York: Knopf, 1984. Written by a member of the staff of the Saint Thomas More Project at Yale, but intended for the general reader. The omission of the word saint in the title seems intentional. Contemporary scholarship has not rallied to the view that Sir Thomas was a man of all seasons.

More, Thomas, Saint. *The Tower Works: Devotional Writings*. Edited by Garry E. Haupt. New Haven: Yale University Press, 1980. A companion volume to *A Dialogue of Comfort*, containing shorter writings composed during More's imprisonment: *A Treatise Upon the Passion; The Sadness of Christ;* and *Instructions and Prayers*.

THE SPIRITUAL EXERCISES OF ST. IGNATIUS LOYOLA

Author: Saint Ignatius Loyola (1491–1556)

Ignatius Loyola was a Spanish mystic who founded the Society of Jesus, the Jesuits, one of the most significant religious orders in the history of the Church. Born of a noble family in the Basque region of northern Spain, Loyola embarked on a military career, intending to spend his life as a soldier. At the battle of Pamplona in 1521, he received a severe leg wound that left him disabled. During a painful period of recovery, Loyola spent long periods in prayer and study of the lives of the saints. Through numerous mystical experiences he concluded that God was calling him to be a soldier for Christ. *The Spiritual Exercises* are the result of his profound spiritual experiences and his concern to impart the disciplined life of the Spirit to others. He spent several years in study and contemplation, with an extended period (1528–1535) in Paris. There in 1534, Loyola and six of his friends constituted the Society of Jesus with a concern to extend apostolic witness wherever they went.

Type and subject of work: Manual of spiritual discipline that serves as the foundation of Jesuit religious life

First published: 1548

MAJOR THEMES

The spiritual life is a life of rigorous discipline.
The Christian disciple must reflect continuously upon the life, death, and resurrection of Christ.

Continued self-examinations are necessary for spiritual growth.
The imitation of Christ is the essence of Christian discipleship.
Meditation on the incarnation prepares the soul for spiritual experience.
The experience of divine love is the ultimate goal of Christian spirituality.
Prayer is the means to greater intimacy with God.
All devotion is a means to conformity to the image of Christ.

In 1540 Pope Paul III approved the Jesuits as an official order of the Roman Catholic church, with Loyola as its first "general." *The Spiritual Exercises*, written as early as the 1520s, but revised throughout his life, served as a guide to the spiritual life of the Jesuit order. It has become a textbook for spiritual renewal and discipline used by persons throughout the Church.

The materials that make up *The Spiritual Exercises* were written over a period of several years and grew out of the religious devotion and idealism of Loyola himself. They represent a handbook of Christian spirituality intended to move the faithful to ever-increasing maturity through moral reflection, meditation, and discipline. Just as the worldly soldier prepares for warfare through an unending series of drills and exercises, the Christian soldier must prepare for the battle against evil. *The Exercises* are, therefore, a training manual for life in the Spirit. By following this organized spiritual method, the Christian grows and matures in the faith and knowledge of the Lord.

The book is divided into four basic sections, each to be practiced for one week. The actual time spent on each exercise may vary from a month to a few days. There is freedom to extend or restrict the time available for the observance.

The Exercises begins with a brief introductory session that provides "directions" for understanding the nature of the material and preparing the heart of the pilgrim for spiritual reflection. These introductory directions are aimed at purifying the person of sin and worldly distractions. Each exercise seeks to lead the believer to continuous reflection on the life, death, and resurrection of Jesus Christ to the end that Christ's love may be experienced anew.

The instructions also suggest that the spiritual exercises are best observed under the guidance of a retreat master or spiritual mentor. In fact, younger Christians require such direction for the proper use of the exercises. Special instructions to the "master of the Exercises" are provided throughout the book.

The first week is a time of spiritual purgation and preparation. In this section Loyola defines the purpose of the *Exercises* as intended to help the seeker "to conquer himself and to regulate his life so that he will not be influenced in his decisions by any inordinate attachment."

The pilgrim thus learns to practice Christian discipline in such a way as to reject everything that might distract from Christ.

Spiritual renewal, therefore, begins with self-examination. The chief end of human beings is to "praise, reverence and serve God." Any activity that helped achieve that goal was acceptable for the Christian. Any activity that inhibited the goal was unacceptable.

The "exercitants" (those who practice the *Exercises*) are called upon to examine their lives with utmost honesty and intensity. No sin, mortal or venial, is to be overlooked. One is "to ask the grace to know my sins and to free myself from them."

The first *Exercise* also establishes some basic spiritual steps that are repeated in all other sections of the book. These include the "preparatory prayer" and the first and second "prelude." The preparatory prayer is an invocation of divine grace upon the individual that all "intentions, actions and works" may be completely devoted to the service and praise of God. The first prelude calls the participant to focus mental attention upon a particular place (location) in which the object or event of contemplation occurs. The mind thus moves back in time to significant moments in the life of the Virgin or Christ. The exercitant may be asked to create a mental image of Mary receiving the annunciation, or of Christ in the carpenter shop, on the cross, or by the seashore.

The second prelude involves supplication, asking God for what one wants, needs, or desires. Such desires are not whimsical or self-centered but are prompted by the specific subject matter of the exercise. When reflecting on the resurrection one asks for joy. When meditating on the crucifixion one seeks sorrow and tears.

Participants are required to devote a portion of every day to the examining of the conscience—morning, noon, and evening. Explicit instructions are given regarding the process of confession and repentance in the continuing life of the Christian.

The use of the imagination is a major factor in the spiritual discipline of the exercises. Exercitants are required to use their imagination throughout. In the meditation on hell, for example, the reader is urged to feel the heat, smell the brimstone, and hear the screams of the damned. On another occasion, one is to imagine being bound in chains, and standing before God in judgment. Through the intensity of visualization, the believer moves to spiritual sensations. The spiritual life involves the discipline of the mind.

The second week of the exercises involves meditation on the kingdom of Christ. During this week the *imitatio Christi*, the imitation of Christ, is urged upon the participant. Through reflection on Christ, his birth and activity in the world, the Christian learns to imitate his life. Meditation on the incarnation and the nativity provide spiritual insight into the nature of Christ, his humanity and divinity. In fact, Loyola suggests that the pilgrim read passages from *The Imitation of Christ* by Thomas à Kempis or from the classic *Lives of the Saints* during this week of meditation.

In considering the incarnation, participants meditate on the many peoples of the world, their sins and sorrows, and the desire of God to save them. In preparing for the incarnation, the individual considers "what I should say to the Three Divine Persons, or the eternal Word Incarnate, or to His Mother and our Lady." Those who wish to explore the nature of Christ's divinity are asked to imagine "the infinite fragrance and sweetness of Divinity" in order to secure "spiritual profit."

The intensity of the meditation is evident in the "observation" that the exercise on the incarnation be observed at midnight, daybreak, at mass, at vespers, and before supper, each time for at least one hour. Instructions acknowledge that the pilgrims will experience exhaustion, physical and spiritual, after the first full week of activities. Thus some exceptions might be made: The midnight observance may be omitted.

This week of exercises also focuses on the virtues of the kingdom life. Meditations concentrate on "the two standards" for human behavior, Christ and Satan. One reflects on the evils of the demonic as contrasted with the beauty of Christ. On the same day the exercitant concentrates on "the three classes of men" and the question of attachment to the things of this world. The end of such meditations is that persons shall learn how to act as God inspires them. Those who know Christ have "broken all the attachments," desiring only those things that God permits.

After reflection on specific occurrences in the life of Jesus, the exercises turn to the "three modes of humility." Each marks a steady progression to a higher degree of humility and self-denial.

During the second week Loyola gives serious attention to the role of free will and "choice" in spiritual life. How does one make choices to marry or remain celibate, or to discern the will of God in all things? Proper choices may be good or indifferent and may be accomplished only as God acts on the human will "to reveal to my spirit what I should do to best promote His praise and glory in the matter of choice." Such decisions are best made when one has cultivated enough other spiritual disciplines to experience "a time of tranquility" when the soul acts "freely and calmly" in using its divine resources.

The third week of exercises is directed toward meditation on the sufferings of Christ. Exercitants reflect on the events that led up to Christ's death—the Last Supper, the Garden, his arrest and trials, his crucifixion and burial. Using the imagination, the pilgrim returns to the places and events of Christ's passion, the road from Bethany to Jerusalem, the upper room, the house of Pilate, the hill of Golgotha, the sepulcher of his burial.

Rules for the use of food and drink and the practice of fasting are included in this section. Food is never to be a distraction from the life of the Spirit. Even while eating, the Christian should focus concentration on the spiritual realm, contemplating Christ's presence at meals, the lives of the saints, and the need for temperance in all things.

The fourth and final week requires contemplation of the resurrection of Christ and the experience of divine love, the ultimate goal of all Christian spirituality. Through these exercises the believer discovers the wholeness of faith and unity with God. Contemplation becomes a means of attaining divine love expressed in "deeds rather than words."

A portion of this chapter is devoted to the three methods of prayer, each leading to greater intimacy with God. The first method involves moral contemplation, using the Ten Commandments, the seven capital (deadly) sins, and the five senses as guides for purification of the self. The second method of prayer involves careful contemplation of each word of such selected prayers as the "Our Father" (Lord's Prayer), the "Hail Mary," and the Creed (Apostles'). Instructions include the position of prayer, kneeling or sitting, with eyes closed or focused on one spot, and the considerations for each word of the prayer. The third method involves a "rhythmical recitation," a process of breathing out the same selected prayers in "rhythmical measure." The major portion of this final exercise, however, is given to meditation on the "mysteries" of Christ's life, from the annunciation to his resurrection appearances. These reflections are taken directly from the text of the Gospels.

The book concludes with a section containing various rules for Christian living. These include rules for discernment of spirits, for distribution of alms, and for proper "thinking with the church." The section on discerning the spirits gives particular attention to periods of "desolation" that may overtake the Christian. Loyola advises that during such times one should avoid all rash behavior and continue to stand firm in the faith. The Spirit brings consolation, not confusion, during such stressful times. Christians should also understand the nature of the enemy, Satan, and how he acts to entrap them. He works in secrecy, "like a false lover who wishes to remain hidden" and as an "angel of light" who entices the soul to his own evil "designs and wickedness."

"Rules for thinking with the church" provide advice on proper mental attitudes in the "Church Militant." Loyola recommends frequent participation in worship and reception of the most holy sacrament at least once a year, preferably once each week. He also urges conformity to Church doctrine and the careful study of the doctors of the Church (theology). This devotion, like all others in the *Exercises*, provides a means of continued conformity of the soul to the image of Christ.

The Spiritual Exercises of Saint Ignatius provides the seeker with a manual of vigorous military discipline in the spiritual life. It is a guide to Christian maturity that offers instruction in the freedom of the Spirit within the security of religious structure. It is a classic of the Church's devotional life.

William J. Leonard

RECOMMENDED READING

Edition used: *The Spiritual Exercises of St. Ignatius.* Translated by Anthony Mottola. Garden City, N.Y.: Doubleday, Image Books, 1964.

Barthel, Manfred. *The Jesuits.* New York: Morrow, 1982. A history of the Jesuit order from its beginning to the present.

Loyola, Ignatius. *The Autobiography of St. Ignatius Loyola.* New York: Harper & Row, 1974. A spiritual autobiography.

Wulf, Fredrich. *Ignatius of Loyola, His Personality and Spiritual Heritage, 1556–1956.* Saint Louis: Institute of Jesuit Resources, 1977. Essays on Ignatius and the Jesuits on the 400th anniversary of his death.

THE NAMES OF CHRIST

Author: Fray Luis Ponce de León (c. 1527–1591)
Born into a well-to-do family, with friends at court, and whose father became a judge in Granada, Luis Ponce de León was well educated at the schools of Madrid, Valladolid, and Salamanca. He professed in the Augustinian convent of Salamanca in 1544. He did further studies at Alcalá and then at Toledo. From Cipriano de la Huerga at Alcalá he learned Hebrew, and in 1588 he was awarded the degree of master of theology. The following year he was elevated to the chair of Thomas Aquinas's philosophical and theological thought. A brilliant linguist, he was arrested and imprisoned in 1572 for five years on charges of heresy and of translating the Song of Songs into Spanish. He was released in 1576, and appointed to a new chair. Allusions to his sufferings are made in his book, *The Names of Christ*, which he completed in 1583. He is also known for his poems, and in 1588 he edited the works of Teresa of Ávila. In 1591, he completed his translation of *The Book of Job*.

Type and subject of work: A history of salvation written in the form of a dialogue of three friends, developed in three books, each ending in a lyrical meditation or poem

First published: 1583; book three, 1585; final posthumous edition, 1595

MAJOR THEMES

Each name of God is like a diamond, revealing the multifaceted mystery of the being of God.
Wisdom for human beings is the knowledge of Christ.

Meditate on the names of Christ: Branch, Face of God, the Way, the Shepherd, Mountain, Everlasting Father, Arm of God, King, Prince of Peace, Husband, Son of God, Lamb, Beloved, Jesus.

The name Jesus, Christ's true and proper name, means health and salvation, and expresses the sweetness of his character, as well as the power and the glory.

In the dedication of his work to Don Pedro Portocarrero, principal of the University of Salamanca (1555–1557, 1566–1567) and member of the Inquisition, León points out that it is God's intent to make the Scriptures comprehensible for everybody. Hence the importance of new and vernacular translations. There is a need to communicate sound doctrine in the language of the people. And what better way could there be to communicate the Scriptures and sound doctrine than to meditate on some of the names of Christ in Scripture, as expressive of his saving acts in history, so that we can begin to appreciate the greatness of God, in Christ? While the names of Christ are innumerable, the writer selects ten that reflect upon Christ's humanity, and to which he added four more later.

León chooses "Bud" as the first name of Christ (Isa. 33:15, Jer. 33:15; Zech. 6:12), to touch upon the character of Christ's new birth, and the fruitage it brought forth. As "the Face of God," Christ came to reveal God, and also to be "a perfect model of humility." Yet it is like standing on the shore of a vast ocean, limitless in its exploration. So Christ is "the Way" (John 14:6), the way of salvation (Ps. 67:2), anticipated by the prophet (Isa. 35:8–10). He likewise directs our way in his commandments. As "the Shepherd," whom he claims to be (John 10:11), he nourishes and feeds his flock, and gathers the scattered flock. This title reflects Christ's love and tenderness for others. He rules by feeding the flock.

Christ as "the Mountain" is the ruler over all (Isa. 2:2), the fullness of all things. As such he is a refuge for the afflicted and the poor. In Daniel's vision Christ becomes as a great mountain that fills the whole earth (Dan. 2:34–35). To accept his sovereignty, however, we need to "be born a second time after we were born and left our mother's womb," as Jesus affirmed to Nicodemus. Then we begin to know God also as "the Everlasting Father" (Isa. 9:6), reforming and recreating us to be conformed to the image of his Son, no longer "in Adam," but now "in Christ."

In book two, Luis de León shifts the scene of the reading of Sabino's manuscript to a small island where in a forest stream they cool their feet and listen further to his meditations on Christ. As "the Arm of the Lord" (Isa. 52:10, 53:1), Christ is our strength, our shield, our defense. As the promised Messiah, he preaches good news to the poor, heals the brokenhearted, proclaims freedom to the captives, and releases the prisoner from darkness (Isa. 61:1-2), as he did originally in the Exodus. As "King," he was prophesied by Zechariah 9:9. But his sovereignty is over the poor and those needing the vindication of his sovereign grace. As "Prince of Peace," the shining stars in the heavens proclaim his benefits of harmony and peace. Only Christ can bring about this transformation of serenity in our hearts. As "Husband," Christ is head of the Church, who brings such joy to this relationship, and who will one day consummate the union forever. Looking at the writings of the church fathers, Juliano develops this theme of union with Christ.

In book three, Luis de León explains his purpose in writing a scholarly work not in Latin but in Spanish. He appeals to a wide audience, he writes, not to be popular but to express as widely as possible the glories of Christ. (This approach was a new departure in his day, when the Bible was a closed book because it was in the Latin Vulgate version.)

The third scene is set once more in the island grove. The friends agree to choose a name in turn that appeals to each. Juliano begins by choosing the title, "Son of God," and they discuss together the divine nature of Christ, in the incarnation. Marcelo chooses "the Lamb," to described the meekness and suffering of Christ, and then proceeds to meditate upon Christ as "the Beloved," because of the deep love we have for him. If we do so, how much more do the angelic hosts, and how, eternally so, does the Father! The discussion then focuses on how we can keep Christ's friendship.

Finally, the climax of the friends' meditation centers upon "Jesus," Christ's personal name. But like the facets of a diamond, so a word study of *Dabar* as an acrostic of the character of Jesus, reveals his manifold character. Bernard of Clairvaux had also meditated on the names of Jesus, and those meditations Luis de León takes up also and quotes. All this is dwelt upon, says Marcelo, because "our aim as Christians is to become like Christ, to hold Christ in us while we become like Him." As in a vast ocean, Christ is all in all, where we find the essence of life for all the world. Sabino then concludes the meditation with a hymn to celebrate the names of Christ.

> O soul of mine, let us praise God
> And all that's light in thee,
> Celebrate today His Holy Name
> His blessed Memory.
> An army of stars parades above,
> Mankind unfolds her story,
> And stars and men, made one at last,
> Sing only of Thy glory.

In this ingenious way, Luis de León weaves together many strands in his meditative tapestry. First, he uses the dialogue of friends as the genre for theology. On one occasion, the three friends agree that the pastoral scene of their walk on the island is a better setting than the classroom of scholasticism. Second, salvation history is the realization of God's presence in history. So the names of God are viewed as theophanies. Making his presence realizable in space and time involves the occurrence of domestic, daily events, as on one occasion when a small bird is attacked by two vicious crows, which interrupts the friends' discourse. Third, there is the awakening of "eternal longings" in the hearts of the three friends, to encourage each other in their desires for God, which are infinite. Fourth, there is the companionship and authority of the Fathers who are quoted extensively. Their meditations on Christ involve also the communion of saints. Fifth, there is the use of the oblique, a roundabout way of describing the ineffable and the mysterious, to arouse awe and wonder. Finally, the spiritual and emotional effects of encountering are discussed, since no one can experience God without being changed by God.

James M. Houston

RECOMMENDED READING

Edition used: León, Luis Ponce de. *The Names of Christ*. Translation and introduction by Manuel Duran and William Klubach. Preface by J. Ferrater Mora. Classics of Western Spirituality. New York: Paulist Press, 1984. A clear and careful edition.

Barnstone, Willis, trans. *The Unknown Light: The Poems of Fray Luis de León*. Albany: State University of New York Press, 1979. This edition makes León's mystical poems accessible to the English-reading public.

Bell, Aubrey, F.G. *Luis de León*. Oxford: Oxford University Press, 1925. A useful biography that places León in the cultural and religious context afforded by the Golden Age of Spain.

Kottman, Kal A. *Law and Apocalypse: The Moral Thought of Luis de León*. The Hague: Martinus Nyhoff, 1972. León's ideas on the principles of human conduct are related to his Christian stance.

Welch, Robert T. *Introduction to the Spiritual Doctrine of Fray Luis de León*. Washington, D.C.: Augustinian Press, 1951. León's spiritual ideology is examined intellectually.

ASCENT OF MOUNT CARMEL
AND
DARK NIGHT OF THE SOUL

Author: Saint John of the Cross (1542–1591)
The intellectual, poetical, and mystical were graciously fused in the most celebrated of Catholic mystical theologians. Born into a poor family, Juan de Yepes received his early education through the generosity of a patron who recognized the youth's exceptional intellectual and spiritual gifts. The young man entered the Carmelite order in 1563 and in the following year began studies at the University of Salamanca. Shortly after ordination in 1567 he met Saint Teresa of Ávila who urged him to join her Reform, which he did a year later. He served the Discalced Reform as a teacher, administrator, and spiritual director, suffering at times the worst of religious politics that set Calced and Discalced at odds, pitting brother against brother even within the Reform movement. He was imprisoned twice by the Calced and ultimately stripped of administrative office by the Discalced, spending his last days in the order's poorest houses. He died from an ill-treated infection that spread throughout his body, to the last a gentle, loving man. He was canonized in 1726. His poetry—which many literary critics consider the finest in the Spanish language—occasioned the prose commentaries that are the bulk of his mystical writings. *The Ascent of Mount Carmel* and *Dark Night of the Soul* are an explication of "Dark Night of the Soul," while the *Spiritual Canticle* (begun in 1578– 1579) and *Living Flame of Love* (1585) explain poems of the same titles.

Type and subject of work: Theological explanation of the apophatic journey of the soul to union with God

First transcribed: c. 1587

MAJOR THEMES

In the apophatic way, also known as the **via negativa,** *the soul increasingly detaches herself and is detached from the specific and knowable until in utter detachment she knows only that which is dark, confused, and general, which is God.*

The journey is traced in terms of the sensual and spiritual parts of the soul as well as active and passive consciousness.

Night is the image for the journey of purgation or detachment.

The stages of night are active purgation of the senses, passive purgation of the senses, active purgation of the spirit, and passive purgation of the spirit.

Actively and passively purged in the sensual and spiritual parts, the soul is transformed by God so that her will is conformed to God's will.

Saint John of the Cross drew upon the long tradition of apophatic mysticism to chart the ascent of Mount Carmel, which is his image for the ascent of the soul to God. There is reason to believe that Saint John was familiar not only with the writings of the early apophatic mystic, Dionysius the Areopagite, but also such later ones as Eckhart and Ruysbroeck. Saint John, however, provides a precise, comprehensive, and elegant description of the way of unknowing that is missing in preceding texts.

Although the *Ascent of Mount Carmel* and *Dark Night of the Soul* appear as two volumes with different titles, they constitute a single treatise on one poem. The recommended order for reading them is:

1. Active purgation of the senses: *Ascent*, Book One
2. Passive purgation of the senses: *Dark Night*, Book One
3. Active purgation of the spirit: *Ascent*, Books Two and Three
4. Passive purgation of the spirit: *Dark Night*, Book Two

It is well to begin the "ascent" with chapter five of book two of the *Ascent of Mount Carmel* wherein Saint John defines substantial union and mystical or transforming union. The former is natural union with God whereby the soul is able to exist; the latter is supernatural in that the transformation of the soul, whereby her will is brought into conformity with the will of God, is effected through grace. *Substantial* union is the union of essence while *transforming* union is the union of likeness.

Saint John suggests that the purpose of the Christian life is to experience mystical union; all Christians, therefore, are called to ascend the mount.

Saint John's mystical map assumes that God is totally other than the soul and yet can be known by the soul. Granted that God is not like the soul, the soul cannot rely on what is like her to know and love God. Since all means must be proportioned to the end, and since the end is the unknown, the soul must travel by the unknown to the unknown. Thus the ascent is a leaving behind and being detached from that which is known, meaning that which is like the soul, in order to travel by the unknown (the unlike) into the unknown (the unlike) which is God. Night is the image for the journey wherein the soul is deprived of desire for worldly things, dispossessed of natural understandings of God and plunged into Divine Darkness.

There is only one night, but there are stages in the night. In the first part of the night, the Active Night of the Senses, the soul strives actively to rid herself of desires that come in a natural way through the five exterior senses and the interior senses of the imagination and fancy. Unless desires are purged, the soul will suffer *privative* desire: The more she fills herself with desire for things, the more she is deprived of God. She will also suffer five *positive* effects: She is wearied, tormented, darkened, defiled, and weakened. The main point that Saint John makes is that it is our craving for things rather than the things themselves that hinders the ascent.

The soul is unable to accomplish the purgation of the senses. God perfects the work in a more intense darkness known as the Passive Night of the Senses. Saint John describes passive purgation in terms of the spiritual imperfections that afflict beginners: pride, avarice, luxury, wrath, gluttony, envy, and sloth. These chapters reveal the author's spiritual perceptiveness, sharpened not only by reflection on his own journey but also by years of service as spiritual director to novices, brothers, priests, and nuns. He knew firsthand, for example, the grave obstacle of pride that blocked the ascent of beginners who flaunted their piety, looked to confessors for praise, and were impatient with their own faults; or the extremes of bodily penance in which the gluttonous indulged while in pursuit of spiritual sweetness.

Spiritual sweetness, that is, the good feelings the soul experiences in meditation and devotion, must cede to dryness if the ascent is to continue. In a chapter of stunning clarity Saint John sets forth three signs by which to discern if the absence of sweetness in spiritual activities is caused by the soul's own lukewarmness or is God's way of leading her into a more delicate mode of prayer. Had Saint John left no more than this one chapter (nine), his place in mystical literature would be assured. The first sign is that the soul finds no pleasure in God or things created; the second is that the soul is anguished because without spiritual sweetness she thinks she is not serving God but backsliding; the third is that she cannot meditate or use her imagination in prayer, devotion, and reading. If the three signs exist together, they mark the transition from meditation to contemplation, from active consciousness to passive, from the natural to the supernatural, from the known to the unknown. The proper response to the experience of aridity that is indicated by the co-existence of the three signs is to rest in peace and do nothing except remain attentive to the darkness. God infuses love into the soul in ways too subtle for the senses to grasp. Infused loving, however, is discernible in the effects of humility, charity, increased virtue, remembrance of God, and liberty of spirit. Now, as the poem sings, the house (of the senses) is at rest.

The climb becomes steeper and darker as the soul becomes ever more aware of the need to cleanse herself of attachments, not only to natural understandings but also to supernatural ones. Chapter ten of the second book of the *Ascent of Mount Carmel* is the necessary introduction to all of book two, which treats purgation of understanding, and book three, purgation of memory and will.

Saint John's explanation of the two kinds of understanding, natural and supernatural, derives from the process of knowing wherein we gather information about an exterior reality through the senses, store the data in the imagination as images, and conceptualize the images. If the elements of exterior reality, senses, imagination, images, understanding, and concepts are present or active, the mode and content of knowing/understanding are natural. If one of more of the elements are absent, the mode of understanding is supernatural, but the content is not necessarily supernatural.

For example, if a person is present at the crucifixion of Jesus Christ, sees the event with the eyes, stores images in the imagination, and conceptualizes the images as the execution of a man, the knowing is natural in mode and content. This knowing John calls corporeal natural understanding. If the exterior reality of the crucifixion is absent, the phenomenon is a corporeal supernatural understanding, supernatural in mode in that the first element is missing but not in content because that which is seen in a supernatural way is nonetheless specific and distinct, hence natural (that is, a man executed by crucifixion).

If the image of the crucifixion is impressed directly on the imagination without benefit of the exterior reality or use of senses, the phenomenon is a supernatural imaginary vision, supernatural in mode in that the elements of exterior reality and senses are absent but not in content because that which is seen in the imagination (a man executed by crucifixion) is nonetheless specific and distinct, hence natural.

If the exterior reality of the crucifixion, the senses, the imagination, and the understanding are absent or not active, and if the understandings are given to the understanding in the form of distinct, clear visions, revelations or locutions—that is, they can be articulated in the form of concepts—the phenomenon is a supernatural spiritual understanding, supernatural in mode in that said elements are absent, but not in content because that which is understood in the understanding in the guise of a vision or revelation or locution is nonetheless specific and distinct, hence natural.

If, however, the vision or revelation or locution is not distinct—as, for example, is the case of an angel or an event prophesied—but is dark and confused, and if the dark, confused understanding leaves the soul quiet, desirous to do God's will, and inwardly convinced of being present to God, even though she does not see or imagine or understand anything clear and specific, then the content as well as the mode of understanding are supernatural.

The summit of Mount Carmel is dark, confused, and general understanding, for the summit is God; to human reason God is darkness. All that is not dark, confused, and general is to be dispossessed in the ascent; the soul is not to depend on anything specific, hence natural, to mediate that which is not specific, hence supernatural.

Throughout the rigorous treatment of these kinds of understandings, Saint John states repeatedly the case against depending on specific and distinct knowledge. Surely he was painfully aware of the precipitous plunges suffered by contemporaries who mistook their visions of angels and prophecies of the future for the Divine Darkness that, for Saint John, must overwhelm the traveler if God is to be met in the transforming love of mystical union.

The structure of understanding outlined in the second book of the *Ascent of Mount Carmel* is the foundation for the active purgation of memory and will that follows in the third book. Just as one acquires knowledge, so it is remembered; hence the purging of memory of natural and supernatural understandings in the order established in the preceding book. The rest of book three is devoted to cleansing the ill of affections of joy, hope, grief, and fear. Saint John breaks off discussion after defining temporal, natural, sensual, moral, supernatural, and spiritual joys, describing the evils of attachment to them and benefits of purging attachment. Saint John has made his case against attachment so thoroughly that by this time further explanation would be tedious. The point of purgation is clear.

Night, however, is not over. The mount is steeper and darker than ever. The soul feels bound for desolation. If she was disconsolate in the Passive Night of the Senses, what she is made to endure in the Passive Night of the Spirit leaves her gasping and groaning. Gone are consolations: The understanding is dark; the will, dry; memory, empty. In vain she labors to meditate and read; in vain she seeks comfort from spiritual directors. She feels abandoned by friends, books, devotions, by whatever once served to bring alive God's presence. And she feels abandoned by God, cast into a cell of dark solitude, her only companion Darkness itself. She cannot see that God is dispossessing her of cravings, desires, and attachments, whatever form they take—and Saint John hastens to advise that the way is individual, beset with unique difficulties such that no person, only God, can illumine the way. But God's illumination the soul cannot see in the blackness of night as God blinds the eyes of natural understanding, annihilating her with respect to how and what she knows, remembers, and wants.

Thus God secretly instructs the soul, lighting her with divine wisdom. But the more she is illumined by God with God, the more her natural faculties are darkened. She cannot see the Light that is darkness to her faculties.

So the soul suffers. She undergoes. She is passionate. Paradoxically, her suffering—her passion—is her love for God and God's love for her, for she would not suffer if God were not present to her beyond her natural understanding and if she did not yearn with all her being to love and know God as God is. In the awful darkness come moments of relief, fleeting yet sufficient to sustain her, when she discerns God in the sudden enflaming of her will to love. Emboldened, she runs in search of her Beloved.

In darkest night, faculties and senses purged, freed from attachments to the natural, the soul is freed to love God and know God, not as she thought or expected God to be, but as God is. Securely, secretly, joyously, she runs up the dark slopes to be touched again and again by God, to seize him, hold him fast and be held, to soar upward to her Beloved, the house of her spirit and senses now at rest.

Mary E. Giles

RECOMMENDED READING

Edition used: John of the Cross, Saint. *Ascent of Mount Carmel.* Translated by E. Allison Peers. New York: Doubleday, Image Books, 1958. *Dark Night of the Soul.* Translated by E. Allison Peers. New York: Doubleday, Image Books, 1959.

Dicken, E. W. Trueman. *The Crucible of Love.* New York: Sheed & Ward, 1963. Although the study was published more than twenty years ago, it remains the indispensable introduction to the mystical theology of Saint John of the Cross and Saint Teresa of Ávila.

John of the Cross, Saint. *Spiritual Canticle* and *Living Flame of Love,* available in two excellent translations: *The Collected Works of St. John of the Cross.* Translated by Kieran Kavanaugh, O.C.D. and Otilio Rodgríguez, O.C.D. Washington, D.C.: ICS Publications, 1979. *The Works of St. John of the Cross.*

Translated by E. Allison Peers. 3 vols. London, 1934–1935. The translations by E. Allison Peers are also available in paperback editions published by Doubleday under the Image Books imprint.

Stein, Edith. *The Science of the Cross.* London, 1960. A lucidly beautiful entry into the theology of the cross which for this martyred nun became a lived reality.

INTERIOR CASTLE

———

Author: Saint Teresa of Ávila (1515–1582)
Lacking the formal theological study that routinely was denied women
in sixteenth-century Spain, Teresa de Cepeda y Ahumada was an unlikely candidate to lead a thoroughgoing reform of the Carmelite order and
write masterpieces of mystical literature. A stunning conversion after
twenty years of spiritual vacillation as a nun was the beginning of a journey in prayer and religious reform to which she remained true until her
death. Her extraordinary administrative and literary talents and the love
of God that informed all her activities have inspired women and men
from her day to the present. The Catholic church canonized her in 1622,
and in this century she, with Catherine of Siena, was declared the first
woman doctor of the Church. Her major works include the *Life*
(1562–1565), *Way of Perfection* (1565), the *Foundations* (1573), and the *Interior Castle*. With the exception of the *Foundations*, which was published
first in the Brussels edition of 1605, these works were published first in
1588 at Salamanca.

Type and subject of work: Descriptive treatise on the mystical journey
of the soul to union with God

First published: 1588

MAJOR THEMES

The interior castle is the soul where God takes his delight.
The castle contains seven mansions in each of which are many rooms.
The beginner enters the castle by means of mental prayer.

In the first three mansions the beginner actively labors to cultivate virtues and rid herself of imperfections.

The transition from the purgative way of the first three mansions to the illuminative way of the fourth and fifth occurs with passive recollection, the first manifestation of supernatural prayer.

The Prayer of Quiet is the increased quieting of the senses and faculties in the fourth mansion.

The Sleep of the Faculties expresses the deepening passivity of the soul with respect to God in the fifth mansion.

The Spiritual Betrothal in the sixth mansion is the transition into the unitive way.

The fullness of the unitive way is experienced in the Spiritual Marriage in the seventh mansion.

Experiential rather than theological in tone and written in a style that is lively, anecdotal, and rich in imagery, the *Interior Castle* has appealed to countless pilgrims on the inner way. That Teresa was not trained in the Scholasticism of her day is to the reader's benefit, for her experiences are not cast in the theological jargon that obscures many treatises written in her time.

The image of the soul as a castle came, she says, in answer to prayer when, in obedience to her confessor, she sought to begin an explanation of the soul's journey to God. She holds firm to the image throughout the work, returning to it again and again when she strays from the subject to comment on a matter that has just occurred to her.

She perceives the interior journey in terms of prayer. One cannot even begin the journey unless one practices mental prayer, which requires concentrating on the meaning of words said aloud or to oneself. In affirming the necessity of mental prayer, Teresa was bold, for mental prayer was associated with the heretical *alumbrados,* many of whom were women. In the eyes of the Inquisition the practice and teaching of mental prayer by a woman was sufficient grounds to call her before the church officials. Yet Teresa insisted that no true inner journey could take place without thinking about the words one said; thus she urged her nuns—for whom she wrote—to use their minds.

In the first three mansions, which correspond to the purgative way, mental prayer, devotional reading, edifying conversation, and good works are means of actively purging imperfections and building virtues. Progress is discernible by the degree to which the soul is humble and charitable and the senses and faculties are quieted in prayer. In charting the soul's journey, Teresa referred to the lower part of the soul with its five exterior senses and interior senses of imagination and fancy and the higher part with its faculties of memory, understanding, and will. In the beginning stages the soul enjoys spiritual sweetness, which are the good feelings that come during devotion, prayer, reading, conversation, and doing good works. Toward the end of the third mansion, however, spiritual sweetness dries up with the result that the soul cannot understand what is happening and fears that she is not progressing. Teresa assures us that times of aridity indicate progress in that God is speaking to the soul in ways that are too subtle to register on the senses and emotions.

The Prayer of Recollection, which Teresa treats in the third chapter of the fourth mansion, marks the transition from the purgative way of beginners to the illuminative way of proficients. The major difference in consciousness between the purgative and illuminative ways is that in the former the soul is primarily aware of striving to please God whereas in the second, the subject of mansions four and five, she is aware of being made pleasing to God. Note that Teresa treats the Prayer of Recollection out of order, placing it in the third chapter rather than the first; the error is not unexpected given the fact that she wrote hurriedly and often late at night or in the midst of other business.

Recollection, like mental prayer, is a term that appears harmless, but in Teresa's day it was fraught with polemic. Earlier in the century arguments between advocates of the prayer of recollection (*recogimiento*) on the one hand and abandon (*dejamiento*) on the other caused bitter division among Christians who in general favored the interiorized Christianity that had been inspired by Erasmus. In the case of the Franciscan order the dispute turned brother against brother. Ultimately the Inquisition declared the prayer of abandon a heretical practice because its advocates abandoned themselves or surrendered themselves to God's grace in the belief that nothing they did could bring them into divine favor. Recollection was made famous by Francisco do Osuna who in his *Third Spiritual Alphabet* (1527) used the term for prayer in general as well as a specific manifestation of prayer. Osuna's was the first treatise on prayer that Teresa read; thus it is not surprising to find her conversant with the term and the passive nature of prayer that it evokes. Recollection is supernatural in that, without willing it, the soul closes her eyes and feels a temple of solitude being built up about her. Teresa compares the recollected soul to a hedgehog (one of several Teresian images also found in Osuna's text), the senses and faculties gathered together so as not to disturb her. Teresa stresses, however, that the soul cannot recollect herself at will as does the hedgehog. She is passive; recollection is a gift; loving is infused.

The remaining chapters in the fourth mansion describe a deepening recollection that is called the Prayer of Quiet. Now the soul is watered abundantly without effort on her part; she feels peace, quiet, and humility, and her faculties are absorbed and amazed at what is happening to her. Teresa cautions toward the end of the discussion that the soul not strive for the spiritual consolation of passive prayer, for God, who alone can bestow the Prayer of Quiet, knows what is best for each soul. The soul's desire should be simply to imitate the Lord.

The Sleep of the Faculties is the term for prayer in the fifth mansion as the soul becomes so deeply recollected that God enters her center without using the door of the senses or faculties. In this mansion Teresa compares the soul to the silkworm that is transformed into a butterfly. The soul is so changed by the intense experience of being quieted in prayer that she longs to suffer and even die for God. She realizes, however, that her will is not yet conformed to God's will, and lest she become overconfident, she is reminded to improve in charity. Teresa is commonsensical in that she knew only too well both from her own experience and from that of others the dangers of self-delusion, pride, and zealousness. Thus in mansions four and five when the soul receives gifts of infused prayer and love, she warns repeatedly not to trust in oneself but in God and to grow in love for neighbor.

The transition from the illuminative way to the unitive way is expressed in the Spiritual Betrothal that is described in the sixth mansion. This mansion is the most perilous of the inner journey. Teresa describes in startling detail the extraordinary phenomena of wounds of love, rapture, flights of the spirit, and jubilation of the soul that she herself experienced for several years. The danger is to assume that the experiences are necessary to perfection. The reader is reminded that in the matter of these phenomena Teresa's writing is descriptive rather than prescriptive. Her friend and director, Saint John of the Cross, was adamant in his belief that relying on extraordinary phenomena hinders the soul rather than helps her.

Teresa also describes and explains understandings that come to the soul during a rapture, for example, or a flight of the spirit. She employs the categories of corporeal, imaginary, and intellectual/spiritual to define the kinds of visions and locutions that she experienced. She also provides valuable criteria for determining if the understandings are genuine, that is, if their source is God rather than the soul's weakness or selfish expectations. If the vision occurs unexpectedly and if its effects are positive—the soul is at peace, joyous, and humble as opposed to restless and prideful—its source is God.

Teresa sounds another cautionary note in the middle chapter of the sixth mansion as she stresses the continuing need to meditate on the Sacred Humanity. Her advice originates in a debate that circulated in her day as to whether the contemplative had further need of meditation once she was graced with infused love. Teresa clearly did not agree that the gift of infused prayer or contemplation lessened the need to make active use of the mind by meditating on the life and example of Jesus Christ.

Another theme that recurs throughout the sixth mansion is suffering. Reflective of the suffering that she herself endured—when others either derided her or acclaimed her a saint because of her visions; or when inept confessors misled her; or physical infirmities beset her; or when earthly consolations lost their appeal; or spiritual consolations dried up—Teresa sees the soul in the sixth mansion suspended between two worlds. Ultimately her advice is the same as in previous mansions: Do charitable works and trust in God.

A spiritual vision of the Trinity is Teresa's entry into the Spiritual Marriage of the seventh mansion. Anguish, restlessness, and longing are transformed into the tranquil certitude of resting habitually in God's presence. The previous highs of rapture and lows of aridity vanish as the active Martha and contemplative Mary live harmoniously. The mystical state is realized wherein the soul is transformed, her will brought into conformity with the will of God. Prayer, which Teresa elsewhere says is simply talking with God, has been transformed from such events as a moment of recollection or an hour of rapture into an uninterrupted conversation with her Beloved Companion.

Mary E. Giles

RECOMMENDED READING

Edition used: Teresa of Ávila, Saint. *Interior Castle.* Translated by E. Allison Peers. Garden City, N.Y.: Doubleday, Image Books, 1961.

Dicken, E. W. Trueman. *The Crucible of Love.* New York: Sheed & Ward, 1963. This is necessary reading for the mystical theology of both Saint Teresa and Saint John of the Cross.

Teresa of Ávila, Saint. *Life, Way of Perfection,* and *Foundations,* available in two excellent translations: *The Collected Works of St. Teresa of Ávila.* Translated by Kieran Kavanaugh, O.C.D. and Otilio Rodríguez, O.C.D. 3 vols. Washington, D.C.: ICS Publications, 1976, 1980, 1985. *The Works of St. Teresa.* Translated by E. Allison Peers. 3 vols. London, 1951. The translation of the *Life* by E. Allison Peers is also available in a paperback edition published by Doubleday under the Image Books imprint, 1960.

THE RULE OF PERFECTION

Author: Benedict Canfield (1562–1611)

Benedict was the religious name of William Fitch, born in Canfield, Essex. Having gone to London to study law and been converted from a life of dissipation through reading Catholic books, he went to Douai in northern France to study theology. In 1586 he entered the Capuchin order and was sent to Paris and to Italy to study. It was in his capacity as master of novices that he developed the method of contemplation later published as *The Rule of Perfection. The Rule,* published several times during the seventeenth century, was later forgotten, so that Aldous Huxley, in 1940, said that it was "very hard to come by, in any edition or language." Happily the book has now been republished in a critical edition by Presses Universitaires de France.

Type and subject of work: Compendium of asceticism and contemplation

First published: 1608

MAJOR THEMES

Whatever stage of life one has attained to, the rule for one's spiritual development reduces to following "the will of God."

The exterior will of God, known to us in laws and in reason, is the rule for beginners, engaged in a life of activity.

The interior will of God, present in the soul, is the rule for the proficient, engaged in contemplation.

The essential will of God, which governs the hidden movements of the soul, is the rule for the perfect, who live in communion with God.

Benedict Canfield (Brother Benet, as he signs himself) lived in the great age (the Baroque) when artists, scientists, and philosophers all thought themselves obliged to comprehend the greatest possible amount of detail within an immediately discernible whole. Thus, when Benet titles his book *The Rule of Perfection Reduced to the Sole Point of the Will of God*, we must not think of him as throwing out what others have taught but rather as offering a multiple-service category in which everything worth keeping is not merely kept but is exhibited in its essence. Other books setting forth the way to serve God commonly have a chapter on the will of God, says Benet, and then go on to other topics; but this book pursues only the will of God, making it "the beginning, the progress, and ending, of the whole spiritual life," giving precepts for everyone, showing the means to knowing it both in our outward calling and in our contemplative life, and ultimately showing that the will of God is God's own self.

Benet accepted the conventional division of Christians into three classes: beginners, proficients, and perfect. Accordingly, as he expounds it, the will of God is threefold. We can speak of an exterior will directing the active life of beginners on the path to perfection; of an interior will discerned in the contemplative life of proficients; and of an essential will serving as goal and fulfillment of the perfect. Canfield designed a frontispiece for his book to illustrate his scheme. On the lower part of the page is a picture of Gethsemane, with Christ ready to receive the cup of suffering, with the disciples asleep behind him, and with soldiers in the background. The subscription is, "Not my will but thine." On the upper part of the page is a diagram showing the sun with its rays illuminating three concentric circles of devout faces designated, according to their distance from the sun, as perfect, contemplative, and active. In the center, in Hebrew characters, is the name Jehovah. At the perimeter is a circle composed of scythes, spades, mallets, and other tools, including a quill and an inkwell. Benet's book, as Aldous Huxley suggests, could be looked upon as a commentary on this symbolical frontispiece.

Of the three parts that make up *The Rule*, the first part, "Concerning the exterior will of God, containing the active life," is quite businesslike. In chapter two, the rule—which is, that all our works and actions should be done only for the will of God and because he wills them—is treated as if it were a hypothesis that needed to be proved. It is tested against a list of eleven Christian perfections drawn from various sources, mostly biblical: self-renunciation, resignation, purity of heart, presence of God, knowledge of self, knowledge of God, annihilation, union, contemplation, love of God, and transformation. For example, Jesus' words, "He that will follow me, let him renounce himself," are included in the exercise of the will of God, seeing that one cannot make God's will one's rule without renouncing oneself, that is, one's own will. Again, the words of the Psalmist concerning God's presence, when he says, "I always have God in my sight because he assists at my right hand lest I should be moved," are included in the exercise of the will of God because the will of God is God himself, "so that when by doing his will we have it present, we must have God present."

In chapter five, the exterior will is specified as "the divine pleasure known by the law, and by reason." In order for us to discern our duties in respect to these, Benet suggests that everything that we are to do or endure falls into one of three classes: things commanded, things forbidden, things indifferent. There is no special difficulty with the first two classes, once they are understood to include not only written laws of the state and the Church but also social customs and commands of parents and of other superiors. But the third class, things indifferent, is further subdivided according as things are agreeable, disagreeable, or neither. As concerns things indifferent, then, two further rules are given: that we are to mortify the flesh; and that whatever we do, we must do it with the intention of fulfilling God's will. This last consideration, moreover, applies as well to what is commanded and what is prohibited, since what is important in the mystical way is not the public peace but the perfection of the soul.

One can detect the hand of a lawyer in this first part. But what mainly distinguishes it from a work of casuistry is that, like the *Spiritual Exercises* of Saint Ignatius Loyola, it provides rules for training the soul. These are denominated "the six degrees of Solomon's throne," after the account given in 3 Kings 10, where Solomon is said to have built a throne of ivory, covered with gold, which had six degrees. In Benet's allegorical presentation, there are six degrees of perfection in the Christian's intention when he or she says, "I will do this for the only will of God." The first degree, called "actually," means bringing God's will consciously to mind. The second degree, called "only," means having in mind no other end than God's will. The third, "willingly," means giving one's full consent. And so on, up to the sixth, "speedily." Solomon is a type of Christ, and the steps of his throne are a further representation of the mystical ladder reaching from earth to heaven. The modern reader could let it go at that—but not Benet, who turns now to the Song of Solomon to show that each of the six degrees that he has formulated in practical terms is allegorically present in the conversation between the soul and her heavenly Spouse. For example, when the Bridegroom in the Song says, "Put me as a signet upon thy heart, and as a signet upon thine arm," we are to understand that Christ desires his bride to be mindful of him, that she have an "actual remembrance of him; which actual remembrance is the first degree called 'actuality.' "

More helpful from our point of view is the ascetic scheme (chapter seventeen) introduced as "A particular means for beginners how to enter into the practice of this rule, and how a man may keep himself therein, and greatly fructify and go forward in the same." The practical problem, Benet recognizes, is that even in this first part, the will of God consists largely in right intentions, but that these, being interior, are difficult for the beginner to lay hold of. Benet suggests that the soul desiring to become holy make it a daily practice to renounce or mortify itself a certain number of times throughout the day, starting with the five senses. For example, one might resolve to mortify the sense of taste by giving up a tempting dish, or one might mortify the sense of hearing by foregoing a musical treat, saying with the Psalmist, "I will voluntarily offer up a sacrifice unto thee." Or, the exercise may be reversed, and some disagreeable experience deliberately undergone, as when Saint Francis kissed the leper out of charity. Other powers may be beaten down in a similar way, notably "the will in all her intemperate passions and disordinate affections," but also the intellect, wherein, says Benet, all manner of vain thoughts reside. Although this practice is given for beginners, others may find weaknesses cropping up and to control them voluntarily undertake each day a number of mortifications, "renouncing themselves therein for the will of God," always keeping in view the ivory throne of pure intention "where God great Solomon sitteth."

Part one, by far the most readable section of *The Rule*, concludes with three appendixes, of which the first (chapter eighteen) should be mentioned. Titled "Two errors which may happen in this exercise," it presents two allegories meant to keep the active and contemplative stages of life in balance. The first is the story of Jacob's two wives, of whom it is told that having first been given Leah, afterward, when he was given Rachel, he despised the first. This, says Benet, should warn those who have reached the stage of contemplation not to despise the active stage, for he says, no one can be perfect in contemplation without continual mortification of the self. The second allegory is the story of Mary and Martha found in Saint Luke's gospel. Here the danger is the opposite; for there are those who have so great an affection for the active life —which, according to Benet, includes intellectual activity—that, like Martha, they complain of the seeming idleness of contemplatives, though these have chosen the better part.

The second part, "Concerning the interior will of God, containing the contemplative life," is but half the length of the first, although it could have been made twice as long. (Benet himself mentions that he has arbitrarily limited himself to five heads although any number readily come to mind.) What chiefly characterizes the interior will of God is that it is perceived as dwelling within the soul once the active self attains the point of intending to think and do only the will of God. Such purity of intention (Solomon's throne) is a choice that the soul has made, having rejected the creature in order to embrace the Creator "by a true, faithful, and simple regard of the will of God." Memory, understanding, and all the other faculties are suspended by this act; and, in the inner quiet that it brings, God's "secret operation and inward touch" fill the soul with unspeakable joy.

Benet calls the first degree of contemplation "manifestation" and he expounds it largely by means of Old Testament poetry, notably passages from the Psalms and from the Song of Solomon. Having experienced the presence of God within herself, the soul needs hardly to be encouraged to "plunge herself more deeply into the will of God," which, as she does so, discloses itself to her in four further degrees: admiration, humiliation, exultation, and elevation—a classification apparently suggested to Benet by his reading of Saint Bonaventura's *Journey of the Mind to God* (or *The Mind's Road to God*). Of these five degrees the second is most important. Admiration here has the sense of wonder and astonishment. It follows from the discovery of God's greatness, of humankind's nothingness, and of the familiarity that God allows between himself and his creature. These are truths that the soul knew formerly by hearsay: Now she knows them "by a general and simple view and by her inhesion to God." The soul that has attained to this degree is not only extremely amazed, but departs out of herself "so far forth as falling thereby into a trance or ecstasy, languishing for love." Humiliation follows understandably from admiration, and exultation follows from humiliation, as in the *Magnificat*. Elevation, though spoken of as the fifth degree, is not properly speaking a higher step in the spiritual ascent, but is the union of the will with God following from the other degrees. In her exaltation the soul is so seized upon by God as no longer to have dominion over herself, adhering to God as unfailingly as the circumference of a circle does to the center, the branch to the vine, and the part to the whole, "and so is perfectly become one and the same spirit with God."

In the final chapter of part two, Benet reminds the reader that distinctions are of no use to souls that have attained to contemplation. This part of the book, he says, is written for "souls that have no yet tasted the same, and which without such divisions are not able to comprehend it." God's will is not divided any more than is the light of the sun, which, however, may be distinguished according to the degree of its coming into the world. "Even so the divine will discovers itself in one degree of light to beginners, in another to proficients, and in a third to the perfect."

The third part of *The Rule*, "Concerning the essential will of God, pertaining to the perfect life," is as long as the other two parts combined, and far more technical, so much so that those who have not attained to enlightenment are advised by the author to leave it alone. Without flattering ourselves in this regard, we may at least go so far as to indicate the salient features of part three.

There is no great difficulty in understanding chapter one, in which Benet explains what he means by the essential will of God and argues that it is one with God himself. The essential will of God is abstract spirit or life, apprehensible neither through the senses nor the understanding. Since it is presumed to be present in all of God's works, one can ask how it differs from the interior will known to the contemplative. The answer is found mainly in the pronouns *I* and *my*. The interior will, although stripped of almost every relic of the personal, hence the human, is still bound, very subtly, to sensitive life, being in this minute degree active, whereas the essential will is completely without any trace of form or image, hence entirely passive. For the rest, chapter one is a theological exercise, proving what, in the author's view, is self-evident, namely, that the will of God is God.

Chapter two makes the point, fundamental to the life of the perfect, that there are no human means for reaching the essential will; so, what remains to be done, says Benet, is to show "the means of arriving at it without means. For," he continues, "be assured that no act, meditation, thought, aspiration, or operation is of any use, and that no discourse, exercise or teaching can mediate between the soul and this essential will or essence of God, but rather that the will itself, without any means, must draw us to itself and make itself the object of our sight and contemplation."

Chapters three to fifteen in part three we are content to leave alone. They have to do with two "non-means," familiar no doubt to mystics, whereby the soul reaches union with its Maker. Chapters sixteen to twenty-one have to do with contemplating God in the passion of our Lord. This is another story. Scholars argue as to whether Benet wrote these chapters, nothing that they demand a return to images and feelings, which is difficult to reconcile with the whole tenor of *The Rule*. Recent scholars, however, tend to agree that Benet wrote these chapters and meant them to occupy their present place in his book. The explanation they give is that Benet was himself devoted to this subject of meditation and that in his experience it was needed to counterbalance the impersonality of the type of mysticism that Christianity took over from the Greeks.

Jean H. Faurot

RECOMMENDED READING

Edition used: Benoit de Canfield. *La Regle de Perfection—The Rule of Perfection.* Critical edition edited by Jean Orcibal. Paris: Presses Universitaires de

France, 1982. French and English text, except for part three, of which Canfield seems not to have completed the English version.

Huxley, Aldous. *Grey Eminence: A Study in Religion and Politics.* New York and London: Harper & Bros., 1941. Fascinating study of a Capuchin monk making history as assistant to Cardinal Richelieu, the red eminence. Tells of Father Joseph's training under Father Benedict, how he became a master of novices, wrote his own *Introduction to the Spiritual Life,* served as a provincial of his order—all of this alongside his government service. Contains, besides a study of Canfield's place in the religious life of his times, a useful summary of *The Rule of Perfection* (pp. 88–92), including a reproduction of the frontispiece. The most convenient introduction in English to Benedict Canfield.

Stephen, Leslie, ed. "Canfield, Benedict." In *Dictionary of National Biography,* 8:409f. London: Smith, Elder, & Co., 1986. One column of biography. Mentions, in addition to *The Rule of Perfection,* a small work published at London in 1878, *The Holy Will of God: A Short Rule of Perfection.*

FOUR BOOKS ON TRUE CHRISTIANITY

Author: Johann Arndt (1555–1621)

The son of a Lutheran pastor, Johann Arndt had studied theology in the best universities, but he had found more satisfaction in Thomas à Kempis's *The Imitation of Christ*, the *Sermons* of Johann Tauler, and the *Theologia Germanica* than in the disputations that went on in the schools and were carried into the pulpit. Although he became a zealous pastor and served during his last years as a church superintendent, Arndt was a center of controversy because of the emphasis that he placed on conversion and on holy living.

Type and subject of work: Discourses on practical piety

First published: 1605–1610

MAJOR THEMES

A true Christian is a child of God in whom the image of the Father has been restored through union with Christ.

A true Christian patterns his or her life on Christ's humanity.

The kingdom of God is an internal good that true Christians carry within their souls.

The fellowship with God as experienced by the true Christian is a foretaste of eternal life.

Broadly speaking, *True Christianity* represents an attempt (remarkably successful in the long run) to bring what Fredrich von Hügel called the mystical element back into the mainstream of Lutheran Christianity.

During the late Middle Ages, spiritual fellowships flourished among the German peoples as they did nowhere else in Europe, but in the years immediately following the Reformation the Lutheran churches were preoccupied with the doctrinal and institutional elements of religion and tended to neglect the interior life. Arndt, while he adhered faithfully to the principles of Lutheran theology and recognized, to a point, the need for writing and preaching against sects and heresies, complained that alongside "the many heavy disputations, polemical sermons, writings, and tracts, Christian life, true repentance, godliness, and Christian love are almost forgotten." *True Christianity* was an attempt to redress the balance. Its four books are not so much a connected discourse as a collection of tracts, brief expositions of biblical texts, sermon notes, and occasional finished sermons. It is repetitious but seldom dull. The headings of the four books (*Of Scripture, Of Christ, Of Conscience,* and *Of Nature*) would seem to have come to him as an afterthought.

Book one, which was published by itself, deserves the title later given to the expanded work. Expressions such as "true repentance," "true faith," "true knowledge," and "true life-work" abound. We hear much in this book about the "true Christian," who is known by his life and not by his profession. "He who wishes to be a true Christian must endeavor to let one see Christ in him, in his love, humility, and graciousness, for no one can be a Christian in whom Christ does not live." The opposite of the true Christian, for Arndt, is not specifically the false Christian, but rather "the child of this world," and he has but little occasion to speak of false Christianity. But in a day when churches were state institutions, when everybody who was anybody was a member in good standing, it was necessary to warn against the presumptuous who thought that they could have their sins forgiven without forsaking them. "Ah, you deluded, false Christian," he writes of those who thought that all they need do was to believe that Christ died for humankind's justification; "God's Word has not taught you that thus you will become holy. No apostle or prophet preached so, but they [your pastors] preach so. If you wish to have forgiveness of sins you must be repentant and leave your sins, have sorrow for your sins and believe in Christ." Good Lutheran that he was, Arndt developed his theme within the framework of Adam's sin and Christ's obedience: As a result of the former, humanity has ceased to be the image of God and become the image of Satan; as a result of the latter, it is changed back into the image of God. Lutherans generally understood the image or reflection of God, mentioned in Genesis, as the perfect conformity of the human mind and will with that of the Holy Trinity. What set Arndt apart was that, whereas his brethren regarded the restoration of God's image purely as a work of God, Arndt thought of it as something that requires our constant attention. "The whole of the

Christian life upon earth," he writes, at the end of book one, "is nothing and can be nothing other than a raising up of the image of God in the believer. Thereby, he continually lives in the new birth and the old birth is daily extinguished and mortified in him."

The theme of book two is Christian discipleship, which involves denying oneself, taking up one's cross, and following in Christ's steps. As Arndt interprets these words, they have to do not so much with our outward as with our inward walk. The true cross is the daily mortification of the old person and the daily resurrection of the new. Christ's person, his life on earth, his passion, death, and resurrection become symbols of the mystical ascent. Beginning with Christ's human nature we rise to his divinity. "We climb up as on a true ladder to heaven into the true heart of God, and we rest in love." Humility, holy poverty, and sorrow are the first rungs of this ladder.

Next comes prayer, which has three stages. Progress in prayer opens the heart to love—the believer's love for God and the mystery of God's love for us—and this leads to song and praise. But the highest rung is patience—waiting and hoping for deliverance, with grace to endure suffering. "Christ made suffering a sanctifying thing, and eternal glory follows upon suffering." Prayer, however, is central to the whole project of destroying unbelief, pride, covetousness, and anger—the image of Satan—and of restoring faith, humility, love, and patience—the image of God. Before the Fall, we lacked nothing; after the Fall we lack everything and must seek what we lack in continual prayer. Our model here is the prayer that Christ gave to his disciples. In praying it, we ask that God's name be praised and our own pride laid low, that his kingdom come and Satan's be overthrown, that his will be done and ours reduced to nothing. In addition, we pray for the goods of body and soul that we need in this life and the one to come.

This kind of prayer Arndt describes as "a conversation with God, a piece of the inner spiritual, heavenly life, the characteristic and mark of a faithful Christian's heart, a continual movement of the Holy Spirit." Such prayer may be public or private. Because it takes place in the heart it may engage us in any place whatever we may be doing. For Arndt, however, as for others in the tradition of German mysticism, this kind of prayer is but the first stage in the believer's communion with God. As one advances in spiritual discipline, external or articulate prayer rises to internal or meditative prayer. One is awakened to God's presence, to his love of his creatures and his wish to hear us and make us participants of his immeasurable goodness. Moreover, on occasion, internal prayer is crowned by supernatural prayer, in which "the mind is filled with God's love through true faith so that it can think of nothing other than God," and is filled with a "good above all goods," and a "joy above all joys." It all happens in an instant, says Arndt; but by comparison with it, external prayer is like a penny alongside a thousand-mark goldpiece, for in this instant the soul is completely united with God in knowledge and love.

Book three was intended by its author for more advanced Christians. Corresponding to the stages of natural life, there are stages in the Christian life: Repentance and faith correspond to youth; discipleship to middle age; perfection to ripe old age. Here, in effect, Arndt makes his boldest effort to revive in the churches of his day the devotional outlook and spiritual discipline that had been inspired by Meister Eckhardt and by Jan van Ruysbroeck. One might describe it as a monasticism without vows. It called for giving up the world, though not necessarily for leaving one's station in the world, and for finding the full satisfaction for one's life in God and in his favors.

Arndt's central thought is that the heart of the enlightened Christian is God's throne room: The Lord of the universe, who is present in all his works, enters in a special way into the heart of the believer. "There, in his own image and likeness, he enacts those works that he himself is." But God cannot reveal himself except in a heart that has been emptied of all cares and is perfectly at rest. "The eternal wisdom of God is so delicate in its work that it can accept nothing that belongs to a creature. He does not rest, and works in you insofar as his work can be brought about and you do not hinder it." Arndt does not suggest that this is the only way to seek God nor that everyone is suited to pursue this way. There is the external active way followed by Martha, which consists in the practice of Christian works. But Mary chose the better way, which is internal and passive. It "occurs when a man enters into the ground of his heart and there realizes [that] the kingdom of God is in us, that God himself is in us with all his goodness, that he is nearer to us and more internal than the soul is to itself." This, says Arndt, is Christian perfection, the internal Sabbath of the soul. Contrary to what is popularly believed, perfection is not a state of spiritual self-glorification, but rather a knowledge of one's nothingness, heartfelt compassion for one's neighbor, and a love of God that is as continuous and complete as life in this world allows.

Book four seems to have been written for the Marthas of the world. Not many experience mystical union in this life; and if the Marys say, "You don't know what you are missing," the Marthas are sure to answer, "So what?" In any case, book four exhibits a more commonsense view of things. Arndt turns to nature (including human beings) to see what lessons it hold for the believer. This is not a particularly remarkable performance on his part: Mostly he does not observe nature but comments on the six days of creation, mentioning Saint Ambrose and Saint Basil as the predecessors. We are invited to meditate on God's wisdom and goodness, to learn the proper subordination of the lower creatures to humankind and of humankind to its Maker. In addition to the wonders we find there, nature furnishes a rich language of symbols with which we can represent to ourselves the mysteries of God's own being.

A modern reader cannot but ask whether Arndt was aware of the astonishing new views of nature that were then being put forward by such men as Francis Bacon and Galileo Galilei; but if he was, he had no interest in trying to apply them or to refute them. Nature interests him only as a further witness to religious and moral truths. The purpose of the fourth book, he explains, is to show "how the Scripture, Christ, man, and the whole of nature agree and how everything in one eternal living source, which is God himself, flows together and leads to God." Incidentally, it is here for the first time that we understand the point of the titles that he has given to the different books: *Of Scripture, Of Christ, Of Conscience,* and *Of Nature.*

In the ten years between the publication of the *Four Books on True Christianity* and his death, Arndt composed two additional books, which were henceforth incorporated in the whole, bringing it to some fifteen hundred pages in length. Books five and six bear no title and may be thought of as forming an apologia. Arndt's writings, although they enjoyed wide popularity, also created resentment, particularly in official circles. So far as this was a response to his charges of worldliness and hypocrisy, he did not bother to reply. But in part, undoubtedly, it rested on the sincere belief that Arndt was turning back the clock and throwing away the gains made by the Reformation. This, he thought, was a misunderstanding. There were two main points to be made. The first had to do with the doctrine of justification by faith alone; the second, with the mystical union of the believer to God.

As to the first, Arndt conceded that the so-called reformers before the Reformation, including Tauler and Thomas à Kempis, were not always clear on the distinction between the faith that justifies the sinner in God's eyes and the love that follows from that faith. Martin Luther's enduring insight had been that it is beyond the capacity of human beings to achieve the righteousness that they know they ought to achieve, but that this righteousness was achieved by Christ and that, as God planned it, those who trust in Christ having nothing more to worry about on that score. This is not to say that those who look to Christ for forgiveness of their sins are not obliged to obey Christ's commandments. Luther had put it succinctly: "Faith alone justifies; but faith never occurs alone." Arndt understood the issue and was in agreement with the official theology. But, as modern scholars agree, Arndt's emphasis fell in a different place, so that no matter what assurances he tried to give, he was taken to be in the wrong. In effect what he says is that, though you need forgiveness above all else and though forgiveness is free, the only way you can be sure that you are forgiven is to love much. That was exactly the qualification that drove the young Luther to distraction.

The other main set of objections that Arndt felt obliged to meet arose from the prominence that he gave to the believer's experience of union with God. Not many Christians had experienced any sense of union, whereas many were convinced that union with God, although perfectly real, is not the kind of thing that can be experienced. For these, the mystical union is a fact in the spiritual world. It was accomplished through the mystery of the incarnation and through the incorporation of believers into the mystery of the Church. The mystics seemed to be talking about something different. In the fifth book of *True Christianity*, Arndt deals at length with the ways in which one can be said to be in union with God—the presence in each person of God's image is one way, everyone's possession of God's covenant-word another, and so forth. Particularly he elaborates the poetic image of the Song of Solomon, which Lutherans generally understood to be an allegory of Christ's marriage to the Church. (Arndt takes it as the marriage of Christ and the individual believer.) In any case, what was precious to Arndt and to his followers was no longer merely the belief that Christ is like a husband to his Church but, rather, the emotions accompanying the belief. More and more what we call religious experience became the center of Christian life and practice. "The souls of those who fear God cannot be satisfied unless they have God himself ... If we are to experience only a small beginning of this blessedness in this life, our union with the highest Good is a good indication of it. Spiritual joy and the taste of divine sweetness are witnesses to it ... Therefore, dear soul, prepare yourself, that your heart may be God's dwelling place. Unite yourself with God in this life ... He who is united with God through true conversion in this mortal life before the soul leaves [the body] will remain united with God in the immortal life in all eternity."

Jean H. Faurot

RECOMMENDED READING

Edition used: Arndt, Johann. *True Christianity.* Translation and Introduction by Peter Erb. New York: Paulist Press, 1979. An abridgment, with selections from all six books. The Introduction and Notes are concerned with Arndt's debt to his predecessors.

Heick, Otto W. *A History of Christian Thought.* 2 vols. Vol. 1, p. 471. Philadelphia: Fortress Press, 1965. A Lutheran work.

INTRODUCTION TO THE DEVOUT LIFE *AND* ON THE LOVE OF GOD

Author: Saint Francis de Sales (1567–1622)
Upon returning to his native France after studying in Italy, in law and theology, Francis rejected a promising career in service to his state in order to become a priest. In response to the Protestant Reformation, he worked to win back Calvinists to Catholicism in Chablais when it was regained by the duke of Savoy. Some 72,000 converts are ascribed to Francis's efforts, which were made at serious personal risk. In 1599 he was ordered to accept the appointment as bishop to Geneva. He died in Lyons and was declared a saint in 1665 by Pope Alexander VII.

Type and subject of work: Instruction, primarily for non-clergy, on attaining spiritual perfection

First published: *Introduction to the Devout Life*, 1609, *On the Love of God*, 1616

MAJOR THEMES

Union with God can be attained by all.
Prayer and the sacraments along with subordination of the will and obedience are important elements in seeking perfection.

Love of God is the key virtue.
There are practical steps for achieving spiritual growth.

In his preface to *Introduction to the Devout Life* the author says that what follows in the book is nothing that predecessors have not said before him. His bouquet differs from their flowers, however, because his arrangement is different. Most earlier writers, Francis notes, addressed their work to persons who had withdrawn from the world, whereas the intention now is to present these words of instruction to "those who live in towns, in families or at court." He tells of the plan of his book, which is in five parts: first, to convert Philothea (his presumed reader) from her simple desire to solid resolution, which he hopes to do through his emphasis on the sacraments and prayer (in the second section); the third section contains a discussion of the several virtues most necessary to spiritual advancement; the next part attempts to expose to her some of the snares by which her enemies might trip her up; and in the last segment she is shown how to regain her strength through refreshing herself by retiring a little, examining herself, and reflecting on Jesus, the saints, and other spiritual topics.

Francis begins the body of this work by observing that devout souls ascend to God more promptly than those whose efforts are on their deeds alone. Devotion is not meant exclusively for the monks and clergy but is compatible with every calling in life. He then tells of the importance of a guide to conduct one through the rigors of the search for God and the need for obedience to that teacher. The initial need is for the purification of one's soul, and particularly from mortal sin. A good confessor is important here, he stresses. Then should come the renunciation of the attraction to sinful things.

Next come meditations that are suggested by the writer to be used in purifying one's soul. There are ten of these (each is about two pages long): First we are to consider our own, individual creation, "from when you were not yet in the world" and the great gift that each life is; second, we are to reflect on the purpose for which we were created, with gratitude for the opportunity to love and serve God; God's benefits are the subject of the next meditation—things like gifts of the mind, healthy bodies, spiritual graces; reflections on sin follow, and the fifth meditation is on death (here Francis suggests that Philothea consider her life from the perspective of her deathbed); personal judgment and hell are the sixth and seventh meditations, with one on Paradise succeeding those; the ninth is titled "By Way of Election and Choice of Paradise"; and the final is on the choice that a soul makes concerning the devout life. These brief reflections are followed by advice on how to make a good confession; then there is the admonition to purify ourselves from the attraction to venial sins and all evil inclinations.

Part two of this volume contains various instructions as to how the soul can be elevated to God by the practice of prayer and the experience of the sacraments. Mental prayer, particularly that centered on the Passion of Jesus, is the most efficacious, Francis advises. He also recommends some of the traditional prayers of the Church, including the Our Father, Hail Mary, *Credo*, the rosary, litanies, and so forth.

The writer urges several steps of preparation for meditation. These include putting oneself consciously in the presence of God, invoking his assistance reverently, and focusing intently on the entire mystery that one has chosen as the subject of this particular meditation. He cautions that after the period of meditation there is a need for appropriate transition to return to workaday activities. He also cautions the person who prays not to be discouraged if a certain dryness is experienced during meditation. The important point is to persevere nevertheless. This is followed with advice on morning meditation, the evening exercise plus examination of conscience, how to use shorter prayers (aspirations, ejaculations), how one ought to attend mass, the need to honor and invoke saints and angels, and on the reception of holy communion.

The longest section of this book is part three, which contains instructions concerning the practice of virtues. Francis suggests that the exercise of one particular virtue, when not practiced at the expense of others, will help to properly order the spirit. When a vice tempts us, we must learn to embrace its opposite virtue; he writes of the need of all for the virtue of patience, even in the light of false personal attack. The value of humility is then shown as "the true sun of all other virtues; and meekness is discussed—meekness toward both our neighbors and ourselves. Chastity is presented as a virtue that makes people almost equal to angels. Poverty of spirit, even among riches, is to be strived for, and he counsels how to practice real poverty even if one is wealthy. Then he urges the practice real poverty even if one is wealthy. Then he urges the practice of the richness of spirit even in the midst of true economic poverty.

A warning follows: While love holds first place among the soul's passions, friendship is the most dangerous love of all and one must scrutinize the basis of each friendship. A distinction is made between foolish friendship and that which is true, and he especially has reference to relationships between people of different sexes. The spiritual value of solitude receives attention and there is a chapter on "Of Decency in Attire." Modesty in word, respect for others, and the temptation to slander people are discussed, as is the need for caution in recreation and games (dice and cards, for example, are dangerous, as is dancing).

Instructions for the married are included in this portion of the work, matrimony being "the nursery of Christianity." Love in wedlock is to be more than the human love that heathens accorded their spouses; the relationship of the married is to be that of Christ to his Church. Advice to widows and virgins closes out part three.

The fourth part of Saint Francis's volume is where he counsels against the most frequent temptations. People should learn to disregard the censures of worldly persons, he insists, since theirs is but empty babbling. Courage is presented as a requisite for the devout life. He also talks of the nature of temptations and consoles his reader with the assurance that feeling tempted is no sin but the evil results only from the consenting to temptation. It is important, he reminds Philothea, that she not put herself knowingly in a situation that could become sinful: That in itself puts one in the state of sin. The best remedy against sin is to open your heart to your spiritual director and communicate your problems to that person. With the exception of sin, anxiety is the greatest evil that can befall the soul; thus it is of great import to find peace of soul. Sadness, too, should find relief in prayer. Difficulties will arise—they have come to the greatest of God's servants—so no one should be surprised if they too have to suffer some of them.

Exercises and instructions designed to renew the soul and confirm her in devotion make up the fifth and final portion of this classic. It is the shortest segment of the volume. A devout person should annually renew her good resolutions. Just as clocks (in his time) have to be wound up, so does one's spirit. He tells of ways to examine the soul on its advancement and he offers ten questions to assist in the examination of one's soul, questions concerning one's state of sin, attitude toward Jesus, how one speaks to God, regards the saints, and honors God through one's work. How one is in relation to one's neighbor is also to be questioned. The way toward perfection is not easy, but it is clearly the most important way.

Published seven years after his *Introduction to the Devout Life*, Saint Francis's two-volume *Treatise on the Love of God* has proven a popular work as well. It is divided into twelve books with the first four, broadly speaking, providing the fundamentals of his approach to loving God and the other eight books containing an application of that approach. We read in the preface that this book is addressed to those who are advanced in devotion.

Book one is a preparation for what is to follow. God has given the will dominion over all of the soul's other faculties and the sensual appetite. But love rules all of the affections and passions, and also the will. God's love dominates all other loves and true love aspires to spiritual union. Francis shows that charity is most certainly a form of love. We each have a natural inclination to love God although we do not have the power in ourselves to love God above all else. Still, he remarks, our natural tendency toward God is not useless.

Something of God's nature and how he loves us is found in book two. God exercises supernatural power over his rational creatures and he distributes diverse graces to human beings. God wants us to love him and when we fail to do so that reflects on us, not on God's goodness. We are free to accept or reject God's inspirations.

The third book is titled "On the Progress and Perfection of Love," and develops the idea that while eternal union with God cannot be achieved in this life, a desire for such union is necessary if it is to be gained in the hereafter.

In book four we read of the possibilities for failure in our love for God, the danger always being with us for as long as we are alive because we can lose sanctifying grace through our actions.

The second part of this work begins with the fifth book, which deals with complacence and benevolence, the two chief exercises of sacred love. God himself "plants the loving complacence that we have in his goodness and on which we feed ourselves," Francis writes, adding later that benevolence is exercised in the supreme praise of God. The sixth book is on the exercise of love in prayer. The author devotes his thoughts to mystical theology (identical with prayer), meditation (the first degree of prayer), and the distinction between meditation (attentive, repeated thought) and contemplation (unmixed permanent attention with unified view, made without effort). He then concentrates on the love of God in prayer.

The soul's union with God, perfected in prayer, is the focus of book seven. Love as the life of the soul is discussed and Francis tells how some, particularly the Virgin Mary, died a sweet death due to divine love. In the next book he writes of how God's commandments, counsels, and inspirations help us to conform our wills to the will of God. Each of us is obligated to love, though not all in the same manner. Again, as in his other writings, he recommends the virtue of obedience to the church and its hierarchy. Book nine is titled "Concerning the Love of Submission, by Which Our Will Is United to God's Good Pleasure." This may be effected through trials, through resignation, even by a holy indifference. A will dead to itself, Francis teaches, lives purely in the will of God.

The great commandment to love God above all things is the subject of the tenth book. We need to love God's goodness more than we love ourselves, and the instructions of certain saints are shown by way of example. The penultimate book treats of the supreme authority of sacred love, which reigns over all virtues, acts, and perfections of the soul. This section ends with remarks on sadness, which is not contributive to spiritual advance. The saint asks rhetorically, "How can it help holy charity, since joy is ranked next to charity?" The final book contains counsels with regard to the soul's progress in holy love. We must have a continual desire to love, he urges, and he closes the book by teaching that Calvary, the passion and death of Jesus, embodies the true school of love.

Harry James Cargas

RECOMMENDED READING

Editions used: Francis de Sales, Saint. *Introduction to the Devout Life.* Translated by John K. Ryan. Garden City, N.Y.: Doubleday, Image Books, 1955. *On the Love of God.* Translated by John K. Ryan. 2 vols. Garden City, N.Y.: Image Books, 1963.

Bremond, Henri. *Devout Humanism.* Translated by K. L. Montgomery. London: Society for Promoting Christian Knowledge, 1928. A history of the development of devotional attitudes in France during Saint Francis's time.

Pius XI. *Rerum Omnium.* In *Encyclicals of Pope Pius XI.* By James H. Ryan. St. Louis: B. Herder, 1927. The papal letter published in 1923 marking the third century of Saint Francis's death.

THE WAY TO CHRIST

Author: Jacob Boehme (1575–1624)

In his twenty-fifth year, Jacob Boehme, a cobbler, saw in a vision the origin of all things. When the manuscript in which he tried to expound the vision (later named "The Aurora") came to the attention of the local pastor, he was forbidden by the civil authority to write anything more. This was 1612. Although he complied, he became the center of a growing circle of admirers, kept up a wide correspondence, and was active in a secret brotherhood. Except for village schooling he was self-taught; but among his friends were persons of quality who lent him books and introduced him to theosophical and alchemical writings. About 1619 he resumed writing and allowed his manuscripts to circulate. *The Way to Christ*, comprising three short devotional pieces, is the only one of his manuscripts that was published during his lifetime. Written in 1622, it shows him turning back from theosophical speculation to the tradition of German mysticism represented by the *Sermons* of Johann Tauler and by the *Theologia Germanica*. While Boehme intended no break with official Lutheranism it is clear that his affinities lay elsewhere; and it comes as no surprise that English Behmenists allied themselves with the Quaker movement. Boehme's best-known work is a spiritual commentary on the book of Genesis titled *Mysterium Magnum*.

Type and subject of work: Tracts on the mystical way

First published: 1624

MAJOR THEMES

True repentance is a lifelong struggle between the good and the evil forces in human beings.

In true resignation, egocentric knowing and willing is replaced by God's love.

Only as Christ restores to a soul the divine vitality lost to humankind in Adam's fall can this renewal take place.

Heaven and hell are not places that human beings enter after death but present states of their souls.

Jacob Boehme's *The Way to Christ* originally consisted of three tracts: "Of True Repentance," "Of True Resignation," and "Of Regeneration." In subsequent editions, from three to five additional tracts written during the same period were always included. The period was one of revivalist intensity: Boehme himself had experienced a new illumination and had assumed the role of a lay evangelist. The three tracts that made up the original collection were clearly intended for the newly converted. The same might be said of the "Dialogue Between an Enlightened and an Unenlightened Soul" (1624). "The Supersensual Life" (1622), on the other hand, was addressed to the mature disciple.

"Of True Repentance," as the author wrote to a friend, was the outgrowth of a new conversion that Boehme himself had lately experienced. "As this tract will lead you to the *Praxis,* you will experience its good since it was born through the fire of an anguishable twig, and it was and still is my own process through which I have attained the Pearl of divine knowledge." It is an awkward composition. Addressing persons who feel an inclination to repent but were unable to act, he begins by recounting reasons for repenting and follows these with various considerations that ought to lead one to take the needed steps, among them the enormity of the Fall. Consider, he says, "the noble image in which God fashioned [human beings] to his likeness." (Boehme is thinking not so much of Adam as of the Heavenly Man, rival of Lucifer, described in the *Cabala.*) Then consider what the human being has become instead, "a formless grub, like a hellish worm or abominable animal, an enemy to God, to heaven, and to all holy angels and men; and that his intercourse is—and forever shall be—with devils and hellish worms in gruesome darkness." Boehme intersperses persuasion with prayer and through the whole he weaves an allegory of the soul engaged in knightly combat, hoping to receive a crown from the hand of the Virgin Sophia. What is the Way? Even the same as Evangelist showed Christian (though Boehme never achieves anything approaching John Bunyan's pathos): "He who does not forsake wife, children ... even his earthly life, is not worthy of me." "Gracious reader, this is no joke," Boehme warns; "Better to be judged early in youth before the Devil has bastioned his robber's castle in the soul!" And of the Sophia-tale: "Dear reader, Do not consider this an untrue myth. This is the ... sum and substance of Sacred Scriptures ... clearly presented to the eyes just as it became known to the author, for this has been his whole process."

In "Of True Resignation," the second tract, Boehme makes use of a term (*Gelassenheit*, from *lassen*, leave alone) that Tauler had helped to popularize. In more ordinary speech, what is here demanded is humility, or, as the Psalmist expressed it, "a broken and a contrite heart." The examples of Lucifer and of Archetypal Man show what happens when God grants reason to even the most promising of his creatures. Reason is the best of treasures, but "we also see that in our technically trained men, when they acquire the light of external reason as their own, nothing results but pride." Boehme translates into his own jargon Christ's parable about the unclean spirit which, returning to finding his old quarters empty and garnished, reoccupies them together with seven other spirits more foul than himself. Says Boehme: "As the creaturely will-spirit rises with the rational light into the center, that is, into selfhood, and begins self- delusion, it again departs from God's light. Now the Devil finds a gate opening up into him, and a garnished house, i.e. rational light, for habitation. Then he appropriates to himself the seven forms of the life-properties which have departed from God into selfhood. Then he becomes self-conscious and sets his desire into the inclination towards his own self and into a false imagination." In short, those who think that the light of reason is sufficient for salvation are easy game for the Devil. Instead of looking to external reason, one must descend into oneself and become dead to the world, resign oneself to Christ, and do what Christ wishes to do with his own instrument. This is the *praxis*; but Boehme is always ready with the *theoria*. The question how the creature can have any will at all, as distinct from that of its Maker, was one that Boehme was prepared to answer. There are two poles in God, as Boehme had been shown: his Love-will and his Wrath-will. These same two poles are present in every creature also. When God created Lucifer and Heavenly Man (a glorious androgynous being) he did so out of love and looked for love in response. The rest of the story is well known: The two splendid creatures got what they chose—and what they still choose even when they are aware of the error of their choice. For Lucifer there is no hope. For the human race, the only hope lies in appropriating Christ's Passion. "Any meditative scheme leading to God" is fruitless apart from a regeneration of the mind; and for that to take place, the soul must "envelop its will in Christ's death, so that the soul's mind no longer wills sin."

The third tract, "Of Regeneration or the New Birth," is concerned with the conflict that Christians experience within themselves as a result of their union with Christ. How can one be the Temple of God and at the same time a sinful mortal? To answer this question, Boehme must go back to the beginning and explain how man was created (Scripture doesn't tell all!); how he "stood in heaven as well as in the external world" (this was paradise); how the Devil overcame man through his imagination; how man originally begat offspring in the way God created heaven and earth (by fiat); how Adam slept (for the first time!), therein exchanging his angelic life for the life of a beast. Desolation followed, but also a covenant, which was fulfilled when "the divine Vitality introduced heavenly, living essence, and reawakened the distorted essence in Mary's seed and brought it to life." Much of the tract is directed against false Christians and against the "stone churches," which is not surprising in view of the slanders he endured from the pulpits. Their preaching and sacraments would be good, he says, if spiritually used. But how many there were who had attended church for decades, heard the sermons, received the sacraments, and been absolved, but remained as much beasts and children of the Devil as before! "A true Christian brings his holy church into the congregation; his heart is the true church in which one should practice the worship of God."

"A Dialogue Between an Enlightened and an Unenlightened Soul" has the makings of a morality play. Soul, in her innocence, leaves paradise in order to satisfy her curiosity about the world of creatures. The Devil offers his services and promises her all knowledge and power on condition that she break off from God and focus her desires on the serpent image. This image (which is the circle formed by the serpent biting its own tail, and also the magical fire-wheel of Mercury) ignited Soul's egocentric passions, thereby liberating Arrogance, Avarice, Envy, and Wrath—the very "foundation of Hell." So, Soul began to rule on earth in a bestial manner. Then Soul met Christ, who had come into the world to destroy the works of the Devil. When Christ offered to free Soul from her wormlike image, Soul repented and sought God's grace. But the properties of the astral spirit that the Devil had formed in her would not let her will remain with God. Meanwhile, the Devil reappeared and drew her back into worldly things. "What are you troubling yourself about? Just look how the world lives in joy! Hasn't Christ paid the ransom and satisfied for all men? All you need to do is to comfort yourself that it has happened ... Don't you ever think what will happen to you if you become so melancholy and insane? You will be everybody's fool." Soul was disconsolate. She decided to forsake the world and engage in charitable works—but to no avail. Then Troubled Soul met Enlightened Soul, who assured her that there was an ointment that would remove the serpent image and restore the paradisal image. "You yourself shall do nothing except surrender your self-centered, self-calculating will.

Then your evil qualities will weaken and begin to die, and you will sink your own will back into the One out of which you originally came." After Englightened Soul preached her a long sermon on following Christ and walking the straight way, Troubled Soul resolved to forsake her egocentric will and to surrender to Christ. Bewailing her wormlike form and the presence in her of the four passions, she embraced the death of Christ as her own and, permeated by God's love, broke into joyful prayer. "The marriage-feast of the Lamb was now celebrated, and the espousal of the noble Sophia with the Soul. The signet ring of Christ's Victory was impressed upon her essence and she was received again as a child and heir of God."

The tract is interesting mainly because in it one can overhear the arguments and discussions, admonitions and counsels, that must have engaged Boehme and his friends in their evangelical activities.

"Of the Supersensual Life: A Dialogue Between a Scholar and His Master," dated 1622, was obviously written for Boehme's more intellectual friends. "How," the disciple asks, "may I come to the supersensual life so that I can see God and hear him speak?" The master answers: "When you can leap for a moment into that where no creature dwells then you can hear what God speaks." Salvation, in this dialogue, is presented less as a matter of embracing Christ's death than of sinking oneself into the No-thing out of which everything has come and to which it will return. Human beings fell when they separated themselves from the All, emerging as ego-centered selves in the midst of a world of severed things known to them through sensible images. In this condition, they rule externally over other creatures, led by the desires of their bestial nature. If one wants to see and hear God, one must forsake the world of images and no longer desire to claim things as one's own. Then one becomes like all things—a no-thing among no-things.

There follows an example of what Boehme calls his "deep writing." The talk has turned to love, which, the master says, is a no-thing. He explains that all things have emerged from one source, the Supersensual Unconditioned (*Ungrund*). Because it is potentially all things the Source is actually no-thing. God's being and that of his creatures are things, differentiated in virtue of an order superimposed on the *Ungrund*—but only the limited degree of order that the *Ungrund* can receive. Hence, there remains in God himself and in each of his creatures a residual no-thingness. In this no-thingness love resides, but also hate; for, one member of a pair of opposites cannot exist without the other. Human beings, for example, must love the divine that is within them but must hate the I-ness that has raised itself against God. This consideration helps the master explain to the disciple why it is that though so many people seek love, so few are able to find it. "Though Love offers itself to them it can find no place within them to live, for the imaginativeness of selfish inclinations wants to own it. But Love flees, for it lives only in the no-thing, and therefore the ego-centric will cannot find it." It also helps the master answer the disciple's questions about heaven and hell. These are not places but states of men's souls. Heaven operates everywhere, for it is "nothing more than a manifestation of the Eternal One wherein all works and wills in love." Hell is its countèrpart: It is active everywhere God and love are excluded. "What then is an angel," asks the disciple, "and what is man's soul, that they become manifest in God's love or in his wrath?" The master's explanation is that they are projections of God's knowledge into objects of his love. "They come out of the eternal ground from which Light and darkness arise. As darkness lies in the employment of ego-centric desire, so Light consists in a similar willing with God." As for one's body, and the visible world in general, they are external manifestations of the inner spiritual world, whether good or evil. With this in mind, the master is able to answer the disciple's questions concerning life beyond the grave, the resurrection of the body, the Last Judgment, and the eternal separation of the children of darkness from the children of light. But one last question: "Why does God allow such strife in this time?" There must be strife for life to exist and for wisdom to become manifest and for joy to triumph. "For this the Eternal One assumed sensibility and divisibility, and by sensibility brought itself forth again through death into the mighty Kingdom of Joy, so that there might be an eternal play in the endless unity."

Thus the master spoke, and each interpreted him as each was able.

Jean H. Faurot

RECOMMENDED READING

Edition used: Boehme, Jacob. *The Way to Christ.* Translated by John Joseph Stoudt. Forward by Rufus M. Jones. London: John M. Watkins, 1953. Includes seven tracts, and a helpful introduction by the translator.

———. *Six Theosophic Points and Other Writings.* Introductory essay, "Ungrund and Freedom," by Nicolas Berdyaev. Ann Arbor: University of Michigan Press, 1958. Most convenient introduction to Boehme's general philosophical position.

Jones, Rufus M. *Spiritual Reformers in the 16th and 17th Centuries.* London: Macmillan, 1909. Chapters 9 through 12 contain an introduction to Boehme's life and thought and to his influence in England, by a noted modern Quaker.

Stoudt, John Joseph. *Sunrise to Eternity: A Study in Jacob Boehme's Life.* Preface by Paul Tillich. Philadelphia: University of Pennsylvania Press, 1957. Traces the growth of Boehme's thought, which is seen as a new, personalist type of mysticism. Useful mainly for biographical details.

DEVOTIONS UPON EMERGENT OCCASIONS

Author: John Donne (1572–1631)

A great poet in an age of great poetry and a great preacher in an age of great preaching, Donne studied at Oxford and at Lincoln's Inn; joined the famous expedition to Cadiz (1596); aspired to preferment at court until James I pressed him into Anglican orders (1615); and was appointed dean to London's Saint Paul's (1621) where he served until his death. His meditative imagination is evident in both his religious poetry and his prose. Among his best-known works are the two *Anniversaries* (1611, 1612), the *Divine Poems* (1633), and "Death's Duel," the most celebrated of his 160 extant sermons.

Type and subject of work: Meditative literature

First published: 1624

MAJOR THEMES

Sudden illness occasions the thought of life's variableness and of the soul's imminent danger in face of the body's death.

Meditations on the misery of the human condition, on spiritual impotency and isolation, and on the mysterious ways of God confront the self with its own spiritual destiny.

Meditative insight reveals to the soul a God who multiplies aid for human spiritual assistance and above all makes us ministers in mutual assistance to one another in Christ and Christ's body, the Church.

"No man is an island." However familiar this observation, few except students of English literature would recognize it as coming from Donne's *Devotions Upon Emergent Occasions*. That may be because today Donne is remembered more for his metaphysical poetry than for his spiritual exercises, and we are more inclined to think of a rakish Jack Donne than of an earnest dean of London's Saint Paul's Cathedral and author of the *Devotions*. Nevertheless, the dean had the temperament of the poet, and his spiritual exercises exhibited the imaginative concreteness, intellectual tautness, and dramatic immediacy of his poetry. As in the poetry, puns and metaphors abound; images build on images; analogies and correspondences between the material and the spiritual world are discovered and elaborated. Even the poetry's familiar themes are evident: the transience of human existence, the illusory character of the phenomenal world, and the ubiquity of death and dissolution.

There was, however, no work with more personal immediacy for Donne than the *Devotions*. Their circumstance was a sudden sickness, thought to have been either typhus or relapsing fever, that brought him near death in the winter of 1523. Donne was then in his third year as Saint Paul's dean and in the tenth year of his ministry. Not that Donne had aspired to church or pulpit. He contemplated holy orders at first reluctantly and then principally at the urging of the king, James I. Nevertheless, the interpretation he gave to this first vocational crisis is consistent with the thoroughness with which he gave himself to the Church. "[T]hou who hadst put that desire into [the King's] heart didst also put into mine, an obedience to it." His almost exclusive occupation with sacred themes after his ordination indicates how earnest he was when in his own words he turned from "the mistress of my youth, Poesie, to the wife of mine age, Divinity." Because he believed himself called to God's service, the serious illness of his fifty-first year had a vocational as well as a personal significance for the author. "Why callest thou me from my calling?" "In the door of the grave, this sickbed, no Man shall hear me praise thee." The author's "calling" to the Church intermingles with thoughts about the soul's vocation and final destiny.

So vividly presented are the successive stages of the sickness that one is tempted to take the contemporary biographer Issak Walton at his word, that the *Devotions* were composed on the sickbed. The probability is that they were written during Donne's convalescence. The work consisted of a dedication to Prince Charles, later king; the Latin *Stationes* or table of contents in the shape of a poem; and the text proper, containing twenty-three devotions, which are further divided into Meditations, Expostulations, and Prayers. The Meditations open each devotion with a report on the sickness or with a reflection on the human condition; the Expostulations anatomize the soul's spiritual condition; and the Prayers express the soul's willing conformity to God's proceedings. Collectively, the devotions chart the disease and its treatment over the twenty-three days of sickness, beginning with the first evident alteration in the patient's condition. Almost as if making diary entries, Donne details each day. The patient takes to his bed; the physician is called. Other physicians are brought in for consultation, and these are joined by the king's own physician. The disease worsens imperceptibly; a cordial is administered for the heart, and pigeons are applied to the feet to draw off humors from the head. Spots appear and the crisis deepens. Tolling bells of a nearby church signal the death of a neighbor. The physicians detect hopeful signs, and at last the patient rises from bed, as Lazarus from the grave, but with warning of the danger of relapsing.

The Meditations thus detail the patient's physical state or his treatment; they take the body as a type or figure for the self and the human condition, and they usually reflect not directly on religious themes but on secular ones. The third meditation, for example, focuses on the patient taking to his bed, on the likeness of the grave to the sickbed, and on the contrariness between the prone position of the sick and the natural upright position to which God created us. The Renaissance commonplace that "man is a little world" is the motif for the fourth meditation. How much greater than nature are human beings, whose thoughts reach around the globe and from earth to heaven, and how strange it is that they have need of physicians, when even wild creatures are physicians to themselves. At every point, we are confronted by our paradoxical nature, at once a wonder of the world and a fickle, variable thing, prone to sudden alteration, dissolution, decay, and decomposition. "Let [the self] be a world," we read in the eighth meditation, "and him self be the land, and misery the sea." The waters of the sea swell above the hills, whelming kings and commoners alike, for all are dust, "coagulated and kneaded into earth, by tears."

The Meditations take measure of the human condition: "Variable, and therefore miserable condition of man!" And, throughout, the human condition is discovered in the condition of the human body, the principal analogue for the meditator's larger text, God's Second Book, the historical world of time and space. The Expostulations repeat the themes or the motifs of the Meditations for, in Donne's words, "the body dost effigiate my soul to me." The Expostulations, however, are more passionate, more urgent than the Meditations. In the Expostulations, for example, the meditator exegetes Scripture and anatomizes the spirit's health: The soul hangs in the balance. Thus, nature's inconstancy is the theme of a meditation arising from the sudden weakening of the body's faculties with the first approach of the sickness; the expostulation turns on the soul's vulnerability. His prostrate body occasions a meditation on human dignity; the expostulation focuses on spiritual impotency. The prospect of universal ruin accompanies the "insensible" or imperceptible progress of the disease; the expostulation wrestles with Eve's temptation and Adam's sin, with the serpent within the human heart and the lie that conceals the heart's guilt.

The devotions progress from a general meditation in the first section to the soul's concrete expostulation of God in the second, from thoughts on the condition of humankind to the private afflictions of the individual soul, from contemplation of the world of humanity to an anxiety about the state of the spirit. A resultant energy and passionate intensity characterize Donne's exegesis of God's Third Book, the Bible, in the middle section of each devotion, and this level of intensity sets these spiritual exercises apart from most traditional meditations. Rather than spiritual colloquies, the soul's conversations with God, the Expostulations take the form (as the Latin of "expostulation" indicates) of urgent demands or passionate interrogations. The biblical text is interrogated for answers to the exegete's own bewilderment in face of the text's ambiguities or the soul's doubts and uncertainties. In the sixth devotion, for example, the patient marks the apprehension in his physician and the mounting fear in himself. In the expostulation he searches Scripture to resolve his mind that fear need not be evidence of despair. He reads in Scripture that "fear is a stifling spirit," and asks: "Shall a fear of thee take away my devotion to thee?" He discovers also that fear of the Lord is the beginning of wisdom and that a holy fear is an antidote against "inordinate fear." From start to finish, the exegete scrutinizes biblical texts and presses God for a clarification of his meaning ("Dost thou command me to speak to thee, and command me to fear thee?"), pressing the demand at times very near complaint, "too near murmuring." In the end, the questions are answered, the ambiguities and doubts are resolved, and the Expostulations attain a kind of equilibrium in what amounts to an intellectual assurance, propaedeutic to the affective or emotional acceptance of the Prayers, which conclude each devotion.

Taken separately the Expostulations move from ambiguity and doubt to clarity and assurance. Collectively, they chart the soul's conversion from a self-preoccupation and a "care" for its own preservation to a concern for the neighbor, from anxiety and fear to patience and assurance. And by the sixth devotion, absorption with sin, God's anger, spiritual impotency, and isolation have been somewhat mollified intellectually—if not affectively—by an acceptance of a wholesome fear of the Lord. In the seventh devotion we hear also of the "multiplication" of divine assistances and of Donne's profound dependency on the Church and its sacraments. We become aware too that the spiritual exercises, while they are intensely personal, are not private. The Church is never far from the meditator's mind nor are the sacraments—confession, baptism, Eucharist—ever without a place in his devotion. Even confinement to the sickbed in the second devotion causes Donne anxious concern for his soul's safety. "It is not a recusancy," protesting his absence from church, "for I would come [to thy holy temple], but an excommunication, I must not come." Thus, when the seventh devotion notes the consultation of his physicians, the meditator's mind turns to God's manner of proceeding with the soul afflicted with spiritual disease. "Thy way from the beginning," he announces, "is multiplication of thy helps." Helps multiply for the assistance of human weakness, but not as schismatics multiply. God's health-giving Word is not to be sought among "comers or conventicles or schismatical singularies but from the association and communion of thy Catholic church." Divine assistance is multiple, though the Church principally administers that assistance in the form of the divine Word and sacraments. Donne's own personal Easter—"my quickening in this world, and my immortal establishing in the next"—is in fact associated with the reappropriation and interiorization of the Church's sacramental life during the course of the spiritual exercises. Though confined to a sickbed, he experiences anew the sacraments that chasten, quicken, and communicate Christ's mystical body to the diseased soul.

Donne's universalism is also the expression of this Catholic view of the Church. At the *Devotions'* spiritual center, in devotion seventeen, the meditator hears the bells of a nearby church, tolling the passing of one who, perhaps like Donne, had fallen victim of the fever that swept through London. Earlier, in the seventh devotion, preoccupation with the self had been temporarily interrupted with thought for the need of others more destitute and with great reason to complain of aloneness, and the meditator interrogates himself: "Is not my Meditation rather to be inclined another way, to condole, and communicate their distress, who have none [to aid them]?" Now the enlarging of this meditation in the seventeenth devotion comes about when thoughts of the neighbor, audibly present to the meditator in the bells, are joined with thoughts of the universal fellowship of Christians in the mystical body of Christ. The Church, he says, is universal; "so are all her actions; all that she does belongs to all." The baptism of a child—"That action concerns me; for that child is thereby connected to that body which is my head too." The burial of a man—"That action concerns me." All of humankind is of "one author, and is one volume" and in the last day God will "bind up all our scattered leaves again for that library where every book shall lie open to one another." And, as if by anticipation of that eschatological age, where "every book shall be open to one another," we are given Donne's consummate expression of universalism and Christian charity: "No man is an island, entire of itself; every man is a piece of the continent, a part of the main. If a clod be washed away by the sea, Europe is the less, as well as if a promontory were, as well as if a manor of thy friend's or of thine own were: any man's death diminishes me, because I am involved in mankind, and therefore never send to know for whom the bell tolls; it tolls for thee." Here is no gloomy obsession with death but rather confirmation that even in seeming isolation, the isolation of a sick man's closet, God has us speak to and serve one another.

After the Meditations and the Expostulations, where the emotional experience of the devotions is sustained by taut historical description, argument, and exegesis, the Prayers give us the measured assurance of one who is planted firmly in the Church. Beginning with an invocation to the eternal and gracious God, the Prayers call to mind God's mercy and eternal ways and make petition for the soul's needs. Above all, the meditator asks for a will obedient to God's directives and for the soul's conformity to Christ's example. And in the seventeenth prayer the meditator, having given thanks for divine instruction mediated through "this sad and funeral bell," makes priestly intercession for the one, "the voice of whose bell hath called me to this devotion." The meditator's prayers, in short, revolve on God's mercy and God's power to communicate grace to the members of his Church, and by stages the meditator arrives at an ever-deepening conviction that his sickness is a "correction" and a preparation of his spirit, that it might be "conformed to thy will."

In conforming the soul to the pattern of Christ's affliction, Donne does not promise a spirituality of safe harbor. Yet, though the waters of destruction mount, the Church, a type of the Ark, is envisioned as a refuge when the flood grows "too deep for us." Like Noah, members of Christ's mystical body have God's Word and the divine sacraments, rising above the Flood's destruction, and in a personal confession of gratitude the meditator says "to the top of these hills, thou hast brought me." Still the rigor of the spiritual exercise does not dissipate with the prospect of recovery. And in the last devotion Donne asks for assistance against presumptuous security, mindful that, as his physicians counsel watchfulness against the fever's recurrence, so strict vigilance is also wise counsel against a future lapsing of the spirit from grace.

Thomas E. Helm

RECOMMENDED READING

Edition used: Donne, John. *Devotions Upon Emergent Occasions: Together with Death's Duel.* Ann Arbor: University of Michigan Press, 1959.

Mueller, Janel. Introduction to *Donne's Prebend Sermons.* Cambridge: Harvard University Press, 1971. The superb introduction treats the sermons from the period following Donne's illness, a period informed by Donne's conviction that he had been restored to health so that he could preach.

Raspa, Anthony. Introduction to *Devotions Upon Emergent Occasions*. Montreal and London: McGill-Queen's University Press, 1975. Provides an interesting review of the scholarly conjecture concerning Donne's illness and an excellent discussion of Donne and the meditative tradition.

Weber, Joan. *Contrary Music: The Prose Style of John Donne*. Madison: University of Wisconsin Press, 1963. An insightful discussion of Donne's religious prose with a concluding section on the *Devotions* and its tripartite division.

THE TEMPLE

Author: George Herbert (1593–1633)

George Herbert was born into a noble family; his elder brother was Lord Herbert. George became public orator at Cambridge University in 1620, and he was a friend of the crown prince. The death of King James in 1625 turned his attention to spiritual matters, much influenced by the godly community of Nicholas Ferrar in Little Gidding. Herbert relinquished his worldly opportunities, and for the last three years of his life he pastored a small church at Bremerton, near Salisbury. His famous account of a pastoral model, *A Priest to the Temple: or the Country Parson*, was published posthumously in 1652. *The Temple*, a volume of his lyrical poems, embodies expressions of his personal struggles of faith and was used as a device of pastoral teaching.

Type and subject of work: Spiritual poetry

First published: 1633, with a preface by his friend, Nicholas Ferrar

MAJOR THEMES

The role of a pastor is to act as Christ's deputy, to reduce human arrogance, and to guide the individual believer to God.

Praying is more important than preaching.

The spiritual needs of human souls can be satisfied only through the exercise of the Christian virtues.

The contradictions and inconsistencies of life are resolved by a faith that leads one to God.

Just as the *Book of Common Prayer* sets the frame for the corporate devotion and worship of Anglicanism, so Herbert collects his poems of a lifetime into an architectural setting with its "porch," "supreliminary" (a passageway into the main sanctuary), and the church "proper," with its "altar" providing the focus for worship. As Herbert cites from Psalm 29:9, "in His Temple, does every man speak of His Honor," so the life of the Christian is subsumed within a corporate sharing in the faith, fellowship, and ordinances of the Church.

Seeing the need of unity in all of one's life before God, Herbert identifies, in the first section of his poems, the individual's need of right conduct before God. In the second section Herbert seeks to deepen the Christian's life by reviewing the spiritual virtues. In the third section, possibly composed before the poet's scheme for *The Temple* has been formulated, Herbert traces the history of the "Church Militant." Thus the book has a threefold structure in considering the significance of the symbols of the church architecture, the virtues of the Christian life, and the events of the Church's history.

The simplicity of Herbert's poems is deceptive, as each of the 162 poems has very varied patterns of line and rhyme. Self- reflection and scriptural meditation are inextricably bound together for the poet, for as Jesus told the tempter, "Man shall not live by bread alone, but by every word that proceeds from the mouth of God" (Matt. 4:4). Accordingly, Herbert offers a number of explicitly biblical poems that meditate on some verse or thought of the Bible, and frequently in *The Temple* God's words— "Thy words"—become the poet's—"my words"—to guide human beings beyond their own, blind, inadequate resources, to know the will of *God*.

Like Solomon, Herbert prefaces his collection with a prayer of dedication: "Lord, my first fruits present themselves to Thee;/Yet not mine neither: for from Thee they came." His first poem in the opening section, "The Church Porch," is entitled "Perirrhanterium," the Greek term for the instrument used for sprinkling holy water, to suggest that the poem is a preparatory ritual of cleansing before entering "the Church" section of *The Temple*. For remember "when once thy foot enters the Church, be bare/God is more there, than thou; for thou are there/only by His permission." Likewise, contrary to the Puritan tradition that makes so much of the sermon, "resort to sermons, but to prayers most:/praying is the end of preaching"!

In "the Church," we enter the major collection of the poems. Appropriately, we begin with "the Altar," "made of a heart and cemented with tears" of the supplicant. "The Sacrifice" then follows, the focus of worship being on Christ, whose refrain is repeated in sixty-four verses, "was ever grief like Mine?" The conclusion is, "never was grief like Mine." "Thanksgiving" then spells out the spirit of gratitude in the worshiper.

Other lenten themes follow through to "The Passion" of Good Friday, and the Resurrection of Easter. "Baptism," "Sin," and "Repentance" follow.

Major elements of the life of the Christian then are delineated: "Faith," "Prayer," "Holy Communion," "Love," "The Tempter," "The Holy Scriptures," "Grace," and "Affliction." It is as if the Lord himself teaches us between his risen appearance at Easter and his ascension at Pentecost. After this seasonal rhythm of devotional training, there follows the daily rhythm of worship in "Matins," and "Evensong," and the habitual problems of "Sin." "Church Monuments," "Church Music," "Church Lock and Key," "Church Floor," and "The Windows" all add their contribution to the maturing character of the Christian, so that "doctrine and life" combine and anneal as one faith in the Lord.

There follows the need to cultivate the virtues of the Christian life: "Contentment," "Humility," "Frailty," "Constancy," the serenity of "The Star," the restful composure of "Sunday," the depression of "Avarice," and the exercise of self-"Denial." Further recitations bring us to "Christmas," and once more to "Lent." Biblical poems follow, such as "Colossians 3:3," "The Pearl" (Matt. 13:45), "The Quip" (Ps. 38:15), "Love Unknown" (Ps. 51), "Ephesians 4:30," "Praise II" (Ps. 116), "Self-Condemnation" (Luke 23:18–19), "Mary Magdalene" (Luke 7:37–38), "The Odor, 2 Corinthians 2:15–16," and "The Rose" (Song of Songs 2:1). However, the range of emotional and spiritual experiences and needs that Herbert articulates is impossible to do full justice to in such a summary. He concludes with "Love (III)," "Love bade me welcome: yet my soul drew back,/guilty of dust and sin," a poem that Simone Weil thought was the most beautiful in the English language. At the end of the Anglican service of Holy Communion the *Gloria in excelsis* is sung, and with these words, "Glory be to God on high, and on earth/peace, good will towards men," Herbert concludes "The Church."

The third section, "The Church Militant," celebrates the presence of God's provident deeds in history, commencing with the Patriarchs and Old Testament times. Then it proceeds to trace the impact of Christianity on the classical world, the Reformation, to the present time. The collection closes with the words: "Blessed be God alone,/Thrice blessed Three in One."

In the collection of poems, Herbert is doing many things. At one level he is autobiographical, expressing his personal realization of what it means to be a priest in God's house. Sometimes, as in "The Quip," the poet is defenseless before his assailants, with only the repeated reply on his lips, "But Thou shalt answer, Lord, for me." In "The Sign," the poet knows the depth to which he must yield himself to God. As a pastor, he reminds himself, "Christ purg'd His temple; so must thou thy heart." Indeed, "look to thy actions well:/for churches are either our heav'n or hell."

At another level, Herbert represents the claims and value of the visible church. In "The Invitation," all are invited to share in the communion "Supper," to a feast which is God himself. For "where is All, there All should be." In the "Church Militant," having described the corruption of past false institutions, Herbert anticipates "then shall Religion to America flee:/They have their times of Gospel, ev'n as we." But he believes it will be accepted by dint of their poverty,"for gold and grace did never yet agree:/Religion always sides with poverty."

At a third level, Herbert senses the contradictions of life, of nature and grace, of continuity and renewal, of humankind's natural existence and God's purposes. In day-to-day living, balance and theological resolution are needed, in the experience of faith by tension. In "Vanitie," he sees the immediate presence of eternal life within a fleeting world of death. In "The Tempter (II)" he suffers the inconsistencies of life. In "The Glimpse" he lives with spiritual desertion. But tension is resolved when I can see "My life is hid in Him that is my treasure." So Herbert sees theology in practice, as a daily challenge. For as "The Forerunners" reiterates, "Thou art still my God." The mystery of God's presence is life's resolution.

James M. Houston

RECOMMENDED READING

Edition used: Hutchinson, F. E., ed. *The Works of George Herbert.* Oxford: Clarendon Press, 1941. This is the standard text.

Summers, Claude T., and Ted-Larry Pebworth. *"Too Rich to Clothe the Sunne": Essays on George Herbert.* Pittsburgh: University of Pittsburgh Press, 1980. Sympathetic essays on Herbert's Christian faith in his poems.

Thekla, Sister. *George Herbert, Idea and Image: A Study of "The Temple."* Normanby, Yorks, England: Greek Orthodox Monastery, 1974. This is a Christian appreciation of *The Temple*, in contrast to many fine scholarly works on George Herbert that do not have this theological perspective.

Wall, John N., ed. *George Herbert, The Country Parson, The Temple.* New York: Paulist Press, 1981. Has useful introduction.

RELIGIO MEDICI

Author: Sir Thomas Browne (1605–1682)
Born into an upper-middle-class London family, Thomas Browne attended Westminster school and received his arts degrees from Oxford. Choosing medicine as a career, he studied at universities in Montpellier, Padua, and Leyden, from the last of which he received his doctorate in medicine. In due time he settled into a medical practice at Norwich. Pacific in disposition and a confirmed royalist throughout the Civil War, he was knighted when Charles II visited Norwich in 1671. *Religio Medici* came into being about 1635, intended only for the author's "private exercise and satisfaction"; and, although manuscript copies circulated freely, Browne did not see fit to authorize its publication until after pirated editions had appeared.

Type and subject of work: Musings on humanity's place in creation

First published: 1642–1643

MAJOR THEMES

Man is the true "amphibium" because he joins the visible and the invisible worlds.

Although God is unknowable, his eternity and his wisdom are evident in nature and in history.

Human existence would be intolerable if we did not know that we shall die.

What happens to the soul at death each person determines for oneself.

A title may be more illuminating than the book, though this is hardly true of *Religio Medici*, "The Religion of a Physician." It happens that the author was a physician; but so far as the book is concerned he might as well have been a poet or a prime minister. What matters is that he was a layman of some culture and great genius, who approached religion from a fresh point of view. Being outside the pastoral office he did not have constantly to weigh his expressions; and, having no standing with professional theologians, he did not have to cover the whole subject. Browne writes only about what happens to excite him. He says, for example, that there is no salvation for those who do not believe in Christ, but he puts forward no theory of the atonement of the sacraments, because what interests him at the moment of writing is the fate of Socrates and other noble pagans. Similarly, he dwells at length on the thesis that everything in the world is determined by God's wisdom and power, but he omits all discussion of the related problems of evil and the freedom of the will.

The book is composed of separate paragraphs (numbered sections), each about one page in length. That many of these are only remotely connected with religion supports the view that the book originated as a kind of writer's diary. Browne's discussions of demons, magic, and witchcraft sound as if they were written when the budding author had just returned from the tavern and wanted to record the best parts of his conversation. His treatment of biblical puzzles is on about the same level: For example, will the famous rib go to Adam or to Eve at the resurrection of the dead? Browne makes several attempts at versification; and there are thoughtful essays on subjects such as almsgiving. Nothing indicates the order in which the paragraphs were written, for when he decided to make them into a book he arranged them roughly according to content, putting first those that deal with the world at large and toward the end those that deal with humanity and its salvation. In addition, he wrote several new paragraphs, which he put at the beginning to serve as a kind of apologia: People might not think of him as a religious man, he says, because his profession speaks against it and because he personally lacks zeal for the sectarian disputes that characterized the age. So, he wants to make his position clear. While he supports the Reformation he sees no need for scurrility between the opposing parties. "We have reformed from them," he says, "not against them." When in Catholic countries, he is not averse from worshipping in local churches, being a natural lover of ceremony, though an enemy of superstition. In all, the moderation of the Church of England squares with his conscience, and, as for questions of doctrine and polity, he has a ready formula: "Where the Scripture is silent, the Church is my text: where that speaks, 'tis but my comment; where there is a joint silence of both, I borrow not the rules of my religion from Rome or Geneva, but the dictates of my own reason."

Browne's philosophy is not antagonistic to religion. As he views it, the world is a hierarchy, with human beings occupying an interesting position as the lowest of the spirits and the highest of the brutes. Much of Browne's piety arises from his consciousness of being a microcosm, a part of "the great and true Amphibium" that joins the two worlds. "The world," he says, "was made to be inhabited by beasts, but studied and contemplated by man: 'tis the debt of our reason we owe unto God, and the homage we pay for not being beasts; without this the world is still as though it had not been, or as it was before the sixth day when as yet there was not a creature that could conceive or say there was a world." On these grounds, he counted it a privilege that, as a student of nature, he was able to "return the duty of a devout and learned admiration," unlike "those vulgar heads, that rudely stare about, and with a gross rusticity admire God's works."

"Christianity Not Mysterious" was the title of a book by the deist, John Toland (1670–1722). This is one of those titles that tells everything. Browne was the opposite of a deist. In an exuberant frame he complains that to his taste the Bible contains too few miracles. "I love to lose myself in a mystery," he writes; "to pursue my reason to an *O altitudo!* (Rom. 11:33 Vulg.). 'Tis my solitary recreation to pose my apprehension with those involved enigmas and riddles of the trinity, with incarnation, and resurrection. I can answer all the objections of Satan and my rebellious reason with that odd resolution I learned of Tertullian, *Certum est quia impossibile est.*" Browne does not discuss these great mysteries in his exercise book; but he does set down his musings on God's more manifest attributes, notably his eternity and his wisdom.

The thought of the former, he says, confounds our understanding; "for, who can speak of eternity without a solecism, or think thereof without an ecstasy?" If eternity is real, then time and everything in it are diminished. "This visible world is but a picture of the invisible, wherein as in a portrait, things are not truly, but in equivocal shapes, and as they counterfeit some more real substance in that invisible fabric." What Christ said, "Before Abraham was I am," anyone can say. Predestination poses no problem because in God there are no tenses. "The world was before the creation, and at an end before it had a beginning; and thus was I dead before I was alive; though my grave be in England, my dying place was Paradise: and Eve miscarried of me before she conceiv'd of Cain."

But though God's eternity numbs our thinking, his other "mighty attribute," wisdom, stimulates devotion. We can trace it, says Browne, in God's two-fold providence: in nature and in history.

Browne's special temperament shows itself in his respect for living things. That nature does nothing in vain is, he says, the one indisputable axiom in philosophy, which he interprets to mean that there are no gaps and no misfits in God's workmanship. By what logic, he asks, do people say that a toad or an elephant is ugly or grotesque when its outer shape is the best expression of its inward form? In every creature God's wisdom is shown forth; and, like King Solomon, Thomas Browne is happy to go to school to the bee, the spider, and the ant. Browne accepted the traditional four causes, but he held that these are secondary and that they serve only as implements in the hands of the First Cause, who uses them to achieve his goal. "In brief, all things are artificial, for nature is the art of God."

Nature Browne calls "the ordinary and open way of his providence." People can investigate it and learn its order well enough to predict the future. This is not the case with the particular providence whereby God governs the affairs of people and of nations. If God's causal power in nature resembles a straight line, that by which he directs human history is serpentine. But here no less than in nature his hand may be discerned. "Surely there are in every man's life certain rubs, doublings, and wrenches which pass a while under the effects of chance, but at the last, well examined, prove the mere hand of God." Browne does not believe in chance. God's hand determines the fall of the dice at a gaming table. That Pharaoh's daughter found the baby Moses was part of God's eternal plan. Nor was it an accident when Spain's Armada was destroyed by contrary winds. Browne admits that there is a cycle in the affairs of nations—if one is to rise another must fall—but this must not be ascribed to a fickle fortune.

Not all of Browne's thoughts are taken up with the word around him. Contrary to what we might expect in a physician, Browne is highly introspective, and he finds life on the whole quite unsatisfactory. We are surprised to hear a physician praising death as the one thing without which life would not be bearable. Longevity might appeal to us, he says, if with increased years came moral improvement; but in fact all the vices of our youth grow worse as we grow older. Browne is not burdened with a sense of guilt, being confident of God's forgiveness; still, he is dejected that so many infirmities and vices are woven into his nature. He notes especially how quickly affection is dissolved. "Let us assize the love of our parents, the affection of our wives and children, and they are all dumb shows and dreams without reality, truth, or constancy." "Certainly there is no happiness within this circle of flesh, nor is it in the optics of these eyes to behold felicity; the first day of our jubilee is death."

In other paragraphs Browne is more cheerful. Writing about his ability to get along with people, he says that there is no such thing as a bad man, if you take each man at his best. "There is no man's mind of such discordant and jarring a temper to which a tuneable disposition may not strike a harmony." Moreover, he adds, no man is alone, for as a microcosm each of us "carries the whole world about him." After a brief discussion of sexuality and female pulchritude, he takes up the subject of beauty in paintings and in music. "For there is music wherever there is a harmony, order, or proportion . . . In brief, it is a sensible fit of that Harmony which intellectually sounds in the ears of God." From harmony he turns to the world's discords, to the malignant aspects of nature, to plagues, famines, unseasonable winters. Too many in the medical profession, he admits, "secretly implore and wish for these." Not Browne, who is ashamed that his profession owes its origin to Adam's fall. But the same, he notes, is true of the other two noble professions—law and divinity; and he draws what comfort he can from the fact that as a doctor he can do more to cure stones and gout than lawyers and preachers are able to do about dishonesty and pride.

It is Browne's quiet despair, no doubt, that leads him "to look beyond the body and cast an eye upon the soul . . . wherein we all do place our last felicity." That there is "a piece of divinity" in us, that each one bears the image of God, is told us by nature as well as by the Scriptures. But we are not to have it in perfection until we slough off our flesh and enter the last world, "that proper *ubi* of spirits." When and how that shall be is the subject of several paragraphs. Browne plays at length with the notion that "our estranged and divided ashes shall unite again," citing reports of experiments in which, under chemical treatment, ashes of plants have been revived; and the belief that human forms, being independent of matter, may withdraw from the elements waiting the command of God to "call them out by their single individuals" was compatible with his understanding of nature. But Browne can hardly have attached much importance to the resurrection of the body. More characteristically he speaks of souls as passing at death to "those two contrary and incompatible places we call heaven and hell." The difficulty here is to think of disembodied spirits as occupying space. "Briefly, where the soul hath the full measure and complement of happiness, where the boundless appetite of that spirit remains completely satisfied, that it can neither desire addition nor alteration, that I think is truly heaven." Since this can be only where God manifests himself, heaven must reside within men's souls. Likewise hell, if it is "worthy to stand in diameter with heaven." "The heart of man is the place the devil dwells in." Nor does the Devil have to be there: "A distracted conscience here is a shadow or introduction to hell hereafter." We can only pity persons who, with merciful intention, destroy themselves. The Devil would destroy himself if he could, but because that is impossible his sufferings are endless.

Browne spells all this out in the language of mystical theology. God, who is all goodness, can love nothing but himself. When God created the world he did it for no other end than his own glory. Honor, being an external adjunct, is the only virtue that God is without; and if we neglect to love and praise him, we miss the end for which we were created. We are happy when we love truly, and we love truly when we rejoice that God's will is done. "That wherein God himself is happy, the holy angels are happy, in whose defect the devils are unhappy; that dare I call happiness; . . . whatsoever else the world terms happiness . . . is to me a delusion."

We could conclude on this note, as Browne meant his readers to do, having placed this paragraph at the end of his book. It is important, however, for the reader to be apprised of an earlier paragraph in which Browne comes close to despairing of any knowledge at all. What do Aristotle and Plato do but teach us that "we do but learn today what our better advanced judgments will unteach us tomorrow"? "Most wise heads at last prove skeptics and "stand like *Janus* in the field of knowledge." Accordingly, Browne says that he has one philosophy—that taught in the schools—which he uses when he has to appeal to other people's reason, and a quite different philosophy—one drawn from his own experience—whereby he tries to satisfy himself. In *Religio Medici*, it would seem, we are treated to some of each.

Browne was young and unmarried when he wrote his masterpiece. Later he was a model husband and father and in time became Norwich's most celebrated citizen, "an object of worship for young disciples and remote admirers," as Edmund Goss puts it, who goes on to describe Sir Thomas walking in the cathedral close with one or two companions listening to his conversation. "His talk was grave, perhaps continuous . . . We know that he was not facetious nor a merry companion . . . We know, too, that he had a rare genius for friendship, and it displayed itself in a warm and tender sympathy for those younger than himself."

Jean H. Faurot

RECOMMENDED READING

Edition used: Browne, Sir Thomas. *Religio Medici and Other Works.* Edited by L. C. Martin. Oxford: Clarendon Press, 1964. Critical edition with archaic spelling. I have retained the syntax but modernized spelling and punctuation. Easy-to-use commentary at end of book.

Bennett, Joan. *Sir Thomas Browne: A Man of Achievement in Literature.* Cambridge: Cambridge University Press, 1962. Chapters 3 and 4 outline and explain *Religio Medici.*

Coleridge, Samuel Taylor. *The Collected Works.* Edited by George Whalley. Vol. 12: *Marginalia I*, pp. 743–758. Princeton, N.J.: Princeton University Press, 1980. Passages from *Religio Medici*, with Coleridge's appreciative comments.

Dunn, William P. *Sir Thomas Browne: A Study in Religious Philosophy.* Minneapolis: University of Minnesota Press, 1950. Intellectual background. Of use mainly to advanced students.

Gosse, Edmund. *Sir Thomas Browne.* London: Macmillan, 1905. The life and work of Sir Thomas by a well-known literary critic. Includes interpretation of *Religio Medici.*

Roston, Murray. "The 'Doubting' Thomas." In *Approaches to Sir Thomas Browne*, pp. 69–80. Edited by C. A. Patrides. Columbia: University of Missouri Press, 1982. Argues that Browne achieved a healthy balance between the realities of this world and the mysteries of the next.

PRIVATE DEVOTIONS

Author: Lancelot Andrewes (1555–1626)

The oldest child in a large London family, Lancelot Andrewes would have been apprenticed to a craft had not one of his early teachers persuaded his parents of the boy's exceptional abilities and guided him along the way that led to a scholarship at Cambridge. Andrewes's life story is mainly a record of academic and ecclesiastical appointments. Although as a bishop and a noted preacher, he was much in the public eye, his inclinations lay in the direction of study and prayer.

Type and subject of work: Devotional manual

First published: 1648

MAJOR THEMES

Christians are favored in having a rich devotional heritage of psalms, liturgies, breviaries, and prayerbooks.

Devotional life must be ordered according to hours, weeks, and seasons.

We improve our prayers when we discriminate between kinds of prayer and keep in mind their various uses.

Prayers should embrace both the needs of individuals and the broader concerns of the Church and of humankind.

Lancelot Andrewes's *Private Devotions* (Latin: *Preces Privatae*) is fittingly titled "private." Composed in Latin, Greek, and Hebrew, the product of Andrewes's devotional fervor and his idiosyncratic habits of mind, it can hardly have been intended for the use of other people. The book did, however, appear in translation at an early date, and it has been retranslated many times, continuing to enjoy a certain popularity even today, owing to the sensitive and intelligent arrangement, translation, and annotation of the work by Canon F. E. Brightman.

Andrewes compiled the book from existing books of devotion. However, it is not in any sense a mere collection of prayers and meditations. The best way to form an idea of it is to think of a person who has prayed extemporaneously all his life, but whose prayers over the years have become saturated with biblical expressions so that they seem to be taken from a book. Such persons were common enough at one time. That, basically, is what Andrewes was doing, except that, like many bookish people, he could not think consecutively without pen and paper, and with the further exception that he was familiar with other materials besides the Holy Scriptures, such as the Book of Common Prayer, the Latin Missal, breviaries, writings of the Fathers, *mediaeval horae* (books of hours), synagogue prayerbooks, and so on. From none of these does he quote at any length, but he borrows snippets and then pastes them together to form a collage. Each page of the book is laid out as the material demands, with short lines, and long, and large areas of blank space. Andrewes favored condensation, and some pages are little more than columns of words and short phrases joined by braces. It remains a notebook. Its purpose is to serve as a reminder of the number of things the world is full of and concerning which we should be happy sometimes, other times distressed, but never indifferent, and of which we should be mindful when we turn our thoughts toward God.

Among the jottings at the beginning of the book are several outlines or "schemes of prayer," in which Andrewes enumerates the varieties of prayer, guided by the injunction of the apostle Paul: Let supplications, prayers, thanksgiving, and intercession be made. Prayer, he notes, in the first of these schemes, is either petition or thanksgiving; if petition, either for ourselves or for others; if for ourselves, either deprecation ("spare us") or precation ("grant us"). In the second scheme he divides intercession in a similar fashion: either confession or petition; if confession, either of sins or of praise. The fifth scheme is comprehensive consisting of nine heads: address, confession of sins, confession of faith, confession of benefits (praise and thanksgiving are included here), deprecation, comprecation, intercession, blessing, and commendation. Brightman has followed this scheme in preparing his edition of the *Devotions*. Perhaps the best way to get an overview of the book is to think of the first part as determined by the *times* of prayer, and the second by the *concerns* of prayer.

More than one hundred pages are given to what Brightman calls "Daily Prayers." First there is "The Dial"—eighteen stanzas marking the hours by biblical events: "Thou who for us men and for our salvation wast born at dead of night: give us daily to be born again by the renewing of the Holy Ghost, till Christ be formed in us unto a perfect man, and save us . . . Thou who at the ninth hour for us sinners and for our sins didst taste of death: mortify in us our earthly members and whatsoever is contrary to thy will, and save us . . ." "The Dial" is a finished piece of work; and so are most of the others that make up this first part. Here we find three morning prayers and three evening prayers. Typically they cover three or four of the divisions mentioned above but not all nine.

Between the morning and evening prayers is a special section of daily prayers, one for each day of the week, each divided into ten sections. Perhaps it is wrong to suggest that some of these prayers are not finished, but the fact is that they do not all read like prayers. For Andrewes's purposes it was sufficient to list objects of devotion. The Tuesday prayer, for example, under "Deprecation" simply lists: imagination, error, trespass, sin, transgression, iniquity, abomination; and under "Comprecation" lists: carefulness, clearing of self, indignation, fear, vehement desire, zeal, revenge. And so on, through the rest of the prayer. Students of Andrewes's writings point out that compression is one of the characteristics of his style, that he uses it to attract attention and achieve intensity. But that would apply more to public address than to private prayer. It is more useful to remember that private devotions do not have to conform to rules of grammar and syntax, and that a word or phrase may do as well as a sentence. If we think of the book as intended for more general use, we have to remember that it was never finished, and that individual prayers should be thought of as specimens. This, at least, is Brightman's suggestion.

The most interesting feature of the "Morning Prayers for a Week" is the use that Andrewes makes of symbols and types. Each prayer corresponds to one of the days of creation. Thus, Sunday commemorates the creation of light, the resurrection of Christ, and the sending of the Holy Spirit, while Saturday commemorates the rest from creation, the burial of Christ, cessation from sin, and the souls of the departed. Brightman has drawn up a table that makes clear at a glance the acts of penitence, of deprecation, of intercession, of thanksgiving, and so forth, for each day. But one must read the prayers to get a proper sense of the way in which Andrewes's thoughts range throughout the world of nature, the history of the race, and the stages of individual lives.

The remaining two-thirds of the book is divided according to content. A major section is concerned with prayers of penitence. A scheme of penitence, which breaks the subject into three parts—contrition, confession, and satisfaction—is followed by numerous acts of penitence, of pleading, and of confession of weakness. Some of the acts of penitence run to over twelve pages in length. The first, for example, develops the following heads: address, pleading, confession, aggravation of sin, kinds of sin, contrition, petition for mercy, pleading of the divine mercy, purpose of amendment, confession of weakness, petition for help, and comfortable words.

The language is drawn mostly from Scripture, and, taken with the marginal references, forms what Brightman calls a kind of "devotional concordance to the Bible." Some pages are lists of words that each reader must color for himself: for example, "omission, commission, of the heart, of the mouth, against God, against neighbor, against our own body, unwitting, witting, unwilling, willing, old, recent." Other pages are colored for us: "Look upon me, o Lord, look upon me with those eyes wherewith Magdalene at the feast, Peter in the hall, the robber on the rood; that with Peter I may weep, with the robber I may acknowledge, with Magdalene I may love, may love Thee much, very much, as to whom very many sins have been forgiven."

The section given over to praise, blessing, and thanksgiving might well be called "How to give thanks to God without being pharisaical." The solution, as one might surmise, is to join one's praises to those of the innumerable company of the redeemed. "Let thy works praise Thee, o God: and let thy saints give thanks unto Thee . . . I, an unworthy sinner; but would God I were devout and grateful unto Thee." Most of the devotions in this section are impersonal acts of praise. The longest of these begins with the creation of the world, lists universal characteristics of the human condition—"birth, nurture, preservation, government, education, civil estate, religion"— takes up the history of redemption from "the promise of the Seed" to "the holy incarnation"; follows the life of Jesus Christ "from the cratch to the cross" in minute detail; relives the passion, burial, resurrection, appearance, and ascension; and concludes with the acts of the Holy Spirit in the history of the New Testament Church. There is no room for Pharisaism in these prayers. But there follow four "particular thanksgivings," each of moderate length, in which Andrewes reviews his own life and circumstances. For example, "Blessed art Thou, o God, who didst create me . . . a living soul and not aught insensible, a man not a brute, a civil man not a barbarian, free and not a thrall, . . . lettered and not a mechanic, a Christian and not a paynim," and so forth. Thanksgiving begins at home and if sincere can hardly be distinguished from what, in some other connection, might be called self-congratulation. Hence, there is need for a further prayer, "Conclusion and Thanksgiving," in which Andrewes confesses amazement, asking what return such a "dead dog as I am" can render to God, and praying that God will enable him to offer the glory that is due to God's name.

Under the headings "Deprecation," "Comprecation," and "Intercession," Brightman distributes what are sometimes called bidding prayers. In "A Deprecation of the Divine Wrath," Andrewes prays first that God's "most righteous indignation" may be turned away from himself; then he continues, "Let it be turned away from my parents, brothers, sisters, my reverend lord, and my family, relations, friends, neighborhood, country, the whole Christian people. Amen." This short prayer is followed by two litanies of deprecation, punctuated by the refrain: "Destroy not; deliver us." The prayers of comprecation are mostly asking for grace, but there are prayers for plenty, for peace, for unity, for national prosperity, and for a safe journey. There is a short "Grace Before Meat," which beautifully illustrates Andrewes's method of composition, because each phrase is drawn from a different part of the Bible. "Thou that givest food to all flesh,/which feedest the young ravens that cry unto Thee;/and hast nourished us from our youth up;/fill our hearts with food and gladness/and establish our heart with thy grace." The section headed "Intercession" has at the beginning "A Scheme of General Intercession," drawn from three liturgies of the Eastern church. The prayers give a prominent place to the union of the churches, to the conversion of Jews, Turks, and paynims; but, facing in a different direction, they also remember the poor, the sick, and the brokenhearted, and mention deliverance from famine, plague, and war; nor do they omit the interests of the English Commonwealth, its king, parliament, municipalities, army, fleet, "yeoman, merchantmen, handicraftsmen, even down to sordid crafts and the beggars."

Andrewes is known to have spent up to five hours a day in his private devotions. There have been others who have specialized in wordless prayer. Andrewes was an exemplary specialist in vocal prayer, finding humankind's highest achievement in rising from habitual sloth to the full stretch of human awareness.

Jean H. Faurot

Recommended Reading

Edition used: Andrewes, Lancelot. *The Preces Privatae.* Translated and with an Introduction by F. E. Brightman. London: Metheun & Co., 1903. Republished with an essay, "Lancelot Andrewes," by T. S. Eliot, under the title *The Private Devotions of Lancelot Andrewes.* New York: Meridian Books, 1961. Valuable introduction by Brightman. Eliot's essay is often cited as having helped revive interest in Andrewes's work.

Frere, W. H. *The English Church in the Reigns of Elizabeth and James I*. London: Macmillan, 1904. See Index for references to Andrewes's role in shaping the Anglican church.

Owen, Trevor A. *Lancelot Andrewes*. Boston: Twayne, 1981. Helpful survey of Andrewes's life and work, with a discussion of *The Preces*, pp. 50–59.

Webber, Joan. "Celebration of Word and World in Lancelot Andrewes' Style." *In Seventeenth Century Prose*, pp. 336–354. Edited by Santley E. Fish. New York: Oxford University Press, 1971. Interesting account of the "witty" or "metaphysical style" of Andrewes and of Donne.

The Saints' Everlasting Rest

Author: Richard Baxter (1615–1691)
Attracted early to Puritan ideas and discipline, Richard Baxter gained distinction as pastor of Kidderminster (1641–1642 and 1647–1660) and army chaplain (1645–1647). His Nonconformist views, however, led to his removal from ministry in the Church of England during the Restoration (1660 and after) and finally to imprisonment (1686). Baxter composed *The Saints' Everlasting Rest* in 1648 while recovering from serious illness. A popular preacher and writer, he guided many other Puritans through books such as *The Reformed Pastor* (1656) and *The Call to the Unconverted* (1657). His autobiographical *Reliquiae Baxterianae* appeared posthumously (1696).

Type and subject of work: Treatise on spiritual formation for life after death

First published: 1650

Major Themes

The chief end of human beings is to obtain "the saints' everlasting rest," that is, heavenly bliss.

This rest can be obtained only by the people of God, who can have assurance from God's promises set forth in Scriptures.

The people of God, therefore, ought to seek this rest with the greatest seriousness, knowing they can have assurance.

> *Although salvation is a gift of God, the faithful can prepare themselves by continuous meditation on heaven, the control of which lies in human reason.*

Like other Puritan treatises such as Lewis Bayly's *The Practice of Piety*, John Dent's *The Plain Man's Pathway to Heaven*, and John Bunyan's *The Pilgrim's Progress*, this work urges readers to spend their time on earth in preparation for heaven. Composed during a prolonged period of illness, it offers practical counsel on meditation remarkably like Ignatius Loyola's *Spiritual Exercises* (published in 1540), save for reservations regarding the use of imagination on Scriptures. Baxter would approve imaging of hell or heaven, but he feared that imagination applied to Scriptures would lead to distortion.

Originally eight hundred pages long, *The Saints' Everlasting Rest* consists of four parts. The first is an eloquent exhortation to make the saints' rest of Hebrews 4:9 ("There remains therefore a rest to the people of God") the major occupation of Christian life. As Baxter envisioned it, the rest would mean cessation from constant striving, perfect freedom from evil, the highest degree of personal perfection, enjoyment of God (the chief good), and integration of all the human faculties in this endeavor. Baxter undergirded his appeals with rational arguments, but he laid greatest stress on the excellences of the rest. It would bring relief from sin, suffering, temptations of Satan and the world, persecutions, divisions and dissensions, participation in suffering of others or of ourselves, labor, and experience of God's absence.

The second part of *The Saints' Everlasting Rest* wrestles with the problem of assurance that figured so prominently in Protestant and Puritan thinking. Baxter readily accepted Calvin's conviction that God's promises alone supply the grounds for assurance. Accordingly he argues that the Scriptures, repository of the promises, prove the certain truth of the rest. Although he never obtained a university degree, he revealed here the thoroughness of his own method and the subtlety of his mind when he proceeded to argue the reliability of Scriptures themselves. In his view neither Scriptures nor faith can be approached naively. Scriptures must be differentiated like wheat and husk. That Scriptures are the Word of God is proven, however, from miracles, content, fulfillment of prophecy, and human need.

Elaborating on his chief text, Baxter argued that the everlasting rest is the possession only of the people of God and is not enjoyed on earth but "remains." Somewhat surprisingly, he was careful not to confine the people of God to the Elect, as Hyper-Calvinists did. Those who fail to enter God's rest have themselves and not God to blame, for God has given freedom of choice and wooed them from the beginning. The fact that the rest is not yet enjoyed is not only because God wanted it that way but because it is natural. Human beings would not keep striving toward perfection were they to obtain its benefits now. Contrary to some, however, Baxter argued that they can enjoy heavenly bliss even before the final resurrection.

The fourth part delineates four ways in which the concept of the saints' everlasting rest can be applied and instructs various groups of the faithful in its use. The first use is to confront the wicked with the awful consequences of losing the rest: loss of personal perfections that belong to the saints, loss of God himself, loss of spiritual affections by which the saints enjoy God, and loss of the company of angels and saints. Not only will they lose all these blessings, their perceptions will be heightened in such a way that they will experience still greater torment over the loss and find even earthly hopes and desires stifled.

The second use of the concept is to reprove the general neglect of the rest and excite people to a diligent search for it. Baxter singled out for rebuke the worldly-minded who cannot spare time, the profane multitude, the lazy and self-deceiving "professors" of religion, and the negligent godly (magistrates, ministers, and people), prodding them with about fifty rational considerations, thoughts, or questions: Can one ignore anything of such moment as to whether one would go to heaven or hell? Would any person neglect human duties that bore such consequences? Consider the time.

The third use of the concept is to persuade those who lack confidence to "try their title" to the rest and to direct them in this trial. Baxter grapples here again with the most vexing issue in Reformed and Puritan theology. The Puritans urged people to self-examination to discover whether or not they were among the Elect. They supplied a method for doing so, namely, to let Scriptures (over which they pored hour after hour) dart into their minds at random. For those who received positive signals this method could be reassuring. But what about those like John Bunyan who got negative ones? Small wonder many refused to start such a contest!

In this matter Baxter showed once again he was not a thoroughgoing Calvinist, conceding Catholics may have been right when they refused to speak of absolute assurance. His self-examination included reflection upon the sincerity of our acts, both moral and physical, temperament or disposition of heart, and habits. Like a good spiritual guide, he urged leniency, recognizing that assurance comes in various degrees. Perfect assurance cannot be obtained on earth; doubt always remains. Yet Scriptures give ample assurance when they tell us that whoever believes sincerely will be saved, as they do in many places. The major hindrances to examination, therefore, come from Satan, from wicked persons, or from our own hearts.

Baxter, a consummate guide himself while a pastor at Kidderminster, offers specific directions for self-examination, including marks for determining sincerity, the keynote in Puritan thought and life. The major marks are: "love for the children of God because they are such," to be the same in secret as one is in public, to love preaching that leads to holiness, to have no known sin with which one would not part.

The fourth use of this concept is to inform us why the people of God must suffer so much in this life. A frail and sickly person himself most of his life, Baxter spoke from experience when he insisted that afflictions, if viewed from the end of life, could be useful in keeping one headed toward the goal and even in discovering in the depths some foretaste of the future rest.

The fifth use of the concept is to encourage those who have been assured of the rest to help others obtain the same. Baxter, speaking and ministering "as a dying man to dying men," set a high standard as a mentor. His instructions emphasized the need for fine-tuning in approaching persons with the exhortation to undertake the trial. Above all, he insisted, it should be done sincerely, lovingly, plainly, seriously, and yet prudently and discreetly. He knew, too, the hesitancy of most to undertake this, so he laid a special responsibility upon ministers and parents.

The fourth part of *The Saints' Everlasting Rest* is a treatise on meditation described by Baxter as "a directory for the getting and keeping of the heart in heaven." The longest section of the book, it begins with two negative notes—reproval of expectations of rest on earth and of dread of dying. Baxter displayed here a keen awareness of the natural human tendencies and put together a procedure for dealing with them. Like Ignatius Loyola, he suggested rational "considerations" to argue a case against earthly happiness. To make any creature or created thing our rest, he said, is idolatrous. It contradicts the purpose of God in creation. Thence it can only result in God's displeasure and wrath. We, therefore, will lose the benefit and pleasure even of our earthly labors and experiences. Baxter advanced similar considerations to counter fear of dying. We should examine whether such reluctance does not indicate secret infidelity, coldness of love, desire to go on sinning, vanity, dissembling, or the like. Contrariwise we should consider that if we were not to die, we would never know true happiness, the glory of God freely given, or other joys of heaven. Rather, we would continue in the sufferings of earthly life with all of its dread.

Baxter next expounded on considerations that can motivate us to seek the rest of heaven. Having a heart set on heaven is the chief evidence of sincerity and the working of saving grace in one's soul, the noblest aspect of Christian disposition, the nearest and truest way to live in comfort, an excellent preservative against temptations, a way to invigorate all other graces and to inspire one to perform one's duties, and a cordial in all afflictions. Persons who live with their minds set on heaven profit all those whose lives touch theirs and honor God. Those who do not focus on heaven disobey God's command. Should anything else occupy our heart's attention? Is anything else of comparable worth?

Baxter knew that many things hindered attention to the saints' everlasting rest: living in a known unmortified sin, an earthly mind, the company of ungodly and sensual persons, too frequent disputes about matters of little consequence, a proud and lofty spirit, willful laziness and slothfulness of spirit, or contentedness with preparation for the heavenly life without ever tasting the thing itself. To deal with such difficulties, he offered several countermeasures: viewing heaven as our only treasure, striving to know it as our happiness, thinking about how near it is both in place and in time, spending much time talking about it, stirring up affections to be nearer heaven, taking advantage of whatever we see or experience to arouse the soul to the approaching rest, praising God much in song or prayer, recalling the infinite love of God, paying heed to the "drawings" of the Spirit, and caring for physical health so as to maintain cheerfulness of spirit.

Baxter defines meditation as "the set and solemn acting of all the powers of the soul." In explaining this statement he underscored the fact that meditation is a rational activity over which we have control but that requires complete ("all") powers of concentration. Citing Bernard of Clairvaux, he noted that we use both intellect and affection in meditation. As in heaven, so also here, we must enjoy God with both mind and heart. We must not leave such an activity to chance but must do it of "set and solemn" purpose. As to time, it should be set and constant, frequent, and seasonable. Like other Puritans, Baxter emphasized sabbath-time, that is, worship on the Lord's Day. As to place, it should be private, but otherwise accommodated to one's particular personal needs. As to disposition, the heart must be worthy for God to dwell in it and as serious as possible.

Baxter, like Loyola, made "consideration," "reasoning the case with ourselves," the chief instrument for moving the soul. Consideration opens the door between head and heart, presents matters of importance to the affections in the most persuasive way, puts reason "on the throne of the soul," brings it from reflection into action, and keeps blowing over coals of affection until they burn brightly. Although Baxter shared Puritan reserve regarding affections, he had confidence in rational controls that the mind could exert when it brought everything before Scriptures for judgment. Affections that we should major on in meditation are love, desire, hope, courage or boldness, and joy.

From theory Baxter proceeded to a practical demonstration. Citing Augustine, Bernard, and others, he illustrated how he would proceed from soliloquy, arguing a case with his own soul, to dialogue with God. Once again, he listed some arguments to heighten and intensify the endeavor. *The Saints' Everlasting Rest* ends with a long sample meditation to aid the "unskillful."

E. Glenn Hinson

RECOMMENDED READING

Edition used: Baxter, Richard. *The Saints' Everlasting Rest.* The Ancient and Modern Library of Theological Literature. London: Griffith, Farran, Okeden & Welsh, 1887.

———. *The Autobiography of Richard Baxter.* Everyman's Library. London: Dent, 1931; New York: Dutton, 1931. A spiritual autobiography typical of Puritans.

———. *A Call to the Unconverted.* Grand Rapids, Mich.: Zondervan, 1953. Revealing of Baxter's spiritual sensitivities.

———. *Gildas Salvianus: The Reformed Pastor, 1656.* 2d ed. Edited by John T. Wilkinson. London: Epworth Press, 1950. Baxter's classic on pastoral ministry.

Kerrys, Charles F. *A Pastoral Triumph: The Story of Richard Baxter and His Ministry at Kidderminster.* New York: Macmillan, 1948.

Ladell, A. R. *Richard Baxter: Puritan and Mystic.* London: Society for Promoting Christian Knowledge, 1925.

THE RULE AND EXERCISES OF HOLY LIVING AND HOLY DYING

Author: Jeremy Taylor (1613–1667)

Jeremy Taylor's fortunes were closely tied to those of the Anglican church during the fateful years of the Civil Wars and the Protectorate. A protégé of Archbishop William Laud and a chaplain to Charles I, Taylor was fortunate, after the fall of the monarchy, to find sanctuary as chaplain in the Welsh household of Lord and Lady Carbery, whose estate was named golden Grove. Later a position was found for him in Northen Ireland; and when the monarchy was restored, he ruled as bishop in those parts. The two books here reviewed were written at Golden Grove at a time when the fortunes of the Anglican order seemed desperate. They were intended as helps for laymen deprived of clerical ministrations. Well versed in classical literature and a keen observer of nature and of humankind, Taylor was mainly celebrated for his rhetorical gifts.

Type and subject of work: Handbooks for Christian living

First published: Holy Living, 1650; Holy Dying, 1651

MAJOR THEMES

God's offer of salvation to penitent sinners includes the requirement that believers live holy lives.

Holy living includes temperance and justice as well as godliness.

Because our brief lives issue on eternity, those who strive for holiness must submit to a severe regimen.

A holy life includes the trials and sufferings of sickness and death.

The Rule and Exercises of Holy Living and *The Rule and Exercises of Holy Dying* were intended as aids to self-examination and self-improvement, under the assumption that one fulfills one's purpose on earth when one brings a whole life as a glad offering to God. Jeremy Taylor uses the word *holy* much as we use the word *religious,* to signify a life given over to God. There are, according to Taylor, degrees of holiness on earth, just as there are degrees of blessedness in heaven; but who should and who should not be called holy is not his concern, which is, rather, to correct the common supposition that holiness has to do only with churchgoing and private devotions and to show the various ways in which one's entire life must be changed when a person undertakes to become a Christian. The two books somewhat overlap. When he wrote *Holy Living* Taylor had no intention of writing *Holy Dying.* The latter was undertaken at the suggestion of his patroness, Lady Carbery, who had then entered upon her final illness, and adds to the first only a more detailed consideration of the trials, duties, and services that accompany sickness and the approach of death. Taylor, who insists that earthly life is a preparation for eternity, rejects in strong terms the view that a person may safely postpone religion until his or her life is nearly over.

Taylor was a great methodizer, not to say methodist—although John and Charles Wesley made no secret of their debt to his writings. Christians who have made holiness their guiding star have always felt the importance of method, and Taylor's expression, "rule and exercises," is intentionally reminiscent of monastic rule and discipline. Indeed, *Holy Living* is a typical example of the so-called Protestant ethic, which came into existence when the notion of the religious life or Christian vocation, hitherto applied to persons entering monastic orders, was extended to include persons who remained in "the world" and undertook to realize the ideals of Christianity in their secular callings. *Holy Living* makes this explicit. According to Taylor, one's whole duty is comprised in responsibilities to one's own person, to one's fellow human beings, and to God. Citing what he calls the arithmetic of the apostle Paul, who enjoined believers to live "soberly, righteously, and godly in this present world," Taylor heads his main divisions "Sobriety," "Justice," and "Religion." Moreover he adds his own arithmetic to that of the apostle. The student once heard to complain of an instructor, "He just hints all around and doesn't number things," would have appreciated these books.

Chapter one, "Considerations of the General Instruments and Means Serving to a Holy Life, by Way of Introduction," has three parts: care of one's time; purity of intention; and practice of the presence of God. To take the third of these as an example, there are six ways in which God may be said to be present; there are ten rules for exercising this consideration; and there are five benefits of this exercise. It is the rules that receive the most emphasis, the first of which we may take as an example: "Let this actual thought often return, that God is omnipresent, filling every place; and say with David, 'Whither shall I go from thy spirit . . . ?' This thought by being frequent will make an habitual dread and reverence towards God, and fear, in all thy actions. For it is a great necessity and engagement to do unblameably when we act before the Judge who is infallible in His sentence, all-knowing in His information, severe in His anger, powerful in His providence, and intolerable in His wrath and indignation." Another example: "God is in the bowels of thy brother; refresh them when he needs it, and then you give your alms in the presence of God, and to God; and He feels the relief which thou providest for thy brother."

Chapter two, "Of Christian Sobriety," has to do with what later moralists have called self-regarding virtues. Taylor treats first of libidinous desires (food, alcohol, and sex), and second of egoistic desires (pride, honor, and ambition). He writes about the former pretty much in the tone of a Dutch uncle, and we are reminded by the critics that he was mainly writing for people who lived in the great houses and that he had but little contact with the commonality. His method remains numerical. There are five evil consequences of voluptuousness, three degrees of sobriety, and six rules for suppressing the evil and effecting its cure. And so forth. We might add that the supposed uncle happens to be a classical scholar, and that, edifying as it may have been to anxious souls such as those of John Wesley and his friends in the Holy Club at Oxford, the book could hardly have won the wide readership on which its standing as a classic rests solely on the basis of its suitability for religious instruction. It must also have appealed to many for such curious items as what Alexander told the queen of Caria, and for the miracle that happened to the body of Epiphemius (to take two random examples of the sort of thing that appears on nearly every page). Schooled in renaissance humanism, Taylor had all the pagan authors at his fingertips as well as the church fathers and such modern writers as Saint Francis de Sales. Much of this material was taboo to Roundheads, but it was welcomed by Cavaliers and (especially) by their ladies.

Chapter three, "Of Christian Justice," includes all persons' duties to their fellows. From Greek antiquity, two kinds of justice had been distinguished: distributive, having to do with one's relations to superiors, inferiors, and equals; and commutative, having to do with the exchange of things needful. Taylor finds a biblical basis for the former in such texts as "Render to all their dues," and "As every man hath received the gift, so let him minister the same one to another as good stewards." Under this head he considers all acts and duties of subjects to authorities, of children to elders, and of servants to masters, but also the provision owed by superiors to those over whom they have the rule. His text for commutative justice is, "Whatsoever ye would that men should do to you, even so do to them." This kind of justice he breaks down into two parts: negotiation, or civil contract; and restitution, arising out of faults connected with a precedent contract. The emphasis on contract has a modern sound about it; but the emphasis on ranks and estates belongs to the old order, as appears especially in the section, "Acts and obedience to all our superiors," item twelve, to wit: "Lift not up thy hand against thy prince or parent, upon what pretence soever; but bear all personal affronts and inconveniences at their hands, and seek no remedy but by patience and piety, yielding and praying, or absenting thyself."

From the first, Taylor had distinguished between religion as inclusive of personal and public morality, and religion as direct intercourse between the believer and God. This latter he treats of in chapter four, "Of the Christian Religion." As he divides this subject, there are three internal actions of the Christian religion (faith, hope, love), three external actions (reading and preaching the Word, fasting, keeping holy days), and four mixed actions (prayer, almsgiving, repentance, and receiving the sacrament). The approach is inclusive. In contrast to the Puritans, who followed the principle that religious practices having no precedent in the New Testament should be eliminated, Taylor makes it his policy to avoid sharp breaks with the past and to do everything in moderation. Taylor's main concern in this chapter is to prevent religion from becoming idle sentiment on the one hand and soulless formality on the other. Special mention should be made of his exposition of the two parts of Christian love—love of god and love of neighbor. There is no religion, though there may be sobriety and justice, without love of God, which, according to Taylor, has two motives: God's perfection and God's beneficence. Ordinarily people are first moved to love God by their experience of his beneficence; afterwards, they "love the spring for its own excellency, passing from passion to reason, from thanking to adoring, from sense to spirit, from considering ourselves to union with God." Curiously, to our thinking, Taylor reserves consideration of love to our neighbors until he comes to the section on almsgiving. But this is reasonable, considering that love to others is a mixed activity or it is nothing: The external act is barren without the holy intention, and the intention is less than holy unless it results in an appropriate act. To persons of our legalistic and egalitarian formation, there is something patronizing about giving alms and something humiliating in having to receive them—unless they are funneled through an anonymous agency. But, not to repeat what has been said already about the social class for whom Taylor was writing, it should be noted that under almsgiving Taylor includes every kind of help that a person can render to one more needy than himself. In Taylor's catalogue, there are corporal alms, ranging from providing the sick with medicine to paying a maiden's dowry; spiritual alms almost no less diverse, among which are mentioned defending the oppressed and correcting and chastising the refractory; and a third kind, mixed, which includes erecting schools and finding employment for the unbusied. One could add that Jeremy Taylor and hundreds like him owed their chances for an education to wealthy patrons.

The Rule and Exercises of Holy Dying is not simply an afterthought. In some ways it is a rethinking of *Holy Living,* a deepening and intensifying of earlier insights resulting from the author's assistance at the death of his patroness and, within weeks, that of his own wife. There is still plenty of rhetoric, particularly in chapter one, "General Considerations Preparatory to Death," where Taylor finds a place to record everything he has ever read on the brevity and wretchedness of human life and on the devices that thoughtful men have used to prepare themselves for the inevitable. Here and in chapter two, where he passes on from resolutions to practice, he is addressing people in good health with unaltered prospects, pressing them to face up to life's final issue while there is still time to do something about it. Daily examination is, he says, the best way to keep little sins from growing into big ones, and to keep unconfessed sins from piling up. What, he asks, is worse than to approach death with an accumulated treasure of wrath and to have no bank of good works? Warning his readers not to believe those who teach that heaven is a cheap purchase, he insists that, in offering salvation through Jesus Christ, God contracted for a holy life. "A resolving to repent upon our death-bed is the greatest mockery of God in the world, and the most contradictory to all his excellent designs of mercy and holiness; for therefore He threatened us with hell if we did not, and He promised heaven if we did live a holy life; and a late repentance promises heaven to us on other conditions, even when we have lived wickedly."

Chapters three and four take up sickness as a forerunner of death, and consider what the invalid must do by way of putting his affairs in order. The final chapter, "The Visitation of the Sick," is addressed mainly to clergy. Of the special trials that the sick must be prepared to face, impatience and fear of death receive special attention. But perhaps of more interest to those of us not yet prostrated is a section on the advantages of illness. Sickness can be turned into a cause for praise if we view it as a kind of dressing room in which the soul is stripped of vanity and pride and clothed for immortality; or, to change the figure, as a gymnasium for exercising certain virtues. "It is the agony in which men are tried for a crown." "And so God dresses us for heaven. He loves to see us struggling with a disease, and resisting the devil, and contesting against the weakness of nature, and against hope to believe in hope, resigning ourselves to God's will, praying Him to choose for us, and dying in all things but faith and its blessed consequences."

A prominent feature of the book has not been mentioned. Both parts abound in beautifully written prayers. Each chapter concludes with prayers suited to its special concerns, and each book with a whole section consisting of prayers.

Jean H. Faurot

RECOMMENDED READING

Edition used: Taylor, Jeremy. *The Whole Works.* Edited by Reginald Heber. 10 vols. Vol. 3: *The Rule and Exercises of Holy Living and Dying.* London: Longman, Brown, Green, & Longman, 1850. Reprinted New York: Hildescheim, 1969.

Gosse, Edmund. *Jeremy Taylor.* English Men of Letters Series. New York: Macmillan, 1904. Republished Grosse Pointe, Mich.: Scholarly Press, 1968. The well-known English critic studies Taylor's writings in a biographical context. See especially chapter 3, "Retirement at Golden Grove."

Mitchell, W. Fraser. *English Pulpit Oratory from Andrewes to Tillotson,* pp. 242–254. London: Macmillan, 1943. Standard work. Emphasis on literary side.

Taylor, Jeremy. *The Golden Grove: Selected Passages from the Sermons and Writings of Jeremy Taylor.* Edited and with an Introduction by Logan Pearsall Smith. Oxford: Clarendon Press, 1930. Excellent fifty-page introduction. Taylor is praised for his occasionally inspired style of writing.

PENSÉES

Author: Blaise Pascal (1623–1662)
This French thinker's life was as brilliant as it was brief. Mathematician, physicist, and inventor, Pascal experienced a decisive religious conversion on the night of November 23, 1654. That experience led to his most famous work, *Pensées*. Consisting of a large body of notes, the work was unfinished and published posthumously. At times compared to Søren Kierkegaard, Pascal is often regarded as one of the first Christian existentialists.

Type and subject of work: Intended to explore the human condition and to answer objections against Christianity, this book has a fragmentary form, which gives it the flavor of an intellectual-spiritual diary.

First published: 1670

MAJOR THEMES

Essential though it is, reason cannot provide the answers we seek; on the contrary, the human desire for truth exposes the limitations of mathematics, science, and philosophy.

We seek happiness but cannot find it apart from a faithful relation to God.

God's existence cannot be proved by human thought. It is reasonable, however, to wager that God does exist.

The God who redeems human beings is not the God of "the philosophers and scholars" but the biblical God of Abraham, Isaac, Jacob, and Jesus.

Friendship, love, work, and play—all of those realities give us good reasons for living. The problem is that those elements are not the only ones we experience. Untimely death stalks us. Love and friendship cannot always resist the onslaughts that threaten them. Apparently senseless accidents intrude, and natural or human violence reduces our fondest accomplishments to rubble. Seemingly without rhyme or reason, our best-laid plans come to naught. True, if we study them a second time, those events often make a kind of sense. They do not appear in a vacuum but are the outcomes of causes and effects that occurred before. Nonetheless, they still strike us as catastrophes, leaving us to feel that life lacks the overall sense it ought to possess. Humanity's place in the scheme of things, let alone that of any single individual, seems immensely fragile when life can be tossed about so capriciously. Our existence may even be swallowed up eventually by a void that reduces everything to empty silence. Such lines of thought never haunted a thinker more than they did Blaise Pascal.

Meditating on the thought of the famous philosopher René Descartes (1596–1650), his older French contemporary, Pascal once remarked that "all philosophy is not worth one hour of pain." On another occasion he concluded that "to make light of philosophy is to be a true philosopher." One might wonder whether a person who said such things could really be a philosopher. Yet Pascal certainly belongs in that category, for he was deeply moved by the experiences that cause us to wonder whether life makes sense. Particularly in his *Pensées* Pascal tried to fathom life's meanings. He probably wrote as much for himself as for a public audience, but his aphoristic style makes the author of this spiritual classic a memorable and eminently quotable thinker.

During the night of November 23, 1654, Pascal experienced a profound religious conversion. Thereafter he always carried with him a description of the event: "From about 10:30 at night, until about 12:30. FIRE. God of Abraham, God of Isaac, God of Jacob, not of the philosophers and of the learned. Certitude, certitude, feeling, joy, peace. God of Jesus Christ ... Jesus Christ. ... Let me never be separated from Him." Pascal went on to write his *Pensées* and thereby became one of the most passionate defenders of the Christian faith. His reflections also contain much insight about human existence in general, because Pascal emphasized that the human condition is largely one of finitude, uncertainty, and considerable misery. Those convictions also account for his suspicion of philosophy. It might do what is natural in catering to our yearning for certainty, he argued, but philosophy also misleads us by suggesting that reason, even in its mathematical and scientific guise, can provide such stability.

When we ask, "Does life make sense?" Pascal's *Pensées* does not offer a systematic response. Instead, Pascal grasps the moods that bring that issue to the fore, states only what is essential, and leaves the rest to the reader to elaborate. One of those moods involves the significance of death. Most people would rather not think about that issue, Pascal admits, and we become experts at fending it off. But it remains before us, as Pascal uses the following scene to suggest: "Let us imagine a number of men in chains, and all condemned to death, where some are killed each day in the sight of the others, and those who remain see their own fate in that of their fellows and wait their turn, looking at each other sorrowfully and without hope. It is an image of the condition of man."

Our condition creates related moods and issues, too. At one point, for example, Pascal's thoughts moved in the following direction: "When I consider the short duration of my life, swallowed up in the eternity before and after, the little space which I fill, and even can see, engulfed in the infinite immensity of spaces of which I am ignorant, and which know me not, I am frightened, and am astonished at being here rather than there, why now rather than then. Who has put me here? By whose order and direction have this time and place been allotted to me?" Such passages indicate the kinds of issues that emerge for Pascal when he asks whether life makes sense. They also suggest how the insights of mathematical and scientific reason may combine with those of existential concern to advance an intense effort by a keen mind to appropriate honestly the hope religion offers.

Pascal's best-known contribution to religious philosophy is called "Pascal's Wager." In the section of his *Pensées* devoted to it, he speaks about the search for God. For Pascal that search *is* the quest for meaning in life, not least of all because God provides the hope that we can be redeemed from misery and death. The question of one's immortality is of particularly great consequence. If only death awaits even the noblest lives, we will possess no lasting satisfaction. To have only doubt is a great burden where such questions are concerned, but even worse is a failure to try moving beyond that condition. As Pascal's conversion experience suggests, he thought that religious experience could convey a kind of certitude, at least in the moment of its happening. But he recognized, too, that life goes on and is never completely immune to doubt and uncertainty. Where the meaning of life is at stake, Pascal understood, we are dealing with faith, which means that the risk of making and sustaining a commitment is present.

Pascal argues that we ought to bet religiously that life does make sense. That wager, he underscored, is about God's existence and purposes. For if God does not exist, life's meaning will at best be tragic and at worst simply annihilated. We ought to wager that God exists, asserts Pascal, and live accordingly. To do so, he contends, is not irrational but exactly the opposite. In our human situation it is not given to us to demonstrate that God exists, and yet an analysis of our predicament suggests that faith in God is sensible.

The importance of the latter claim is clarified when Pascal writes that "man is but a reed, the most feeble thing in nature; but he is a thinking reed. . . . Thought constitutes the greatness of man." Pascal believes that reason is limited, but it must not be disparaged, for "all our dignity consists . . . in thought." For Pascal, religious faith is a further expression of human dignity. The thoughtful person, Pascal believes, will see that the wager makes sense: "Let us weigh the gain and the loss in wagering that God is. Let us estimate these two chances. If you gain, you gain all; if you lose, you lose nothing. Wager, then, without hesitation that He is." The clincher in this argument, Pascal believes, is that this wager is forced. Not to choose is also a choice, for a decision is made by refusing to try, to enter in, to venture. Lack of belief excludes one from the benefits of faith. This situation has an either/or quality. We have to choose.

Having distinguished between the God of philosophers and scholars and the God of Abraham, Isaac, Jacob, and Jesus, Pascal elaborates his convictions about God and God's relation to humankind. As a Christian, Pascal affirms that his religion teaches two essential truths: There is a God we can know; there is also a corruption in human nature that renders us unworthy. But God is "a God of love," adds Pascal, and God will "fill the soul and heart of those whom He possesses." Such claims, however, are not rationally demonstrable. On the contrary, religion often places us in a precarious position, saying that people are in "darkness and estranged from God." Religion pushes reason to its limits, but, Pascal asserts in one of his most famous lines, "the heart has its reasons, which reason does not know." He goes on to argue that primarily the heart, not reason, experiences God. Indeed faith is characterized by heartfelt experience of God.

As Pascal saw it, one's decision as to whether life makes sense does not depend ultimately on reason alone but at least as much on one's willingness to act when confronted by a forced wager. This is Pascal's fundamental spiritual point. He argues that this situation need not offend reason. Indeed, defining life as meaningful is no greater affront to reason than the opposite decision. One has everything to gain and nothing to lose, at least in the long run, by believing. An eternity of happiness is at stake.

In fact, when forced to gamble, the paradox is that the *reasonable* action is to let choice transcend reason in order to allow oneself to be possessed by God. According to Pascal, those who demand certainty prior to commitment fail to understand the human situation. If one objects that religion is too uncertain and God too difficult, while sufficient meaning can be found without entanglement in the vagaries of either, Pascal thinks the issue of life beyond death is crucial where life's significance is concerned. He finds it hard to conceive that death is not the end for us unless a loving God exists.

"To deny, to believe, and to doubt well," Pascal thought, "are to a man what the race is to a horse." Pascal likens life to a game, but one that should be played out earnestly. To do so takes one beyond reason, for "the last proceeding of reason is to recognize that there is an infinity of things beyond it." Played well, the game of life teaches reason to trust the heart. Yet that result can occur only when we give reason its due as well. Each has its own order. In searching for meaning in life, Pascal recommends that we must be careful not to confuse the two or try to reduce one to the other. Life might be simpler if we could do the latter, but Pascal insists that this is impossible. There are two levels, two ways of proceeding. They can supplement each other, but they do not always blend. We must learn to live with both and discount neither. It is this complexity that forces us to wager where the meaning of life is concerned.

When we ask, "Does life make sense?" Pascal's first reply is: "Not of itself and not on its own." Life does not come with built-in answers for our questions, in spite of hopes that it will. But for Pascal this outcome does not mean that life has no meaning in itself. Nor does it follow, as some philosophers assert, that all meaning is dependent on us and varies with each person. Pascal thinks life has meaning in itself, but our awareness of and participation in it are not assured unless we gamble. We must make the wager. Then the purpose of life may become clear.

John K. Roth

RECOMMENDED READING

Edition used: Pascal, Blaise. *Pensées.* Translated by W. F. Trotter. Introduction by T. S. Eliot. New York: Dutton, 1958.

Krailsheimer, A. J. *Pascal.* New York: Hill & Wang, 1980. A brief but insightful overview arguing that "Pascal and the *Pensées* are incontrovertibly important today," that "Pascal's life is inseparable from his work, in particular the *Pensées*, and that habits of mind originally acquired in a scientific context persisted after his conversion."

Nelson, Robert J. *Pascal: Adversary and Advocate.* Cambridge: Harvard University Press, 1981. This work analyzes Pascal's life and thought, focusing on their "tormented awareness that existence forces the question upon us: How, then, shall we live?"

Pascal, Blaise. *The Provincial Letters.* Translated by A. J. Krailsheimer. New York: Penguin Books, 1967. Widely read and controversial when they appeared in 1656–1657, the letters by Pascal that make up this work satirized Jesuit theology and defended the Jansenists against heresy charges. The book was put on the Index in 1657.

Rescher, Nicholas. *Pascal's Wager: A Study of Practical Reasoning in Philosophical Theology.* Notre Dame, Ind.: University of Notre Dame Press, 1985. Concerned only secondarily with "the concrete historical setting of Pascal's own thought and writing," the work by a prominent American philosopher specifically scrutinizes the line of thought in "Pascal's Wager."

PIA DESIDERIA

Author: Philipp Jakob Spener (1635–1705)
Born near Strassburg to pious Lutheran parents, Spener grew up in an atmosphere dominated by the spirituality of Johann Arndt (1555–1621). Following his studies, he entered the ministry with a program that called for Bible studies among the laity, the development of lay leadership in the Church, the use of small groups for mutual edification and correction, and the renewal of seminary education. He has been called "the Father of German Pietism." Few of his works have been translated into English.

Type and subject of work: Call to piety and for renewal in the Church and in seminary education.

First published: 1675

MAJOR THEMES

The Church, the body of Christ, "is now afflicted with distress and sickness."
As a result, those who are concerned and are open to edification must help discover and correct any shortcomings.

The Church's corrupt conditions are caused by defects in the three basic classes in society: the civil authorities, the clergy, and the "common people."

To improve the Church, six steps are necessary: (1) The Bible must be used more extensively; (2) the priesthood of all believers must be emphasized and practiced diligently; (3) the emphasis in faith must be on practice; (4) Christians must be gracious in controversies with heretics and unbelievers; (5) the clergy must be limited to those of high calling and earnest lives (this can be assured

through a reform of the universities that touches both professors and students);
(6) preaching must be intended to bring about "faith and its fruits" in the lives of
the hearers, rather than to demonstrate the erudition of the preacher.

In his greeting, Philipp Jakob Spener laments the current "distress and sickness" that afflicts the Church. In the wake of the Thirty Years' War Germany was devastated, entire villages having been completely wiped out. Morality was at a low ebb, and the Lutheran church, as perceived by those in the Arndt-Spener school of thought, was constricted by a hard confessionalism and debilitated by a clergy more intent upon demonstrating their erudition in the pulpit and polemicizing against the Reformed, Roman Catholic, and Anabaptist wings of the Church than with edifying their listeners. Added to this were the charges that the laity were ignorant not only of orthodox faith, but particularly of orthodox practice. Tension arose between those interested in the personal piety of every person in the Church and those primarily concerned with securing correct doctrine. In 1675 *Pia Desideria* appeared and set loose a controversy that has left the term *Pietist* an insult to this day. Spener lamented this tension to the day of his death.

Spener's book, originally a preface to a collection of Johann Arndt's sermons, is addressed primarily to those concerned with the well-being of the Church and open to his suggestions. His attempt at Church renewal begins with identifying the sources of the Church's problems, namely, corruption in all three classes of society.

Spener cites the failure of the civil authorities to remember that God has given them power in order to advance the kingdom of God. Even the best of them are mainly concerned with "maintaining the traditional pure religion and preventing the introduction of false religion," too often out of concern for their own well-being. This is hardly sufficient in a society in which the civil powers are responsible for the spiritual well-being of their subjects.

The clergy (a "thoroughly corrupt" estate) likewise is self-seeking, hypocritical, and hedonistic when in fact self-denial is "the first practical principle of Christianity." This is especially dangerous since the laity assume that if the clergy manifest a certain kind of behavior it must be acceptable Christianity.

Spener laments that those concerned more with doctrinally orthodox faith than with personal, living faith tend to accuse the more devoted believers of being members of secret mystic sects, while they are in fact blind to the terrible condition of the Church. Their contentiousness is a blot upon the Church and betrays their ignorance of true Christianity which is made up of a godly life rather than of disputation.

Spener then goes on, quoting theologians from the early Church through Luther to his own period, to repudiate the idea that scholasticism is the center of the Christian faith. This preoccupation with theological nit-picking is more dangerous than it may seem, Spener argues, since it diverts one's attention from God. Thus one ends up speculating and thinking *about* God rather than concentrating on living with and pleasing God.

This theologizing ultimately is self-defeating, in that in turning the pastor from God, it also renders the pastor ignorant, since "divine illumination can[not] be grasped by human ingenuity."

The third estate, the common people, is characterized by nominal Christianity. The majority of the people no longer recognize that sins are actually sins. Drunkenness and lawsuits, for example, were considered routine parts of life.

Spener also claims that greed and acquisition have become the impulses behind one's vocation rather than making money to spend for the glory of God and the benefit of one's neighbor. He then goes on to promote sacrificial giving to the extent of giving all one owns if necessary.

In what was a controversial section, Spener affirms that we are saved solely by the grace of God through faith, and "would rather give up our life and the whole world than yield the smallest part of it." He goes on, however, to claim that those who persist in evil ways and avoid good works cannot expect to be saved. Nonetheless, the equally dangerous illusion exists that one can be saved through churchly things: baptism, church attendance, confession, and receiving the Lord's Supper. In this Spener was echoing charges already made against members of the Lutheran church by, among others, Heinrich Mueller who called the baptismal, the pulpit, the confessional, and the altar "the four dumb idols of the church."

There must be a give and take between the usual churchly practices and trust in God. The believer is saved by God and then participates in worship, with an eye to being transformed and strengthened in faith and love by the living God whom the faithful encounter therein.

As senior minister of Frankfurt (am Main), Spener was aware that one result of defects among the Lutherans was offense to the rather large Jewish population of that city. They and others could not believe that Christians consider Christ to be God, since Christians are so disobedient to his commands. Or they concluded that Jesus must have been a wicked man if his followers lead such dissolute and evil lives.

The solution, then, is to recognize, lament, repent of, and change the wretched conditions that plague the Church. Spener places special emphasis upon *changing* these conditions. He refutes those who would ignore the problems lest enemies of the Church capitalize on these revelations and confessions. Christians should instead be moved to encourage one another and transform the Church. Anyone "who is the Lord's" must surely lend a helping hand in this cause.

The possibility exists for better conditions in the Church. This would be facilitated by the demise of the Roman Catholic church, but since this is not in the foreseeable future, Lutherans must do what they can. The current conditions are to be accepted in love and patience rather than responded to with anger, since perfection will be realized only in heaven. Nonetheless, the Christian is constrained to seek perfection in this life while at the same time accepting his or her inability to achieve it. This is to the Christian both a word of encouragement and of comfort.

If the Church is to be purified, there must be some way of training prospective members and especially of encouraging them in a godly life. To this end Spener has six proposals:

(1) That "thought should be given to a more extensive use of the Word of God among us." That is, the Bible, especially the New Testament, should be read aloud daily in the home. Particularly revolutionary is Spener's suggestion that the Church "reintroduce the ancient and apostolic kind of church meeting." Here, in small groups made up of pastor and laypersons, questions and even doubts could be raised in an accepting environment intended to glorify God and to enlighten and encourage the participants. This idea, although promoted by the senior minister of the city, was greeted initially by many clergy with hostility and suspicion. They anticipated schism and heresy.

(2) Spener also proposed "the establishment and diligent exercise of the spiritual priesthood." That is, "all spiritual functions are open to all Christians without exception." The realization of this idea will break the slothfulness of the laity, the "presumptuous monopoly" of the clergy, and will lead to the renewal of the Church. By "spiritual functions" Spener did *not* mean administering the sacraments or the *public* exercise of these functions. Rather he intended that laypersons would lead Bible studies, admonish, comfort, and chastise one another (including the pastor), pray, and undertake other tasks normally left to the pastors.

(3) Spener stressed that Christian faith is more than knowledge, "for Christianity consists rather of practice." This practice is made up of seeking ways to love one's neighbor, being sensitive to situations as they present themselves, and searching one's heart to see if the behavior is prompted by good motives. The Pietists felt that a faith understood solely or primarily as assent to doctrines had contributed greatly to the lamentable condition of the Church.

(4) Because of the coexistence of Reformed, Lutheran, Roman Catholic, and Anabaptist churches, as well as a multitude of sectarian groups,

polemic and dispute were the order of the day. Even the most irenic church leaders felt no qualms about trying to lure people into their own denominations.

Thus Spener proposed that "we must beware how we conduct ourselves in religious controversies with believers and heretics." We should above all pray that God would enlighten them; we should be good examples, point out firmly but gently the correctness of our position and the weaknesses of theirs, and regard them with heartfelt love. While disputation is necessary to arrive at truth, we will achieve unity only by repentance and holiness.

Thus Spener concludes that "not all disputation is useful and good" and that even proper disputation needs the "holy love of God." Even the erring can love and serve God.

(5) Pastors bear the greatest burden in the reform of the Church and thus must be true Christians. This entails, however, a reform of the universities (in Germany, pastors are trained for the most part at universities). To this end the pursuit of academic honors and recognition must be downplayed, the typical student life of brawling and carousing must end, and the schools must become workshops of the Holy Spirit for student and professor alike, since "study without piety is worthless."

Professors should concern themselves not only with lectures, but with the students' lives as well. With insight that sounds familiar to modern ears, Spener suggests that the curriculum be tailored to the gifts and needs of the individual students.

(6) The education of pastors should be oriented toward the practical disciplines, with an emphasis on preaching as a tool for facilitating faith and sanctification. Since the outer person manifests the inner, preaching should be aimed chiefly at the transformation of the inner person.

Spener's book was met with a sympathetic echo until the various offenders realized its implications for them. *Pia Desideria* is a manifestation of Pietism at its best, in that it is brutally honest, irenic, and deeply concerned with the well-being of the Church. It reflects the basic Pietist tenet that renewed individuals will transform Church and society, and that true Christianity is reflected in fallen yet faithful individuals living for God's glory and neighbor's good.

Gary R. Sattler

RECOMMENDED READING

Edition used: Spener, Philip Jacob. *Pia Desideria*. Translated, edited, and with an Introduction by Theodore G. Tappert. Philadelphia: Fortress Press, 1964. Brown, Dale. *Understanding Pietism*. Grand Rapids, Mich.: Eerdmans, 1978. An

introduction to the basic tents of the Pietist movement in Germany, referring chiefly to Spener and August Hermann Francke (1663–1727).

Richards, Marie. *Philipp Jacob Spener/August Hermann Francke.* Philadelphia:
Lutheran Publication Society, 1897. A short work with an introduction to
and translations of works by Spener and Francke.

Wildenhahn, Karl. *Pictures from the Life of Spener.* Translated by G. A. Wenzel.
Philadelphia: J. Frederick Smith, 1879. A historical novel sympathetic to Pietism, tracing the rise of the movement through the life of one of its
founders.

THE PILGRIM'S PROGRESS *AND* GRACE ABOUNDING TO THE CHIEF OF SINNERS

Author: John Bunyan (1628–1688)

Born in the heyday of Puritanism in England, Bunyan developed a hypersensitive religious conscience that even in childhood "did scare and affrighten me with fearful dreams." When he reached adulthood, his struggle increased, leading to depression and despair. At about age twenty-five, however, he began to discover the sufficiency of divine grace in the context of the little church in Bedford of which he became pastor. During the Restoration under Charles II (1660–1685), he spent twelve and a half years in prison for refusal to cease unlicensed preaching. There he initiated his writing career. During the first six years in jail, he composed nine books, during the second only two, but eighty altogether. His most famous work, *The Pilgrim's Progress*, was probably written during a six-month incarceration in 1675, when the Parliament issued the Test Act.

Type and subject of works: Grace Abounding to the Chief of Sinners is a spiritual autobiography; *The Pilgrim's Progress* is an allegorical rendition of the same subject matter, to which Bunyan later (in 1685) appended an account of the pilgrimage of Christian's wife and family.

First published: Grace Abounding to the Chief of Sinners, 1667; *The Pilgrim's Progress,* 1678

Major Themes

God's grace is sufficient to enable the Christian to remain faithful during the arduous pilgrimage from life to death.

The goal of Christian life is the heavenly city, and life here and now is only a preparation to which the faithful must commit themselves unreservedly.

The Bible is the main guide for the journey, but other persons (the Church) will also offer vital encouragement and assistance.

True religion consists in deed rather than in word.

Grace Abounding to the Chief of Sinners, Bunyan's "relation of the merciful working of God upon my soul," is a seventeenth-century *Confessions*. In it the Bedford handyman recounted only in an incidental way his external biography, for his concern, like Augustine's, was to tell how "great sins do draw out great grace." Although Bunyan, like other Puritans, had imbibed deeply of Calvinist or reformed theology, he revealed also a profound dependence on the more experiential thinking of Martin Luther, whose *Commentary on Galatians* etched itself deeply on his mind and heart precisely because it accorded so well with his own battle with doubt and guilt.

According to *Grace Abounding*, Bunyan, born in Elstow (two miles from Bedford) in 1628, had dreams in childhood that "did scare and affright" him. By the age of nine or ten he was experiencing already the spiritual distress and despair concerning sin that brought him to the brink of suicide as he approached adulthood. Although he lapsed occasionally into such "worldly" pursuits as a game of "cat" or bell ringing, he did little more than dabble in serious sins.

Serving two years in Cromwell's "New Model" army (1644–1646), he became still more serious about religion as a consequence of near scrapes with death. When he married after leaving the army, his wife presented him with two Puritan classics—Arthur Dent's *The Plain Man's Pathway to Heaven* (1602) and Lewis Bayly's *The Practice of Piety* (1610)—which impressed upon him the need for serious searching to see whether or not he was among the "elect." The Puritans devised a method for this. The devout saturated themselves with Scriptures and then counted on random passages to dart into their minds to confirm or deny whether they were among the saved or damned. To those who received favorable responses, this would supply powerful assurance—*the* central concern of Calvinists and their major objection to Roman Catholic theology and practice—but woe to those who got negative ones.

Bunyan heard both reassuring and devastating words. His moods rose and fell in thunderous waves. The passage in Hebrews 12 about Esau selling his birthright for a bit of food pulled him down again and again. He feared he had committed the unpardonable sin, selling his Christian birthright. Fortunately, as he told the tale, God's grace won the titanic struggle for a soul. The little congregation at Bedford, especially the pastor John Gifford, listened sympathetically to his cries and encouraged him. The preface to Luther's *Commentary on Galatians* handled his experience so largely and profoundly he felt it had been written out of his own heart. Then, sitting in the little congregation he would later serve as pastor, 2 Corinthians 12:9, "My grace is sufficient for thee," darted three times into his mind, "and, O me-thought that every word was a mighty word for me; as *my*, and *grace*, and *sufficient*, and *for thee*; they were then, and sometimes are still, far bigger than others be." The battle did not end there. His skiff still bobbed up and down on both small and big waves. He prayed that the two key texts—about Esau and about grace—would enter his mind and fight it out. They did, and grace won!

To this gripping soul narrative Bunyan added accounts of his call to ministry in 1653 and of his imprisonment in 1660. In the latter Bunyan spoke movingly about his costly decision to accept prison rather than stop preaching. He left to the care of his young wife four children—one blind daughter "nearer my heart than all I had besides." Thought of their hardships broke his heart. Yet he took the leap of faith, declaring, "if God doth not come in, I will leap off the Ladder even blindfold into Eternitie, sink or swim, come heaven, come hell; Lord Jesus, if thou wilt catch me, do; if not, I will venture for thy Name."

The Pilgrim's Progress from This World to That Which Is to Come presents in symbolical or allegorical form what *Grace Abounding* discloses in narrative form. Here Bunyan strove to dramatize, as the full title of the book makes clear, the pilgrimage that a Christian must undertake to get safely "from this world to that which is to come." Saturated with scriptural language, metaphors, and ideas in the style characteristic of "mechanick preachers" of the seventeenth century, he expounded a typically Puritan message in an unpuritan manner. Indeed, he confessed in his "Apology," he hesitated for a while to publish lest he offend Puritan sensitivities about using allegory, but he received enough encouragement to go ahead anyway.

Although *The Pilgrim's Progress* lends itself nicely to Jungian analysis, it can be properly understood only within the framework of Puritan theology. In the Puritan's view, the most urgent human concern is salvation, that is, to go to heaven. Although salvation is a free gift of God, it requires nonetheless a complete detachment from all earthly ties and single-minded preoccupation with heavenly concerns during this life. The way is difficult and few make it through from the City of Destruction to the Heavenly Jerusalem, for all kinds of dangers lurk along the path.

In Bunyan's imaginative story, Christian, warned by Evangelist and his own reading of Scriptures to flee the "wrath to come," forsook a wife and four children (the same number Bunyan left behind when he went to prison in 1660) when they refused to go with him, chidings and ridicule of neighbors notwithstanding. Though two neighbors, Obstinate and Pliable, tried to drag him back by force, he managed to make it through the Slough of Despond and past Mr. Worldly-Wiseman, who counseled him against Evangelist's preaching, to the Strait Gate through which one must pass to go to the Celestial City. Good Will opened the Gate for him when he discovered Christian's brokenhearted repentance for sin.

Entering the Gate, Christian made his way to Interpreter's House (suggested perhaps by the church at Bedford) where Interpreter enlightened him from Scriptures about the difficulties of the journey and explained how he could overcome them. Rested and illumined thus, he headed directly to the Cross, where the heavy burden of sin and guilt he bore fell immediately from his back. Though he proceeded with greater confidence without his burden, he faced difficulty all along the way, constantly tempted to leave the path by such figures as Simple, Sloth, Formalist, Hypocrisie, Timorous, and Mistrust. Resting after an arduous climb up the Hill Difficulty, he read from his Roll (the Scriptures) for encouragement, then placed it under his head and went to sleep. When he awakened, he went off without the Roll and had to return "with sorrow" to find it, for he could not reach the Celestial City without it.

At the Porter's Lodge Watchful, Piety, Prudence, and Charity supplied much-needed encouragement and armed him, still fearful for the rest of the journey, with Sword, Shield, Helmet, Breastplate, All-Prayer, and Shoes that would not wear out. They also showed him a vision of the Delectable Mountains of Immanuel's Land within sight of the Celestial City. Thus outfitted, he overcame Apollyon (the Destroyer) in hand-to-hand combat. All-Prayer enabled him to pass unharmed through the Valley of the Shadow of Death that winds just above Hell itself. Here Christian overtook Faithful, who shared with him the cost of discipleship. Along the way, they encountered Talkative, whose faith "hath no place in his heart, or house, or conversation," but rather "all he hath lieth in his *tongue*, and his Religion is to make a noise *therewith*." Extended conversation with Talkative gave Christian and Faithful a chance to explain what true religion consisted of: an experimental confession of faith in Christ; a life answerable to that confession, that is, a life of holiness; and, above all, the practice of faith.

Upset with the peevishness of the pilgrims, Talkative bid them farewell. Once again, Evangelist appeared and encouraged them just in time, for they now came to Vanity Fair, which had claimed the lives of many faithful pilgrims. The Fair offered for sale all sorts of worldly merchandise from the world over. Not unexpectedly, fairgoers took offense at the clothing, speech, and disdain for their wares. Consequently they beat Christian and Faithful, smeared them with dirt, and locked them in a cage to ridicule them. When the brash pair preached and won some converts, Judge Hate-good and a jury composed of no-goods of Vanity tried and condemned Faithful to death. Christian, however, though remanded to prison for a time, managed to escape.

No sooner had he lost Faithful than Christian was joined by Hopeful for the last leg of his journey. Deceptive company and dangerous temptations still lurked along the way, trying to lure them astray. They nearly perished at Doubting-Castle, owned by the Giant Despair and his wife Diffidence, but Hopeful helped Christian overcome his depression by recalling previous victories. Just when the giant was ready to pull them to pieces, Christian found a key in his bosom, called Promise, that would open any lock in Doubting-Castle. From thence, they came quickly to the Delectable Mountains and within sight of the Celestial City.

Shepherds—Knowledge, Experience, Watchful, and Sincere—fed them and directed them to the right path, warning them to beware of flatterers and not to sleep on the Enchanted Ground. Ignorance joined them, thinking he could enter the Celestial City even though he had not passed through the Strait Gate, and kept them company the rest of the way. Little-faith, a good man from the town of Sincere, joined them too in time to get a lecture about Esau's selling of his birthright and about the courage of Christian. Flatterer nearly diverted them from the way, but Christian and Hopeful passed through the Enchanted Ground without going to sleep and entered safely into Beulah Land where angels met them.

One danger stood between them and the Celestial City, the River of Death. Their hope in Jesus Christ, however, gave them courage to pass through to the other side. Ignorance reached the very gates of the heavenly Jerusalem and was thrown into outer darkness because he had entered as a thief and robber. Only the Pilgrims who had come by the way of the Wicket Gate were welcomed in.

The story of Christiana which Bunyan added to his classic in 1685 seems by design *déjà vu*. Although he proposed to fill in some blanks in the original with this addendum, he really repeated his main theme of the Christian pilgrimage—this time one somewhat more placid than his own. With just a few exceptions personae are the same: Timorous, Obstinate, Pliable, Interpreter, Simple, Sloth, Formalist, Hypocrisy, Watchful, Giant Despair and his wife Diffidence, and Valiant-for-Truth. Greatheart, however, who played a nominal role in Christian's saga, became the hero and guide in Christiana's, lending the male power Puritan sensibilities required a woman to have on a dangerous journey. He, rather than Christiana, fought the major battles. Places were also familiar: the

City of Destruction, the Slough of Despond, the Strait Gate, Interpreter's House, the Hill Difficulty, the Valley of the Shadow of Death, Vanity Fair, Doubting-Castle, the Delectable Mountains, Beulah Land, the Enchanted Ground, the River of Death, and the Celestial City. Yet Christiana's journey itself lacked the terror and the sheer drama of Christian's. Indeed, by this time Bunyan seemed ready to open heaven's gates more readily for those who would claim some morsel of sincerity such as Mercie, a neighbor who trailed along more on Christiana's credentials than on her own, or Feeblemind and Fearing, whose fear of God more than any special courage confirmed their faith. None of the pilgrims had to pay the price Faithful did; the age of persecution had passed.

E. Glenn Hinson

RECOMMENDED READING

Edition used: Bunyan, John, *Grace Abounding to the Chief of Sinners* and *The Pilgrim's Progress from This World to That Which Is to Come.* Edited by Roger Sharrock. London: Oxford University Press, 1966.

Bunyan, John. *The Miscellaneous Works of John Bunyan.* Edited by Roger Sharrock. Vol. 2: *The Doctrine of the Law and Grace Unfolded and I Will Pray with the Spirit.* Edited by Richard L. Greaves. Oxford: Clarendon Press, 1976. Key themes in Bunyan's thought can be seen here.

Greaves, Richard L. *John Bunyan.* Grand Rapids, Mich.: Eerdmans, 1969. An excellent critical study relating Bunyan to the Lutherans as well as the Reformed tradition.

Harding, M. Esther. *Journey into Self.* New York: Longmans, Green & Co., 1956. A Jungian analysis of *Pilgrim's Progress.*

A Short and Very Easy Method of Prayer

Author: Madame Guyon (1648–1717)

Suffering an unhappy childhood, and married at sixteen, thereby becoming Madame Guyon, Jeanne-Marie Bouvier de la Motte was converted to deep faith in 1668. She withdrew from the worldly life of the aristocracy to make known to others what she had learned personally of the spiritual life. In 1685 she published her *Short and Very Easy Method of Prayer*, for which she was imprisoned in 1688 on suspicion of heresy. Through this experience she became acquainted with Cardinal Fénelon, on whom she was to have much influence. She was imprisoned again, in the Bastille (1698–1702). Among her other works is *Spiritual Torments, an Autobiography* (1683), which she circulated in manuscript for her initiates. Altogether, her collected works were published in forty volumes, posthumously.

Type and subject of work: Spiritual instruction, with an emphasis on prayer

First published: 1685 (*Moyen court et très facile pour l'oraison*)

Major Themes

Prayer is the state of the heart in which it is united to God in faith and love. Interpret the Lord's Prayer in your own heart; in the Lord's Prayer, God gives himself to us, to guide us and empower us to pray.

Inward holiness is the true regulator of the outward life.

The heart of prayer is the prayer of silence, when the only request of the soul is the unspoken desire, "Thy will be done."

The focus of prayer remains, simply, to speak and teach the primacy of Jesus Christ in the depths of one's being.

The whole controversy in which Bossuet, bishop of Meaux, challenged Fénelon, archbishop of Cambrai, over quietism, and Madame Guyon in particular, was discreditable and confusing. Anyone reading her famous book that was banned by the Church of Rome in 1699 will see that its subsequent popularity among Protestants in the eighteenth century and onward was a result of its insistence upon self-abandonment to God's will.

Prayer is the key to knowing God, Madame Guyon insists. But it is a style of prayer she calls "the prayer of simplicity," for it comes from the heart. It is our response to God, knowing that his desire to give himself to us is far greater than any desire we may have towards God. Begin then, she urges, by praying over some passage of the Scriptures to find the Lord there. Then allow your heart to be still in his presence. Do not try to imagine what or who God is like. Simply admit his presence into your heart.

From this first level of simple waiting in God's presence, you can now move to a second level of what she calls "the prayer of simplicity." This will not come until you have spent much time in the first stage, of quietly resting in his presence. Also, have a believing heart so that you are not discouraged in changing course in your devotions. Do not try to be self-conscious of what you are doing, in exploring the depths of Jesus Christ. For praying with a believing heart is more important than any reflections upon the experience of prayer. Come then with a heart full of love for Christ, she urges.

For Madame Guyon prayer is an act of the heart and its objective is union with God in faith and love. She sought to make available to all Christians an easy way of prayer that would lead to the contemplation of God. She argued that prayer and religion are the same thing, but she was distressed to find that for many persons the only exercise of prayer is in the rote recitation of the Lord's Prayer. She urged her readers to begin by meditating on the whole meaning of the Lord's Prayer; she calls upon all believers to go beyond the mere recital of the prayer and to interpret the prayer in their own hearts. In the Lord's Prayer, she insisted, God gives himself to us, to guide us and to empower us to pray.

Devotional reading and meditation will also help, she wrote. By these practices one will be brought into the presence of God. At first, she cautions, one will be preoccupied with one's own feelings in prayer, but as one abandons all things to experience the will of God alone, one will learn that consecration is the heart of prayer.

In many ways you will be tested concerning self-abandonment, she writes, but always remember that inward holiness is the true regulator of the outward life. Gradually you will experience growth in faith and love, she assures her readers; the conscience will become increasingly more sensitive, though the struggle against temptation will continue as long as you need to deepen the experience of self-abandonment.

The heart of prayer, according to Madame Guyon, is the prayer of silence, when the only request of the soul is the unspoken desire, "Thy will be done." A total dependence on God takes over as one's dynamic principle and the outcome of the prayer of silence is divine union with God.

Learn to see why you may go through periods of spiritual "dry spells." God may be hiding himself from you, she writes, because God wants to arouse you from spiritual laziness to desire him more fervently. You will experience aridity of soul, she tells us; it is God's way of dealing with you. Our response in such periods should be the exercise of patient love, in self-denial, humiliation, and self-abandonment.

Until now perhaps, she continues, you have seen the need to pray one or two or more times a day. But if incessant prayer is to mark your life, then you need to be prepared for a radical change of your natural temperament. This new attitude toward yourself and toward your Lord also comes when you are prepared to go deeper, much deeper, into experiencing Jesus Christ. "Abandonment" is the key to this spiritual growth. It is the casting away of all your needs, even spiritual needs. It is the casting away of all your cares and desires, other than for God himself (Matt. 6:32, 34; Prov. 3:6; 16:3; Ps. 37:5). Forget your past, Madame Guyon writes; be devoted, moment by moment instead, to the will of God. Your life is now the declaration of God's will in everything about you.

Suffering will enter your life, she cautions us. It may reveal that you had secret expectations of the life of self-abandonment. Sometimes you will bear the cross of Christ in weakness, sometimes in strength. So how you respond to suffering will then become important. Do you feel abandoned by God? If so, be comforted to realize that it is by abandonment that he actually reveals himself to us. He will leave an imprint upon us that begins to change us. So in all the distress, simply go on loving him, she writes; the result of such a life will be godliness, a godly walk with the Lord.

Madame Guyon realized that not everyone is able to develop a severe ascetic attitude to outward things. But we can all turn inwardly toward the Lord, she suggests. So center upon God, as filings to a magnet, she urges, and you will find that the more your heart is centered upon God, the more he cleanses it. Then you will find the Lord takes full possession of you, in continual prayer, the prayer of silence before him. You will also begin to experience complete rest before the Lord. Remember self-effort brings restlessness, so be rebuked by the words of the prophet: "You have wearied yourselves in the multiplicity of your ways, and have not said, 'Let us rest in peace'" (Isa. 57:10). Gradually then, you will make this inner peace a daily, constant experience also. For the prayer becomes his presence, there, always, she assures us.

Silence before God begins to take on new meaning, Madame Guyon writes. Because we see our carnal natures are so opposed to God, we must silence them in his presence. But since God's nature is to reveal, to be the Word, if we listen to him, we allow God to be in our hearts. To listen to God attentively, then, is to welcome him into our hearts. We also allow the entire soul to be open before God, so that we enter more deeply into confession and repentance before him. Moreover, if we are seeking to live a life where we have no needs, then if we pray any petitions, *he* must pray through us; *he* must be the prayer! Of course, distractions and temptations will still come to trouble us, but instead of being preoccupied with them, which only makes them worse, simply turn away from them, she advises.

In conclusion, Madame Guyon appealed to Christian workers. If only new converts were reached in their hearts and introduced to real prayers leading to experiencing the presence of Jesus Christ, then many more would go on to become true disciples. But inexpressible damage has been done to so many who have never experienced this inner, spiritual relationship with Jesus Christ.

There is an intensity about Madame Guyon's writing that reflects her own unjust sufferings, calumny, and imprisonment. For that reason, the book has sometimes had an unhealthy appeal to those who felt politically maltreated, and it can be abused as a political manifesto for the ecclesiastically disenfranchised. This is unfortunate, because as a personal work of devotion, to give counsel to those seeking a deeper experience of prayer, the *Short and Very Easy Method of Prayer* is a wonderful statement of personal devotion.

James M. Houston

RECOMMENDED READING

Edition used: Guyon, Jeanne. *Experiencing the Depths of Jesus Christ.* Edited by Gene Edwards. Goleta, Calif.: Christian Books, 1975. An abridged, rewritten version of her *Short and Very Easy Method of Prayer.* "The Little Flock Movement" has also published her *Spiritual Writings* and *Union with God* in similar fashion.

Upham, T. C. *The Life of Madame Guyon.* Greenwood, S.C.: Attic Press, 1961. Originally published in 1905. A sympathetic biography with an emphasis on the spiritual life.

THE PRACTICE OF THE PRESENCE OF GOD

Author: Brother Lawrence (Nicholas Herman, 1611–1691)
Nicholas Herman was born in Lorraine about 1611. After serving in the army and in the household of the treasurer of the exchequer, in middle age he entered the Discalced Carmelite order and received the name of Brother Lawrence of the Resurrection. After some years of trial, he came to experience the Presence of God, which remained with him through his daily chores as cook and cobbler. Abbé Joseph de Beaufort visited Brother and after Lawrence's death wrote a memoir based on their conversations and Brother's letters, publishing it in 1692 under Herman's name as *The Practice of the Presence of God*.

Type and subject of work: Reports on conversations and some letters, setting forth a practical way of spirituality

First published: 1692

MAJOR THEMES

The way of faith is the way of the Church and is sufficient to bring us to a high degree of perfection.

To go to God we do not need art or science but only a heart resolutely determined to apply itself to nothing but him or others for his sake—to love him alone.

Our sanctification is found in doing for God's sake what we commonly do for our own sake.

The whole substance of religion is faith, hope, and charity; everything else is a means to this end.

Prayer is a sense of the Presence of God.

We should establish in ourselves a sense of the Presence of God by continually talking to him.

The Practice of the Presence of God is the spiritual heritage of a simple, unlearned lay-brother, gathered together by a learned priest. Brother Lawrence had been pursuing his simple way for a decade or more when the Abbé de Beaufort visited him. In the course of 1666, the abbé had four conversations (August 3, September 28, November 22 and 25) with the lay-brother and wrote in a brief and clear report the main points of Brother's spiritual way. After Brother's demise, he gathered up what letters he could find, and published them along with his reports. To the fourth report he added a few details he learned from others about Brother's spiritual teaching.

What is outstanding in the spiritual legacy of Brother Lawrence is the simplicity and directness with which he approaches God. The whole of his way is summed up at the beginning of the report of the fourth conversation:

> He told me that all consists *in one hearty renunciation* of everything which does not lead us to God in order that we may accustom ourselves to a continual conversation with Him, with freedom and in simplicity. That we need only to recognize God intimately present with us, and to address ourselves to Him every moment, that we may beg His assistance for knowing His will in things doubtful, and for rightly performing [those] which we plainly see He requires of us; offering them to Him before we do them, and giving Him thanks when we have done.

Through personal experience, at the age of eighteen, Nicholas Herman, later Brother Lawrence, came to know the providence and power of God. There was always a great awkwardness about Nicholas, which he considered a personal failing. In middle age he entered religious life in a strict order to do penance for what he considered his many faults. His first four years (the report says four; in a later letter Brother says ten) were troubled by a sure sense of damnation. In spite of this he still tried to love God faithfully and fully. In time he came to see that his trouble came from his lack of faith or confidence in God's great love. He allowed his sins to come between him and God. Once he entered into a deeper trust he found liberty and joy. He expected this state to pass, but he abided in trust and so abided in joy and peace. At times he wished he had more to suffer for God. He did continue to fail at times but he humbly turned his failures over to the Lord for healing and went on in trust.

Brother Lawrence turned everything into prayer by simply talking to God as he went about his tasks, even those he found disagreeable, such as business trips and fifteen years' service in the kitchen. His way was so simple that he needed no director but only a confessor. Attempts at getting direction left him only more confused. Methods of prayer did not help him nor did ascetical practices. He lived an ascetical life and found that the shortest way to God is by the continual practice of love, doing all things for him.

Brother Lawrence realized that acts of understanding were of comparatively little value; it was acts of the will that counted, loving and enjoying God. The foundation of the spiritual life, for him, was a profound reverence for God.

Living in the present, he had no care for the future, counting on God to give him what he needed when he needed it; nor did he remember the past. He sought to remain always in the present in the Presence. He strove to do all for the Love of God. He found more consolation and devotion in doing his ordinary occupations than at the community devotions, which often left him dry. Brother felt that many are impeded in spiritual progress because they keep to penances and particular spiritual practices long after they are useful for the individual. To go to God we do not need abilities or lots of learning. The key is a heart that is absolutely determined to apply itself to God and to do other things only insofar as God wants. It is not a question of undertaking special practices. Rather it is doing the things we would ordinarily do, but instead of doing them for our own sakes, we do them for God's sake. There is no dichotomy between prayer time and work time. We are as strictly obliged to adhere to God by action in the time of action as by prayer in the time of prayer. Indeed, all is prayer, for prayer is but the sense of the Presence of God, surrendering ourselves to him in the midst of prayers or work.

When we first enter upon the spiritual life, Brother tells us, we should consider and examine to the bottom who we are. Then we are to turn our minds to God to impress deeply on our hearts God's existence, not by studied reasoning or elaborate meditations but by devout sentiments and submission to the lights of faith. Then with resolve, we endeavor to live in a continual sense of God's Presence. By continually returning to God by deliberate acts, this sense becomes habitual and the Presence of God "is rendered as it were *natural* to us."

Brother began his active duties with this prayer:

O my God, since Thou are with me, and I must now, in obedience to Thy commands, apply my mind to these outward things, I beseech Thee to grant me the grace to continue in Thy Presence; and to this end do Thou prosper me with Thy assistance, receive all my works, and possess all my affections.

As he continued his work, he continued his familiar conversation with his Maker. At the end of work he examined himself on how he had remained faithful. If he did well, he thanked God; if poorly, he asked pardon and, without discouragement, went on in the Presence of God.

The result of this practice was that his soul was "filled with joys so continual, and sometimes so transcendent, that he is forced to use means to moderate them, and to prevent their appearing outwardly" (from a letter Brother wrote to a mother superior on June 1, 1682, almost ten years before his death).

Brother Lawrence encouraged others in this practice by word and by powerful example. *The Practice of the Presence of God* contains sixteen brief letters, all but one addressed to women, mostly religious women or nuns. These collected were written in the last years of his life, 1682–1691, as he moved into his eighties. The last was written a week before he died. The one letter written to a priest lays out his whole spiritual path for the priest's examination, for he was keenly aware that the simply way in which he walked did not correspond to the stages and methods others taught.

In his letters to the women, Brother sometimes speaks of his own experience as though it were that of someone else. When he is more self-revealing, he cautions the recipient against sharing the letter with others. He gives much practical instruction in this simple way to holiness and happiness. He bewails the blindness that holds back most from enjoying the Divine Presence. He encourages and congratulates his correspondents who have been striving to be continually present to God.

M. Basil Pennington

RECOMMENDED READING

Edition used: Lawrence, Brother (Nicholas Herman). *The Practice of the Presence of God.* Nashville: Abingdon Press, 1975.

Caussade, Jean-Pierre de. *Self-Abandonment to Divine Providence.* Translated by Algar Thorold. Revised by John Joyce, S.J. Introduction by David Knowles. Springfield, Ind.: Templegate, 1959. This is a presentation of much the same teaching, but adapted to a later and more complex age. (See the article on this book in this volume.)

Johnston, William. *Christian Mysticism Today.* San Francisco: Harper & Row, 1984. This concise, up-to-date survey of Christian mysticism puts Brother Lawrence's contribution in its full context.

Lawrence of the Resurrection, Brother. *The Practice of the Presence of God.* Introduction by John J. Delaney. Foreword by Henri J. M. Nouwen. New York: Doubleday, Image Books, 1977. An inexpensive paperback edition with a good introduction by John Delaney.

THE JOURNAL OF GEORGE FOX

Author: George Fox (1624–1691)

A child of devout parents, George Fox shared the Puritan concern for heartfelt inward piety and outward reform but not their emphasis on Scriptures or total depravity. Claiming divine leading, in 1643 he began an itinerant prophetic ministry that eventually attracted a significant following not only among the masses but among England's elite such as William Penn and Robert Barclay. His thunderous attacks on the Church of England and refusal to abide by such customs as "hat honor" (removing the hat in the presence of nobility) generated strong opposition and resulted in a series of imprisonments. A strong and persistent person, however, Fox refused to bend to his opponents. He did not himself keep a journal, but rather dictated to others. In 1674 or 1675 he related his biography to his stepson-in-law, Thomas Lower. He died January 13, 1691.

Type and subject of work: Spiritual autobiography

First published: 1694

MAJOR THEMES

There is a Light Within that shows human beings what is evil and in which they may find unity; this "Light" is the divine made sufficiently available to humankind.

Salvation involves turning to the Light, to Christ, which is both within and also transcendent, and it is open to all, not just an "elect."

The Light Within does not conflict with Scriptures, for the Scriptures were a product of the Light, but it alone has infallible authority.

The saints on earth may find unity in the Light such as they will experience in heaven; applied here and now, this unity necessitates treating other persons equally.

William Penn's preface to Thomas Ellwood's edition of the *Journal* (1694) depicted Fox as "a strong man, a new and heavenly-minded man, a divine and a naturalist, and all of God Almighty's making." Defending the master against detractors, he called attention to Fox's unusual insight into persons (confirmed by the type of persons who chose to follow him), his extraordinary gifts in interpreting Scriptures, his potency in prayer, his innocence and selflessness, his tirelessness in spreading his message and in service of others, and his penchant for organization and leadership.

Like other Quaker journals, Fox's served an apologetic purpose, that is, to project Fox as a model of the behavior of Friends which, if imitated, could improve the human condition. Far from being a daily log of events, the "journal" presented vignettes that could illustrate the main features of this remarkable person and the movement that began. The main body of the work recorded Fox's life and work up to 1674; the remainder filled out the last years with letters and other data.

Fox related in the first part as much of his early life as would inform readers and thus praise God concerning "the dealings of the Lord with me, and the various exercises, trials, and troubles through which he led me in order to prepare and fit me for the work unto which he had appointed me." His chief object would appear to have been to establish his character in response to criticism. Neighbors called his father "Righteous Christer." His mother, Mary Lago, was "of the stock of the martyrs." Early on, he developed "a gravity and stayedness of mind and spirit not usual in children" and by age eleven "knew pureness and righteousness" in the sense of acting faithfully both "inwardly to God and outwardly to man." Acquaintances commented, "If George says 'Verily' there is no altering him."

At nineteen Fox experienced a shock that triggered his prophetic ministry. At a local fair one of his cousins and a friend, both professing Christians, asked him to drink part of a jug of beer with them but then, as the alcohol took effect, teased him, demanding that whoever refused to drink should pay the entire cost. Not one for games, Fox threw down a groat and departed abruptly. Deeply disturbed, he perceived a calling to "forsake all, both young and old, and keep out of all, and be as a stranger unto all." For the next several years he became a "seeker," agonizing day and night in a quest for "heavenly wisdom." He experienced a series of "openings" or "considerations." Education at Oxford or Cambridge was "not enough to make a man fit to be a minister of Christ." The God who made heaven and earth does not dwell in temples or churches but in people's hearts. God anoints one inwardly to interpret Scriptures and to teach. Women have souls just as men do and thus should be treated as equals. Not surprisingly, Fox reported, his first associated was a woman named Elizabeth Hooten, who joined him in 1647.

Nowhere that Fox turned—whether to priests of the Church of England or to dissenters—could he find any who, as he expressed it, "could speak to my condition." Near despair after four years of wandering, he heard a voice say, "There is one, even Christ Jesus, that can speak to thy condition." He found this confirmed experimentally as he initiated his remarkable prophetic ministry in 1647. Vivid mystical experiences prepared him boldly to articulate his appeal for a devout and holy life. First a trickle and then a flood of conversions occurred, as Fox urged his hearers to turn from darkness to the Light of Christ within. However, he soon set off opposition, for he coupled his message with a social protest against doffing his hat and saying "thee" and "thou" without respect to class or station. "O, the rage and scorn, the heat and fury that arose! Oh, the blows, punchings, beatings, and imprisonments that we underwent for not putting off our hats to men!" But Fox did not relent. He warned schoolteachers to tutor their charges in sobriety and thundered against "steeplehouses" and "hireling" priests.

At Nottingham in 1649 Fox was hauled off to prison for the first time when he interrupted a congregation at worship and preached that God does not dwell in a temple made with hands. The local sheriff, however, was so touched by him after a few days that he took Fox into his own home and began a ministry somewhat like Fox's. This inflamed the local magistrates so much they had Fox arrested and taken to the common prison again. At Mansfield-Woodhouse his assault on superficial religion resulted in a horrible beating by the parishioners, but the magistrate set him free and he recovered with amazing rapidity. As he met such opposition, Fox was strengthened by what would appear to have been mystical experiences. At Coventry, for instance, he claimed that he "was ravished with the sense of the love of God and greatly strengthened in my inward man." At Derby in October 1650 he was sentenced to six months in prison for continued disturbances and his claim that Christ had taken away all his sin. In Fox's trial Justice Bennet was the first to call the Friends "Quakers" because they bid other people to tremble. A cell did not stop Fox. His witness to prisoners and his jailer earned him some freedom of movement within a mile radius around the jail. He also wrote, initiating what became a powerful facet of the Quaker witness as "publishers of Truth," but his directness tended to work against him and lengthened his sentences.

Many of the social views Fox espoused have a modern ring. For example, he opposed capital punishment (for stealing cattle, money, or other things) as opposed to the mercy of God taught by Scriptures.

Undeterred by nearly a year in prison, Fox continued to travel all over the midlands and the northern part of England proclaiming his controversial message. Attacks continued, but Fox also won converts from all classes, enough to cause some priests to flee and lock the churches. A critical stage was reached in 1652. Fox's converts in that year included Francis Howgill, a key defender of the Friends until his death in 1669, Edward Burrough (1634–1662), who died in Newgate prison, and Margaret Fell, who married Fox in 1659. The Fell estate, Swarthmoor, soon became a center for Fox's rapidly growing movement. Judge Fell (d. 1658), though never a follower, protected Fox and the Friends, seeking warrants for the arrest of a mob that mugged Fox at Ulverston after he interrupted the worship in the "steeplehouse." He also aided Fox in a defense of his views at Lancaster sessions. Fox appropriately called him "very serviceable to the Truth."

The central portion of Fox's *Journal* has a somewhat repetitious character: bold witness, winning of some, harassment and persecution by others, imprisonment and abuse by authorities; yet the Friends' movement spread despite all, as Fox would say, as "the power of the Lord went over all." In 1654 Fox, a genius at organization, dispatched a notable troop of preachers all over England—Francis Howgill, Edward Burrough, John Camm, John Audland, Richard Hubberthorne, George Whitehead, Thomas Holme, and others—with instructions to place their trust in the Light Within. The Quakers encountered opposition from many sources besides the established Church—Ranters, who frequently disrupted meetings; Baptists, who looked upon the Friends' view of Scriptures as heretical; Oliver Cromwell, who though he favored independents and admired Fox, did not know what to do with disruptions caused by the Quaker "publishers of Truth." After 1655 Cromwell increasingly ignored Fox' pleas for protection.

The Friends' movement suffered severe damage as a result of James Nayler, at one time a major proclaimer of the Quaker way, getting caught up in what Fox called "imaginations" and leading some off in a rebellion that resulted in his death. Fox openly repudiated him in September of 1656. Persecution also evidently increased, for Fox complained that no one could describe what Quakers underwent in that time.

In 1657 Fox itinerated through Wales. Indicative of his own confidence in "the power over all," he claimed credit for adequate rain in areas where many had joined the Friends and blamed drought on disbelief in other areas. There he seems to have encountered less opposition than in England. He rebuked Cromwell when the latter appealed for aid for Protestant refugees from Poland and Bohemia while the Protector himself persecuted Protestants in England. The situation did not improve during the brief rule of Richard Cromwell (1658–1660). Fox welcomed the restoration of the monarchy. Rumors circulated that Friends would take up arms to fight for Charles II, but Fox urged them everywhere to "keep out of the powers of the earth that run into wars and fightings, which make not for peace but go from that."

The return of Charles (May 25, 1660) did not bring immediate relief to the harried Quakers. Fox was arrested almost immediately at Swarthmoor and taken to Lancaster, where he was charged as "a disturber of the peace of the nation, a common enemy to His Majesty our lord the King, a chief upholder of the Quakers' sect," and a fomenter of insurrections. Fox denied the charges vigorously, citing Quaker pacifism. Margaret Fell also interceded but, now that Judge Fell had died, with little effect. Fox then applied directly to King Charles and obtained his release after twenty weeks in Lancaster prison. The Friends, who had suffered impounding of property and imprisonment for refusal to pay tithes to the Church in Cromwell's day, fared better under the monarchy at first. An uprising of Fifth Monarchy people, however, occasioned a new outburst of persecution, to which the Quakers responded in January 1661 with a *"Declaration from the harmless and innocent people of God, called Quakers, against all plotters and fighters in the world, . . ."* in which they articulated a pacifist stance. As a consequence, King Charles acquitted them of complicity with the rebels and set them free. At the intercession of Edward Burroughs the king also commanded that execution of Quakers in New England (begun in 1659) be halted.

In 1661 Quakers initiated visits outside the British Isles. Fox himself continued his activities throughout England, organizing his following through Monthly as well as Quarterly Meetings in 1667. Like other dissenters, the Quakers suffered again under the Second Coventicle Act (1670). Fox himself, his health damaged by frequent beatings and imprisonment in dreadful conditions, lost both hearing and sight for a brief time but recovered sufficiently to visit North America, although he suffered frequent illness the rest of his life.

From 1671 on, Fox's *Journal* had to be continued by reconstruction from various sources. (Thomas Ellwood put together a narrative as though written by Fox, but John L. Nickalls, the current editor, has simply incorporated the letters, Fox's American travel diary for October 1671 until April 11, 1673, and other materials. Fox's autobiography ended in 1675. The Nickalls edition replaces Ellwood's narrative with a supplementary account of Fox's last years composed by Henry J. Cadbury.)

Fox spent a couple of years at Swarthmoor (1675–1677), then started traveling again despite severe physical problems. In July of 1677 he departed for the continent, visiting Friends in Germany and Holland, and, upon returning in 1678, resumed his itinerary around England. He made a second visit to Holland in 1684.

E. Glenn Hinson

RECOMMENDED READING

Edition used: Nickalls, John L., ed. *The Journal of George Fox*. London: Religious Society of Friends, 1975. A more accurate edition than that originally edited by John Ellwood.

Jones, Rufus. *George Fox: Seeker and Friend*. New York and London: Harper & Bros., 1930. An excellent biography by a key interpreter of early Quakerism.

King, Rachel Hadley. *George Fox and the Light Within, 1650–1660*. Philadelphia: Friends Books Store, 1940. An insightful analysis of this central concept in Fox's thought and life.

Monagham, Hanna Darlington. *"Dear George": George Fox, Man and Prophet*. Philadelphia: Franklin, 1970. A critical biography.

CHRISTIAN PERFECTION

Author: François de Salignac de La Mothe Fénelon (1651–1715)
Prominent in the court of Louis XIV as tutor to the duke of Burgundy
(heir presumptive), Fénelon was named archbishop of Cambrai in 1695.
Meanwhile he had fallen under the influence of Mme. Jeanne-Marie
Bouvier de la Motte Guyon (1648–1717) of Quietist persuasions, whom
he defended against the anti-mystical party in the court headed by Jacques Bénigne Bossuet, bishop of Meaux. When Fénelon's *Maxims of the
Saints* (1697), a clarification and defense of Quietism, was condemned by
Pope Innocent XII (with the comment that Fénelon erred by loving God
too much, Bossuet by loving man too little), Fénelon was banished by
Louis to his diocese, where he earned the reputation of being an ideal
pastor. *Christian Perfection* is the English edition of a collection of letters
and addresses dating over a period of many years, Fénelon's correspondence with Mme. Françoise de Maintenon (initially governess of Louis's
children, later Louis's wife) accounting for approximately a third of the
text.

Type and subject of work: Spiritual letters and minor works

First published: 1704–1717

MAJOR THEMES

God appoints suffering to those whom he loves.
The purpose of suffering is to strip the individual of self-love.
Human perfection consists in the disinterested love of God.
The way for one to attain this end is unconditional faith.

This important collection of short writings by François de Fénelon can serve as a handbook of spiritual instruction. Its theme is how an earnest Christian, enmeshed in the affairs of the world, can make some progress along the way marked out by the great mystics and ascetics. The undertaking was familiar enough with the religious orders, but Fénelon's writings were meant for the laity, mostly persons of rank, who had the problem of living their religion in places like Versailles. The papers here collected are of a private character except for three or four that were presumably memoranda for talks. As the book is a hodgepodge, readers must arrange the material with their own concerns in mind; but it may be of help to recognize at the start that each piece has a particular point to make, usually in answer to a question put to Fénelon in his capacity of director of consciences.

An early letter deals with the problem of amusements. Mme. de Maintenon, first lady of France, complains of having to fritter away hours in foolish games. Fénelon, warning her against the false piety which assumes that we can serve God only by a gloomy life, calls her back to the ideal of detachment, remarking how simple and serene life can be when one is totally surrendered to God's will. A person's duties, he says, are defined by the place in which Providence has placed him or her, and he urges her to make a point of preserving a gay and sociable humor when she is in company, giving up the notion that there are more important things that she could be doing. When one is converted and wishes to reform one's life, says Fénelon, God does not ordinarily alter the person's outward condition but instead demands a change within. "What he asks is a will which will no longer be divided between himself and his creatures, a will pliant in his hands, which wants without reservation everything which he wants, and which never, under any pretext, wants anything which he does not want."

Another question is, What does mortification mean for a person of wealth and influence? Every preacher talked about cross-bearing and mortification, and Madame refers to it repeatedly. Fénelon's answer is that all the vexations that she mentions to him as arising out of her position in court are mortifications. A person cannot mortify herself: She can only yield to the mortifications with which God afflicts those whom he loves. "God is ingenious in making us crosses." The poor, with their crosses of lead and iron, can hardly understand that there are also crosses of gold and precious stones. "He makes them of all the things which we like the best, and turns them to bitterness." What God aims at is the destruction of the "I," the self. God despoils us from without when he takes away the things we cherish; then he attacks us from within, destroying our egos. This last "stripping" is the most painful, but it is an indication that one is well advanced on the Christian way. In the nature of the case, the self must cooperate with God in the outward mortification of the senses, yet to the degree that this work is successful the soul is inflated with a sense of its virtue; hence, God must attack the self in its depths, showing it its own wretchedness and reducing it to nothing. "All that is left to it is the desire to cling to nothing, and to let God act without reservation."

A question that Fénelon must have heard on many occasions is, Are you not making God pretty severe? A person has a general confession, attends mass with fair regularity, does some reading, and says prayers. Surely God is not going to refuse such honest efforts! Fénelon, in a piece called "Semi-Conversions," describes the conventional Christian as one who is ready to love God if God will be satisfied with ceremonies and not ask one to give up any advantage, especially one's reputation in the beau monde. Persons of this sort, says Fénelon, are afraid of losing what they think of as their liberty, but they err, not knowing either God or themselves. They think of God as tyrannizing over them and think of the world as offering them freedom, when the opposite is the case. What the world promises dissolves into humiliation and boredom, but no promise of God has ever failed. "He will take from us that which makes us unhappy. He will make us do what we are doing every day, simple and reasonable things which we are doing badly . . . and will make us do them well, by inspiring us to do them to obey him."

Either Mme. de Maintenon or one of her friends wants to know how to deal with "a sort of sadness which constricts and oppresses the heart." Fénelon offers two rules. The first rule is to fight it actively. This may mean giving up some of her activities as being too much for her strength, gaining thereby more time for prayer and reading, but also for conversation and other forms of relaxation. She needs someone to whom she can unburden herself: Sorrow kept to oneself breaks the heart. The second rule, however, is not to resist the involuntary feeling of sadness. "Discouragements within us make us go faster than all else in the way of faith." They are God's means of destroying our self-confidence. We take a giant step toward perfection when we lose the taste for our own goodness.

But what about the joys and consolations concerning which one reads in so many religious books? In Fénelon's opinion, the books are misleading. Religious life is plagued with illusions and none more fatal than to "live as though we were seeing paradise wide open." Joyful experiences and extraordinary visions flatter our self-love and in this way take the place of God. "It is only pure faith which saves from illusion." When one loves God without asking to feel his presence and trusts him without asking to see the way, "this dim nakedness leaves no hold for our own will and our senses, which are the source of all illusion." But are those books wrong that tell us to "practice the presence of God"? Not at all. But practicing God's presence is not the same as feeling it. We practice it when we accustom ourselves to "short, simple and frequent liftings of the heart to God." We can do this in company and when we are about our work. "This is the true way to act in the presence of God, and to become familiar with it."

Is it wrong, then, to think of God as dwelling within us? The question was raised by Mme. de Maintenon and draws a long response from Fénelon, perhaps because he recognized its implications for the government's policy toward quietists and others who insisted that God has not to be sought for because he dwells already in the heart. The Bible is clear, says Fénelon: The Holy Spirit dwells in us, prays for us as we do not know how to pray, speaks to us in silence, and so unites us to himself that we are "one spirit with God." Theologians usually forget this because they suppose that we are enlightened from the outside. Does this mean that Christians are inspired? Yes, but not in the same way as the prophets of old times. Inspiration is of two kinds. That which came to the prophets was full of light and certainty, because it announced God's plan for saving humankind. The inspiration that comes to believers is without light or certainty. It has to do entirely with winning our love away from the creature and back to the Creator. Persons who really want to know what is involved in following the great saints must learn to recognize the thousand little ways we have of resisting God's will; for example, being too outspoken in company, being suspicious without reason, and being irresolute over some trifle. "Flexibility and promptness in yielding to these promptings of the Spirit is what advances souls most. Those who are noble enough never to hesitate soon make incredible progress. The others reason, and never lack reasons to keep them from doing what they have at heart."

A question that Fénelon handles with particular care is, What has gone wrong when a person no longer finds joy in prayer? Fénelon's answer is that nothing has gone wrong. When a person gets past the porch of prayer and enters the sanctuary, the feelings and images that filled the soul when it first turned to God are left behind. This may be a critical moment. Saint Theresa of Ávila remarked that many stop praying just when prayer begins to be real. To get straightened out, one should keep in mind that pure prayer is singleness of will. There are other faculties of the soul—sensation, memory, imagination, reason—but the will is the center. It is with the will that one prays, and one prays best when the other faculties are at rest. To pray well is to want what God wants, to attach one's will to his. Those who have achieved this union have reached perfection. The dryness that people complain of is the desert through which the Christian must travel on the way to that goal. God deprives Christians of the confidence that they have been accustomed to place in themselves and in others, until they learn to put all their trust in God. "O how good it is," says Fénelon, "to follow in the way marked by the blessed John of the Cross, who wants us to believe while we yet do not see, and to love without trying to feel."

What then is perfection? Fénelon touches on this question in a passage titled "How one should love God, or Fidelity in little things." Most Christians want to divide their hearts, giving part to God and keeping part for themselves. They are always pulled in two directions. Christian perfection is pure or unmixed love. It consists in singleness of will—in loving God only, and in loving him "purely for love of him, without any idea of self-interest." Our love for ourselves and for other creatures involves feeling and imagination and is a form of enjoyment, hence of self-love. But since the love of God is not colored by the imagination, it is not an affection. One loves God when one's will conforms to God's will, when one wants everything that God wants, and does not want anything that God does not want. "We are perfectly satisfied when his will is accomplished, and we find in God's good pleasure an inexhaustible source of peace and consolation."

Is such perfection visionary and delusive? Fénelon does not think that it is. Certainly not many achieve it in this life, but it would be presumptuous of us to doubt the testimony of the great saints of the ages who acknowledge this love and through it have reached "the highest degree of spiritual life." Other Christians seem to approach perfection in greater or less degree. How do we recognize it? Through the waning of self-love. Two distinguishing marks are simplicity and humility.

Simplicity, as Fénelon thinks of it, is a matter of not being self-conscious. One cannot make progress in the spiritual life while constantly asking oneself how one is progressing. "Simplicity is a rightness of soul which cuts away all useless turning back upon ourselves and upon our behavior." Fénelon underscores his point by contrasting simplicity with sincerity. The sincere, because they want nothing that they do not believe to be true, are constantly reliving their lives, fearful that they have said or done too much. We find such people inhibited and artificial. God does too. He would rather have us less perfect than have us constantly looking at ourselves like a beautiful woman constantly "making up before the mirror." Recognize your fault, but when you stumble get up cheerfully and resume your path. As Saint Paul says, "We no longer judge ourselves, and we are not afraid of being judged."

Humility is similar to simplicity in its diminution of self-love. It is concerned with truth, not with the superficial truth of human judgments, but with the ultimate truth that God is all and the individual is nothing. There is an outer humility that some people practice. But acts of humility are not marks of perfection, because the more we think we are lowering ourselves, the more we are persuaded of our own elevation. Inner humility is an expression of entire disinterestedness. The truly humble person does not feel any difference between what is beneath one's dignity and what is not, or between whether one is being insulted or being complimented. Another way of putting it would be to say that one is humble when one loves oneself as one loves one's neighbor, "never thinking voluntarily of self, or at least only thinking of it as we should think of another person."

Fénelon's definition of perfection as pure or disinterested love of God did not go unchallenged. The Church teaches that the soul naturally seeks beatitude and that it is found only in knowing and loving God. Is it, then, possible, as Fénelon's account of the Christian ideal would seem to imply, for a person to love God without regard to this beatitude? And, if not, how can we say that one's love for God should be unmixed with any love of self? In a piece called "Pure Love," Fénelon distinguishes two ways of loving God: one, to love him primarily on account of his goodness, but with a side-glance at our own blessedness as a sustaining motive; the other, to love God solely on account of his goodness, with no regard for our own blessedness. It is obvious, says Fénelon, that only the second of these perfectly fulfills "the unique relationship of the creature to his end, since it yields nothing to the creature [and] everything to God alone." Fénelon has no intention of denying that God promises eternal blessedness to those who love God: He is merely concerned with putting first things first. But suppose, he asks, there were no promise of eternal bliss: Would it still be our duty to love God with all our heart? Yes, he replies. And would it be possible? Certainly, with the help of God's grace, without which, in any case, no sinner can love God as he ought.

Jean H. Faurot

RECOMMENDED READING

Edition used: Fénelon, François. *Christian Perfection*. Edited and with a Preface by Charles F. Whiston. Translated by Mildred Whitney Stillman. New York: Harper & Bros., 1947.

Davis, James Harris. *Fénelon*. Boston: Twayne, 1979. Useful introduction to the man and his work. Views Fénelon as a literary figure. Chapter 4, "The Mystic Call" (pp. 74–89), introduces the French school of mysticism, with its talk of abandonment, pure love, annihilation, and perfection.

De la Bedoyère, Michael. *The Archbishop and the Lady: Fénelon and Madame Guyon*. London: Collins, 1956. Readable, informative life of Mme. Guyon with full-length portraits of her friends, true and false. A sympathetic account of Fénelon's role in the tragic story.

Janet, Paul. *Fénelon: His Life and Works*. Translated from the French (1889) by Victor Leuliette. London: Pitman, 1914. Reissued Port Washington, N.Y.: Kennikat Press, 1970. Popular treatment by a celebrated professor of philosophy. Commends Fénelon more for his program for reforming the world than for his spiritual counsels.

Knox, Ronald A. *Enthusiasm: A Chapter in the History of Religion with Special Reference to the 17th and 18th Centuries.* Oxford: Clarendon Press, 1952. Chapters 11 and 14 (pp. 231–355) treat of Quietism, which the author regards, along with other forms of perfectionism, as a destabilizing element in the history of the Church. Chapter 14, "Madame Guyon and the Battle of the Olympians," is a balanced discussion of the issue between Fénelon and Bossuet.

A Serious Call to a Devout and Holy Life

Author: William Law (1686–1761)

Refusing to pledge allegiance to the House of Hanover in 1714, William Law lost his fellowship at Cambridge and retired to King's Cliffe. There he lived "the devout and holy life" to which he exhorted others in the classic bearing his name. This book inspired the "Holy Club" at Oxford in which John and Charles Wesley laid out the main lines for their evangelical revival in England. Although John Wesley subsequently parted ways with Law as the latter became increasingly infatuated with Jacob Boehme's theosophy, the effect of *A Serious Call to a Devout and Holy Life* remained.

Type and subject of work: A rational defense of a program of spiritual discipline

First published: 1728

Major Themes

Devotion entails the dedication of the whole and not just a part of one's life to God.

Most Christians fall short of true devotion because they do not intend to please God in all they do.

Although God is merciful to those who sin out of ignorance, we cannot expect him to be so tolerant of those who lack the intention to avoid sinning, as

Scriptures amply attest.

> *All Christians, therefore, are obligated to order their everyday lives in such a way as to turn them into continual service of God.*
>
> *Persons who have leisure time have a special obligation to devote themselves to God to a higher degree, living for God "at all times" and "in all places"; this duty includes proper religious use of estates and fortunes as well as time.*
>
> *Religious exercises, such as prayers, represent only a small part of devotion to God, and unless common life matches prayers, they are nothing but "lip labour" or, worse still, hypocrisy.*
>
> *True devotion will bring peace and happiness, for it reduces desires to such things as nature and reason require and thus removes those that torment an uncontrolled heart.*
>
> *Christians ought to be disciplined in their life of prayer, and if apprehensions and perceptions of God are right, they will do so readily.*

Responding to the challenge that the Age of Reason posed for Christian faith and practice, William Law crafted a tight, rational argument for "a devout and holy life." Devotion, as he defined it, should involve all of life—living according to God's will and not for one's own selfish desires. If religion covers all of life, then it follows that Christians must observe rules that govern all their actions and not merely times of worship. Scriptures do not contain a single instruction regarding worship, but almost every verse gives something on the ordinary actions of life. If we do not practice humility, self-denial, renunciation of the world, poverty of spirit, and heavenly affection, therefore, we do not live as Christians.

Sad to say, many who call themselves Christians do not incorporate these traits into daily living. What is the difference, he asks, between Leo, who shows little regard for religion per se but lives a respectable life, and Eusebius, who has a huge appetite for religious things and can't stop talking about religion but doesn't differ from Leo as regards his everyday life?

Why don't Christians live devout lives? Law asks. We can plead neither ignorance nor inability, for we have the same knowledge and the same Spirit early Christians did. What prevents us, rather, is a lack of intention to do this.

Failure of intention puts us in real spiritual danger. Although we have ample assurance of God's mercy when we sin unavoidably, we cannot count on that when we sin because of a lack of intention, as many Scriptures prove. Scriptures show "that our salvation depends upon the sincerity and perfection of our endeavours to obtain it."

Law's main contention is that we can please God only by intending and devoting all of life to God's glory and honor. God takes no more delight in one station or position than another. His concern rather is that we offer reasonable service in whatever place we occupy in singleness of heart and thus live lives of reason and piety.

A person of leisure himself after his retirement from Cambridge, Law believed such persons held a special responsibility to devote themselves to God in a higher degree. The freer one is from pursuit of necessities, the more one should "imitate the higher perfections of angels." Law continues, "As we have always the same natures, and are everywhere the servants of the same God, as every place is equally full of His presence, and everything is equally His gift, so we must always act according to the reason of our nature; we must do everything as the servants of God; we must live in every place as in His presence; we must use everything as that ought to be used which belongs to God."

Law applied the same rationale to use of estates and fortunes, expending his own for care of others. The humble, meek, devout, just, or faithful person is not one who has done acts of humility, meekness, devotion, justice, or fidelity now and then, but one who "lives in the habitual exercise of these virtues." In the matter of estates or fortunes, it is not enough to deny oneself of needless expenses or be moderate and frugal *sometimes* so as to aid the needy; we must do so *at all times.* Unwise use of one's estate corrupts both mind and heart. As Flavia, perfect example of the self-centered rich person, illustrated, religion exists only in the head; it has no place in the heart.

Although Law will not go so far as to say that such a person as Flavia cannot be saved, he judges that "she has no grounds from Scripture to think she is in the way of salvation" since her whole life conflicts with the "tempers and practices which the Gospel has made necessary to salvation." On the opposite side, wise and pious use of an estate leads to perfection in all the virtues attendant on the Christian life. As Miranda, perfect example of the other-directed person, shows, right stewardship of money and time will benefit both ourselves and other persons.

From the beginning on, Law writes, there have been two orders of Christians—those who feared and served God in secular vocations and those who devoted themselves to voluntary poverty, virginity, devotion, and withdrawal so they might live wholly for God. Nevertheless, all orders of Christians are obliged to devotes themselves to God in all things; to do otherwise is contrary to Christian nature and rebellion against God. Rebellion in any form is equally odious to God. To forsake prayer is no worse than forsaking other responsibilities, for prayer is only a small part of devotion. Unless our lives match our prayers, the latter are at best only "lip labour" and at worst pure hypocrisy.

The end products of the devout and holy life, Law argued, will be peace and happiness. Peace and happiness become possible as we reduce desires to what nature and reason require, control passions by the rule of religion, and remove ourselves "from that infinity of wants and vexations which torment every heart that is left to itself." Persons who do not regulate their lives by strict piety resort to all sorts of poor contrivances to secure happiness, but they cannot succeed since they do what is contrary to nature. Even the most regular kind of life suffers miseries, wants, and emptiness when it lacks piety. On this the whole world is a book of instruction.

In the second part of *A Serious Call to a Devout and Holy Life* (chapters nineteen through twenty-four), Law deals with times and hours of prayer. The reason he relegated prayer to the second place should be self-evident in light of his understanding of devotion as living out our commitment to God in all of life and prayer as only "the smallest part" of devotion. No one should deduce from that statement, however, that Law took prayer lightly. "Prayer," he insisted, "is the nearest approach to God, and the highest enjoyments of Him that we are capable of in this life." We, therefore, must pursue it with all the energy we can muster.

True to his Anglican heritage, Law drew his understanding and proposals for the practice of prayer from the early Church. In imitation of early Christian custom he urged prayer five times daily with a specific focus for each: praise and thanksgiving on arising, humility at the third hour (9:00 a.m.), universal love with intercessions at the sixth (12:00 noon), resignation at the ninth (3:00 p.m.), and particular confession of sins and self-examination in the evening. Throughout he stressed discipline. Christians should not sleep too much, for instance, "because it gives a softness and idleness to your soul" and conflicts with the spirit of true devotion. They should begin with forms of prayer at all the regular times. If in praying they "break forth into new and higher strains of devotion," then they should abandon the forms. It is good to have both fixed and free elements. In later years Law emphasized mystical elements much more than he did here.

Law did not dwell at length on the mechanics of prayer, but he suggested a few simple matters that he deemed important. (1) Shut the eyes and, in a brief period of silence, "let the soul place itself in the presence of God." (2) Always pray in the same place. (3) At the beginning recall God's attributes with various expressions so as to remind yourself of God's greatness and power. (4) Combine fixed elements for each time of prayer with spontaneous petitions.

For the early morning praise and thanksgiving in which we try to develop "right apprehension and right affections toward God," the whole aim of devotion, Law urged chanting and singing of Psalms, for nothing "so clears a way for your prayers, . . . disperses dulness of heart, . . . purifies the soul from poor and little passions, . . . opens heaven, or carries your heart so near it" as the Psalms. Reading or merely reciting Psalms will not suffice to lift up the praises a heart that serves God will feel. Singing is the natural way to express joy. Use of imagination will put one in the proper frame of mind for singing.

Like the medieval saints, Law too perceived humility as a precondition for communion with God and proposed that prayer at 9:00 A.M. focus on it. A prayer for humility may loosen the bonds of sin, reform the heart, and draw down divine grace upon us. We should not think any day safe without putting ourselves in this posture and calling on God to assist us in maintaining it. Humility does not consist in excessive self-deprecation but "in a true and just sense of our weakness, misery, and sin." It is not easy, however, to live in a spirit of humility, for it means we are dead to the world and alive to Christ in us. Being Christian requires nothing less than "absolute conformity to that spirit which Christ showed in the mysterious sacrifice of Himself upon the cross." We must not think of Christ as acting as substitute for us but as "our representative acting in our name" and enabling us to join with him as persons acceptable to God. Education also makes it difficult sometimes to practice humility. Therefore, Christians must make an effort to secure the kind of education that fosters humility.

For noontime prayer Law recommended concentration on universal love with intercession as a primary act of it. No "principle of the heart" is more acceptable to God than "a fervent universal love of all mankind, wishing and praying for their happiness," for none is more like God. We must not play favorites when it comes to compassion. All orders of persons must intercede, for nothing makes us love others so much as praying for them. It is not only "the best arbitrator of all differences, the best promoter of true friendship, the best cure and preservative against all unkind tempers, all angry and haughty passions," but also it enables us to discover "the true state of our own hearts."

For the ninth hour Law recommended resignation and conformity to the will of God. Resignation entails "a cheerful approbation and thankful acceptance of everything that comes from God." Such approbation should cover both God's general providence over the world and his particular providence over us.

Finally, in the evening prayer, Law advised, we should take inventory of all we have done from the beginning of the day. We must not gloss over our sins if we wish to be cleansed and renewed. The more exact the confession, the greater the compunction and sorrow of heart. At bedtime it is good to pray again regarding death.

E. Glenn Hinson

RECOMMENDED READING

Edition used: Law, William. *A Serious Call to a Devout and Holy Life.* Grand Rapids, Mich.: Eerdmans, 1966.

———. *Works.* 9 vols. London: Printed for J. Richardson, 1762.

Overton, J. H. *William Law: Non-juror and Mystic.* London: Longmans, Green & Co., 1881. An old but still useful biography.

Walker, A. K. *William Law: His Life and Work.* London: Society for Promoting Christian Knowledge, 1973. An excellent critical biography.

A Treatise Concerning Religious Affections

Author: Jonathan Edwards (1703–1758)

An early convert to Calvinism, Jonathan Edwards was ordained minister of First Church, Northampton, Massachusetts, in 1727, and through such provocative sermons as "God Glorified in Man's Dependence" (1731), "A Divine and Supernatural Light" (1733), and "Justification by Faith Alone" (1734) became a central figure in the religious revival in New England that came to be known as the "Great Awakening." Among his other important works are *Freedom of the Will* (1754), *The Great Christian Doctrine of Original Sin Defended* (1758), and *The Nature of True Virtue* (1765).

Type and subject of work: Philosophical essay on the conditions of true religion and genuine piety

First published: 1746

Major Themes

True religion consists, for the most part, in the true religious affections.

Affections are positive and negative inclinations of the soul; among the former are love, desire, hope, joy, gratitude, and complacence; among the latter are hatred, fear, anger, and grief.

Love is the paramount religious affection.

The preeminent virtue of Jesus Christ was expressed in the exercise of the holy affections.

Among circumstances that cannot be taken as signs of true grace in persons having religious affections are their making fluent and fervent religious protestations, their spending much time in worship and other religious activities, their confidence about their own piety, and their happening to be pleasing to the truly godly.

Although there is no way of being certain about the piety of persons, there are twelve signs of the true religious affections: (1) They arise from spiritual, supernatural, and divine influences; (2) they are grounded in the excellence of divine things; (3) they are founded on the appeal of the moral excellence of divine things; (4) they arise from the mind's enlightened understanding of divine things; (5) they are attended with a reasonable and spiritual conviction of the reality of divine things; (6) they are associated with honest humility; (7) they accompany a spiritual transformation; (8) they promote the spirit of love that Christ made evident; (9) they soften the heart; (10) they exhibit a beautiful symmetry and proportion; (11) they lead to an increase in the spiritual appetite for holiness; and (12) they have their exercise and fruit in Christian practice.

In the preface to his *Treatise Concerning Religious Affections,* Jonathan Edwards contends that there is no more important question than that concerning the distinguishing features of those who are truly religious and pious. The practical problem of distinguishing the truly pious from the fervent pretenders to piety arose in the spiritual excitement of the Great Awakening, a revival of religious enthusiasm in which it became difficult, if not impossible, to separate the truly holy from those whose emotional intensity and frenetic activity gave them the appearance but not the reality of virtue and piety.

Edwards was troubled, both spiritually and intellectually, by the confusion of emotionalism with true virtue. "There is indeed something very mysterious in it," he writes, "that so much good, and so much bad, should be mixed together in the church of God." But, mysterious as it is, the coexistence of the true and the false in religion is something that must be acknowledged. "'Tis no new thing," he adds, "that much false religion should prevail, at a time of great reviving of true religion; and that at such a time, multitudes of hypocrites should spring up among true saints."

The problem for Edwards, then, was that of distinguishing true religion from false, genuine piety from the counterfeit, sainthood from hypocrisy, and Christian spirituality from religious zealousness.

Edwards begins the task of resolving the problem by remarking on the love and joy of the Christian victims of religious persecution to whom Peter (in 1 Pet. 1:8) wrote (with reference to Christ), "Whom having not seen, ye love; in whom, though now ye see him not, yet believing, ye rejoice with joy unspeakable, and full of glory." Although the persecuted Christians did not see Christ, they loved him; although they suffered, they knew the joy of loving the divine. These religious affections—love and joy—founded in the divine, sustained and spiritually transformed these early Christians and thus were signs of their true piety, arising from the grace of God.

Edwards's reflections on Christian love and joy lead to the statement of his central proposition: "True religion, in great part, consists in holy affections."

In writing of the "affections," Edwards was not referring to sentiments, feelings, or passions; he was writing of the "inclination and will" of the soul, the active tendency to embrace some things and turn away from others. He conceived of the spiritual affections pragmatically; he regarded them as dispositions to act, as established inclinations showing themselves in action.

A distinction is drawn by Edwards between the soul's *understanding*, which is dependent upon perception and speculation, and the soul's *inclination*, its capacity and tendency to approve or reject, to like or dislike, to be *for* some things and *against* others. When an inclination determines action, it may be called "will," and when the mind is affected by inclinations, it may be called "heart." The religious affections, then, are active inclinations affecting the will and the heart; and when they do so under the influence of the divine, they are true religious affections.

Since the affections are either positive or negative—either inclinations to approve or inclinations to reject—they involve either a "cleaving to . . . or seeking" something or, on the other hand, a being averse to or opposed to something. Of the inclinations *for* something, Edwards gives as examples love, desire, hope, joy, gratitude, and complacence; as examples of inclinations *against* something, he cites hatred, fear, anger, grief, and the like.

Some of the affections, Edwards points out, involve both positive and negative inclinations. Pity, for example, involves a positive inclination toward the sufferer and a negative inclination toward the suffering.

Although the religious affections are often of the mixed sort, involving love of the divine and hatred of sin and of Satanic influences, the love of God, that is, love directed toward the divine, is "the chief of the affections, and fountain of all other affections." The two commandments given by Christ—to love God and, accordingly, to love one's neighbor—"comprehend all the duty prescribed," Edwards writes. Thus, "the essence of all true religion lies in holy love."

In support of his general doctrine that true religion consists in the holy affections, Edwards emphasizes "vigorous and lively actings"; our wills and inclinations, he writes, must be "strongly exercised." The affections are springs of human action, to be sure, but unless that action be earnest and enlist all our strength, it cannot be a sign of true piety.

Edwards argues that it is of no help in determining whether a person having religious affections has *true* religious affections, signs of true piety, to discover that the religious affections are intense ("in a very high degree"); nor is it significant if the affections appear to have bodily effects, such as trembling or fainting. Further, if someone having religious affections is "fluent, fervent and abundant" in talking about religious matters, it does not follow that such a person is truly pious, or not: Fervent protestations prove nothing. Nor does the fact that religious affections may arise in a person without any effort on that person's part prove that the affections are supernaturally and divinely caused—nor that they are not. Finally, even if passages of Scripture come to mind and give rise to religious affections, nothing is shown either way about the truth of the affections.

One might suppose that the appearance of love could be taken to be significant in appraising the religious affections, but although love is "the chief of the graces of God's spirit," Edwards writes, it can be counterfeited, and hence no mere appearance of love proves that the reality of spiritual love is present.

Nor, Edwards continues, can one determine whether or not religious affections are "gracious," signs of God's grace, by noticing that, in a given case, the affections are many and varied, or that some persons experience comfort and joy after awakenings of conscience, or that people spend a great deal of time in zealous religious activity, or that they have their mouths full of praise for God, or that they are confident that their experience has a divine origin, or that what they do is pleasing to the truly godly.

If all these presumed indicators of true religion are false signs, what signs are reliable? Edwards offers twelve signs of holy affections, but he warns that no set of signs could enable anyone to determine with certainty whether someone enjoys true affections. The difficulty is not with the signs but with the use of them, with seeing clearly whether or not the signs are present. Nevertheless, the signs are useful in seeking understanding even though they can hardly be employed to convince hypocrites.

The true affections, first of all, arise from influences that are "spiritual, supernatural and divine." Edwards states that "true saints" are "spiritual persons," and he explains that by a "spiritual" person is meant one in opposition to a *natural* person, the latter being without benefit of the influence of the Spirit of God. To be spiritual is to be of the Spirit of God, and true spirituality consists in being affected by God's grace.

The second sign of the true affections is that they have as their objective ground the excellence of divine things, not any benefit that might come to the person and thereby satisfy self-love. That is, God is loved as God and because of the glory and excellence of God, not because God might benefit those who love him.

One may take it as a sign of true affections that they are based on a love of the "beauty and sweetness" of the "moral excellency" of divine things. By "moral excellency," Edwards means what we might call "spiritual" excellency, for the morality with which he is concerned does not relate to the practical benefits of certain modes of conduct in society but to the requirements of holiness or virtue. The moral excellency of God *is* God's holiness; to love God for his holiness is to find his moral excellency beautiful and sweet and, hence, to take delight in that holiness.

The fourth sign of the true affections is that they arise from an enlightenment of the mind that consists in a true spiritual understanding of divine things. Spiritual understanding, Edwards avers, involves "a sense of the heart," a heartfelt sense of spiritual beauty. Such understanding is not speculative; it involves a "taste" of the moral beauty of divine things—that is, a sense of their reality and a delight in their apprehension.

The spiritual conviction of the reality of divine things is a fifth sign of the true religious affections, provided that the conviction is "reasonable," that is, that it arises from a spiritual understanding, a sense of the excellence and beauty of the divine.

Gracious affections, Edwards writes, "are attended with evangelical humiliation," the sixth sign of the true affections. Edwards explains that by "evangelical humiliation" is meant "a sense that a Christian has of his own utter insufficiency, despicableness, and odiousness, with an answerable frame of heart." Again, to be significant, the sense of one's insufficiency must proceed not from the natural observation that one is limited in various ways but from a spiritual understanding of the difference between the perfections of God and the imperfections of the self, an understanding achieved through the influence of the Spirit of God.

The seventh sign of the true religious affections is that they are accompanied by a transformation of the soul brought about through spiritual understanding. Such transformation or "change of nature" is abiding; it is the permanent effect of the encounter with the Spirit.

If the religious affections promote "the lamblike, dovelike spirit and temper of Jesus Christ," their doing so is a sign of their being true and holy religious affections.

The ninth sign is that the religious affections soften the heart; they lead to a tenderness of spirit. Persons so affected become as little children.

The truly gracious affections are proportionate to their objects; they exhibit "beautiful symmetry." Some persons make a great show of loving God, but they show little love or benevolence in their relationships to other persons: In such persons there is an imbalance of concerns, a disproportion that is a sign of false affections.

True affections give rise to an increase in spiritual appetite: "The more a true saint loves God with a gracious love, the more he desires to love him, and the more uneasy is he at his want of love to him." The increase in spiritual longing is Edwards's eleventh sign of the true affections.

The twelfth and final sign discussed by Edwards involves Christian practice: "Gracious and holy affections have their exercise and fruit in Christian practice."

Christian practice, Edwards emphasizes, is "the chief of all the signs of grace"; it is the "principal sign" by which one can determine the truth or falsity of religious affections. Edwards argues at great length in support of this final definitive sign; he quotes extensively from Scripture, and he places special emphasis on Christ's insistence that "Ye shall know them by their fruits" (Matt. 7:16). Unless the religious affections make a profound and Christian difference in practice, they are not signs of true piety.

Although Edwards offers twelve signs of the true affections and, hence, of true religion, the argument for any one is but a special emphasis on a feature of a basic argument that covers them all; the spirit of a person may, through God's grace, be affected by the Spirit of God; the sense of God gives rise to the holy affections; the holy affections, in turn, are springs of actions that reflect the beauty and holiness of their divine inspiration. To be truly religious and pious, then, is to be transformed by the religious affections arising from and reflecting the moral excellence of divine things: It is to love God.

Ian P. McGreal

RECOMMENDED READING

Edition used: Edwards, Jonathan. *The Works of Jonathan Edwards.* Edited by Perry Miller. Vol. 2: *Religious Affections.* Edited by John E. Smith. New Haven: Yale University Press, 1959.

———. *The Works of Jonathan Edwards.* Edited by Perry Miller. Vol. 1: *Freedom of the Will.* Edited by Paul Ramsey. New Haven: Yale University Press, 1957. First published, 1754. Edwards's philosophical masterpiece argues for Calvinism, against Arminianism, and for the doctrine that freedom of the will is not only compatible with determinism but requires it.

———. *The Nature of True Virtue.* Foreword by William K. Frankena. Ann Arbor: University of Michigan Press, 1960. First published, 1765 (written in 1755). A considered statement, consistent with Edwards's *Treatise Concerning*

Religious Affections, arguing that true virtue consists in benevolence to being in general, that is, "love to God," and consequently that "virtue is the beauty of the qualities and exercises of the heart."

Simonson, Harold P. *Theologian of the Heart.* Grand Rapids, Mich.: Eerdmans, 1974. A careful, detailed, and rewarding study of Edwards's conviction that virtue requires a "sense of the heart" as affected by the grace and glory of God.

NINE PUBLIC LECTURES

Author: Nicholaus Ludwig Count von Zinzendorf (1700–1760)
Born in Dresden and educated as a youth at the Pietist schools in Halle,
Zinzendorf founded the "Moravian Brethren" at Herrnhut. Ever faithful to the Lutheran church despite its deep suspicions that he was an
"innovator," he proclaimed a simple "religion of the heart" and was interested in ecumenism and evangelization. He exercised some influence
on John Wesley, whose "strangely warm" religious experience occurred
at a meeting of Moravians in 1738.

Type and subject of work: A collection of nine sermons preached in the
Brethren's Chapel in London in 1746

First published: 1748

MAJOR THEMES

*Christianity is troubled with much nonsensical speculation when simple
faith is all that is required.*

*The Lord's Prayer is a treasure intended for Christians, and can inspire them
to evangelization.*

The goal of preaching the gospel is the evangelization of the world.

*Faith is also love for the Savior as response to one's need and as knowledge
of Christ.*

*That which gives the believer greatest joy is not power, but the knowledge
that he or she is a child of God.*

A human soul is in and of itself blessed because it is created for salvation and needs only respond to God.

The essential Christian is one who ever appeals not to one's denomination but to one's being in Christ, and who behaves in the world not according to rules of morality, but with Christ in heart and mind.

In his preface, Zinzendorf notes that he has addressed these sermons to a number of supporters and friends in England who had spent three months in Germany, visiting the Moravian settlement.

In lecture one, "That the Prayer to the Father of Jesus Christ Can Be Prayed by No One but Children of God," he stresses that those who avoid God have great freedom concerning their own lives. As soon as they begin to busy themselves with God, however, "then He begins to be serious." Thus to call upon God's name without truly caring to know God is to invite judgment. This is done almost innocently, for example, in lands in which people are forced to attend church, worship certain ways, and accept certain doctrines (such as the Trinity, which is far beyond humanity's ken and is an intrusion into divine mystery).

It is enough if a soul simply knows God as Creator and Husband, knows the Savior and studies him. As Jesus came as God incarnate, as a simple human being, let us be satisfied to love God in simple fashion and leave complicated speculation to those who do not love their Savior.

Zinzendorf's second lecture, "Concerning the Simple Meaning and the Great Idea of the Lord's Prayer," covers the entire prayer, which must surely appear as a paradox to those who do not yet know God. In the Lord's Prayer Jesus intends to point out, as for the first time in history, that God's primary role is that of Father. Thus God deserves divine honor as Father and should be proclaimed as such.

In the petition "Thy Kingdom come," we remember that besides those predestined as the firstfruits, any sinner can be snatched from sin by Christ. The Church should become visible and lively in its redemption.

Zinzendorf interprets "Thy will be done . . ." as a plea to God to give Christians knowledge of and strength to do God's will in high spirits.

The next petition has to do with "supernatural bread," that is, the body and blood of Jesus received in faith. Zinzendorf expressly repudiates any reference to natural bread, which God has promised to the believer.

The fifth petition refers "precisely [to] the sins of omission," the sin of being believers who have not done all they can. Even as we have lacked integrity and faithfulness toward God, so we must overlook what others owe us and "not take things too strictly."

"Lead us not into temptation" is simply another way of asking God not to let us fall so far into temptation that we have difficulty freeing ourselves.

The final petition is a request that God would snatch us out of Satan's jaws in those times when we fall too far into pride.

At this point Zinzendorf reflects on the basic duties of all Christians to love God, do God's will, and share their enormous spiritual wealth with the world, wealth that will move them first to sorrow, then to joy at such great salvation.

In lecture three, "Concerning the Proper Purpose of the Preaching of the Gospel," Zinzendorf stresses the evangelistic element of preaching. The sermon need not concern itself with the "how" of conversion, but rather must be an invitation that describes the beauty of the Bridegroom.

In this, Zinzendorf is criticizing the Methodists for their custom of describing how people have come, and are to come, to faith. He stresses that this is God's concern; ours is simply to issue invitations.

In "Concerning Saving Faith," the fourth lecture, we are told that in Scripture "faith is [often] called love." Thus there is no saving faith that is not at the same time a deep love for the Savior. "Faith-in-distress" is the faith of persons who call upon God in their misery, and such faith is a great gift since all people experience misery and sorrow, while "faith-in-love" is found both in persons who simply know their Savior and in those who also proclaim him. Faith is as simple as choosing to believe because one wishes to, because it gives joy.

Lecture five, "That Aspect of Faith Which Actually Makes One So Blessedly Happy," distinguishes between a faith that believes things, as in a faith in miracles, and saving faith, which is a trusting response to God. Zinzendorf claims that being a child of God, belonging to heaven, not doing miracles is the true joy of faith. Belief saves.

One does not first straighten out his or her life, one does not first give intellectual assent; rather, one is awakened by the Holy Spirit and gives oneself over to the Savior. It is "never the responsibility of the preacher that one is awakened, but rather the Holy Spirit acted" some time, if even for a split second, to awaken the listener first. It is then that the hearer receives the gospel as something of immediate interest rather than as distant news. And in that moment of receiving and believing the listener becomes a believer.

Zinzendorf makes much of authenticity; as one is, so one should respond to Christ. If we are sad or perplexed we should not try to escape our consternation "by some strange means" (including devotional writings and even Scripture), but rather ought to wait upon the Holy Spirit as we are.

In his sixth lecture, "That It Is Blessedness and Happiness to Be a Human Soul," Zinzendorf begins with a brief warning against forcing people's consciences, a theme that is basic to Zinzendorf and that crops up throughout his works. For one thing, it is impossible; for another, humanity lives in the paradox of free will and election.

The message of this sermon, however, is the blessedness of the human soul in and of itself. That is, all human souls "are designed for salvation." Still, one can reject salvation, as happened with Christ in John 1:11. For the human soul, while needing the prompting of the Holy Spirit, nonetheless has the freedom to choose. It is like this: "First, He comes; secondly, He is or is not received." Should a person entertain a serious thought of the Savior, he or she can rejoice, for this is a sign of the Holy Spirit; Christ is indeed there and needs only be received. "Complicated ideas" about the means of conversion are absolutely unnecessary. We need simply say yes. This eliminates all fear about whether one is doing "everything just right." In this Zinzendorf was responding to the elaborate schemes of conversion that had proliferated among the pietistic groups (such as the Methodists). Nonetheless, in the end, it is not our concern with *how* to be saved that holds us back; rather, it is our pride, which will not let us accept salvation without somehow contributing to it. Only our simple acceptance of Christ will unite the denominations and the souls in them.

In lecture seven, "On the Essential Character and Circumstances of the Life of a Christian," Zinzendorf stresses that it is not denominational loyalty, but appeal to one's being in Christ that makes up the genuine character of the Christian. The text for this sermon, or lecture, is John 21:16, "Do you love me?"

This simple question is for Zinzendorf the crux of the matter. Denominations are acceptable in that they provide people with different points of view. As grounds for condemnation and hostility, however, they are abominations. Christ is not the founder of our religion, but rather is our husband. This is an interpersonal category, not an intellectual or doctrinal one.

Because love, not reason, is the basis of faith, Zinzendorf begs theologians to stop representing Christianity as being reasonable, as being common sense. Our faith is inherently "foolish." The work of the gospel is not to convince us of its wisdom, but to etch Christ upon our hearts.

This relational thinking applies to our lives as Christians as well. Christ appears to us and we choose to respond. To this end, lists of moral precepts, rules, and regulations are unnecessary. With Christ ever before us, one look from him is sufficient to let us know the nature of our thoughts and deeds. Thus we are people not of denominations, "wisdom," or rules, but of Christ.

"Concerning the Blessed Happiness of Sincere and Upright Hearts," lecture eight, is concerned with salvation and what constitutes an "upright heart." As soon as Christ comes to a person and sets him or her free, it is up to the individual to choose what master is to be followed.

It is frequently thought that a person of upright heart is one who is honest and refrains from sinning, when the truth is that a person of upright heart is actually one who senses the pull of God and, forgetting everything but the Savior, responds. Again stressing honesty and authenticity, Zinzendorf describes the upright person as one who accepts reality, "takes things as they are," and rushes to meet the Christ who has revealed himself.

In lecture nine, "That Which, Properly Speaking, Can Secure Us from All Fear, Danger, and Harm," Zinzendorf emphasizes the immediacy of Christ to every believer. This constitutes the true "communion of saints," not the Anglican or Lutheran or whatever denomination. We too quickly trust in things that can be lost, such as understanding of doctrine, our senses, Bibles, our memories, friends, and so forth. These can all be taken away from us by injury, fire, or other accidents, but Christ not only cannot be taken away from us, he loves us so much that he *cannot*, as it were, leave us. The problem is not his; rather, "That they do not hold fast to Him, that is the fault."

It is our great error that we do not perceive how close Christ is to us. "The shirt on our back is not nearer to us than He is; the heart in our body is not nearer to us than He is." Yet this can be remedied in a flash; we need simply return to him. It also means that while Satan may torment us, he cannot defeat us or draw too near. The best way to be assured of salvation and to be rid of Satan?: "The best way is that the soul be near its head."

Although Zinzendorf ranges wide in his nine sermons, or lectures, he constantly recurs to the themes of God-initiated grace, freedom of conscience, simple faith in God as opposed to the schemes and artifices of denominations and theologians, personal relationship with God in Christ as opposed to intellectual assent or works, righteousness, personal honesty and authenticity, and sharing the Good News. We might say that the last line of Zinzendorf's ninth lecture sums up best his message to all: "[In] short, I can be nowhere better than in His arms."

Gary R. Sattler

Recommended Reading

Edition used: Zinzendorf, Nicholaus Ludwig, Count von. *Nine Public Lectures on Important Subjects in Religion.* Translated and edited by George W. Forell. Iowa City: University of Iowa Press, 1973.

James, Hunter. *The Quiet People of the Land.* Winston-Salem, N.C.: Old Salem,

Inc., 1976. A well-researched yet lively and informative depiction of the experiences of a Moravian community in America.

Lewis, A. J. *Zinzendorf the Ecumenical Pioneer.* Philadelphia: Westminster Press, 1962. A short and sympathetic introduction to the person and work of Zinzendorf.

THE LIFE OF DAVID BRAINERD

Author: Jonathan Edwards (1703–1768)
Based on the *Diary* of David Brainerd (1718–1747), *The Life of David Brainerd* is essentially the work of Jonathan Edwards, Brainerd's mentor and chief interpreter of the "Great Awakening." Brainerd died in Edwards's home, cared for in his last days by the latter's daughter, Jerusha. Brainerd left his papers in Edwards's hands to dispose of "as he thought would be most for God's glory, and the interest of Religion." Edwards, pastor of the parish church in Northampton, Massachusetts, condensed and made selections from a much larger *Diary*. He found in Brainerd's experience with the Indians support for his controversial proposals concerning church discipline that led to his expulsion from his parish in 1750. Brainerd supplied him with a paradigm of saintliness made evident in deed as well as in word. By way of comments, summaries, and especially his long "Reflections on the Preceding Memoirs," Edwards illustrated the criteria of holiness he had set forth in his seminal work on *Religious Affections* in 1746.

Type and subject of work: Spiritual autobiography and biography

First published: 1749

MAJOR THEMES

True religion and virtue are set forth by example as well as doctrine, for they have to do, above all, with affections.

True experimental religion arises from immediate divine influences, super-

naturally enlightens and convinces the individual, and powerfully impresses, quickens, sanctifies, and governs the heart.

True religion avoids charismatic enthusiasms that defy rational control.

Although conversion is entirely supernatural, a work of grace and not human effort, persons genuinely converted will strive earnestly and constantly for perfection to the end of their lives.

The hand of Jonathan Edwards is visible in the selection and editing of the Brainerd *Diary*, but the devout Calvinist pastor did not leave interpretation solely in the hands of readers. In both a preface and "An Appendix Containing Some Reflections and Observations on the Preceding Memoirs of Mr. Brainerd" he laid out some principles that he wished them to discern in the life of his model.

In the preface Edwards noted that true religion and virtue could be represented and recommended to the world either by doctrine and precept or by instance and example. Scriptures supply specimens of both. Edwards singled out David Brainerd for his "distinguished natural abilities, "unusual services as a minster of the gospel, deep concern for "the various extraordinary effects and unusual appearances" of the Awakening in New England, extensive acquaintance with "the subjects of the late religious operations" all over the British Empire, "peculiar opportunity of acquaintance with the false appearances and counterfeits of religion," and work as "the instrument of a most remarkable awakening, and an exceeding wonderful and abiding alteration and moral transformation of such subjects as do peculiarly render the change rare and astonishing." He promised that the *Life* would disclose not only the external circumstances and behavior of Brainerd "but also what passed in his own heart, the wonderful change that he experienced in his mind and disposition, the manner in which that change was brought to pass, how it continued, what were its consequences in his inward frames, thoughts, affections and secret exercises, through many vicissitudes and trials, . . . and also how all ended at last, in his sentiments, frame and behavior, during a long illness, and what were the affects of his religion in dying circumstances, or in the last stages of his dying illness."

Although Edwards was self-consciously putting Brainerd forward as the model par excellence of the piety of the Awakening, he took pains to anticipate sharp darts hurled at the spirituality he espoused. Edwards admitted that by disposition Brainerd suffered from melancholy and dejection of spirit. Such a disposition, however, did not disqualify his religious experience, for he was a person possessed of "a penetrating genius, of clear thought, of close reasoning, and a very exact judgment and knowledge of things in divinity, but especially in things appertaining to inward experimental religion." He abhorred excesses and was not himself given to imagination. His own religious impressions, views, and affections differed vastly from enthusiasms. Edwards also allowed that criticism for "being *excessive in his labors*" and failing to take care of his health was legitimate, but noted that Brainerd himself had confessed his error in this. Yet neither these faults nor other imperfections that he shared with saints of other ages should detract from the fact that Brainerd was "a remarkable instance of true and eminent Christian piety in heart and practice" that would be worthy of imitation.

Edwards arranged his excerpts from Brainerd's *Diary* in eight parts. Part one covers the years from his birth at Haddam, Connecticut, on April 20, 1718, until he was expelled from Yale in the winter of 1741–1742. Typical of Puritans, Brainerd focused almost exclusively on his religious pilgrimage. At age seven or eight he "became something concerned for my soul and terrified at the thoughts of death, and was driven to the performance of duties." His zeal, however, soon dampened, and did not revive until a "mortal sickness" struck Haddam when he was thirteen, claiming his mother, among others. At this point he hoped for conversion without knowing what it meant, but he again let his religious concern die down after a brief period of fervor. The next several years he continued "a round of secret duty" (fasting and prayer), but had not yet put down a solid foundation. At about age twenty he grew serious about his education, "became very strict and watchful" over his thoughts, words, and actions, and decided to devote himself to the ministry. Apprenticing himself to the pastor of the church in Haddam, he abandoned youthful company, associated only with "grave elderly people," and devoted himself to a regimen "now exceeding regular and full of religion." In line with Puritan counsels he read the Bible through twice in one year, spent much time in secret prayer every day, listened to sermons with rapt attention, met privately with other young persons on Sunday evenings for religious exercises, and, in brief, acted like "a very good Pharisee."

In 1738 Brainerd experienced what he regarded as a genuine conversion. True to Calvinist theology, it began suddenly with "such a sense of my danger and the wrath of God, that I stood amazed and my former good frames, that I had pleased myself with, all presently vanished." Months of agony followed as Brainerd sought to submit himself fully and completely to God with no thought of his own merit and to receive salvation as a free gift. He found several things disturbing: the strictness of the divine law, faith alone as the condition of salvation, what faith was, and the sovereignty of God, namely, that God could save or damn him at will. After months of struggle "'unspeakable glory' seemed to open to the view and apprehension of my soul" on July 12, 1739. "Glory," he explained, did not mean "any external brightness" but "a new inward apprehension or view that I had of God;

such as I never had before, nor anything that I had the least remembrance of it."

In September Brainerd entered Yale College, fearful he "should not be able to lead a life of strict religion in the midst of so many temptations." The worst did not materialize immediately, for he "enjoyed full assurance of his favor" in that period. Despite the demands of study and physical illness, he often enjoyed "unspeakable sweetness and delight in God." Illness caused him to drop out of college in the fall of 1740, but he returned in November. Unfortunately, Jonathan Edwards reported, Brainerd got caught up in "intemperate indiscreet zeal" of the Awakening as it reached its peak. Refusal to make a public apology for criticism of one of the professors for lack of (experiential) grace led to his expulsion from Yale and a major turn in his vocation.

Part two shifts from general biographical form to daily entries from Brainerd's diary, beginning April 1, 1742. From his crushing experience at Yale on, Brainerd obviously suffered severe depression lightened by occasionally profound religious experiences. Continuing his study with other ministers, he tried to satisfy an insatiable appetite for holiness and spent much time in intercession for "lost souls" and for advancement of the kingdom of God. Out of this came his extremely brief but remarkable career as a missionary among the Indians, first at Kaunaumeek (parts four and five) and then at Crossweeksung, where he had his most spectacular success (parts six and seven). Except for his entries about his work at Crossweeksung in part seven, the material is highly repetitious-—dejection and discouragement followed by divine uplift and comfort. Brainerd constantly doubted his worthiness to be a minister or missionary even after appointment by the Society for Propagating Christian Knowledge (November 1742). Meantime, his health failing, he dwelt often like a latter-day desert father on his longing for death and the purity of heart to which he aspired in order to see God.

Brainerd's success at Crossweeksung lightened his otherwise somber spirit. Acquainted by this time with the Indian language, he preached to them much more effectively than he had to those at Kaunaumeek, and the Indians did not fail to notice his obvious sincerity. Almost constantly ill by 1744, he confessed increasing dependence on divine grace and pled for greater holiness. Beginning in August 1745, revival swept the settlement with "the irresistible force of a mighty torrent" in fulfillment, Brainerd believed, of Zechariah 12:10-12. Hundreds were converted in the year following. Brainerd carefully reported specific stories to establish the authenticity of the phenomena that he himself could scarcely comprehend. For the society that supported his work he defended what was happening in journal notes such as the following (for December 15, 1745): "The impressions made by the Word of God upon the audience appeared solid, rational, and deep, worthy of the

solemn truths by means of which they were produced, and far from being the effects of any sudden fright or groundless perturbation of
mind." He alluded at length to one woman's experience of ecstasy in
connection with her conversion, which he judged fully genuine, accompanied by her outward behavior as "a most tender, broken-hearted, affectionate, devout, and humble Christian, as exemplary in life and
conversation as any person in my congregation."

Part eight records the final year of Brainerd's life. His health drain-
ing away with tuberculosis, he made fewer and fewer entries in his diary. In May of 1747 he had to leave Crossweeksung and come to live in
Northampton in the Edwardses' home. Despite his suffering, he perceived that "the essence of religion consisted in the soul's conformity to
God, and acting above all selfish views, for his glory, longing to be for
him, to live to him, and please and honor him in all things" and concluded that, his faults and humility notwithstanding, he approached
this standard. By late August Brainerd had become almost too weak to
write, so most comments came from the pen of Edwards from that point
until Brainerd died on October 9.

Edwards's lengthy appendix draws out the major points he wanted
readers to draw from the *Life*. (1) On the nature of true religion: For
Brainerd conversion was only the *beginning* of God's work in the heart;
the Spirit continues to stir up effort from within and to increase "holy
affections." At the same time Brainerd diligently avoided "zeal, not according to knowledge" and imagination which could deceive and lead
astray. His heart's desire was holiness; humility characterized him
throughout his life. (2) It is possible to distinguish authentic from spurious religious phenomena. (3) True experimental religion exemplified
by Brainerd clearly differs from "vain, pernicious enthusiasm," above
all, in his complete resignation to God. (4) Genuine conversion is a supernatural work of divine grace and not a human contrivance (versus
Arminianism). Brainerd's religion conformed completely to the "Cal-
vinistical scheme." Brainerd offers a great model for (5) ministers and (6)
laypersons alike in his self-denial and dependence on God. (7) He set an
example in his prayers and endeavors for the advancement and enlarge-
ment of the kingdom of Christ. (8) Finally, "the special and remarkable
disposal of divine Providence" is visible in his final illness and death.

E. Glenn Hinson

RECOMMENDED READING

Edition used: Edwards, Jonathan. *Works of Jonathan Edwards.* Edited by Norman
Pettit. Vol. 7: *The Life of David Brainerd.* New Haven and London: Yale University Press, 1985.

Brainerd, David. *Memoirs of the Rev. David Brainerd; Missionary to the Indians.* Edited by Jonathan Edwards and Sereno Edwards Dwight. New Haven, Conn.: S. Converse, 1822. Brainerd's report on his work among the Indians.

Clebsch, William A. *American Religious Thought: A History.* Chicago: University of Chicago Press, 1973. This book will supply some insight into Jonathan Edwards's interest in Brainerd.

A Plain Account
of Christian Perfection

Author: John Wesley (1703–1791)

The circuit rider in American history was usually a Methodist; but it would be a mistake to superimpose our image of the frontier evangelist on the founder of Methodism, who, for all his traveling and out-of-doors preaching, was an Oxford don who had taken Anglican orders. During their university days, John and his brother Charles (the hymn writer) were leaders in a group known as the Holy Club, devoted to charitable works and to holy living. Nothing in the regimen of this pious band gives any hint of the great popular revival movement with which the names of the Wesleys and of George Whitefield (another member of the Holy Club) are so closely connected. The exception might be a certain mystical and ascetical ideal of Christian living that, in Wesley's view, was an essential part of the Anglican tradition and that he fought to retain in the societies that he founded, often in opposition to other evangelical leaders, including Whitefield.

Type and subject of work: Documentation of Wesley's adherence to the perfectionist ideal

First published: 1766

MAJOR THEMES

To be a Christian is to have the mind of Christ and to live in entire conformity to his example.

Holiness is a habitual state of the soul so renewed as to be "perfect even as

the Father in Heaven is perfect."

The sincere convert to Christianity is perfect from the beginning in the sense that he cannot commit sin; the more advanced convert is perfect in the sense that he has no evil thoughts or desires.

The higher perfection is directly attested to a person by the abiding presence of the Holy Spirit within him.

John Wesley is remembered chiefly as a man of action. Of his writings only the *Journal* has excited general interest, and that less for its literary qualities than for the story it narrates. Excerpts from the *Journal* were published serially as part of his attempt to allay prejudice and to promote understanding. *A Plain Account of Christian Perfection* may be thought of as a supplement to the published *Journal.* In the 1760s some people were saying that Wesley had shifted his ground on the matter of Christian perfection. This provided him an occasion to publish the cumulative record. The main statements from which he quotes are: his first published sermon, "Circumcision of the Heart"; a tract, "The Character of a Methodist"; another published sermon, "Christian Perfection"; and two booklets, *Thoughts on Christian Perfection,* and *Further Thoughts on Christian Perfection.* Excerpts and summaries from these are pieced together chronologically and are interspersed with hymns, personal recollections, and reports of conferences and conversations. Because the purpose of the book is to show that his stand on perfectionism remained the same throughout his ministry, one is prepared for a good deal of repetition. On the other hand, Wesley's teaching does not seem to have been quite as uniform as he claimed. It has been said of Wesley that, although he was an insatiable reader (he read as he traveled on horseback), he was never a close reader; and one gets the impression that he was not a close reader of what he himself had written.

The *Plain Account* begins with Wesley's youthful resolves. He was twenty-two when, reading Jeremy Taylor's *Holy Living and Dying,* he was persuaded of the importance of purity of intention and of the need to dedicate every part of his life to God. This resolve was strengthened when he went on to read Thomas à Kempis and William Law. Studying the Bible in this light, he saw the "indispensable necessity of having the mind which was in Christ" and of "an entire inward and outward conformity to our Master." His sermon "Circumcision of the Heart" (1733) belongs to this first period. In it he defines holiness as a habitual state of the soul, so renewed as to be "perfect as the Father in heaven is perfect." The first and great commandment is said to contain all the virtues. The one thing that God desires of us is the living sacrifice of the heart that he has chosen. No creature is to share our love for God, for he is a jealous God. "Desire not to live but to praise his name; let all your thoughts, words, and works tend to his glory."

When we turn to Wesley's next publication, "The Character of a Methodist" (1739), we are on different ground. These are not the vaporings of an Oxford fellow but the manifesto of an evangelist answerable for his vocation. As a Methodist, Wesley does not sigh after perfection, he vaunts it—a Methodist prays without ceasing. In retirement or in company, his heart is ever with the Lord. He loves his neighbor as himself, including his enemies. His heart is purified from envy, malice, and every unkind temper. He keeps all the commandments with all his might.

Other leaders in the evangelical revival were not long in voicing their opposition to these claims. In response, Wesley published the sermon "Christian Perfection" (1740). Drawing heavily from the Bible, Wesley allowed that Christians are not perfect in the sense of committing no mistakes, but he argued that intention is all that counts. Sins have to be intentional. Even newborn Christians are perfect in that they do not commit sins, while more adult Christians are perfect in the higher sense of being freed from evil desires. "It remains, then, that Christians are saved in this world from all sin, from all unrighteousness; that they are now in such as sense perfect, as not to commit sin, and to be freed from evil thoughts and tempers." Much in the same tenor is the preface that Wesley wrote for a book of hymns (1741). Christians are freed from pride; they feel it is not they that speak or act but God in them. They no longer desire anything for themselves, neither possessions nor relief from pain. It is impossible for them to entertain evil thoughts. Their minds do not wander when they pray. They are free from all fear and doubt. Temptations fly about them, but their souls are unmovable. Then, as if making a new start, Wesley allows that the change does not come all at once: God's work is partly instantaneous, partly gradual—at one moment the believer received a clear sense of forgiveness, at another the abiding witness of the Holy Spirit, at another a clean heart. There are times of lamentation mixed with times of rejoicing. On occasion God lets them see all the abominations of pride and self-will that are hidden in their hearts; but "in the midst of this fiery trial . . . they feel after a full renewal," and God, observing their desire, visits them anew with his Son and with the Holy Spirit. Wesley appends a footnote (1765) calling attention to what he had said in 1741 about the hidden corruption of the heart, to prove to his critics that he had even then been mindful of the believer's possible deficiency of self-knowledge.

In 1744, at the first annual Methodist conference, an early session was given to considering "the doctrine of sanctification or perfection." Owing to the presence in early Methodism of Calvinist and Arminian parties, the statements agreed to are little more than scriptural texts that speak of God saving Israel from all uncleanness, and of Christ giving himself that his Church might be without spot and wrinkle. Wesley mentions successive conferences where the issue hung fire. That of 1758 was memorable as subscribing to the distinction between intentional and unintentional transgressions of the law and in acknowledging that unintentional transgressions require atonement as much as intentional. This is the starting point for Wesley's *Thoughts on Christian Perfection* (1759). The work is conciliatory. Wesley goes so far as to say that "sinless perfection" is a phrase he avoids using because some people use the word *sin* carelessly to include involuntary as well as voluntary transgressions. The rest of the book is devoted to problems that perfectionism poses for the pastoral ministry. Methodist preachers, usually self-taught laymen, are advised not only of their duty to preach the necessity for holiness but also of their responsibility for counseling those who believe that they have received this blessing. Some of the questions dealt with seem trivial, such as whether one who has reached perfection will prefer pleasing food to unpleasing, and whether the children of perfect parents will be born without sin. More serious is the question of how one can tell whether a person is perfect. Wesley's answer is not very different from that of other spiritual advisers: I know that this person is not a liar, and if he says that he feels no sin but all love and that he has the witness of the Holy Spirit, then I ought in all reason to believe him.

A letter from one of Wesley's London converts serves well to illustrate the experiences of one passing from justifying faith to what came to be known as the second blessing. Jane Cooper wrote Wesley, May 2, 1761, relating her prayers and distresses. Moved by his sermon on the text, "We wait for the hope of righteousness," she began to wait and pray for the blessing. With the music of Handel's *Messiah* running through her head, she appropriated to herself the prophecy, "The Lord whom ye seek shall suddenly come to his temple" and sit there "as a refining fire." She felt as if she were nothing and enjoyed great quiet, but was not sure whether God had destroyed her sin. She conversed with friends, opened the Bible at random and read, "The unbeliever shall be cast into a lake of fire" and again, "Be not affrighted: ye seek Jesus. He goeth before you into Galilee." One of her friends reminded her that God is no respecter of persons; and in a moment she found full salvation. "I saw Jesus altogether lovely; and knew he was mine in all his offices." Some six months later Jane Cooper died; but Wesley is able to append a letter from one who was witness of her last days. In spite of strong convulsions and extreme pain she was reasonable to the end. Her last words were, "My Jesus is all in all to me: glory be to Him through time and eternity."

Further Thoughts on Christian Perfection (1763) was Wesley's response to the extravagances of a revival that had visited London the previous year. Earlier he had issued a tract called "Cautions and Directions Given to the Greatest Professors in the Methodist Societies," warning preachers against pride, enthusiasm, antinomianism, and other dangers that he saw in store. *Further Thoughts* incorporates this tract, while addressing itself also to substantive issues. Questions that had earlier been debated by preachers at the annual conferences were now being argued by everyone. The book is heavy on the side of doctrine. Classical Protestantism had distinguished between justification (pardon of sins through faith in Christ's atoning death) and sanctification (the inner working of the Holy Spirit), holding that the former is instantaneous and the latter gradual. Wesley, like the German pietists from the time of Johann Arndt, complained that the clergy neglected to preach sanctification, thereby making Christianity seem too easy. This was no doubt a legitimate complaint; nevertheless, in refusing to deal publicly with questions concerning the work of the Spirit in each person's soul, the established churches steered clear of much futile controversy. Wesley held that in most cases sanctification proceeds gradually and that the believer attains complete holiness only in the instant preceding his death; but he insisted, both on the basis of Scripture and on the evidence of his own pastoral experience, that some are entirely sanctified soon after their conversion. It was inevitable that many would ask, How can I know? In answer, Wesley could only refer to the inner testimony of the Holy Spirit. But there were endless questions: for example, whether one could be mistaken about the witness; whether the witness could be lost even though a person remained in a state of grace; and, indeed, whether one can fall out of a state of grace. All of these questions Wesley answered in the affirmative. "Have any a testimony from the Spirit that they shall never sin? We know not what God may vouchsafe to some particular persons; but we do not find any general state described in Scripture, from which a man cannot draw back to sin." This explains the emphasis that Wesley placed on deathbed behavior and last words.

Further Thoughts concludes with a series of "reflections," which Wesley recommends to his readers for "deep and frequent consideration, next to the Holy Scriptures." These are interesting mainly because they echo a long mystical tradition. "The best helps to growth in grace are the ill usage, the affronts, and the losses which befall us." "True resignation consists in a thorough conformity to the whole will of God. . . . In order to do this, we have only to embrace all events, good and bad, as His will." "To abandon all, to strip one's self of all, in order to seek and to follow Jesus Christ naked to Bethlehem. . . . to Calvary, where He died on the cross, is so great a mercy, that neither the thing, nor the knowledge of it, is given to any, but through faith in the Son of God." "True humility is a kind of self-annihilation; and this is the center of all virtues." "Prayer continues in the desire of the heart, though the understanding be employed on outward things." "God does not love men that are inconstant, nor good works that are intermitted. Nothing is pleasing to Him but what has a semblance of His own immutability." And much more in this vein. As a popular evangelist, Wesley spoke ill of mysticism, even in so honored a person as William Law. But in his early years Wesley had visited Law, and on Law's recommendation he had read widely in mystical theology, both ancient and modern. Thus, it is not surprising that we find here passages reminiscent of mystical writers. All that is surprising is that they are appended to a work written long after he had cut himself off from this tradition—unless, as seems likely, these are reflections penned by Wesley in his Holy Club days. If this is the case, and if some of the reflections are lifted, in whole or in part, from mystical authors, we understand somewhat better how Wesley can place them next to the Scriptures. In any case, their appearance at the end of his last published work on Perfection provides an unintentional evidence of the underlying unity of Wesley's convictions through the years.

Jean H. Faurot

RECOMMENDED READING

Edition used: Wesley, John. *A Plain Account of Christian Perfection.* London: Epworth Press, 1952.

Flew, R. Newton. *The Idea of Perfection in Christian Theology: An Historical Study of the Christian Ideal for the Present Life.* Oxford: Clarendon Press, 1934. Holds that despite appearances to the contrary, Quakerism, Pietism, and Methodism were a return to a more Catholic view of Christianity obscured by the Protestant Reformation. Chapter 19, "Methodism," while deeply sympathetic with Wesley's teaching, makes most of criticisms that occur to the reader of *A Plain Account.*

Knox, R. A. *Enthusiasm: A Chapter in the History of Religion with Special Reference to the XVII and XVIII Centuries.* Oxford: Clarendon Press, 1950. Chapters 18 through 21 (pp. 422–548) are on Wesley and Methodism. Critical but respectful treatment of Wesley by an English monsignor.

Wesley, John. *Selections from the Journal.* Edited by Hugh Martin. London: S.C.M. Press, 1955. Based on the "standard" *Journal,* deciphered in 1909. Previously only those parts considered by their author as useful to his cause had been available. Called Wesley's "most picturesque biography."

————. [Selections.] Edited by Albert C. Outler. New York: Oxford University Press, 1964; paperback, 1980. Representative letters, theological statements, and polemical writings, with helpful introductory material by the editor. Contains the sermon "Christian Perfection," and "Thoughts on Christian Perfection."

THE JOURNAL
OF JOHN WOOLMAN

Author: John Woolman (1720–1772)
Born in a rural Quaker community in New Jersey, John Woolman exercised an itinerant ministry that took him throughout the American colonies, and, at the end of his life, to England. Though he was a tailor by trade and ran a successful dry-goods shop at Mount Holly, New Jersey, Woolman's central concern was to serve as a channel for divine love for all creatures, including the poor and oppressed. He visited fellow Quakers in the Southern colonies, convincing them of the evils of slaveholding, and in addition to his journal wrote a number of pamphlets, including *A Plea for the Poor* and *Some Considerations on the Keeping of Negroes.*

Type and subject of work: Spiritual autobiography exhibiting a unique blend if individual piety and social concern

First published: 1774

MAJOR THEMES

Though obedience to God is often demanding and difficult, there is divine help and consolation for those who will accept the way of the cross.

Discernment arising from disciplined practice is necessary for continually recognizing the movement of God's Spirit.

Among the many snares that can divert the believer from the true path is the

desire for wealth and luxury.

The simple, unencumbered life style is most consistent with the gospel calling, and abandoning simplicity leads to many oppressive practices.

Attentiveness to the divine voice will often put one at odds with customs and traditions that support the oppression of others.

Cultivation of a compassion for others is needed to combat natural tendencies toward selfishness that block the flow of God's love.

The overwhelming impression that greets the reader of John Woolman's *Journal* is of a life intent on obedience to God. With a sense of urgency and passionate concern, Woolman repeatedly accepted the hard way he believed God was placing before him, preferring it to the less demanding well-traveled paths. For him, the supreme danger was to block the divine work by allowing worldly desires to crowd out the "pure, universal love" that God would have govern us. He was never in doubt that for the Christian the way to be followed would be filled with difficulties, but he was equally convinced that learning to bear the cross opened the door to spiritual refreshment and inner peace.

Woolman's account of his own life reveals a constant struggle to hear the voice of God. He tells of an experience early in his life at a Quaker silent worship service. In such services, the custom was to wait in silence until the Spirit of God led one or more worshipers to minister audibly to the group. During one service, Woolman records that he spoke some words, "but not keeping close to the Divine opening, I said more than was required of me." He was deeply troubled by his failure to attune himself with the Spirit's leadership, and it was six weeks before he felt free to speak again in a service. Woolman describes the experience as a discipline that strengthened him to "distinguish the pure spirit which inwardly moves upon the heart."

This incident illustrates the tenderness of Woolman's conscience. Whether the issue is of great importance or relatively trivial, he is intent on guarding against motivations and actions that are contrary to the work of God. Later in life, after returning from a dangerous journey to visit the Indians, Woolman records that he had been striving during the trip to arrive at a place of "perfect resignation" and careful "lest I should admit any degree of selfishness."

The concern for inner purity arises in part from a firm conviction of the dangers facing the believer. Toward the end of his life, Woolman writes, "O, how great is the danger of departing from the pure feeling of that which leadeth safely!" Christ is a sure guide, but the follower must be constantly vigilant, wary of the snares in the path. Often Woolman writes of his concern for young people who may be led astray by attractions that point them away from the true path. At times he sounds unnecessarily ascetic, reacting strongly to what many people would be inclined to think of as innocent frivolities. There may be truth in this reaction, but we need to read Woolman's warnings against the backdrop of his keen awareness of the human potential for wickedness and of the eternal spiritual dangers. Perhaps Woolman is overscrupulous about "youthful vanities" and "merriment," but perhaps he sometimes sees what is most likely to be missed by an age that finds it hard to believe that there is a narrow path that is easy to lose.

In his own life Woolman exhibits a remarkable sensitivity to the many ways one may be pulled away from spiritual concerns. High on his list was the desire to make money. From observation he concluded that "with an increase of wealth the desire of wealth increased." Furthermore, he learned by experience that business interests can absorb excessive amounts of time and attention if this is allowed. This may sound like the sort of conclusion one would expect from a man who was too spiritual to be of much use in practical economic matters. But in fact Woolman reports he had both a talent and a "natural inclination" toward business affairs. Besides his trade as a tailor, he was involved in selling retail goods. His trade increased each year and he diversified successfully until "the way to a large business appeared open." But, reports Woolman, "I felt a stop in my mind." Seeing that the growth of his business involved him "in cumbering affairs," he deliberately took steps to decrease its size.

This decision is closely related to one of Woolman's fundamental convictions, that people live best when they abandon the concern for unnecessary luxuries and content themselves with a simple life style. In his own business, Woolman made it a practice to "buy and sell things really useful." He was not eager to be involved with unnecessary luxuries or "superfluities," regardless of whether they might sell well. Woolman reports that whenever he carried such items, "I found it weaken me as a Christian." He was concerned neither to indulge in that which might draw him away from "the voice of the true Shepherd" nor to be an instrument for fanning the flame in others of the lust for more things.

In Woolman's view the inordinate desire for unnecessary luxuries was a major cause of a number of social ills. When writing of a visit to the Indians, he noted that the addiction to wealth was responsible for such oppressive practices as getting the Indians to sell their land for "trifling considerations" and inducing them to trade skins and furs on which they "depend for subsistence" for liquor that did them great harm.

Similarly, it is the unwillingness to be satisfied with a simple life style that Woolman finds at the root of the great evil of slavery. For Woolman, fighting the injustice of slavery was a passionate concern to which he devoted a lifetime of effort. An early experience brought home to him the reality of slaveholding. As a young man he was asked by his employer to draw up a bill of sale for a woman while the buyer waited. Woolman felt uneasy at the recognition that it was a fellow human being who was to be sold. At the same time, he believed he had a duty to do as his employer directed. Finally, he reports, he gave way "through weakness" and wrote the bill of sale. Yet he was troubled enough to tell both his employer and the buyer he believed the practice of slave-keeping inconsistent with Christianity.

Part of the agony of this decision arose from the fact that both buyer and seller were members of Woolman's own religious community, the Society of Friends. While Woolman's conviction of the evil of slaveholding was not unique, it should be remembered that the practice was widely accepted and even defended by many fellow believers. From this time on, the mission of awakening the conscience of Friends to the evil of slavery became a central task in Woolman's life. Traveling throughout New England and in the Southern colonies, he spoke to Quaker slaveholders about the inconsistency of the practice with the Christian faith.

This form of ministry was not easy for Woolman. He records repeatedly his reluctance to confront those he visited. But he felt a task had been laid upon him by God, and often he could not rest easy until he had delivered the message. He speaks of feeling his mind "released from a burden" after humbly and tenderly laying the word of God before others, and, following Ezekiel, he compares his task to that of a watchman. One who accepts the work of warning the people will be faced with constant temptations to avoid the task or do it in a wrong spirit. Not least among the dangers to this ministry are the "snares of prosperity and outside friendship."

The genuine servant of God must be attentive to the divine voice and open to new wisdom from him. Woolman's attempt to do this often brought him into conflict with custom and accepted practice. He became convinced, for example, that the custom of wearing dyed hats and garments and "wearing more clothes in summer than are useful" was inconsistent with God's intended simplicity. To act on the basis of this conviction was difficult because it would mean standing out from others in an embarrassing way. Furthermore, his going against accepted custom could easily be misunderstood because it "savored of an affected singularity." Woolman found the uniqueness of his appearance to be a trial, particularly when friends unsure of his motives "grew shy" of him. Despite the suffering, he experienced "inward consolation" and was confirmed in the conviction that "things though small in themselves, being clearly enjoined by Divine authority become great things to us."

In a similar spirit, Woolman refrained from the use of things that he believed supported oppression or unnecessary luxury. Hearing of the treatment of slaves in the West Indies, he refused to use products connected with the practice. He writes, "I . . . declined to gratify my palate with those sugars." Similarly, Woolman judged it wrong to pay a tax to support war even though ne knew it would mean the confiscation of his goods. He notes that members of his Society usually paid the tax despite their pacifist views, and that going against the common practice was "exceedingly disagreeable." On the other hand, to go against his conscience was even "more dreadful." When during the war Woolman was required by authorities to quarter a soldier in his house, after deliberation he accepted the soldier, but he went out of his way to refuse payment and to explain why.

For Woolman, many occasions became opportunities for bearing testimony to his convictions. Trying to act in things great and small in a manner consistent with the calling of the gospel was often a difficult trial. But time and again he accepted inconvenience, discomfort, and financial loss as a way of maintaining his integrity. In matters that most would probably think too small to make an issue of, Woolman labored to bring his actions into conformity with the will of God.

Underlying these efforts is a firm conviction that God is actively involved in the affairs of life. For Woolman, the attitude of looking for the divine intention became second nature. On several occasions he interpreted his own illness as a means through which God wanted to teach him something. Difficulties were often regarded as chastisements intended for his purification. He even refers to smallpox as "a messenger from the Almighty, to be an assistant in the cause of virtue." During one illness he felt the need for greater purification and consequently felt no desire for health "until the design of my correction was answered." When there was complete surrender and resignation to God's purposes, inward as well as outward healing could come.

Throughout the experience of various trials to faith, Woolman is acutely aware of the refreshment of God's love. He speaks constantly of the grace and mercy of God and the sufficiency of his help. The sense of duty and judgment comes across so strongly in Woolman's writings that it is easy to miss the fact that Woolman's commitment is also a response to his sense of the goodness and love of God. For Woolman, however, the judgment of God on unrighteousness is not something separate or in conflict with God's love and kindness. His judgment is an expression of a providential concern. The necessity of standing strict guard over our desires and concerns arises from the need to keep a clear path for his light to shine within us.

God's tender concern for all creatures becomes for Woolman a motivation to cultivate his own concern. He gives as a partial reason for one of his journeys "that by so travelling I may have a more lively feeling of the condition of the oppressed slaves." Throughout his life Woolman labored to keep alive his awareness of the poor, the dispossessed, and the oppressed. He became "desirous to embrace every opportunity of being inwardly acquainted with the hardships and difficulties of my fellow-creatures." This was not simply an academic exercise. It was a crucial preparation for one who desired to be used as an instrument to spread God's righteousness. Only an appreciation of the situation of others can prepare one to put aside the "spirit of selfishness" to which all are naturally inclined.

Woolman was never content with pious feelings divorced from consistent practice. His commitment to "universal love" led him to repudiate all actions conflicting with the well-being of his fellow creatures. Faithfulness to this vision often meant personal sacrifice, but for Woolman acceptance of personal loss was a small price compared to the danger of blocking God's work with selfish motives. He saw the task of life as a matter of disentangling oneself from temporal concerns that crowd out the movement of Divine Love. Renouncing the desires or wealth, power, or comfort meant opening channels through which God's love could flow.

While people may disagree with particular conclusions Woolman draws, it is hard not to admire his concern to bring together confession and practice. Within the literature of Christian spirituality, he stands out as a model for those who strive to make of their lives a unified whole.

David M. Holley

RECOMMENDED READING

Edition used: Woolman, John. *The Journal of John Woolman and A Plea for the Poor.* The John Greenleaf Whittier Edition text with an Introduction by Frederick B. Tolles. Secaucus, N.J.: Citadel Press, 1972.

Cady, Edwin H. *John Woolman.* New York: Washington Square Press, 1965. This volume in the Great American Thinkers series sets Woolman's life and work in their historical context, and contains a helpful bibliography including some of the more recent works on the American Quaker community and its historical influence.

Whitney, Janet. *John Woolman, American Quaker.* Boston: Little, Brown, 1942. The definitive Woolman biography, readable and based on copious research, if somewhat colored by the author's imagination.

Woolman, John. *The Journal and Essays of John Woolman.* Edited from the original manuscripts with a biographical introduction by Amelia Mott Gummere. New York: Macmillan, 1922. Contains the complete texts of Woolman's writings, plus a lengthy biographical sketch, as well as many other Woolman documents (correspondence, ledgers, and so forth).

SONGS OF INNOCENCE AND OF EXPERIENCE

Author: William Blake (1757–1827)

William Blake, born on November 28, 1757, whose father was a London hosier, had a number of experiences as a child that he took to be revelations of God's mysteries. He began his training as an artist at the age of ten, in Henry Pars's drawing school. At fourteen, he became an apprentice to the engraver James Basire. He had already written a number of poems. By 1778 he had established himself as an engraver, and in 1782 he married Catherine Boucher, who not only encouraged him in his literary and artistic efforts but also became his associate in the art of engraving. He wrote a number of prophetic works, illustrated numerous volumes by which he acquired a reputation as an outstanding designer and engraver, and employed his artistry as poet and illustrator to express his spiritual insights. He died in London on August 12, 1827.

Type and subject of work: Lyrical poetry on the spiritual condition from the perspectives of the very young and of the more experienced

First published: Songs of Innocence, 1789; Songs of Experience, 1794

MAJOR THEMES

The very young in their innocence, even when suffering, recognize, accept, and delight in the presence of God.

The innocent know the joys of love and sympathy, both human and divine.

The older, more experienced witnesses to God's presence and power recognize and to some degree exhibit human selfishness and know evil as the darkness of the soul in alienation from God.

But, like the innocent, experienced souls are affected by God's power and will, and they glory in the drama of life under God.

William Blake himself used as a subtitle of his *Songs of Innocence and of Experience* (which he illustrated and printed in 1794), "Shewing the Two Contrary States of the Human Soul." Ever since, critics have debated the question of whether Blake intended to present the insoluble paradox of the human encounter with God or simply to cast into verse the contrasting experiences of the innocent and the experienced.

If one considers Blake's own moving experience as a child that he attributed to his innocent awareness of God's presence in the world and if, further, one realizes that the experiences of the very young are hardly worth a sympathetic rendering if they are nullified by the experiences of the older and the wiser, then one must take Blake as a visionary poet who knew God both as a child and as a man, wondering throughout at God's power and his glory, while comforted throughout by God's love.

One is tempted to suppose that there is a discernible division between innocence and experience and that Blake used his poetry to mark and define the difference. But the experience of the young and innocent is, after all, experience in the course of the movement toward evil and the struggle against evil, while the experience of the older, which includes the experience of guilt, is lightened by a kind of innocent wonder at God's love and forgiveness.

If, then, one adds to the constant of human innocence and experience, both present at once and in confusion, the illuminating fact that Blake switched poems back and forth from the one collection to the other, himself confused—or, perhaps, struck—by the ambiguity of the human encounter with God in God's world, one comes to the conviction that whether a song is one of innocence or of experience, it is of the contrary states of the human soul.

In the introductory poem to *Songs of Innocence*, Blake writes of a laughing child "on a cloud," who called upon him to write happy songs "that all may read" and that "Every child may joy to hear." The image is pastoral and Blake is piping when he sees the child. The image of the piping poet anticipates the image of the good shepherd.

For the most part, the *Songs of Innocence* are celebrations of the Shepherd in his loving care of the lamb. One realizes through the child's experience that relative to God's care, all persons are lambs; relative to his knowledge, will, and power, all persons are innocent. The child's celebration of God's love is for all persons, both the innocent and the experienced; here, in the mouths of babes, are the truths experience has forgotten.

Thus, in his first poem, "The Shepherd," Blake writes that the Shepherd "shall follow his sheep all the day," that "he hears the lambs [sic] innocent call," and that "He is watchful while they are in peace."

But human beings are not simply lambs. In "The Ecchoing Green" (Blake's spelling), the initial image is of the sun's rising, the happy skies, the singing birds, the ringing bells, and the children's sporting on the green. But under the oak the old folk sit and, although laughing at the children's play, remember, surely with some regret, that "Such such were the joys, / When we all girls and boys, / In our youth time were seen, / On the Ecchoing Green." The children become weary, the sun descends, the sports have an end, and there is no more playing "On the darkening Green."

The human adventure, then, is from childhood to age, from innocence to experience, from light to darkness, from spontaneous joy to profound sorrow. This human passage, inevitable but both threatening and promising at once, is anticipated in the image of the children's returning to the laps of their parents as the playing ends and the green darkens.

Another kind of cloud, here symbolic not of the course of nature but of the inevitability of confusion and suffering, is thrown over innocence in Blake's poem "The Little Black Boy." The poem begins, "My mother bore me in the southern wild, / And I am black, but O! my soul is white, / White as an angel is the English child: / But I am black as if bereav'd of light." The child's mother tells him that "we are put on earth a little space, / That we may learn to bear the beams of love." And she promises him that "when our souls have learn'd the heat to bear / The cloud will vanish . . . " and the child responds that when "I from black and he from white cloud free," he and the English boy will play joyfully around the tent of God: "I'll shade him from the heat till he can bear, / To lean in joy upon our fathers knee. / And then I'll stand and stroke his silver hair, / And be like him and he will then love me."

Surely there is the experience of suffering in this poem, and there is also the affirmation of faith by which the clouds of human prejudice are dispelled. Innocence anticipates the shock of experience and the recovery through God's love.

Again, injustice intrudes upon the innocent, as portrayed in "The Chimney Sweeper." The young sweep reports that after his mother died, his father sold him "while yet my tongue, / Could scarcely cry weep weep weep weep. / So your chimneys I sweep and in soot I sleep." The poem tells of Tom Dacre, whose hair "curl'd like a lambs back" is shaved off so that soot cannot spoil it, dreaming of thousands of chimney sweeps locked in black coffins but liberated by "an Angel who had a bright key. . . ." The boys run leaping and laughing across the green plain to wash in the river and "shine in the Sun." They "rise upon clouds, and sport in the wind," and the Angel promises Tom that if he were a good boy he would "have God for his father and never want joy." The dream ends, and Tom rises in the dark to do his work, but he is happy and warmed by the faith that "if all do their duty, they need not fear harm."

In "The Lamb" Blake expresses the mystery of creation as grasped by the simple faith of innocence. Here the light side of creation provides a background for the dark side later to be expressed in "The Tyger." "Little Lamb who made thee / Dost thou know who made thee?" asks the child—and answers: "Little Lamb I'll tell thee, / Little Lamb I'll tell thee; / He is called by thy name, / For he calls himself a Lamb. . . . " The poem concludes, "I a child and thou a lamb, / We are called by his name. / Little Lamb God bless thee, / Little Lamb God bless thee."

But he who made the lamb made the tiger, and Blake's "Tyger," in the Songs of Experience, strikes one with the mysterious creative power of God. Experience is helpless in the effort to understand the awesome signs of God's creative will. In the image of the tiger beauty and evil seem to be inextricably interrelated, but the incomprehensibility of divine creation suggests the wonder of paradoxical resolution through the dramatic workings-out of the limitless power that made the tiger possible.

"Tyger Tyger, burning bright, / In the forests of the night; / What immortal hand or eye, / Could frame thy fearful symmetry?" So the poem begins, and it is evident from the beginning that the question is not the metaphysical one of who or what created the tiger; the essential question is *why* the tiger was created. Surely God created all and, hence, the tiger. But "Did he smile his work to see? / Did he who made the Lamb make thee?" Experience wants an explanation but must be content with the God-revealing mystery of the tiger's fiery brain and heart.

There is something threatening, dark, and even evil in the image of the tiger. The tiger burns bright; the fire burns in the tiger's eyes; the tiger was somehow wrought on an anvil: "What the hand, dare seize the fire? / . . . What the hammer? what the chain, / In what furnace was thy brain? / What the anvil? what dread grasp, / Dare its deadly terrors clasp?" At the creation of the tiger " . . . the stars threw down their spears / And water'd heaven with their tears . . . ."

Blake's celebration of God's power through the image of the tiger is perhaps also a celebration of the possibility of love's triumph over evil. The very power that made the tiger also, and perhaps in the same act, made the lamb. The possibility of love is also the possibility of the violation of love; the power that makes evil awful is the same power that makes love awesome. The tiger is a natural beast, of course, but Blake's genius endows the tiger with the aura of the supernatural and with all the ambiguity of the human being so created as to be capable of either destructive or purifying fire.

When the tiger appears in "Night," from *Songs of Innocence,* it appears in its natural condition, along with wolves, as howling for sheep as prey. The poem presents an image of protecting angels: As night comes, the angels visit and bless the birds and beasts, and "pour sleep on their head." But—"When wolves and tygers howl for prey / They pitying stand and weep; / Seeking to drive their thirst away, / And keep them from the sheep. . . ." Despite the effort of the angels, the beasts may "rush dreadful," but the promise of the poem is that the angels will receive each spirit and escort it to the new world of eternal love, a world in which the lion (also, in the natural world, a beast of prey) will lie down with the lamb and, under the influence of divine love, guard the fold. What is true of the lion, one may presume to be true of the tiger: The possibility of love is inherent even in the dreadful.

Just as paradoxical imagery is used in both the *Songs of Innocence* and the *Songs of Experience* to present and resolve what has been called the problem of evil, so such imagery is used to present and resolve the problem of sexual love, an aspect of the problem of evil that stems from the power of human freedom.

In the *Songs of Innocence* a deceptively simple poem, "The Blossom," portrays sexual intercourse in a telling, although again ambiguous, way: "Merry Merry Sparrow / Under leaves so green / A happy Blossom / Sees you swift as arrow / Seek your cradle narrow / Near my Bosom." The next stanza, which completes the poem, is addressed to "Pretty Pretty Robin," and here the happy blossom "Hears you sobbing sobbing . . ." However one might account for the "sobbing sobbing," whether it be a kind of sadness evinced, a kind of joy, or a kind of act, the element of something in some way negative is introduced.

When one moves to the *Songs of Experience,* whatever is or can be negative in sexual love is acknowledged and little of the positive remains, as in "The Sick Rose":

> O Rose thou art sick.
> The invisible worm,
> That flies in the night
> In the howling storm:
>
> Has found out thy bed
> Of crimson joy:
> And his dark secret love
> Does thy life destroy.

Throughout his poems Blake recognizes the positive, light, creative aspects of nature and of the human being—and also the negative, dark, and destructive aspects. The innocent respond to and delight in the brighter side; the experienced know, partly through self-knowledge, the darker—the possibility of negating the positive values made possible by the divine. This recognition, however, has its positive aspect: Through knowing humanity's misuse of power, freedom, and one another, one knows also, through experience, how one can consciously return to the kind of world the innocent see but cannot realize.

Ian P. McGreal

RECOMMENDED READING

Edition used: Blake, William. *Songs of Innocence and of Experience.* New York: Orion Press, 1967 (in association with Trianon Press, Paris).

Bentley, G. E. Jr., and Martin K. Nurmi. *A Blake Bibliography: Annotated Lists of Works, Studies, and Blakeana.* Minneapolis: University of Minnesota Press, 1964. A definitive bibliography of writings by and about Blake. Includes a helpful introductory essay on the history of Blake scholarship.

Gillham, D. G. *Blake's Contrary States: The "Songs of Innocence and of Experience" as Dramatic Poems.* Cambridge: Cambridge University Press, 1966. A perceptive analysis of Blake's *Songs* in defense of the thesis that Blake dramatically expressed the contrasting attitudes of self-interest and sympathetic concern.

Paley, Morton D., ed. *Twentieth Century Interpretations of "Songs of Innocence and of Experience."* Englewood Cliffs, N.J.: Prentice-Hall, 1969. A brilliant collection of critical essays by such writers as S. Foster Damon, Northrop Frye, Joseph H. Wicksteed, and Mark Schorer. The essays appear under the headings "Interpretations" and "View Points."

REAL CHRISTIANITY

Author: William Wilberforce (1759–1833)

Born into a wealthy family of merchants in Hull, William Wilberforce was educated at Cambridge University, became a member of Parliament at twenty-one, and was a lifelong friend of the prime minister, William Pitt. He became a Christian in 1785, and moved to Clapham to join a prominent group of Christian politicians and business leaders, "the Clapham Sect." With these friends, Wilberforce led the attack on the abolition of slavery. They founded the settlement of Sierra Leone in 1787 to absorb freed slaves. Legal trading of slaves from West Africa was stopped by the 1807 Act. Portugal followed suit in 1810. The final act of abolition in the British Empire took place the week of his death. Wilberforce's second major concern was to raise the moral tone of the ruling class, with his book *A Practical View . . . Real Christianity*, first published in 1797. It remained a best-seller for more than fifty years, and was translated into French, Italian, Spanish, Dutch, and German.

Type and subject of work: An evangelical effort, directed to the ruling classes in England

First published: 1797

MAJOR THEMES

The prevailing religious practices of the higher and middle classes in England contrast with the spirit of true Christianity.

Christianity consists not simply in churchgoing but in the exercise of a spirit

that is the antithesis of selfishness, is based upon humility, and is lived out in every aspect of society and its duties.

The true Christian walks by faith, purifies the heart, and focuses on the interior life before God.

Measure your growth as a Christian by your growth in love to God and your neighbor.

The full title of William Wilberforce's *Real Christianity* was "A Practical View of the Prevailing Religious System of Professed Christians in the Higher and Middle Classes in This Country, Contrasted with REAL CHRISTIANITY." A religious book by a politician was unheard of, and coming at a time of national emergency, the effect was dramatic, and the book was read by most of the national leaders. The work marked the beginning of the influence of Evangelicalism upon the ruling classes.

Wilberforce's approach was practical. Christianity calls for more than churchgoing; it is an expression of spirit and character, and its principles should be lived out in every aspect of society and its duties. Christianity calls for the antithesis of selfishness and, consequently, for the reversal of current practice. In seven chapters Wilberforce describes the inadequate notions of the importance of Christianity commonly held, as well as the false notions of the corruption of human nature and the defective practice of nominal churchgoers. He then outlines the true doctrines of "real Christianity," with practical advice as to how people who take their faith seriously live their lives. Recognize, warned Wilberforce, that the decline of real Christianity is a national disaster and that there is the earnest need for prayer for a national revival.

Since Wilberforce's purpose in writing this book was to arouse the nation, it is both a forthright and a conciliatory exposure of the false attitudes and defective practices of professed Christians. These are contrasted with what is delineated in the Bible and evidenced in the spirit of sincere Christians. It was a new approach, skillfully handled by a public orator who knew how to move people without offending them. For Wilberforce writes in humility and earnestness. He is comprehensive in his exposé of what is false, and practical in seeking an alternative perspective. He appeals to the heart, as well as to the mind. Wilberforce's own public spirit, his national concerns, his high visibility in the abolition of slavery, made it a powerful book in its time, a force for religious revival. It went far to accredit real Christianity to statesmen and politicians. It charged the ruling class with their personal needs of religious integrity. It deeply affected the younger clergy, looking for a true message to communicate. It provided a new model for devotional writers to take. And having such a spokesman encouraged the faithful servants of Christ.

Wilberforce's first charge is that moralism has replaced real Christian faith. For "their opinions on the subject of religion are not formed from the perusal of the Word of God. The Bible lies on the shelf unopened." The prevailing assumption is that sincerity is enough in itself. So there is naïveté concerning human nature: The depravity of humanity is overlooked. Furthermore, in the moralistic view the reality of a personal devil is denied and the pride of humanity is overlooked and misunderstood. Consequently, there is also an inadequate appreciation of the character of Christ as Savior. If the seriousness of sin is not accepted, writes Wilberforce, then the Savior is rejected also. One has only to look at Church history to see the crimes perpetrated in the name of religion, to see the corruption of the human heart. The absence of true religion is substituted for by warm feelings, rationalism, zeal, "do-goodism," and much else. But a personal knowledge of God the Savior, who has saved us by his own death and resurrection, is unknown.

The tendency to create one's own system of religiosity, of "churchianity" instead of real Christianity, also implies a misconception of the Holy Spirit, Wilberforce insists. We tend naturally to believe that all that is necessary is to "do the best you can." Scripture, however, teaches us that "of ourselves we can do nothing," that by nature "we are the children of wrath," and that only God's Holy Spirit can give us new birth, "creating us anew in Christ Jesus." Mistaken notions of repentance abound, of being sorry for what has happened, perhaps, without a daily conversion that only God's Spirit can give to us. "Pray earnestly, then, that we may be filled with *joy* and *peace* in believing, that we may abound in *hope* through the power of the Holy Ghost."

The false notions concerning the Holy Spirit lead to the assumption that if we merely have some superficial notion of what Christianity is about, and avoid the more flagrant sins, then everything will be all right. Conformity, conventions, and the reduction of faith to a mere word are presumed to be sufficient. But the morality of the gospel rejects such superficiality. Nothing can be more comprehensive that what Scripture teaches: "Whatsoever you do in word or deed, do *all* in the name of the Lord Jesus"; "Be you *perfect* as your Father in heaven is perfect." Holiness is commanded of us, writes Wilberforce. The effect of the Holy Spirit upon us is to appear "in *all* goodness, and righteousness, and truth." The apostle prays that his beloved converts will "be *filled* with *all* the fullness of God." The awesome standard of God's morality is that, relying upon the promises of the Redeemer to repenting sinners, they now devote themselves unreservedly and consistently to God. They become the implacable enemies of sin, and the master principle of their lives is to honor and glorify God. The prerogative of Christianity is "to bring into captivity every thought to the obedience of Christ."

The true Christian "walks by faith, and not by sight." So the natural tendencies of temperament, the satisfaction of the natural affections, the public applause and popularity of the world, have no place in the life of a Christian. The true Christian is not looking for earthly rewards, the distinctions given by others, nor for advancement in this world. "It is the distinguishing glory of Christianity not to rest satisfied with superficial appearances, but to rectify the motives, and purify the heart," writes Wilberforce. The Christian's focus is upon the interior life before God; such believers watch themselves in small as well as in great acts, in small as well as in great duties. Again Wilberforce emphasizes the fatal error of not distinguishing the true religion of the heart from the mere morality of the conventional life. Unless, then, we are "looking unto Jesus," we have the fatal flaw of being ignorant of the doctrines of the faith.

Wilberforce concludes with some practical hints to the repentant reader. Do not think you have overcome sin because you have walked away from a particular vice, he enjoins. We cannot be realistic enough about being sinners before God. Do not be "almost persuaded" about the truths of the Bible. Follow through all insights you are given. Rely on the promises of God who "works in you both to will and to do of His good pleasure." Measure your growth as a Christian by your growth in love, to God and your fellow human beings. Self-seeking, base, and financial motives in serving others are false. Only true love is true, for "God is love." Take seriously, devotedly, the cause of the gospel. There can be no half-hearted believers in real Christianity. Passionate concern for God is needed at all times in history.

James M. Houston

RECOMMENDED READING

Edition used: Wilberforce, William. *A Practical View . . . Real Christianity.* Introductory essay by Daniel Wilson. New York: Crocker & Brewster, 1829.

Lean, Garth. *God's Politician: William Wilberforce's Struggle.* London: Darton, Langmen & Todd, 1980. An interesting biographical account of Wilberforce's evangelical effort.

Pollock, John. *William Wilberforce.* New York: St. Martin's Press, Lion Aslan Paperbacks, 1978. A popular biography.

Wilberforce, William. *Real Christianity.* Portland, Oreg.: Multnomah Press, 1983. An abridged version, rewritten by James M. Houston, and with an introductory essay by Senator Mark Hatfield.

PRACTICAL PIETY

Author: Hannah More (1765–1833)
One of five unmarried sisters, Hannah was one of the most remarkable women in the English society of her time. In her youth, her interest was in drama and literature, and she was well known in the circles of David Garrick, Samuel Johnson, Joshua Reynolds, and others of the *literati*. She wrote some plays and ballads. She became the confidante of political figures such as Horace Walpole. In the 1780s, her philanthropic interests in the abolition of slavery drew her into the circle of the Evangelicals, William Cowper, John Newton (in 1780), and especially William Wilberforce (in 1786) and the Clapham Sect. She aided in the development of the Sunday School Movement. She became the propagandist of the Clapham Sect, writing hundreds of pamphlets. She argued that as women had inferior education to men, the only area in which women were equal to men, if not superior, was in religion. Hence, she argued, the further education of women could be seen as the furtherance of Christianity. She became one of the best-known writers of her time. Her collected works were published in eleven volumes in 1853. Four of her devotional works were *Practical Piety* (1811), *Christian Morals* (1812), *Character and Practical Writings of St. Paul* (1815), and *Reflections on Prayer* (1819).

Type and subject of work: A devotional essay applying the spirit of Christianity to the conduct of life

First published: 1811

Major Themes

Dedication of life to Christ is the demand of true religion.

Christianity, as "the religion of the heart," is practical religion; it is expressed in deeds, in character, and in duties well performed.

True religion is relevant to the times and needs of society, but it springs from a life of prayer, a devotional spirit, and the love of God.

To love God is to be acquainted with him in every daily circumstance and to see God's claims universally around us.

The full title of *Practical Piety* is: *Practical Piety; or, the Influence of the Religion of the Heart on the Conduct of Life.* Hannah More wrote the work to remind her readers of what the Christian faith demanded. She saw the dangers of the Christian faith to be a broadness of doctrine on the one hand and a narrow bigotry on the other. She regarded Christianity as carrying with it evidence of its God-given origin: Its author is God; it was foretold, confirmed by miracles, satisfied by the blood of Christ, made sublime in its worship and service, and in the exposure of evil. Yet it is much more than a perfect rule for life, for it has the power to change lives, to make them Christlike. It focuses upon the heart, so that inward devotedness to God takes place.

Hannah More was sixty-six years old when she wrote this book, as one "who must die soon, to Christians who must die certainly." She writes her book, cognizant of the writings of men such as George Horne, Jeremy Taylor, George Herbert, Archbishop Leighton, Bishop Joseph Hall, Bishop Usher, John Howe, Richard Baxter, Bishops Ridley, Jewel, and Hooper, the Reformers, and church fathers such as Chrysostom and Augustine.

It is clear from Scripture, argued Hannah More, that God intends us to cultivate the inner being for him. "He would never have said—'give me your heart'—'seek my face'—'add to your faith virtue'—'have a right heart and a right spirit' "—if these had not been enjoined as practicable duties. Such commands are also promises of what God will do in us. Since the happiness of a Christian does not lie in feelings but in a real and radical change within us, we should strive for that change.

Indeed, all the doctrines of the gospel are practical principles, she writes; they are life-giving and they call for practical changes in our lives. So we can never be said to be real Christians without becoming transformed people. Practical Christianity is "exercising ourselves unto godliness." (Here Hannah More was no doubt mindful of the book one of her closest friends, William Wilberforce, had written in 1797, *Real Christianity*.)

Prayer, she says, is the application of want to him who alone can relieve it; the voice of sin to him who alone can pardon it. So it is the urgency of need, the prostration of humility, the fervency of penitence, the confidence of trust. But of all aspects of prayer, adoration is the noblest. As a guide to self-knowledge, prayer is the art of understanding, both of the mind and of the heart. For this it requires the prayerful use of Scripture, so that it is applied constantly. But we can be too preoccupied with sin, so in prayer we should be also much more occupied with the character of God and communion with him. For a sincere love of God will make us thankful, encourage our supplications, and make us responsive to the will of God.

The cultivation of a devotional spirit needs to be habitual and requires avoidance of all things negative to its culture. Our reading habits and choice of books are important, she argues. Prayer, too, should be considered more than *art*; it should lead us to have a *spirit* of prayer, so that we "pray without ceasing." Miscalculation of the true value of lasting qualities is one of the greatest errors of our moral life, since we tend to lavish undue attention upon passing things. So we need the perpetual use of prayer to make right evaluations.

The primary law of our faith is to "love the Lord thy God with all thy heart." This must take some tangible form in specific action, More insists. We love God when we vindicate him before others who deny or defile him; we do so in faithful duties; and we do so when we act with *all* our heart, consecrating every faculty to him. So we also acknowledge the hand of God in the daily circumstances of life. We have to do so, however, not by our own low standards, but by appeal to his character. He then makes us see our weaknesses and seek his strength.

There is a common tendency to reason that many Scriptural injunctions are culturally conditioned, that they belong to the early Church rather than to us today. We need to focus upon the universal requirements of the Christian faith, and obey them wholeheartedly, More writes. For the world's enmity to God remains constant, and our sinful hearts remain with the same tendencies. So standards of right and wrong remain consistent, despite our varying cultures. Old and New Testaments demand the same thing—"be ye holy, for I the Lord your God am holy."

Little faults need attention as much as big faults, so procrastination, indecision, idleness, vanity, sulkiness, triviality, all need attention in self-examination. Indeed, Hannah More devotes much attention to self-examination, self-love, and poor behavior with non-Christians.

Moral vigilance is therefore a vital need for the cultivation of a devout heart before God, she argues. For while the person of the world does not see the essential corruption of the heart, the Christian should recognize it all the time. To be constantly suspicious of one's own intents, desires, and actions generates a moral caution that is humbling and yet realistic. Knowing our natural bent, we shall be more discerning of true or false zeal, which is such an important aspect of our character. Then we shall be better equipped to live with an eternal dimension, and by the truths of God; then we shall live in daily repentance; then we shall die well, as we have lived well; then we shall endure sufferings with a due sense of their importance and relevance to our moral well-being.

Thus, in twenty-one chapters, Hannah More spells out the constituents of the Christian character. Depth and focus are given to the injunction to live according to the religion of the heart through the vicissitudes of the human condition. The book is a portrait of what Hannah More sought to be herself. She had innumerable friends as devoted to her as she had been to others. Her correspondence was enormous, and her influence was felt throughout the British Empire. For she was absorbed in the emancipation of slavery and in the extension of overseas missions, and she had a deep influence in the personal lives of such persons as David Garrick, Horace Walpole, William Wilberforce, and Lord Macauley. She was indeed, a great woman of saintly influence.

James M. Houston

RECOMMENDED READING

Edition used: More, Hannah. *Practical Piety: or, the Influence of the Religion of the Heart on the Conduct of the Life.* Boston: Munroe & Francis, 1811.

Jones, M. G. *Hannah More.* Cambridge: Cambridge University Press, 1952. This is a critical but not unsympathetic critique of her life.

More, Hannah. *Memoirs of the Life and Correspondence of Mrs. Hannah More.* Edited by William Roberts. 2 vols. London: R. B. Seeley & Sons, 1834. Provides a personal expression of More's pervasive spirituality.

LECTURES ON REVIVALS OF RELIGION

Author: Charles Grandison Finney (1792–1875)
The foremost revivalist of the nineteenth century, Finney was born in Connecticut and reared in upstate New York. While studying law, he underwent a religious conversion and began to study for the ministry. Ordained a Presbyterian, he conducted numerous revivals in upstate New York and in New England before becoming a Congregationalist and president of Oberlin College in Ohio, the first coeducational college. Other writings by Finney include *Lectures to Professing Christians* (1836–1837, 1878), which were also first printed in the *New York Evangelist* and in which he first outlined his views on Christian perfection; *Letters on Revivals* (1845); *Lectures on Systematic Theology* (1846, 1851, 1878); and *Sermons on Gospel Themes* (1876).

Type and subject of work: A practical study of revivalism: what it is, how revivals can be promoted, and how they can be hindered

First published: 1835

MAJOR THEMES

Religion is the result of human effort.
A revival is the result of the right use of the proper means.
God created us with free will; we are free moral agents.
Conversion is not something to wait upon God to do, but something for us to do.

If we are unsaved it is because we are unwilling, not because we are unable to be saved.

Charles Grandison Finney was the greatest revival preacher of the nineteenth century. His "New Measures" revivalism revolutionized American religion during the Second Great Awakening.

Jonathan Edwards described the beginning of the First Great Awakening in a book titled *A Faithful Narrative of the Surprising Work of God in the Conversion of Many Hundred Souls in Northampton* (1737). For Edwards, a revival was a surprise, a miracle. The Puritans believed that conversion came only to the Elect; all that one could do was wait to see if one would be a recipient of God's grace.

"Religion is something to *do*, not something to *wait for*," according to Finney. He himself had a sudden conversion on October 10, 1821, and he approached the ministry as he had the study of law. As he says in these *Lectures*, "The object of the ministry is to get all the people to feel that the devil has no right to rule this world, but that they ought to give themselves to God, and vote in the Lord Jesus Christ as the governor of the universe." He approached a congregation as he would a jury; he laid out the facts and told them the choice was theirs, now. He advises a minister to "preach just as he would talk, if he wishes to be fully understood. . . . The minister ought to do as the lawyer does when he wants to make a jury understand him perfectly. He uses a style perfectly colloquial." After all, Finney writes, *"human agency is just as indispensable to a revival as divine agency."*

After a very successful career holding revivals in upstate New York and then in all of the major cities of the East Coast, Finney became pastor of Chatham Chapel in New York City in 1832. The first of these twenty-two Friday night lectures on "Revivals of Religion" was published in the *New York Evangelist* on December 6, 1834. They were collected in book form in May 1835.

Finney began by arguing that *"Religion is the work of man. It is something for man to do."* A revival is *not* a miracle, but "the result of the *right* use of the appropriate means." For Finney the appropriate means were his "new measures": protracted meetings, the anxious bench, the anxious meeting, colloquial preaching, praying for people by name, and most controversial of all, allowing women to pray in mixed assemblies.

Finney began with a strong belief in free will. To say that human beings do not have a free will, are not able to respond to the gospel "slanders God . . . charging him with infinite tyranny, in commanding men to do that which they have no power to do." Since God has commanded us to repent of our sins, that "is the highest possible evidence that we can do it . . . equivalent to an oath that we can do it. He has no right to command, unless we have power to obey." Thus "conversion consists in the right employment of the sinner's own agency." In conversion the sinner apprehends the truth and wills to obey it, turns from selfishness to benevolence, from willing his or her own self-gratification to willing the highest good for all.

Finney said that he believed in total depravity, but it certainly was not the traditional Calvinist interpretation. He defined it not as a "disease" of transmitted guilt, nor any constitutional inability to obey God, nor any inherited fault that predisposed all to sinful choices. He believed that infants possess the original nature of Adam, but that they sin because the temptations to selfishness are so great in the world. Infants, he said, are neither sinful nor holy until they become moral agents and disobey the moral law of God.

One of Finney's most famous sermons was titled "Sinners Bound to Change Their Own Hearts." As he says in the *Lectures*, the sinners' "cannot" consists in their unwillingness and not in their inability. "We, as moral agents, have the power to obey God, and are perfectly bound to obey, and the reason we do not is, that we are unwilling." A sinner's problem is not hardness of heart but stubbornness of will: "It is not a question of *feeling* but of *willing* and *acting* . . . WILLING to obey Christ is to be a Christian."

Finney evaluated his ministry and that of others on one basis: success. One lecture is titled "A Wise Minister Will Be Successful" and his text is Proverbs 11:30—"he that winneth souls is wise." He noted that most churches were sleepy and cold at heart; many ministers did not even know it, let alone know how to wake them up, nor set them to work once they were awake. Revivalists have often been charged with psychologically manipulating their audiences. Finney believed that a good minister should understand "the laws of the mind" and put them to good use. Not seminary trained himself, Finney often criticized more educated ministers. In these *Lectures* he asks, "When young men come out from the seminaries, are they fit to go into a revival?" The obvious answer is no. He declares that there is a "grand defect in educating ministers." Some he had seen "could not manage a prayer meeting, so as to make it profitable or interesting." He believed that ministers should be those who had experienced a religious conversion themselves and felt called to the ministry. That experience and call were validated by the effectiveness of their ministry, that is, by the number of sinners they won to Christ.

Finney also measured the propriety of his new measures by their success. He says that "when the blessing evidently follows the introduction of the *measure itself*, the proof is unanswerable, that the measure is wise." If God blesses a measure with the salvation of souls, then it must be sanctioned by God. To criticize it is to think oneself wiser than God.

Throughout the book Finney uses a number of illustrations from his own career. Often it is the story of a layperson who heard the call of revival and the minister who lacked faith. Women figure prominently in these examples, contrary to the social conventions of his day.

After defining what a revival is, suggesting how to promote it, giving instructions in how to pray for revival, and showing how ministers and churches can win sinners to Christ, Finney lectures on what hinders revivals. Since God is dependent on the use of human means, people can hinder revival. If a church believes a revival is going to stop, it will. Or if Christians become mechanical in their promotion of revival or stop working at it, revival will cease. Finney's meetings were usually inclusive, so he warns denominations against putting their own specific interests forward. Revivals are also hindered by failure to give God the credit or to remember one's dependence on the Holy Spirit.

Finney was the first to include temperance as an integral part of his revival preaching. He lists "resistance to the Temperance Reformation" as a specific hindrance to revival. And even though it was very controversial, he declared that "revivals are hindered when ministers and *churches take wrong ground in regard to any question involving human rights.*" He specifically names the issue of slavery. He cites the example of John Newton (1721–1807), who worked on slave ships but became opposed to slavery after God convicted him of its evil. As Finney says, "it is a subject upon which [Christians] cannot be silent without guilt." The New York Anti-Slavery Society had been formed in the Chatham Street Chapel October 2, 1833; the American Anti-Slavery Society grew from that and often held its conventions there. He urged churches to "take right ground in regard to politics" and "on the subject of slavery." Both those who sell liquor and those who hold slaves should be barred from the church.

Finney gives directions for dealing with sinners. Basically they should be told to repent, believe the gospel, give their hearts to God, submit to God, and choose whom they will serve. "All they have to do is to *accept* salvation"; they do not have to make themselves better. Nor do they have to suffer for a long time under conviction to atone for their sins or wait for different feelings. When a person is truly willing to be a Christian and chooses to be a Christian, that person *is* a Christian.

Finney concludes by noting that "there is no such thing as standing still in religion." One either grows in grace or one is in declension. Later he began to teach a type of sanctification that was labeled "Oberlin Perfectionism" because he believed that people needed to be encouraged to continue growing in the Christian life.

Nancy A. Hardesty

RECOMMENDED READING

Edition used: Finney, Charles Grandison. *Lectures on Revivals of Religion.* Edited by William G. McLoughlin. Cambridge: Harvard University Press, Belknap Press, 1960. The definitive text.

Cross, Whitney. *The Burned-Over District.* New York: Harper & Row, Harper Torchbooks, 1950. Details the milieu in which Finney's revivals took place and outlines their impact.

Dayton, Donald. *Discovering an Evangelical Heritage.* New York: Harper & Row, 1976. A series of essays analyzing Finney and his compatriots.

Finney, Charles Grandison. *Memoirs.* New York: A. S. Barnes & Co., 1870. Finney's own account of his life.

———. *Reflections on Revival.* Compiled by Donald Dayton. Minneapolis: Bethany Fellowship, 1979. A full reprint of his *Letters on Revivals.* Outlines his social views.

———. *Revivals, Awakenings, and Reform.* Chicago: University of Chicago Press, 1978. The best analysis of how revivalism fits into the American story and social history in general.

McLoughlin, William G. *Modern Revivalism.* New York: Ronald Press Co., 1959. Good analysis of revivalism with major emphasis on Finney.

Smith, Timothy L. *Revivalism and Social Reform.* Nashville: Abingdon Press, 1957. The classic treatment of the Second Great Awakening and Finney's role in it.

THE DIVINITY SCHOOL ADDRESS

Author: Ralph Waldo Emerson (1803–1882)
Breaking with the theological traditions of Puritan forebears and affronting many Unitarian contemporaries, Ralph Waldo Emerson began his work in controversy and became perhaps the most influential thinker in the American cultural tradition. As preacher, poet, lecturer, and essayist over the course of his career, he sought to articulate a new vision of spirit in the world and a conduct of life appropriate for the citizenry of the young nation. Other major works include his *Nature* (1836), "The American Scholar" (1837), *Essays: First Series* (1841), *Second Series* (1844), and *Representative Men* (1850).

Type and subject of work: A lecture on the need for new forms of religious vision and new revelations of spirit

First published: 1838

MAJOR THEMES

The world is infused with currents of spirit, emanating from Supreme Being, to which all people have direct access if they will turn themselves to the ways the world answers to the cravings of the human soul.

To sense the presence of this divine law in the natural order is to awaken the genuine religious sentiment, and to participate in such a perfect world of spirit is to grasp new "miracles," new sources of revelation.

Jesus Christ was the only one who fully practiced the religious sentiment and grasped the divine law, who followed out the ultimate reaches of the soul, and who thus participated in the Supreme Mind, but all others have such possibilities open to them in a world permeated with influences of divinity.

All people have within them the same capacity of soul, but that spiritual potential is dimmed in an age that fails to comprehend the great unrealized dominion of humankind.

Historical Christianity errs when it assumes or teaches or practices the idea that such possibilities, centrally evident in Jesus Christ, ended in nature and history with him, and a new kind of preaching is called for that recognizes this "doctrine of soul" and that urges a corresponding conduct of worship in a world understood in its complete spiritual dimensions.

With the publication of *Nature* in 1936, Ralph Waldo Emerson found himself the center of controversy with the Unitarian community at Harvard. In the introduction to that essay, he had insisted that his contemporaries discover their own "original relation to the universe" instead of living out the history of the forefathers' understanding. Those "dry bones" of the past ought to be discarded, he declared, in favor of a "religion of revelation to us" in which one could behold God and nature face to face in a new immediacy of spiritual life. And, in the remainder of the essay, he outlined a vision of the created order in which currents of divinity, stemming from an "Over-Soul," were immanent in the natural world and described a form of the essential human "self," the soul, and the forms of its potency and striving that could take possession of such a world for those people daring enough to seize such possibilities for personal spiritual fulfillment.

In more particular terms, as a "self" enjoyed its most glorious prospects, Emerson argued, it would ascend through the world of nature by approaching it not only for its "commodity," its practical uses, and not only for its "Beauty," its aesthetic and moral uses, but for its "Spirit," its revelation to the self of that presence of world-soul that corresponded to the human soul. Thus would the human spirit be nurtured by self-reliance, the active independent seeking of the soul in the realm of direct experience, through the medium of intuition, for that which would answer it and on which it was ultimately dependent, the immanence of spirit.

This early, visionary piece of writing, foundational for virtually every feature of Emerson's subsequent thinking, removed him from his intellectual and religious lineage in the American Puritan tradition and disaffected all but the most radical members of the Unitarian community he served in his own generation.

Thus, when Emerson was approached in 1838 to speak to the senior class at the Harvard Divinity School, the invitation came neither from the Unitarian clergy nor from the officers of the school but, rather, from the seniors themselves, eager to get a look at this challenging new figure on the New England scene. For controversy, he did not disappoint them: The challenge to the doctrinal tradition, generalized and muted in *Nature*, now became decidedly more specific; the hints in the earlier essay about divine capacity in humans were now spelled out more explicitly; the new vision, proposed in broad cultural terms in 1836, was directed during that July of 1838 to inspire a particular community of religious belief.

If the senior divinity students might have been stirred by the speech and if it was highly regarded by men such as William Ellery Channing and Theodore Parker, many others, however, resented this little talk, entitled simply "An Address." If for his part Emerson had delivered a clear remedy for the overemphasis on formalist and rationalist aspects of religion (which he spotted most especially in Unitarianism and which he would elsewhere refer to as its "pale negations"), and if he had done so in what he thought a congenial and constructive manner, one prominent Unitarian, Andrews Norton, vigorously attacked the address as "the latest form of infidelity," expressing a sentiment apparently shared widely among the clergy since only after nearly three decades was Emerson invited again to address the Harvard community.

Planning his talk (later to be called "The Divinity School Address") fully in continuity with the vision of the world articulated in Nature, Emerson opens his remarks with a melodious description of the New England summer and suggests how the plenitude and beauty of nature, its breadth and variety, invite the participation of human life in such abundance. But he quickly turns from the questions of subduing the world for the realm of commodity and of enjoying the world at the level of beauty in order to raise the question of "the laws which traverse the universe" and which contain and unite all of its "infinite relations."

This is the ultimate question the human spirit has sought to answer, Emerson insists, because the human intuition of the spiritual unity of the world has always been the source of morality and worship. To sense the unifying laws of the world is also to have an "insight of the perfections of the laws of the soul" which insight, in turn, leads to "the sentiment of virtue" as the soul seeks to live in harmony with the universal principles of life. If the human soul realizes its implication in the spirit of the universe, it attempts to practice that "reverence and delight in the presence of . . . divine laws" that constitute moral essence. But the intuition of these spiritual laws also leads the open soul to the perception that "all things proceed out of the same spirit," to the recognition of "the sublime creed that the world is not the product of manifold power, but of one will, of one mind; and that one mind is everywhere active" in the created order. With the perception of this "law of laws," there is awakened "the religious sentiment" that is both "divine and deifying" because it makes the human soul illimitable in its communion with this Supreme Mind. While the Supreme Mind cannot be fully comprehended by human rationality, it can be approached through the intuitions of a human soul enlarged by worship.

To be opened to and infused by the divine law of the natural world is to exhibit such worship and to practice faith in "the doctrine of soul," which gives full release to the moral and religious sentiments potential in all people. While these sentiments have been embodied fully and uniquely only in Jesus Christ, they are capable of realization by everyone, Emerson thinks, even if now all seem to struggle in darkness and limitation. Were people to enter the world fully open to the currents of spirit flowing through it, they might move in delight and reverence and worship through a confluence of divine spirit with human spirit, and this new conduct of piety would bring to them "the privilege of the immeasurable mind" to seize a world brimming with the miracles of natural life "in the blowing clover and falling rain," a world now seen as revelatory of spirit at every turn, a world forever to be beheld in astonishment by that form of human response to which that world corresponds and for which it is made perfect.

This vision of the world, the doctrine of soul at its heart, and the new conduct of life it would create, were yet to be born in his time, Emerson believes, because the age was suffering under a lower estimate of human spiritual potential and under forms of religious understanding and practice that clouded the spiritual horizons. Only one man, Jesus Christ, has ever been true to the doctrine of soul, Emerson argues: Jesus "saw with open eye the mystery of the soul. . . . He saw that God incarnates himself in man, and evermore goes forth anew to take possession of his World." What was open to Jesus, the realization of God in him, is open to all people because the principle of incarnation is structured into the divine laws of the world, Emerson notes, but "alone in all history he [Jesus] estimated the greatness of man." Such an estimate cannot be taught to the rational understanding; it can arrive only through the example of those who have themselves intuited the spiritual unity of the universe by worshiping within the doctrine of soul. Sadly, however, the ages have not followed the soul-principle evident in Jesus Christ but have instead followed his "tropes" to worship with "a doctrine of church."

Thus, historical Christianity itself has erred in two considerable ways, Emerson declares, which further prevent the recognition of people that they have and can do all that Jesus had and did, that by "coming again to themselves, or to God in themselves, can they grow forevermore." First, Christianity errs by confusing the *person* of Jesus with the soul of Jesus. In such a misunderstanding, people are urged to subordinate their own natures to the person of Christ and are not inspired to recognize that the capacity of soul in Christ is duplicated in themselves, in their essential selves, their souls, given by the divine mind for the venturous reach for complete spiritual fulfillment. "The soul knows no persons," Emerson boldly states, and the invitation to the soul is for "every man to expand to the full circle of the universe," not to shackle the self in imitation of another. The second defect of the Christian Church is a related one. By emphasizing the unique person of Christ, Emerson points out, "men have come to speak of the revelation as somewhat long ago given and done, as if God were [now] dead." So long as the Supreme Mind flows through the world of nature and history, however, the principle of revelation centered in Jesus Christ must be seen as a continuing principle—indeed a divine law—that beckons the soul to enter into that "original relation to the universe" Emerson craved in *Nature*. To regard revelation as having gone out of the world after Jesus is to cripple efforts to make the doctrine of the illimitable soul the wellspring of religion and society. Such an "injury to faith throttles the preacher," Emerson thinks, and gives the Church "an uncertain and inarticulate voice."

With these errors of historical Christianity exposed, Emerson becomes more explicitly mindful of his audience, a group of young men poised to take up the vocations of Christian ministry. He challenges them directly: "In how many churches, by how many prophets, tell me, is man made sensible that he is an infinite Soul; that the heavens and earth are passing into his mind; that he is drinking forever the soul of God?" The pulpit has been usurped by formalists, Emerson argues, while the necessities of the age require a preacher "on whom the soul descends, through whom the soul speaks." At a moment in which "the need was never greater of new revelation," the pulpit was being mounted too often by those as yet unawakened to the real presence of spirit in the world, by those cloaked so securely in the doctrinal garments of the Church that they remained untouched by those miraculous currents of life that answer to the struggle of soul for the realization of spirit. Against this deformity in the ministry, Emerson tells the divinity students, the new preacher must "live with the privilege of the immeasurable mind," must not confuse the soul with the Church, must deal with men and women in the immediacy of their experience, which would be to "acquaint . . . [them] at first hand with Deity" by now cheering "their waiting, fainting hearts . . . with new hope and new revelation." In order to accomplish this, he asserts, the young preachers will need to "cast behind . . . all conformity" in favor of their own souls' intuitions of the laws in the world of divine immanence. "I shall look for the New Teacher," Emerson closes, "that shall follow so far those shining laws that he shall see them come full circle; shall see their rounding complete grace; shall see the world to be a mirror of the soul."

Finally, then, Emerson sought in "The Divinity School Address" to

instill in the ministers of the young American nation a sense of the revelatory dimensions of the abundantly spiritual world he thought
awaited their possession. In this, he spoke with a vibrancy of soul, a
hope of heart, an attitude of spiritual conviction, that made him less interested in being accredited in terms of the doctrinal measurements of
historical Christianity and more committed to respond out of his own
sense of life's mysterious plenitude and humankind's potential spiritual
dominion. Above all, he thirsted for an immediacy in spiritual existence.
And, at the last, although he would vaunt the enlarged soul over any
constricted sense of the person, Emerson's own passionate voice proposed him as the "New Teacher," captivated by the doctrine of soul and
poised to find revelation restored to nature and history.

Rowland A. Sherrill

RECOMMENDED READING

Edition used: Emerson, Ralph Waldo. "An Address." In *The Complete Essays
and Other Writings*. Edited, with a biographical introduction by Brooks At-
kinson. New York: Random House, 1940. This book in The Modern Library
series is an accessible collection of the major essays and lectures and other
selections from Emerson's work.

Allen, Gay Wilson. *Waldo Emerson: A Biography*. New York: Viking Press, 1981.
Allen's magisterial critical biography treats Emerson's thought in the con-
texts both of the age and of the personal life-history with which Emerson's
ideas were so deeply intertwined.

Robinson, David. *Apostle of Culture: Emerson as Preacher and Lecturer*. Philadelphia: University of Pennsylvania Press, 1982. Following out the evolution
of Emerson's thought over the course of his career, Robinson studies the
shifts of mode involved in Emerson's movement from preacher, to lecturer,
to essayist.

THE WAY OF HOLINESS

Author: Phoebe Palmer (1807–1874)
A lifelong Methodist, Palmer became the mother of the Holiness and
Pentecostal churches through her teaching of holiness as a "second
blessing." She and her sister Sarah founded the Tuesday Meeting for the
Promotion of Holiness in their New York City home in 1835; it contin-
ued until 1896. With her husband Walter Palmer, a physician, Palmer
held religious meetings in the United States, Canada, and the British
Isles (which they toured from 1859 to 1863). In 1864 they bought the
Guide to Holiness, and Phoebe became its editor.

Type and subject of work: Biblical theology, devoted to the question of
how one might attain holiness or sanctification

First published: 1843

MAJOR THEMES

*Sanctification can be a distinct and instantaneous work, just as salvation is.
One must simply "lay one's all on the altar" (surrender all to God).*

*Because "the alter sanctifies the gift" and Jesus Christ is the altar, the person
is sanctified.*

*Because God's word is true and divine promises are sure, one can thus claim
sanctification, regardless of one's feelings.*

John Wesley in his *Plain Account of Christian Perfection* and other works taught that sanctification, Christian perfection, or, as he preferred to call it, perfect love, was the goal of the Christian life. If one commits oneself to Christian growth, sanctification begins subsequent to justification. Some, he admitted, appear to attain entire sanctification or perfect love before death, though he himself never felt that he had so matured.

The teaching became a point of controversy with the Calvinist Methodists led by Selina Countess of Huntingdon and George Whitefield. It was defended and exhibited by John and Mary Bosanquet Fletcher. In time, it became less popular with American Methodists. Phoebe Palmer, along with Oberlin Perfectionists Charles Finney and Asa Mahan, resurrected the doctrine, modified it, and nurtured numerous new branches on the Wesleyan family tree.

The Way of Holiness begins with an anecdote. Palmer once heard a gentleman ask "whether there is not a *shorter* way of getting into this way of holiness than some of our . . . brethren apprehend?" (He probably was referring to the Methodists.) Her immediate response was, "Yes, brother, THERE IS A SHORTER WAY! O! I am sure this long waiting and struggling with the powers of darkness is not necessary. There is a shorter way." After prayer and Bible study, she began to preach it.

She begins with the premise that God was serious when God commanded: "Be ye holy" (Matt. 5:48). Thus, "God requires that I should *now* be holy . . . God requires *present* holiness." The fact that God has commanded it guarantees that it is possible.

The first step is to form "the determination to consecrate all upon the altar of sacrifice to God, with the resolve to 'enter into the bonds of an everlasting covenant to be wholly the Lord's for time and eternity,' and then acting in conformity with this decision, *actually laying all upon the altar.*"

She deduced from a reading of Exodus 29:37, Matthew 23:19, and Romans 12:1–2 that Christ was the altar and that the altar sanctified the gift (this "altar terminology" caused some controversy; the reasoning is somewhat convoluted). Thus once one laid one's all upon the altar, then "by the most unequivocal Scripture testimony," one was compelled to *believe* that the sacrifice became 'holy and acceptable,' and virtually the *Lord's property,* even by virtue of the sanctity of the *altar* upon which it was laid, and continued 'holy and acceptable,' so long as kept inviolably upon this hallowed altar." "By the removal of this offering from off this *hallowing* altar, she would *cease to be holy.*" Thus a continuous act of faith is required.

Following Charles Finney's lead in asserting that cooperative human action was necessary to spiritual growth, "she apprehended that nothing *but the blood of Jesus* could *sanctify* and *cleanse* from sin, yet she was also scripturally assured that it was needful for the recipient of this grace, as a worker together with God" to bring the gift to the altar and lay it there. *"Man must act,"* she wrote.

John Wesley had demanded testimony and proof that someone's life had indeed changed before he accounted them sanctified. Thus Palmer raises the hypothetical question: "Shall I *venture* upon these declarations without *previously* realizing a change sufficient to warrant such conclusions?" Palmer's reply was "Venture *now,* merely because they stand thus recorded in the *written word!*" Since *"faith is taking God at his word,"* if one meets the conditions—lays all upon the altar—one is guaranteed the results—one is holy. One does not have to have any particular emotional experience or wait to see if one's life exhibits certain hallmarks. One can simply claim holiness; to do less is to doubt God's word, according to Palmer.

She describes her own experience in the space of a few sentences: "O, Lord, I call heaven and earth to witness that I *now lay body, soul, and spirit,* with *all these redeemed powers, upon thine altar, to be for ever* THINE! 'Tis DONE! Thou has promised to receive me! Thou canst not be un-faithful! *Thou dost receive me now!* From this time henceforth I *am thine —wholly thine!"*

In the second part of the book, titled "Notes by the Way," Palmer details her own experience and that of others in the "way of holiness." At age thirteen she had begun to seek salvation and joined the local Methodist church. Shortly thereafter she had an experience of God's presence in which "the place seemed to shine with the glory of God . . . . All was light, joy, and peace." She took as her motto in life, "Holiness unto the Lord," a phrase that became the watchword of the Holiness churches.

Many of the examples are drawn from Palmer's work as the teacher of a Bible class, a distributor of tracts, and a speaker at camp meetings. She speaks of her dreams in which God revealed truth to her. She also gives thanks for her daughter, so precious after two sons had died in infancy. She particularly regretted that she had hesitated to baptize her firstborn because she understood that as an acknowledgment that she was giving him up to God. She felt that God took the child back rather than accepting him as a free-will offering. Although Palmer taught that holiness was a "second-blessing" experience, received the moment one surrendered to God, it is clear from her own life that, for some time before she experienced holiness and even after she had experienced it, the Christian life was a continuous struggle.

Her life and work exemplify a dictum found often in nineteenth-century religious literature: "God *requires* you should be useful, and has not left the matter optional with yourself." One must aim not only to save one's own soul, but also the souls of others. One must also constantly testify to one's experience if one hopes to retain it. In sharing one's experience with others, one grows.

Palmer ends the book with an account of her elder daughter's conversion. She explained to her "how she might *retain* the blessing": "It was by giving your heart away to God that you received a new heart; and the only way to keep it is to keep giving."

Palmer develops her view of holiness in several other works. *Faith and Its Effects: Fragments from My Portfolio* (1848) is a series of letters to various people in which she gives spiritual guidance. *Present to My Christian Friend on Entire Devotion to God* (1845) begins with the assertion that "if you are not a *holy* Christian, you are not a *Bible* Christian." She proceeds to cite chapter and verse to support her teachings on holiness. Although Palmer's work is clearly in the classical and Wesleyan traditions of perfection, she repeatedly declares that "THE BIBLE, THE BLESSED BIBLE, IS THE TEXTBOOK. Not Wesley, not Fletcher, not Finney, not Mahan, not Upham, not Mrs. Phoebe Palmer, but the Bible—the holy BIBLE, is the first and last, and in the midst always. The BIBLE is the standard, the groundwork, the platform, the creed." She buttresses her argument with testimonies from converts and with endorsements by leading ministers. While her "altar terminology" was controversial, her work gained the support of many of the leading ministers and theologians of the Methodist church and other denominations.

Nancy A. Hardesty

RECOMMENDED READING

Edition used: Palmer, Phoebe. *The Way of Holiness.* New York: Printed for the Author, 1854.

Dieter, Melvin E. *The Holiness Revival of the Nineteenth Century.* Metuchen, N. J.: Scarecrow Press, 1980. Excellent historical treatment of the movement in which Palmer was a central figure.

Hardesty, Nancy A. *Women Called to Witness: Evangelical Feminism in the Nineteenth Century.* Nashville: Abingdon Press, 1984. Shows Palmer's connection with the women's rights movement.

Jones, Charles Edwin. *Perfectionist Persuasion: The Holiness Movement and American Methodism, 1867–1936.* Metuchen, N. J.: Scarecrow Press, 1974. Another historical analysis of Palmer and the Holiness movement and its relationship to the Methodist Episcopal church.

Smith, Timothy. *Revivalism and Social Reform.* Nashville: Abingdon Press, 1957. The classic study of revivalism and social reform. Sets Palmer's Holiness movement alongside Charles Finney's Oberlin Perfectionism.

Syman, Vincent. *The Holiness-Pentecostal Movement in the United States.* Grand Rapids, Mich.: Eerdmans, 1971. The history of how the Holiness movement gave birth to modern Pentecostalism at the turn of the twentieth century.

Purity of Heart Is to Will One Thing

Author: Søren Kierkegaard (1813–1855)

The seventh son of a wealthy wool-merchant, Søren Kierkegaard resided all his life in the large family dwelling in central Copenhagen, where he was prominent as a literary figure. An unhappy love affair, quarrels with other writers and, in his last years, with the Church—all documented in lengthy journals—make up the story of his life. Graduated in theology, he put off taking orders (Lutheran); still, an overriding sense of what the gospel can mean to those who embrace it with faith and love led him to sandwich in between his various poetical and philosophical writings a number of "Edifying Discourses," of which the present book is a memorable example.

Type and subject of work: Meditations in preparation for the office of Confession

First published: 1847

Major Themes

Only persons who will the Good can be said to will one thing.

If one is to be sincere in willing the Good, one's will must be stripped of the entanglements of self-interest.

A person who wills the Good in sincerity must be willing to do all or to suffer all for the Good.

One wills the Good by obeying the voice of conscience, which speaks in time with the authority of eternity.

Purity of Heart Is to Will One Thing is a penitential sermon intended to accompany the office of Confession. To be sure, it is an amplified sermon, not meant to be preached but to be read; still, it is a sermon, with a text, appropriate divisions, long somnolent stretches, and a conclusion exhorting the reader to change his or her ways. The sermon, which enjoins holiness, deserves a place in the literature of Christian perfection. "Purity of heart," Søren Kierkegaard's name for holiness, is conceived as right willing, that is, willing the Good, or what God wills—"the one thing needful."

The text comes from James 4:8: "Draw nigh to God and He will draw nigh to you. Cleanse your hands, ye sinners; and purify your hearts ye double-minded." "Double-minded" (Greek *dipsychos*, a term peculiar to Jewish-Christian Wisdom Literature) means doubting, wavering, uncertain, and, especially, division of interest between the world and God. Appropriately in a preconfessional sermon, the preacher's main concern is to expose double-mindedness (or, as we might say, bad faith, not in the sense of deceiving others but in the deeper sense of deceiving oneself). In any case, the opposite of double-mindedness, that is, willing one thing, does not lend itself to any elaboration. For Kierkegaard , it is equivalent to obeying the secret voice of conscience.

The divisions of the sermon (obscured by extraneous section headings in the American version) are conveniently stated by the author in more places than one. The argument falls into two main parts: a shorter part in which it is maintained that to will one thing one must lift one's eyes to the heavens, for there is nothing on earth that can be willed with an undivided will; and a much longer part in which typical duplicities that creep into the creaturely will when it tries to conform itself to the will of the Creator are systematically exposed. In this second part, the author further distinguishes between willing and doing. The problem when one tries to will what heaven wills is that self-interest keeps creeping in; similarly, when one tries to do what heaven wills, all the shifts and expediencies familiar to us in business clothes turn up again in cassock and gown.

The first, relatively short, part of the sermon, called "Willing the Good," is of interest mainly in view of the claim of secular humanists that doubters can give meaning and weight to their lives by willing one thing without any reference to the Good. Select a cause, give it your all, and save your soul in so doing. Whether it is the best cause will always be debatable, but all that you need ask is whether it is a cause with which you have enough affinity to be authentic in the role you will be undertaking to play. A life is too precious to waste in drifting with the tide. Be somebody! Maybe you will find out that you are strong enough not even to need a cause to lean on. Choose your goal and follow it ruthlessly to the end!

How far does willing one thing—any one thing—equal purity of heart? Suppose the extreme case, Kierkegaard proposes. Can the unmitigated seeker after pleasure or wealth or power win a halo merely in virtue of the consistency with which the goal is pursued? No doubt such a person can—in the eyes of the double-minded. If halos were for average persons to bestow, quite possibly they would immortalize great sinners who have done what the bestower would sneakingly have liked to do. But questions arise. When one devotes oneself to pleasure or power or wealth or fame, is that person in fact willing one thing? First, may that person not be mistaken about the world? How can anyone will one thing in a world where everything changes, often into its opposite? "Carried to its extreme limit," says Kierkegaard, "what is pleasure other than disgust? What is earthly honor at its dizzy pinnacle other than contempt for existence? What are riches, the highest superabundance of riches, other than poverty?" Second, is not such a person's conception of self mistaken? One may imagine, perhaps, that one is self-made, the only one strong enough to overcome the indolence and mediocrity that enslaves the human spirit. But in thinking so one is surely deluded. And, Kierkegaard remarks, "if you should meet him in what he himself would call a weak moment, but which, alas, you would have to call a better moment," you might find him envying "that man of single purpose who even in all his frailty still wills the Good."

The second, much longer, part of the sermon is called "Willing the Good in Truth." It is addressed to upright souls, to conventional Christians, to those who, like the Pharisee in the parable, are in the habit of addressing God with a certain complacency, and who are not like other people—extortioners, unjust, adulterers, or even like yon publican. Its purpose is to show that good people ought not to get into the habit of approaching God too familiarly, not because of minor lapses but because of what might appear to one standing on the other side as treachery or double-dealing.

In division A of this second part, the sermon appeals to the hearers to get themselves together: "If it be possible for a man to will the Good in truth, then he must be at one with himself in willing to renounce all double-mindedness." In developing this point, the preacher suggests that we ask ourselves whether we serve the Good with a single eye or with an eye out for rewards and punishments. Only briefly does Kierkegaard touch the question traditional to mystical theology as to whether perfect love of God requires that a person set aside all thought of eternal beatitude. Mainly, under rewards and punishments, Kierkegaard is thinking of the here-and-now question of whether serving the Good can or ought to be independent of one's business and social interests. The double-mindedness here involved is fairly gross, although not always easy to root out. Kierkegaard compares it to the predicament of the man who loves a beautiful heiress: Would he love her as much if she were poor and ugly? More subtle than the outright question of rewards and punishments (or gains and losses) is the case in which an ambition person, with an eye out for the main chance, is transfixed with a vision of the Good, and henceforth makes the service of the Good a career. He or she may become a great person, a universal benefactor. But the question remains, with what will does that person serve the Good: Is the Good never subservient to personal ambition? With persons less capable of holding to a single course in life, double-mindedness is more likely to take the form of compromise. There is the person who is sometimes called a Sunday Christian. Such a person has, says the preacher, "a living feeling for the Good." If one speaks to such a person of God's love and providence, especially if one does so in a poetic fashion, the person is deeply moved. But when an occasion presents itself in which that person might serve as an instrument of God's love and providence, it will probably find him or her engrossed in private affairs.

In division B of this second part, the sermon appeals for total commitment. "If a man shall will the Good in truth, then he must be willing to do all for the Good or be willing to suffer all for the Good." The "or" is important. Admittedly, doers of the good will have to suffer, but their suffering has some point to it. The word *or* reminds us that, besides persons who are fitted for an active life and who can serve the Good outwardly, there are many who are not fitted for an active life and who can serve the Good only inwardly. What doers and sufferers have in common is indicated by the word "all." Whichever their lot, they must do or suffer all for the Good.

In treating of the active life, Kierkegaard minimizes the difference between various callings. For some, doing all means giving up a place in the world, leaving possessions, not even turning back to bury a father. But for others, it may mean assuming wealth and power and managing these faithfully. As regards the Good, there is no difference between these callings, nor is the difficulty or magnitude of the task worthy of any note. Remember the widow's mite. Quarreling and comparisons involve double-mindedness. But this is a minor point. Kierkegaard's main concern in this section is the danger that arises whenever one tries to realize the Good in the temporal order. He calls it cleverness. "In its given reality the temporal order is in conflict with the Eternal." But cleverness makes its appearance. Remember Jesus' temptations. By altering the Good here and there the clever one can win the world's good will. Many will join together under the conviction that the Good, instead of being something that human beings need, is something that stands in need of humankind. So, the clever one is able to accomplish something in the world. But, asks the preacher, does memory never visit the popular idol? "Can you remember the deceptive turn you gave the thing, by which you won the blind masses? . . . Very well. Let it rest. No one shall get to know. . . . But eternally, eternally it will continue to be remembered."

But now, what has the sermon to say to the sufferer—to "the person whom nature, from the very outset, as we humans are tempted to say, wronged, one who from birth was singled out by useless suffering: a burden to others; almost a burden to himself; and yes, what is worse, to be a born objection to the goodness of Providence"? Kierkegaard is thinking, no doubt, of the physically afflicted; but in his opinion the physical distress is less a problem than the mental anguish of being forever cut off from a happy life on earth. We laud the joys of childhood, of youth, of domestic life, says the preacher; but for the sufferer there is no happy childhood: If he is asked, "Why do you not play with the others?" he turns away. At the time of love, nobody loves him; and when anyone is friendly he knows that it is from compassion. So, he withdraws from life. Even at death, the handful of mourners say to each other that it is a blessing. He did, indeed, take part in life, says the preacher, in that he lived; but one thing he never knew, and that was "to be able to give and to receive 'like for like.'" What has the sermon to say to the true sufferer? It will not mock him by saying, "You too can accomplish something- —for others." But it will say, in truth, "You can still do—the highest thing of all. You can will to suffer all and thereby be committed to the Good. Oh, blessed justice, that the true sufferer can unconditionally do the highest quite as well as fortune's favorite child!" Indeed, says Kierkegaard, it is from the sufferer and not from the outward achiever that we learn most profoundly and most reliably what the highest is.

Such, in skeletal form, is the sermon. If one is to draw near to God one must do so by sincerely willing to be holy even as God is holy.

But Kierkegaard has introduced the sermon with a long meditation on the time for confession, and has followed it by what is almost another discourse reminding the reader of the necessity for decision. In these two additional parts, which one may bring together under the expression, "the eleventh hour," Kierkegaard touches on the central theme of his philosophy, namely, human beings' consciousness of eternity, together with the dread that it causes in their hearts and the decision which it holds continually before them. King Solomon said, "For everything there is a season" (Eccles. 3:1); so, it is natural for us to suppose that there is a season for remorse and repentance just as there is a season for rejoicing and for sorrow. But the eleventh hour is not a season but an understanding of life that should accompany us in every season. "It is a silent, daily anxiety," says Kierkegaard. Every hour is appropriate for confession, and confession is always the eleventh hour. That it is an hour of decision is Kierkegaard's concluding word. God "has set eternity in the heart" is another of Solomon's sayings (Eccles. 3:11). God has installed in each of us the voice of conscience with "its eternal right to be the exclusive voice." The preacher is no more than a prompter. He has nothing to tell his hearers beyond reminding them of their own inner voice, which the voices of the crowd make it difficult to hear. Eternity, says Kierkegaard, scatters the crowd, giving to the individual infinite weight. Viewed in another manner, conscience is the presence in the temporal order that is prepared to change a nullity into an individual through decision. The talk does not ask you to withdraw from life, from a useful calling, from agreeable society. It does demand that you be eternally concerned, that you bring not merely your life goal under the aegis of the Good but also the means by which you hope to achieve this goal. And, once again, to you who suffer: Solomon says, "Sorrow is better than laughter; for by the sadness of the countenance, the heart is made better" (Eccles. 7:3). Hence, the talk asks you, How has your condition changed? But this is not a question about the state of your health: The talk will not be diverted into that channel. It asks rather "whether you now live in such a way that you truthfully will only one thing." "Not a change in suffering (for even if it is changed, it can only be a finite change), but in you, an infinite change in you from good to better." You may be denied sympathy: People may be afraid to mention your suffering. But do not feel bitter about this. Ask only whether at your grave those standing by, instead of mumbling prayers of thanks that the sufferer is dead, will say, "The content of his life was suffering, yet his life has put many to shame."

Jean H. Faurot

Recommended Reading

Edition used: Kierkegaard, Søren. *Purity of Heart Is to Will One Thing.* Translated from the Danish with an Introductory Essay by Douglas V. Steere. New York: Harper & Bros., 1938.

———. *The Living Thoughts of Kierkegaard.* Presented by W. H. Auden. Bloomington: Indiana University Press, 1952. Selections arranged under such topics as The Present Age; Aesthetics, Ethics, Religion; The Subjective Thinker, Sin and Dread; and Christ the Offense. Includes an appreciative introduction.

Rogness, Alvin N. "Kierkegaard, Søren Aabye." In *The Encyclopedia of the Lutheran Church,* 2:1208–1210. Edited by J. Bodensieck. Minneapolis: Augsburg, 1965. Helpful for understanding Kierkegaard's relation to his contemporaries as well as his influence on twentieth-century existentialism.

Rohde, Peter. *Søren Kierkegaard: An Introduction to His Life and Philosophy.* Translated with a Foreword by Alan M. Williams. London: George Allen & Unwin, 1963 (from Danish 1959). For the general reader. Sound insights.

Stendahl, Brita K. *Søren Kierkegaard.* Boston: Twayne, 1976. Convenient review of the writings. Up-to-date bibliography. Most substantial general introduction to Kierkegaard's thought.

Thomte, Reidar. *Kierkegaard's Philosophy of Religion.* Princeton, N.J.: Princeton University Press, 1948. The development of Kierkegaard's religious thought. See pp. 154–157 for a survey of the present work.

CHRISTIAN NURTURE

Author: Horace Bushnell (1802–1876)
Even as a divinity student at Yale during a transitional period of American religious history, Horace Bushnell gave evidence of the contribution he would make to Christian life and thought. There, resisting the reigning "New Haven theology," he began the uneasy relationship with Protestant orthodoxy that would characterize the remainder of his career, including his pastorate of nearly three decades at the North Church of Hartford, Connecticut. Other major works of this prolific writer are *God in Christ* (1849), *Christ in Theology* (1851), *Nature and the Supernatural* (1858), and *The Vicarious Sacrifice* (1866).

Type and subject of work: Theological treatise on the nature and necessity of Christian education of children

First published: 1860

MAJOR THEMES

The Calvinist tenet of "original sin" and of the innate depravity even of children fails to correspond with the full possibilities of Christian experience because it depends on the contradictory idea that children can only grow up in sinfulness with the hope of being converted when they reach maturity.

Although children might be inclined to corruption if left only to the world of nature, they might also be reared in the bosom of true Christian families which themselves can be understood as the medium for the cultivation of piety in children.

Infant baptism, grounded on the teachings of the apostles, signals the organ-ic spiritual connection of the family with God; in absorbing a child into the nur-ture of Christian experience, parents exert that influence of genuine piety that builds Christian character.

The possibility of such nurture, less a technique of formal instruction than an experiential matter of the communications received intuitively by the child through a community of goodness, flows from God through the parents to form the child in spirit, thus revealing a means for redemption through "family religion."

The effects of such nurture, found in Christian communion, work to extend the Christian family, to enhance the harmony of life, and to extend the kingdom of God.

From the time as a young man when Horace Bushnell read Samuel Taylor Coleridge's "Aids to Reflection," he struggled against the domi-nant Protestant theology of the first half of the nineteenth century in America and its insistence on the Calvinist doctrine of "innate deprav-ity" and on the possession of religious truth only through rationality. Coleridge helped him to understand a powerfully organic and intuitive character of spiritual life that could not be captured in precise rationalist language, and, with this understanding, Bushnell found himself pitted as a divinity student at Yale against the views of the most notable figure of the reigning "New Haven theology," Nathaniel William Taylor. Lat-er, after taking a doctor of divinity degree from Wesleyan, this clash led Bushnell to write two "Discourses on Christian Nurture," published in 1847 and later supplemented for the book *Christian Nurture* to be pub-lished in 1860. In these writings, Bushnell defended the rightfulness of a theory of Christian education and growth against what he thought were the pernicious effects on Christianity of the prevailing Protestant attitude toward children.

Enthralled by the doctrine of "original sin," orthodoxy left itself lit-tle choice but to regard infants as part of and prey to the world of corrup-tion, Bushnell claims. This doctrine meant that children were born and lived in an unregenerate state until and unless a moment of dramatic conversion overtook them, conquered them, frequently in a revivalist setting, for their elected place in God's plan of redemption. Such a scheme vividly marked out the occasion of "new life" and profoundly pointed out the sovereignty of the transcendent God, Bushnell readily admitted, but he worried that with these doctrines, revival and conver-sion experiences had become the whole of religion and that such a Christianity had become wholly a "religion of conquest." Further, as a young pastor at the North Church in Hartford, Connecticut, he won-dered if this emphasis on sudden, individualistic conversions, to be hoped for as God willed and in God's time, did not lead even the most devoutly Christian parents to practice a kind of "ostrich nurture," neglecting proper attentiveness to the ways Christian life might provide resources for a child's more gradual growth in spiritual character.

Faced with these theoretical and practical concerns, then, Bushnell sought in *Christian Nurture* both to encourage a form of Christian education of children and to provide the logical and theological underpinnings for it that he hoped would transform ideas of Christian life in his age. His treatise, then, is presented in two major sections—the first on the "doctrine" of Christian nurture, including his 1847 discourses on the subject, and the second on the "mode" of this spiritual education, including practical instructions for a "family religion" that he sees as the "sphere of grace" for the life of children. Throughout the work, Bushnell's main objective is to explore the possibility and the effect of having a child, from birth, "grow up as a Christian, and never know himself as being otherwise." This true idea of Christian education could emerge, Bushnell is convinced, with a new view of Christianity as "a religion of love and growth" that would supplant, or at least supplement, the "religion of conquest" aimed solely at vanquishing individual souls in abrupt conversion experiences.

Bushnell's conception of Christianity as a religion of nurture and growth stems from his understanding of God's divine love. A loving God would not, as the most severe Calvinists seemed to believe, commit children only to be born in an unregenerate state without also providing the possibility and the means for their regeneration. The doctrine of "original sin" has no biblical foundations, Bushnell argues, while the rightness of "infant baptism," despised by the Calvinists, has clear precedents in Scripture. On the basis of Scripture and early Christian tradition, then, Bushnell concludes that God instituted with his people a means for entrance and growth into Christian life that would extend the kingdom. Although his more complete views on the "divine logic" at work in this plan of redemption would be worked out later in *God in Christ* and in *The Vicarious Sacrifice*, even the early discourses on Christian nurture make clear Bushnell's understanding that Christ, communicating God's love, introduces to humanity a redemptive principle. This, in turn, means for Bushnell that Christian life permits and even requires bringing children into the sphere of such a principle: "Since Christ and the Divine Love, communicated through him, are become the food of . . . [the Christian parents'] life, what will they so naturally seek as to have their children partakers with them, heirs with them, in the grace of life?"

Thus, Bushnell sees an organic communication of love from God, through Christ, to Christian parents, that might embrace the child in the bosom of Christian love and cultivate in the child the growth of Christian character. As all social relations are organic, so too is the relationship of God with his people, a fact for Bushnell that made the Christian family a "sphere of grace" for the protection of the child against a corrupting "sphere of nature." To baptize the infant is to signal the beginning of the process of spiritual communication, to enact symbolically the organic spiritual communion at the source of Christian understanding and experience. Within the containing circle of family piety, the child enters a world of Christian nurture and love, the very atmosphere of a natural education in Christian character. Never being able to remember a time when he or she was not religious, the child will need no sudden conversion in later years.

Bushnell's idea of the nature of such nurture is definitive in his understanding of genuine Christian piety. Indebted not only to romantic theories of organic life but to the Scottish commonsense philosophy influential in the America of his time, Bushnell insists that proper nurture or education is a matter of gentle influences, appropriate examples, an environment of graceful and harmonious family life, which the child absorbs through quiet suasion, through the media of impressions, associations, and intuitions. Although formal instruction in the realm of religion might play a part, the more important element is the child's full exposure to, experience of, and participation in the daily actions of harmony and grace within the fold of love: Indeed, for Bushnell, these influences of piety, these organic inflowings of spirit, are surely more irresistible for the child than the sterner stuff of training in doctrine as the child participates in them in a way somehow more unaware. The proper parental piety that is both the wellspring of childhood nurture and the genuine piety of Christian life, then, appears not simply in adherence to tenets of faith, nor in the solemnity of expression Bushnell refers to as "longitude of face"; it is, rather, the expression of mature Christian character in love, joy, goodness, and commitment through which the realizing presence of God becomes known.

Although Bushnell devotes major sections of *Christian Nurture* to practical advice on proper childhood education—from discipline and instruction to dress and table manners—the organic and intuitional communications of spiritual life, the dynamics of "family grace," are for him the central forces and media of childhood nurture and the cultivation of Christian character, and such character, for him, reveals itself not only, and not most importantly, in displays of moral rectitude but also in the influences of existence lived in full spiritual communion. Genuinely Christian character in parents, expressive of communications of divine love, comprises and presents the possibilities of childhood nurture, for Bushnell, to be located in a "family religion."

Bushnell argues that family religion should not be a substitute for the Church community. Indeed, Bushnell's beliefs concerning the spiritual communication of God with his people, as it appears profoundly in "family grace," were equally a conviction for Bushnell about the nature of the Christian community. With it, he wants to understand the Church in terms of its organic character and to view it as an extended example of the spiritual unities he believed could be realized in the immediate family. The Church, he argues, should not be seen as a group of Christians who happen to have families but, rather, as a fully Christian family. Thus, when a child goes out of the home of the parents into the broader, surrounding community of belief, he or she only enters an extended family existence—a wider "sphere of grace," a larger world of nurture—that should duplicate the cultivating influences of piety found in the home.

With a recognition of the organic nature of the Church as a family and with a realization of the interdependence of persons within this framework of nurture, Bushnell believed, the failures of an "over-intense individualism" in Protestant life might find a remedy and children might no longer be lost under that "atomizing scheme of piety" that placed them in lonely exile from the Christian family for the moment of conversion. To educate a child in the personal family until genuinely Christian character becomes a "habit in the soul" is to ensure the movement of the child toward the full Christian family, the Church, and to advance the kingdom of God. It is not by the conquest of souls alone but also by deepest nurture of tender affections, Bushnell insists, that Christianity will grow in the world. Finally for him, then, "Home and religion are kindred words; names both of love and reverence; home, because it is the seat of religion; religion, because it is the sacred element of home." From the baptism of the infant to the realization of the kingdom, the family is the vital symbol and center of spiritual life.

Rowland A. Sherrill

RECOMMENDED READING

Edition used: Bushnell, Horace. *Christian Nurture.* Introduction by Luther A. Weigle. New Haven: Yale University Press, 1967.

———. *Nature and the Supernatural as Together Constituting the One System of God.* 3d ed.; reprinted. New York: AMS Press, 1973. In this work, Bushnell extends the themes of "nurture" to propose under a theory of symbols how the natural world appears as a medium for divine revelation and as a resource for human redemption.

———. *The Vicarious Sacrifice Grounded in Principles Interpreted by Human Analogies.* New York: Scribner, 1907. Bushnell argues that Christ's suffering and death for humankind should be understood in terms of the capacity of humanity as well as divinity for natural love, a vicarious love that bridges the gap between God and fallen humanity.

Cross, Barbara M. *Horace Bushnell: Minister to a Changing America.* Chicago: University of Chicago Press, 1958. This study interprets religious and cultural influences, especially romanticism, on Bushnell's thought as he shaped and was shaped by the character of his age.

Smith, David L. *Symbolism and Growth: The Religious Thought of Horace Bushnell.* Chico, Ca.: Scholars Press, 1981. Smith argues that the central and unifying element in all of Bushnell's major theological writings is a theory of communication.

SELF-ABANDONMENT TO DIVINE PROVIDENCE

Author: Jean-Pierre de Caussade (1675–1751)
Very little is known of Caussade's life. He entered the Jesuit novitiate in Toulouse (1693) and was ordained priest in 1705. He was much appreciated as a teacher and professor, giving conferences for many years to the nuns of the Order of the Visitation at Nancy. He published one book in 1741, *Instructions spiritualles*, translated as *On Prayer*, in form of dialogues, in keeping with the doctrinal position of Bossuet, bishop of Meaux, the enemy of Archbishop Fénelon. So Caussade was never accused of quietism. His teaching was dependent on the works of Francis de Sales and John of the Cross. Materials he had given the sisters of the Order of the Visitation were collated after his death by the Jesuit, H. Ramière, and published as *Abandonment to Divine Providence* in 1861.

Type and subject of work: A treatise on self-abandonment written for those in contemplative practice

First published: 1851 (*L'Abandon à la Providence Divine*)

MAJOR THEMES

Christian perfection is achieved with self-abandonment.
The indwelling Triune God enters our lives as we abandon ourselves to him, so that Christ is formed in the depths of our hearts.
In the process of detachment, the intellect must give way to faith, while the

senses need to yield and become the instruments of God's will.

Trials and suffering only help to deepen the experience of self-abandonment.

The more we are deprived naturally, the more we gain supernaturally.

The Abandonment to Divine Providence that Father Henri Ramière reconstructed and published in 1861 was supposedly collated from two series of letters written by Caussade, arranged by one of the nuns at Nancy, but with some material omitted by Ramière. It was not until 1966 that the text of the original manuscript was translated by Michel Olphe-Galliard, S.J. This was translated into English by Mrs. Kitty Muggeridge, with the title, "The Sacrament of Every Day," which is one of the dominant themes within the subject matter of self-abandonment. In 1981, Olphe-Galliard returned to the matter of authorship, agreeing with Louis Hilaire, who in 1853 had argued that the book was unsound and could not be the work of Caussade. However, it is difficult to believe that this is not the work of Caussade, though it is debatable how much material of the original letters of spiritual direction made by him is kept in the text. The work itself is an important and influential treatise on spiritual discipline.

When Caussade says that the key to all spiritual truth is self-abandonment, he is exposing himself to the accusation of quietism associated with Madame Guyon and her friend François Fénelon. But he protected himself in three ways. First, the material he used to direct the sisters of the Visitation at Nancy was not published in his lifetime. Second, the one book he did publish as *Spiritual Instructions* (1741) repeatedly invoked the orthodoxy of Bossuet to support his views. Third, in *Self-Abandonment to Divine Providence*, Caussade neatly distinguishes the *virtue* of self-abandonment, a virtue universally claimed of all Christians, from the *state* of self-abandonment that may be peculiarly manifested by only a few of God's saints. This distinction is important.

Caussade warns against the busyness of a hectic piety, of being perpetually engaged in meditation upon meditation, prayer upon prayer. For he was writing in a time when devotion was becoming baroque in its wealth and complexity. Instead, there was the need of progressive inner simplification. For this growing complexity in devotion could lead either to discouragement or one's placing trust in good works of piety rather than in the grace of God; it could become an inner variety of spiritual pride, probably unconscious, yet a form of spiritual narcissism. For it could subtly lead to self-preoccupation, even in attending to the things of God.

Faithfulness to the ways of God, writes Caussade, will help us to see in every moment, in every duty, ways in which the self-abandonment to

God's will can be manifested. It is the spirit of Mary, "let it be according to Thy will." This spirit will be revealed in daily tasks so that God will show himself in the humblest things to the humble, while the great will never see God working, even in the great events. This is the essence then of holiness—to be faithful to God in all, positively obedient and passively acceptant. All else, whether devotional reading, the understanding of the mind, or any other human action, is merely instrumental to submission and faithfulness.

Interior peace will follow from this submissiveness. This peace will enable us to put up with anything that naturally disturbs us—the food we eat, the people we meet, the frustrations of our own feelings. We must be detached, even from feeling self-detached, Caussade urges. There is no particular path we should follow; we should simply seek the way of self-abandonment, which is most likely to be realized in small, unimportant ways of acting.

But instead of being *our* virtue, self-abandonment, we discover, is God's work in us. So we live a life of faith, writes Caussade, trusting God most greatly in the smallest circumstances and trivial details of our daily lives. As in the past, so now, Jesus Christ is "the same, yesterday, today, and forever." The book of life, seen in the Scriptures, continues also in our everyday existence. The revelation of the present moment is an ever freshly-springing source of sanctity. So no longer will I enshrine the will of God within the narrow covers of a book, but embrace it in everything I meet, as bread to nourish me, soap to cleanse me, fire to purify me, Caussade writes. But God alone can do this, he adds; so he alone is my Teacher, Master, Father, and Love.

This, then, is the *virtue* of self-abandonment that all Christians should cultivate. But some have entered deeply into a *state* of self-abandonment. This is expressive of the intensity with which God dwells in the soul, so that it has nothing more of its own. In this profound state, it leaves all good works, all conscious practices of devotion, and methods of prayer, to be guided alone by God in faith, hope, and love, united in one action, one desire, one all-encompassing surrender. God becomes the sole business of the soul. All vicissitudes of the soul are included in this one experience, surrender to God.

To abandon oneself! This is the great duty that encompasses the whole of the spiritual life, in complete self-forgetfulness. So beyond all cares and anxieties, all weaknesses of mind or aridity of spirit, seeing God is the sole pleasure of the soul. This is seen in the present moment, in the immediate task to hand. If God wishes more of you, he will make it plain. So the one thing only, is to allow God to act and do as he wishes with you. It is this that requires great faith, to be implicit and immediate in obedience to him. Nothing more is required of us than to be like an artist's canvas, on which God can paint the picture he wants.

Taking such an attitude will bring its trials. People who are reputed to be wise will criticize. The apparent uselessness and the external defects of such a course of action will cause questions and doubts. Contemptible in the sight of others, there will come inward humiliation also. To walk humbly and simply the way God has traced for us is so little in our own sight, and before the world. Surrender to the will of God is such an obscure thing, hidden from all except God.

Finally, Caussade sees that such a task of self-abandonment is assisted by the fatherliness of God. But the experience is the reverse of what we may think. For the less we may believe that God is supporting us, actually the more he is doing so. In the darkness, his presence is warmly felt, though without illumination, so that the "songs of the night" he gives are in darkness. Moreover, the more God seems to be stripping away the soul, the more he is actually giving to it. Likewise, the more random appears the behavior, the more God is actually guiding; the more defenseless the soul appears, the more it is protected with the *whole* armor of God. So enemies are no longer to be feared, but seen as instruments that God uses.

All this occurs, for the only instruments God can use are the weak and the humble, submissive to his divine will. True devotion, then, is simply acceptance of the divine order. Herein lies the power that overcomes the world, and is victorious over all the principalities of evil. It is this that turns the world upside down. For our life, even our interior life, does not belong to us, but to the will of God.

James M. Houston

RECOMMENDED READING

Edition used: Caussade, Jean-Pierre de, S.J. *Self-Abandonment to Divine Providence.* Translated by Algar Thorld. Revised by Father John Joyce, S.J. London: Collins, 1971.

———. *The Sacrament of Every Day.* Translated by Kitty Muggeridge. San Francisco: Harper & Row, 1984. This is the most up-to-date translation of the spiritual dialogues on contemplative prayer.

THE CHRISTIAN'S SECRET OF A HAPPY LIFE

Author: Hannah Whitall Smith (1832–1911)
A birthright Philadelphia Quaker, Smith was introduced to holiness
teachings by Methodists. She wrote *The Christian's Secret of a Happy Life*
in installments to aid the circulation of a paper started by her husband,
Robert Pearsall Smith. Along with William and Mary Boardman, the
Smiths became leaders in England of the "Higher Life Movement." In
1874 Robert toured the Continent, and together they led huge meetings
in England. But suddenly Robert was disgraced, and they retired to New
Jersey. Robert became increasingly bitter, but Hannah preserved her
faith, continued her writing, and was able to counsel many people. They
later moved to England, where she was confidante to her son-in-law
Bertrand Russell and many of the Bloomsbury set, into which her grand-
daughters married.

Type and subject of work: A practical study of how to live the higher
Christian life; in the holiness and Keswick traditions

First published: 1870

MAJOR THEMES

Perfection, holiness, is scriptural and possible.
Our part is to trust, and God's part is to work.
The chief characteristics of the higher life are entire surrender to God and

perfect trust in God, resulting in victory over sin and perfect peace within.

We must let Christ bear our burdens and manage our affairs instead of trying to do it ourselves.

We enter into this life by entire abandonment and absolute faith; attainment is not the result of works, but a gift of God's grace.

Holiness is not a place but a way, a day-by-day walk.

Smith begins *The Christian's Secret of a Happy Life* by noting that most Christians feel instinctively that a life of inward rest and outward victory is their birthright, yet most live a roller-coaster life of failure, repentance, brief victory, and then failure again. They ask, Is this all?

Smith declares that we can be sure of one thing: that Jesus came to save us now, "in this life, from the power and dominion of sin" and to make us more than conquerors through divine power. The words of Scripture are unequivocal. Our victory is not to be partial or temporary, but complete and absolute.

However, sanctification or holy living is not something we can do ourselves: Our part is to trust; God's part is to work. Our goal is to be delivered from the power of sin and to be made perfect in every good work to do the will of God. "A real work is to be wrought in us and upon us" as Scripture teaches. Surrender and trust are all that we can do. God does the work of transforming us. The clay is not expected to do the potter's work.

From the moment we surrender fully to God, we are holy before God; yet as we allow God to work in our lives we become more and more fully capable of the service for which God is fitting us. Or as Smith says, "The little babe may be all that a babe could be, or ought to be, and may therefore perfectly please its mother; and yet it is very far from being what that mother would wish it to be when the years of maturity shall come." Sanctification is God's work in us as we, by an act of faith, place ourselves in God's hands and by continuing acts of faith, keep ourselves there. "Our part is the trusting; it is [God's] to accomplish the results."

In speaking of the Higher Life, Smith prefers to speak of the "life hid with Christ in God." Its chief characteristics are entire surrender to God and perfect trust in God. This results in victory over sin and complete rest of soul. It is allowing God to bear our burdens and manage our affairs, rather than thinking we can do it all ourselves.

We must turn over all to God, Smith urges, beginning with ourselves and then everything else—our health, our work, our families, our futures, our present. Everything must be surrendered to God. We must live by faith, as children in our Father's house.

"This blessed life must not be looked upon in any sense as an attainment, but as an obtainment," she writes; "We cannot earn it, we cannot climb up to it, we cannot win it; we can do nothing but ask for it and receive it." It is God's gift to us in Jesus Christ. In order to enter into this life, we must abandon ourselves to God. Smith also uses the word *consecration* to mean "entire surrender of the whole being to God." She notes that God does not respond by making us miserable, as many seem to fear God will do, but showers us with divine love.

Faith follows surrender. In salvation we had faith that God forgave our sins; in sanctification we have faith that God can and will deliver us from the power of sin. In salvation Christ became our Redeemer; in sanctification Christ becomes our life. Smith points out that theologically and juridically we have the whole package from the moment of conversion; experimentally we have only what we claim by faith.

The second part of the book deals with difficulties, questions about consecration, faith, the will, doubts, temptation, and failure. Concerning consecration, Smith notes that once we have surrendered something to God, we can be sure that God accepts it. Our part is done, the rest is God's. She quotes Phoebe Palmer in saying that "the altar sanctifies the gift." Once an offering is laid on the altar it becomes God's and it becomes holy, made holy not by the giver's state of mind but by God.

Concerning faith, Smith points out how we continually trust people and technology in our daily lives, and yet we hesitate to trust an omnipotent God who loved us enough to die for us. Trust, she notes, is an active energy.

Although our emotions may fluctuate, we are in control of our wills and can actively surrender them to God. When we turn our wills over to God, we accept the will of God, which is always focused on our highest welfare.

Concerning guidance, Smith declares that God reveals the divine will to us in four ways: through Scripture, through providential circumstances, through the convictions of our own judgment, and through impressions made on our minds by the Holy Spirit.

Smith warns that temptations do not disappear after one enters the life of faith; indeed they multiply tenfold. But temptation is not sin; it is only an invitation to sin. We succumb when we become discouraged. Yet most discouragement comes from our wounded self-love. True humility can recognize its own utter weakness and foolishness, its absolute need for God. Rather than be discouraged, we should dive deeper into God and trust more fully.

While sin is not longer necessary for the sanctified person, sin is still possible. Sometimes we fail and commit conscious, known sin. Holiness is a walk, not a state; a way, not a place. "Sanctification is not a thing to be picked up at a certain stage of our experience, and forever after possessed, but it is a life to be lived day by day, and hour by hour," she writes. "'Up, sanctify the people,' is always God's command. 'Lie down and be discouraged,' is always our temptation." When we sin, we should immediately return to God and ask forgiveness.

The third part of *The Christian's Secret of a Happy Life* is devoted to describing the results: liberty, growth, service, joy, and union with God. When we fully surrender our lives to God, we are no longer in bondage to sin. We are at liberty to be fully ourselves. God nurtures our growth and offers us fulfilling service. The practical results in daily life include a quietness of spirit, calmness in the midst of turmoil, sweetness under provocation, an absence of worry, deliverance from care and fear, and a deep abiding joy. The sanctified soul finds itself becoming one in character with God.

Nancy A. Hardesty

RECOMMENDED READING

Edition used: Smith, Hannah Whitall. *The Christian's Secret of a Happy Life.* Old Tappan, N.J.: Fleming H. Revell Co., Spire Books, 1942.

Parker, Robert Allerton. *The Transatlantic Smiths.* New York: Random House, 1959. Biography of the Smith family.

Smith, Logan Pearsall. *Unforgotten Years.* Boston: Little, Brown, 1939. Hannah's son's musings on his early family life.

Smith, Timothy. *Revivalism and Social Reform.* Nashville: Abingdon Press, 1957. This classic historical study sets the stage for Smith's work and details her and Robert's early ministry.

Strachey, Ray [Rachel]. *A Quaker Grandmother: Hannah Whitall Smith.* New York: Fleming H. Revell Co., 1914. Hannah's granddaughter remembers the woman who reared her after her mother deserted her and her sister.

THE WAY OF A PILGRIM

Author: Unknown

Although we do not know the author's name, he appears to be a Russian peasant, writing prior to the liberation of the serfs in 1861. A reference to the Crimean War of 1853 gives another clue to the book's vintage. It was first discovered in the possession of a monk at Mount Athos. It is sometimes published along with another account by the same author, *The Pilgrim Continues His Way*.

Type and subject of work: A narrative of a pilgrim's spiritual life and his discovery of the "Jesus Prayer" and how to pray without ceasing

First published: 1884

MAJOR THEMES

To pray without ceasing is possible.

The interior Prayer of Jesus is a constant uninterrupted calling upon the divine Name of Jesus with the lips, in the spirit, and in the heart.

The prayer consists of these words: "Lord Jesus Christ, have mercy on me."

The literal title of this book in Russian can be translated "Candid Narratives of a Pilgrim to His Spiritual Father." The book begins, "By the grace of God I am a Christian man, by my actions a great sinner, and by calling a homeless wanderer of the humblest birth who roams from place to place." It is a report given to his spiritual director.

In the fourth chapter the Pilgrim tells us that he was born in a village near Orel. His parents died when he was two; he and an older brother were reared by their grandparents, who owned a small inn. When he was young his brother pushed him into a stove, and his left arm was injured so badly that he could never use it. His grandfather taught him to read, and a clerk who often stayed at the inn taught him to write. The older brother ran off and became an alcoholic, so the grandfather left the Pilgrim the inn and his money. He married a fine young woman, and they were happy until the jealous brother robbed them of the money and set the inn, their home, on fire. Left with nothing, they found a small hut and lived on income from the wife's work until she died two years later of a fever.

The book begins with the Pilgrim's report that on the twenty-fourth Sunday after Pentecost he went to church and heard in a reading from 1 Thessalonians (5:17) the words "Pray without ceasing." He began to ponder how that could be done and where he could find someone to teach him to do it. He began to go to churches where famous preachers held forth. He heard a number of fine sermons, but none answered his questions.

He heard of a devout man in another village, so he went there and asked his questions. The man told him that "ceaseless interior prayer is a continual yearning of the human spirit towards God" and advised him simply to pray more and more fervently. But this advice did not satisfy the Pilgrim. He walked 125 miles to the provincial capital, where he stopped at a monastery and asked the abbot, but still found no answer.

Eventually he found a monk who introduced him to *The Philokalia*, "The Love of Spiritual Beauty," a book of writings on prayer and devotion by Fathers of the Eastern Orthodox church over a period of eleven centuries. He learned from the monk that "the continuous interior Prayer of Jesus is a constant uninterrupted calling upon the divine Name of Jesus with the lips, in the spirit, in the heart; while forming a mental picture of His constant presence, and imploring his grace, during every occupation, at all times, in all places, even during sleep. The appeal is couched in these terms, 'Lord Jesus Christ have mercy on me.'" The monk told him that if he did this for a time, he would find that he could no longer live without it and the prayer would continue to voice itself within of its own accord.

The monk read to him the instruction of Saint Symeon the New Theologian, who advised: "Sit down alone and in silence. Lower your head, shut your eyes, breathe out gently and imagine yourself looking into your own heart. Carry ... your thoughts, from your head to your heart. As you breathe out, say 'Lord Jesus Christ, have mercy on me.' Say it moving your lips gently, or simply say it in your mind. Try to put all other thoughts aside. Be calm, be patient, and repeat the process very frequently." The Pilgrim and the *starets* (a Russian monk noted for his great piety, long experience in the spiritual life, and with a gift for spiritual direction) talked all night long. Since pilgrims could stop at the monastery for only three days, the Pilgrim found a job for the summer tending a garden in a nearby village so that he could continue to learn from the *starets's* counsel.

To begin with, he said the prayer three thousand times a day. At first it was hard, but after several days it became natural, so the *starets* suggested that he say it six thousand times a day. For a week the Pilgrim did that and found that if he stopped he felt as if he had lost something. But when he resumed saying the prayer, "it went on easily and joyously."

After ten days he was advised to increase the repetition to twelve thousand times. The first day that took him until late evening; the second day it was easier. He counted the times with the aid of a rosary and by this time the thumb of his left hand hurt and his wrist was inflamed, but he continued. Finally, early one morning the prayer woke him up; he could say no other prayers but that, and when he said it he was filled with joy and relief. He spent the whole day "in a state of greatest contentment." When he told the *starets*, the monk gave him permission to say the prayer as often as he wished and as often as he could.

He passed a wonderful summer, very peaceful and happy. But at the end of the summer the *starets* died and the Pilgrim's job ended. He began to wander again. He decided to use the money he had earned to buy his own copy of *The Philokalia*. He feared that he would fall prey to the mere charms of the prayer and his feelings, so he studied *The Philokalia* to check out his perceptions and feelings.

He would walk as much as forty-four miles a day, with his Bible and copy of *The Philokalia* in his breast pocket. After a while he felt he wanted a more settled place to study his books, and so he set off for the tomb of Saint Innocent in Irkutsk, Siberia. He began to walk at night and sit and read by day. One night two thieves hit him on the head and stole his books. He was heartbroken, but his *starets* appeared in a dream and reminded him that he should be detached from all worldly things. Eventually he saw the two thieves with a group of convicts under military guard, so he got his books back. The officer in charge told him how reading the Gospels faithfully had cured him of alcoholism.

He found a hut in the forest where he spent another summer. When in his reading and meditation he came to an impasse, his *starets* would appear in a dream and instruct him. Once the *starets* in the dream marked a page with charcoal. When he awoke, the book that had been under his pillow was on the table, open to the proper passage, with a mark in the margin and a piece of charcoal on the table beside it.

He began to realize that "interior prayer bears fruit in three ways: in the Spirit, in the feelings, and in revelations. In the first, for instance, is the sweetness of the love of God, inward peace, gladness of mind, purity of thought, and the sweet remembrance of God. In the second, the pleasant warmth of the heart, fullness of delight in all one's limbs, the joyous 'bubbling' in the heart, lightness and courage, the joy of living, power not to feel sickness and sorrow. And in the last, light given to the mind, understanding of Holy Scripture, knowledge of the speech of created things, freedom from fuss and vanity, knowledge of the joy of the inner life, and finally certainty of the nearness of God and of His love for us."

The book records his wanderings: his encounters with men, women, children, and animals, and the counsel that he gave and received. Once his legs were frozen after he went through the ice trying to cross a creek. A peasant concocted a remedy that cured him. In gratitude he soon had the opportunity to help a woman who had a bone lodged in her throat—his *starets* appeared in a dream and gave him the remedy. His fame spread and soon he had to get away, back to his wandering, in order to have time for prayer and study.

He once advised a man to set the words of the prayer to his heart beats: "Lord," "Jesus," "Christ," "have mercy," "on me." Or to match it to his breathing, "Lord Jesus Christ" as one inhales, "have mercy on me" as one exhales.

From Irkutsk, he vowed to set out for Jerusalem. That is where *The Way of the Pilgrim* ends, but in *The Pilgrim Continues His Way* we learn that he did not get to Jerusalem. He continued his travels in Russia. From a traveling Greek monk from Mount Athos he learned the Greek version of the prayer, which is "Lord Jesus Christ, Son of God, have mercy on me, a sinner." The book continues with his accounts of conversations in which he shared with others the benefits of the Jesus Prayer and in which others shared with him their spiritual experiences.

Nancy A. Hardesty

RECOMMENDED READING

Edition used: French, R. M., ed. *The Way of a Pilgrim and the Pilgrim Continues His Way.* New York: Seabury Press, 1965. Good critical edition with helpful introduction. Other editions contain only *The Way of a Pilgrim* without *The Pilgrim Continues His Way.*

THE STORY OF A SOUL

Author: Saint Thérèse of Lisieux (1873-1897)

Marie François Thérèse Martin was born in Alençon, France, and moved to Lisieux at an early age. She lost her mother when she was still quite young and was reared by her father and sisters in economically comfortable surroundings. From an early age she was attracted to Jesus and to the convent life of the Carmelite order, which she was permitted to enter at age fifteen. Three of her sisters left the world for that same convent. While outwardly Thérèse appeared to lead a life devoid of adventure, she sacrificed continually to gain spiritual perfection and, according to her own account, suffered both physical and mental anguish. She saw her role as that of following the "little way," doing the simple things to perfection. She wrote her autobiography in obedience to orders from her religious superiors. Her death came at age twenty-four. She was declared a saint in 1925.

Type and subject of work: Essays of spiritual instruction

First published: 1899

MAJOR THEMES

Grace is offered, proportionally, but totally, to everyone.
Suffering is an important path to holiness.
Love is the basis of all spirituality.
It is essential to do even the smallest things for God.
Humility is an important factor in the growth toward spiritual perfection.

The Story of a Soul is actually composed of three separate manuscripts, written for three different people. The first, set down mainly in 1895, is the longest section. The second, written in September of the next year, is quite brief. In 1897 Thérèse wrote what were to become the final chapters. She wrote under obedience because she was told to do so in her convent when it was decided that her words would prove edifying for others.

The first portion of the manuscript was written for Mother Agnes of Jesus, Thérèse's blood sister as well as convent companion, the woman who edited her younger sibling's writings and who was for a time the religious superior at that institution. She was also Thérèse's surrogate mother for several years since their parent died while Thérèse was quite young.

The future saint begins her work by telling how she had often wondered why some persons received more grace from God than others. But God showed her how he created in variety, as with flowers. Some are lilies or roses; others are smaller violets or daisies. Yet each has a place to fill, and if every little flower were to wish to be a rose, nature would lose her adornments. Further, God's love is shown as much through a little soul that allies itself completely with his grace as through a larger one.

Identifying herself with the little flower (a title Thérèse has in Catholic tradition), the writer tells the story of her early life. Her affectionate mother died when she was not yet five. Her father was a warm, loving man whose life was grounded in his Catholicism. He and her sisters cared for Thérèse very kindly. The young child was early convinced that spiritual perfection was attained in large part through suffering and that obedience to God's will also was very important.

She saw her most youthful period as a very happy time, one in which the whole world smiled on her. But a new period was to come next, one of suffering, which the writer tells us was appropriate for someone who was to become a spouse of Jesus so young. This next portion of her childhood was marked by the illness and death of her mother. She remembers her father's sorrow, her kissing the corpse of her dead mother, and his selecting her sister Pauline (now the Mother Agnes to whom this segment is written) to be her new mother.

Thérèse recalls how her joy left her at her mother's death, how she wept a great deal, and how she felt secure only within the intimacy of her family. Pauline taught the girl to read, and the first word Thérèse was able to make out was "heaven." We learn how the child loved making little altars, which she would enjoy decorating and showing to her father. She tells of making her first confession and of how this sacrament always gave her a foretaste of eternal happiness.

Once, when she asked Pauline about what might be a disproportionate amount of glory for some in heaven, the older sister had her fill two different-sized glasses with water and asked her which was fuller—this illustrating how each person may be completely glorified. At age eight and a half Thérèse was rather troubled by a fourteen-year-old girl who teased her, but love at home helped her to overcome this trial. Even at this age Thérèse turned to contemplation as a means of communicating with God.

At nine the child told the head of the Carmelite convent that she would like to become a nun there but was told that sixteen was the minimum age for entering. When Pauline became Sister Agnes there, Thérèse was saddened by the separation, and for several months Thérèse was quite ill and her family thought that she might die. Her sufferings included frightening hallucinations. In these memoirs she attributes her recovery to a miraculous cure. Later, as an adult, Thérèse came to believe that it took much suffering for one to become holy.

The next step on her spiritual journey was the making of her first communion. Her sister Marie helped to prepare her for three months and then continued such instruction before each important Church feast day, at which times the young girl was allowed to receive the sacrament. This was followed by a training for confirmation. During this period Thérèse was a day-boarder at school where her lessons went very well and where, during playtime, she was content to watch from a distance while others engaged in their games. She wrote that she thought about serious things; that was what she liked doing most of all.

Claiming that Jesus knew that she was too weak a creature to resist temptation, Thérèse says that she had none and therefore cannot take any credit for resisting any. She did, however, experience being overcome by scruples. Her most commonplace thoughts and acts were the source of great worry and anxiety. This made her so ill that she had to leave school at thirteen. She was then tutored, and while at her teacher's house she overheard compliments about herself, words that she felt it would have been better not to hear.

On reflection, Thérèse recognized that she was far too sensitive a child. But at Christmas she was to have a complete conversion, as she called it. Her father was upset over her babylike responses to holiday gifts, and when she reacted in a totally new manner, without tears, her life was changed to one of much greater happiness. This marks the beginning of the third stage of her childhood, she notes: The first was the years before her mother's death; the second, the period between that event and this conversion.

At this time a notorious murderer was to be hanged and he appeared unrepentant. When, moments before his execution he made a visible act of faith, Thérèse, who had asked for a sign from God to show her the man had changed (she had been praying intensely for this), felt her intercession was accepted. Her reading at this time consisted almost exclusively of Thomas à Kempis's *Imitation of Christ*. She had not yet discovered the hidden treasures of the Gospels.

Now, at fourteen, only Pauline encouraged Thérèse to pursue her desire to enter Carmel, but soon after another sister, Céline, supported the teenager as well. Finally their father did not oppose her either: He plucked a tiny flower and gave it to her, and she saw this as symbolic of herself. But Pauline had to give Thérèse the bad news that Carmel's superior would not allow the girl to enter until age twenty-one. She and her father then went to ask the bishop for his assistance, and he agreed at least to talk to the superior. He said it was the only time he had experienced a father's eagerness to equal the daughter's regarding entrance into religious life.

Then her father took Thérèse and Céline on a long trip. They went to Rome where they saw grand monuments and treasures of art, and stood on the very soil on which some of the apostles trod. There she encountered some priests who, much to the young girl's surprise, exhibited human weaknesses. This was a revelation to her. Prior to the Eternal City, however, the three made other stops, Switzerland among them. There the profusion of nature's grandeur profoundly moved Thérèse.

In Milan, the child was impressed by the works of man. She found Venice a melancholy city for all its splendor, and in Padua and Bologna she venerated saints' relics. In Rome Thérèse wanted to kiss the ground of the Arena where so many Christians were martyred, and she was disappointed to learn that the original soil was some twenty-six feet below the now raised surface. The highlight of the tour was a large group audience with Pope Leo XIII.

It was with the successor to Peter that Thérèse felt she would have the best chance of getting permission to enter the convent early. People in the audience were warned not to speak with the pope, and Thérèse felt the tension rise in her. She was not only planning to disregard the instruction but she had to do so in front of a large crowd, with cardinals, archbishops, and bishops present.

When she blurted out her plea to enter religious life at age fifteen, the pope responded by saying that she should do what the superiors decide. But the child continued to beg and the pope simply placed his hand on her head. Despite her disappointment and tears, Thérèse felt a peace in her heart, though she records that "all the rest was bitterness."

The family visited other Italian cities. When they returned home Thérèse received a letter from Mother Superior saying that the bishop had authorized her entry into Carmel. She went to her "blessed prison" on April 9, 1888. The Reverend Mother treated her with great severity, frequently scolding her for minor things. Later, however, the author was to be thankful for such rigorous training. Had she become the pet of the community, she realized, it would have been harmful to her spiritual growth.

Thérèse professed that she had come to Carmel to save souls and above all else to pray for priests. She immediately felt the richness of the convent life although her joy was tempered by her father's illness. It was during this period that she developed a love for ugly and inconvenient things such as a jug that was chipped in many places. She writes that she concentrated her efforts on little hidden acts of virtue such as folding the nuns' choir mantles when they had forgotten to do so.

An account of her day of profession as a nun follows. This day was preceded by a brief period of doubt about her vocation but her doubt was soon dispelled. Thérèse's father was so ill that he could not attend the ceremony. An epidemic of influenza attacked the convent and a number of the women there died, and this took much of Thérèse's attention. Then her father died. This last unhappiness was succeeded by a more joyous event, however: Thérèse's sister Céline entered the same Carmelite convent. Here the author concludes her remarks to her Sister Agnes with words of her devotion to Jesus and gratitude for his love.

The next chapters are dedicated to Mother Marie de Gonzague and were written in obedience to her order. Thérèse says that the greatest thing that the Lord has shown her is how insignificant she is. She indicates that the continuous suffering that she experiences she now faces with peace and joy rather than with the bitterness of an earlier period. She relates her months-long illness that brought her a happy anticipation for heaven. But she did not ask God for the favor of being allowed to die young although she believed that she would. However, if it were God's will that she continue on this earth in order to serve others, she would gladly do so, at Carmel or at various missionary locations such as Hanoi, Saigon, or wherever God chose to send her.

Thérèse expressed her regret for loving her convent companions imperfectly, not as Jesus loves them. And she says she will never judge them or anyone uncharitably since she fears God's judgment on her.

We read of Thérèse's being appointed to be the spiritual directress of the novices, and this caused her to learn much about human nature and about herself. She preferred being corrected to correcting others, but she tried to do her duty as was necessary. She also writes about her simple approach to prayer. And she tried to work at being of spiritual service, particularly to whichever nuns she found to be especially unpleasant. Again she stresses that hers is "the little way" of serving God.

The final chapter here is written for Sister Marie of the Sacred Heart who, like Mother Agnes, was a sister by birth to Thérèse. Though her life appears to be one of consolation, Thérèse writes that this is not the case. Her great joy, however, is in the love of God. She records a vision she had of her own mother who told her that they would be joined together in paradise soon and that God was very much pleased with her. Yet she longs for even more torments at the hands of Christ's persecutors so that she may work for God in this way. She sees herself, without complaint, as a victim for love.

Although Thérèse realizes that preaching the gospel or becoming a martyr are beyond her, she expresses satisfaction with the lesser role granted her. She will scatter her flowers by suffering and rejoicing for love. Writing in prayer to Christ, she ends with the key word of her life, "Love."

Harry James Cargas

RECOMMENDED READING

Edition used: *Autobiography of St. Thérèse of Lisieux.* Translated by Ronald Knox. New York: Kenedy, 1958.

Combes, Abbé, ed. *Collected Letters of Saint Thérèse of Lisieux.* Translated by F. J. Sheed. New York: Sheed & Ward, 1949. Letters to family and friends from earliest youth to very near her death.

Corres, Ida Friederike. *The Hidden Face.* New York: Pantheon Books, 1959. A study of the subject's life and spirituality.

Sackville-West, Vita. *The Eagle and the Dove.* London: Michael Joseph, 1943. An analysis of the contrasting spirituality of two saints, Thérèse of Lisieux and Teresa of Ávila by a major British writer.

THE GRACES OF INTERIOR PRAYER

Author: R. P. Augustine Poulain (1836–1919)

R. P. Augustine Poulain was born in Paris, December 15, 1836. He entered the Society of Jesus in 1858. After completing his studies, he taught mathematics at Metz and Angers. *The Graces of Interior Prayer* went through nine editions in Poulain's lifetime and prompted a renewal of interest in mysticism. He died in Paris on July 19, 1919.

Type and subject of work: Practical treatise on mysticism concerning the stages of mystic union

First published: 1901 (*Des grâces d'oraison*)

MAJOR THEMES

Mystic prayer is distinguishable from ordinary prayer in that, although both depend upon God's grace, in the mystic prayer God intervenes to produce supernatural acts or states that are in no way the result of one's own effort.

There are four kinds of ordinary prayer: vocal, meditative, affective, and simple; the latter two go beyond reason, on the way to mystic union.

Mystic union has four states: the prayer of quiet or repose, full or semiecstatic union, ecstatic union, and transforming union.

All four stages or degrees of mystic union involve the soul's being affected by the divine, but only in the last stage is the soul transformed.

Transformation of the soul occurs when, through God's grace, a person be-

*comes like God through participation in his nature; the soul becomes permanent-
ly conscious of divine cooperation in the exercise of its higher faculties.*

In the preface to the English translation by Leonora L. Yorke Smith of Augustine Poulain's *The Graces of Interior Prayer* (6th ed., 1911), the Reverend Daniel Considine, S.J., describes the book as "an example of modern scientific methods applied to a subject—mysticism—that critics outside the Church commonly regard as a mere form of brain-weakness peculiar to pious persons . . . " and then asks, "Is there to be found in the interior life of devout souls, in their intercourse with their Maker, a life more intimate still—a secret door opening into a world still further withdrawn from sense, where very few may enter, but where the chosen ones have a sight and feeling of God, and enjoy His presence not less, but more really than we apprehend objects with our bodily senses?" Considine's answer is that Poulain's book "is a survey of the Kingdom of Prayer in all its length and breadth, in its lowest as well as its most perfect forms. The interior life is seen to be a process, an orderly evolution, of which we can outline the laws and mark the successive stages."

The author himself, in the preface to the first edition, describes his aim as that of writing a "purely practical treatise on Mysticism," and he adds, "I wished as far as possible to give very clear and very accurate *descriptions*, as well as very plain *rules of conduct*."

Poulain, like Considine, describes his method as "scientific," but he emphasizes that it is scientific in that it belongs within what may be called "the *descriptive school*," and he contrasts the descriptive procedure with that of "the *speculative school*," which "endeavours to systematize all facts theologically by connecting them with the study of grace, of man's faculties, of the gifts of the Holy Spirit, etc."

Accordingly, Poulain addresses himself to "those souls who are beginning to receive the mystic graces and who do not know how to find their way in this new world" and "to those also who are *drawing near* and who have entered into the adjacent states."

The book, then, Poulain continues, must be practical; it must offer descriptions of mystical states and spiritual progress by which persons for whom the mystical experience presents a "new world" can immediately recognize themselves. The rules of conduct to be offered (as guides to spiritual "experimentation") are to serve as "formulae, easy to *remember and to apply*."

Poulain calls attention to his having studied for forty years the matters with which has book is concerned. His sources, he tells us, are not only "quantities of treatises" but also interrogations with "persons possessing the graces of interior prayer," as well as with those who were "under the illusion" that they, too, possessed these graces. (He points out that acquaintance with those suffering from such illusions is also useful.)

The book offers no ascetic counsels, Poulain warns, for it is concerned with mysticism, not asceticism. Nevertheless, the emphasis on the mystical graces is not intended to suggest that those who know the experience of being graced by God in their interior life are free from the necessity of aiming at spiritual perfection by following the paths of active duty "trodden by Christ and followed by all the saints."

The mystical graces are not sanctity, Poulain avers; such graces must be received with humility and manifested by generosity of spirit. Those who merely dream of enjoying the mystical graces and who thereby divert themselves from the paths of ordinary duty will be disappointed: "The souls called by God to the higher ways are precisely those who, acknowledging themselves to be the most unworthy, are chiefly occupied with the task of doing their very best in the ordinary paths."

In part one of his book, "Mysticism: Some Preliminary Questions," Poulain offers some fundamental definitions and distinguishes four degrees of ordinary prayer. "Mystic" or "extraordinary" prayer is prayer involving "supernatural acts or states which our own industry is powerless to produce, *even in a low degree, even momentarily.*" Some supernatural acts can be the results of one's own efforts—acts of contrition or meritorious acts—but acts described as "mystic" occur only because of God's special intervention; no acts of human will can accomplish such acts even to a low degree or momentarily. In ordinary prayer only faith makes one aware that the act of ordinary prayer is supernatural and not a purely natural act; in mystic prayer, on the other hand, "something shows more or less clearly that God is intervening." To illuminate this point, Poulain offers an example, a "clear and simple case," as he does throughout the book: ". . . at Lourdes, Bernadette has an apparition of the Blessed Virgin; and not only is the fact supernatural, but it is *manifestly* so. It is, therefore, a mystic fact."

Poulain distinguishes four degrees of ordinary prayer: *vocal* prayer, *meditation, affective* prayer, and the prayer of *simple regard* or of *simplicity.* He concerns himself exclusively with the latter two degrees because the former two, both of which involve reasoning, have been dealt with extensively by others.

By "affective" prayer is meant mental prayer in which the affections or sentiments (such as love, gratitude, contrition) outbalance thoughts and arguments. When the intuitive aspect replaces reasoning and a dominant thought prevails over a variety of affects and the use of words, the prayer has become one of "simple regard." These two types of prayer—the affective and simple regard—differing in the degree of the affections and discursive thought, have been considered by some to be mystical prayers, but Poulain argues that since anyone can at will accomplish these degrees of prayer, they are not mystic: they are not realized only through God's intervention and participation.

To prove the existence and show the nature of the prayer of simple regard or simplicity, Poulain offers a series of "extracts," quotations from those who have reported their experiences in prayer. (Throughout the book there are such extracts, consisting of relevant and illuminating passages from the writings of the saints and other spiritually profound persons; this device gives a moving spiritual dimension to Poulain's analytical account of the stages or degrees of prayer.) For example, Father Nouet writes that as prayer "perfects itself, it discards reasonings, and being content with a simple glance, with a *sweet remembrance* of God and of Jesus Christ, His only Son, it produces many loving affections according to the various motions it receives from the Holy Ghost. But when it has arrived at the highest point of perfection, *it simplifies its affections equally with its lights.*"

Poulain concludes the first part of his work with a survey of the advantages and disadvantages of affective and simple prayers, and he offers three rules of conduct for those who experience difficulty in meditation. The first rule is not to force oneself to reflections, vocal prayers, or petitions for which one has no inclination, but to be content with the prayer of simplicity. The second rule is to yield to the inclinations to act in a particular way while praying. "To sum up," writes Poulain, "there are two contrary excesses to be avoided: forcing ourselves to perform a variety of acts, seeing in those acts the ideal prayer; and compelling ourselves systematically to repose, as the quietists do."

The third rule of conduct concerning meditation is to take advantage of opportunities for instruction or for arousing the will.

In part two, "Some General Ideas About the Mystic Union," Poulain begins by dividing the mystical graces into two classes, those that consist in the manifestation of God himself in the act of mystic union, and those that consist in the manifestation of created objects, such as the Blessed Virgin, an angel, or past or future facts concerning creatures.

Poulain then proceeds to distinguish four stages or degrees of the mystic union: (1) the *prayer of quiet,* an incomplete mystic union involving repose; (2) the *full or semiecstatic union,* the prayer of union; (3) *the ecstatic union,* ecstasy; and (4) the *transforming union,* the "spiritual marriage of the soul with God."

The first three degrees of union differ in degrees of intensity as the soul, while yet untransformed, is variously affected by the divine. In the prayer of quiet one may still be distracted despite the divine action; in full union, although the soul is fully occupied with the divine object, the body is stil capable of sensing and acting; in ecstatic union, the state of full ecstasy, bodily action and sensing are hardly possible and one cannot at will come out of the prayer.

Poulain continues his discussion of the mystic union by calling attention to its two fundamental characters: God's presence is *felt*, and God gives knowledge of his presence through the *spiritual senses*.

There is spiritual seeing and hearing, Poulain argues, pointing out that most persons accept these analogies to bodily sensing, but perhaps the most significant kind of spiritual sensing is spiritual *touching*. Poulain writes: ". . . that which constitutes the common basis of all the various degrees of the mystic union is that the spiritual impression by which God makes known His presence, manifests Him in the manner, as it were, of something *interior* which penetrates the soul." The author defends his use of the expression "interior touch" by claiming that no other term so accurately suggests the impression made by God in his penetration of the soul. God manifests himself through an interior unity, Poulain contends, and one is aware of this spiritual presence as one is aware of the presence of one's own body. (Poulain provides an illuminating extract from Father Thomassin: "We grasp God by an *interior* and secret *touch*; we feel Him thus, reposing in us, as it were, in a very intimate manner . . . the soul feels God and *touches* Him.")

In addition to the two principal features of the mystic union—that God is felt, and that he is felt through a spiritual sensing—there are ten subsidiary features cited by Poulain: (1) The mystic union does not depend on one's will; (2) the knowledge of God in mystic union is obscure and confuses; (3) the mode of communication is partially incomprehensible; (4) the union is not produced by reasonings, considerations, or sensible images; (5) it varies in intensity; (6) it demands less effort than meditation; (7) it is accompanied by sentiments of love, repose, pleasure, and, often, suffering; (8) in inclines the soul to different virtues; (9) it acts upon the body and is acted upon; (10) it impedes interior acts of the will by binding one to the reception of what God gives.

Poulain turns in part three to a detailed discussion of the four stages of mystic union. A prefatory chapter concerns Saint John of the Cross's "two nights of the soul," two successive states of prayer, forming the borderland between ordinary prayer and mystic union.

The first night of the soul, called by Saint John "the night of the senses," is a prayer of simplicity involving five elements: It is habitually *arid* (in that the mind is powerless to reason or to imagine); it involves a *memory of God* that is "*simple, confused*, and general, returning with a singular *persistence* which is *independent of the will*"; the memory of God is accompanied by a *painful need* for closer union with God; there is a *distaste for all things of the senses*, a privation of all desire (hence, a "night of the senses," a dark night of the soul); it has a *hidden aspect* consisting in *God's beginning the action* that takes place in the prayer of quiet but "in too slight a degree for us to be conscious of it."

According to Poulain, the "second night of the soul," as described by Saint John of the Cross, is a "second purgatory," a series of mystic states falling short of the spiritual marriage, containing both joy and suffering. The second night is at the line between ordinary prayer and mystic union; it involves God's secretly teaching the soul without any effort on the soul's part. Such infused contemplation causes spiritual darkness, Saint John writes, because it deprives the soul of its natural perceptions. In the *Ascent of Mount Carmel,* Saint John writes that God infuses into the soul "a new understanding of God in God, the human understanding being set aside, and a new love of God in God."

The goal of all mystic unions, Poulain writes, is the fourth degree or stage of mystic union: the spiritual marriage, the transforming union. This union has three principal elements: it is almost permanent; it involves a transformation of the higher faculties; and it brings about "a permanent intellectual vision of the Blessed Trinity or of some divine attribute." The transformation consists in the creature's becoming "like unto God" through participation in God's nature as God cooperates in the exercise of the higher operations of the soul.

In his account of the transforming union Poulain relies primarily on the testimony of Saint John of the Cross and Saint Teresa of Ávila. Numerous extracts illuminate the analysis, giving dramatic life to an account that is otherwise systematic, intellectual, and pedagogical. For example, Poulain includes the following passage from Saint Teresa's *Interior Castle:* "You will learn how His Majesty ratifies these espousals; probably this is done when He ravishes my soul by ecstasies, so depriving it of its faculties; if the use of these were retained, I think the sight of its close vicinity to so mighty a sovereign would probably deprive the body of life." And Saint John writes in *The Living Flame of God,* "The soul now *being one* with God *is itself God* by participation. . . . It loves God *by means of* God."

With the account of the transforming union Poulain concludes what might be called the heart of his book. As he begins to discuss revelations and visions, he writes, "From the point of view of sanctification, these graces are of much less importance than the mystic union." The account of revelations (also supported by numerous extracts) is followed by a review of the various kinds of trials sent to contemplatives. The book concludes with the discussion of some supplementary questions concerning mysticism. Here Poulain prescribes the qualities necessary for a spiritual director. He then goes on to discuss quietism, the rarity or frequency of mystic states, terminology, and scientific methods in descriptive mysticism.

Ian P. McGreal

RECOMMENDED READING

Edition used: Poulain, Augustine. *The Graces of Interior Prayer.* 6th ed. Translated by Leonora L. Yorke Smith. Introduction by Rev. Daniel Considine, S.J. London: Paul, Trench, Trübner, 1911.

John of the Cross, Saint. *The Ascent of Mount Camel.* (See the article on this book in this volume.)

Teresa of Ávila, Saint. *The Interior Castle.* (See the article on this book in this volume.)

The preceding two books are cited by Poulain and represent the kind of experience he was concerned to analyze and explain.

THE VARIETIES OF RELIGIOUS EXPERIENCE

Author: William James (1842–1910)

William James was the son of Henry James, an American Swedenborgian, and the brother of Henry James, Jr., the American novelist. James was trained as a physician, but turned to psychology and later to philosophy. His contribution to psychology, *The Principles of Psychology* (1890), has become a classic in the field. James early became the most popular spokesman of the American philosophical movement, pragmatism. The present work was his Gifford Lectures. Among his other important philosophical works are: *The Will to Believe* (1897), *Pragmatism* (1907), *The Meaning of Truth* (1909), and *Essays in Radical Empiricism* (1912).

Type and subject of work: Psychological and philosophical lectures on the reports of religious experiences

First published: 1902

MAJOR THEMES

Neurological and physiological conditions are as irrelevant in evaluating a person's religious experiences as they are in evaluating a scientist's physical hypothesis.

Religious experiences should be evaluated in terms of their philosophical reasonableness and moral helpfulness.

A person's psychological makeup contributes to the more specific character-

istics of a person's religious experiences, and this accounts for the variety among religious experiences.

An examination of the reports of religious experience discloses three general beliefs and two psychological characteristics. The beliefs are: (1) the visible world is part of a more spiritual universe from which it draws its significance; (2) that union or harmonious relations with that higher universe is our true end; and (3) that prayer or communion with the spirit thereof is a process in which spirit energy produces effects within the phenomenal world. The two psychological characteristics are: (1) a new zest that adds itself like a gift to life; and (2) an assurance of safety and a temper of peace, and in relation to others, a preponderance of loving affection.

The differences between religious beliefs are differences in over-beliefs, the way in which the vaguer and more general beliefs are made specific and the spiritual is related to the cosmos.

Religious experiences are primarily concerned with individual feelings and destinies, but this is not to be deplored; such experiences deal with realities in the completest sense of that term.

William James begins his series of lectures by characterizing the kind of study and the subject matter with which he is concerned. His concern is a psychological study of religious experiences, but he is not concerned with the physiological and neurological conditions that may underlie religious experiences. Such conditions, he argues, underlie all mental states, and consequently, are irrelevant in describing and evaluating religious experience. In fact, they are as irrelevant in evaluating religious opinions as they are in evaluating opinions in the natural sciences and in the industrial arts. No one accepts or rejects an opinion in the sciences on the basis of the author's neurological type, and the same should be the case with religious opinions. James readily admits that many striking religious personalities are eccentric, even pathological; but such personalities, for this kind of study, function as microscopes and enlarge, for easier viewing, the subject matter of religious experience. The criteria for the evaluation of the experiences, however, must be kept distinct from these pathological considerations. Immediate luminousness, or philosophical reasonableness, and moral helpfulness James takes to be the only two relevant criteria for evaluating the religious phenomena with which he is concerned.

As for delimiting the subject matter as such, that is, deciding which experiences are to be called religious, James eschews an attempt to define the term *religion* as such. He is not concerned with "the essence of religion," but with describing and evaluating those experiences usually classified as religious. He is, likewise, not concerned with the institutional aspects of religion, but with the personal aspects. He ignores the ecclesiastical organization with its rituals and creeds, its systematic theologies, and its ideas about the gods, and confines himself to examining "the feelings, acts, and experiences of individual men in their solitude, so far as they apprehend themselves to stand in relation to whatever they may consider the divine."

The term *the divine* is here taken to refer to what one considers the most primal, enveloping, and real, and religion is the person's attitudes and reactions to it. James wishes "the divine" to be interpreted broadly enough to include the godless, or quasi-godless, religion of an Emersonian optimism and a Buddhistic pessimism. On the other hand, James does not wish to include, as religious, all attitudes concerned with a total reaction to life, for this would make the subject matter too broad and strain the ordinary use of language. After all, there are trifling and sneering attitudes toward the whole of life, attitudes that would hardly qualify as religious. "There is something solemn, serious, and tender," he tells us, "about any attitude which we denominate religious. If glad, it must not grin nor snicker; if sad, it must not scream or curse." As a consequence, James limits "the divine" to "the most primal, enveloping and real which an individual feels impelled to respond to solemnly and gravely, and neither by a curse nor a jest."

James is still not quite satisfied, however, with his characterization of the religious attitude, for it does not clearly distinguish the religious attitude from what might be called the purely moral, such as the stoic attitude. The solemn and serious reaction and attitude of the religious person is distinguished by an element of joy or happiness. It is not a simple joy that results from a person's being liberated from oppressive moods; it is a solemn joy, or happiness, that embraces within it the negative, or tragic, side of life and holds it in check. The religious reaction and attitude, which is the subject of these lectures, as a consequence, has a depth and strength that is lacking in the purely moral.

After delimiting the kind of experiences with which he is concerned in his study, James turns to the testimony concerning concrete religious experiences, and this occupies the bulk of his lectures. The amount, as well as the variety, of the testimony that he has collected is phenomenal and any summary will appear a lifeless skeleton compared to the richness of his concrete cases and his own colorful commentary. In this main section, however, James is primarily concerned with reporting what religious persons concretely describe, not with an evaluation of the experiences. These experiences by and large involve a sense of an unseen reality—that is, a reality that is not present to the special and particular senses—yet these experiences are as convincing to the person who has them as any direct sensible experience can be. In fact, one could say, James tells us, that "the life of religion . . . consists of the belief that there is an unseen order, and that our supreme good lies in harmoniously adjusting ourselves thereto." It is with this sense of the unseen and the variety of reactions to it that James is concerned here, not with the various ways in which the unseen has been conceptualized. The latter are creedal and theological, and, consequently, primarily institutional concerns. His concern is with the concrete personal experiences, including the reactions of the person having the experience. In addition to the solemnity, seriousness, and joy that he sees characterizing these experiences in general, James finds a variety of reactions—and consequently, "varieties of religious experience."

It is an underlying thesis of these lectures that this variety of reactions to the divine, and consequently, the varieties of religious experience, is due to the varieties of human personality. The solemn joy of which we spoke earlier will exemplify a continuum of responses depending, for example, on how sanguine or somber the personality of the person experiencing is. For the two extremes here, the more optimistic one and the more pessimistic one, James coined the colorful phrases "the healthy-minded" ("the once born") and "the sick soul" ("the twice born"). Either extreme can be quasi-pathological, he tells us; but it is the extremes that interest James for, as was mentioned earlier, there one can see the religious reactions enlarged.

The healthy-minded, or optimistic, response can be either immediate and involuntary, or systematic and voluntary. In either case, the person looks on all things, finds them good, and refuses to admit their badness or ignores their presence. "The sanguine and healthy-minded," he writes, "live on the sunny side of their misery-line, the depressed and melancholy [the sick souls] live beyond it, in darkness and apprehension." He includes among his collection of reports of the sick souls, experiences of the vanity of all mortal things, a very deep sense of sin, and a general panic fear of the universe. To the sick soul, the healthy-minded appears blind and shallow; to the healthy-minded, the sick soul appears unmanly and diseased. It is only natural to expect these two extreme types of personality to react to the presence of the divine in quite different ways.

Having already suggested that the sick soul perhaps has a deeper sensitivity to evil in the universe and, as a consequence, perhaps a deeper religious insight, James devotes three lectures to the "divided self" and the process of its unification and conversion, summarizing and quoting from the testimonies concerning these experiences and loosely classifying them in terms such as "sudden" or "prolonged" and "unconscious and involuntary" or "conscious and voluntary." From the wealth of testimony, James finds three general characteristics of the converted state: The first is the loss of all worry, the sense that ultimately all is well with one, and a willingness to be, even though outer conditions may remain the same; the second is the sense of perceiving truths that one did not know before; and the third is that the world itself appears to undergo an objective change, a newness seems to beautify every object. The converted state is almost the precise opposite of the state of "the sick soul" or "the divided self."

In the fact that James devotes three lectures to saintliness and two more to the value of saintliness one can observe something of James's pragmatic interest in religious experience. He has told us that immediate luminousness, or philosophical reasonableness, and moral helpfulness were the only relevant criteria of evaluation. Saintliness, the "fruits of genuine religion," and frequently the fruit of conversion, provides the factor in religious experience for the application of the "moral helpfulness" criterion to religious experience. Consequently, saintliness is very important for James in evaluating religious experience, and he devotes five lectures just to this one topic, by far the most allotted to any one topic in the series. In examining the lives of the conventional religious saints, James finds that the saintly characteristics are frequently taken to excess, excesses of devotion, purity, charity, and asceticism. These excesses, however, are, he thinks, the result of an imbalance within the individual due to a weakness of the intellect.

James now turns to the possible data for the other criterion of evaluation of religious experience, namely, immediate luminousness, or philosophical reasonableness, and he devotes two lectures to mystical experiences and one to religious philosophy. James lists four marks for what he takes as mystical states: ineffability, noetic quality, transiency, and passivity. By their very nature, these experiences, James concludes, are invulnerable: The mystic has been there, the nonmystic has not. By virtue of this same fact, however, the experiences can have no authority over the nonmystic. What these experiences can do is to offer us a hypothesis of another world or of a wider world than is given to us in sensation. But then, James points out, the religious experiences of the nonmystic also offer us such a hypothesis. Consequently, mystical experiences offer us no more for the application of the criterion of philosophical reasonableness than religious experience in general does.

What James appears to mean by "religious philosophy" is a philosophical attempt to prove or to justify religious belief by some form of coercive argument. Here James is probably more emphatic than at any other point in his series of lectures: "We must conclude that the attempt to demonstrate by purely intellectual processes the truth of the deliverances of direct religious experience is absolutely hopeless." The history of the apparent failure of this attempt is perhaps now well known. Before giving us, however, his own conclusions concerning the evaluation of this vast testimony concerning the phenomenon of religious experience, James treats in one lecture a number of more minor elements in religious experiences, such as aesthetic elements, sacrifice, confession, prayer, and automatism.

As James looks at the reports of religious experiences of the previous lectures, he finds them containing three general beliefs and two psychological characteristics. The beliefs are: (1) that the visible world is a part of a more spiritual universe from which it draws its chief significance; (2) that union, or harmonious relations, with that higher universe is our true end; and (3) that prayer or communion with the spirit thereof is a process in which spiritual energy produces effects, psychological or material, within the phenomenal world.

The two psychological characteristics are: (1) a new zest that adds itself like a gift to life; and (2) an assurance of safety and a temper of peace, and, in relation to others, a preponderance of loving affection.

Before evaluating these beliefs and psychological characteristics, James considers the position that religion, from the standpoint of modern science, is an anachronism because of its concern with personal destiny and the preponderance of feeling involved. He rejects this thesis on the grounds that it is precisely here that we deal with realities in the completest sense of the term. "Individuality is founded in feeling; and the recesses of feeling, the darker, blinder strata of character, are the only places in the world in which we catch real fact in the making, and directly perceive how events happen, and how work is actually done."

As suggested earlier, the psychological characteristics are evaluated on the basis of their moral helpfulness; but James here raises the question of the objective "truth" of the religious beliefs, the philosophical problem of evaluation. They must at least, he suggests, be in harmony with our scientific beliefs and not conflict with them. This James finds to be the case with these three general religious beliefs in their above vague formulation. He takes the existence of such a spiritual universe to be a hypothesis evoked to explain the religious effects, particularly the above two psychological characteristics. Here he falls back on what he calls "the instinctive belief of mankind," that something is real if it has real effects. To be a good hypothesis, however, the beliefs must be spelled out and related to facts other than the ones the hypothesis is invoked to explain. It is in the spelling out of the religious hypothesis in more specific ways, which he terms "over-beliefs," that we find the religious beliefs frequently conflicting with each other and with our accepted scientific beliefs.

Bowman L. Clarke

RECOMMENDED READING

Edition used: James, William. *The Varieties of Religious Experience.* Edited with an Introduction by Martin E. Marty. New York: Penguin Books, 1982.

———. *The Meaning of Truth.* New York: Longmans, Green & Co., 1909. This is James's more mature and systematic position on truth, which is quite relevant to his suggestions at the end of the present work and *The Will to Believe and Other Essays.*

———. *The Will to Believe and Other Essays in Popular Philosophy.* New York: Dover, 1956. Particularly in the essay entitled, "The Will to Believe," we find James virtually taking up where he disappointedly left off in the present work, with an evaluation of the truth of religious beliefs.

THE DOUBLE SEARCH: STUDIES IN ATONEMENT AND PRAYER

Author: Rufus Jones (1863–1948)

Author of fifty-seven books and numerous short writings, Rufus Jones was renowned in his lifetime as a Quaker, a mystic, a philosopher, and a social activist. He was born to a family of Maine farmers that had identified itself with intense Quaker piety for generations. Jones recalled of his childhood that "religion was a vital part of the air we breathed." Although his family celebrated God's love above all else, they inculcated obedience and guilt. One of the most somber turning points in his religious life occurred after he had abandoned his farm chores for a day of swimming and his mother put him in his room "in the silence with God." As an adult, Jones recast such childhood experiences into an unsystematic but emotionally charged religious psychology. He studied philosophy and religion at Haverford, Heidelberg, Oxford, and Harvard and was instrumental in revitalizing Quaker mysticism in the light of New Thought psychology. His mysticism was emphatically moralistic and led toward social action. He founded the American Friends Service Committee and served as its chairman and honorary chairman from its inception in 1917 to his death in 1948.

Type and subject of work: Meditation on the relationship between God and each person

First published: 1906

Major Themes

One does not seek God alone; God is equally fervent in His search for each human being.

This double search is represented in the person of Christ; Christ is both God reaching down toward humankind and humankind reaching up toward God.

The double search is characterized by atonement and prayer: Atonement is the process by which God loves and suffers with us and, in so doing, compels our devotion; prayer is the process by which we open ourselves to God and, in so doing, establish fellowship with Him.

At the outset of *The Double Search,* Jones invokes the myth in Plato's *Symposium* that man in his original nature was a round being with four legs, four arms, one head, and two faces. Plato defines love between human beings as the longing to return to this original state in which each human being was perfectly joined to another. While Plato argues that there is another, higher love, namely, the soul's longing to return to eternal Truth, Jones believes that our love for God is radically similar to our love for other people. Thus Plato's parable of human love can also be taken as a parable of religious love. God and humanity were originally one being, a "Divine whole" divided at human birth by the emergence of our individuality. God longs to be reunited with us as much as we long to be reunited with God. Christ represents the fulfillment of this double search; Christ is the round man in whom God and humanity are one.

Jones believes that his view of Christ is not undermined by modern science or biblical criticism. While other views of Christ are called into question by scientific rejections of supernatural claims and by literary critical rejections of the simple unity of biblical texts, Jones believes that his approach avoids these problems. His approach to Christ is psychological; more particularly, it is an expression of the psychology of New Thought that has been popular in America since the mid-nineteenth century. Like Ralph Waldo Emerson, the father of New Thought, Jones regards the historical Christ primarily as an example of how persons can realize the presence of God in their own lives. He believes that the outward, historical revelation of Christ is an important guide to God, much as Beethoven and Mozart are important instructors in music. But Christ is fundamentally an inward reality for Jones. The incarnation is an ongoing psychological event.

Like Mary Baker Eddy, who is the most famous proponent of New Thought, Jones understands Christ as the idea of divine love. He further believes that having the idea of divine love enables man to represent Christ to others. Also like Eddy, Jones believes that religious idealism amplifies without contradicting modern science. But while Eddy focused on the health-giving effects of Christian idealism, in *The Double Search* Jones is primarily interested in reflecting on the role that God and Christ play in the human psyche. He defines God as the spiritual Personality that human persons develop through their love of God. He uses the term *Christ* as a means of discussing the evolution of the human personality.

Viewed in relation to the evolution of human society, Christ represents the historical moment when humankind became fully aware of God as the ideal toward which it should rightly strive. Jones believes that the Hebrew prophets were dimly aware of this Christ ideal but that their primitive culture prevented them from fully realizing this ideal. The birth of Christ represents a new era of cultural maturity. Christ is the great divide in the history of human evolution. He embodies humanity's successful striving for the ideal self that pulls it out of its lower nature.

The spiritual evolution of humankind is the result of cooperating forces. On the one side, as we strive for an ideal self, we push ourselves upward. God is this ideal self. On the other, by opening ourselves to the compelling force of our ideal self, we are drawn upward by its embrace. This is the point Jones continually reiterates: the uplifting pull of the ideal self cooperates with our effort to push ourselves upward from below. Human beings' efforts to improve themselves are met by spiritual cooperation from above; God is always reaching down to draw us upward. Jones pictures God as a universal force permeating human personalities, much as sunlight permeates the natural world, infusing all organisms with the power of life. Just as in the natural world the capacity to absorb sunlight differentiates a giant oak from a daisy, so in the human world, persons who open themselves fully to God and his uplifting love grow spiritually stronger and more loving than persons who absorb less of his love.

Some confusion results from the fact that Jones sometimes speaks of God as the Divine Other and of his love as a force outside the individual, and at other times he speaks of God and his love as aspects of human personality. Although by identifying him as the person's ideal self, Jones implies that God can be understood in terms of human psychology, he ultimately relinquishes this line of thought in favor of mysticism. His experiences of God's love are so fundamental to his worldview that, like other mystics, he ultimately defines himself and others in terms of God.

In his chapter on Christian atonement, Jones defines sin as our disobedience of our own good intentions. He believes that persons seek deliverance from the selfish drives that prevent them from following their own visions of goodness. He argues furthermore that sin corrupts not only the sinner but also the sinner's view of God. The idea of an angry God who demands appeasement is the erroneous but inevitable by-product of the guilt persons feel when they fail to obey the higher principles they know to be right.

The correlation between religious faith and childhood experiences of parental authority is essential to Jones's religious views. In his chapter on the atonement, he compares the disobedient and frightened child's desire to appease his father with the primitive religious belief that an angry deity requires human sacrifice. In both cases the felt experience of sin colors perceptions of authority, causing it to seem stern and distant rather than warm and loving. Although Jones interprets primitive religious fear in terms of childhood guilt and compares a sinner's relation to God with a child's relation to its father, he stops short of discussing the possible relationship between guilt and love.

From the perspective of Jones's mysticism, the gospel dissolves the pagan fear of God and reveals him to be an inherently loving and tender Father. This does not mean that the Christian God either blinks at disobedience or does not require repentance for sin. The divine Father no more overlooks sin than any responsible parent overlooks errancy in a child. But like the remonstrances of every loving parent, God's corrections and rebukes are expressions of his love for his children. God actually suffers with his children just as other parents suffer with their children when they fail.

The idea that our sin draws down God's suffering is essential to Jones's whole view of the relationship between God and man. Jones believes that sin is not confined to the sinner; every act of sin affects every other part of the organic whole that God and humanity comprise. When a person sins, God reacts; he feels the sin himself and suffers on behalf of the sinner. Thus Jones identifies God's love with vicarious suffering. Furthermore, he believes that this suffering defines holiness. Holiness always involves sacrificial acts in behalf of others. Holiness is the vicarious suffering that is spiritual love.

In the final analysis, holiness is a means of compelling holiness in others. While Jones rejects the idea that God demands human sacrifice as appeasement, he argues that God willingly sacrifices himself for humanity and that everyone who realizes this is compelled by that sacrifice. He also argues that we represent God to each other by acts of holiness that embody vicarious suffering. This process of being compelled by the vicarious sufferings of another is not a matter of involuntary assent, but compels our active and total responsivity. The realization that God sacrifices himself for us prompts a radical transformation in our will and stimulates a lifelong faith in the goodness of God. Although Jones does not discuss it fully, guilt plays an essential role in the internal logic of this religious psychology and is not limited to its primitive phases. Just as a child's love for its father can be stimulated by the guilt it feels when the father suffers on its behalf, so guilt is essential to the underlying process by which human beings feel compelled to return the love of their divine Father.

In the final chapter of *The Double Search,* Jones turns to the subject of prayer. He defines prayer as the opening of the soul to God and argues that the effort to communicate with God elicits his response and actually establishes fellowship with him. Jones objects to the idea that prayer is an effort to interrupt the chain of physical causation, and he welcomes scientific critiques of such primitive conceptions. In Jones's view, prayer is not a means to some utilitarian end, but an end in itself. Prayer is the spontaneous outreach of the soul toward the circle of life beyond itself. Although opening the soul to larger forces of energy may have utilitarian benefits, such as increased health or perspicacity, the real meaning of prayer is in the act of praying itself. The process by which one opens oneself to God is its own reward.

In Jones's view, there can be no subjective need without "an objective stimulus which has stimulated the need." Extended theologically, this view translates into the theory that longing for communication with God is proof of the existence of his Personhood and of his capacity to communicate with us. The soul's outreach toward God inevitably leads to enjoyment of immediate fellowship with him. Prayer in its highest form is "actual social fellowship." God is not a lonely sovereign but a Person who, like all other persons, exists in relation to other persons.

Interwoven throughout Jones's testimony to the organic social relationship between God and human beings are statements about the organic spiritual relationships among human beings. The theory that social relationships are central to the spiritual life is the theme of Jones's influential *Social Law in the Spiritual World* (1904), to which he refers the reader of *The Double Search* for philosophic groundwork. In Jones's mysticism, the ties between God and humanity are often manifest in relationships among persons. He believes that we find God in our relationships with other human beings. Thus social life is essential to the mystic's apprehension of God.

Amanda Porterfield

RECOMMENDED READING

Edition used: Jones, Rufus Matthew. *The Double Search; Studies in Atonement and Prayer.* Philadelphia and Chicago: John C. Winston Co., 1937.

Fuller, Robert C. *Mesmerism and the American Cure of Souls.* Philadelphia: University of Pennsylvania Press, 1982. An excellent study of the close relationship between psychological theory and American religious thought in the late nineteenth and early twentieth centuries.

Jones, Rufus. *The Later Periods of Quakerism*. London: Macmillan, 1921. An important study of the history of Quaker spirituality.

———. *Social Law in the Spiritual World: Studies in Human and Divine Inter-Relationship*. Philadelphia: J. C. Winston Co., 1904. A pioneer study in New Thought exploring the relationship between mysticism and social life.

Meyer, Donald. *The Positive Thinkers*. Garden City, N.Y.: Doubleday, 1965. A good overview of the history and issues involved in the New Thought tradition from Emerson to Norman Vincent Peale.

Rufus Jones Speaks to Our Time: An Anthology. Edited by Harry Emerson Fosdick, New York: Macmillan, 1961. A good collection of excerpts from Jones's writings organized by religious themes.

THE MYSTICAL ELEMENT OF RELIGION

Author: Baron Friedrich von Hügel (1852–1925)
The son of an Austrian diplomat and a Scottish gentlewoman, Friedrich von Hügel spent his childhood and youth mainly on the Continent. His marriage to Lady Mary Herbert, a recent convert, drew him into English Catholic circles, among whom he established himself as a moderating influence. A prolific writer, Hügel summed up his thought in *The Reality of God* (1931). Numerous essays, addresses, and letters are available in print, including the popular *Letters from Baron Friedrich von Hügel to a Niece* (1928).

Type and subject of work: Critical biography

First published: 1908

MAJOR THEMES

Mysticism is an essential element of a developed religion.

The properties of mysticism are best studied in the lives of individual mystics.

The traditional lives of mystics are commonly overlaid with legends, and must be subjected to historical criticism.

Because those who have enjoyed a full mystical experience frequently suffer from mental and nervous illness, care must be taken to distinguish symptoms of illness from spiritual insights.

The life of Catherine of Genoa is especially suitable for such a study.

Friedrich von Hügel's interest in Catherine Fiesca Adorna (1447–1510), known to history as Saint Catherine of Genoa, began in 1884 when he picked up a copy of her life and teachings at the British Museum; but fourteen years elapsed before he published a small book on questions suggested by her life, and another ten years before the present two-volume work appeared. Why, one might ask, was this relatively minor saint chosen as the subject of such a monumental work? Among the reasons that the author puts forward are: She represents not the Middle Ages nor the Counter-Reformation from which the more notable mystics have come, but the high tide of the Italian Renaissance; she was never a member of a religious order and owed almost nothing to spiritual directors; she was highly intelligent and able to interpret her own experience in the light not merely of Scripture but also of Renaissance Platonism. As has been said, she was the perfect heroine for a Victorian novel and Hügel was the complete Victorian.

The book is divided into three parts. Part one, "Introduction," is instructive mainly as setting forth the three elements that the author believes are essential in a religion that is to meet our needs. The first or historical element corresponds to the needs of childhood, which demand that religion be founded on fact and embodied in a social institution. The second or intellectual element corresponds to the needs of youth, when the argumentative and reflective capacities come into play and eventuate in a system of doctrine and a view of the world. The third or experimental element corresponds to the needs of maturity, when belief and reason ripen into volition and action, and when religion is felt rather than seen and argued about. The author returns to these elements in his conclusion.

In Part two, "Biography," Hügel takes up the life and teaching of the saint and the beginnings of her official cultus. As a beautiful girl of sixteen, Catherine was married by her aristocratic family to Giuliano Adorno, the wealthy but irresponsible scion of a rival clan. The marriage was unhappy; but ten years of loneliness and of frantic activity went by before, in a moment of transport, "she was drawn away from the miseries of the world; and, as it were beside herself, she kept crying out within herself: 'No more world; no more sins!'" For four years she lived as a penitent, giving herself to menial tasks among the poor, wearing a hair shirt, and moving with downcast eyes, seemingly dead to all around her. Meanwhile, Giuliano had suffered financial ruin and had become a convert, and they moved from their palace to a humble house near the great hospital of the Pammatone where they ministered to the sick and the poor. Later they moved into the hospital, living without pay and at their own expense, Catherine serving as matron for a number of years, including the plague year 1493 during which she caught the fever as a result of kissing the lips of a dying woman. In 1497 Giuliano died, and Catherine, although still living within the hospital, was gradually forced by illness to give up her work. During these last years of her life she had a small following of disciples; and these, when she died, arranged for her to be buried, not beside her husband as she had desired, but in the pilgrimage church of San Nicolo.

It is to two of these disciples that we owe the *Life and Doctrine*, published in Genoa in 1551, but based on material gathered by Ettore Vernazzo (1470?–1524), a notary who helped Catherine during the plague and who devoted the remainder of his life to charitable work—a competent man of the world and a true saint; and by Don Cattaneo Marabotto (1450?–1528), a secular priest, honest and competent, who was Catherine's confessor for the last ten years of her life. Vernazzo's daughter Battista (1497–1587), an able and saintly woman, seems to have taken the work in hand and given it final shape. According to Hügel, only a small part of the book is narrative, the rest being discourses by the saint; and while it contains brief passages that must have been recorded when they were spoken, most of the book is secondary so that the whole is "largely insipid and monotonous." The two "works" usually attributed to Saint Catherine are from the same hands: The *Treatise on Purgatory* is a seventeen-page excerpt from the life, and the *Spiritual Dialogue* is a composition of Battista Vernazza designed to systematize the teachings found in the Life.

Apart from the desire to record her teaching, Catherine's biographers were guided by two main interests. One was to put on record divine favors. These were not many. On one occasion, when asked by Vernazzo to narrate graces shown to her, she replied that it was impossible to describe her interior experiences and that "as to exterior things, few or none had taken place in her case." Still, it was reported that she would lie on the ground for hours in a state of trance, that during her fasts (forty days twice a year) her stomach rejected food, that she could tell unconsecrated from consecrated wine, and that the hand with which Don Cattaneo blessed the elements had for her a sweet odor. The other main concern was to put in a favorable light certain of Catherine's departures from conventional piety: that she took communion daily, that she went for years without confessing to a priest, that she did not take advantage of indulgences, and that she would not pray to saints. Both of these concerns were important in the eyes of the cult that grew up soon after Catherine's death, notably after her body was found not to have undergone decay.

Hügel goes into every detail. Of Catherine's absorption in prayer he notes that from the time of her conversion until her health failed (some twenty-six years of active life) these absorptions (she did not like the word *ecstasy*), which occurred almost daily and lasted up to six hours, were controlled by herself although they came and went so quickly as to seem involuntary. Often they were occasioned by her reception of the Eucharist, together with which they constituted her chief source of spiritual growth. In Hügel's judgment she seems to have experienced only one form of absorption, that which is known as the Prayer of Quiet. These, he says, "are treated substantially as times when the conscious region of her soul, a region always relatively shallow, sinks down into the ever-present deep regions of subconsciousness; and hence as experiences which can only be described indirectly,—in their effects, as traced by and in the conscious soul, after its rising up again . . . to its more ordinary condition." Hügel denies that Catherine's teachings are "pneumatic," in the sense that they were given to her during these absorptions. Rather, he suggests, the soul itself was fed on these occasions, and its capacities for intellectual expression were increased when she returned to ordinary consciousness. He further notes that in Catherine's later years, when she was no longer able to work and when the rhythm of her life was broken, her protracted absorptions diminished and, toward the end, were interspersed with a different kind of trance, outwardly indistinguishable from her healthy absorptions, but which she recognized as alien and complained that they did her harm. It was, however, in the last year of her life that she was granted what was perhaps the most stirring of all her experiences. "There came upon her an insupportable fire of infinite love; and she declared that there had been shown to her one single spark (scintilla) of Pure Love, and that this had been but for a short moment; and that, had it lasted longer, she would have expired because of its great force." According to Hügel this "scintilla-experience," the richest in her life, must be kept in mind if we are to understand her most profound teachings. Yet essentially it was no different in kind from her earlier experiences, being at once "a grace addressed to, and an act performed by her spiritual nature —God's Spirit stimulating and sustaining hers. . . . It was a gift of herself by herself to God; and yet her very power and determination to give herself were rendered possible and became actual through the accompanying gift of God."

Catherine was never a teacher in the formal sense. What her followers called her doctrine is simply a compilation of detached sayings without context. To aid in deciding which are authentic, Hügel used the tests of rhythm, simplicity, and originality. (We are told that she often "made rhymed sayings in her joy.") The sayings, while touching many matters and giving vent to many moods, are all true to Catherine's central experience of God's unifying love, and can easily be grouped under the great theological heads of God and Creation, Sin and Redemption, and Last Things.

For Catherine, God is a "living fountain of goodness." All creatures participate in this goodness even when they are in mortal sin; otherwise they would perish. God, she says, seems to have "nothing else to do than to unite Himself to us." As for man, "lift sin off from his shoulders and then allow the good of God to act." True self-love is love of God, and all other love is self-hatred. It is nonsensical to say that God is offended by our acts; say rather that we damage ourselves. God is the true center of each rational creature. "My *Me* is God, . . . not by simple participation but by a true transformation of my Being."

How there can be evil in the presence of an all-loving God is not easy to understand, especially for those who are consumed with the thirst for unity that Catherine shares with all the Neoplatonist school, for reality constitutes a graduated series with the sensible world at the bottom and with God at the top. "Listen," she says, "to what Fra Jacapone says in one of his *Lauds:* 'True elevation is in heaven; earthly lowness leads to the soul's destruction.'" On this view, everything is good in its place; evil is merely displacement. But this solution to the problem does not represent Catherine's better thinking, for she recognized in self-determining creatures not only the varying degrees of goodness but also the capacity for self-making and self-marring. Indeed, nothing is more characteristic of her own experience than the continuous awareness of her own bad side, which must be fought with and subdued again and again. With the aid of God's grace one makes progress but never attains to perfection. Time and again she had thought her love was complete, but when she saw more clearly she was aware of great imperfections. "God-Love was determined to achieve the whole only little by little, for the sake of preserving my physical life, and so as to keep my behavior tolerable for those with whom I lived."

Catherine's doctrine of Last Things is closely connected with her teachings concerning Sin and Redemption. There is no break between our present life and our life after the body's death. While still in the flesh, the penitent soul experiences God's love as refining fire, even as souls in purgatory are cleansed of such stains as remain after death. Voluntary acceptance of the suffering necessarily attaching to the pleasure-seeking of the false self renders suffering wholesome. Impenitent souls are those who have so far unmade themselves as to be no longer capable of recognizing God's love. To these nothing remains but to endure the pain, although even in these there must remain a residue of moral goodness that cannot but mitigate what they have to bear. This is hell; and it is the same whether it be experienced here or hereafter.

Part three, titled "Critical," is a wide-ranging survey of scientific and philosophical opinions as they bear on religion in general and on mysticism in particular. There are interesting comparisons between Saint Catherine (canonized in 1737) and other mystics, most notably

Saint Teresa of Ávila; learned discussions of Pseudo-Dionysius and other Neoplatonists; and a sympathetic presentation of quietism (Madame Guyon) and the doctrine of pure love (Fénelon). Catherine's doctrines are discussed at length and compared not merely with received doctrines of the Church but also with the teachings of many of Hügel's contemporaries. Hügel saw no difficulty in reconciling mysticism and science, insisting that, as over against various schools of Idealism, it is a leading characteristic of Catholic teaching to insist on the full reality of the "determinist Thing" alongside the freedom of Spirit—a principle he finds illustrated in Catherine's karmalike doctrine of purgation.

As was mentioned in connection with part one, Hügel holds that there are three main elements of religion corresponding to three main forces of the soul. In his final summary he returns to these, arguing that although each of them is necessary to a true religion, any one of them divorced from the other two is destructive of itself and of religion. For example, institutionalism led to the Spanish Inquisition, rationalism to the Goddess of Reason being installed at Notre Dame of Paris, and emotionalism to the apocalyptic orgies of the Münster Anabaptists. Even where the imbalance does not reach these proportions, it leaves the church weak and divided, as in the parties of the Church of England: High, Broad, and Low Church.

Mysticism, which is one manifestation of the third or experimental element of religion, is as susceptible as the other elements of exaggeration and abuse. This is apparent when, as sometimes happens among followers of Pseudo-Dionysius, love of God is thought of as competing with love of God's creatures, and the inference is drawn that God is not loved until he is loved alone. But in contrast to exclusive mysticism of this kind there is an inclusive mysticism that places God not alongside his creatures but behind them "as the light which shines through a crystal and lends it whatever lustre it may have." This latter recognizes the necessity of diverse types of souls and finds in the kingdom of God the "means of an ever more distinct articulation, within an ever more fruitful interaction, of the various gifts, vocations, and types of souls which constitute its society." Among inclusive mystics, says Hügel, in spite of the uncertainty on many points of her life and of defects in her natural character and limited opportunity, the Saint of Genoa "shines forth . . . with a penetrating attractiveness, rarely matched, hardly surpassed, by Saints and Heroes of . . . more massive gifts and actions."

Jean H. Faurot

RECOMMENDED READING

Edition used: Hügel, Baron Friedrich von. *The Mystical Element of Religion.* 2 vols. London: Dent, 1908. Reprinted 1927.

Bedoyère, Michael de la. *The Life of Baron von Hügel.* London: Dent, 1951. A full-length biography including a full account of his role in the Modernist controversy as a friend and correspondent of Alfred Loisy and of George Tyrell.

Whelan, Joseph P. *The Spirituality of Friedrich von Hügel.* New York: Paulist Press, 1972. Von Hügel's teachings concerning Christ, God, and the Church as they help to illuminate the problem of sanctity in the modern world.

MYSTICISM

Author: Evelyn Underhill (1875–1941)

British mystic, writer, and retreat leader, Evelyn Underhill was born into a middle-class family in which there was no particular emphasis on religion. But even in her early writings she showed an absorption in the imagery and sense of the Christian spirit. After a visit to a convent in 1907 she was converted and although at first inclined to join the Roman Catholic church, she remained with the Church of England and became fully committed in 1921. In her work she emphasized the importance of worship, the course and spirit of Western mysticism, pacifism, the ministry of spiritual direction, and spiritual retreats.

Type and subject of work: Historical and analytical account of the mystical spiritual life

First published: 1911

MAJOR THEMES

The mystical life develops through five distinct stages:

1. Awakening, in which one makes a commitment to seek God with all of the heart;

2. Purgation, in which one, realizing one's own finitude and imperfections, seeks to become detached from all sensible things through discipline and mortification;

3. Illumination, in which God gives the soul various "consolations" as encouragement—voices, visions, trances;

4. The Dark Night of the Soul, in which all sense of God's presence vanishes, and the mystic must struggle on toward the goal of faith;

5. Union, in which the soul is united with God.

The heart of Evelyn Underhill's *Mysticism* is her extensive analysis of the highest examples of the spiritual life, primarily the great mystics of the Middle Ages. Her description of the mystical way has become normative.

She begins with the awakening of the self to a consciousness of Divine Reality. This experience, usually abrupt and well recognized, is accompanied by feelings of intense joy. She suggests that it is an intense form of "conversion" or "sanctification." It is usually a crisis experience. She cites the example of Francis of Assisi, who went into the church of San Damiano to pray and, "having been smitten by unwonted visitations, found himself another man than he who had gone in." Some people like George Fox, founder of the Quakers, however, have a more gradual experience. In awakening, the person surrenders totally to God, and a passionate love for God, for the Absolute, is born.

As Underhill says, "the business and method of Mysticism is Love." According to "An Epistle of Discretion," probably by the same anonymous author as *The Cloud of Unknowing*, God "may not be known by reason, [God] may not be gotten by thought, nor concluded by understanding; but [God] may be loved and chosen with the true lovely will of thine heart." Or as John of Ruysbroeck put it, "where intelligence must rest without, love and desire can enter in."

The process of purification, purgation, begins. The soul, meeting God, realizes its sinfulness, its willfulness. Catherine of Genoa's first response to her vision of God's unmeasured love was "No more world! no more sin!" The first steps are contrition and repentance. According to Richard of Saint Victor, though, the "essence of purgation is self-simplification."

The perpetual process of purification has both negative and positive sides. The first is detachment, the stripping away or purging of all that is superfluous, illusionary, or distracting. It is the essence of the "evangelical counsels": poverty, chastity, and obedience. Many, though not all, of the great mystics have been members of religious orders or have adopted monastic practices, at least during this period of their lives. Underhill defines poverty as "a breaking down of [humanity's] inveterate habit of trying to rest in, or take seriously, things which are 'less than God': *i.e.*, which do not possess the character of reality."

The more positive or active side is mortification, the changing of one's character, the forming of new habits. It is a dying and finding new life. According to John Tauler, "this dying has many degrees, and so has this life. A man might die a thousand deaths in one day and find at once a joyful life corresponding to each of them." Asceticism for the mystics is a means to an end, not an end in itself. Henry Suso practiced extreme mortification for sixteen years, and then "on a certain Whitsun Day a heavenly messenger appeared to him, and ordered him in God's name to continue no more." So he ceased at once "and threw all the instruments of his sufferings ... into a river." Catherine of Genoa went through a penitential period of four years, constantly haunted by a sense of sin, and then in an instant it seemed as though her sins were cast into the sea and she was free. In modern terms, their attitude toward spiritual disciplines was simply "No pain, no gain." Their goal was freedom from the world, freedom from self-will.

Interspersed with purgation is illumination, God's revelations of the divine. Some called it *Ludus Amoris*, the game of love that God plays with the seeking soul. The mystic is consoled by glimpses of the Divine Reality. Though a sense of self remains, and thus a distance from God, the soul is treated to moments of transcendence, rapture, ecstasy. Some experience a total oneness with nature. Others hear voices or celestial music, see visions, feel heat or stabbing joy, write automatically. This is not the unitive state because the self remains separate and intact and the moments of illumination are measured.

This state is not to be sought for its ecstasies or clutched as though it could be selfishly preserved. Underhill is careful to note that true mystics seek God alone, and not spiritual thrills. She criticizes Madame Guyon as "basking like a pious tabby cat in the beams of the Uncreated Light." The purpose of illumination is to call the soul onward in its quest. Quoting Ruysbroeck: "Here there begins an eternal hunger, which shall never more be satisfied. It is the inward craving and hankering of the affective power and created spirit after an Uncreated Good."

The pious soul is now tuned to recollection, quiet, and contemplation, topics to which Underhill devotes several chapters. This is the mystic's education of the faculty of concentration, the power of spiritual attention. This is where the mystic ascends the ladder toward heaven, practices "degrees of prayer." This is not petition but the yearning of the soul for God. Recollection begins in meditation and develops into interior silence or simplicity. This melts into true Quiet. This deepens into ordinary contemplation and then into the contemplation proper, which is passive union with God. The "personality is not lost: only its hard edge is gone," says Underhill.

However, as the mystic travels toward union, he or she must cross the desert, that period of blankness and stagnation known as the Dark Night of the Soul, so named by John of the Cross. All consolations are withdrawn. Often the person is assailed by slanders and trials without, doubts and temptations within. It is the final purgation of selfhood, "self-naughting." The aspiring soul must struggle on, usually on the basis of naked faith and sheer will. All sense of God's presence is gone. A sense of one's hopeless and helpless imperfection weighs heavily, and there is complete emotional exhaustion, spiritual aridity. Sometimes death seems preferable to struggle. The goal is total surrender and utter humility. Those who persevere may obtain union with God, the unitive life. Underhill underscores the "may" because it is a gift from God's grace, not the result of a person's work or willing. The mystics teach that the lessons of the way are just as valuable as the attainment; thus the soul who strives and does not attain union is also blessed.

Union is often described under the metaphor of spiritual marriage between the soul and God. Richard of Saint Victor described the result: "When the soul is plunged in the fire of divine love, like iron, it first loses its blackness, and then growing to white heat, it becomes like unto the fires itself. And lastly, it grows liquid, and losing its nature is transmuted into an utterly different quality of being."

The result is not passive exaltation but energetic action. Joan of Arc led the armies of France. Catherine of Genoa administered hospitals; Catherine of Siena became a peacemaker between warring states; Teresa of Ávila reformed her order. Francis of Assisi became God's troubadour. Many mystics wrote of their insights and counseled those in need of spiritual nurture. They led productive lives of balanced wholeness.

Underhill begins *Mysticism* with a discussion of the philosophical basis for mysticism, an understanding of the universe as constituted on two levels: that of the physical senses and that of the spiritual realm. She does not analyze nor critique at any length, however, the Neoplatonism on which most understandings of mysticism have been based. Her interest is more psychological than philosophical or theological.

In looking at the psychological aspects of the mystical life, Underhill notes with the author of *The Cloud of Unknowing* that "By love [God] may be gotten and holden, but by thought of understanding, never." Throughout she stresses the psychological maturity and balance that has characterized the great mystics.

One of the most attractive features of the book is an appendix that gives the history of mysticism in outline form, citing all the great mystics, their dates, relationships to each other, and their principal ideas. The high points of mysticism were in the eleventh and fourteenth centuries. A bibliography follows with a listing of the major works by each mystic of note. Another feature of this book that appeals to the student is the outline at the beginning of each chapter. These allow the reader to follow the continuity of Underhill's argument and then to read more deeply in the sections with special appeal or to find parts one has previously read. Since this is a rather massive book, the help is welcome.

Underhill amplified her ideas in a number of other books, namely

The Mystic Way (1913), *Practical Mysticism* (1915), *The Essentials of Mysticism* (1920), *The Life of the Spirit and Life of Today* (1922), and *Man and the Supernatural* (1927). Examples of her spiritual guidance given to retreat participants are found in *Concerning the Inner Light* (1926), *The Golden Sequence* (1933), and *The Mystery of Sacrifice* (1933). Her other major work was *Worship* (1938).

Nancy A. Hardesty

RECOMMENDED READING

Edition used: Underhill, Evelyn. *Mysticism.* New York: Dutton, 1961.

Cropper, Margaret. *Life of Evelyn Underhill.* New York: Harper & Bros., 1958. An absorbing spiritual biography.

Williams, Charles, ed. *The Letters of Evelyn Underhill.* London: Longmans, Green & Co., 1943. Underhill's letters reveal the pervasiveness of her spiritual preoccupations.

THE POEMS OF
GERARD MANLEY HOPKINS

Author: Gerard Manley Hopkins (1844–1889)

The eldest of nine children of a well-to-do middle-class family, Hopkins proved to be an outstanding student. He alienated family and friends, however, when he converted from Anglicanism to Catholicism under John Henry Cardinal Newman. He joined the Society of Jesus in 1868 and became a priest nine years later. He served in several slum parishes before becoming a classics professor in Dublin. He studied music and painting and wrote poetry, almost none of which was published until several decades after his death. He shared his verse with his poet-friend Robert Bridges through a correspondence of many years. A breakdown shortly before his death may have resulted from the tension in his life, which he considered nearly unresolvable, between his wanting to be a poet and his striving for sanctity.

Type and subject of work: Spiritually expressive poetry

First published: 1918

MAJOR THEMES

The world is filled with the grandeur of God.

All reality is interconnected: God, humanity, and the universe are inseparable.

Each person and each object in the world is unique and glorifies God in its uniqueness.

The revelation of individual uniqueness is found in the energy that each people or object emits.

To understand Hopkins's poetry, the reader must know something of his poetic theory. His three main concepts are found in the terms *inscape, instress,* and *sprung rhythm.* The first two terms are closely related. By *instress,* a term that Hopkins coined, is meant the principle of physical uniqueness that an object (natural or artistic) has that distinguishes it from all else that is, was, or shall be. It has its basis in the term *haecceitas,* as used by the Catholic philosopher Duns Scotus (d. 1308), which is sometimes translated as "thisness." *Inscape* may be defined as the outward manifestation of the interior integrity of a thing.

Instress is described in terms of energy: the force by which inscape is revealed. Instress is that which acts on the mind of the beholder in such a way as to allow the beholder to comprehend the inscape. It is, as Hopkins himself wrote, the energy by which "all things are upheld."

Sprung rhythm is another term invented by the Jesuit. It is a difficult concept that commentators have tried to make comprehensible, not always with success. Sprung (or abrupt) rhythm is measured by feet of one to four syllables in length, regularly, although for certain effects any number of unstressed syllables may be used. If there is but one syllable, it receives the stress. If there are more syllables, the stress is on the first and different sorts of feet will result. There are four possibilities: a monosyllable, accentual trochee, dactyl, and first paeon. In this respect, sprung rhythm differs from running rhythm because sprung rhythm may use rests, monosyllabic feet, and the first paeon, whereas running rhythm, if it is scanned from the first stress in a line, can be made up only of trochees and dactyls. "Sprung rhythm" is meant by Hopkins to convey emotionally charged speech.

Perhaps Hopkins's best use of sprung rhythm may be found in his famed sonnet, "The Windhover." The poem, named after a small hawk, a kestrel, known for hovering in the wind, is subtitled "To Christ Our Lord" to emphasize its religious orientation. It is set in the morning, when the narrator first sights the bird. Hopkins names the winged creature by the more aristocratic term (which he significantly capitalizes), *Falcon* and calls it "daylight's dauphin" to stress its royalty. The creature circles in air and when it seems to come into conflict with the wind in a kind of crisis, the bird experiences ecstasy in a movement resembling a skater's figure eight, a movement combining hurl and glide. The bird's control enables it to overcome the wind's force, intelligence defeating physicality, as it were. And this skill excites the narrator: "My heart in hiding / Stirred for a bird,—the achieve of, the mastery of the thing!" The triumph over the blind force of nature is exhilarating.

Thus the first eight lines of this sonnet come to a close. In the sestet, Hopkins summarizes the hawk's attributes—its beauty, courage, and energy—all of which "buckle," a deliberately ambiguous term suggesting both a collapse (or submission) and a fastening together. The poem closes with an acknowledgement of the almost dangerous beauty of the bird that, in its violence, may reflect the ambiguity of the crucifixion —violence culminating in salvation.

"The Windhover" exemplifies much that is in Hopkins's work. The bird is one of his favorite images taken from nature. The hawk gives glory to God by being fully itself, but in the poem the image also suggests Christ as well as one who would use Christ as a model for life, probably the narrator of the poem. The bird is a Christlike image of self-sacrifice and in being true to itself is shown as part of the great unity of the cosmos. Everything is connected with everything, and the incorporating energy for this is signified in the concept of inscape, which reconciles the individuated creature with the rest of the universe.

Theologically, for this priest, that is what Christ does for all. Other aspects of the Victorian's religious beliefs are found in his longest poem, based on a historical ship-sinking, "The Wreck of the Deutschland." The transport went down with five Franciscan nuns among the victims. The work is in thirty-five stanzas which are divided into four sections. The first ten stanzas make up part one and feature the poet's ideas on the nature of God and on humanity's need to worship him. Much of Hopkins's approach is influenced by his understanding of *The Spiritual Exercises* (1548) of Ignatius Loyola, the founder of the Jesuit order. The prime motivation of Ignatius's volume could be summarized thusly: The glory of God brings forth a reverence in his creatures, and Christ's love, seen through the Redemption, instills in our hearts the unselfish service of the Second Person of the divine Trinity.

As the poem proceeds, the poet describes the ship as leaving port and then getting into trouble. He also renders the situation of various people on board. Hopkins portrays a journey from haven to heaven (the final haven) since humanity's shipwreck in this earthly existence is inevitable. One of the nuns stands out, being very tall, and our attention is drawn to her and to her act of faith. And in a typically Hopkinslike gesture, he personalizes the poem: "Sister, a sister calling / A master, her master and mine!—" He then remarks on the need we have to offer ourselves in sacrifice as Christ did. The nun knows intuitively what the poet has uncovered through reflection, that life is a trial, a period of purgation. We must be prepared to succeed by failure.

The last four stanzas emphasize submission to God, praise of the Father with a request to the tall nun to intercede for us with God. "Let him easter in us . . . " It is thus a poem about death, ending on a note of triumph with the promise of resurrection. God's mastery and mercy are woven themes in this poem as they are in the Ignatian *Spiritual Exercises.* Elements found in "The Wreck of the Deutschland" that are evident in much of Hopkins's verse include the use of alliteration, the repetition of words and ideas, the juxtaposition of terms of seemingly mutual exclusion ("wild-worst / Best"), the use of unusual words ("thew," "voe"), and the hyphenated or compound creations ("the dappled-with-damson west," "Eastnortheast").

"Pied Beauty" is one of the Englishman's shorter efforts and also indicates an Ignatian influence. It begins with a recognition of God's glory and ends with the simple charge: "Praise him." The motto of the Jesuit order, as formulated by its founder, is *"Ad majorem Dei Gloriam"* (To the greater glory of God) and there is another Jesuit motto, "Laus Deo semper" (Praise be to God always). The poet expresses joy in all of creation, the colorful skies, fish, wind-falls from chestnut trees, birds, the work of man, life in nature. The only authentic reaction to all of this awesome being is "Praise him."

It should not be thought, however, that Hopkins wrote from a spiritually comfortable soul. His poetry often exhibited the tension he experienced between his religious faith and his poetic skills. His work reflects pain and joy, excitement and agonized interpretation. The poet experimented in how exactly to present his thoughts and moods, frequently having to invent new words, unique verbal combinations, and hyphenations and to revive words long out of use. Influenced by both Welsh and medieval verse traditions, Hopkins was determined to render meaning and feeling through his highly personalized view of poetic language.

The music of his poems was developed through use of alliteration, internal rhyme, and repeated syllables as well as words. The first two lines of "The Windhover" illustrate this:

I caught this morning morning's minion, king-
   dom of daylight's dauphin, dapple-dawn-drawn Falcon, in his
      riding

It has been noted by critics that the arrangement of Hopkins's words is not based on that of ordinary speech but is rather for the effect of communicating meaning and tone. This tends to give a high energy level to his poetry when read aloud. It has further been said that the priest's interest in painting contributes to his concern for beauty and the form that establishes it. This is reinforced by his attraction to John Duns Scotus's philosophy with its emphasis on the uniqueness of each individual person and object. It is not difficult, then, to see how Hopkins came to develop his theories of inscape and instress.

One can readily observe that many of Hopkins's poems deal with his response to nature and the relationship of God, human beings, and the universe (a relationship that the contemporary Spanish-Indian Catholic theologian and philosopher Raimundo Panikkar was to call "cosmo-theandrism"). But Hopkins's approach did not always demonstrate a full confidence in his spirituality, and some of his poems seem to indicate a tortured doubt and a relentless harshness, particularly in a later group of poems known as the "terrible" sonnets.

One such composition contains a near-despairing question of God, who is addressed almost formally as "sir." "Why do sinners' ways prosper? and why must Disappointment all I endeavour end?" The narrator of the poem goes further to wonder aloud how, if God were his enemy rather than his friend, life would be any worse than it now is.

A poem of far greater hope and one that is among the most critically appreciated of Hopkins's productions is titled "The Leaden Echo and the Golden Echo." The first part, "The Leaden Echo," develops the echo theme (not surprisingly, through repetition of sound as well as of sentiment) to illustrate the fear of mortality. Nothing can be done to keep aging at bay is the lament, and this section ends with "to despair, to despair, / Despair, despair, despair, despair." But "The Golden Echo" segment beings with a saving word that echoes partially the awesome sounds preceding: "Spare!" Here is a long stanza of resurrection, salvation, and hope. The poem ends thus: "Yonder, yes yonder, yonder, / Yonder." This indicates direction and is clearly contrary to the close of the initial stanza. The golden echo may be seen to be, in fact, not an echo at all but something original—perhaps as Christ is to Adam.

This leads us back to a consideration of another of the "terrible" sonnets, which editors have labeled "Carrion Comfort." Here, the priest personifies despair in his opening line. In the face of the temptation to cry "*I can no more*" the persona makes the absolute assertion, "I can!" If nothing else, he insists, he can "not choose not to be," which contains its own echo—of Hamlet's famed soliloquy. So after addressing the personified Despair, the narrator turns to speak to Christ who, initially at least, is terrifying to him. There is a questioning here of the rude treatment God gives his creature, but then the comparison is made to John the Baptist's preaching where a wind will winnow the wheat, leaving the chaff for the unquenchable fire.

The sestet of this sonnet begins most economically, by summarizing what went before in one word: "Why?" This is answered immediately, directly: "That my chaff might fly; my grain lie, sheer and clear." But it is more complicated than that, the complexity being introduced by the very next word, "Nay." Not only is the speaker purified but he is strengthened by accepting God's chastisement. He kisses not only the rod of correction but the hand of God holding it. But whom, then, is he to cheer? Should he cheer Christ or himself who fought Christ? The suggestion may be that the struggle itself, the "wrestling with- (my God!) my God," is a purificatory act. Certainly the titanic mental struggle with the ultimately awesome adversary is not an action of the lukewarm, the kind of person who will be spewed forth on Judgment Day.

Critics have found that Hopkins, while living in the era of Victorian literature in England, is a very contemporary poet today. One critic has noted that Hopkins led poetry forward by taking it back to its primal linguistic beginnings. His verbal daring is celebrated now as going far beyond what any other nineteenth-century writer of English verse came close to attempting. His poetry is seen as offering a kind of meeting place for orthodox Catholic theology and secular poetry—an inestimable feat, perhaps on the level of achievement in verse of a Teilhard de Chardin in science.

It is arguable how much symbolism Hopkins employs. There are certain readers who claim he uses almost none at all, while others seem to make penetrating analyses of his symbolism. Echoes of Shakespeare appear throughout Hopkins's work although his original use of such materials is stunning. The work of the Jesuit is clearly self-conscious; he appears continually to be asking questions such as "Who am I?" "What is the world?" "What is my place in the world?"

In spite of all of his inventiveness, Hopkins may have entrapped himself in forms; this is possibly why his later poems seem to lose the energy apparent in earlier ones. Personal illness may have contributed to a certain decline as well. One writer has considered Hopkins as self-victimized in a symbol of his own making, that of a restricted bird. His poem "The Caged Skylark" may be read as one of hope but it may also be seen as one that laments humanity's limitations, in spite of an apparently triumphant conclusion. Christianity is a religion of constant struggle for Hopkins, and his poetry clearly reflects his ongoing attempt to discover meaning in that struggle.

Harry James Cargas

RECOMMENDED READING

Edition used: Hopkins, Gerard Manley. *Poems and Prose of Gerard Manley Hopkins.* Edited by W. H. Gardner. Baltimore: Penguin Books, 1956.

Cutter, James Finn. *Inscape.* Pittsburgh: University of Pittsburgh Press, 1973. Here is the best insight into the Christology and poetry of Hopkins.

Hopkins, Gerard Manley. *Letters of Gerard Manley Hopkins to Robert Bridges.* Edited by Claude Colleer Abbott. Oxford: Oxford University Press, 1955. Here is revealed much about Hopkins's poetic theory as well as underlying themes of his verse.

Pick, John. *A Hopkins Reader.* New York: Doubleday, 1966. Contains all of the Jesuit's major poems, journal extracts, and letters on a wide variety of topics, including poetic theory, criticism, and religion.

ST. FRANCIS OF ASSISI

Author: G(ilbert) K(eith) Chesterton (1874–1936)
A dominant figure in English letters during the first third of the twentieth century, Chesterton was known as a champion of the common man. He was born in London on May 29, 1874, and died in Beaconsfield, England, on June 14, 1936. He wrote prolifically—novels, short stories, biographies, literary criticism, religious and philosophical argumentation, economic and political writings, social commentary, detective stories, humorous pieces, plays, and poetry. His near-universal appeal was the result of his great range of interests, incisive wit, and egalitarian vision.

Type and subject of work: A spiritual biography

First published: 1924

MAJOR THEMES

Francis of Assisi, a pampered youth, a romantic ringleader, imbued with military ambition, was transformed by a shocking experience into a "fool for God."

Francis found the secret of life in loving God, in being a servant for others, in becoming the humble "little poor man of Assisi," and in acting out the gospel truths.

For his age and for those to come, Saint Francis became the mirror of Christ.

In this biography of Saint Francis, G. K. Chesterton rekindles for the reader a sense of the early medieval spirit, with its childlike faith, its chivalry, its ethos of fraternity and fair play. He puts himself in the position of the "ordinary modern outsider . . . approaching the great Saint's story through what is . . . picturesque and popular," seeking to understand the human and spiritual dimensions of Francis Bernardone, "who walked the world like the pardon of God."

Writing especially to the skeptics of his own day, the "modern rationalists" who saw religion as only a detached and impersonal philosophy, Chesterton lays bare the personal passion and beauty of a soul submitted in most intimate relationship to God. He explores the seeming paradoxes of Saint Francis: how the joyous poet who sang so eloquently to his Brother Sun could also hide himself like an ascetic in a dark cave; how the saint who was so gentle with friends and animals could be so harsh to his own body; how the troubadour who claimed that love set his heart aflame could so easily withdraw himself from women. And Chesterton concludes that the key to seeking Francis's life as a consistent whole is his love affair with God. A man will hardly go without food in the name of some abstract righteousness; nor will he be lost in prayer for hours on end in relation to an inert consciousness.

The indulged and pampered son of a status-seeking cloth merchant, Francis was the romantic ringleader among the young men of his town. He spent his father's money extravagantly on luxuries for himself and his friends but also in acts of mercy toward the poor. Imbued with romantic visions of military might, he was imprisoned for a year following a local battle and was later turned back from the crusades by sickness and a troubling vision. He returned to Assisi a dispirited, humiliated, and bewildered figure, seeking direction and meaning in life.

While riding in the fields outside the city walls of Assisi, during the aimless days of transition that followed the collapse of his military ambitions, Francis was filled with fear at the sight of a man coming up the road toward him—not the fear that comes from facing an enemy in battle, but the fear of a spirit that wanes helpless in the presence of disease and death. A leper stood before him, decayed and white. Francis's soul stood still. Then, suddenly released in inner freedom and joy, Francis sprang from his horse and threw his arms around the leper and kissed him.

Soon after, while praying before a crucifix in the Church of Saint Damian, Francis heard a voice saying to him, "Francis, seest thou not that my house is in ruins? Go and restore it for me." Again Francis sprang to action, selling his possessions, including several expensive bolts of cloth that he "borrowed" from his father, and physically beginning the rebuilding of the Church of Saint Damian. His father responded by treating his son as a common thief, and Francis hid himself underground in the blackness of a world that had caved in upon him.

In that dark cell, writes Chesterton, "It may be suspected that . . . Francis passed the blackest hours of his life." After his premature return from the crusades he was probably called a coward. After his quarrel with his father about the bolts of cloth he was certainly called a thief. Even those youthful companions who had benefited from his generosity derided him with humorous laughter. The conclusion was all too clear: By the world's standards he had made himself a fool. But in that black cave a turning took place. As he stared at the word *fool* written in luminous letters before him, the word itself began to shine and change so that "when Francis came forth from his cave of vision, he was wearing the same word 'fool' as a feather in his cap; as a crest or even a crown. He would go on being a fool; he would become more and more of a fool; he would be the court fool of the King of Paradise."

Called before the bishop's court, Francis was admonished and asked to return the money to his father. Francis responded: "Up to this time I have called Pietro Bernardone father, but now I am the servant of God. Not only the money, but everything that can be called his I will restore to my father, even the very clothes he has given me." Francis stripped himself of his clothes, laid them at his father's feet, and walked out into the world with nothing but a hair shirt. He was penniless, parentless, vocationless, but bursting with joy and song. The town of Assisi saw, that day, "a camel go in triumph through the eye of a needle" as Francis, in a passion for obedience, moved from belief, to adoration, to imitation of his beloved Lord Christ.

Francis pursued simplicity and poverty with as much enthusiasm as he had pursued battle. He devoured fasting as a hungry person devours food. He plunged after poverty as feverishly as a miner digs for gold. He wanted to be poor because Jesus was poor and because his beloved Master loved the poor. He felt blessed in having nothing because he was free to enjoy everything. Unimpressed by numbers, success, degrees, rank, prestige or status symbols, he chose weakness instead of strength, vulnerability instead of security, truth instead of practicality, honesty instead of influence. He turned the values of his day "holy topsy-turvey," not because this was fashionable, but because it seemed divine common sense. He discovered the pearl of great price, the treasure hidden in the field—the kingdom of God, God himself—the possession of which all other things were worth abandoning; and he held to this heroic, unnatural course from the moment he went forth in his hair shirt, a truly happy man.

Francis called those who followed after him—first the twelve, then hundreds, and finally thousands—"friars minor," which means little unimportant ones. He taught them to see things from the bottom, to accept willingly and joyfully ridicule and public insult, to be gentle and forgiving toward all people. Humility was not a virtue to be sought after, but a natural result of a heart overflowing with the worship of God and a profound respect for *every* creature God had made.

Chesterton presses the egalitarian theme of Saint Francis's life: "Whatever his taste in monsters, he never saw before him a many-headed beast. He only saw the image of God multiplied but never monotonous." What gave Francis his extraordinary appeal was the honor and respect he had for all people: "There was never a man who looked into those brown burning eyes without being certain that Francis was really interested in him," that he himself was being valued and taken seriously and not merely added to the spoils of some religious order. "For he treated the whole mob of men as a mob of kings."

Francis's desire was for his friars minor to live as nomads, mingling with the world without becoming entangled with the world. The bishop of Assisi, and many others, expressed horror at the hard life of the brothers—no comforts, no possessions, sleeping on the ground, eating what they could beg—but Francis's quick reply was that "If we had any possessions, we should need weapons and laws to defend them." He knew that the submissive man could go anywhere, even among the rich or powerful, as long as there was nothing to hold him. Francis wanted his friars to be salt that did not lose its taste and light that kept its power to illuminate, and so the friars were free from the cloister and free from the world. Like small and slippery fishes that could go in and out of the net of medieval culture, they were free; nothing could hold them because they had hold of nothing. Chesterton comments: "You could not threaten to starve a man who was ever striving to fast. You could not ruin him and reduce him to beggary, for he was already a beggar. There was a very lukewarm satisfaction even in beating him with a stick, when he only indulged in little leaps and cries of joy because indignity was his only dignity. You could not put his head in a halter without risk of putting it in a halo." The authority of Francis and his friars was not by force, but by persuasion; it was the authority of submissive servants, persuasive by impotence.

Chesterton sees Francis as a "dramatist capable of acting the whole of his own play." From the first act when he stripped off his clothes and flung them at his father's feet to the last scene when he stretched himself in death on the bare earth in the pattern of the cross, his life was an enacted parable, a dramatic expression of gospel freedom.

Chesterton succeeds in revealing the human and spiritual dimensions of Francis: the human figure bubbling over with the joy and humility that comes from a single-minded love for God; the spiritual life lived wholly and obediently in the power and spirit of the cross of Christ. For Francis the model was always Christ; not the thirteenth-century church, not the movement of renewal he founded, certainly not the prayerful humility others so admired in him—but Christ alone. Chesterton helps the reader see Christ vividly incarnate in the life of Saint Francis.

Douglas H. Gregg

RECOMMENDED READING

Edition used: Chesterton, G. K. *St. Francis of Assisi.* Garden City, N.Y.: Double-day, Image Books, 1957. First published 1924.

———. *The Everlasting Man.* Garden City, N.Y.: Doubleday, Image Books, 1955 (by arrangement with Dodd, Mead; original ed., 1925). Propounds the thesis that Jesus Christ—the incarnation of God, the everlasting man—is not to be compared with other religious figures or myths but stands absolutely unique in time and history.

———. *Orthodoxy.* Garden City, N.Y.: Doubleday, Image Books, 1959 (by arrangement with Dodd, Mead; original ed., 1908). A masterpiece of prose that reveals Chesterton's mature faith as he sets forth his contention that Christian orthodoxy is the only satisfactory answer to the meaning of the universe.

Englebert, Omer. *Saint Francis of Assisi: A Biography.* Abridged ed. Ann Arbor, Mich.: Servant Publications, 1979. Both an acclaimed work of scholarship and an inspiring spiritual classic.

Green, Julien. *God's Fool: The Life and Times of Francis of Assisi.* Translated by Peter Heinegg. San Francisco: Harper & Row, 1985. This biography of Saint Francis fuses solid historical research, literary elegance, and deep religious sensibility into a contemporary, easily accessible work.

Habig, Marion A., ed. *St. Francis of Assisi, Writings and Early Biographies: English Omnibus of the Sources for the Life of St. Francis.* Chicago: Franciscan Herald Press, 1973. The complete sourcebook, including authentic writings of Saint Francis, the earliest biographies by Thomas Celano (1228) and Bonaventura (1263), and other material, along with extensive introductions, historical notes, and bibliography.

Holl, Adolf. *The Last Christian.* Translated by Peter Heinegg. Garden City, N.Y.: Doubleday, 1980. Holl forcefully conveys the radical nature of Saint Francis's life and teaching, seeing him as the last Christian of the premodern world, who rejected the materialistic motivating thrusts behind the forces of progress in the centuries that followed.

OUT OF MY LIFE AND THOUGHT

Author: Albert Schweitzer (1875–1965)

Albert Schweitzer was born on January 14, 1875, in Kaysersberg, Upper Alsace, the son of Louis Schweitzer, an Evangelical pastor, and Adele (*née* Schillinger) Schweitzer. He began the study of the piano at the age of five and of the organ at eight. He studied philosophy and theology at the University of Strassburg and received the Ph.D. in philosophy in 1899 and the licentiate in theology in 1900. After serving as curate at Saint Nicholas in Strassburg and having subsequently been appointed principal of the theological seminary there, he decided on his thirtieth birthday to become a medical doctor and to devote his life to the service of natives in equatorial Africa. In 1912 he married Helene Bresslau, and in the following year he received his medical degree and established his hospital at the Lambaréné, Gabon station of the Paris Missionary Society. The remainder of his life (fifty-two years to follow) was spent in work at Lambaréné, in extensive writing, and in trips to Europe and the United States to present organ recitals and lectures. He played a major role in influencing sentiment against the testing and proliferation of nuclear weapons. Schweitzer received numerous honors and awards, including the Nobel Peace Prize in 1952. He died in Lambaréné on September 4, 1865.

Type and subject of work: Autobiography (to 1931) and review of his principal convictions

First published: *Aus meinem Leben und Denken,* 1931; *Out of My Life and Thought* (translated by C. T. Campion), 1933

MAJOR THEMES

The religion of love Jesus taught makes it clear that ethics is the essence of religion.

It is the destiny of Christianity to develop through a process of spiritualization made evident in the religion of love.

Christians must bring themselves into spiritual relation with the world and become one with it through active service out of a reverence for life.

Elemental thought that penetrates to the nature of things leads to a world- and life-affirmation that stems from an ethics based on the will-to-live and, accordingly, on a reverence for all life.

We experience God in our lives as the will-to-love.

Albert Schweitzer's autobiography is a spiritual autobiography in that it is both an account of spiritual progress and an expression of it. His book could very well have been entitled "Out of My Thought, My Life," for the thinking he calls "elemental" concerns itself with the fundamental conditions and opportunities of life and is itself an expression of the will-to-live. It is Schweitzer's thesis, exemplified in the course of his creative life of service, that elemental thought, in aiming at truth, effects a transition from the will-to-life to the will-to-love. His autobiography is an account spiritualized by just such a process—a course of fundamental thinking leading to the will-to-love and, accordingly, to a religion of love that proves itself in life-affirming service to others.

A gifted organist, philosopher, theologian, pastor, and writer, Schweitzer decided, at the age of thirty, to become a medical doctor and to devote his life to the service of natives of equatorial Africa. He had conceived the idea during his days as a student, and he reports that "It struck me as incomprehensible that I should be allowed to lead such a happy life, while I saw so many people around me wrestling with care and suffering." At Gunsbach in 1896, while on holiday away from the university at Strassburg, Schweitzer decided that he would be justified in living until he was thirty for science and art, and then to devote the remainder of his life to the "direct service of humanity." His decision to become a doctor and to serve in Africa was prompted in the autumn of 1904 by his reading an article on the needs of the Congo mission, published in a magazine of the Paris Missionary Society. A few months later, on his thirtieth birthday, January 14, 1905, he decided on equatorial Africa as his place of service and, despite the opposition of his friends and relatives, began planning to enter medical college. He persevered despite being told that he was throwing away his many talents in order to bury himself in the jungle. He writes that "it moved me strangely to see them [people who passed for Christians] so far from perceiving that the effort to serve the love preached by Jesus may sweep a man into a new course of life."

Schweitzer's account of his life experience (to 1931, when he still had thirty-four years to live) alternates reports of significant events in his life with reviews of his thoughts and commitments. It becomes apparent as one reads that the events of his life stimulated thought, thought gave rise to commitment, and commitment showed itself in action. The thesis he argues is proved in the life he led.

While at Strassburg studying philosophy and theology, Schweitzer undertook an inquiry that later assumed the title *The Quest of the Historical Jesus* (1906). Schweitzer's studies led him to the conclusion that Jesus accepted the late-Jewish Messianic worldview involving the imminent end of the world and the establishment of the kingdom of God. The idea that Jesus held views later shown to be false is repugnant to many Christians, Schweitzer points out, but he argues that the religion of love that Jesus taught need not be dependent upon the worldview in which it first appeared. Although we cannot accept the dogma involved in the late-Jewish Messianic expectation, Schweitzer writes, "the spirituality which lies in this religion of love must gradually, like a refiner's fire, seize upon all ideas which come into communication with it." And hence, he concludes, "it is the destiny of Christianity to develop through a constant process of spiritualization." The religion of love persists whatever the prevailing *Weltanschauung* of any particular period; the spiritual and ethical truth continues to be influential whatever temporal view may clothe it.

Schweitzer and his wife arrived in Lambaréné in the spring of 1913, and the construction of the jungle hospital began. The intensive medical work was interrupted the following year with the beginning of the war in Europe. The Schweitzers were interned at the Lambaréné mission-station, and on the second day of their internment Schweitzer began work on a problem that had occupied his mind for a number of years—the problem of civilization. The product of his labors was to be published under the title *The Philosophy of Civilization* but not until its completion in 1923, when the first two volumes were published.

Having called into question the common opinion that humankind naturally develops in the direction of progress, Schweitzer sought to resolve the problem of restoring civilization. Having realized that "the catastrophe of civilization started from a catastrophe of world-view," he explored the idea of civilization itself. His conclusion was that "the essential element in civilization is the ethical perfecting of the individual and of society as well," that the "will to civilization is . . . the universal will to progress which is conscious of the ethical as the highest value of all." The worldview that is required, then, is one that consists in an ethical affirmation of the world and life. What is needed is "an act of the spirit" whereby progress is understood to be internal, not external; spiritual, not material; life-and world-affirming, not negating.

What Schweitzer sought in order to complete his basic idea of the conditions of true civilization was a fundamental truth, an "elementary and universal conception of the ethical," that would enable the connection between a spiritual worldview and civilization to be realized. For months he grappled with the problem, but it was not until he was traveling upstream on the Ogowe river to visit the ailing wife of a missionary that he suddenly conceived the answer: "Late on the third day, at the very moment when, at sunset, we were making our way through a herd of hippopotamuses, there flashed upon my mind, unforeseen and unsought, the phrase 'Reverence for Life.'"

What is Reverence for Life? Schweitzer asks, and in response he suggests that we look away from the manifold, the product of thought and knowledge, and turn attention to the immediate fact of consciousness, the assertion, "I am life which wills to live, in the midst of life which wills to live." Life-affirmation, Schweitzer writes, is a "spiritual act" by which a person becomes devoted to life with reverence "in order to raise it to its true value."

A "thinking" being, Schweitzer insists, is one who gives to every life the same reverence given one's own. Thus, such a being "accepts as being good: to preserve life, to promote life, to raise to its highest value life which is capable of development; and as being evil: to destroy life, to injure life, to repress life which is capable of development." This principle, stemming from the will-to-live, is the fundamental principle of morality. "The Reverence for Life, therefore," Schweitzer concludes, ". . . contains world-and life-affirmation and the ethical fused together." The spiritual and ethical perfection of humanity becomes the highest ideal.

Schweitzer concludes that the solidarity with all life cannot completely be brought about, for each human being "is subject to the puzzling and horrible law of being obliged to live at the cost of other life, and to incur again and again the guilt of destroying and injuring life." But the thinking, ethical being, Schweitzer adds, "strives to escape whenever possible from this necessity."

The discovery of and commitment to the reverence for life enabled Schweitzer to complete the first two volumes of his *Philosophy of Civilization: The Decay and Restoration of Civilization* and *Civilization and Ethics*, both published in 1923. Schweitzer bemoaned the modern renunciation of thinking. Elemental thinking shows that the will to truth must involve the will to sincerity, and the will to sincerity and truth leads to the reverence for life, which contains within itself resignation (one sees the world as it is, with all its suffering), world-and life-affirmation (one thinks through to a solidarity with other wills-to-live), and the ethical (the call for action issued by love).

Schweitzer describes the worldview that involves reverence for life as an "ethical mysticism." He contends that rational thinking, "if it goes deep, ends of necessity in the non-rational of mysticism." The essential element in Christianity, then, as preached by Jesus, is that "it is only through love that we can attain to communion with God. All living knowledge of God rests upon this foundation: that we experience Him in our lives as Will-to-Love."

Ian P. McGreal

RECOMMENDED READING

Edition used: Schweitzer, Albert. *Out of My Life and Thought: An Autobiography.* Translated by C.T. Campion. New York: Henry Holt & Co., 1933.

Cousins, Norman. *Albert Schweitzer's Mission: Healing and Peace.* New York and London: Norton, 1985. Part 1 is an adaptation of Cousins's *Dr. Schweitzer of Lambaréné* (1960) and provides a sensitive and sympathetic portrait based on a visit Cousins made to the jungle hospital; part 2 contains previously unpublished correspondence involving Schweitzer, Nehru, Eisenhower, Krushchev, Kennedy, and Cousins, and centers about Schweitzer's effort to awaken world consciousness to the catastrophic dangers of nuclear war.

Joy, Charles R., ed. *Albert Schweitzer: An Anthology.* Boston: Beacon Press, 1947; enlarged ed., 1956. Joy has edited an excellent and moving anthology drawn from Schweitzer's most effective writings. It includes a chronological summary of Schweitzer's life (to 1956) and a bibliography.

Schweitzer, Albert. *Civilization and Ethics.* Part 2 of *The Philosophy of Civilization.* Translated by C. T. Campion. New York: Macmillan, 1929. The central spiritual and ethical philosophy is here developed at length.

———. *On the Edge of the Primeval Forest.* Published with *The Forest Hospital at Lambaréné* in 1 vol. Translated by C. T. Campion. New York: Macmillan, 1948. Schweitzer's African reminiscences, dealing in part with the problems of colonization among primitive peoples.

———. *The Quest of the Historical Jesus: A Critical Study of Its Progress from Reimarus to Wrede.* Translated by W. Montgomery. New York: Macmillan, 1945. Insisting on Jesus' messianic worldview, Schweitzer calls attention to his religion of love.

THE ESSENCE
OF SPIRITUAL RELIGION

Author: D. Elton Trueblood (1900–
A Quaker teacher, minister, and author, David Elton Trueblood has been
on the faculty of Earlham College in Indiana since 1946, and currently
holds the title "Professor at Large." His thirty-two books, ranging in
subject from philosophy of religion to family life, attempt to encourage
and guide the seeker in developing a Christian faith that has both religious vitality and intellectual respectability. In 1970, Trueblood founded Yokefellows International, an interdenominational organization of
committed Christians, through which he continues to influence worldwide Christian activities.

Type and subject of work: Apologetic writing intended to describe for
modern people a type of religion to which they can commit themselves

First Published: 1936

MAJOR THEMES

*Underlying the diversity of religious forms is a unified core that could be
called spiritual religion.*

*Spiritual religion is based upon personal experience of the One who sustains
our highest ideals, and is nourished by a mood of worship.*

*The greatest teacher of spiritual religion is Jesus Christ, but those who fully
enter into his teaching discover him to be more than a teacher; he is "Lord and
Master" as well.*

In its highest expression, spiritual religion involves a sacramental view of life, an openness to continual revelation, a recognition of a universal call to ministry, and action in accordance with a belief in the sacredness of human life.

Although religious expression has exhibited a striking diversity, D. Elton Trueblood finds even more impressive a unity underlying the multitude of external forms. Within divergent traditions, persons possessing the deepest insights have displayed a remarkable kinship with one another. Their religious experience takes us to the heart of each tradition, revealing a kind of inner core or essence that contains the highest and best features of religion. Trueblood describes this inner core as "spiritual" religion, in contrast to the ceremonial, creedal, and other external forms distinguishing various sects. These formal aspects of religion vary greatly in value, some being positively harmful, but if we can peel away the surface, we will discover "the genuine religion of the spirit which has existed in all generations." Trueblood's book is an attempt to describe and commend this spiritual religion to his readers.

Before discussing in detail his conception of spiritual religion, Trueblood attempts to develop an understanding of the place of religion in human life. He begins with the observation that our aspirations go beyond the satisfaction of physical needs. We crave beauty and harmony, and we strive to attain moral ideals. These aspirations are either an odd fact about human nature, or they are indications of something that is "rooted in the very nature of things." Within human nature is a strong desire to believe the latter. In particular, many desire to believe in "a Power which sustains us in our finest efforts and aids us in our allegiance to ideal ends." Beyond this desire is the experiential claim made by some of a fellowship with the One who cares about the things that matter most to us. Those who have had this kind of experience think of it as the most important thing in their lives. Religion, then, on Trueblood's account, is the result of "the human desire to believe in a Sustainer of our ideals and the human experience of knowing the Sustainer."

On the foundation of desire and experience, claims Trueblood, a structure of belief is built. Religion is not merely belief, but belief is a crucial feature of religious expression. What a person believes about the nature of things will shape the way that person lives. While beliefs are always inadequate vehicles to give expression to the depths of religious experience, it would be a mistake to try to get along without them. Between the horns of dogmatic narrowness and a tolerance that borders on indifference, we must seek a way that includes both concern for sound belief and a spirit of loving acceptance. Trueblood finds the appropriate attitude to be "critical tolerance." We can allow others the freedom to think differently while still holding to our convictions. This is possible in part because we humbly recognize our limitations and the mysterious complexity of God's ways. For Trueblood, belief is the outer shell, not the inner substance, but genuine spiritual religion requires the best outer shell we can find.

While religion is a universal phenomenon, it does not arise in abstract generality, but rather in particular embodiments. For the Western world, the most important of these is Christianity. The central figure in Christianity, Jesus Christ, is held in "almost universal esteem." Given the prevalence of confused and even false objects of admiration, Trueblood finds it remarkable that there should be so much agreement in assessments of Jesus. Trueblood sees Jesus as a supreme illustration of "spiritual inwardness." The religion of Jesus is primarily a matter of "worshipping God and being like Him, that is, completely and powerfully loving." Jesus opposed the degeneration of religion into excessive concern with externals, fighting against ceremonialism, creedalism, and legalism. Correctness of doctrine or ceremony or outward act is no substitute for a heart that is right with God.

Ironically, Christianity furnishes many examples of the very things Jesus opposed, Trueblood concedes. Nevertheless, he points out that many have concluded that when Christianity is true to its source, it is "superior to any other religion," and that Jesus is a "unique fact in the world." The portrait of him in the Gospels is irresistibly attractive, and many have found that their own experience of spiritual inwardness is nourished not only by attention to what he taught, but by an awareness of the teacher. Jesus comes to be experienced as more than the one who brought a message of spiritual religion; he is found to be "Lord and Master."

Trueblood argues that if our religion is to be mature, we must develop an understanding of God that moves beyond thinking in magical terms of a being subject to our manipulation or in material terms of a localized being with some physical embodiment. God is to be conceived as entirely spiritual. We know ourselves to be something more than our bodies, and when we think about the deepest reality we should realize that here is a "Principle, Power, or Person who differs from matter as we differ from matter." The reality that we are best acquainted with in our own case becomes the key for interpreting the basic nature of things. We must of course recognize the significant differences between our awareness of ourselves as spiritual beings and our thought about God. God is not conditioned or limited as we are. Nevertheless, Trueblood contends that our own experience of love and fellowship with one another gives us a clue as to what the nature of divine love, freed from all limitations, is like.

Genuine spiritual religion requires the confidence that God is concerned with the welfare of each person. To abandon a childlike faith in God's providence is to abandon the core of any vital religious experience. The primary obstacle to maintaining a belief in providence is the fact of undeserved suffering. While no one has a complete explanation for how recognition of such suffering can be reconciled with belief in God's loving concern, Trueblood claims that the basic religious attitude is contained in the book of Job. It is that "we are too small to understand, and God is working at something bigger than we can appreciate." If we are right in thinking that our moral and religious experiences provide the surest keys to unlock our understanding of the nature of things, the appropriate attitude in the face of unexplained evil is one of childlike trust.

To be conscious of our own nature, says Trueblood, is to be aware of the spiritual realm. Such awareness has produced the conviction of the great religious pioneers that there is something of God in each of us, an insight necessary for spiritual religion. Unless we are spiritual beings, we cannot expect to "commune with a God who is Spirit." It might seem that the claim that we are somehow akin to God smacks both of egoism and anthropomorphism, but the alternative would be a refusal to "interpret the world in terms of the highest we know." A central conviction of spiritual religion is that the division between spirit and that which is not spirit is "the most significant chasm in the universe." Human beings find themselves on both sides of this chasm, and that is the source of both our glory and our shame.

Trueblood conceives of sin as a kind of contradiction within the inner life. We find ourselves holding high ideals and aspirations, yet deliberately going against them. To find salvation, he believes, is to be enabled to embrace genuinely that which one holds to be best. The opposite of salvation is waste, the kind of waste that results from fighting against our own growth and development. Paradoxically, though, we cannot be saved by concentrating on our own development. Individual striving is self-defeating because concern with our own state can be a form of selfishness that blocks our progress. Only by "giving ourselves away" in an act of trust exercised absolutely and unconditionally can we find salvation. Salvation is given to us from outside ourselves, but it is not given until we surrender ourselves. For Trueblood, salvation through Christ means that "the Person we meet in the Gospels is the one who stirs us to the act of trust and loyalty on which salvation rests." Many have testified to finding within themselves something of the *"very same* reality that was manifested in Jesus." Trueblood interprets this as the experience of the living Christ.

Genuine experiences of God lead to worship. While worship may sometimes be enhanced by particular acts or words, it should not be identified with observable behavior nor limited to specifically "religious" situations. Trueblood characterizes worship as a mood that involves the whole person. Neither merely an intellectual nor an emotional response, the experience of worship combines the diverse moods of awe and childlike trust. These moods pull us in opposite directions, an awe-inspiring awareness of God's majesty creating a sense of our own insignificance, and a confidence in God's loving care calling forth a sense of our value. Paradoxically, the result is a profound yet mysterious experience.

While the experience of worship cannot be forced or demanded, church services are arranged to facilitate worship. Trueblood writes that "great music, harmoniously constructed buildings, ancient words" may help to put us in a state where worship is possible. True to his Quaker roots, however, he also stresses the role of silence in worship. He sees silence as the typical response to genuinely ennobling experiences, in contrast to the usual noise and haste of our lives.

Although individual worship is possible, Trueblood sees worship at its best as a group experience in which we participate together, each person a contributor to the total mood. The appropriate attitude to take toward worship is one of expectancy and wonder, "realizing that a creative venture" is about to begin and that the result is "quite unpredictable." But worship is not to be limited to church services; prayer is a specialized form of worship, and a prayerful spirit can mean throughout the day a mood of "continual worship."

While it is true that no particular outward aid is necessary for worship, it would be a mistake to regard outward aids as unimportant. Creatures with physical bodies require physical media of some kind for spiritual experience, which leads Trueblood to a recognition of the importance of sacraments. Trueblood defines *sacrament* as "a physical means to a spiritual end." Sacraments, he suggests, may be thought of as windows allowing the glory of God to shine in. Various traditions have institutionalized particular sacramental acts, but Trueblood believes the potential for sacramental experience is much greater than officially recognized acts. Humble and ordinary experiences may be filled with sacramental meaning when we recognize their latent potential. This is not to claim that anything is sacramental. That claim risks a loss of distinction between good and evil. However, while maintaining a sense of that which opposes God's will, we can still look at all our experiences as potential windows to God's glory. Even evil things can become sacraments. An attitude of openness to God's presence will reveal signs of holiness in unexpected places.

Along with an extension of our concept of sacrament, Trueblood believes that we need to extend our concept of revelation. Some people are willing to believe that God has spoken in the past, but deny that he still speaks. But if God is not localized in time or space, why should we think that what he communicates is so limited? Furthermore, Trueblood argues, unless we have some experience of God's revelation now, could we even understand a past revelation? The Bible is a remarkable collection full of the "insights of spiritual giants." However, it also contains much that is base and unworthy. The individual reader is forced to regard some aspects as more revelatory than others. However, to make such a judgment or even to judge the Bible more worthy than other sacred writings, one must already have some criterion of revelation. It is because God still speaks to us that we are able to receive his past revelation. A genuinely spiritual religion is open to the fresh light that God continually brings.

This does not mean that we should shut ourselves up in the narrow confines of our individual experience. Trueblood finds it both practically necessary and reasonable to accept the authority of others. Of course, we must select some authorities over others, but the process of doing that is precisely one of confirming authority by tests of reason. There is sometimes good reason to place trust in an authority. This does not produce an absolute certainty free from all doubt, but an authority may be found reliable even when not infallible. We can neither rely on ourselves nor depend blindly on others, but, writes Trueblood, "by a thrust and counterthrust" of individual judgment and trust in others we strive toward truth. In the spiritual life, as in other spheres of life, there are those who may be regarded as authorities, people who have devoted themselves "long and faithfully" to understanding its many facets. In addition to the wisdom of individual masters, there is also wisdom to be found in the group. Ideally, a group of like-minded people can discover more than what its individual members would have found alone. Trueblood sees the group not as simply overriding individual leading, but rather as one of the many possible vehicles for God's revelation.

Individuals can be helped in their spiritual development by a minister who will nourish the seed of God's work that is within the heart. The most important way of doing this, according to Trueblood, is by helping to foster a mood of worship. While we have high aspirations, we need the help of a spiritual guide to remind us "of what it is we really want." The minister is a kind of "spiritual midwife," bringing to birth our capacity for reverence. This requires sensitivity on the minister's part to the people's needs and to the leading of the Holy Spirit.

While there may be some who have the officially designated task of being ministers, Trueblood does not draw a hard and fast distinction between clergy and laity. Instead, he believes that a complete understanding of the Christian message leads directly to the recognition that "all Christians are ministers and that the mere laity is nonexistent." There may be differences in capacity and some efforts may be feeble, but the realization that all followers of Christ have the vocation of minister can raise all life to a new level.

Genuine spiritual religion has practical implications as well. A recognition of the sacredness of all human life should give rise to a sensitivity to forces that debase that sacredness. War, poverty, racial discrimination, and other agents of human suffering must be opposed. As we recognize God's image in each person, we see the necessity of treating all human beings with reverence and respect. Reverence for human life also leads us to try to break down the barriers in economic and social practices that stand in the way of human fulfillment. The natural fruit is a concern for those in need and a missionary spirit devoted to helping others unlock their God-given capacities.

The Essence of Spiritual Religion, like so many of Trueblood's books, is an attempt to respond to the spiritual needs of an age in which people have become doubtful that the Church offers them a viable option. It is also a call to the Church to listen to its own tradition and provide the kind of options that sincere seekers can accept. Trueblood opposes both the mindless dogmatism of those who are content to repeat old formulas and the empty intellectualism of those who would throw off any creed at all. What is needed is a renewed awareness of the heart of religion in individual spiritual experience that at the same time maintains intellectual integrity and social concern. Trueblood holds up a brand of piety that he believes can fill the emptiness of those who thirst for meaningful religious experience, recognizing that we need to listen to the old truths, but in a way that makes sense in our world.

David M. Holley

RECOMMENDED READING

Edition used: Trueblood, D. Elton. *The Essence of Spiritual Religion.* New York: Harper & Row, 1975.

———. *The Best of Elton Trueblood.* Edited and with an Introduction by James Newby. Nashville: Impact Books, 1979. An anthology of topically organized selections that illustrates the development of a number of typical Trueblood themes through his many books.

———. *The Company of the Committed.* New York: Harper & Row, 1961. Probably Trueblood's most widely read book, in which he argues for the necessity of the redemptive fellowship of believers in the conviction that "it is not possible to be Christian alone."

———. *The New Man for Our Times.* New York: Harper & Row, 1970. An attempt to describe an integrated spiritual life characterized by personal piety, intellectual depth, and social concern.

———. *A Place to Stand.* New York: Harper & Row, 1969. An attempt to set forth systematically the essentials of a faith that meets the demands of rational examination. Confidence in Christ is seen as the central postulate furnishing a stable basis for putting together a coherent set of beliefs.

———. *Your Other Vocation.* New York: Harper & Row, 1952. Expands on Trueblood's belief that "all Christians are ministers," that there is no such thing as a "mere layman."

THE COST OF DISCIPLESHIP
AND
LETTERS AND PAPERS FROM PRISON

Author: Dietrich Bonhoeffer (1906–1945)

The son of a psychiatrist teaching at Berlin University, Dietrich Bonhoeffer decided early to enter theology. He served as pastor, lecturer, and theology professor in Spain, America, and England as well as Germany. Bonhoeffer early became an outspoken critic of the Nazi government and an active member of the resistance movement. He was arrested and imprisoned by the Gestapo and two years later hanged. His other important works include *Schöpfung und Fall*, (1933) (*Creation and Fall*, 1959); *Gemeinsames Leben*, 1939 (*Life Together*, 1954); and *Ethik*, 1943 (*Ethics*, 1955).

Type and subject of work: Meditations on what it means to be a Christian disciple in the twentieth century

First published: 1937 (in German, *Nachfolge*); 1951 (in German, *Widerstand und Ergebung: Briefe und Aufzeichnungen aus der Haft*)

Major Themes

Cheap grace is justification of the sin rather than the sinner; what is needed today is costly grace.

Costly grace is obedience to the call to discipleship of Jesus Christ, it is to take up the cross and follow him; this is both grace and law.

The Beatitudes express the works of discipleship; they point to the man on the cross and not to the disciple.

The call to discipleship is also a call to be a messenger proclaiming the kingdom of God.

The call to discipleship is also the call to be baptized and incorporated into the Church, the Body of Christ, the bodily presence of Christ in the world.

The call to be incorporated in the Body of Christ is the call to be imitators of Jesus Christ and, consequently, imitators of God.

The call to be included in the Body of Christ is also the call to be messengers to a secular world, a humanity come of age, which means we must speak of God in secular fashion.

God, as revealed in Christ, is a powerless God who redeems humanity by suffering for humanity.

The Body of Christ, the Church, must be an imitator of Christ by serving and suffering for humanity.

The *Cost of Discipleship* is an exposition of passages of Scripture under four headings: "Grace and Discipleship," "The Sermon on the Mount," "The Messengers," and "The Church of Jesus Christ and the Life of Discipleship." The first begins with a discussion of "cheap grace" versus "costly grace" and can be viewed as setting the theme for the entire work. Cheap grace is the justification of sin, but not the sinner. It is essentially grace without discipleship. Costly grace is the justification of the sinner, the single-minded response of obedience to the call of Jesus to discipleship; it is grace and commandment in one. In responding to the call to discipleship, one must first break with the past, break all allegiances to the world, then follow the living Christ. For one to follow the living Christ is to take up the cross and to forgive as one is forgiven. "Through the call of Jesus," Bonhoeffer tells us, "men become individuals." One does not go out and seek suffering; each person has a cross and one must take up that cross with its own particular suffering and its own particular death.

In the section on the Sermon on the Mount, we find three subsections, each dealing with an aspect of the life of discipleship: its extraordinariness, its hidden character, and its separation. The community of the blessed is the community of the Cross. Where else, he asks, can the poorest, the meekest, the most sorely tried be found, but on the cross at

Golgotha? That community of the blessed is the salt of the world, the light of the world; but it is not the human beings of that community, it is their works, their "poverty, peregrination, meekness, peaceableness, and finally persecution and rejection." It is in these works that the world sees the cross and the community beneath it, and it is these works that are the law of Christ and the fulfillment of the Old Testament law. This law of Christ is a law of love extended to enemies. It is this love that overcomes and takes us along the way of the cross and into the fellowship with the Crucified.

In turning to the hidden character of discipleship in Matthew 6, where we are warned against practicing our piety before men, we have something of a paradox with the extraordinary and visible character of discipleship just described, "the light of the world" and "a city set upon a hill." Bonhoeffer resolves this paradox by telling us first that the good works of discipleship are not to be practiced for the sake of making them visible. Also, he suggests that it is from ourselves that they should be hidden. It is to Christ and to Christ alone that our attention is directed so that the good works of discipleship point to Christ and not to ourselves. In the section on the separation of the disciples, "the great divide," we are admonished not to judge the nondisciple and not to force discipleship on anyone else. The ultimate division, the decision of who is and who is not a disciple, will come on the last day. Our commandment is simply to follow the living Christ. As Bonhoeffer puts it with reference to the Sermon on the Mount, what is called for is "simple surrender and obedience, not interpreting it or applying it, but doing it and obeying it."

In the third section Bonhoeffer turns to the commissioning of the disciples as messengers. The original disciples were sent as messengers first to the house of Israel so that, according to Bonhoeffer, they might reject the message of Christ and thereby open the door to the Gentiles. The disciples are armed with the simple message, "The kingdom of God is at hand," and they are bidden to go in poverty, to indicate their freedom, and to accept lodging and food in that freedom. When their message is rejected, they are to shake the dust from their feet as a sign of the curse that will befall that place, a curse from which they disassociate themselves.

Bonhoeffer also deals with the problem of being a disciple today and uses it to introduce the fourth section, "The Church of Jesus Christ and the Life of Discipleship." The original disciples had the bodily Jesus and his word; today we appear to have only the word. It was through the word and commandment, however, that they recognized the Christ. Today we can recognize the living Christ through the same word and commandment, through the ministry of Word and Sacrament; the original disciples have no advantage over the contemporary disciples. The commandment today is a clear and unambiguous as it was to the original disciples. "Thus the gift Jesus gave to his disciples," Bonhoeffer concludes, "is just as available for us as it was for them. In fact, it is even more readily available for us now . . . because he is glorified, and because the Holy Spirit is with us."

Bonhoeffer now tries to relate the Gospel language of discipleship with the "churchly" language of Saint Paul and the Church. The latter concerns the presence of the risen and glorified Christ rather than the earthly presence of the Lord as does the former. When the earthly Jesus called human beings to follow him, he summoned them to a visible act of obedience. Baptism is such a visible act of obedience and it involves the same breach with the world and dying to the old self; the baptized one is baptized into the visible community of Christ's body. As a member of that community one can still enjoy the bodily presence of Christ.

Bonhoeffer's theology of Christ and the Church here is intriguing. For him, in Adam, who had been both an individual and the representative of the whole human race, humanity had fallen. The incarnate Son of God, the Second Adam, likewise, exists both as himself, an individual, and as redeemed humanity, the Church. To become a member of the Church is to be incorporated literally into the body of the Son of God. As Bonhoeffer points out, "As they contemplated the miracle of the incarnation, the early Fathers passionately contended that while it was true to say that God took human nature upon him, it was wrong to say that he chose a perfect individual man and united himself to him. . . . The Body of Jesus Christ, in which we are taken up with the whole human race, has now become the ground of our salvation." In fact, Bonhoeffer goes so far as to say, "Christ is the Church."

The body of Christ, as the Church, is visible insofar as the Church occupies space. Firstly, it is visible when the congregation is assembled to preach the word and to participate in the sacraments of baptism and the Lord's Supper. Secondly, it is visible in its organization and order. Thirdly, it is visible in the daily life of its members in fellowship and brotherly love, in their world vocations and in positions of worldly authority. He concludes, "That is the Church of the elect, the *Ecclesia*, those who have been *called out*, the Body of Christ on earth, the followers and disciples of Jesus."

Those who are "called out" are called to be saints. Those who answer this call of God in Christ are the saints. They are called by God to be holy, holy like the Holy One. The members of the congregation that composes Christ's body are separated from all things profane and from sin to be God's sanctuary, his dwelling place, the Body of Christ. God dwells in that body with his Holy Spirit. The image lost in the Fall is to be restored in humankind's becoming like Christ. We can become like Christ only because he became like us. Bonhoeffer once again concludes that "we simply are to look away from ourselves to him who has himself accomplished all things for us and to follow him." And those who follow him are destined to bear his image, the image of the incarnate God, the crucified and risen Lord. They can then be called the "imitators of God."

Letters and Papers from Prison is precisely that. It is a collection of letters to friends and relatives, poems, and papers in which Bonhoeffer preserved some of his thoughts while imprisoned and awaiting death at the hands of the Nazis. In these letters and papers we do not find any systematic development of a set of ideas, but mostly questions and suggestive answers, or suggestive lines along which one may look for answers. As Bonhoeffer himself says, "I am led on more by an instinctive feeling for the questions which are bound to crop up rather than by any conclusions I have reached already." However, one gets the feeling when reading this material that there was a book brewing in his mind. Just as one may think of the previous work as a book on the theme of Christ as Lord of the Church, one could think of this new book, which appears to have been brewing in his mind, as one dealing with the theme of Christ as Lord of the world. For it is Christ and the world in the twentieth century and how one can be a disciple of Christ in this century that seems to have been occupying his mind. One of Bonhoeffer's questions raised here, for example, and one that has greatly influenced recent theology, is "How do we speak . . . in secular fashion of God?"

It is the secularization of the world in the twentieth century that seems to preoccupy him. He sees the world with its science and technology as having "come of age," and the world and human beings as having become autonomous. We do not need God as the answer to problems as we once did. This he takes to be a fact with which theology must deal, but he also does not take it to be a bad one. When humanity can resolve its problems itself, to force human beings to rely on God is merely to force them back into adolescence. In the light of this, he calls for a "religionless Christianity," one that does not rest on some a priori religious need of God. "The time when men could be told everything by means of words, whether theological or pious," he tells us, "is over and so is the time of inwardness and conscience, which is to say the time of religion as such."

A religionless Christianity is in contrast to a Christianity that maintains that humanity has problems which only religion can answer. Of religion, he writes, "Religious people speak of God when human perception is (often just from laziness) at an end, or human resources fail: it is always a *deux ex machina* they call to their aid, either for the so called solving of insoluble problems or as support in human failure—always, that is to say, helping our human weakness or on the borders of human existence." This is precisely the role for God that Bonhoeffer takes humanity "come of age" to have rejected. It is the kind of situation, also, that we find reflected in Tillich's method of correlation, which maintains that human reason raises questions that it cannot answer and these questions find their answer in Christianity. This is to base Christianity on a false religious premise. In reference to Tillich's attempt Bonhoeffer remarks, "[Tillich] . . . sought to understand the world better than it understood itself, but it felt entirely *mis*understood and rejected the imputation." If the disciples of Christ are to be messengers, as was called for in Bonhoeffer's previous work, then they must know how to be messengers to humanity "come of age"; otherwise Christ cannot fulfill his role as Lord of the world.

Two things that Bonhoeffer thinks the Church must take seriously if it is to speak to humanity "come of age" are: First, "God is teaching us that we must live as men who can get along very well without him. . . . God is weak and powerless in the world, that is exactly the way, the only way, in which he can help us. Matthew 8:17 makes it crystal-clear that it is not by his omnipotence that Christ helps us, but by his weakness and suffering. . . . This must be the starting point for our "worldly" interpretations." The second is that the Christian Church must see itself as belonging to the world, but as powerless in the world like its Christ and existing for humanity. "She must take part in the social life of the world, not lording over men, but helping and serving them."

Bowman L. Clarke

RECOMMENDED READING

Edition used: Bonhoeffer, Dietrich. *The Cost of Discipleship.* Translated by R. H. Fuller. London: SCM Press, 1959. *Letters and Papers from Prison.* Edited by Eberhard Bethge. Translated by R. H. Fuller. New York: Macmillan, 1962.

———. *Ethics.* Edited by E. Bethge. Translated by H. Horton Smith. London: SCM Press, 1955. Most of this work is an unfinished book on Christian ethics on which Bonhoeffer was working while in prison and is largely contemporaneous with the second work discussed here. The editor, however, has included a number of shorter pieces concerning ethics by Bonhoeffer. Nonetheless one can see some of the problems that concerned Bonhoeffer at the time he was in prison.

———. *Life Together.* Translation and Introduction by John W. Doberstein. New York: Harper & Bros., 1954. This little book is a very readable introduction to Bonhoeffer's thought. It comes between the two works discussed here and continues some of the themes of the first one.

Godsey, John D. *The Theology of Dietrich Bonhoeffer.* Philadelphia: Westminster Press, 1960. This is a good summary of Bonhoeffer's theology in the historical development of his writings. As such it is an equally good source of the story of his life. Unlike some interpreters of Bonhoeffer, the author sees no radical change in Bonhoeffer's theology between the two works discussed here, rather an expansion of concern from Christ as Lord of the Church to Christ as Lord of the world, somewhat as the above discussion.

LETTERS BY A MODERN MYSTIC

Author: Frank C. Laubach (1884–1970)

A Pennsylvanian trained at Princeton, Union Theological Seminary, and Columbia University (Ph.D. in sociology, 1915), Laubach went to the Philippines under the American Board of Foreign Missions. After fourteen years of successful teaching, writing, and administration at Cagayn and Manila, he realized in 1929 his long-standing ambition of settling among the fierce Moros, an Islamic tribe on Mindanao. There, in the village of Lanao, he underwent a remarkable series of experiences of God, and simultaneously developed a technique for reducing the Moro language to writing, with symbols closely correlated to their spoken words. This not only made it possible to teach them to read in only a few hours, but permitted them immediately to teach others. The famous "Each One Teach One" program was born, and with the generalization of his linguistic methods the foundation was laid for his worldwide efforts to promote literacy, beginning with India in 1935. During his last thirty years Laubach was an international presence in literacy, religious, and governmental circles. His personal contacts with President Truman were thought to be partly responsible for "point four" in Truman's inaugural address of 1949, sponsoring a "bold new program . . . for the improvement and growth of underdeveloped areas" of the world.

Type and subject of work: Excerpts from a series of letters dated from January 3, 1930 through January 2, 1932. Though derived from letters, this book is in the lineage of Saint Augustine's *Confessions*, being a narrative of Laubach's ascent into the life of active union with God.

First published: 1937

MAJOR THEMES

Submission to the will of God means cooperation with God in the moment-to-moment activities that make up our daily existence.

This cooperation is achieved through continuous inner conversation with God.

That conversation in turn is, from our side, a matter of keeping God constantly before the mind.

One learns to keep God constantly in mind by experimentation, by trying various experiential devices, until the habit of constant God-thought is established.

Then God permeates the self and transforms its world and its relations to others into God's field of constant action, in which all of the promises of Christ's gospel are realized in abundance of life.

It is possible for all people under all conditions to establish this habit if they make constant effort and experiment within their peculiar circumstances to discover how it can be done.

Two years prior to his transforming experiences of 1930, Laubach found himself profoundly dissatisfied in the realization that after fifteen years as a Christian minister he still was not living his days "in minute by minute effort to follow the will of God." He then began trying to "line up" his actions with the will of God about every few minutes. His confidants at the time told him he was seeking the impossible. But in 1929 he began to try living *all* his waking moments "in conscious listening to the inner voice, asking without ceasing, 'What, Father, do you desire said? What, Father, do you desire done this minute?'" In his view, this is exactly what Jesus did.

Laubach did not fall into the trap of *merely trying* to achieve his goal. Rather, he understood the necessity of *learning how,* of spiritual method. He was, in fact, a very subtle and realistic experimentalist, and regarded himself as fortunate to be living in a "day when psychological experimentation has given a fresh approach to our spiritual problems." Thus he experimented for a few days by taking enough time from each hour to give intensive thought to God. Again, "disgusted with the pettiness and futility of my unled self," he experimented with "feeling God in each movement by an act of will—willing that He shall direct these fingers that now strike this typewriter—willing that He shall pour through my steps as I walk." Again, he wished to "compel his mind" to "open straight out to God." But to attain this mental state often required a long time in the morning. Therefore he determined not to get out of bed "until that mind set, that concentration upon God, is settled." He found that great determination was required to keep the mind on God. But he also found it quickly getting easier, and hoped that "after awhile, perhaps, it will become a habit, and the sense of effort will grow less."

In the most subtle passage in these letters—so far as the "mechanisms" of holding God before the mind are concerned—Laubach deals with the question of whether it is *possible* to have contact with God all the time. Can we think his thoughts all the time? *Must* there not be periods when other things push God out? Laubach's response to this issue should be fully quoted, for it gives us the heart of his understanding of the constant conscious hold on God. Admitting that he once thought there must be periods when God is excluded, he continues:

> . . . But I am changing my view. We can keep two things in mind at once. Indeed we cannot keep one thing in mind more than half a second. Mind is a flowing something. It oscillates. Concentration is merely the continuous return to the same problem from a million angles. We do not think of one thing. We always think of the relationship of at least two things, and more often of three or more things simultaneously. So my problem is this: Can I bring God back in my mind-flow every few seconds so that God shall always be in my mind as an after image, shall always be one of the elements in every concept and percept?
>
> I choose to make the rest of my life an experiment in answering this question.

The tremendous results of this experiment are found in the narrative of these letters. They are elaborated more systematically and practically in the *Game with Minutes* (1961), where the method was reduced to calling God to mind for at least one second out of each minute. But the quotation given contains the psychological principles back of Laubach's method for achieving active union with God, constantly abiding in the abundant life.

Within weeks of beginning his experiments he began to notice differences. By the end of January 1930, and with much still to learn about his method, he had gained a sense of being carried along by God through the hours, of cooperation with God in little things, which he had never felt before. "I need something, and turn around to find it waiting for me. I must work, . . . but there is God working along with me." He discovered by March 9 that *"This hour* can be heaven. *Any* hour for *any* body can be rich as God." In a manner familiar to the mystics of all ages, we find him saying to God: "And God, I scarce see how one could live if his heart held more than mine has had from Thee this past two hours." He experienced difficulties and failures in maintaining his consciousness of God, but in the week ending May 24 he began to experience a further dimension in his conversations with God. In a moment of immersion in natural beauty, "I let my tongue go loose and from it there flowed poetry far more beautiful than any I ever composed. It flowed without pausing and without ever a failing syllable for a half hour." This brought him a deeper awareness of God in beauty and in love.

Reflecting upon the results of two months of strenuous effort to keep God in mind every minute, he exclaims: "This concentration upon God is *strenuous*, but everything else has ceased to be so!" That was especially true of his relations to the Moros, who, seeing the difference in him, took him entirely into their hearts and lives, loving, trusting, and helping him without regard to their cultural and religious differences. Two of the leading Moslem priests went about the area telling their people that Laubach would help them to know God. He never pretended to be anything but a follower of Jesus, but he studied the Bible and the Koran with the priests and the people and prayed in their services with them. Observing this, one priest said, "He is Islam." He replied, "A friend of Islam." But the Islamic emphasis upon constant submission seems to have been one factor prompting him to develop his way of being in constant contact with God. He could not endure to see his practice as a Christian fall below the profession of Islam. The inner transformation was substantial and with real outward effects. "God does work a change. The moment I turn to him it is like turning on an electric current which I feel through my whole being." There is a "real presence" that affects other people directly, and that also makes intercessory prayer an exercise of substantial power in cooperation with God.

In the letters after mid-1930 there is a different range of concerns, which predominantly have to do with various practical aspects of the life in union with God. These are further elaborated and beautifully concretized for the varying conditions of life in *Game with Minutes* —which of course was written to guide others as the *Letters* were not.

Because of Laubach's immense involvement with worldwide social problems, he came to be generally know for his work, not for his inner life. Many of those who have written about him say little about his spiritual side, and obviously do not know what to make of it. But his own words and writings (he published more than fifty books) reveal that he remained primarily a spiritual man—fundamentally living from his moment-to-moment relation to God—to the end of his days. He knew this relation in a way that did not bear many of the external trappings conventionally associated with spirituality. But to observe his effect is to see that he was truly one of those born of the spirit, of the "wind" that invisibly produces visible results (John 3:8).

Dallas A. Willard

RECOMMENDED READING

Edition used: Laubach, Frank C. *Letters by a Modern Mystic.* Foreword by Alden H. Clark. Edited and compiled by Constance E. Padwick. Syracuse, N.Y.: New Readers Press, 1955. First published in 1937.

Edwards, Gene, ed. *Practicing His Presence: Frank Laubach and Brother Lawrence.* Goleta, Calif.: Christian Books, 1973. An instructive comparison.

Laubach, Frank C. *Christ Liveth in Me* and *Game with Minutes.* Westwood, N.J.: Fleming H. Revell Co., 1961. A practical guide to living with God in mind.

———. *Prayer, the Mightiest Force in the World.* Westwood, N.J.: Fleming H. Revell Co., 1951.

———. *The World Is Learning Compassion.* Westwood, N.J.: Fleming H. Revell Co., 1958. Chapter 7 deals with Truman's "Point Four" referred to earlier.

Medary, Marjorie. *Each One Teach One: Frank Laubach, Friend to Millions.* New York: Longmans, Green & Co., 1954. An account of Laubach's linguistic methods.

IF

Author: Amy Wilson Carmichael (1867–1951)
This British poet and missionary to India, who served without furlough for fifty-five years, rescued children at her independent faith mission, known as the Dohnavur Fellowship. She wrote a total of thirty-eight books, thirteen of them after a fall in 1931 rendered her an invalid, though she continued to administrate the mission.

Type and subject of work: A book of epigrams describing the struggle between self-will and divine will

First published: 1938

MAJOR THEMES

God's love is the source of our life, the measure of our failures, and the means of our perfection.
"If I can write an unkind letter, speak an unkind word, think an unkind thought without grief and shame, then I know nothing of Calvary love."

This small book was written during a restless night following a complaint from one of her subordinates about another. Carmichael felt that perhaps she had failed to teach them how to relate to one another with Christlike love. Out of her own prayers for forgiveness and guidance came the affirmations of the first part of the book, written in the form of "If . . ., then I know nothing of Calvary love" sentences. Each sentence came, she declares, "almost as if spoken aloud to the inward ear."

Many of the statements deal particularly with issues of supervision and relationship. For example, "If I am perturbed by the reproach and misunderstanding that may follow action taken for the good of souls for whom I must give account; if I cannot commit the matter and go on in peace and in silence, remembering Gethsemane and the Cross, then I know nothing of Calvary love." Yet all readers will find them challenging and beneficial. For example, "If a sudden jar can cause me to speak an impatient, unloving word, then I know nothing of Calvary love."

In the preface Carmichael notes that "I know nothing of Calvary love" may sound a bit harsh, but explains, "the thought came in this form, and I fear to weaken it." She declares that when one sees one's life and actions in the light of Calvary love, one "feels that indeed all [one] ever knew was nothing, less than nothing."

The second part of the book consists of short meditations on divine love. She begins by admitting that "I have felt these words scorching to write." The problem is that despite the fact that so much of Christian teaching is devoted to love, many are "content with the shallows of love, if indeed such shallows should be called love at all." The more we read of Scripture, the more we "feel our deadly lack."

Influenced by the "Higher Life" movement as expressed in England by the Keswick conferences, Carmichael upholds a lofty view of the Christian life. She says, "If I fear to hold another to the highest because it is so much easier to avoid doing so, then I know nothing of Calvary love." At Keswick in 1890, she heard a phrase that became one of her themes: "Thou wilt perfect that which concerneth me." In the meditations, she notes that God lovingly, patiently "waits till the heart, all weary and sick of itself, turns to its Lord and says, 'Take full possession.'"

We need not plead for God to take possession; we need not wait for God to fill us with divine love: "Love is pressing round us on all sides like air. Cease to resist, and instantly love takes possession." She also reminds her readers that we need not be distressed by past failure or tormented by fear of future failure. God's grace is always available, God's forgiveness eternal.

Ever a realist, Carmichael knows that "the way of love is never any easy way," and suffering will come. Such a time, she suggests, is a time to pray particularly for God's love to sustain. That prayer will be answered, and we will find as always grace for grace. We will draw upon our inheritance as the children of God who is Love.

The key is trust. We must trust God with humble heart and full abandon. We must trust God to clear away any debris that has choked off the channels of God's love to us. We must trust God to perfect us.

Many of her books—such as *Toward Jerusalem* (1936) and *His*

Thoughts Said . . . His Father Said (1949; similar in format to *If*)—are poetry. Others, such as *Gold Cord* (1932) and *Things As They Are* (1904) are about her mission experiences in India. She tells of how God continually supplied the needs of her mission, which included as many as nine hundred persons—children, doctors, nurses, teachers, builders, farmers, craftspersons, and cooks. She never appealed for funds in any way. Yet her mission flourished and expanded.

To those of the mission, she was always known as "Amma," which in Tamil means "mother." She once wrote to one of the mission's supervisors concerning her charges: "Love them dearly. Hold them to the Highest." It summarizes her own way of relating. When asked what they remember of her, everyone who knew her replies, "It was her love."

Nancy A. Hardesty

RECOMMENDED READING

Edition used: Carmichael, Amy. *If*. Grand Rapids, Mich.: Zondervan, Cowman Publication, 1965.

———. *Gold Cord: The Story of a Fellowship*. London: Society for Promoting Christian Knowledge; New York: Macmillan, 1933. A moving account of work with the Dohnavur Fellowship in India.

———. *His Thoughts Said . . . His Father Said*. Dohnavur Fellowship. London: Society for Promoting Christian Knowledge, 1949. A poetic dialogue—man and God—in the style of *If*, emphasizing the problems and rewards of the spiritual life.

———. *Things As They Are: Mission Work in Southern India*. London: Morgan, 1904. An earlier account of work in the mission field.

Elliot, Elisabeth. *A Chance to Die: The Life and Legacy of Amy Carmichael*. Tappan, N.J.: Revell, 1987. A complete biography of a remarkable woman born in the Victorian era. An appreciative but fair and critical account.

Houghton, Frank. *Amy Carmichael of Dohnavur*. Fort Washington, Pa.: Christian Literature Crusade, n.d. Definitive, authorized biography.

THE DESCENT OF THE DOVE

Author: Charles Williams (1895–1945)

Born in London, Charles Williams became a writer, teacher, editor, and lecturer. Despite having no formal degree, he was appointed a lecturer at Oxford and was awarded an honorary degree by the university. He published thirty-eight books, which include novels, poetry, drama, literary criticism, and theology. He is perhaps best known for his supernatural novels, particularly *War in Heaven* (1930), *Descent into Hell* (1937), and *All Hallows' Eve* (1945).

Type and subject of work: A history of the Christian Church interpreted as the activity of the Holy Spirit

First published: 1939

MAJOR THEMES

The history of the Christian Church is the history of the Holy Spirit in its act of the regeneration of humankind; and in its act of regeneration, the Holy Spirit must act under the conditions of our humanity.

The history of the Christian Church represents the co-inherence of the Holy Spirit in the body of the Christian and the co-inherence of its members in the Holy Spirit: The Spirit is in the Church and the Church is in the Spirit.

The nature of the Trinity and the incarnation exemplifies this same principle of co-inherence: God is in a man and humankind is in God.

This same principle is exemplified throughout all of creation, in the natural order as well as the supernatural.

The regeneration of humankind, which is the act of the Holy Spirit, is the restoration of co-inherence in the natural order.

This beautifully written work is not merely the result of an attempt to write a history of the Christian Church from Pentecost to contemporary times; it is intended to be a history of the activity of the Holy Spirit. The name—as well as the subtitle, "The History of the Holy Spirit in the Church"—makes this clear. As a mere history of the two thousand years of the Christian Church, it appears to be an accurate and well-balanced account; but it is the theological framework in which Williams repeats this account that is its major contribution. The very first sentence, "The beginning of Christendom is, strictly, at a point out of time," sets the stage for the recounting within this framework. For Williams the history of Christendom is the history of "an operation of the Holy Ghost towards Christ, under the conditions of our humanity." It is this latter phrase, "under the conditions of our humanity," that gives Williams's account of the history of the Christian Church its evenness, its gracious and balanced nature. W. H. Auden has gone so far in his introduction as to say, perhaps with only slight exaggeration, "Never was there an historian more courteous to all alike." Williams does not have to be defensive in his recounting of "the operation of the Holy Ghost"; for him it is also a human story with all the warts and perversions of human sin, as well as a divine story.

A fair and well-balanced character is seen throughout the work. It is seen in Williams's treatment of the extreme, if not pathological, character of the ascetics, whose way he refers to as "the Negative Way." In recounting, for example, the death of Saint John of the Cross, he inserts parenthetically, "And even he, towards the end, was encouraged to remember that he liked asparagus; our Lord the Spirit is reluctant to allow either of the two great Ways to flourish without some courtesy to the other." Williams's generosity extends to the professed historical enemies of the Church as well. Of the communist movement, as an illustration, he writes, "The Russian persecution, however evil, had at least partly arisen from the intention of saving the poor. . . . Its atheistic societies and its anti-God demonstrations were honestly meant to break the chains of all men; even if they broke the limbs in so doing, it was an unfortunate result of the period of transition." Williams's generosity, however, does not extend to one historical group, the Nazis: "The new racial image . . . admitted no fault and it looked for no Messiahs; it left freedom of conscience on one point only—whether God had created the Nordic Race or whether it grew."

The humanity of the Church is particularly visible in Williams's recounting of the conflicts and schisms within the Church—doctrinal, political, and economic—that have torn the body of Christ asunder. The split between the eastern and western branches of the Church, as well as the Great Schism, are handled against the background of this human element of the Church. With reference to the Protestant Reformation, for example, he writes, "Economics confused the process of the Reformation as they had been partly responsible for the beginning of the Reformation." Human factors enter into the story of the Church as well as the activity of the Holy Spirit. Yet Williams sees the Reformation as "The Renewal of Contrition," which is the title of his chapter on the Reformation. Even that chapter, however, he closes with this sentence, "Contrition indeed was renewed—but not for its own day, only for the day before yesterday."

This humanity of the Church is also recognized, for example, in some of its darker activities, such as those of the Inquisition. Of the Inquisition, Williams writes, "from some points of view it might be regarded as the dark shadow cast, men being what they are, by Corpus Christi." Another dark chapter in the history of the Christian Church, the Children's Crusade, is handled with great sensitivity: "An age like our own of infinite attention to children is defeated by the spectacle. . . . They cross the Alps, they descend on Genoa, on Rome; they wait upon miracles. . . . They excite piety, admiration, greed. The doom closes on them, and they are betrayed. They die of hunger, they are sold as slaves; the capitalists of the day made profit out of them, and it is as if with them some strange quality and capacity of freshness passed from Europe which not all the dogmatic glory of Lateran could revive, nor even the learned subtle piety of the *Pange, lingua* when St. Thomas adored the Sacrament in great verse."

Williams's entire recounting of the story of the Christian Church is framed within his doctrine of co-inherence and exchange, or substitution; he seems to use the latter two words in his writing synonymously. The dedication of The *Descent of the* Dove reads: "For the Companions of the Co-inherence." To the work he has also added a postscript, which is one of the better places in all of Williams's writing for a reader to get an idea of Williams's doctrine of co-inherence. The dedication and the postscript themselves would testify to the importance of Williams's doctrine of co-inherence for his recounting of the operation of the Holy Spirit; but the doctrine is also echoed and used throughout *The Descent of the Dove*, as it is in all of Williams's writings, whether it be a history, a novel, a poem, or a drama. And it is Williams's doctrine of co-inherence that makes possible that tolerance and honesty which was noted in the beginning of this summary.

In the body of this particular work Williams introduces the doctrine of co-inherence very early by recounting the story of Felicitas, a Carthaginian slave who was martyred under Severus. In prison Felicitas bore a child and in her pain she screamed out. A jailer reportedly asked her that if she shrieked at bearing a child, how could she expect to endure the death of a martyr? Felicitas's answer is almost taken as the theme of the work. She is said to have replied, "Now I suffer what I suffer; then another will be in me who will suffer for me, as I shall suffer for him." Here we have the paradigm for Williams's doctrine of co-inherence and exchange, as well as an analogy between natural generation and supernatural regeneration, an analogy that Williams alludes to later in the postscript. Co-inherence is not mere coherence; it is co-*in*herence, the other *in* me, and I *in* the other, each bearing the other's burden, or suffering. It is the latter that constitutes the basis for the co-inherence, that is, the exchange or substitution, the bearing of something of the other. For this idea captured in Felicitas's response to the jailer, Williams grants Felicitas a place among the great African doctors of the Universal Church.

In the center of his work, beginning with the story of Felicitas and ending with the postscript, stands Dante, much as Jesus stands in the center of human history revealing its meaning. Williams's admiration of Dante is no secret; he almost accepts Patmore's evaluation that there has been no religious poet since David, but Dante. Here Williams is not concerned with Dante as a historical figure in the history of the Church; it is with an interpretation of Dante's writings that he is concerned. For he sees Dante as taking the doctrine of co-inherence to be central and functioning on all levels within the natural and supernatural orders, and perhaps more importantly, between the two. Dante's *New Life*, for example, is interpreted primarily as Dante's bearing the burden of Beatrice, particularly her death; it is the Way of Romantic Love. The *Divine Comedy* is interpreted primarily as Beatrice bearing the burden of Dante. The revelation of the divine factor of co-inherence comes to the fore in the third heaven when Dante cries to Folco of Marseilles of Venus, " . . . I in-thee myself as thou dost in-me thyself." Beatrice mediates the Deity to Dante by way of this "in-me" and "in-thee," and it is raised to the supernatural level where the Divine and the human co-inhere. In characterizing Dante's literary work, Williams thus writes, "It begins when a boy and a girl meet in the streets of Florence; it ends when the whole web of interchanging creation pour themselves towards the *Deivirilis* (to borrow a term from the Areopagite) within the point of Godhead."

In his postscript Williams once again returns specifically to the doctrine of co-inherence and the analogy between human generation in the natural order and the regeneration of humankind in the spiritual order, which he sees as the work of the Holy Spirit in time, or history. It is easy to see why he earlier elevated a virtually unknown Carthaginian slave girl to one of the great African doctors of the Universal Church on the basis of the idea captured in her response to the jailor. Williams begins here with human generation as an instance of co-inherence and substitution. In the act of generation, he tells us, a man can have no child unless his seed is received and carried by a woman and a woman can have no child unless she receives and carries the seed of the man. This is for him a mutual act of substitution; the child, he says, literally co-inheres in its mother and this, he points out, is often referred to as "bearing the burden." Williams then immediately speaks of the sacrament of baptism. In its natural co-inherence in the mother, the child co-inheres in an ancient and contemporary guilt. In the act of baptism, the godparents present themselves as substitutes, and in that act the child by spirit is incorporated into the Church; the child now co-inheres in the Church. Co-inherence and exchange, or substitution, is the pattern of the natural as well as the supernatural order. This parallel was, for Williams, also Felicitas's insight.

Dante's insight is likewise not lost in the postscript. For we find that the triune formula of the Deity by which the child is baptized, Father, Son, and Holy Spirit, exemplifies, for Williams, this same pattern of co-inherence and exchange. Each person of the Trinity co-inheres in the others. The incarnation represents this same principle; God was in a human being, but this humanity is also taken up into the Deity. Each bears the other's burden, and the natural order is reconciled with the spiritual order. Williams tells us that in the God-Man God "restored substitution and co-inherence everywhere; up and down the ladder of the great substitution all our lesser substitutions run; within that sublime co-inherence all our lesser co-inherences inhere."

The Descent of the Dove is the story of this restoration of substitution and co-inherence everywhere. The members of the Church co-inhere in each other; they are, as Saint Paul says, one body, each member co-inhering in the other by bearing the other's burden. It is more than that, however; it is the story of the co-inherence of the Spirit and the Church. The Church bears the burden of the Spirit, and the Spirit bears the burden of the humanity of the Church. This is why the Spirit always labors under the burden of "the conditions of our humanity" in its act of the regeneration of humankind. Just as God had to suffer the conditions of humankind in the incarnation, so the Spirit must labor under the conditions of our humanity. The story of the Christian Church is not the story of the Holy Spirit and it is not the story of human beings; it is the story of the co-inherence of the Spirit and humanity in the activity of the regeneration of humankind, or the restoration of co-inherence in humanity as it is exemplified in the Divine Trinity. As Williams suggests in his first sentence, the history of the Christian Church begins outside time; and as he suggests in the postscript, this co-inherence that characterizes the triune Deity, the incarnation and the history of the Church, "is experienced, at their best moments of delight, by lovers and friends."

He closes his work with the suggestion that the apprehension of this order of co-inherence, in nature and in grace, within and without Christendom, should be one of our chief concerns today.

Bowman L. Clarke

RECOMMENDED READING

Edition used: Williams, Charles. *The Descent of the Dove.* Introduction by W. H. Auden. New York: Meridian Books, 1956.

———. *All Hallows Eve.* New York: Pellegrini & Cudahy, 1948. This is one of Williams's more popular supernatural novels in which the spiritual and the natural, the living and the dead intermingle and co-inhere. It is a very good work to get a sense of his doctrine of co-inherence.

———. *The Figure of Beatrice: A Study of Dante.* London: Faber & Faber, 1958. This is Williams's masterpiece on Dante and the role of Beatrice in his works. It is very helpful in understanding his references to Dante above.

———, and C. S. Lewis. *Taliessin Through Logres, The Region of the Summer Stars, and Arthurian Torso.* Grand Rapids, Mich.: Eerdmans, 1974. This volume contains two long poems by Williams that make use of the Arthur legend. These two poems are a good example of his treatment of co-inherence in his poetry. The third piece in the volume is a piece of literary criticism by C. S. Lewis on Williams and his use of the Arthur legend. Lewis also discusses Williams's theory of co-inherence and the use of it in the two poems.

A TESTAMENT OF DEVOTION

Author: Thomas R. Kelly (1893–1941)
A devout Quaker, Kelly was educated at Wilmington College in Ohio, Haverford College, Hartford Theological Seminary, and Harvard University. He taught philosophy at Wilmington College, Earlham College in Richmond, Indiana, and the University of Hawaii, and Haverford College in Pennsylvania. His premature death at age forty-seven cut short a promising academic career.

Type and subject of work: Devotional essays with an emphasis on the interior life

First published: 1941

MAJOR THEMES

Within each person is a Light Within which, if continually yielded to by inward worship and listening, can be the truest guide of life.

By practicing the presence of God we can order our lives on two levels—the active and the interior—at one and the same time and bring them into fruitful interplay.

Being guided by the Light Within results paradoxically in both detachment from the world and reattachment to the world.

The call of Christ is a call to holy obedience, complete and unreserved obedience, which may come by way of profound mystical experience or by gradual surrender; the fruits of holy obedience include humility, holiness, entrance into suffering, and simplicity.

The Blessed Community of loving Christians is an objective reality, not an intellectual fantasy.

Social concern and action ought to emerge from an experience of the Eternal Now penetrating time as we experience life on two levels at the same time.

A Testament of Devotion consists of five addresses delivered by Thomas R. Kelly to Quaker audiences following a remarkable transformation of his life as he wrestled with depression brought on by failure to receive his Ph.D. at Harvard. Kelly himself had readied three of them for publication before his untimely death on January 17, 1941. His colleague at Haverford College, Douglas V. Steere, added two others and wrote the moving "Biographical Memoir" that supplies a key for interpreting his friend's profound and graceful message.

Steere points out that Kelly's life entailed "a passionate and determined quest for adequacy." His father died when he was four, leaving his mother to support him and his sister Mary, first on the farm and then as a stenographer and bookkeeper in Wilmington, Ohio. At Wilmington College, Kelly fostered a passion for the physical sciences, but when he moved to Haverford College in 1913, he came under the spell of Rufus Jones, who fanned a religious spark into a bright flame. Kelly taught for two years at Pickering College, a Quaker preparatory school in Canada. A mission volunteer, he entered Hartford Theological Seminary in 1916, receiving a B.D. in 1919.

When the United States entered the First World War, he volunteered to serve canteen duty in the Y.M.C.A. and then to work among German prisoners of war in England (June 1917–February 1918). After teaching two years at Wilmington College he returned to Hartford to take the Ph.D. in June of 1924. Pursuing an interest ignited during the way, he and his wife, Lael, spent fifteen months in Berlin directing a Quaker center. From there Kelly proceeded to Richmond, Indiana, to teach philosophy at Earlham College. He was not happy at Earlham, however, nor with his own achievements. He aspired to attain an ultimate certification in his field and, with that goal in mind, applied to Harvard for the Ph.D. After completing his residency at Harvard he returned reluctantly to Earlham, pushing himself all the while to complete his thesis in the spring of 1935. A long-standing desire to do mission work in Japan, however, kept tugging at him. In line with that, he accepted a post at the University of Hawaii, where he could assimilate something of the atmosphere of the Orient. His one-year stay there marred by ill health, he welcomed an invitation to teach philosophy at Haverford College. In 1937, however, an "earthquake" shook his foundations. When he took his oral exam at Harvard in defense of his thesis, "Explanation and Reality in the Philosophy of Emile Meyerson," his mind went blank and his examiners failed him without permitting him a second chance. As one might expect of a person who had gotten so close and then failed to grasp the goal on which he had labored seven years, the flood waters rolled over him. For several months Kelly suffered severe depression. But suddenly the cloud lifted. A new Kelly was born. As he described his experience, he was "shaken by the experience of Presence—something that I did not seek, but that *sought* me."

The *new* Kelly spoke in the lectures gathered under the title of *A Testament of Devotion*. Personal experience unquestionably stands behind and verifies in a fresh way central and cherished Quaker verities. Where previously Kelly could have explained and defended these rationally, now he knew them personally and experientially.

In "The Light Within," composed just nine days before he died, Kelly expounded and affirmed the central axiom of George Fox's philosophy: "Deep within us all there is an amazing inner sanctuary of the soul, a holy place, a Divine Center, a speaking Voice, to which we may continuously return." In opposition to the humanistic impulses of our age, Kelly insists that Christ, the living Christ, is the initiator and we the respondents. Our basic response is to be "adoration and joy, thanksgiving and worship, self-surrender and listening."

We will not persist in the sense of Presence, however, Kelly argues, unless we engage in internal disciplines and develop habits of the mind wherein we are attentive to the Light Within. Such disciplines and habits are not the property of any special group; all can have them. All can live life on two levels at once—the exterior and the interior. At first we may alternate between these two, but as we grow and develop in discipline we may live at both levels simultaneously. While we engage in thinking, discussing, seeing, doing external things, at the same time, quietly behind the scenes as it were, we also remain attentive to the Presence. A fruitful interplay between outer and inner thus becomes possible. How can one get in touch with the Light Within? Through mental habits of inward orientation, keeping up a life of secret prayer behind the scenes. Kelly suggests that one use brief ejaculations such as "Thine only. Thine only," or fragments of the Psalms such as "so panteth my soul after Thee, O God." Inward reorientation will result, in time, in an outward one. Paradoxically, we will experience liberation from earthly attachments and renewed attachment. God "plucks the world out of our hearts, loosening the chains of attachment. And He hurls the world into our hearts, where we and He together carry it in infinitely tender love."

Kelly delivered "Holy Obedience" as the annual William Penn Lecture to the Yearly Meeting of Quakers in late March of 1939. While ominous war clouds hovered over the horizon, he directed his hearers to focus their attention on the eternal God of love engaged in his relentless pursuit of humankind and to the life of absolute and complete and holy obedience that he demands. No one should underestimate "the revolutionary explosiveness" of a call for complete obedience, so unlike conventional religion. No one should undertake it without counting the cost. Some come to it by way of profound mystical experience. Kelly spoke knowingly when he said, "It is an overwhelming experience to fall into the hands of the living God, to be invaded to the depths of one's being by His presence, to be, without warning, wholly uprooted from all earth-born securities and assurances, and to be blown by a tempest of unbelievable power which leaves one's old proud self utterly defenseless. . . . One emerges from such soul-shaking, Love-invaded times into more normal states of consciousness. But one knows ever after that the Eternal Lover of the world, the Hound of Heaven, is utterly, utterly real, and that life must henceforth be forever determined by that Real."

Others attain complete obedience by way of step-by-step obedience, Kelly continues. The fruits of holy obedience include humility, holiness, entrance into suffering, and simplicity. Humility does not mean "a brow-beaten, dog-slinking attitude" but a reliance upon the power of God rather than on a slick and weasellike self-pride. This kind of humility makes one bold. Holiness has to do with "purity of heart—absolute honesty, absolute gentleness, absolute self-control, unwearied patience and thoughtfulness" in all circumstances. Suffering is something Americans shun, but suffering can cause a tendering of the soul wherein we learn the truth of the paradox, "Nothing matters; everything matters." Suffering stretches the heart and enlarges it. Through suffering we discover strength we did not know we had. Simplicity lies not in rearrangement of external calendars and programs but in an internal simplification where "life is lived with singleness of eye, from a holy Center where the breath and stillness of Eternity are heavy upon us and we are wholly yielded to Him."

In "The Blessed Community," which also appeared first in 1939, Kelly spoke about the bonds of love that knit Christians together in a fellowship that is beyond any human ties they have known. Here they become "God-enthralled" and "Light-Centered." Old friendships are examined and dissolved and new friendships developed as the "X-ray light of Eternity" discloses the realities that underlie them. Persons outside the fellowship are amazed at the "group Interknittedness of God-enthralled men and women who know one another *in Him*." Even persons within it find it astonishing to be "at home" with kindred souls. Within the fellowship cultural and educational and national and racial differences tumble as persons with "chilly theologies" reveal "glowing hearts." Such fellowship has its grounding in God, "the medium, the matrix, the focus, the solvent." All within it make their way to this single Center, where God coordinates their pliant wills and suffuses them with his glory and joy. The Blessed Community is an objective reality, not an intellectual fantasy. It is deeper than democracy, for its authority rests in God and not in the group. Within it are varied levels of fellowship, yet from each person radiate the bonds of love far and near.

In "The Eternal Now and Social Concern," published in March 1938, Kelly criticized the current tendency "to suppose that the religious life must prove its worth because it changes the social order." The Eternal should judge Time and not-Time, the Eternal. The central message of Friends is that experience of Divine Presence can transform and transfigure all of life. Life can be lived at two levels, but the one that must dominate is the level of the Timeless. When the Divine Presence "steals upon us," all things become new. One walks in the world but at the same time above it. The Eternal Now lifts one above anxiety about past or future, for within it God dwells. Christian do not pay sufficient attention to the double search that is going on in our world. God is the Seeker who enters into our human affairs. He puts a "new song" in our mouths. We experience love, joy, and peace. We live life "beyond fevered strain." Out of this experience of Presence comes a weakening of purely rational approaches as decisions are guided by the Presence. This does not mean a weakening but a strengthening of social concern, for God-guided decisions take away excuses for inaction. Souls are "tendered" toward all creation. Concern is particularized with cosmic tenderness.

Kelly's final essay, "The Simplification of Life," appeared in a symposium on the subject in March 1939. In it he reiterated a theme of other essays, namely, that modern urban life is too hectic and frantic, leaving us weary and unfulfilled. The answer to the problem, however, does not lie in rearranging externals or fleeing from the city. Americans have tried those approaches repeatedly to their disappointment. The answer lies, rather, in slipping into the Center, where we can discover "a life of amazing power and peace and serenity, of integration and confidence and simplified multiplicity," if we really want to. John Woolman models just such a life, in which fellowship with God issues in world-concern.

E. Glenn Hinson

RECOMMENDED READING

Edition used: Kelly, Thomas R. *A Testament of Devotion*. New York: Harper & Row, 1941.

Kelly, Richard M. *Thomas Kelly: A Biography*. New York: Harper & Row, 1966. A biography by the son of Thomas Kelly, this slim book contains long excerpts from letters and papers and fills in some background for interpreting *A Testament of Devotion*.

Kelly, Thomas R. *Reality of the Spiritual World*. Wallingford, Pa.: Pendle Hill, 1942. An additional lecture by Thomas Kelly delivered the second Sunday of January 1941, just before he died, this is Kelly's apology for belief.

THE SCHOOL OF PRAYER

Author: Olive Wyon (1881–1966)

Olive Wyon was born in London, England. She studied at the Church of Scotland Missionary College, Seley Oak Colleges, and King's College, London. She served as education secretary for the Young Women's Christian Association, Birmingham; as assistant editor of *World Dominion;* as tutor and then principal at Church of Scotland Missionary College, Edinburgh. She achieved a considerable reputation as a translator (she spoke French, German, Dutch, and Italian), including some of the notable works of Henrich Brunner, Jacques Ellul, and Ernst Troeltsch. She wrote extensively. Perhaps her most notable works, in addition to *The School of Prayer,* were *The Altar Fire: Reflections on the Sacrament of the Lord's Supper* (1954), *Prayers for Unity Through the Christian Year* (1955–1956), and *Desire for God: A Study of Three Spiritual Classics* (1966). During her career she concentrated on the importance of prayer and community in the development of Christian spirituality. She died in Edinburgh on August 21, 1966.

Type and subject of work: A practical guide to the practice of prayer

First published: 1943

MAJOR THEMES

Prayer and a living faith are inseparable.
God moves us to pray, and through prayer God becomes real for us.
The object of prayer is that God's will be done through us.

God intended that his unity be reflected in the unity of life, and that unity requires that prayer be an essential part of life.

There are fundamental and practical hindrances to prayer; the first can be overcome by correcting false thoughts about God; the second can be overcome by persisting in prayer and relying on the support of God.

Temptations in prayer come from thinking about ourselves; in true worship we rise above ourselves.

Olive Wyon's *School of Prayer* is both an expression of a profound faith and a practical guide to spiritual growth through prayer. In the foreword to her book the author reveals at the outset that she has written for two groups of people: "(*a*) those who are puzzled about people and would like to try it seriously; and (*b*) those who have made several efforts and have been discouraged by their experiences."

Wyon also makes explicit three basic assumptions of her book: (1) that a living faith requires prayer, (2) that although most Christians profess to believe the first assumption, there is a serious discrepancy between theory and practice, and (3) that although prayer is *personal*, it is an expression of spiritual community, of "fellowship within the Body of Christ."

(When reading Olive Wyon's *School of Prayer*, do not pass over her delightful and stirring prologue, "The White Birds." Here is a story of a man "who had a waking dream." In his dream he saw that at the side of each person praying there was a white bird. Some of the birds with difficulty took to their wings and found release to the heavens through open windows near the roof; others made the effort to rise but failed; an ugly bird managed to fly to the open window; another bird lay lifeless beside the one who prayed. These birds, an angel explained, are the outward signs of the prayers: some prayers are true expressions of faith and mount to the heavens; others reflect the personal preoccupations of the ones who pray and cannot get off the ground; the prayer of one who holds a bitter grudge against another is dead to begin with.)

Prayer "is rooted in the reality of God," Wyon writes; we can pray as Christians and know the reality of God because by his death and resurrection, Christ opened the "Kingdom of Heaven to all believers." Therefore the access to God's presence is not the reward of one's own efforts, she declares; that access was gained by Christ through his sacrifice, and the will to pray is affected by God's breathing into us the desire to pray. God continually renews in us the will to pray, and through prayer God becomes real for us.

Some persons suppose that through prayer they can use God for their own purposes, but such a supposition is blasphemous, Wyon writes. The object of prayer becomes clear to us, she says, if we reflect on

Christ's teaching us to pray the Lord's Prayer. The object of prayer, "very simple, very deep, very far-reaching," is "that God's will should be done, in and through and by us." We wait for God not to use him; God waits for us to will that he use us.

Wyon offers a detailed analysis of the spiritual dimensions of the Lord's Prayer. The Lord's Prayer, she claims, "is a complete guide to prayer" because it grew out of Christ's experience as man: "He *lived* the Prayer He taught, gathering it all up in the Final Act, in His Passion."

If the object of prayer is that we conform ourselves to the will of God, that our will be his, then it is clear, the author claims, that prayer should be directed not by one's feelings or one's concern to make progress but simply by one's will to be in union with God. God makes his will known to us, Wyon writes, through general rules that apply to all, at moments of crisis and for special purposes, and through the events that happen day by day. Often it is difficult to discern God's will, but if one is willing to put oneself at God's disposal, his will, particularly in the present moment, becomes clear. (His will may be, however, that one continue to reflect on a certain matter or that one wait for the direction one needs.)

"Wherever life and prayer have been divorced, something is wrong; neither develops aright," Wyon writes. The reason, she explains, is that God intends his unity to be reflected in the whole of life. If one understands the place of prayer in one's life, one thereby unifies one's personality and fulfills the purpose for which we are created.

Wyon emphasizes the close connection between prayer and health. To develop the habits that lead to the health of the body is itself a kind of prayer, the doing of the will of God. And, in turn, when prayer is not self-centered, when while praying we are least conscious of our bodies, and when prayer is not self-willed but receptive, "the strength of God can enter into our souls": prayer brings health to the body.

How is daily life to be redeemed from the sense of triviality? she asks. The answer Wyon gives is that one should start the day with an offering of the day to God, "praying that he will accept and guide and use us." And as the day progresses, she continues, one can get into the habit of relating the practical details of one's life to the will of God by offering up "ejaculatory prayer," short prayers by which the whole of life is lifted to a new level.

Wyon next considers the hindrances to prayer. Hindrances to prayer are of two kinds, she writes: *fundamental* and *practical*. The fundamental type is the most important; "if we go wrong here, we go wrong all along the line."

The first and most damaging *fundamental* hindrance to prayer is a false idea of God, the author states. If one regards God as exacting, tyrannical, fault-finding, or in some way having the features of human beings at their worst, we make prayer as a submission to the will of God impossible. She goes on, " . . . so if we sigh 'Thy will be done' at funerals, but never dream of putting these words on a invitation to a wedding, are we any better than heathen?"

To pray "in spirit and in truth," Olive Wyon writes, we must have confidence in God; we must be sure that he is Love. To be sure that God is Love, she continues, one must turn to Christ: "We *need* Christ in order to be sure that God is Love."

The second fundamental hindrance to prayer, she says, is *"misunderstanding Christ's teaching on prayer as a whole."* To understand Christ's teaching on the Lord's Prayer, four fundamental points should be considered. The phrase "In His Name" signifies that the gift of blessing is asked of God; "we are really praying for the Glory of God and for the accomplishment of His will in us."

The second point is that Christ insisted on the need for *perseverance.* Wyon cites Luke 18:1: "And He spake a parable unto them, that they ought always to pray and not to faint." Christ himself persevered in prayer even when, as a human being, he was dismayed about Judas's treachery and was moved to pray for the soul of the betrayer.

The third point to remember about Christ's teaching on prayer is that he insisted on *forgiveness.* God requires forgiveness, Wyon writes, because "Resentment erects a barrier between ourselves and the love of God, through which the rays of divine healing cannot penetrate."

In his teaching on prayer Christ called for *faith* in God and in prayer. Wyon concedes that faith cannot be secured through one's own efforts, but if one struggles to overcome in oneself hopelessness and apathy, if while praying one seeks the assurance of God, "He will increase in us the spirit and power of prayer."

The *practical* hindrances to prayer include distractions, discouragement, carelessness, and temptations.

Distractions or "wandering thoughts" are common and natural, Wyon claims. Distractions are not sins but occur because of physical fatigue or lack of concentration or the mind's tendency to give rise to vivid mind-pictures. For all distractions, the author advises, the most effective response is a tranquil faith; one works with the will and intellect, as Saint Teresa suggests, and by persistence one quietly returns the heart to God.

Whether the practical hindrance to prayer be discouragement, carelessness, or temptations, the way of resolution is by a will that expresses faith; we cease to think about ourselves and in the effort to turn to God we can count on God's being with us. In true worship, therefore, we rise above ourselves.

Bible reading and meditation on what is read is excellent preparation for prayer, Wyon writes, and she also encourages spiritual reading, the reading of classics that concern themselves with the soul's journey to God.

In a chapter entitled "Prayer and the Spirit of Worship" Wyon repeats ideas that she stresses throughout her book: that the aim of the true Christian life is the worship of God, that prayer is worship, and worship is adoration. Although religion is adoration, she continues, it also involves a personal response "to the Reality which lays its demands upon us." To adore God, to worship him, requires that we offer ourselves to him, and such self-offering is an act of will.

In the school of prayer, Wyon says, God acts on all the pupils, from those in the lowest class to those who are most advanced. There are many ways to pray, and persons learn in various ways and at various speeds, but throughout the process God is working with those who pray, and he facilitates the adoration that consists in conforming one's will to his, in hearkening to whatever call he gives us to move onward.

God has a purpose for us all, Wyon writes, and it is that we come into union with his will so that he may use us all. Thus, true prayer is "cooperation with God"; the soul cannot live without prayer, and the world cannot live without the dedication to the will of God that is achieved through prayer.

Ian P. McGreal

RECOMMENDED READING

Edition used: Wyon, Olive. *The School of Prayer.* New York: Macmillan, 1963.

Baillie, John. *A Diary of Private Prayer.* London: Oxford University Press, 1936. A work recommended by Wyon that she says will "speak to our condition."

Underhill, Evelyn. *Abba: Meditations Based on the Lord's Prayer.* London and New York: Longmans, Green & Co., 1940. Wyon herself discusses the Lord's Prayer in considerable detail, but she recommends the reading of Underhill's book.

Wyon, Olive. *Desire for God: A Study of Three Spiritual Classics.* London: Collins, 1966. Wyon discusses the contributions to Christian spirituality made by the following books: François Fénelon, *Christian Perfection*; John Wesley, *Christian Perfection*; Evelyn Underhill, *The Spiritual Life.*

GOD WAS IN CHRIST

Author: Donald M. Baillie (1887–1954)

A Scottish minister, teacher, and theologian, Donald Baillie blended a personal piety shaped by his Calvinist upbringing with an acute sensitivity to the intentions of both liberal and neo-orthodox theologians. He held the Chair of Systematic Theology at the University of Saint Andrews from 1935 until his death.

Type and subject of work: Theological essay on the person and work of Christ

First published: 1948

MAJOR THEMES

Affirmation of the deity of Christ should not be made in such a way as to minimize his full humanity.

Concern for the "historical Jesus" cannot be surrendered by the believer.

The Christian experience of recognizing God as the source of every good act is a clue to help us understand how Jesus could be both God and man.

Forgiveness is costly to God and the cross is one aspect of a sacrificial act he makes continually.

Recognition that "God was in Christ" furnishes the means by which we are enabled to break the bonds of selfishness and enter a new kind of community.

All Christian spirituality is centered on Jesus Christ. Donald Baillie's *God Was in Christ* is an attempt to understand who Christ is and the significance of his life. Some parts of the book deal with matters of particular concern to professional theologians; other parts are written with the educated, though perhaps theologically unsophisticated, general reader in mind. To both audiences, Baillie would like to affirm the classic teaching of the Church about Christ, and to do so in a way that makes sense. But the book is more than just an academic discussion. By exhibiting how Christian experience helps to illuminate the nature and significance of Christ, Baillie is calling the attentive reader to a revitalization of personal experience and to the fellowship and ministry of the Christian community.

Baillie begins his book with a survey of the theological situation of his day with regard to the doctrine of Christ. Gone are the days when liberal theologians could paint their confident portraits of the "historical Jesus" behind the Gospels. However, the rejection of this approach has not meant a return to precritical approaches to Christology. Things are different in two very important respects. One is an agreement on all sides that the full humanity of Jesus must be taken more seriously. Throughout theological history there has been a tendency to shrink back from or explain away some aspects of Jesus's humanity, treating his life as "a divine life lived in a human body." But theologians who accept the deity of Christ have recognized that they must not let this doctrine push out a recognition that he had a humanity like our own. This has included an acceptance of limits on Jesus' knowledge, an understanding of his miracles as "works of God in response to human faith for which all things are possible," and a recognition of the human characteristics of Jesus' moral and religious experience.

The other important factor on the theological scene, according to Baillie, is a new radicalism with regard to historical studies of the Gospels. Advocates of form criticism attempt by an analysis of the various literary forms in the gospel to uncover the nature and content of early Christian preaching. However, they are extremely skeptical of attempts to get behind the preaching to discover anything about the historical Jesus. Bultmann, a leading advocate of this approach, maintains that we can know "almost nothing concerning the life and personality of Jesus." However, this radical skepticism is coupled with a strong confessional stance, claiming that what is important to us is the Christ of faith given to us in the Gospels, not any historical construct.

Baillie finds acceptance of the full humanity of Christ combined with skepticism about the possibility of historical knowledge to be an inherently unstable position. To hold that God has entered history in a concrete human life but to renounce the possibility of knowing what that life was like is intellectually unsatisfying. While agreeing that the "over-imaginative" liberal attempts at historical construction must be rejected, Baillie holds that the reaction against this program has moved too far in the other direction. If the "Jesus of history" is given up altogether, that amounts to a rejection of Christianity as a historical religion. What is the basis for a faith response if not the conviction that in the historical Jesus is a revelation of God? Historical facts are not sufficient for faith, but without them faith becomes an empty shell. Furthermore, skepticism of the type exhibited among the form critics is based on a number of assumptions that are not obviously true. Among these is the assumption that motives for passing on a story never include a desire to preserve a true account of events that really occurred.

If the need for a historical Jesus is accepted, it is still possible to imagine a different kind of problem: Why complicate the human Jesus found in history with the "theological mystifications" of traditional Christian doctrine? Why can't we simply regard Jesus as the supreme discoverer of God? Part of the answer, says Baillie, lies in the nature of God as described in Jesus' teaching. Jesus described God as one who takes the initiative to seek us out and come to our aid. If this report is correct, we are led to reassess the idea of Jesus as a discoverer. Is God passively waiting to be discovered, or is he rather actively revealing himself in the life of Jesus? In the New Testament accounts, the witness of those who came into contact with him is unmistakably clear that whatever Jesus said or did, "it is really God that did it in Jesus." The most striking example of this is in how Jesus' followers describe his death on the cross. They spoke not of the love of Jesus but of the "God who sent him." None of this makes sense unless we acknowledge some kind of identity between the revealer and the revealed. Christological doctrines are developed in an attempt to say how intimately God is involved in the "phenomenon of Jesus." They answer the question, "Is the redeeming purpose which we find in Jesus part of the very being and essence of God?" The apprehension of God as one who comes to us in Jesus is given expression in the doctrine of the incarnation.

Another reason for thinking the picture of Jesus as the supreme human pathfinder incomplete, according to Baillie, is that it is bound up with an evolutionary philosophy of human progress. Christian faith has always regarded Jesus' life as the center of history, the key event in God's eternal plan. But unless christological doctrines are added, this conviction seems to collapse. We can regard Christ as a high point in human development, but without Christology we have a difficult time making his life the center of a story about divine action from creation to consummation.

Even if we accept the need for a Christology, the doctrine that Jesus is God and man is profoundly mysterious. How is it to be understood? Baillie rejects the claim that we can clarify the matter by denying that

Jesus had a distinct human personality but was "divine Personality assuming human nature." That account tends to lead to a denial of his real humanity. Baillie also rejects the theory that the incarnation may be understood in terms of a temporary laying aside by God of the distinctively divine attributes. This theory describes a metamorphosis rather than an incarnation, and it seems to involve the claim that Jesus is not God and man simultaneously, but successively. Finally, Baillie argues against a Christology based on the model of leadership. This view leaves the essential christological questions unanswered, including the question of who Jesus is and how he is related to God.

Baillie's own attempt to understand the incarnation begins with the recognition that this doctrine contains a paradox that cannot be eliminated. In this respect it is not unique, however, for paradox crops up all through Christian theology. Paradoxes arise, says Baillie, from the fact that "God cannot be comprehended in any human words or in any of the categories of our finite thought." We know God in direct personal relationship, but when we try to express our knowledge in theological statements, as we must, the statements fail to do justice to the reality. Doing theology is like "the attempt to draw a map of the world on a flat surface." There is always a degree of falsification.

Paradoxes arise in several doctrinal statements, but a fundamental paradox that may help to clarify our understanding of the incarnation is what Baillie calls the "paradox of Grace." The center of this paradox is the conviction of a Christian that "every good thing he does is somehow not wrought by himself but by God." This is not an attempt to deny personal responsibility or freedom. The attribution of good works to God is accompanied by a profound conviction of freedom, and wrong choices are accepted as the individual's responsibility. Yet the believer feels that good actions cannot be attributed to personal effort, but to God's grace. This does not mean merely that there is a division of labor with God doing part and the individual doing part. The good in our lives is "all of God." This puzzling experience, says Baillie, furnishes our best clue to understanding the union of God and man in the incarnation. The man who was God incarnate surpasses everyone in "refusing to claim anything for Himself independently and ascribing all the goodness to God." What in other lives is a fragmentary and incomplete experience is in his life "complete and absolute." He is the supreme illustrator of a paradox known to us in Christian experience.

For the Christian, Baillie states, God is the one who "makes absolute demands upon us and offers freely to *give* us all that he demands." The attempt to attain goodness on our own is self-defeating, but when God takes possession of us, we are enabled to obey his commands. Paradoxically, when we are most fully possessed by him we are most completely free and most genuinely ourselves. Similarly, in Christ we find one whose "self consciousness was swallowed up in his deep and humble and continual consciousness of God." In all of his good works he looked not to himself but to the source of all goodness. While his goodness is clearly a human achievement, acceptance of the paradox of grace leads us to regard it as the "human side of a divine reality." Baillie finds that all good in human life is produced by God, and perfect goodness would mean that God was perfectly present. Christ's life was the very life of God and at the same time the life of a man.

The early disciples became convinced that with Jesus something new had entered the world. God was in Christ in a unique way and the reality of the divine presence that came into the world with Christ became available in fuller form through the work of the Holy Spirit. These experiential convictions come to be summed up in the doctrine of the Trinity. Baillie argues that the doctrine "arose out of the historical Incarnation" and "gives us its eternal background in the only possible terms."

Traditional Christian teaching connects the work of Christ with the forgiveness of sins. For some people today, talk about forgiveness seems irrelevant and unnecessary. Is it not better to forget about the past and go on to better things, rather than brooding over what cannot be changed? Baillie replies that the suggested approach is unrealistic; the person who is serious about doing right will inevitably brood over moral failure unless that person has discovered "some deeper secret" of dealing with failures. If we treat our sins lightly, Baillie believes that "we will not go on to better things, but to the same things over again."

Only if our sense of moral failure can be regarded as sin against God, says Baillie, are new possibilities opened. An abstract moral law cannot forgive us, but when we see ourselves as having violated a love that continues to press us and to offer forgiveness, we are able to be more concerned about God than about ourselves. When that happens, the door is open to "release and a new beginning." Seeing God's forgiveness, we are enabled to forgive ourselves and continue striving for better things without either taking our failures lightly or allowing them to undermine our physical and mental well-being.

But if God loves us and wants to forgive us, why should we bring in the idea of an atonement? Baillie's reply is that there is an important difference between "good-natured indulgence and a costly reconciliation." One misinterpretation of divine forgiveness is that God passes off our sins lightly because they do not matter much to him. It is because God cares about us so deeply, says Baillie, that forgiveness becomes "the costliest thing in the world." In the New Testament, the belief that God wants to forgive sins comes together with the belief that atonement is costly in the conviction that God has provided a means of expiation in Christ.

Baillie points out that while there is no agreed upon account in the New Testament of exactly how the sacrifice of Christ brings about reconciliation, it is clearly regarded as a work done by God. We find no contrast between the love of Christ and the wrath of God or suggestion that God is appeased by the cross. Instead it is "God's merciful attitude towards sinners" that is behind the whole process. Baillie suggests that the cross is part of an "eternal divine sin-bearing." It reveals on the historical plane the costly nature of divine forgiveness. This does not mean that the cross is simply a symbol of something else, but that is part of something larger that is not "confined within any one moment of time."

Christ, according to Baillie, is the one who offers himself to God without limit. To do so means "at the same time to love men without limit and so carry the load of their sins." Historically, it was Jesus' love for sinners that most caused offense and brought him into conflict with the authorities. Avoiding the cross would have been possible if he had been willing to give up the activities that aroused such hatred. However, Jesus knew that what they opposed was the very essence of what he was called to do; it was the very same as what God does. Jesus suffering for sinners is an aspect of the suffering of God who loves sinners with an "inexorable love."

When we see how Christ has submitted to the worst because of a love that would not give up, it makes us realize how serious a matter our own sin is and how willing God is to forgive us. The story of Jesus, says Baillie, "makes us willing to bring our sins to God, to see them in His light, and to accept from Him the forgiveness we could never earn." The realization that "God was in Christ" allows us to respond to God's grace and receive his work of reconciliation. Without God's initiative we are locked in an inescapable trap of individual self-centeredness. Through Christ God breaks down the obstacles that stand in the way of a new kind of community built on love. To those who experience this love, God commits the message of reconciliation. Central to that message is the story of "what God has done in Jesus Christ."

David M. Holley

RECOMMENDED READING

Edition used: Baillie, Donald M. *God Was in Christ.* New York: Scribner, 1948.

———. *The Theology of the Sacraments and Other Papers.* Edited and with a biographical essay by John Baillie. New York: Scribner, 1957. Donald Baillie's brother, John Baillie, assembled this collection of five lectures on sacramental theology along with an essay on freedom of the will and a lecture on the preaching of Christian doctrine.

———. *To Whom Shall We Go?* New York: Scribner, 1955. A collection of twenty-five of Baillie's sermons.

THE PURSUIT OF GOD

Author: A(iden) W(ilson) Tozer (1897–1963)
A native of Newburg, Pennsylvania, Tozer was editor of *The Alliance Witness*, the periodical of the Christian and Missionary Alliance Church, for thirteen years. From 1959 until his death he pastored the Avenue Road Church of the C&MA in Toronto. Before that he had ministered to churches in Morgantown, West Virginia; Indianapolis, Indiana; Toledo, Ohio; and Chicago, Illinois. He was vice president of the denomination from 1946 to 1950 and a member of its board of managers from 1941 to 1963. He and his wife Ada had six sons and one daughter. Besides *The Pursuit of God* Tozer authored a number of other books, many of them growing out of his editorial work and preaching. All illustrate his deep understanding of the Christian life and his great familiarity with the riches of the Christian tradition. His works include *The Root of the Righteous* (1955); *The Divine Conquest* (1950); *Born After Midnight* (1963); *Wingspread* (1948), a biography of A. B. Simpson, the founder of Tozer's denomination, the Christian and Missionary Alliance; *The Knowledge of the Holy* (1961); *Christian Book of Mystical Verse* (1963); *Man, the Dwelling Place of God* (1966); *Paths to Power* (1964); and *Keys to the Deeper Life* (1957). (See also Recommended Reading.)

Type and subject of work: A book of instruction on how to live a deeper Christian life

First published: 1948

MAJOR THEMES

Religion is the natural response of creatures to their Creator.

Contemporary conservative Christianity focuses too much on the experience of conversion and arid, propositional theology, rather than on a personal, intimate relationship with God.

God can really be known only through personal experience.

The characteristic shared by great Christians through the ages has been spiritual receptivity.

God is always speaking to us, not only through the Bible.

We must accept God as God is and adjust our lives accordingly, rather than trying to remake God in our image.

A(iden) W(ilson) Tozer was a saint in the mold of Brother Lawrence. He practiced the presence of God while engaged in day-to-day ministry in small churches of the industrial cities of the Northeast. In sermons and editorials, he shared with his parishioners and readers, mostly lower-middle-class working people, the spiritual wealth of the centuries.

Quoting from Augustine of Hippo and John Wesley, Bernard of Clairvaux and David Brainerd, Thomas á Kempis and Spinoza, Lao-tze and Baron von Hügel, Tozer very simply and compellingly urges his readers to seek God, to pursue God. He notes that for many Christians the whole process of religious conversion has become mechanical and spiritless. People do not think of God as a real person, the object of a relationship to be cultivated. They may have a set of intellectual beliefs about God, they may even have read about other people's experiences with God, but the idea of having a serious relationship with God themselves is only a theoretical possibility.

Tozer lays the blame at the feet of contemporary evangelical leaders who are more interested in making a name for themselves than proclaiming the Name of God. They are content to talk about the Christian's judicial standing before God rather than encourage people really to experience the Divine Presence. God is the object of a creed or a philosophical argument, but is not a present reality. As he says, "we are today overrun with orthodox scribes, but the prophets, where are they?" Too many Christians, he writes, fit the following description: "We read our chapter, have our short devotions and rush away, hoping to make up for our deep inward bankruptcy by attending another gospel meeting or listening to another thrilling story told by a religious adventurer lately returned from afar."

Tozer argues that God is available to us; indeed, God made us for communion with the Divine. Only God can satisfy the deepest longings of the human heart. God's presence is our natural habitat. Sin has barred us from the Garden. We are no longer at home in God's presence. Now that relationship is one that we must work to achieve and maintain.

The first step is to want communion with the Divine, to thirst after God as the hart panteth after the water brooks, to use the image from Psalm 42. We must yearn for God. Christ "waits to be wanted." Ours is an age of complexity, but God comes in simplicity. We must strip down to essentials. Indeed, God is all we need. The natural and material gifts, with which God has showered us in abundance, have become hindrances to our spiritual growth. We have become possessive and succumbed to the tyranny of things. We must let go of all things save God. For each person that letting go will come in a different way, but, Tozer reminds us, "we will be brought one by one to the testing place, and we may never know when we are there." If we meet the test, the veil that separates our hearts from God will be rent. The tearing will be painful, we will not give up easily, but if we seek God's presence, the veil will be torn and we will see God face to face.

How do we apprehend God? By looking and believing. God surrounds us in nature, speaks to us through the created world. The presence of God surrounds us, but God is manifest only as we are aware of that presence. What the great saints through the ages have had in common was their "spiritual receptivity." They began with a spiritual awareness, and they cultivated that until it became the supreme goal of their lives. They listened to God.

As Tozer reminds us, "self-expression is inherent in the Godhead." While Tozer is a great student of Scripture and continually draws examples from the Bible, he chides those who think that God spoke in the Book and is mute otherwise. He notes that "God did not write a book and send it by messenger to be read at a distance by unaided minds." God spoke in the Bible and lives in the spoken words. God became human in Christ to speak to humankind. God speaks to us today. Dame Wisdom continues to cry in the streets of the city. "This universal Voice has ever sounded," Tozer concludes.

Faith is our response to that Voice. As Tozer points out, faith is illustrated in Scripture; it is seldom defined. However, we notice that Jesus uses the story of the brass serpent in the book of Numbers to suggest that looking and believing are often simultaneous and synonymous. Tozer defines faith as "the gaze of a soul upon a saving God." If we keep our inner eyes on God, we meet the all-seeing eyes of God.

Tozer cautions that Christians should not neglect the visible means of grace—prayer, Bible study, church attendance, acts of charity. While he is encouraging personal piety, he is not preaching a privatized creed. Indeed, he declares that "social religion is perfected when private religion is purified." He also notes that this is not a way of life only for monks or ministers; it is possible for Christians in every calling to live every day with their eyes on God.

Our goal should be the restoration of the Creator-creature relationship. God is a Person who created persons with whom to be in relation. But God is God and we are not. Too often we try to change God into our own image, rather than seeing God as God and adjusting ourselves accordingly. We must conform ourselves to God, rather than expecting God to conform to our desires. The key is surrender from beginning to end. We must put God first. And as we honor God, God will bless and honor us.

If we surrender to God, writes Tozer, we will find ourselves relieved of a number of burdens: pride, pretense, artificiality. We will become childlike, meek, and rested. We will find our lives healed and whole. We will experience no division between sacred and secular, soul and body. Our lives will be one in God.

Nancy A. Hardesty

RECOMMENDED READING

Edition used: Tozer, A(idan) W(ilson). *The Pursuit of God.* Harrisburg, Pa.: Christian Publications, 1958.

———. *Man, the Dwelling Place of God.* Harrisburg, Pa.: Christian Publications, 1966. An essay on the spiritual life and mystical union.

———. *Ten Sermons on the Voices of God Calling Man.* Edited and compiled by Gerald B. Smith. Tozer Pulpit series, vol. 8. Harrisburg, Pa.: Christian Publications, 1981. Relates to the spiritual life.

JESUS AND THE DISINHERITED

Author: Howard Thurman (1899–1981)
Described as a modern mystic and prophet, Howard Thurman served as
dean of Rankin Chapel and professor of theology at Howard University;
minister of Fellowship Church in San Francisco; and dean of Marsh
Chapel at Boston University. His many publications include: *Meditations
of the Heart* (1953), *The Creative Encounter* (1954), *The Inward Journey*
(1961), and *The Search for Common Ground* (1971).

Type and subject of work: Moral and spiritual reflection on the relationship between religion and racism

First published: 1949

MAJOR THEMES

The religion of Jesus provides hope for society's disinherited.
*In order to understand this hope, the life and teachings of Jesus must be seen
through the eyes of desperate people.*
*As opposed to the options of fear, deception, and hate, the religion of Jesus
offers the possibility of love for desperate people.*
Love is the ability to see and treat every person as a potential neighbor.

In *Jesus and the Disinherited,* Howard Thurman looks at the significance of religion for "people who stand with their backs against the
wall." He is disturbed that religion in general, and Christianity in par-

ticular, is often used to justify the inequitable relationship between the powerful and the weak of society. He writes from his experience as a black American, prompted by the question: Why has Christianity been unable to address discrimination and injustice "on the basis of race, religion and national origin"? For Thurman, this is a profoundly spiritual and moral issue.

Thurman begins by reinterpreting the religion of Jesus. Too often, Christianity has been on the side of the strong rather than the weak. This is ironic, however, since the deepest impulse of the religion inspired by Jesus is to share and be in fellowship with people regardless of their social status. According to Thurman, the crucial issue is to understand what Jesus offered to "the poor, the disinherited, the dispossessed."

Thurman reminds us that Jesus was born a poor Jew. He was a member of a persecuted minority in the Roman world. The unique character and spiritual wisdom of Jesus are understood by looking at his response to this situation in contrast to his contemporaries.

For Jesus the critical problem was Rome. Rome tried to destroy Judaism through assimilation or the use of political and military power. But Jesus was certain that the only way for Rome to succeed was to crush the people's spirit. For this reason, Jesus turned to the "inner life of the individual," because here was the "crucial arena where the issues would determine the destiny of his people."

In seeking a proper attitude toward Rome, Jesus recognized that his people had two options—nonresistance and resistance. Each option had two forms.

One form of nonresistance was to imitate Rome. This was the plan of King Herod and the Sadducees. They tried to look and act like Romans in order to avoid persecution. The other form of nonresistance was to limit contact with Roman culture as much as possible. The Pharisees chose this form. They tried to isolate themselves, hoping to be ignored or overlooked.

If Rome were to be resisted, however, one could follow the way of the Zealot or revolutionary. Rome would be fought with the sword; violence met with violence. Another form of resistance was the one taught and lived by Jesus. This involved a humility of the spirit. Such humility was not weak, for it provided the inner strength that could neither be assimilated nor crushed by the enemy.

It is this form of resistance that gives the religion of Jesus power to inspire courage in the midst of despair. According to Thurman, when such a spirit is nurtured within the oppressed, "fear, hypocrisy, and hatred, the three hounds of hell that track the trail of the disinherited, need have no dominion over them." Thurman examines these three "hounds of hell."

Fear is difficult to define or locate, but it nonetheless permeates the spirit of its victim. Like the fog, it "is nowhere in particular yet everywhere." Fear is created by a threat of violence that ignores self-respect and personal dignity. For example, the disinherited must stay in their place or suffer the consequences. As a result self-respect and dignity are lost, because the disinherited accept the inferior status imposed upon them. The threat of violence is then used as a means of social control.

The starting point for overcoming fear is the discovery that everyone is a child of God. This process of discovery begins with the questions: Who am I? What am I? When the disinherited allow others to answer these questions for them, they are denied dignity and self-respect. As an example, Thurman recalls a story his grandmother told of her childhood as a slave. In the secret religious meetings on the plantation, the black minister would end his sermons with: "You—you are not niggers. You—you are not slaves. You are God's children." The minister had helped his people answer who and what they were.

When one's identity is secured by God, fear is replaced with confidence. No longer is it a confrontation between the weak and the powerful, but a relationship of equals. Self-respect and dignity are restored, and integrity is established because everyone holds a common status before God.

Hypocrisy or deception is used by the weak to protect themselves from the powerful. Such deception is both natural and social. For example, less aggressive animals trick their predators, and individuals often resort to cunning when faced with threatening situations. In their relationship with the powerful, the disinherited often focus attention on trivial matters. In doing this the strong are distracted, and the weak can go about their daily pursuit of survival. Deception is a temporary release from the direct threat of violence.

Deception, however, affects the spiritual and moral well-being of the deceiver. It shapes and molds those who use it, at the expense of honesty and integrity. In short, deception alters what is meant by "truthtelling." According to Thurman, there are three alternatives in response to this situation.

First, one can simply accept the situation. Since the weak never approach the powerful as equals, there is really no option other than deception. Their relationship is one of struggle, in which the goal is to win at any price. "There can be no question of honesty" because the "only thing that counts is victory—or any level on which victory can be achieved." Accepting the situation means that truth has no moral meaning or purpose.

The second alternative is compromise. Truth is based on its consequences. What is "true" for the disinherited is what assists their survival. It is an amoral position, for truth makes no moral claim outside of its usefulness; its meaning and content changes with each situation. Any objective sense of truth is compromised, because survival "becomes the great end, and morality takes its meaning from that center."

The third alternative is a "complete and devastating sincerity." The truth claims both the powerful and the weak. Neither can hide behind the deception, because both stand as equals before God. No longer can the disinherited merely compromise or accept their situation, nor can the strong take refuge behind a pretentious social status.

When deception is replaced with sincerity, there is no longer a desperate struggle between the weak and the powerful but "merely a relationship between human beings." When this occurs it is a time of grace and spiritual victory, because it "marks the supreme moment of human dignity."

The final "hound of hell" Thurman examines is hate. Hatred cannot be defined, but its "anatomy" can be described. There are four stages in the development of hatred.

First, there is a "contact without fellowship" that is "devoid of any of the primary overtures of warmth . . . and genuineness." People interact with one another in a polite but impersonal manner.

Second, these contacts without fellowship create relationships between the weak and powerful that are "strikingly unsympathetic." The pain of the disinherited cannot be truly understood or embraced by the strong, because they cannot see themselves in a position of weakness. A sympathetic response is therefore impossible. Even if there is goodwill, the emotion expressed is usually pity rather than sympathy.

Third, an unsympathetic relationship breeds ill will. Because the powerful do not truly understand the experience of the weak, they hold them in contempt. Due to this ignorance, prejudices arise. Ill will, then, is a vague feeling, but it can nevertheless pervade relationships. It is a poison that can unleash an evil imagination.

Fourth, if ill will is given enough time, it evolves into hate. Hatred is born in the recalling of old injuries and grievances. In plotting to settle old scores, hatred slowly consumes the spirit—disfiguring one's very life. Hatred, however, is self-deceptive. It can be used to justify any cruelty in a quest for vengeance, and yet in the process it becomes a denial of life itself. Ultimately, hatred destroys those who are ruled by it, because the "urgent needs of the personality for creative expression are starved to death."

According to Thurman, the religion of Jesus overcomes fear, deception, and hate because of the centrality of its love-ethic. Every person is a potential neighbor and should be treated with the moral obligation such a relationship demands—that the neighbor be loved "directly, clearly, permitting no barriers between."

A religious attitude based on the love-ethic makes possible legitimate fellowship. All artificial barriers are overcome in such a fellowship, for it is not shaped by social distinctions but reflects a "common sharing of a sense of mutual worth and value." A person's worth is not determined by race or national origin but by one's status as a child of God.

When this divine status is truly embraced, fear, hypocrisy, and hate are replaced with assurance and peace. Ultimately people do not deal with one another from positions of strength or power but as persons equal before God—nothing more; nothing less. Thurman insists, therefore, that all social relationships are based on an inward integrity that is shared by all. When the depth of the soul is touched, a universal spirit that includes all people is found.

Thurman believes that a discipline of the will and spirit is required if the love-ethic is to be accomplished. It is more than a religious theory or attitude, for it is "rooted in concrete experience." A form of this discipline would be to radically forgive in word and deed. Despite the justice of one's indignation, forgiveness must be offered without qualification. If such a forgiving spirit is withheld, the fragile structure of love can give way to fear, deception, and hate. Thurman admits that this is a demanding endeavor that contradicts conventional moral assumptions about human existence. Yet, he insists that this captures the very faith and hope that inspired the religion of Jesus, for in "so great an undertaking it will become increasingly clear that the contradictions of life are not ultimate."

Thurman concludes that fear, deception, and hate are things that destroy and pull people apart. The love-ethic of Jesus provides a way for such destruction to be overcome—a glue that repairs the pieces torn away by the "hounds of hell." This is a proper pattern for living, because "the individual is made up of a creative synthesis of what the man is in all his parts and how he reacts to the living process." The religion of Jesus gives hope to the disinherited, for in such love—in such a synthesis— they are reunited with their rightful inheritance.

Brent P. Waters

RECOMMENDED READING

Edition used: Thurman, Howard. *Jesus and the Disinherited.* Richmond, Ind.: Friends United Press, 1981.

———. *With Head and Heart.* New York: Harcourt Brace Jovanovich, 1979. Thurman's autobiography recounts both his professional career and the events that helped shape his spiritual and religious insights.

WAITING FOR GOD

Author: Simone Weil (1909–1943)

Simone Weil was born in Paris on February 3, 1909, to an agnostic Jewish family. She was graduated in 1931 from the École Normale Supérieure as a teacher of philosophy. In 1934, she took a year's leave from her teaching to take a job at the Renault Works in order to learn through her own experience the hard conditions of the workers there. After another period of teaching she spent several weeks on the Catalonian front sharing the sufferings of the Republican army. She wrote for various journals of the political left and periodically took on manual labor without asking for or receiving any concessions because of her social status, education, or health, which was often poor. In June 1941 she met the Reverend J. M. Perrin, O.P., and through him Gustave Thibon, a Catholic writer, both of whom had a profound influence on her. In 1938 she had undergone a mystical experience in which, as she reported it, "Christ came down and took me," and in letters to Father Perrin she told of this experience and of the anguishing reflections that her persistent spiritual search provoked. In May 1942 she left France with her family to escape from Vichy anti-Semitic policies and went to the United States from Casablanca. She was then asked to work with the French provisional government in London and went there in November 1942. She became ill in England but refused to take the food she needed to survive so that she would not be in a more favored position than the French suffering under the German occupation. She died on August 29, 1943.

Type and subject of work: A collection of letters and essays on the love of God and the spiritual demands of such love

First published: In French: *Attente de Dieu*, 1950; in English (as translated by Emma Craufurd), 1951

MAJOR THEMES

The soul that attentively and with love waits for God is rewarded with a divine pressure or compulsion; to submit to that pressure is to move toward perfection.

God's mercy is manifest in affliction as well as in joy.

We cannot go to God, but if we wait attentively and with love, God will come to us.

If one persists in loving God even while, during extreme affliction, one thinks of oneself as abandoned by God, one will end by knowing the love of God.

The love of neighbors, friends, religious ceremonies, and the beauty of the world are forms of the implicit love of God.

In his introduction to the American edition of *Waiting for God* (the British edition has the title *Waiting on God*), Leslie Fiedler describes Simone Weil as "the Outsider as saint in an age of alienation, our kind of saint." Born into an agnostic Jewish family, she became a political leftist, probably more out of love for the oppressed than from the influence of any political philosophy. She became devoted to God through an entirely unexpected and, were it not for the fact of its happening, incredible mystical experience, one in which, as she described it to Father Perrin, "Christ himself came down and took possession of me."

Despite her mystical encounter with Christ, a spiritual marriage that was repeated frequently when she recited the poem "Love" by George Herbert (the recitation of which had first brought Christ to her) or the Lord's Prayer in Greek, she never was baptized into the Church. She remained outside the Church and insisted (in letters to Father Perrin) that "the will of God is that I should not enter the Church at present." By remaining outside the Church she identified herself with those who through the accidents of personal history lived their lives in suffering and isolation, in poverty and rejection, also outside the Church. Her death from starvation was a consequence of her refusing to eat more than her compatriots who were suffering under the Germans during the occupation of France.

Waiting for God consists of letters and essays sent or entrusted to Father Perrin. Other volumes of her writings have been published in France and then in English translation, including *La pesanteur et la grâce* (1948) (*Gravity and Grace*, 1952); *L'Enracinement* (1949) (*The Need for Roots*, 1952); and *Cahiers* (1951, 1953, 1956) (*The Notebooks of Simone Weil*, 1956).

Simone Weil's letters to Father Perrin are represented by a set of six letters, beginning with one concerned with her hesitations concerning baptism, including her significant "spiritual autobiography," and concluding with her "last thoughts." The essays that follow are "Reflections on the Right Use of School Studies with a View to the Love of God," "The Love of God and Affliction," "Forms of the Implicit Love of God," and "Concerning the Our Father." Together these letters and essays, as presented in *Waiting for God*, enable the reader to come to focus on the unique faith and the brilliant intellect of Simone Weil.

In her letter to Father Perrin concerning baptism (dated January 19, 1942), Weil writes that she has been wondering how to reach the point of conforming herself to God's will. She argues that it is necessary, if one is to clarify the matter, to distinguish three domains: that which is independent of human beings (the past, present, and future beyond the reach of any finite person), that which is under the rule of the will, and that which, although not under the will, is nevertheless in some way and to some degree dependent upon us. As for the first domain—the domain of the facts beyond our power—"everything that comes about is in accordance with the will of God," she argues, and she contends that accordingly we must "love absolutely everything," including evil, our past sins, our sufferings, and "what is by far the most difficult," the sufferings of others.

The second domain is the domain of duty; here the intelligence and the imagination reign.

But in the third domain "we experience the compulsion of God's pressure, on condition that we deserve to experience it." (Here the idea central to her faith and thought is expressed for us: that we are to love God by attending to him, by waiting for him attentively and with love.) "God rewards the soul that thinks of him with attention and love," she writes; " . . . we must go on thinking about God with ever increasing love and attentiveness." God's reward comes in the form of a "compulsion," a "pressure," to which, she declares, "We have to abandon ourselves . . . , to run to the exact spot whither it impels us and not go one step farther, even in the direction of what is good." The culmination of this process of submitting oneself to the divine pressure is reached when "the pressure has taken possession of the whole soul" and "we have attained the state of perfection."

Weil makes it clear to Father Perrin that God has not by his will led her to enter the Church. She suggests that she may not be at the level of spirituality that would be adequate for one to be worthy of the sacraments. But she declares her readiness to submit to the God on whom she attends: "If it is God's will that I should enter the Church, he will impose this will upon me at the exact moment when I shall have come to deserve that he should so impose it," and, again, "But one thing is absolutely certain. It is that if one day it comes about that I love God enough to deserve the grace of baptism, I shall receive this grace on that very day, infallibly, in the form God wills."

The second letter is also concerned with the problem of her entering the Church. Here she expresses her misgivings concerning the Church as a "social structure." She confesses that she is very easily influenced, and that the Church, through its power as a community of enthusiastic persons, might very well have the effect on her of winning her allegiance through her emotions rather than by way of her independent will to love God. She declares that the thought that she might come to regret having been baptized with sentiments "other than those that are fitting" fills her with horror. The degree of her submissiveness to the will of God, the strength of her determination to wait for God to move her, is shown by the following declaration near the end of her letter: "If I had my eternal salvation placed in front of me on this table, and if I only had to stretch out my hand to take it, I would not put out my hand so long as I had not received the order to do so."

Weil's determination to be moved only by God is also expressed in the third letter of the collection in *Waiting for God*, a letter written to Father Perrin on April 16, 1942. She tells him that she will be leaving France at the end of the month, and she writes: "It seems to me as though something were telling me to go. As I am perfectly sure that this is not just emotion, I am abandoning myself to it." Abandonment of this kind (submission to the will of God) will bring her to "the haven," she writes, and she goes on to tell him that, for her, the haven is the Cross. She adds: "If it cannot be given me to deserve one day to share the Cross of Christ, at least may I share that of the good thief." She envies the good thief: "To have been at the side of Christ and in the same state during the crucifixion seems to me a far more enviable privilege than to be at the right hand of glory." (At the close of her next letter, the "spiritual autobiography," she repeats the idea: ". . . every time I think of the crucifixion of Christ I commit the sin of envy.")

In her letter of May 15, 1942, from Marseilles (letter four in the book, entitled "Spiritual Autobiography"), Weil begins her account of what might be called her spiritual pilgrimage by reminding Father Perrin that he brought her neither the Christian inspiration nor to Christ; by the time she met him, "it had been done without the intervention of any human being." She tells him that she had never sought God; for her the "problem of God" was a problem to be let alone. (She was already, one might presume, "waiting for God"; in any case, the tendency on her part to let problems resolve themselves whenever there was nothing she could do about it was later manifest as the tendency to await God's "pressure," to be ready for but not to anticipate his action on her.)

But despite her having put the problem of God aside, she adopted (for as far back as she could remember) the "Christian attitude," and she declares that from childhood "I always had . . . the Christian idea of love for one's neighbor, to which I gave the name of justice."

Through her year's experience in the factory (she tells Father Perrin) she became intimately aware of the *malheur* (the French word is translated as "affliction") of others: ". . . the affliction of others entered into my flesh and my soul." She suddenly came to regard herself and the others in affliction as slaves, and "the conviction was suddenly borne in upon me that Christianity is pre-eminently the religion of slaves, that slaves cannot help belonging to it, and I among others."

In 1937 in Assisi, in the chapel of Santa Maria degli Angeli, "something stronger than I was compelled me for the first time in my life to go down on my knees," she writes Father Perrin. In 1938 she found that during the liturgical services at Solesmes she was "able to rise above" her migraine headaches (from which she often suffered) and to find joy in the service. She realized then "the possibility of loving divine love in the midst of affliction," and she came more and more to understand and to appreciate (and even, in a sense, to share) the passion of Christ.

A reading of George Herbert's "Love" led to her first encounter with God, and she explains that "in this sudden possession of me by Christ, neither my senses nor my imagination had any part; I only felt in the midst of my suffering the presence of a love." She is careful to tell the father that "God in his mercy had prevented me from reading the mystics, so that it should be evident to me that I had not invented this absolutely unexpected contact."

In the close of her autobiographical letter Weil writes to Father Perrin, "Good-by, I wish you all possible good things except the cross; for I do not love my neighbor as myself, you particularly, as you have noticed." (For herself, of course, she wished the cross; she wished to wait in extreme suffering for God, to share the passion of Christ.)

In letter five to "S" (entitled "Her Intellectual Vocation"), she remarks that her vocation requires her to remain outside the Church "in order that I may serve God and the Christian faith in the realm of the intelligence."

The idea that "God's mercy is manifest in affliction as in joy" and that both joy and affliction are signs of the contact with God is developed in her very significant letter of May 26, 1942 (letter six, "Last Thoughts"), again to Father Perrin. After declaring to the father that "in affliction itself . . . the splendor of God's mercy shines," she writes: "If still persevering in our love, we fall to the point where the soul cannot keep back the cry 'My God, why hast thou forsaken me?' if we remain at this point without ceasing to love, we end by touching something that is not affliction, not joy, something that is the central essence . . . : the very love of God."

The letters offer the most direct way of comprehending (to some degree only, of course) the iconoclastic faith of Simone Weil, for they are personal and go directly to the heart of her affliction and her faith. (We know her personal anguish when she describes herself in the letters "Last Thoughts" as "a barren fig tree for Christ" and tells Father Perrin that "for other people, in a sense I do not exist. I am the color of dead leaves, like certain unnoticed insects.")

The essays are valuable, however, as intellect's reading of her faith. In "Reflections on the Right Use of School Studies with a View to the Love of God," Weil develops the central idea that prayer consists of attention and that, accordingly, Christian study is fundamentally a matter of giving full attention and developing the power of attention. "In every school exercise," she writes, "there is a special way of waiting upon truth, setting our hearts upon it, yet not allowing ourselves to go out in search of it," and she underscores the spiritual seriousness of her message by writing: "Only this waiting, this attention, can move the master to treat his slave with such amazing tenderness." Even the love of neighbor requires attentively looking at the neighbor to know the neighbor as one who suffers. If one goes at Latin or geometry with the right kind of attentiveness, she concludes, one may on that account "be better able to give someone in affliction exactly the help required."

The essay "The Love of God and Affliction" is a careful statement of her view that both joy and affliction are necessary if one is to know God, and she describes affliction as "a marvel of divine technique," and adds the reassuring comment that although affliction is the most depressing and painful kind of suffering, if one loves—that is, persists in turning toward God—one finds oneself "nailed to the very center of the universe. It is the true center; . . . it is God." We cannot go to God, she declares, but if we love God whatever our affliction, "Over the infinity of space and time, the infinitely more infinite love of God comes to possess us."

If one is inclined to suppose that Simone Weil was urging an attitude that calls for isolation and self-absorption in the effort to make contact with God, one has only to read her essay "Forms of the Implicit Love of God," in which she argues that the love of God includes and requires love of neighbor, love of the world's order, love of religious practices, and friendship. Although she argues that "contact with God is the true sacrament," she immediately adds that "We can, however, be almost certain that those whose love of God has caused the disappearance of the pure loves belonging to our life here below are no true friends of God."

Ian P. McGreal

RECOMMENDED READING

Edition used: Weil, Simone. *Waiting for God.* Translated by Emma Craufurd. Introduction by Leslie A. Fiedler. New York: Harper & Row, Perennial Library, 1973. Originally published New York: Putnam, 1951. This edition includes an excellent introduction by Leslie Fiedler of Montana State University. It also includes (in addition to the letters and essays mentioned in the review above) a biographical note translated from the French edition.

Cabaud, Jacques. *Simone Weil: A Fellowship in Love.* New York: Channel Press, 1964. Based on careful research and extensive interviews, this biographical account, with its numerous revealing photographs, provides a vivid picture of the dedicated but tortured life of Simone Weil.

Panichas, George A., ed. *The Simone Weil Reader.* New York: David McKay Co., 1977. A well-produced, representative selection of Weil's writings.

Pétrement, Simone. *Simone Weil: A Life.* Translated from the French by Raymond Rosenthal. New York: Pantheon Books, 1976. A monumental biography by one of Simone Weil's closest friends who as a doctor of philosophy and letters is well equipped to handle the sometimes almost elusive thought of Simone Weil. A detailed biographical account, with many photographs.

Rees, Richard. *Simone Weil: A Sketch for a Portrait.* Preface by Harry T. Moore. Carbondale and Edwardsville: Southern Illinois University Press, 1966. Sir Richard Rees's account of Simone Weil's life emphasizes her ideas in an intelligent and sympathetic way.

Weil, Simone. *The Need for Roots.* Translated by Arthur Wills. Preface by T. S. Eliot. New York: Putnam, 1952. Published as *L'Enracinement*, Paris: Gallimard, 1949. A thoughtful but not always successful attempt to develop a Christian social ethics, particularly aimed at France.

———. *Notebooks.* Translated by Arthur Wills. London: Routledge & Kegan Paul, 1956. The *Notebooks* reflect the original and inquisitive intellect of Simone Weil.

THE MEANING OF HOLINESS

Author: Louis Lavelle (1883–1951)
One of the outstanding academic philosophers of his time, Louis Lavelle taught at the University of Paris and held the prestigious chair of philosophy at the College de France (1941– 1951). Most of his writings are of a technical nature and have not been translated into English.

Type and subject of work: Meditations on saints and sainthood

First published: 1951 (French title: *Quatre saints*)

MAJOR THEMES

The saints are those who teach us how to live in the visible world by seeing things invisible.

Saint Francis of Assisi showed that God reveals himself in nature to those who have rid themselves of possessiveness.

Saint John of the Cross was a witness to the way in which God fills the soul that has emptied itself of particular thoughts and desires.

Saint Teresa of Ávila is an example of a life in which the sense of God's presence is the preparation for noble works.

Saint Francis de Sales showed that love invests the world with new meaning and transforms anguish into joy.

Each saint represents an ideal type, witnessing to the variety of human powers and the ways in which they can be used.

Louis Lavelle's outlook on life was similar to that expressed by the poet John Keats, who called the world "a vale of soul-making." Lavelle thought of humanity as existing simultaneously in two worlds—the visible world of nature and the invisible world of spirit—the purpose of one's existence being to use the body and its environment as means for realizing one's spiritual powers. In Lavelle's view, one is not called upon to reject the natural life but to subordinate it rigorously to the requirements of spirit. This is what we can learn from the saint, who has succeeded in transcending the dual order and has combined matter and spirit in a single whole. Saints have not rejected the world as "a vale of tears," nor fled the society of their fellow creatures, nor disowned their own individuality; but they have consulted the will of their Creator and have become creators together with him in their own time and place. God has need for heroes and for sages in his creative undertaking, but especially he has need for saints, with their gift for illuminating the visible world and for helping us "to find out who we are," which is the same as finding out "who we ought to be."

The Meaning of Holiness is a study of the lives of four saints, together with an essay "On Holiness." The four saints chosen by Lavelle are types of men and women whom grace has transformed. They were alike in the total union of their wills with the divine will; but they are helpful to us because of their characteristic differences. Saint Francis of Assisi found God in nature; Saint John of the Cross, in contemplation; Saint Teresa of Ávila, in the union of contemplation and action; and Saint Francis de Sales in the transformation of the human will.

Saint Francis of Assisi is presented to us as one who, by harmonizing nature and grace, inspired a new awakening of spirituality that lasted for over a hundred years, the secret of which, according to Lavelle, lay in the saint's devotion to poverty. Lavelle describes poverty as "a deep science we must master." It "hollows out in our soul a little vacant place which we must continue to enlarge until at length nothing remains but free and empty space for God Himself to fill." This appears, says Lavelle, in the paintings of Giotto representing scenes from the life of Saint Francis, which have about them the same miraculous power that resided in the saint's own person of turning poverty into riches and of spiritualizing material things. In Saint Francis's eyes, nature's gifts are not to be rejected. Instead of finding fault with nature we must learn to recognize the wrong that we do when we turn these blessings into objects of possession. It is not surprising, says Lavelle, that Saint Francis has been regarded by romantics as heralding a break with civilization and a return to nature; but that view is wrong, for Saint Francis loved nature not for itself but as the field of opportunity that God has stretched out between himself and us whereby we can make our way to him. He had no recipe for doing away with toil and suffering, but he saw clearly that a person who finds life irksome in a hut will find it the same in a castle. Joy, he said, is the perfect freedom that comes to those who are no longer slaves to the body and to material possessions, and who have learned to accept both themselves and their fellows. According to Lavelle, there was a penitential side to Saint Francis, a sense of evil in his inmost heart, that is obscured when we think of him solely as "the troubador of God"; nor was his experience one of uninterrupted delight, as we might like to believe. But he could say, "The Good to which I aspire is so great that all my suffering is turned to joy."

It is tempting to say that Saint Francis was an extrovert and that Saint John of the Cross was an introvert. However that may be, such is the variety within the unity of sainthood that whereas Saint Francis looked to nature in order to find God there, Saint John turned away from the world of the senses as the first step toward that renunciation that must take place within the soul and that purification in which the self is rid of all particular thoughts and desires in order for divine truth and love to enter. This is the sense in which Lavelle construes the well-known formula: "To relish everything, to know everything, to possess everything, one must desire nothing, relish nothing, know nothing, possess nothing, be nothing." The "nothingness" here arrived at obliterates the world of objects but does not do away with the powers of willing and thinking that make up the soul itself: These, having been purged, are redirected and enhanced by supernatural means so that intellect is transmuted into faith, imagination into hope, and will into charity. At the peak of contemplation the soul reaches peace and contentment, which, however, must not be thought of as inactivity, for it consists of "loving attentiveness to God," in which the passions of joy and sorrow, hope and fear, are brought under the control of intelligence and will and are redirected to God. Saint John of the Cross was a prince of mystics; but not all mystics are saints; and Saint John saw in the ways that many souls pursue in their effort to be united with God mere projections of the ego. Particularly he warned against visions and voices, maintaining that since the coming of Christ God no longer uses these means of communicating with his children. Nor would he allow that contemplation, worthy though it is, dispenses one from other duties. That is a false mysticism in which the soul falls back into the enjoyment of its own activities and forgets its duty toward its fellow creatures. No one whose will has been truly united with that of God and who has seen created things as God sees them has any other recourse than to join in God's creative work.

Saint Teresa of Ávila and Saint John of the Cross were great friends, closely linked in their efforts to reform the Carmelite order; but we hear her rallying her friend on his single-mindedness. "May the Lord deliver me," she said, "from people who are so spiritual that they wish to turn everything to perfect contemplation, come what may!" He, for his part, was capable of retorting that bodily movements are not only easier to perform than acts of spirit but that they also minister to our vanity because seen by the world. Saint Teresa could speak lightly of contemplation without being misunderstood because she herself was well acquainted with visions and ecstasies, and was quite able to give her account of these. Of the former she said, "Visions of themselves are neither good nor evil: their good or evil depends on the use we make of them." Of the latter, "I seem to see nothing, to say nothing, to have no power of willing; but within me is a spirit which animates, guides and sustains me. . . . Without the aid of any interior or exterior word one is conscious of a Presence nearby." But Saint Teresa regarded these interior graces as merely auxiliary to her long struggle to bring the order back to its principles, a role in which she appears to us, perhaps, less as a saint than as a heroine. Lavelle's point, however, is that it was the constant sense of God's presence that enabled her to overcome the resistance of superiors and ecclesiastics, and that she is exemplary of the way in which contemplation can be translated immediately into action. "She mastered even the most powerful wills without herself having to make any effort of will; such decision, despatch, moderation, balance, energy and achievement bore witness to a supernatural presence which never failed to give her light and strength. Only a state of uninterrupted contemplation could have endowed her with these qualities."

"The Unity of Will and Love" is the caption for Lavelle's meditation on Saint Francis de Sales. Venerated in his own day for his preaching, his confessing, and his part in founding (with Saint Jane de Chantel) the Order of the Visitation, he is remembered today for his writings, in which, according to Lavelle, the "gentleman saint," as he is sometimes called, appears as "the very model of the spiritual director whom we seek or would wish to be in our own regard." His, however, was not the way of contemplation nor the way of heroic action, but a gentler way, better suited to those who must live in the world. "Why build castles in Spain," he would say, "if we have to live in France. . . . How foolish are those who dream of being martyred in the Indies and yet neglect their duty in the state of life to which they have been called." What Lavelle sees as central in the teaching of Saint Francis de Sales is his insistence that the essence of humanity's spirit resides not in knowledge but in love. This, he says, is the only answer to contemporary thinkers whose extended knowledge of the world has led them to conclude that life is an absurd confrontation between nature and the human spirit. As long as we are lacking in love and think of nothing but ourselves life may seem meaningless and even absurd. The mystery of love is that, without changing anything in the world, it invests everything with new meaning and so transforms anguish into joy. Like the earlier Saint Francis, he refused to admit that nature is opposed to grace: As a counselor he tried not to oppose a person's natural inclinations, but instead to find ways of directing them toward their true object; and as the author of the *Treatise on the Love of God* he argued that our wills, although truly our own, become identical with God's all-embracing love when they attain to the point of affirming what God means us to be. Making it clear that harmony of soul does not come without interior discipline, he refused recourse to "force of arms." "When we reach a point where discord is inevitable, we must not break the strings but relax the tension when we become conscious of dissonance; and give ear to detect the source of disharmony, tightening or slackening the strings as our art enjoins."

"On Holiness," the meditation with which the book begins, is not concerned with holiness as an abstract quality, but with sainthood—nothing more, nothing less. Lavelle believes that there are saints, that they are persons to whom the presence of God is particularly real, and that there is a potential saint in each of us (as well as a potential devil). In his meditation on holiness, or sainthood, he tries to draw a composite portrait. The saint lives on the frontier between two worlds, the visible and the invisible. The saint does not repudiate the body nor extinguish natural passions, because it is from these that our higher activities derive their energy. The saint is indifferent to his or her situation in the world, because he or she desires nothing for the self and wills the world only as God has willed it. The saint does not set fellow human beings at a distance in order to concentrate on the spiritual life, because the only spiritual life possible consists in relations with other spiritual beings. These are examples of generalizations that Lavelle draws from his studies.

If there is any one thought that brings these traits together it is that sainthood perfects nature. Those at least of the saints that Lavelle has chosen for study do not view nature as out of kilter nor do they find any wrench within the human soul that love cannot repair. Not that they are especially favored by nature—living among us, saints are not distinguishable from anyone else: They share our common weaknesses and are not without their individual faults. But from time to time they show themselves masters of the world, as though they see things with different eyes, as though behind the impressions that things make on our senses they are aware of inner connections that relate nature to spiritual ends. Things respond to their wills: Where the rest of us see only problems, saints also see solutions.

All of this hangs together with Lavelle's view of the world as consisting essentially of spirits created by God for the end of sharing in the highest Good, which is his own creative love—with nature, including our souls and bodies, serving as material means to this spiritual end. The end remains a mystery; nevertheless, Lavelle believes that in our knowledge of the saints we have intimations of our common destiny. That there is no hard and fast distinction between saints and the rest of us is clear, if only from the fact that no one is a saint (in the high sense of the word) until he or she dies, "for it was death that brought about the spiritual transformation without which [saints] would be mere men like ourselves." Without following Lavelle's line of thought in any detail—it involves his sometimes tortuous account of time and its relation to eternity—we can perhaps learn something from what he says about memory as being the common plane of union between the living and the dead. In memory the deeds of each of us are raised above time, freed from matter, and spiritualized—otherwise they would not enter the knowledge that we have of ourselves. So it is with our memory of the deceased: They remain close to us and exert on us a purer influence than when we lived side by side; all that is perishable disappears, and we are moved by the "significant power," the "living idea," which remains to us as "a soul with which we are in constant communion." Even persons whom we have known only by report, as is true of great saints and heroes, enter our lives and awaken in us ideas that change our view of the world. "We live with them in an invisible world," says Lavelle, "the true world of which the spirits that exist are members, and which is constituted by their mutual and constant inter-relations. Of this other world our visible world is at once the sign and the instrument; it is therefore only natural that when its work is done it should fade away."

Jean H. Faurot

RECOMMENDED READING

Edition used: Lavelle, Louis. *The Meaning of Holiness.* Introduction by Dom Illtyd Trethowan. London: Burns & Oates, 1954. Dom Trethowan, of Downside Abbey, undertakes "to 'place' Lavelle as a thinker and to indicate some guiding lines," drawing from an article by M. J. Lacroix, a translation of which had appeared in *The Downside Review.* Autumn 1953, pp. 372–386.

———. *The Dilemma of Narcissus.* Translated with an Introduction and Notes by William Gairdner. New York: Humanities Press, 1973. Translation of *L'Erreur de Narcisse*, 1939. An essay on purity of heart and its incompatibility with *amour-propre.*

———. "The Three Stages of Metaphysics." In *Philosophical Thought in France and the United States.* Edited by Martin Farber. Buffalo, N.Y.: University of Buffalo, 1950. Best overview of Lavelle's philosophy available in English.

Smith, Colin. *Contemporary French Philosophy.* London: Methuen & Co., 1964. Chapter 1, "The Search for Significance," has selections on J.-P. Sartre, A. Camus, and L. Lavelle.

THE SUN AND THE UMBRELLA

Author: Nels F. S. Ferré (1908–1971)

Born in Sweden to conservative religious parents, Ferré emigrated alone to the United States at age thirteen and supported himself through Boston University, Andover Newton Theological School, and Harvard University, where his theological views were greatly broadened. His first book, *Swedish Contributions to Modern Theology* (1939), announced his lifelong theme of God as *Agape*, other-centered love, which theme Ferré developed during his meteoric academic career in numerous philosophical, theological, ethical, and spiritual books, many of them controversial among more orthodox Christians, for whom he always maintained a special affection. Among his other important books are *Faith and Reason* (1946), *The Christian Understanding of God* (1951), *Christ and the Christian* (1958), and *The Universal Word* (1969).

Type and subject of work: Theological essay, based on a parable, on the temptations of Christians to shield themselves from God

First published: 1953

MAJOR THEMES

Many Christians are shielded from God "under" the figure of Christ, who then becomes for them not mediator and "first born among many brethren," but an "umbrella" shading fearful souls.

The Bible and the Church also are often used to keep God safely remote, "umbrellas" under "umbrellas" that block the healthful and illuminating radiance of God for all the world.

The first challenge for evangelization is the Christian community itself, since the Church needs to be brought to repentance and radical change of attitude.

Jews, too, could more readily accept the one true God, who was once decisively incarnate in Jesus and who thus showed himself to the world as **Agape**, *if only Christians would stop defensively equating "their" Jesus with the eternal Christ.*

A similar appeal could then be made to Hindus and Buddhists, to whom Christianity would appeal as a fulfillment rather than a rival.

Even secularists and Communists can be won—or outrevolutionized—by a Christianity that dares to put away its barriers to completely honest thinking and to abandon its cultural ties to racism, capitalism, and imperialism.

The Sun and the Umbrella, based on a parable that came to Ferré in a prayerful moment one night, was meant to communicate his message as widely as possible. The ironic central parable is about "sunworshipers"—so-called—who nervously fortify themselves in the shade of layers of umbrellas. After coming out from the dim "House of Legality," at the urgings of a young prophet who had learned to live in the light, the prophet's followers found the dazzling sun too much to bear. Thus they put up the first umbrella in honor of the young prophet; then they opened another under it in honor of the holy words they remembered about the Sun; then they placed still a third under the first two in honor of the community that could authoritatively interpret the holy words; then, within the shade of the first three, some raised here and there various other smaller umbrellas to honor special interpretations of particular formulae. Eventually a young man, puzzled at the apparent teaching of the prophet that sunlight itself was good to live in, tried venturing out from under all the umbrellas. Dazzled at first, he gradually learned for himself that it was better than in the shade, and he tried persuading others to try it too. Some dared. Those who did found it so good that they ventured back to tell the rest, not only those clustered under the various umbrellas but also those still back in the House of Legality and those huddled in all the other Houses of the earth; ". . . and the time being ready, there was a great and joyful exodus from all Umbrellas and Houses into the Light. . . ."

The spirituality represented here is daring, free, scornful of the barriers and constraints of tradition. What many Christians find shocking is the declaration that their doctrines of Christ can themselves be barriers against a proper spiritual relationship to God. This position Ferré strongly affirms. Jesus was the young prophet of the parable. "Jesus himself came from the sunlight; he knew it personally and taught it confidently; he lived it thoroughly, died on account of his espousal of it, and lives eternally within its power." But "umbrellas" of doctrine have tended to make Jesus into a barrier rather than a reflector of God. The doctrine of the sinlessness of Jesus, for example, is a myth that not only robs him of his humanity but, worse, robs him of his real victory over sin if he never had to deal with it in himself. Myths generate myths, and the myth of sinlessness requires the myth of the virgin birth to protect Jesus from the full concreteness of history. Likewise, the terrible old myths of atonement by blood sacrifice, of eternal hell, and of second coming, tie Jesus to standards of legality rather than to new truths of spontaneous, abundant love. "The parable of the prodigal son is the heart of Jesus' Evangel, his main view of God," Ferré declares. Theology, by erecting mythic barriers, "denies the naturalness of the love of God." The limitless love of God beams like the effulgent sun upon the whole earth; our greatest human need is to be warmed by that love and to live in its light. To this end Jesus taught, healed—and died. If we honor him properly we shall not cluster under stories about him but shall walk with him into the direct love of God.

Ferré loved the Bible, reading and underlining, praying and meditating, on this book of books. But for him the Bible was not to become a substitute for the direct light of God. It is meant for those who find themselves in the dark; it is to be a means of grace, not a final authority. Ferré recognized that "we have to live as creatures, not as pure spirits, and therefore need the help of Scriptures and institutional religion"; but there is a danger that Christians will cling too tightly to the Scriptures and ascribe to them ultimate rather than penultimate authority. "The use of the Bible as the final authority for Christian truth is idolatry."

Instead, the authority of the Bible is itself to be interpreted by the criterion of the love of God that it manifests as its own highest peak. Then it can never become an "umbrella" between humankind and God's radiance. Once the dawn of radiance is experienced, however, the "useful night light," once needed in a dark place, is no longer necessary and need not be wept for.

The Church, furthermore, for Ferré, ideally constitutes the community of the children of God, in which the children should live in God's active and loving presence. Unfortunately, in practice, the family tends to take the place of the Father. The personal authority of the Holy Spirit is blocked by regulations, organizational structure, and creeds. Instead of the joyful community of sons and daughters of Love, the Church turns into a myopic institution of nominal Christians led by their paid advocates. And as institutional conflicts arise, denominationalism with all its loveless factionalism and rivalry sets in. "Behold with pained astonishment how the Church, the open community in Christ, has become an Umbrella! No weeping of Jesus over Jerusalem can be more deep and tragic than the weeping of his true followers over the Church which bears his name."

Organization is needed, no doubt. "An organized Church life mitigates and militates against irresponsible individualism. We need the organization. Too often, however, the organization identifies its own past with God's present, thus thwarting the Spirit." This is why Ferré both welcomed ecumenical advances toward reunion among Christians and yet remained suspicious of too much ecumenical superstructure. "This search for unity is all to the good provided that it does not create a super-church which usurps the place of personal experience and that of small groups." All in all, therefore, the spiritual situation for Christians is perilous and ripe for radical renewal by the guidance of the Living God.

Critique gives way to visionary enthusiasm in the rest of his book, as Ferré imagines what a spirituality based on the "folding of umbrellas" might mean to Christians, to other religions, and to the secular society of unbelievers and Communists.

The first ones to need "conversion" are the Christians themselves. This follows clearly from the previous critique, and specific themes for the evangelization of the Church follow also. The problem as Ferré sees it is how to help Christians remove their defenses against the Light without allowing the situation to be "warped by a fight," or even to degenerate into a decidedly anti-Christian movement, with followers of the Church of the Living God pitting themselves against, rather than for, the Church as it is.

The only hope, Ferré concludes, is for the Holy Spirit so to move, responding to the loving honesty of those who call on God from outside the ranks of defensive umbrellas, that everything will be transformed. The Church needs a miracle. God is longing to grant one. "The same Holy Spirit is now urgently inviting Himself into our hearts and our humanity. The same Holy Spirit is waiting to turn the world upside up." When the Spirit finally is allowed to enter, the people who call themselves Christian will let God become real to them through personal and family prayer, through ecclesiastical reorganization based on group sharing of God's will for them and of their common property, through the abandonment of divisive creeds, as well as through a decisive turn against war, racism, and exploitation. Only then will the Church truly be the Church. "No slightly improved Christian Church will do. It must be a basically redirected and dominantly motivated community of God's love which is both present and powerful in the world."

As the Holy Spirit transforms Christians and leads them to live directly in the Light, so Christians will be better positioned to lead Jews and Hindus and Buddhists out of their respective "Houses" into the common radiance of God's love. The only legitimate evangelizing of the Jews, Ferré holds, will be on the basis not of converting them into Jesus worshipers but, rather, of showing them God's universal truth and love. Such showing was the main significance of Jesus. "Jesus never was or became God," Ferré declares, and theological formulations to that effect are misconstruals of the incarnation. It is proper to *identify* the eternal Christ with Jesus—God became truly and decisively one with man in the historical Jesus—but we must never *equate* them. "The destiny of our human personalities," like that of Jesus' human personality, "is to be fulfilled by the divine." Thus Jews need not—ought not—to abandon their principled insistence that "Jesus is not God" in order to join the Church of the Living God. Their principle has always been correct. In good conscience, then, Jews may leave their unavailing trust in Legality to order to live in the fulfilling Light that was conclusively but not exclusively present in the Man of Galilee.

Hindus too can find fulfillment of their best insights in the loving evangel of a transformed, nonimperial Christianity. Strands within Hinduism allow the personalism that divine Love entails, and those will be reinforced. Retained also in a new synthesis will be the strong Hindu sense of immanence between self and divine as the proper destiny for all finite selves. What Hinduism needs is a stronger sense of the actual estrangement between creature and creator, in this life, and therefore a stronger awareness of the need for self-transformation as well as self-discovery. What traditional Christianity can learn from Hinduism, in return, is a more adequate treatment of "last things" to replace our spiritually primitive images of heaven and hell. Together, both traditional Christianity and traditional Hinduism can be transformed into Western and Eastern branches of the Church of the Living God.

Buddhist religion, likewise, can be fulfilled in the Light of God's perfect love as shown in history through Jesus. Like Jesus, the Buddha himself sacrificed his well-being for the sake of others. He gave up his personal entrance into *nirvana* in order to remain with his followers and show them the way. Since such compassion is strictly inconsistent with the Buddhist doctrine of self-reliance and noncaring, Buddhists would need to exchange their negative ultimate goal of personal release for the positive goal of Love; but the basis is there for nonimperial evangelizing to Buddhists "if the inclusive love of God becomes our own actual operating message and way of behaving."

Finally, the nonreligious and the antireligious multitudes of our time need the Light of the Living God. In fact no persons are really nonreligious in one sense. "Religion is our relation to reality; and all have that!" But if people choose to relate to reality by reason alone, they are making a faith-judgment that nothing fulfilling exists beyond their rational compass; this faith-judgment can be successfully challenged by those who know the Light of God for themselves; and this challenge is most effectively offered on the field of universal truth itself. Those who have seen the truth need not be defensive at any level of argumentation. Arguments alone, however, may not be able to break through to those who refuse to listen because of fears of having to give up the security of their own prejudices and privileges to live simply in love. For such hardened secularists, the only hope is in the persuasive power of the Holy Spirit and grace.

Likewise hardened may be convinced Communists, who see religion as an opiate against needed struggles for justice. The Church of the Living God needs to share or exceed the passion for earthly justice that is the true portion of the half-truths proclaimed by Communists. But against false portions, such as excessive trust in science, materialism, and the doctrine of economic determinism, a committed counteroffensive of effective love must be launched by those who have dared to step into the Light. By the power of the Holy Spirit, the world can thereby be converted. "If this cannot be done," Ferré wagers, "our faith is false." Thus the lines are boldly drawn for the spirituality of this book. "If totalitarian oppression can permanently crush Christian faith," Ferré concludes, "then God is not real and Christianity is a first-class lie." But first of all Christians need to become genuinely Christian. They need to set aside their own materialism, insecurity, and hypocrisy if the coming test is to be fair. They need to fold their umbrellas. They need to step directly into the Light, just as Jesus taught and lived. They need, in other words, to accept the incarnation within themselves of ultimate Love.

Frederick P. Ferré

RECOMMENDED READING

Edition used: Ferré, Nels F. S. *The Sun and the Umbrella.* New York: Harper & Bros., 1953.

———. *Faith and Reason.* New York: Harper & Bros., 1946. A key methodological work in the series of volumes of theological scholarship directed to an academic readership. It deals with religion and the proper methods of thinking in relation to science and philosophy. Other works in this scholarly series include *Evil and the Christian Faith* (New York: Harper & Bros., 1947), dealing with the problem of evil in the light of adequate Christian thinking; *Christianity and Society* (New York: Harper & Bros., 1950), dealing with the analysis of society and Christian social ethics; *The Christian Understanding of God* (New York: Harper & Bros., 1951), dealing with the radical revolution in theological thought and the illuminating philosophical implications implicit in taking God as infinite Love; *Christ and the Christian* (New York: Harper & Bros., 1958), dealing with detailed issues in Christology in relation to the theological tradition and to the doctrine of God as infinite Love; and *The Universal Word* (Philadelphia: Westminster Press, 1969), dealing with "the fulfilling dimension of truth that can minister to all faiths, within them, among them, and beyond them."

———. *Return to Christianity*. New York: Harper & Bros., 1943. An early volume in a series of spiritual advice-giving books, dealing with the essentials of a vital Christian faith, the basic functions of the Church, and Christian positions on education, economics, and world order. Other books in the series include *Pillars of Faith* (New York: Harper & Bros., 1948), dealing with five central issues—Jesus, Holy Spirit, Church, Bible, and experience—undergirding Christian faith; *Strengthening the Spiritual Life* (New York: Harper & Bros., 1951), dealing with private prayer, family devotions, bad habits, and Christian communication; *Meeting God Through the Bible* (Nashville: The Upper Room, 1954), dealing with the proper interpretation of the Bible; *Making Religion Real* (New York: Harper & Bros., 1955), dealing with spiritual strengthening through thinking, reading, prayer, worship, the family, friendship, giving, and suffering; and *The Finality of Faith and Christianity Among the World Religions* (New York: Harper & Row, 1963), dealing with the dynamic importance of *not* knowing final answers and with the spirituality of worldwide ecumenism.

ON LISTENING TO ANOTHER

Author: Douglas V. Steere (1900–   )

Douglas V. Steere, professor emeritus of philosophy at Haverford College, Haverford, Pennsylvania, is one of the eminent spiritual guides and writers of the twentieth century. He introduced many to some of the great devotional classics with his translation of Søren Kierkegaard's *Purity of Heart,* his editing of selections from Baron Friedrich von Hügel's writings under the title of *Spiritual Counsel and Letters,* and his introduction of five devotional classics in a volume entitled *Doors into Life* (1948). In addition, he offered spiritual guidance through such works as *On Beginning from Within* (1943), *Prayer and Worship* (1938), and *Together in Solitude* (1982). From the 1930s on he led an ecumenical vanguard in constructing bridges between Protestantism and Catholicism and between Christians and non-Christians.

Type and subject of work: Devotional writing

First published: 1955

MAJOR THEMES

Listening is the ground of all true conversation, prayer, worship, vocal ministry, and what Friends call "concerns."

Listening takes place at various levels, but genuine listening exacts a price.

Qualities of a good listener are vulnerability, acceptance, expectancy, and constancy.

Within every conversation the Eternal Listener is also present to clarify and *to confront in an inner encounter; the more conscious a listener is of this Presence, the more disclosure can occur.*

Listening is a key to private prayer and corporate worship where all gather around the Eternal Listener.

Silence enhances the listening process.

In what was delivered in part as the Swarthmore Lecture at the London Yearly Meeting in 1955, Douglas Steere used the common experience of listening and being listened to as a fresh way of laying before his hearers the genius of Quaker worship and vocal ministry. Listening, as he understands it, involves far more than hearing. It is nothing less than a disclosure of the inner person, "where words come from," as the Indian Chief Papunehang exclaimed of John Woolman's prayer delivered in a language he could not understand.

All of us have experienced both listening and not listening, being listened to and not being listened to, in this sense. Steere contends that true listening requires discernment not merely of the external sounds but of what the speaker is trying to communicate that is beyond words, what lies beneath the layer of words at the level of the heart. Every conversation involves more than a speaker and a hearer. It has to do also with what each person meant to say, with what each understood the other to say, and with many other levels of listening. More important still, it involves a spectator listener within each speaker who listens as that person speaks and grasps what is going on at all levels.

Yet deep and genuine listening is rare, Steere claims, for the kind of love that is required for it seldom is present. All listeners experience lapses as a consequence of bored inattention, adverse judgments on what is being revealed or on the person revealing it, and the imposition of one's own subconscious interpretations, unfaced fears, evaded decisions, repressed longings, or hidden aspirations. Here the inward spectator must never let up on vigilance toward the outward listener.

A good listener will be characterized by vulnerability, acceptance, expectancy, and constancy. The critical factor, Steere insists, is openness in the listener, which can create a climate for self-disclosure "where the deepest longings in the heart of the speaker feel safe to reveal themselves, . . . where nothing needs any longer to be concealed." This degree of openness will make a listener vulnerable, for the speaker will know that person has been through some testing, too. Father Damien on Molokai, for instance, put a new note of reality into his ministry to lepers when, after years of service, he began his sermon one Sunday, "We lepers."

The good listener will also *accept* the other person just as that person is, Steere suggests. Acceptance does not mean "toleration born of indifference," but "an interest so alive that judgment is withheld." By *expectancy* the good listener "reaches through" to partially concealed capacities in the speaker "by something that is almost akin to divination." Rufus Jones, for instance, touched such a hidden spring in Thomas Kelly when he went to Haverford to work on a master's degree that Kelly exulted that he was inspired to make his life a miracle.

Good listening depends too on a fourth quality, Steere writes, namely, *constancy,* "an infinite patience grounded in faith in what the person may become." All other qualities, however, circle back to the first—caring enough to risk being involved.

Listening so as to lead another into a condition of disclosure and discovery goes beyond human listening. Over the shoulder of the human listener, as it were, Steere writes, is "the silent presence of the Eternal Listener, the Living God." Steere asks, in penetrating to the depths of another, "do we not disclose the thinness of the filament that separates [persons] listening openly to one another, and that of God intently listening to each soul?" As Kierkegaard points out in *Purity of Heart,* the listener stands alone on the stage with God as the audience while the deliverer of the message prompts from offstage in the wings. Psalm 139 reminds us that we can conceal nothing from the Eternal Listener, and it is the presence of this Listener that clarifies and discloses. Such is the point Dostoevsky makes in the Grand Inquisitor scene of *The Brothers Karamazov* as Jesus stands silent before the accusations of the Inquisitor until his listening "penetrates to the core of the Cardinal and reduces him to silence."

The Eternal Listener has exemplified the qualities of vulnerability, acceptance, expectancy, and constancy. He entered flesh and blood and went to the cross to demonstrate how much he cared. As Abbé Huvelin once told Friedrich von Hügel, no Sermon on the Mount could ever have secured our redemption; God had to arrange this by dying so as to convince us he cared supremely. Jesus modeled acceptance, expectancy, and constancy. Steere asks, can one find any starker demonstration of unqualified *acceptance* than Jesus' association with tax-collectors, prostitutes, and outcasts of Jewish society? Or of *expectancy* in what his acceptance did to the impetuous, vacillating Peter, Mary Magdalene, or Zacchaeus? Or of *constancy* as he rallied the dismayed, fearful, scattered, fleeing band of followers to send them out as witnesses?

What really matters, Steere comments, is not what the listener is but what the listener *is* in what he or she *does.* In encounter with a human listener, a speaker is never unaware of the judgment upon his or her life by the listener, nor can the listener resist judging the speaker. However, it is encounter with the Eternal Listener that really matters, Steere claims, for this Listener's very existence, if not ignored, "rebukes and clamps down the evil and calls out and underlines the good, drawing

from the visible participants, things they did not know they possessed."
On the Emmaus Road, for instance, Jesus set the hearts of his two companions to glowing. As Bernard of Clairvaux expresses it, the Living Listener "seems able to take fearlessly the speakers' own diseased
irradiations, lethal though they may be, to absorb them, and to transform them." The more conscious the human listener is of the effect of
the Living Listener, the more certain that person becomes "that only the
cleansing radiations of an utterly loving and charitable one will do."
The Living Listener's presence totally alters the situation.

This is especially true of prayer, Steere contends. Prayer may begin
as a soliloquy, for human beings must begin where they are. What veter-
ans in prayer counsel is that we persist until we stop talking and start
listening. The situation in corporate worship is similar. Worshipers
gather with a heavy load, their minds far from worshiping. Worship,
after all, is for the weary and heavy laden. What matters is that the
Divine Listener changes these cares, reorders them, drops them into the
background, and reduces them to silence as worshipers become still
enough to hear God. The test of worship or vocal ministry rests in its
ability to draw worshipers to an attentive awareness of the Living Listener until they themselves become listeners.

The Quaker form of corporate renewal may appear strange to many
but, Steere writes, "the living Listener's magnetic transforming caring is
present and able to meet [the worshipers'] needs and to draw the wor-
shippers into his service." Quaker worship has its own set of problems,
but it does not experience some of those experienced in either Free Protestant or liturgical churches. In laying aside traditional patterns, Quakers place immense responsibility upon the shoulders of each listener to
praise, give thanks, confess sins and receive forgiveness, offer petitions
or make intercessions, and yield to what God requires. The danger is
that this freedom may lead to an abandonment of discipline or cause
lapses into artificial reliance on cold psychological devices.

Quaker corporate worship requires both voluntary and involuntary
attention to the subject of worship. The more one knows of the subject,
the better the concentration, Steere remarks. Concentration upon the
Divine Listener is the small part the worshiper can and must perform if
the service is to be fruitful. Quakers do not speak much about their voluntary acts of attention because they recognize "the drastic variations
in temperament and personal needs in so intimate a matter as coming
into the presence of God." Readying oneself in silence, however, is as
natural in preparing to enter the presence of God as it is to prepare oneself to meet a distinguished person. Sitting quietly in the midst of other
silent worshipers helps restore attention as inner and outer distractions
tug away at the mind. Most Friends know it is futile to fight against distractions or be despondent about them, for all persons, no matter how

saintly, experience them. By accepting, acknowledging, and quietly ignoring them, they fade into the background. Some enfold them into a prayer. Others reflect on what the distractions might communicate. Most ignore them and return to the Center.

Thankfulness to God for himself, his love, his constancy, and his caring passes naturally into adoration. Regular contact with the Bible and Jesus' life, ministry, death, and resurrection may supply ample reasons for such thankfulness. Such an experience, however, leads to "no snug coziness." Adoration, rather, stirs a desire to penetrate further the abyss of being that is the living God.

Quakers enter the service not just as private worshipers but in a company of worshipers. They know something of the needs of their fellow worshipers and of the world and are thus brought into intercession for them. Steere contends that if we do not bring others before God, then the leading of the spirit "has neither sincerity nor deep intent behind it." In intercession we often realize how little we care and how much God cares and how long he has cared. From thence we offer what we are and what we have to God. "To leave a meeting without this offering is to leave too soon."

What begins as a voluntary act of guided attention may be lifted up, Steere says, and "drawn irresistibly by the living power of the all tender One whom we confront in worship." Here the query becomes "Did you finally find the Listener taking over?"

Quaker worship often concludes without a vocal ministry and has demonstrated again and again that a company of worshipers can receive a message without words from the Word, Steere writes. Protestant services suffer from wordiness and a forensic character. Friends have always preferred deeds above words. Nevertheless, words do carry power and authority when they "come up fresh and breathless, come up still moist and glistening from the sea of existence." What is spoken must come from the source itself. Quakers have wrestled from the beginning with the problem of the relation of words to the Word. Sometimes they have lapsed into conversational-type homilies or ethical counsels, only to rediscover that a prophetic ministry is a listening ministry. The eighteenth-century Quaker Quietists such as Job Scott protested the ministry of words not "freshly tempered, hammered out, and reshaped in the powerful forge of the silent listening meeting." The fire for vocal ministry is laid by reading the Bible and other great literature, prayer, writing, and using the power of reason. Ultimately it is a matter of the worshipers' own personal commitment to the Inward Guide and the welfare of those for whom they cared. What turns the worshiper into a minister is the disclosure before the Living Listener. Inward caring for others and inward disclosure of their conditions and needs are the most important preparation for speaking. Here one learns to trim away nonessentials. Quaker worship has not fulfilled its purpose until worshipers put themselves at the disposal of the Listener and one's fellow human beings for whom God cares. It is here that Friends discover "concerns," "a costly inner leading to some act that in the course of its fulfillment may take the very life of the one it engages." Friends know the meaning of Meister Eckhart's remark that "a person can only spend in good works what he/she earns in contemplation." All depends on openness to the Divine Listener.

E. Glenn Hinson

RECOMMENDED READING

Edition used: Steere, Douglas V. *On Listening to Another.* New York: Harper & Row, 1964.

Hinson, E. Glenn. "Douglas V. Steere: Irradiator of the Beams of Love." *Christian Century,* 102 (April 24, 1985).

Steere, Douglas V. *On Beginning from Within.* New York: Harper & Row, 1943. An essay on the need for saints in modern society to effect spiritual renewal.

———. *Doors into Life from Five Devotional Classics.* New York: Harper & Bros., 1948. Introductions to *The Imitation of Christ,* Francis de Sales's *Introduction to the Devout Life,* John Woolman's *Journal,* Søren Kierkegaard's *Purity of Heart,* and Friedrich von Hügel's *Selected Letters.*

———. *Prayer and Worship.* New York: Association Press, 1938. An essay on the relationship between private and public prayer.

———. *Together in Solitude.* New York: Crossroad, 1982. A collection of essays, including the remarkably insightful "On Being Present Where You Are."

THE PRISON MEDITATIONS OF FATHER ALFRED DELP

Author: Alfred Delp (1907–1945)

Father Delp was born in Mannheim, Germany. He joined the Jesuits when he was nineteen, after having become a convert to Catholicism. He was editor of *Stimmen der Zeit* from 1939 until 1942 when the Nazis suppressed the publication. In 1943 he joined in the work of the Kreisau Circle, an anti-Nazi group devoted to planning a new social order built on the principles of Christianity. Delp joined the circle at the invitation of Count von Moltke, and with Moltke he stood trial for treason and was sentenced to be executed. The execution took place in Plotzensee prison on February 2, 1945.

Type and subject of work: Writings from a condemned Christian whose last days provide keen insights into the nature of our modern spiritual situation

First published: 1956 (*Im Angesicht des Todes*)

MAJOR THEMES

An honest appraisal of modern Western humankind leads to the conclusion that humanity today is profoundly godless and seemingly incapable of knowing God.

The present task is to help create the fundamental conditions that will reestablish living contact with God, who alone can give meaning and purpose to life.

This regeneration must come from God, is to be received by the believer, and is inextricably bound to a renewal of the entire social order.

The principles of Christian spirituality revealed in *The Prison Meditations of Father Alfred Delp* are wrapped in the personal experiences of a man sentenced to die by the Nazis. Alfred Delp and a group of his friends were arrested by the Gestapo in 1944. He had joined a secret group called the Kreisau Circle who expected Hitler's defeat and were planning a new social order to be built on Christian lines after World War II. These "rechristianising intentions" were considered heresy. Charges that he was part of a plot to assassinate Hitler were dropped; the trial was plainly a religious one. Delp maintained that he was condemned because he "happened to be, and chose to remain, a Jesuit." After a mock trial and a perfunctory sentencing he was executed in Plotzensee prison on February 2, 1945.

The insights that he gained during his last months of life have universal validity for contemporary Christian spirituality. They are bare and unsentimental; he had no time for extraneous matters. As he awaited the executioner's certain but unscheduled arrival he wrote:

> On this ultimate peak of existence at which I have arrived many ordinary words seem to have lost the meaning they used to have for me and I have now come to see them in quite a different sense. Some I don't even care to use at all any more; they belong to the past which already is far away. Here I am, on the edge of my cliff, waiting for the thrust that will send me over. In this solitude time has grown wings—angels' wings; I can almost sense the soft current as they cleave the air, keeping their distance because of the immense height. And the noises from below are softened and quietened—I hear them rather as the distant murmur of a stream tossing and tumbling in a narrow gorge.

What he could see from the cliff's edge is recorded for us in excerpts from his diary; meditations on Advent, Christmas, and Epiphany; some short essays; reflections on the Lord's Prayer and a pentecostal liturgy; and in his parting words after the death sentence. These writings, written in the face of Nazi terror, peer deep into the dark heart of modern evil and point unfailingly to the saving reality of faith in God.

Father Delp's description of his time is disturbingly realistic for our own. From "the very shadow of the scaffold" Father Delp saw that his world had entered a new era which has as its recurring theme a humanity that is profoundly godless, no longer even capable of knowing God. Drowned by the noises of everyday life, forbidden by restrictions, lost in the hurry of "progress," stifled by authority, misled by fear, the ordinary person's "spiritual mechanism has rusted and become practically useless." He portrayed Western humanity as "spiritually homeless, naked and exposed." The modern world seems "incapable of being God-conscious." Ground down by the totalitarian machinery of a ruthless nation-state, Father Delp had no illusions about the strength of human evil in the modern age.

The Church was not spared by the critique coming from the shackled priest in solitary confinement. He wrote:

> But recently the man turning to the Church for enlightenment has all too often found only a tired man to receive him—a man who then had the dishonesty to hide his fatigue under pious words and fervent gestures. At some future date the honest historian will have some bitter things to say about the contribution made by the churches to the creation of the mass-mind, of collectivism, dictatorships and so on.

Admitting that the Church was no longer one of the controlling powers in human affairs, Delp urged believers to leave the familiar territory of religious habit and a privileged clergy. He found himself surrounded by "mechanical 'believers' who 'believe' in everything, in every ceremony, every ritual—but know nothing whatever about the living God."

Father Delp's meditations are not just the cynical analyses of a doomed man; they are a message of hope despite the harsh realities portrayed. Indeed the very shock that arises when one knows what one is capable of, as well as the "failings of humanity as a whole" are essential elements in the journey to renewed contact with God. Two things must be accepted unreservedly according to Delp: first, "that life is both powerless and futile in so far as by itself it has neither purpose nor fulfillment"; and second, "it must be recognised that it is God's alliance with man, his being on our side, ranging himself with us that corrects this state of meaningless futility." The recognition of our separation from God is Delp's most important message, for it helps us to realize that only by the direct intervention of God "who breaks the fetters, absolves the guilt and bestows the inevitable blessing" can humankind recognize its true identity. "The essential requirement is that man must wake up to the truth about himself." In the unfolding of history, even the dark history of the 1940s, this word of truth is carried into effect.

Once that recognition of the true state of affairs occurs, persons are free to turn away from "passionate preoccupation with self" and turn toward God. Delp's suffering led him to see that thinking only in terms of self destroys self. The "happy" alternative is that one "needs the eternal, the infinite." The hunger and thirst and awareness of lack turn life into "a continuous Advent" that is hope itself. As humankind turns toward God, consciously trying to make contact with him, we find we are no longer on our own. Freedom is restored for real contact with the living God. This surrender of self Delp calls "God-conscious humanism."

The conversion of a soul is an act of God and requires an inner turning but it does not take place in a vacuum. For the reestablishment of contact with God to occur a new social order is demanded. "As long as human beings have to exist in inhuman and unworthy conditions the majority will succumb to them and nothing will make them either pray or think." The spiritual insights that Delp found in his isolation are to be applied to all of life, to the whole human race. Only then are they valid for the prisoner of God-forsakenness.

Delp believed that every human being required space to grow in. This space includes an "existence minimum" of living space, stable government, and adequate nourishment; an ethical minimum of honesty in society, dedication to the search for truth, and a sense of service; and a "minimum of transcendence"—an ultimate goal to live toward. Delp sums these up "in the words respect, awe, devotion, love, freedom, law." Individually they are expressed in character; collectively in family, community, economy.

In themselves these insights are valuable and good, but the force of Alfred Delp's writing is the personal incarnation of this spirituality. The principles expressed by one who was forced to test their validity in the face of death carry the force of truth. His struggles and doubt are there in black and white. Near the end he wrote, "So is it madness to hope—or conceit, or cowardice, or grace?" but he also added, "One thing is gradually becoming clear—I must surrender myself completely." This process of surrender to God worked out before our eyes in his writings is a treasure for all Christians who seek God in a seemingly godless age. He concluded his wrestling with these words: "I will honestly and patiently await God's will. I will trust him till they come to fetch me. I will do my best to ensure that this blessing, too, shall not find me broken and in despair."

William Loyd Allen

RECOMMENDED READING

Edition used: Delp, Father Alfred. *The Prison Meditations of Father Alfred Delp.* Introduction by Thomas Merton. New York: Herder & Herder, 1963. (First published in German as *Im Angesicht des Todes* by Jesf Knecht, 1956.) Father Delp's meditations on Christianity, the pervasiveness of sin, and death are most rewarding if read in their entirety. Thomas Merton's introduction, written in 1962, is a thoughtful and challenging statement, an affirmation of faith that is at the same time a word of warning to those who fail to realize the dangers of division in the nuclear age.

THE DIVINE MILIEU

Author: Pierre Teilhard de Chardin (1881–1955)
Teilhard's father was a farmer interested in geology, a subject that was to fascinate the son for the rest of his life. Ordained a priest in 1912, Teilhard chose to serve as a stretcher-bearer, proving very courageous, rather than as a chaplain in World War I. After study in Cairo and teaching in Paris, the Jesuit spent a number of years doing paleontological and geological research in China. He returned to France in 1946 amid theological controversy. Since Teilhard was forbidden by religious superiors to publish during his lifetime, important works, such as *The Phenomenon of Man* (1955), *The Divine Milieu* (1957), *The Future of Man* (1959), and *Science and Christ* (1965) all appeared after his death on Easter Sunday, 1955.

Type and subject of work: Essay on the interior life from a Christian evolutionist's viewpoint

First published: 1957

MAJOR THEMES

The earth is Christ's body.
The human endeavor is to be sanctified through embracing rather than rejecting the world.
Both our activities and our passivities can be sanctified.
Attachment and detachment are not adversarial experiences.
The divine milieu is in the communion of Christians in the Universal Christ.

Teilhard's well-known book *The Phenomenon of Man* contains the core of his scientific thought; *The Divine Milieu* is its counterpart on the spiritual level. It is a meditation book for intellectuals and is addressed primarily to those who waver rather than to Christians who are firmly established in their beliefs. However, as the author writes in the preface, there is not much in this book on moral evil and sin. Teilhard assumes that he is dealing here with souls who have already turned away from such errors. The subject to be treated in these pages is actual, supernaturalized human beings, seen in the restricted realm of *conscious* psychology.

Humankind is involved in a collective awakening, Teilhard notes in his introduction. This will inevitably have a profound religious influence on humanity. Teilhard sets out to consider human beings in the double aspect of their experience: active and passive—that which the person does and that which is undergone.

Part one, "The Divinisation of Our Activities," begins with a note that what is most divine in God is that "we are nothing apart from him." All persons are impelled by the will to be and to grow; the particular problem that the Christian faces is to sanctify one's actions. How is one to make important contributions to the world, though, when we are constantly warned by spiritual writers to preserve an attitude of detachment toward the world? Thee are three responses, traditionally, to this dilemma, according to Teilhard. One is to center oneself on specifically religious acts; another is to devote oneself to strictly secular pursuits; finally, and usually, one merely throws up one's hands at the inability to understand the problem and makes a weak compromise that results in one's belonging neither wholly to God nor wholly to things.

All three responses are dangerous, Teilhard writes. But there is a fourth way to resolve the situation that will provide mutual nourishment for love of God and a healthy love for the world. This will combine a striving for detachment with a striving for development. There are two solutions that can be employed when facing this Christian problem of the divinization of human activity. The first is an incomplete solution and is based on the concept that our actions have no value except in the intentions that motivate them. But this is not fully satisfactory because this does not give hope for the resurrection of our bodies.

The more satisfactory solution is found in this: that all work, all striving, cooperates to complete the world in Christ Jesus. Teilhard illustrates this point by use of a syllogism. At the heart of the universe, every soul exists for God; but all reality exists for our souls; therefore, all reality exists, through our souls, for God. God's creation, after all, was not completed long ago; it is a continuing process and we serve to complete it by what we do. The task is no less than bringing Christ to fulfillment.

The divine so permeates our every energy that our action is the most appropriate milieu for embracing it. In action we cleave to God's creative power, we coincide with it and prolong it. There is a specifically Christian perfection to human endeavor. We cripple our lives if we see work as only an encumbrance. Because of the incarnation of Christ, nothing on this earth is profane for those who see properly. Too many Christians are not conscious enough of the responsibilities to God that we have for our lives.

There is, of course, the need for detachment through action, Teilhard adds. By its very nature work may be seen as an important factor in detachment. First, work indicates an effort beyond inertia. Then, too, it is always accompanied by painful birth pangs. The worker becomes more avid in his or her efforts, wanting to blaze new paths, to create more widely. Thus one belongs no longer exclusively to oneself but the spirit of the universe gradually insinuates itself in the person. The Christian, as described in this section, is at once the most detached and the most attached of human beings.

"The Divinisation of Our Passivities" is the title and content of part two. In the encounter between humanity and God, Teilhard writes, humanity—because it is the lesser—must receive rather than give. Our passivities comprise half of our existence, as has been said earlier, but it is important to realize that the passive parts of our lives are immeasurably wider and deeper than the active.

Growth itself is essentially passive, is undergone. Teilhard writes that we probably undergo life more than we undergo death. All of our desires to realize ourselves are charged with God's influence. But the forces of diminishment are our true passivities and we should recognize their twofold origins: those passivities whose origin lies within us and those whose origin is found outside ourselves. The passage of time is an important diminishment; death is the consummation of all our diminishments. But we can overcome death by finding God in it. We must ask ourselves how our deaths may be integrated into God's milieu.

One of the most difficult of all mysteries is found in the problem of attempting to reconcile our failures with creative goodness, Teilhard argues. Providence may be seen as turning evil into good in three main ways. Occasionally one of our failures will divert our energies into another channel that will be a more virtuous one. Sometimes the loss we experience will cause us to turn, out of frustration, to less material areas. The third and most common way, because we see diminishment all around us, almost continually, is by uniting with God and transfiguring our sufferings within the context of a loving annihilation and union. God carves out a hollowness in us in order to make room for his entrance into our innermost being. Thus everything can be taken up again to be recast in God, even our failures.

In a separate section, "Some General Remarks on Christian Asceticism," Teilhard appends a conclusion to the first two parts of his treatise. He thinks that the question very often facing people is not well put when dichotomies are implied. For example, when someone asks if activity or passivity is better for the Christian, the question is unfair because misleading. Other contrasts are set up as well: growth or diminishment; development or curtailment; possession or renunciation. Why, Teilhard responds, should we separate what should be recognized as two natural phases of a single effort? We must develop ourselves and take possession of the world *in order to be;* he advises us that once that is achieved, the time to think about renunciation has come, as well as the time to begin diminishment for the sake of being in God. This is the way to complete Christian asceticism, Teilhard contends.

Previous writings on spiritual perfection usually fail to emphasize enough the need for self-development first. This is a serious flaw, Teilhard believes. The effort of humanity, even in what are incorrectly felt to be solely secular areas, must assume a holy and unifying function. In the Gospel, Christ says that we should leave our possessions and follow him. We must do penance as a way of organizing and of liberating the baser forces within ourselves. But we have no right to diminish ourselves solely for the sake of self-diminishment. The general rhythm of the life of a Christian indicates that development and renunciation, attachment and detachment, are not mutually exclusive. They are, rather, harmonized, like inhalation and exhalation.

What is true of individuals is true of the Church, as well, which goes through phases in her existence. At times she projects a great care in the duties of her earthly tasks, at other periods she emphasizes the transcendental nature of her activities.

The section on asceticism ends with the typically Teilhardian view of the spiritual power of matter. To despise matter, as the Manichaean heretics did, is to err gravely, he contends. Matter can represent a continual aspiration toward failure, but by its nature, and particularly by Christ's incarnation (wherein he took on a physical, material existence), matter can be a partner in the quest for spiritual perfection. And, just like humanity, the world has a path to follow to reach its final goal.

"The Divine Milieu" is the heading for part three, implying as it does that it is toward this point that what has gone before has prepared us. This may be seen as Teilhard's major mystical statement. According to his account, all created things are penetrated by the divine. The world is, in truth, a holy place. The basic attribute of the divine milieu is the ease with which it is able to gather into harmony within itself various qualities that appear to be contradictory.

God shows himself everywhere as a universal milieu, Teilhard argues, because God is the ultimate point toward which all realities tend or, to use an important word for Teilhard, "converge." Regardless of the tremendous size of this divine milieu, it is in fact a center in which all for which we strive is reunited. We should, therefore, attempt to establish ourselves in that divine milieu. And, the French theologian insists, one who travels in this center is not a pantheist. Our God, he assures us, preserves the individuality of things in their fulfillment, whereas in pantheism they would lose their differentiation.

This true spiritual milieu is formed by the divine omnipresence, Teilhard writes. It is charged with sanctifying grace, the fundamental sap of the world. The great communion is found in the universal Christ; there is a profound identification of the Son of man and the divine Eucharist. Teilhard suggests that not only are all the communions of a lifetime one single communion and all the communions of all now living a single communion, but all the communions of all who have lived and who will live are but one single act of adoration.

When we come to realize that the divine milieu has been revealed to us it is possible to make a pair of important observations, Teilhard suggests. First, the manifestation of the divine causes no apparent changes on the outward nature of things as perceived by our senses—though their meanings may be accentuated. Second, the persistence of the revelation is guaranteed by Christ himself. No power can keep us from the accompanying joys.

Individual growth in the divine milieu stems from purity, faith, and fidelity. Purity is not merely a negative, an abstention, but an impulse introduced by the love of God. One's purity is measured by the intensity of the attraction pulling one to the divine center. Faith is not a mere intellectual exercise but rather a belief in God that is charged with total trust in goodness. If one believes, then everything is illuminated with the light of understanding. What we thought was chance is seen as order, and suffering is recognized as the caress of God. Through fidelity, one situates and maintains oneself in God. If a person has this quality, greater desire follows lesser ones, and eventually self-denial will gain ascendancy over pleasure.

Teilhard argues in closing that it is through love that the divine milieu will be intensified. Christian charity is the conscious cohesion of souls engendered by their convergence, communally in Jesus Christ. There is a tendency toward fusion among the good, and in this association their ardor increases. In fact, Teilhard concludes, the history of God's kingdom is a history of reunion.

In the epilogue, "In Expectation of the Parousia," Teilhard writes of segregation (of the evil elements) and aggregation (of the good). There will come a time, the Gospels promise, when the tensions that are accumulating between humanity and God "will touch the limits prescribed by the possibilities of the world. And then will come the end." Such, he says, will be the consummation of the divine milieu. The enchantments of the earth, we thus see, will not harm us because we can see, in truth, it is the body of Jesus who is and who is coming.

Harry James Cargas

RECOMMENDED READING

Edition used: Teilhard de Chardin, Pierre. *The Divine Milieu.* Translated by Bernard Wall. New York: Harper & Bros., 1960.

Cuenot, Claude. *Teilhard de Chardin.* Translated by Vicent Colimore. Edited by René Hague. Baltimore: Helicon, 1965. The best biographical study of Teilhard to date.

Teilhard de Chardin, Pierre. *The Future of Man.* Translated by Norman Denny. New York: Harper & Row, 1964. Teilhard's reflections on the direction and goal of the world.

———. *The Phenomenon of Man.* Translated by Bernard Wall. New York: Harper & Bros., 1959. A scientific and philosophical inquiry into the spiritual meaning of evolution.

Shadow of the Almighty: the Life and Testament of Jim Elliot

Author: Elisabeth Elliot (1926–   )

Elisabeth Elliot was born in Brussels, Belgium, the child of missionary parents. Reared in New Jersey and Florida, she attended Wheaton College with a major in Greek. After training for missionary service, she went to Ecuador in 1952 under appointment from the Christian Missions in Many Lands organization. In 1953, after a courtship of over five years, she married Jim Elliot. Their child, Valerie, was born in 1955. In January 1956, Jim Elliot and four other missionaries were killed by a group of Auca Indians whom they were attempting to evangelize. "Betty" Elliot remained in Ecuador and was among the first missionaries to establish relations with the Aucas and instruct them in Christian faith. Her first book, *Through the Gates of Splendor* (1957), detailed the events leading up to her husband's death.

Type and subject of work: An account of spiritual pilgrimage, as told through letters, diaries, journals, and other writings

First published: 1958

MAJOR THEMES

Genuine religion is found in direct experience with God.

The Christian mission is to take the gospel to the entire world.

Private prayer and Bible study are necessary to the cultivation of the spiritual life.

Conformity to the life of Christ is the goal of Christian spirituality.

Though experiences vary, every Christian must encounter Christ in conversion.

The conversion of sinners is the chief end of the gospel.

Spirituality should be active, not passive.

All Christians should be willing to sacrifice their lives for the sake of the gospel.

Jim Elliot's life exemplified the spirituality of conservative evangelicalism in America during the second half of the twentieth century. His journals reflect the individualism and personal piety of a religious experience grounded in a personal relationship with Jesus Christ. His missionary zeal was based on a concern to preach the gospel "to all nations" (Matt. 28:19) and to take the Word of God where it had never been heard before.

Born in Portland, Oregon, in 1927, Elliot was one of four children. His mother was a chiropractor, his father an evangelist. Nurtured in a Christian home, Elliot was converted at the age of six. Christianity thus became the most powerful force in his life and the source of his overwhelming concern for personal evangelism. During his high school years he was known for his abilities to "win persons to Christ" and his youthful efforts as a "Hellfire and Brimstone" preacher. He also loved "adventure"—camping, biking, hunting, and other wilderness experiences. This desire for adventure made him "extremely wary of women, fearing that they only intended to lure a man from his goals." This concern that "domestication" and family responsibilities would distract him from his spiritual calling was a continuing issue for Elliot and the reason that he deferred marriage until he was twenty-six.

Personally, Elliot was an energetic, gregarious man with a magnetic personality and natural leadership abilities. He also revealed a strong element of nonconformity, evident in his disgust for the stuffiness of traditional religion. His intent was not to be religious but to experience the presence of God. In 1945, at the close of his first year at Wheaton College, he wrote, "How wonderful to know that Christianity is more than a padded pew or a dim cathedral, but that it is a real, living, daily experience which goes on from grace to grace."

At Wheaton, Elliot was already convinced of a divine call to Christian missions. That sense of direction provided him with a "singleness of purpose" directed toward evangelism and missions. His daily spiritual, mental, and physical regimen reflected a rigorous effort to discipline himself in preparation for Christian service. His personal spirituality was cultivated through daily periods of private prayer, meditation, and extensive study of the Bible. He was particularly careful to memorize extensive passages of Scripture and to "claim the promises" they provided in his own life. While in college Elliot questioned those academic requirements that might distract Christians from their evangelical task, leaving them "puffed up" and proud (1 Cor. 8:1). He suggested that "culture"—art, concerts, opera, and politics— might turn persons away from the "humble life" of the Master. He wrote "I do not disparage wisdom—that comes from God, not from Ph.D.'s." His concern was not for grades or degrees but for spiritual experience. His desire was not for a B.A., but an "A.U.G.," "approved unto God." Academic pursuits, dating, sports, and other activities were secondary to his primary spiritual calling: "Nothing but Christ."

In January 1948, Elliot began a spiritual diary that he kept until his death. It provides much of the material for the book and, like many such works, it reveals the spiritual heights and depths of the author. In it he confesses his sins and failures, while testifying to a profound relationship with God. His concern was not for systems of dogma but for continuing communication with the Divine. Indeed, he warned that the obsessive dogmatism of both Fundamentalism and "papism" could find no justification in Scripture. Elliot was a conservative-evangelical Christian with a commitment to the literal application of Scripture in daily life. Yet throughout his journal he chides his Fundamentalist friends for their obsession with doctrinal uniformity at the expense of spiritual freedom.

The spontaneity of Elliot's spirituality made him theologically unpredictable. Though a political conservative, he was a life-long conscientious objector, first espousing that view as a high school student during World War II. Elliot remained a conscientious objector all his life, insisting that the principle of nonresistance was demonstrated dramatically on the cross of Christ. While relentless in his concern for evangelism, Elliot repudiated the idea that all conversion was dramatic and immediate. He insisted that his own conversion had occurred over a period of several years. God had many ways of bringing persons to faith. He concluded, "I think we alter-callers often perform [spiritual] abortions in our haste to see results." The fullness of the Spirit was "not instantaneous but progressive" as believers immersed themselves in the Word and presence of God.

Elliot's spirituality also influenced his attitude toward material possessions. He rejected the rabid materialism of postwar America, content to live with the barest necessities. Possessions complicated the life of the Christian, turning one's eyes from Christ to the things of this world. He wrote that the "wisest life is the simplest one, lived in the fulfillment of only the basic requirements of life—shelter, food, covering, and a bed." This effort to simplify his life also created a dilemma concerning marriage. Should he remain a "eunuch" for the kingdom's sake? His journals give evidence of his continued struggles with the flesh, and with his indecisiveness concerning marriage to "Betty." Marriage brought responsibilities that diverted attention from missions. They were married, however, agreeing to limit their earthly possessions so as to remain as unrestricted as possible.

Anything, including religion, that interfered with Christ's mission was unacceptable. Elliot prayed, "O God, save me from a life of barrenness, following a formal pattern of ethics, and give instead that vital contact of soul with Thy divine life that fruit may be produced." Spiritual experience was not an end in itself, but the source of strength for accomplishing the conversion of sinners.

This intense desire to proclaim the Christian message was the allpervasive goal of Elliot's spiritual pilgrimage. His journal reveals the evolution of his call from a basic realization that God was leading him into Christian missions to the absolute assurance that he must take Christianity to those who had never heard it before. There were persons, tribes, and peoples "who are not yet included in the singing hearts. . . . Hence my burden for cultural groups as yet untouched." His special calling was to reach those whose spiritual ignorance had never been broken. In preparation for missionary life Elliot studied the life and work of David Brainerd, the young colonial American who had sacrificed himself as a missionary to the Indians. He was moved by the story of Ragland, pioneer to South India, and Hudson Taylor, founder of the China Inland mission. The spirituality of these men as well as their missionary accomplishments had a major impact on Elliot's own spiritual life. His spiritual experiences, like those of Brainerd, reveal periods of ecstatic encounter with God and times of spiritual emptiness. His diaries indicate his own continued struggle against sin and doubt, pride and selfishness. On one occasion, after his impassioned preaching produced no response, he wrote, "Came home questioning the Father's goodness." He was "rebuked," he said, with the realization that God withheld his blessing in wisdom, not in spite. He had not asked clearly or purely enough to receive the blessing.

Elliot's spirituality was decisively "active" in nature. He was no isolated contemplative but poured all his energy into the missionary task. To read the journal is to sense Elliot's desire to expend himself in the pursuit of the gospel. Less energetic persons simply could not keep up.

It is that spiritual activism that he passed on to those who heard and believed. Elliot clearly believed that all Christians were called to declare the gospel. In America, he was continually critical of those Christians who professed a support for "missions" but would not participate in the missionary tasks. He wrote that young men were entering secular professions because they did not "feel called" to a mission field. "We don't need a call; we need a kick in the pants. We must begin thinking in terms of 'going out' and stop weeping because 'they won't come in.'" He urged American Christians not merely to talk and pray about missions but to carry the gospel to all persons. As a missionary he encouraged new converts to take leadership roles in church life. He was concerned that the Indian church develop indigenous leadership as soon as possible. His efforts to translate the Bible into previously unwritten languages were related to his belief that only as the native peoples understood the Word could the indigenous church develop.

As a missionary, he sought to develop a spirituality that could be expressed in the unique cultural context of the native people. While working among the Quechua Indians of Ecuador he developed a simple communion service in which native Christians were encouraged to sing, pray, and preach as they gathered at Christ's table.

Elliot's compelling sense of personal Christian commitment dominates the book. It is a spirituality of absolute sacrifice and service. For Elliot, the gospel was a life of intense devotion to Christ and unreserved dedication to humanity. During his college days he established a covenant with God that involved two possibilities: "either glorify Himself to the utmost in me or slay me." Elliot would not have a spirituality that was "second best." He would know only "a life of sacrificial sonship or heaven—soon." In fact, the possibility of martyrdom in the cause of the gospel is an underlying theme of much of his writing. The book begins with what seems to have been one of his favorite sayings, "He is no fool who gives what he cannot keep to gain what he cannot lose."

Jim Elliot was a young man when he died at the hands of the Auca Indians in the jungles of Ecuador in 1956. The intensity of his devotion and the spiritual insights of his writing served as an inspiration for a generation of evangelical young people who accepted the "call" to Christian and missionary service. *The Shadow of the Almighty* is an extraordinary source of spiritual insight and missionary fervor evident within the twentieth-century Church.

William J. Leonard

RECOMMENDED READING

Edition used: Elliot, Elisabeth. *Shadow of the Almighty: The Life and Testament of Jim Elliot*. New York: Harper & Bros., 1958.

———. *The Savage, My Kinsman.* New York: Harper & Bros., 1961. An account of Elliot's work with the Auca Indians of Ecuador.

———. *Through Gates of Splendor.* New York: Harper & Bros., 1957. The details of Jim Elliot's encounter and subsequent death at the hands of Auca Indians of Ecuador.

New Seeds of Contemplation

Author: Thomas Merton (1915–1968)
Thomas Merton was born in the Midi in France and educated in France, England, and the United States. The story of his conversion to the Catholic faith and of his entrance in 1941 into the Cistercian Abbey of Gethsemani (Kentucky), told in his autobiography, *The Seven Storey Mountain* (1948), brought him to international prominence. The publication of his poems, articles, books, and letters did not cease with his accidental death in 1968, but continues to come forth from an extraordinarily rich spiritual legacy.

Type and subject of work: Practical theological reflection on the interior life and the contemplative experience

First published: 1962

Major Themes

Contemplation is the union of our mind and will with God in an act of pure love that brings us into obscure contact with him as he really is.

Christian contemplation—the religious apprehension of God through a life in God and sonship—supersedes every other form and experience of contemplation whether in art, philosophy, theology, or liturgy.

The "spiritual life" is the perfectly balanced life in which the body with its passions and instincts, the mind with its reasoning and its obedience to principle, and the spirit with its passive illumination by the Light and Love of God, form one complete person who is in God and with God and from God and for God.

The first step to contemplation is faith; and faith begins with an assent to Christ teaching through his Church.

We read the Gospels not merely to get a picture or an idea of Christ but to enter in and pass through the words of revelation to establish, by faith, a vital contact with the Christ who dwells in our souls as God.

Far from being essentially opposed to each other, interior contemplation and external activity are two aspects of the same love of God.

New Seeds of Contemplation is an update of an earlier work, modified and expanded in light of the author's experience of others' solitude and his own additional contemplative experience. Merton always considered this one of his best works. It is a collection of more or less connected thoughts and ideas and aphorisms about the interior life, along the lines of Pascal's *Pensées* or the *Cautelas* of Saint John of the Cross. He is strongly influenced by the latter and by the twelfth-century Cistercian fathers, especially Saint Bernard of Clairvaux. Merton deliberately uses a language in accord with Catholic theology and has no desire to deviate from the Tradition.

- The interior life and the contemplative experience are for Merton what we most of all need. He sees contemplation as the highest expression of our intellectual and spiritual life. In the course of the book he gives many descriptive definitions of contemplation: "knowing beyond knowing," "a vivid realization of the fact that life and being in us proceed from an invisible, transcendental and infinitely abundant source," "an ascent to a supremely active passivity in understanding and love," "the work of a love that transcends all satisfaction and all experience to rest in the night of pure and naked faith," "the union of our mind and will with God in an act of pure love that brings us into obscure contact with Him as He really is."

Christian contemplation—the religious apprehension of God through a life in God and sonship—supersedes every other form and experience of contemplation whether in art, philosophy, theology, or liturgy. The only way to get rid of misconceptions about contemplation is to experience it, Merton writes. It is not a function of the external self; it cannot be taught nor clearly explained. The "I" that works in the world, thinks about itself, observes its own reactions, and talks about itself, is not the true "I" or the real self, but the "empirical self." "I think, therefore I am" is the statement of an alienated person. For the contemplative there is only "I am."

Contemplative intuition has nothing to do with temperament, according to Merton. Nor is it to be identified with a charismatic gift. The certitude it brings does not free us from all anguish or doubt. Indeed, there is no evil in anything created by God, nor can anything of his become an obstacle to our union with him. God looks at us from the depths of his own infinite actuality, which is everywhere and in everything, and his seeing us gives us a new being and a new mind in which we also discover him. This begins at baptism, but it does not take on practical meaning for us until we become capable of conscious acts of love.

The "spiritual life," then, is the perfectly balanced life in which the body with its passions and instincts, the mind with its reasoning and its obedience to principle, and the spirit with its passive illumination by the Light and Love of God, form one complete person who is in God and with God and from God and for God.

The first step to contemplation is faith, Merton assures us, and faith begins with an assent to Christ teaching through his Church. It demands a fundamental act of renunciation that accepts the necessity of starting out on the way to God under the guidance of others. This acceptance can be paid for only by sacrifice. Ultimately, only a gift of God can teach us the difference between the dry outer crust of formality that the Church sometimes acquires from the human natures that compose it, and the living inner current of Divine Life that is the only real Catholic tradition.

We read the Gospels not merely to get a picture or idea of Christ but to enter in and pass through the words of revelation to establish, by faith, a vital contact with the Christ who dwells in our souls as God. According to Merton, the mere name of Jesus or the indistinct, unanalyzed notion of Christ is enough to keep the faith fully occupied in a simple and loving awareness of God who is really present in our souls by the gift of his personal love. This loving awareness is a thing more real and more valuable by far than anything we can arrive at by our interior senses alone, for the picture of Jesus we may have in our imagination remains nothing but a picture, while the love that his grace produces in our hearts can bring us into direct contact with him as he really is.

But before this begins, Merton writes, we ordinarily have to labor to prepare ourselves in our own way and with the help of his grace, by deepening our knowledge and love of God in meditation and active forms of prayer, as well as by setting our wills free from attachment to created things. Attachment to spiritual things is just as much an attachment as inordinate desires and attachment to worldly goods. They all make contemplation difficult and even impossible. The way to God lies through deep darkness in which all knowledge and all created wisdom and all pleasure and prudence and all human hope and human joy are defeated and annulled by the overwhelming purity of the light and the presence of God.

It is more ordinary for the spirit to learn contemplation from God not in a sudden flash but imperceptibly, by very gradual steps. As a matter of fact, according to Merton, without the groundwork of long and patient trial and slow progress in the darkness of pure faith, contemplation will never be learned at all. The real purpose of meditation is to teach us how to free ourselves from created things and temporal concerns and enter into a conscious and loving contract with God in which we are disposed to receive from God the help we know we need, and to pay God the praise and honor and thanksgiving and love that it is our joy to give.

Compared with the pure and peaceful comprehension of love in which the contemplative is permitted to see the truth not so much by seeing it as by being absorbed within it, ordinary ways of seeing and knowing are full of blindness, labor, and uncertainty. Through contemplative union with God we become a "new man." This new person, spiritually and mystically one identity, is at once Christ and myself. We receive him in the "inspiration" of secret love, and we give him to others in the outgoing of our own charity.

Far from being essentially opposed to each other, interior contemplation and external activity are two aspects of the same love of God. But the activity of contemplatives is born of their contemplation and must resemble it. Everything one does outside of contemplation reflects the luminous tranquillity of the interior life. Ultimately the secret of all this is perfect abandonment to the will of God in things we cannot control and perfect obedience to him in everything that depends on our own wills, so that in all things, in our interior life and in our outward works, we desire only one thing, the fulfillment of God's will. Merton remains ever concrete and down-to-earth in his contemplative attitude. He relates it to communism and property rights and everyday duties. "The contemplative needs to be properly fed, clothed and housed. But he also needs to share something of the hardship of the poor. He needs to be able to identify himself honestly and sincerely with the poor, to be able to look at life through their eyes, and to do this because he is really one of them."

Merton's Catholicism is most evident in the role he gives to the Blessed Virgin Mary: "In the actual living human person who is the Virgin Mother of Christ are all the poverty and all the wisdom of all the saints. It all came to them through her, and is in her. The sanctity of all the saints is a participation in her sanctity, because in the order he established God wills that all graces come to men through Mary. . . . The emptiness and interior solitude and peace without which we cannot be filled with God were given by Him to Mary in order that she might receive Him into the world by offering Him the hospitality of a being that was perfectly pure, perfectly silent, perfectly at rest, perfectly at peace, and centered in utter humility."

As a son of Saint Benedict, Merton gives humility its due place: "It is almost impossible to over estimate the value of true humility and its power in the spiritual life. . . . In perfect humility, all selfishness disappears and your soul no longer lives for itself or in itself for God: and it is lost and submerged in Him and transformed into Him."

In the end there seem to be no distinctions: "For in the depths of contemplative prayer there seems to be no division between subject and object, and there is no reason to make any statement either about God or about oneself. He IS and this reality absorbs everything else." For this we are made, so says Merton, to enter fully into the being and joy of the Lord.

M. Basil Pennington

RECOMMENDED READING

Edition used: Merton, Thomas. *New Seeds of Contemplation.* New York: New Directions, 1972.

Hart, Patrick, ed. *The Message of Thomas Merton.* Cistercian Studies Series, vol. 42. Kalamazoo, Mich.: Cistercian Publications, 1981. Twelve studies on Merton by the leading scholars in the field, edited, with an introduction, by Merton's secretary. The first study, by Merton's last abbot, is most relevant to our work here.

———. *Thomas Merton/Monk. A Monastic Tribute.* Cistercian Studies Series, vol. 52. Kalamazoo, Mich.: Cistercian Publications, 1983. Nineteen reflections on Merton by fellow monks and others who knew him well, along with the homily Abbot Flavian preached at his funeral and an Afterword by Rosemary Haughton. A bibliography lists the thirty-nine books published by Merton in his lifetime and twenty-one of his posthumous works.

Merton, Thomas. *The Hidden Ground of Love.* Edited by William H. Shannon. New York: Farrar, Straus & Giroux, 1985. This first volume of the collected letters of Merton includes those on religious experience and social concern. These more candid and personal writings of the author complement the works he carefully prepared for publication. Shannon has a good preface and introduction.

———. *The Seven Storey Mountain.* New York: Harcourt, Brace & Co., 1948. Merton later repudiated some of the attitudes prevalent in this book, but it remains a classic, a conversion story with which multitudes have been able to identify.

Mott, Michael. *The Seven Mountains of Thomas Merton.* Boston: Houghton Mifflin, 1984. The authorized biography of Thomas Merton (the authorization entitling the author to use otherwise reserved material), this is the most complete and satisfying life of Merton yet produced. It contains a twenty-page bibliography and some interesting pictures.

MARKINGS

Author: Dag Hammarskjöld (1905–1961)
Hammarskjöld was born in Johköping, Sweden, and died near Ndola, Rhodesia, on September 18, 1961, in a plane crash while flying there to negotiate a cease-fire between United Nations and Katanga forces. The son of the Swedish prime minister during World War I, Hammarskjöld studied law and economics at the University of Uppsala and Stockholm. After serving as secretary and chairman of the board of governors of the Bank of Sweden, he became under secretary of the Swedish department of finance. In 1946 he entered the foreign ministry as financial adviser. In 1951 he was vice chairman of the Swedish delegation to the United Nations. In 1952 he became chairman, and in 1953 he was elected secretary-general of the UN. He was reelected in 1957.

Type and subject of work: Spiritual diary

First published: 1964

MAJOR THEMES

Genuine religion is an inner experience of the Divine.
God is the source of all spiritual life.
In sacrifice and suffering, particularly the suffering of Christ, we discover the meaning of life.
Jesus is our best example of life lived to its fullest and best.
Fear of death and loneliness, inescapable elements of life, can be the source of spiritual insight and development.

Faith is a struggle that always involves an element of risk.

In self-surrender and service to others, human beings discover their true destiny.

The Mystic Way provides liberation for service and relationships.

After Hammarskjöld's untimely death in 1961, the manuscript of his *Vägmärken*, or *Markings*, was discovered in his New York residence. Attached to it was a letter to his friend Leif Belfrage, the Swedish under secretary for foreign affairs. In the letter, Hammarskjöld gives his friend permission to pursue the publication of the diary. The writing was begun, he said, "without thought of anybody else reading it," but the situation changed as he became a more public person. Thus, he concludes, "These entries provide the only true 'profile' that can be drawn." They were written "for myself, not for the public," as a part of "my negotiations with myself—and with God."

Hammarskjöld began the journal sometime in 1925 and his last entry was made August 24, 1961, only a few weeks before his death, September 18, 1961.

The major portion of *Markings* was written during the 1950s, that period when Hammarskjöld was secretary-general of the United Nations. Exact dates of entries do not appear until 1953. Most are simply listed under particular years.

While common themes appear throughout the work, there is no systematic method behind the essays. Rather, these writings reflect various day-to-day insights and meditations of a spiritually sensitive person. Hammarskjöld does not refer extensively to contemporary events or persons. The diary was not an outlet for his secret denunciation of enemies or movements in the world. It is a written account of his spiritual pilgrimage expressed within the struggles and celebrations of life. The entries vary in style, content, and length. Most are brief comments born of a particular moment of inspiration or contemplation. Citations give some indication as to Hammarskjöld's interest in poetry, literature, and theology. Most of the Scripture references are taken from the Psalms and the Gospels.

Other quotations are taken from the classic mystical literature of the Church and from a variety of poets. Mystics include Meister Eckhart, Saint John of the Cross, and Julian of Norwich. Eckhart, the fourteenth-century German mystic, seems to have been a particular favorite. Hammarskjöld also refers to numerous poets, among them Saint John Perse, whose work he translated into Swedish. Hammarskjöld's style is sometimes heavy, sometimes obscure. Even the briefest of the entries often seem to be written in a type of blank verse, and a strong poetic element runs throughout the book. He was particularly influenced by the *haiku*, that characteristically Japanese form of blank verse. Most of the entries for 1959, for example, are written in the form of *haiku*. One of them reads:

> For him who has faith
> The last miracle
> Shall be greater than the first.

Hammarskjöld's religion, at least as *Markings* reveals it, seems profoundly private, even secret, in its primary orientation. It is a religious experience anchored in the intimacy of the self with the Divine. It is also a deeply ethical faith that insists on right behavior and right relationship with others, not as a formal legalism but as a quality of life.

While the essays are not organized thematically, there are recurring themes. The God to whom Hammarskjöld commits himself is a personal deity, transcendent in his holiness but intimate in his presence with his creation. He is not the God of dogma and doctrine but the God of direct encounter. Although specific references to God occur intermittently in the journal, the practice of the presence of God permeates the work. God is the source of all spiritual enlightenment. Hammarskjöld is less concerned that concepts of God be orthodox than that they be personal. He writes: "God does not die on the day when we cease to believe in a personal deity, but we die on the day when our lives cease to be illumined by a steady radiance, of a wonder, the source of which is beyond all reason." It is experience with God himself that is the essence of true religion. It is in union with God that one discovers life itself. To lose self in God is to discover self as it was intended to be. "I am the vessel. The draught is God's. And God is the thirsty one."

Hammarskjöld's mysticism is clearly Christocentric. It is Christ who reveals what God is like. This idea seems less exclusive than inclusive. It is not Christianity that Hammarskjöld seeks but Christ himself, "the Way" that leads to a deeper knowledge with God and the model for all life. Hammarskjöld seems most concerned about the sufferings of Christ as a clue to understanding the nature of all suffering. His references to Christ continually relate to suffering, sacrifice, and the cross. He writes, "He who has surrendered himself to it knows that the Way ends on the Cross—even when it leads through the jubilation of Gennesaret or the triumphal entry into Jerusalem."

Jesus represented humanity and mystical religion at its best. His association with the outcasts and the public sinners was evidence that he saw the worth of all persons, whatever their condition.

Jesus' Passion is but one element in another of Hammarskjöld's continuing concerns: death. "The inaccessible solitude of death" is a topic that occurs repeatedly throughout *Markings*. Death is at once friend and enemy, to be feared and welcomed by human beings. How does one "die rightly"? he asks. A few entries reflect on the question of suicide and the search for death; others call for courage in the face of death, while still others examine the relationship between death and loneliness.

Loneliness is one of the constant issues that Hammarskjöld explores. Loneliness is "a blast from the storm center of death." Solitude is an inescapable reminder of that most solitary moment, death. Yet loneliness is also a spiritual asset. It can be "a communion" that broadens our vision of reality. For Hammarskjöld such loneliness was "inescapable" from which only death could bring deliverance. Through loneliness one looks for faith—faith that is always a "risk." Faith is allowing "the inner" to have precedence over "the outer" nature of life. It is not a quality that can be described or analyzed. To act in faith is to experience miracles. Yet human nature often confuses the miracle with the faith, and in doing so risks the loss of faith. Faith, he writes, "is not derived from nor created, nor carried by anything except its own reality." Life, therefore, is the arena in which we search for and struggle with faith.

As he reflects on the meaning of life, Hammarskjöld reveals a sense of destiny, if not fatalism. He indicates that those who fail to take "the way which could have been theirs will be lost eternally." The sense of destiny means recognizing that your life is not your own but belongs to God and through him to other persons. Our destiny is to live for God and others. Self-centeredness is the great destructive force of human life. Destiny is not something lost in the past or anticipated in the future. He insisted that "your duty, your reward—your destiny— are *here and now.*" Hammarskjöld seems to have had a powerful sense of destiny in his own life.

The sense of destiny enables persons to accept life as a gift and recognize the necessity of humility. Humility is found in simply accepting one's self. Such worth is not found in being better than anyone else, but in accepting ourselves as we are. "To be humble is *not to make comparisons.*"

Hammarskjöld seems to have struggled with humility throughout his life. Several journal entries contain suggestions for dealing with pride and public acclaim. He reveals a particular mistrust of those artificial social occasions where persons meet together but fail to communicate. Several of the *Markings* entries bemoan the observance of "sociability," around which persons exchange meaningless trivialities without really responding to one another. He warns against those practices that give the false impression of community while actually promoting "the hell of spiritual death."

Ethical behavior is another continuing theme of *Markings.* References to right action, duty, and proper moral and spiritual conduct occur throughout the book. "Goodness," he believed, was one of life's simple attributes, a willingness to "live for others." It was found in right relationship with others. Yet his sense of virtue is less an elaborate code of behavior than a way of life. Goodness and morality begin, not with the "great" commitments of one's life, but with the "little" ones. Before we can declare our love for "the masses of humanity, we must reveal that love for specific individuals. Through self-sacrifice and self-giving the individual discovers true freedom beyond religious dogmas or moral codes. The experience of the transcendent, the willingness to surrender self to God and others provides liberation from the need to live "with the herd." It is "the freedom of the continual farewell, the hourly self-surrender" that leads to "self-realization."

It is in that sense of limitation and surrender that Hammarskjöld claimed to have discovered the real meaning of life. In an entry dated Whitsunday, 1961, he reflected on that unknown moment when "I did answer *yes* to someone—or something—and from that hour I was certain that existence is meaningful and that . . . my life, in self-surrender, had a goal." It was a Way that brought the liberating grace of humility and the experience of the Cross.

Thus Dag Hammarskjöld discovered the Mystic Way. It was a mysticism he described as "self-surrender without self-destruction," a way that required the courage to go on whether anyone else might follow. It was a mysticism not limited to abstract speculation, but evident in the here and now, a mystery lived in the immediate moment, "a stillness in the midst of other human beings." This sense of the transcendent, the ability to experience God amid the struggles of life is the central theme of Hammarskjöld's *Markings*. It is a practical, active mysticism that is expressed tangibly in human relationships and daily life. It provides a liberation for a genuine service to humanity that is based not on accumulating power or reputation but on sincere service to others. Such a quality of life was not inherent in human life, but was a gift from God. Thus the mystic was a "recipient," one who was "grateful for being allowed to listen, to observe, to understand." We do not seek the Mystic Way; it seeks us. In discovering that, we discover ourselves.

Markings is a classic of modern spirituality. It represents the private spiritual journey of a very public individual.

One of Hammarskjöld's brief poems provides a fitting memorial:

> Alone in his secret growth,
> He found a kinship
> With all growing things.

William J. Leonard

RECOMMENDED READING

Edition used: Hammarskjöld, Dag. *Markings*. Translated from Swedish by Leif
Sjöberg and W. H. Auden. New York: Knopf, 1965.

Van Dusen, Henry Atney. *Dag Hammarskjöld: The Statesman and His Faith*. New
York: Harper & Row, 1967. This book provides a basic biography of Hammarskjöld, with particular attention to the relationship between his political attitudes and his religious commitment.

STRENGTH TO LOVE

Author: Martin Luther King, Jr. (1929–1968)
Awarded the Nobel Peace Prize in 1964, this black clergyman labored for racial equality in his native United States and throughout the world. Heading the Southern Christian Leadership Conference, King practiced a philosophy of nonviolent resistance and civil disobedience. He was also a masterful preacher, orator, and writer. His other important books include: *Stride Toward Freedom* (1958) and *Why We Can't Wait* (1964), the latter including his famous "Letter from Birmingham Jail." King was assassinated in Memphis, Tennessee, on April 4, 1968.

Type and subject of work: A series of sermons—some written in Georgia jails—preached by King from 1955 to 1963 during the civil rights struggle in the United States

First published: 1964

MAJOR THEMES

As exemplified in Jesus Christ, love is the most durable power in the world.

The universe is governed by a loving, personal God who is the companion of those who struggle for justice.

Evil cannot permanently organize itself, for it contains the seeds of its own destruction.

In the life, death, and resurrection of Jesus, we see that unearned suffering is redemptive and that evil is overcome with good.

God is able to subdue all evil, but God calls on humankind to cooperate in this

task and strengthens those who do so.

When combined with Mahatma Gandhi's method of nonviolent resistance, the Christian doctrine of love is a potent force in the struggle for freedom.

Well over seventy million human beings have been uprooted, enslaved, or killed in the twentieth century alone. What happened to those victims? Is death—utter annihilation—their end? How should we appraise such wasting of human life? Considering such questions as these moves one to reflect on the significance of evil. Why does it exist? Where does it lead? Can evil be overcome? Raising his voice against a world that wasted human life through racial hatred, poverty, and violence, Martin Luther King, Jr., spent his life wrestling with those questions in word and deed.

King outlined part of the problem of evil in his "Letter from Birmingham Jail" (April 16, 1963): "Lamentably, it is an historical fact that privileged groups seldom give up their privileges voluntarily. Individuals may see the moral light and voluntarily give up their unjust posture; but, as Reinhold Niebuhr has reminded us, groups are more immoral than individuals. We know through painful experience that freedom is never voluntarily given by the oppressor; it must be demanded by the oppressed." Later, on August 28, 1963, King spoke at a massive civil rights rally in Washington, D.C. He proclaimed that "in spite of the difficulties and frustrations of the moment, I still have a dream. It is a dream deeply rooted in the American dream. I have a dream that one day this nation will rise up and live out the true meaning of its creed: 'We hold these truths to be self-evident: that all men are created equal.'" His dream, King concluded, was that "when we let freedom ring, when we let it ring from every village and every hamlet, from every state and every city, we will be able to speed up that day when all of God's children, black men and white men, Jews and Gentiles, Protestants and Catholics, will be able to join hands and sing in the words of that old Negro spiritual, 'Free at last! Free at last! Thank God almighty, we are free at last!'"

As an orator and a spiritual-political leader for his nation, Martin Luther King, Jr., may never have had a finer moment than on that summer day in the American capital. The point is arguable, however, because the Sunday sermons that King preached regularly were brilliant and inspiring, too. Urged to publish a sampling of them from the period 1955–1963, King expressed misgivings because "a sermon is not an essay to be read but a discourse to be heard." Nevertheless, the publication of *Strength to Love* more than fulfilled his hope that "a message may come to life for readers of these printed words."

King's sermons make clear that evil is activity, sometimes inactivity, and thus a manifestation of power. Evil powers are those that *waste*. That is, evil happens whenever power is used to ruin or squander life, or whenever it is not used to forestall those results. The kind of evil that most concerned King ignores and violates the worth of individuals. Everyone inflicts that sort of pain to some degree. Yet some people, and especially some societies, are more perverse than others. We measure them by the extent to which their actions waste human existence.

As he combated evil, King found it meaningful to affirm his love for life in Christian terms. Through Jesus, preached King, God gives reason to trust that life beyond death is in the future for people of faith. But God also intends that this hope should give us courage to take action now for justice, dignity, and freedom. Affirming that the world and human life are God's creation, King saw God at work in the world, striving with men and women to achieve a community in which racism has no place. The fatherhood of God, King frequently emphasized, implies the interdependence—the brotherhood and sisterhood—of humankind. All people, wrote King, "are caught in an inescapable network of mutuality, tied in a single garment of destiny. Whatever affects one directly affects all indirectly. I can never be what I ought to be until you are what you ought to be, and you can never be what you ought to be until I am what I ought to be."

Within this framework of God's love and human interdependence, King attempted to determine evil's significance. Nothing is more obvious, he thought, than the presence of evil in the universe, its chief manifestation being our brutalizing tendency to hate and oppress each other. King saw every person's existence as a mixture of and a struggle between good and evil. Created in God's image, human life is good, but it is also stained and shattered by destructive powers. King had no comprehensive theory that ultimately explained why evil exists, although he did point to humanity's abuse of freedom as a crucial factor. Instead he focused on the structure of evil, on God's action and our human responsibility in coping with it.

"Evil," asserted King, "carries the seed of its own destruction." Its forces are powerful and stubborn, never voluntarily relinquishing their hold. But, King argued, "evil cannot permanently organize itself." Its nature is to divide, separate, and negate. This structure suggests a sense in which evil is self-destructive. It will not destroy itself completely, he admitted. New obstacles will impede us repeatedly. The consuming force of evil, however, does not exist unchecked. Internally unstable, it is capable of being subdued by the powers of goodness—justice, freedom, and especially love—which remain vital however threatened they may be at times. "Looking back," King could say as he surveyed the battle against American racism, "we see the forces of segregation gradually dying on the seashore."

As for God's action and humanity's responsibility in coping with evil, King held that God is committed to freedom. God permits evil as part of the price to be paid for freedom in the world, but he also contended that God did not will—directly or indirectly—any specific instance of evil. God's commitment to freedom, however, does have some important ramifications for the way in which God permits evil to exist. For that commitment means not only that people can diverge from the course of action that God wants them to pursue but also that trying to discern and follow God's will entails conscious choices. Furthermore, if divergence from the will of God occurs, God does not always use every available means to set things right.

Not that God is unconcerned about justice, insisted King. God is committed to justice but within the context of freedom. God's purpose for human life seems to entail our attempt to establish a community of love through our creative use of freedom, which includes both controlling the potential for evil in human existence and atoning for evil actions that do occur. "Therefore," King contended, "God cannot at the same time impose his will upon his children and also maintain his purpose for man." Yet God will not allow human beings to make a total shambles of creation. Evil is kept in check partly by its very nature. Moreover, although God will not do for us what we can do for ourselves, when people turn to God in faith, they can renew courage and strength to attempt what is just and good.

The universe is formed and finally controlled by the love of God. That love's reality and power, moreover, are revealed with special clarity in the life, death, and resurrection of Jesus. Love builds up and transforms life for the good. It also conquers death; the grave is not our end. "Love," said King, "is the most durable power in the world. This creative force, so beautifully exemplified in the life of our Christ, is the most potent instrument available in mankind's quest for peace and security."

If only men and women will give themselves to love, the universe is structured to favor that ideal. Conversely, King was also convinced that hate and violence breed more of the same even if they sow the seeds of their own destruction at the same time. The forces of evil must not be allowed to do business as usual; resistance to them is indispensable. As he pursued the cause of racial justice, King urged his followers to take up nonviolent resistance and civil disobedience. The authority of these strategies, he asserted, resides in their ability to expose and thwart evil without sacrificing persons. Suffering may be experienced in the course of such resistance, but this suffering is redemptive. It can strike the human conscience and thus produce a defense of freedom and justice. Such suffering can also lead to repentance in those who cause it.

No matter how much he had reason to despair, King retained a deep and abiding faith in the goodness and power of God. "Our God is able," he liked to say, a conviction that provided the title for one of the most popular sermons in *Strength to Love*. At the same time, King always stressed God's decision to create persons with freedom and to respect the integrity and power that freedom entails. God gives us power and then respects it. Such a God, underscored King, is one who takes risks. Such a God recognizes that things may not always function smoothly and that injustices may occur, perhaps even on a massive scale. This God apparently has a high degree of patience and self-control. When things are not going well, God could intervene directly and dramatically. But if King is correct, God's actions in the world are more indirect and subtle. God instills courage when people ask in faith, and God gives renewed strength when people trust and call upon God to support righteous ends. But the kingdom of God for us is "not yet," and for now this life remains a scene of struggle and suffering. Improvements, however, are possible. Oppression can be relieved. Freedom and justice can be extended when, with God's help, we find strength to love.

Reviewing the racial strife that wracked Birmingham, Alabama, in the 1960s, King once observed that it was not the brutality of bad people but the silence of good people that was the greater tragedy. As a religious man, King knew that some forms of silence show a healthy respect for forces beyond our control while others can restore human energies and prepare them for effective use—the life of prayer and the retreat for quiet meditation are not to be ignored. But King also understood that silence can mean failure of nerve in facing issues that do have solutions. He counted on concerned men and women to keep trying their best, not only with words but with actions. Evil is mighty, but King added that God is good and almighty. He wanted that conviction to motivate the love that is needed if we are to create a just society and thereby vindicate God's decision to respect human freedom.

John K. Roth

RECOMMENDED READING

Edition used: King, Martin Luther, Jr. *Strength to Love.* New York: Harper & Row, 1963.

Ansbro, John J. *Martin Luther King, Jr.: The Making of a Mind.* Maryknoll, N.Y.: Orbis Books, 1982. Analyzes King's thought, particularly his strategy of nonviolence, with special reference to the formative philosophical and religious influences on his outlook.

Lincoln, C. Eric, ed. *Martin Luther King, Jr.: A Profile.* New York: Hill & Wang, 1984. Useful insights into King's life and thought are brought together by a leading interpreter of black religious experience in the United States.

Oates, Stephen B. *Let the Trumpet Sound: The Life of Martin Luther King, Jr.* New York: Harper & Row, 1982. A carefully done biography of a skilled scholar and writer.

Washington, James M., ed. *A Testament of Hope: The Essential Writings of Martin Luther King, Jr.* San Francisco: Harper & Row, 1986. A splendid collection, including public speeches, interviews, articles, excerpts from books (including *Strength to Love*), and autobiographical reflections. Includes a selected bibliography.

Witherspoon, William Roger. *Martin Luther King, Jr. . . . To the Mountaintop.* Garden City, N.Y.: Doubleday, 1985. Combines biography, oral history, and photojournalism to produce a dramatic picture of King and his impact.

LETTERS TO MALCOLM: CHIEFLY ON PRAYER

Author: C(live) S(taples) Lewis (1898–1963)

Born into a conservative Christian home, C. S. ("Jack") Lewis abandoned his faith at the age of nine because of his bitter disappointment with petitionary prayer (and the promises made about it) at the time of his mother's death from cancer. After twenty-three years as a thoroughgoing atheist, he was converted to Anglicanism through the books of George MacDonald and G. K. Chesterton and the human agency of, among others, J. R. R. Tolkien. For the rest of his life, Lewis devoted his extracurricular activity (his discipline was Renaissance and Medieval literature) to highly imaginative apologetical, moral, and spiritual writing and to direction through letter-writing. Among his other important works are *The Screwtape Letters* (1940), *Beyond Personality* (1944), *The Great Divorce* (1945), the seven *Chronicles of Narnia* (1950–1956), and *The Weight of Glory* (1980).

Type and subject of work: Twenty-two fictional letters addressed by the author to a friend who has asked him to engage in a correspondence dedicated to discussing problems in prayer and other religious issues in the early 1960s

First published: 1964

MAJOR THEMES

What happens when we pray is that we allow ourselves to be known as persons before God; in prayer we unveil before God.

We learn, first, to tolerate and then to welcome God's loving gaze and touch.

Prayer is personal contact between incomplete persons and God; in this contact he shows himself to us and, un-self-aware, we become persons.

Petition, penitence, thanksgiving, and adoration are the traditional four forms in which this growth as persons through personal contact with God takes place.

Prayer is the beginning of heaven.

Letters to Malcolm: Chiefly on Prayer has no discernible organization, largely because Lewis intended it to have the quality of "occasional-ness" that a real correspondence would have. There are, however, two thematic clusters of five letters each: the problem and problems of petitionary prayer (seven–eleven) and the practice of contemplative prayer (twelve–sixteen). The first six letters then serve as distinguishing the types of prayer and as defining prayer; and the last six concern issues provoked by the foregoing discussions.

Letter one gets liturgical or corporate prayer "out of the way," not dismissively but because Lewis wishes to avoid ecumenical controversy. For him, liturgy is almost a lens through which one sees God. As a consequence, the rites and language of worship should remain virtually stable; otherwise, the shifting lens will attract attention to itself and away from its object. Any revision must be made slowly and carefully. The language of prayer (letter two) is secondary: it channels "the worship or penitence or petition." Wordless prayer is an ideal that only God enables. Praying in our own words can sometimes lead to either overfamiliarity with God or the narrowing of our affections. Both of these dangers can sometimes be avoided by using ready-made prayer, especially the Lord's Prayer (letter five; more below). After a few considerations about praying to or with the saints, letter three discusses the roles of time and the body in prayer, the best time being when the body is most awake.

Using distinctions and definitions Lewis developed in earlier essays ("Work and Prayer" [1945], "On 'Special Providences' " [1947], "Petitionary Prayer: A Problem Without an Answer" [1953], and "The Efficacy of Prayer" [1959]), his letter four represents the height of his thinking about the Prayer Situation: what happens when we pray. What happens is that we allow ourselves to be known (or to treat ourselves) as persons before God. In prayer we unveil before God. We learn, first, to tolerate and, then, to welcome God's loving gaze and touch. Prayer is, then, personal contact between incomplete persons and God; in this contact he shows himself to us and, un-self-aware, we become persons. This process begins when we show God who we are now and what we honestly want. Whatever desires we have must be the subject of our prayers.

Letter five picks up a thread of conversation dropped in letter three, the practice Lewis shares with his fictional friend Malcolm of "festooning" each of the seven petitions of the Lord's Prayer. Lewis tropes the petitions thus: (1) I join all the angels and saints in hallowing thy name; (2) may thy kingdom, there in obedient nature, there in the lives of the most obedient humans and, there in heaven, come *here*; (3) may thy will be endured, obeyed, and celebrated; (4) give us all we need for today; (5) help us go on forgiving and confessing; (6 and 7) and "spare us, where possible, from all crises, whether of temptation or affliction," and even from all of my previous silly prayers. After an excursus on the meaning of religion, letter six adds a codicil to Lewis's festoon of the fifth petition: Help us to ignore an uneasy conscience or uneasy feelings that either vaguely accuse or vaguely approve and to go about our business.

Letter seven introduces as formal a discussion of the validity of petitionary prayer as the literary conceit of a fictional correspondence provides. Here Lewis dispenses with both deterministic arguments against the possibility of meaning in any petitions: Either everything is predictable (and petitionary prayer is thus an illusion) or everything is unpredictable (leaving us free to ask, yes, but God unfree not to respond). This abstract discussion is broken into by the concrete problem of a threat to the life of Malcolm's son, George (letter eight). This crisis occasions real anxiety; prayer at such a time is a form of anguish. Such anxiety and anguish are a share in the passion of Christ. When we are not in crisis, we can return (letter nine) to the abstract argument and say at least that our prayers are granted from the beginning of time and thus are part of the plan of God who is above time. More concretely and in order to avoid any notion of magic, it is better to say that our prayers, like our sins, are taken into account by the providential and creative act of God. What being "taken into account" means (letter ten) is that our prayers are always heard (and that is what we really want) even if they have to be refused. Prayer is the conscious contribution of every pray-er to the course of events that is building the new heavens and the new earth; it is the purpose for which all else is created. But what about refused prayer, especially the prayer of Jesus in Gethsemane (letter eleven), in light of the extravagant promises made in Scripture about the prayer of unwavering faith (Mark 11:24 and James 1:6)? There seems to be a hierarchy of petitioners: The lowest is the suitor (and Jesus descends to this place in his agony), then the servant, then the friend, and finally the fellow-worker with God. It is only to the last, and to them rarely, that God gives the gift of such faith.

Letter twelve begins the second thematic cluster, devoted to mystical prayer, which (put negatively) is a "temporary shattering of our ordinary spatial and temporal consciousness and of our discursive intellect." In this aspect the mysticisms of all world religions are the same, departures; as voyages, they differ in the landfalls. Christian mysticism depends on the "motives, skill, and constancy of the voyager, and on the grace of God." This letter concludes with a flashback to the previous theme: Praying for others or oneself must not become a substitute for doing for them or for oneself.

Letter thirteen deals with the fear that all prayer might be only soliloquy by reminding us that, in our best praying, God is speaking to God. That is, the goal of the spiritual life is the union of our will with God's. As made things, we are manifestations of God's power; as remade persons, we are subjects of God's grace (letter fourteen). The real work of the spiritual life is to awaken and to remain awake to the presence of God everywhere in everything. This presence may be experienced with servile fear (God is neither safe nor tame) or with true fear (God is the ultimate desirable) or, as in letter fifteen, with simple spontaneity (God is altogether trustworthy). Some Christians may start their spiritual lives in such simplicity but for most it is the goal. Most of us must begin with the labor of meditation. This form of prayer seeks to become awake to the real presence of God, first, by piercing the façades of self and surroundings to that which sustains both; second, by choosing to abide in the awareness of our Sustainer; and, third, by speaking from one's deepest self to the God who is ever calling us into being and personhood.

This form of meditation is different from imaginative contemplation (letter sixteen), which is spiritually valuable for those whose visual imagination is weak and in need of stimulation. Mental images are especially useful when they are fugitive and fragmentary because it is then that they mediate the qualities of the basically unimaginable Reality we are seeking to contemplate.

Our sensual and esthetic pleasures can likewise be channels of adoration (and not just occasions for thanksgiving) of the God at whose right hand are pleasures forevermore (letter seventeen). There are, however, four obstacles to this kind of adoration: (1) inattention, (2) attending to the gift and forgetting the Giver, (3) greed for more ("the fatal word *Encore*"), and (4) conceit over our spiritual sensitivity. This adoration in the small pleasures of life is a school for learning to worship God in all of life, a preparation for the joy that is "the serious business of heaven."

Penitential prayer admits of similar degrees (letter eighteen), from the lowest attempts to placate an angry God to the highest attempts to restore a broken, loving relationship. At both ends of this spectrum, the received language of the Christian tradition preserves two central truths about this kind of prayer: (1) Talk about the wrath and the pardon of God, though admittedly analogous, guards the interpersonal character of our relationship with God; and (2) talk about *acts* of penitence steers us away from the danger of trying (and, worse, managing) to stir up perpetual feelings of sorrow for our sins.

Letter nineteen returns to letter seventeen's theme of adoration long enough to add a discussion of its public character ("even in private, adoration should be communal—'with angels and archangels and all the company' "). This occasions a reflection on the meaning, but not the theology, of Holy Communion. Theology is not usually very nourishing, even if it is the theology of spiritual nourishment. However one defines what happens at Eucharist, "Here [in the bread and wine] a hand from the hidden country touches not only my soul but my body." This description hearkens back to letter four's emphasis on all prayer as personal contact.

Though it sometimes takes decades of prayer, especially the prayer to forgive someone who has hurt us or the prayer to conquer an evil habit, answers to such prayers do come (letter twenty). We can even pray for the dead, those in purgatory and those in heaven. The former will know our compassion and forgiveness and the latter, our encouragement in their "continually more ecstatic self-surrender" to a "perpetual increase of beatitude."

Meanwhile, on this side of the door of death, prayer is often an irksome duty (letter twenty-one), a school of surrender: We must say our prayers whether we feel devout or not, longing for the day when we will do with delight what today is unappealing. Prayer is ultimately grounded in the hope of the resurrection of the body and the life of the world to come (letter twenty-two).

Paul F. Ford

RECOMMENDED READING

Edition used: Lewis, C. S. *Letters to Malcolm: Chiefly on Prayer*. New York: Harcourt, Brace & World, 1964.

———. *Beyond Personality*. New York: Macmillan, 1944 (also as bk. 4 of *Mere Christianity*, New York: Macmillan, 1952). Expanded versions of wartime BBC talks, these chapters deal with the spiritual life, especially prayer, as each person's way to become a real personality.

———. "The Efficacy of Prayer." In *The World's Last Night and Other Essays*. New York: Harcourt, Brace & World, 1960. This 1959 essay contains Lewis's most concise definition of prayer and clears up often-encountered problems with petitionary prayer.

―――. *George MacDonald: An Anthology.* Edited with a Preface by C. S. Lewis. New York: Macmillan, 1947. George MacDonald (1824–1905), the most significant influence on Lewis, was a Scottish Nonconformist minister whose sense of the compassion and the fatherhood of God so offended his hyper-Calvinist congregation that they first lowered his salary and then fired him outright. Thereafter he made a living for himself and his family as a poet, fantasist, novelist, and lecturer. Seventy percent of Lewis's anthology of 365 extracts from MacDonald's writings are from the latter's *Unspoken Sermons.* Lewis's preface is invaluable both for its concise assessment of MacDonald's theology and spirituality and for its acknowledgment of the role of spiritual fatherhood MacDonald exercised in Lewis's spiritual life. This is the one essential book to be read by anyone wishing to understand C. S. Lewis.

―――. *The Great Divorce.* New York: Macmillan, 1945. Souls on a day's holiday from Hell take a bus trip to Heaven and each receives a chance to abandon the sin that has condemned it to Hell. This book can be seen as the "companion volume on discernment" to *The Screwtape Letters* in that it gives a heaven's-eye-view of the temptation process.

―――. "On 'Special Providences.' " In *Miracles: A Preliminary Study.* New York: Macmillan, 1978. This brief essay is a discussion of the philosophical problems involved in petitionary prayer.

―――. "Petitionary Prayer: A Problem Without an Answer." In *Christian Reflections.* Edited by Walter Hooper. Grand Rapids, Mich.: Eerdmans, 1967. This address to clergy summarizes Lewis's scriptural and theological problems with petitionary prayer.

―――. *Reflections on the Psalms.* New York: Harcourt, Brace & World, 1958. This book can be seen as the "companion volume on prayer" to *Letters to Malcolm* in that it deals with the use of Scripture in prayer and other problems.

―――. *The Screwtape Letters and Screwtape Proposes a Toast.* New York: Macmillan, 1962. A theology of discernment in thirty-one fictional letters and one after-dinner speech written or dictated by a senior devil to a novice tempter about tested methods in winning the novice's charge, a British, city-dwelling man, newly converted at the outbreak of World War II. The correspondence falls into three sections: (1) Letters one–twelve are full of strategies to prevent the Christian life from taking root in the patient's life chiefly by means of the World; (2) letters thirteen–twenty-two discuss ways to remove or uproot the patient's Christian life by using the temptations of the Flesh; and (3) letters twenty-three–thirty-one disclose the Devil's methods of corrupting the Christian life by the process of subtle deception. The "companion volume" for this work is *The Great Divorce.*

―――. *The Weight of Glory and Other Addresses.* Edited by Walter Hooper. New York: Macmillan, 1980. The title essay, considered by most students of

Lewis's work to be the single greatest essay he ever wrote, treats of the reality and nature of life of the world to come.

———. "Work and Prayer." In *God in the Dock*. Edited by Walter Hooper. Grand Rapids, Mich.: Eerdmans, 1970. A four-page essay summarizing Lewis's theology of petitionary prayer.

THE HEALING GIFTS
OF THE SPIRIT

Author: Agnes White Sanford (1897–   )
Sanford, a writer, lecturer, and healer, was born November 4, 1897, in
Kashing, China, to Presbyterian missionary parents Hugh and Augusta
White. After studying at the Peace Institute and Agnes Scott College in
Decatur, Georgia, she returned to teach in China. There she met and
married Edgar L. Sanford in 1923. After their first child was born, they
moved to New Jersey, where her husband served as rector of an Episcopal church for twenty-three years. They had three children: Edgar, Virginia, and John. They were cofounders of the School of Pastoral Care in
Northborough, Massachusetts, in 1955. After her husband's death, she
retired to Monrovia, California. She bought a house on the San Andreas
Fault because she felt called to pray for the safe and peaceful movement
of the earth.

Type and subject of work: A book on healing: physical, emotional, and
spiritual

First published: 1966

MAJOR THEMES

God's power is real.
Physical, emotional, and spiritual healing is available to us through the work
of the Holy Spirit.

The *"healing of memories"* from a person's past can aid in achieving phys-
ical, emotional, and spiritual healing.
Healing is only answered prayer and anyone can learn to pray.
God is love.
Baptism of the Holy Spirit results in power.

Sanford begins *The Healing Gifts of the Spirit* by telling a bit of her
own story, a fuller version of which is found in her autobiography,
Sealed Orders (1972). Here she simply notes that as a young mother in
Moorestown, New Jersey, she became very depressed, fearful, and para-
lyzed. It seemed as though "the pilot light of the soul" had gone out. In
The Healing Light (1947) she tells how a minister came and prayed for her
child's healing. That incident opened here eyes to the possibility of
healing, but it was another whole year before she sought healing for
herself.

One thing she advises throughout this book for both the person
seeking healing and for the person seeking to be a healing channel is to
get in touch with nature, with creativity, and with God the Creator. She
urges readers "to open our lives to God's creation and to His creativity."
Sanford is very process-oriented in her understanding of the working of
the Spirit.

She declares that *"God's power is real."* She speaks of tapping into that
power through the prayer of faith, which is "not a magic formula, but is
quite simply a prayer with a definite objective and with the belief that
this definite need will be met." The energy of creation is still available
for personal healing. She suggests that one not dwell in prayer on the
disease but picture the person whole and harmonious. She declares that
one should give thanks for healing before one sees outward evidence of
it.

Many make healing prayers contingent. They pray "if it be thy
will." Sanford says that one should pray that a person be healed "according to God's will" because Scripture declares that it is God's will that all
be healed. She suggests that one should teach others to pray for themselves rather than praying for them, though often one teaches by model-
ing such prayer. She cites two reasons for this. One is so that persons
will be able to continue healing prayers for themselves when absent
from the healer. And two, sick persons have an intuitive sense of their
own process and they may not be ready at this point to pray for and receive healing of those deeper causes of illness. They need to have the
tools available to deal with those deeper causes when they eventually
surface.

Healing prayer is found not only within the church or from ordained ministers. It is something available to all Christians for daily use.

And it is something to be used not only for oneself but also for the good of others. "God's power is an expanding power," she writes. One need not fear scarcity.

For years one of her own ministries was as a member of a small prayer group in her husband's church. They worked very quietly. Before each service they entered the sanctuary and prayed that all would be done in harmony with God's will. They noted the appearance of persons entering the church, and they prayed for those who seemed troubled or sick or angry. They served as an intercessory prayer group for the sick of the parish and often carried to Holy Communion a special intention for those in need of healing. Sanford says that the church was devoid of quarrels, jealousy, or hatred.

She criticizes, however, those prayer groups who think of themselves as having the Holy Spirit whereas others do not. She notes that "the holy Spirit can *have you* but He *cannot be had*." She also criticizes those who see all ills as demons in need of exorcism. While she experienced demonic power in China and continued to believe in it, she calls many of the appeals to the demonic a "most convenient alibi for all our failures in understanding." If a person expresses belief or fear that he or she is possessed, then one can pray for that, but if one just has a feeling that someone may be troubled by a demon, Sanford advises silent prayer for protection and then silent exorcism, remanding the foreign spirit over to Jesus so that he may deal with it.

In discussing the gift of wisdom, Sanford notes that "healing is only answered prayer. . . . And anyone can learn to pray." Yet one needs wisdom in discerning God's guidance concerning specific healing needs and the proper timing of our prayers. She confesses that the first time she prayed for a person's healing, he was not healed. She felt like a failure but realized that God had not told her to pray for that particular person but only to learn how to pray for such people.

Throughout the book she speaks of God's love. She suggests that love is not only another gift of the Holy Spirit but "the over-all enveloping blood stream of God, permeating all the gifts." Resentment may easily be the source of disease. She suggests that one can act lovingly even when one does not feel loving. Forgiveness is the key to letting go of resentments. When a person says that he or she feels unworthy of God's gifts, God expects that person to *get* worthy by giving up the resentments and asking for healing.

Sanford suggests that in appropriating God's love one project one's love to Christ and then pray for his love to envelop the person being prayed for. "Thus the feeling of love that reached the sufferer would be the love of Christ and not merely my inadequate personal affection."

The gift of knowledge is needed to probe what is troubling "the deep mind," Sanford's term for the unconscious. If one listens to God's voice within, God will reveal what the problems are. She notes that this information sometimes is given in dreams.

Much of the book, in various ways, is devoted to the "healing of memories." "This *is redemption*. This is the saving of the soul," writes Sanford. She suggests that by oneself or with the help of another person, one take Jesus back into those painful situations in the past and allow Jesus to change that situation— healing the pain, dissolving the fear, meeting the unmet needs, redeeming that situation.

Power is the secret of the baptism of the Holy Spirit. Sanford quotes Acts 1:8 in which Jesus promised his disciples enduement with power. When she was led to pray for the Holy Spirit, she found "the very gifts that Jesus Himself promised and therefore the primary gifts out of which grew all the specialized gifts listed by Saint Paul": "the joy of the Lord (John 15:11), which brought with it such a tingling of joy all over the body that we were instantly healed of our physical ills; second, the gift of the peace that passes understanding (John 14:27) because it does not depend on earthly circumstances . . . ; and third, the gift of truth (John 14:17), an inner power to guide one into right decisions and toward an understanding of things beyond [human] sight."

Toward the end of the book, Sanford discusses the controversial gift of tongues. She notes that speaking in tongues can be distracting; one can get excited about the phenomenon rather than about the Spirit itself. Tongues cannot be identified as the sole mark of the Spirit, since the practice does not always correlate with evidence of the fruits of the Spirit mentioned in Galatians 5:22–23.

Sanford's attitude toward the gifts of the Holy Spirit can be summarized in her own words: "The gifts of the Spirit are not put up in separate compartments or isolated in cellophane wrappings. They weave together and work together in a natural way." God gives the gifts to meet human needs and desires. All are valuable in healing one's own ills and helping one to become a healing channel for others.

Agnes Sanford's first book was *The Healing Light* (1947). Other books concerning healing are *The Healing Power of the Bible* (1969) and *Behold Your God* (1958; reprinted as *The Healing Touch of God* in 1983). Other books by Sanford include *O, Watchman!* (1951), *Let's Believe* (1954), *Twice Seven Words* (1970), *Route One* (1975), and *Creation Waits* (1977). She also wrote several novels including *Dreams Are for Tomorrow* (1963), *Lost Shepherd* (1953), *The Rising River* (1968), and *The Second Mrs. Wu* (1965). Healing is often a theme in her novels as well.

Nancy A. Hardesty

RECOMMENDED READING

Edition used: Sanford, Agnes Mary (White). *The Healing Gifts of the Spirit.* Philadelphia: Lippincott, 1966.

———. *Sealed Orders.* Plainfield, N.J.: Logos International, 1972. Very illuminating autobiography.

BEGINNING TO PRAY

Author: Anthony Bloom (1914–   )
Born in Lausanne, Switzerland, Bloom spent his childhood in Persia where his father was a Russian diplomat. After the Revolution, the family settled in Paris in 1920, where Bloom was educated. His undergraduate studies were in physics, chemistry, and biology, after which he studied medicine. After serving as an officer in the French army until the fall of France, he worked as a surgeon in a Paris hospital while aiding the Resistance. He took monastic vows in 1943 (though he had previously taken vows secretly) and he was ordained in 1948. In 1949 he was sent to England as Orthodox chaplain to the Fellowship of Saint Alban and Saint Sergius. In 1950 he became vicar of the Russian Patriarchal parish in London. Consecrated bishop in 1958 and archbishop in 1962, he was put in charge of the Russian church in Great Britain and Ireland. In 1963 he was appointed exarch to the patriarch of Moscow in Western Europe, and in 1966 raised to the rank of metropolitan. He has been quite active in international ecumenical affairs.

Type and subject of work: A treatise on learning to pray

First published: 1970

MAJOR THEMES

Prayer is an encounter and a relationship.
Humility comes from the Latin word humus, *which means "fertile soil."*
We must live in sobriety, enslaved to nothing.

We must find words for prayer that are worthy of God and worthy of us.

We must find names to address God that are consonant with our relationship to God.

Prayers should not only be memorized, they should be lived.

It is useless to pray for God to do something in us that we are unwilling to do.

We experience God most intensely when our despair is most intense.

Anthony Bloom was in his mid-teens before he met Christ. His childhood had been difficult. Uprooted and stateless, his family had been splintered and he was sent to various boarding schools. But when he was fifteen, the family finally regrouped in Paris under a common roof, and he was totally happy and contented for the first time. But God still had no part in his life; indeed, he was hostile to religious faith.

One day a member of a Russian youth organization to which he belonged asked him to attend a meeting at which a Russian priest had been asked to speak. He resisted but went out of group loyalty. He vowed not to listen, but found himself confronted with a picture of Christianity that was totally repulsive. He hurried home and asked his mother for a copy of the Bible to see if the priest had been correct. He counted the chapters in the Gospels to make sure he was reading the shortest one. But before he had read three chapters of Mark, he was intensely aware of a Presence standing across the desk from him. He knew it was Christ. And the reality of that Presence never left him.

Bloom begins this small book of lectures with the assumption that God is absent. Of course, God is never really absent, but for many people there is that sense that God is no longer present to them. That reminds us that prayer is an encounter, a relationship with a Person. And relationships cannot be forced. They must grow in mutual freedom. We have little room to complain when we are absent from God much more than God is ever absent from us.

To open ourselves to God is also to risk confrontation, judgment. Many times when we begin to pray, we are not yet ready to meet God face to face, and God does us a favor in not responding. When we look at the Gospels, we find people much greater than ourselves who hesitated to meet Jesus. We, like they, may want something *from* God, but we may not really want to see God in person. We may harbor secret sins that we are not ready to have seen by God. Despite our bent knees and lifted hands, we may not yet have our hearts and minds tuned in to God at all.

When we begin to pray, we must be ready to meet God face to face, ready to admit that we are sinners, ready to surrender to God, to seek God's will and be willing to follow it. Bloom reminds us of the words of Paul, "My power is manifest in weakness." It is not the weakness of sin and alienation from God, but the suppleness of one who is surrendered totally to God's direction, a sail responsive to God's wind. We come to God in humility, as fertile soil receptive to the seeds that God plants in us, receptive to the growth that God engenders within us.

Beginning to pray is knocking on the door, which means that we are still outside the kingdom of God, perhaps totally, perhaps just relatively. We must understand where we are and where the door is before we knock. We are outsiders, continually seeking to know God at deeper levels. Bloom quotes John Chrysostom, who said: "Find the door of your heart, you will discover it is the door of the kingdom of God."

We must also remember that we begin in poverty although we have received great riches from God. All that we possess is a gift from God, and we control nothing that is in our possession. When we close our hand around some possession, we lose the use of that hand. We cannot live a life of prayer until we have two hands to raise Godward, a heart open for God to fill with love.

The words we use in prayer are important, Bloom emphasizes. He suggests that just as we choose our words carefully in important relationships with other people, so we should choose our words carefully with God. We should find prayers with which we feel comfortable, prayers worthy of God and worthy of us, words that express exactly what is in our hearts. This does not mean that we must find lofty expressions, intellectual or elegant phrases, but we need to express honestly and clearly what we want to say to God. We must offer God truly the words that we have in our heart.

We should pray words that we can say wholeheartedly, and we should take time to pray when we can give full attention to God. We should aim our prayers, not at some far-off God in the heavens, but to the God nearby, indeed the God within. And we should listen to God's response.

Bloom describes three types of prayer. Spontaneous prayer is the kind that gushes out of our souls either when we are vividly aware of God's presence or when we are in mortal danger or the depths of despair. But to imagine that one can sustain spontaneous prayer throughout life, Bloom calls a "childish delusion." When we cannot pray spontaneously, we can pray with conviction. We can draw on the rich panoply of prayers written down through the ages by Christians past. Memorized, these prayers come to us and support us when we are so exhausted or depressed or numb that we cannot find words of our own. These prayers, however, are not meant to be a "polite madrigal" offered to God when we give God a moment; they should become a completely interwoven part of our lives.

A third type of prayer, which Bloom describes, is the classic "Jesus Prayer." He defines the type as "short vocal prayers which are very short, extremely intense in their content and wide so that they can contain as many meanings as possible." It is a continuous way of prayer that becomes a "walking stick" throughout the day, throughout life. It is the continuous repetition of the phrase, "Lord Jesus Christ, son of God, have mercy on me a sinner." (See the article on *The Way of the Pilgrim* for a further explanation.) He calls it a "prayer of stability" because it is not discursive. It brings the person face to face with God through profession of faith in God. This confession of Christ's lordship is an implicit commitment to God's will.

We need to meditate on the richness of the words we use in prayer. Bloom cites a relationship that the Greek Fathers saw between *eleison* and the olive tree and olive oil. He suggests that when we pray *"Kyrie eleison,"* "Lord, have mercy," we think of those times when the olive is spoken of in Scripture—the olive branch that the dove brought to Noah suggesting that God's wrath was at an end, the olive oil that the Good Samaritan poured into the wounds of the man who had been robbed, and so on.

The words of prayer are words of commitment. We need not ask God to do something if we are as yet unwilling to do it. Christ died for us, but there comes a time when we must take up our own cross. God cannot free us from temptations to which we intend to yield. Thus prayer and action must match.

We meet God most deeply when we have experienced the depths. "Very often," Bloom warns, "we do not find sufficient intensity in our prayer, sufficient conviction, sufficient faith, because our despair is not deep enough." We want God in addition to all the other things we have; we do not want God alone.

We must also meet God in the present—not the future or the past. Thus we must shut out future and past and concentrate on the present, which is not easy to do in our fast-paced world. We must train ourselves to lay aside all our distractions, to simply stop our world, and enter into God's presence. That is the meaning of silence: We meet God in the present with past and future stilled.

Prayer begins when we begin to think of God in second person rather than third person terms, when we address God by name rather than talking about God. We call our friends by name; so too with God. Bloom suggests we find the names of God that are most meaningful in terms of our relationship to God.

Nancy A. Hardesty

RECOMMENDED READING

Edition used: Bloom, Anthony. *Beginning to Pray.* New York: Paulist Press, 1970.

———. *Courage to Pray.* New York: Paulist Press, 1973. Another classic on the same topic by the same author; a development of the ideas first presented in *Beginning to Pray.*

PRAYER AND MODERN MAN

Author: Jacques Ellul (1912–   )
A leading Protestant theologian, Jacques Ellul has been professor of law
and history at the University of Bordeaux. Among his more than thirty
books are: *The Meaning of the City* (1970), *The Presence of the Kingdom*
(1948), *The Betrayal of the West* (1976), and *The Technological System* (1977).

Type and subject of work: A critical reflection on the meaning of prayer
in modern society.

First published: 1970

MAJOR THEMES

*There are many popular misunderstandings about the meaning of prayer in
modern society.*
*Prayer is not practiced by modern people partly because of these
misunderstandings.*
The only valid reason for prayer is that it is commanded by God.
True prayer requires a form of combat with both God and society.

Jacques Ellul warns the reader that *Prayer and Modern Man* is "not a
book of piety." Ellul does not offer suggestions on how to pray, nor does
he theologically explain the meaning of prayer. Rather, Ellul is concerned that prayer has largely vanished from modern society. He tries to

answer the questions: What mistakes has society made regarding prayer? What are the obstacles to prayer?

Ellul begins by reviewing several "intimate and reassuring view of prayer" that reflect fundamental misunderstandings. For example, he rejects any notion of prayer as gesture, sentimentality, or magic. Prayer is more than the pious clasping of hands, the "sugar-coated" words of children, or the expectation that God grants specific requests. It is instead an "act of complete self-giving" to God.

Without this self-giving, prayer is empty, banal, or irresponsible. Empty prayer is seen in the "obligatory" invocation that opens a church meeting, or in a liturgy that evolves into "vain repetitions." Banal prayer is prayer reduced to technique. Ellul ridicules the idea that prayer is a "heavenly telephone" providing a direct line to God, or that it is a matter of relaxation that makes the person feel better. Furthermore, prayer is irresponsible when one assumes that God responds through divine fiat. For Ellul, the effects of prayer do not occur *"ex nihilo,"* but require a relationship between the individual and God that leads to action.

The prayer of resignation is another mistaken view of prayer. This view claims that since God's will is superior, one merely requests "thy will be done." For Ellul, this is a prayer of convenience and cowardice, an excuse not to pray since God's will cannot be changed. It reflects a lack of faith, because it assumes the "impossibility of communication with God or of cooperating with him."

According to Ellul, these views of prayer indicate popular ideas within the life of the Church but do not tell us what prayer is. More thoughtful and disciplined reflection is needed. To begin with, the "fragile foundations of prayer" must be examined.

Ellul argues there are two traditional reasons for praying—a natural foundation and a theological foundation. Neither foundation, however, provided an adequate basis for prayer in modern society.

The natural foundation for prayer is rooted in the fact that people have always prayed in order to "invoke the aid of a divinity." Prayers springs from the heart and is directed to the "Unknown." In turn, the "Unknown" hears and understands. Because of a natural sense of awe and wonder, people cannot help but pray.

Ellul points out, however, that not all cultures pray. Anthropologists have discovered societies where prayer is absent. Therefore, what Western culture calls "prayer" is not a universal phenomenon. In addition, psychologists have shown that prayer is often a mere projection of fears and anxieties. Once an individual has overcome anxiety (through therapy or maturity), there is no longer any need for prayer. Ellul concludes that the natural foundation for prayer is inadequate, because "it is transitory and does not carry any weight." Our knowledge about human nature changes over time and does not provide a lasting or trustworthy reason for prayer.

The theological foundation for prayer is the belief that prayer is a way to discover a sense of purpose and virtue. Through prayer one glimpses a larger purpose, then recognizes the possibility for virtuous behavior. In addition, prayer is a way to affirm God's participation in human life. Through prayer one embraces God's salvation, which is always "coming to us."

Ellul argues that the theological foundation for prayer does not encourage modern people to pray. Such concepts as purpose, virtue, and grace are foreign to modern thinking and experience. It is, however, more than a matter of updating old vocabulary. If classic theological terms cannot motivate people to pray, there is no reason why modern synonyms will be any more successful. The theological foundation for prayer is inadequate since it cannot explain why people do not pray nor why they should pray. In short, prayer has no modern meaning because people no longer pray.

Ellul believes there are sociological and theological reasons why modern people do not pray. The sociological reason is based on the premise that since we "now live in a desacralized, secularized, lay world," prayer has no useful function. The realm of mystery has been eliminated by science, and technology has replaced a dependence upon the divine. This has created a climate of reason and skepticism where trust is placed in appearances and success, rather than in God. Prayer is not useful in a pragmatic and secular world since its power is not obvious or measurable. Prayer is not practiced in the modern world, because it does not accomplish any*thing*.

Ellul maintains that rather than providing a reason for not praying, theology justifies this fact as the will of God. Theology agrees with modern society that prayer has little utility and is, therefore, not valuable. The reason is that humanity has come of age. Previously people lived in an age of scarcity, and prayer was a way to express hope or beg a favor from God. People thought of themselves as children requiring God's care, rather than as mature adults. Any prayer directed toward "God the Father" reinforced this immature dependence and should be rejected. Consequently, the "death of God" (a popular school of theological thought when Ellul wrote this book) should be greeted with praise, since humanity has taken responsibility for its own fate.

This theological justification to ignore prayer betrays the core of Christian faith, Ellul argues. If God is not to be encountered through prayer, then Christianity is reduced to a shallow and temporal morality instead of a faith that captures one's entire being. People can no longer strive to accomplish what their faith requires and compels them to do, because ultimately it has no object or content. Without the need, or even the possibility, of prayer, faith cannot be sustained.

Is there, then, a reason why anyone should pray? Ellul insists that the only reason lies in the fact that prayer is commanded by God. "'Watch and pray'; that is the sole reason for praying which remains for modern man." Such prayer is not offered for benefit but out of obedience to God. It is not based on natural or theological foundations but on faith. Such prayer has its own particular set of demands and consequences.

God's command to pray is, unlike cold and objective legal language, always a "personal word" directed toward the believer. What the Scriptures said in the past is also delivered to the reader in the present—"the word spoken to someone else in another age is really spoken to me now." It "touches" people in their present circumstances and requires a response. Prayer, therefore, is the material with which people weave their world together. The command to pray is a calling for vigilance in order that faith might continue on earth.

God's command to pray is not a duty but a responsibility. Prayer is not a matter of compulsion but an expression of faith on the part of the believer. Through prayer, gratitude is offered to God, and, in turn, one is empowered to act upon one's faith in life's daily affairs. Prayer is a "mirror" in which we "see ourselves as God sees us."

For Ellul, three characteristics of prayer grow out of obedience to God's command. First, God answers all prayers even if this is not easily recognized. The answer to prayer is often the growth of an inner strength that enables us to work along with God in the life of the world. Second, in prayer the faithful are united throughout time. Christians both past and present share a common hope. Since prayer transcends time, a "true history" is assured and confidence in the future provided. Third, prayer makes us "watchful" and helps us to see what must be done in the world. It helps us attend to what God is doing, and what is required of us in helping to establish God's will on earth.

Prayer that is "obedient to the commandment and based on nothing else" requires courage on the part of the believer. It demands fortitude and patience, because it puts us and God to the test. In addition, "there is no oneness" between God and the world because of a broken relationship. Instead, the world strives against God, and people must battle with themselves and with God to overcome this estrangement. For these reasons prayer takes on a combative nature. According to Ellul, there are three forms of prayerful combat.

First, there is a "combat against the self." Prayer provides a point of focus for restoring wholeness within our scattered being. We fight against forces that pull us in different directions in order that God might restore us. Such prayer, however, is not aimed toward our own welfare but toward the glory of God. The self, which is separated from God, is not overcome by giving in to one's self but by giving the self completely to God. Only by making God central to prayer can one's self be conquered and oneness restored.

Second, prayer is a struggle, or combat, that urges us into acts of faithfulness. Since God acts in the world, we strive or wrestle with God in order that things might be other than they are. But there are severe consequences in such prayer. One's life is at stake, because we put ourselves and God to the test in order that "God might manifest himself and that we might be committed unreservedly and without limit." Paradoxically, in this moment we are both separated from *and* in communion with God.

Finally, prayer is a combat against hopelessness. It is the ultimate act of hope for it enables us to live as if God's kingdom were already established. Prayer demands that we be involved with society, because it is within the world that the kingdom is at work. But our prayers must be specific and concrete; our striving must not be vague, for we work along with God. In short, prayer is a radical act of nonconformity and faithfulness—we are in the world but not of it.

Ellul concludes that through prayer we help create a divine history and future. In prayerful dialogue with God, the oneness of creation is restored. Prayer is the victory over the death that threatens the modern world from every quarter. As Ellul warns his reader, prayer is not an act of piety but the giving of oneself to the creator—the source of all life. It is nothing less than a "combat against death and nothingness, so that we might pick up once again the thread of life."

Brent P. Waters

RECOMMENDED READING

Edition used: Ellul, Jacques. *Prayer and Modern Man.* Translated by C. Edward Hopkin. New York: Seabury Press, 1970.
———. *The Presence of the Kingdom.* Translated by Olive Wyon. New York: Seabury Press, 1967. This early work examines how Christian faith influences the life and work of the Christian in the modern world.

A SERIOUS CALL TO A CONTEMPLATIVE LIFE-STYLE

Author: E. Glenn Hinson (1931–   )
E. Glenn Hinson is professor of church history at Southern Baptist Theological Seminary in Louisville. Along with the B.D. and Th.D. degrees from that institution he holds a D.Phil. from Oxford University, London.

Type and subject of work: Essay on leading a spiritual life fully committed to God while living in a technological and secular society

First published: 1974

MAJOR THEMES

The great problem in living a life fully committed to God in all areas is experiencing God in the midst of a secularized society.

The beginning of an answer is to see God's place in the picture as one who is personal, loving, and continually active in all of life.

The Christian's devotion is "sacralizing"—making sacred—human activities by choosing through contemplation to participate in those activities that increase love of God and of neighbor, thus becoming one with God's ongoing creativity.

Contemplation—prayer—is therefore not one activity among many but a style of life that orders all activities according to their place in the will of God.

The contemplative life-style will lead to the simplification in which the *proper use of time and things will become clearer as one "centers down," discovering one's true relationship to God who is personal and active in all aspects of life.*

The development of a devotional style that will affect the whole of one's life requires the disciplined use of devotional aids, despite the danger of substituting the means for the end.

For E. Glenn Hinson devotion is not a set of religious rituals partitioned off from the rest of life. Authentic devotion encompasses the whole of life; devotional activities are those that "contribute something to the enhancement and fulfillment of the larger commitment" to God.

Hinson believes the problem of devotion for the modern age is secularization, the relegation of religious activity to smaller and smaller areas of life. He points out the impact of this secularization process in the areas of central institutions, the clock, the calendar, and the locus of authority. In the Middle Ages the church steeple was the center of community life; the church bells divided the hours into times of prayer; the calendar was regulated by holy days centering on Christian events; and the church debated and resolved all matters of real importance from birth to death, from past to future. Though the depth of this influence varied, almost all of human activity bore the "stamp of the ecclesiastical institution." In the modern era, however, business buildings such as the Sears Tower are the most visible structures; the hours of the day are set according to the needs of the worker's time clock; the calendar's holidays are primarily days off from work and focal points of commercial interest; and the real authorities in life are the "experts" with scientific and technological training.

Hinson describes the church and religion as having been edged out onto the periphery of life. Along with them the sense of transcendence, the experience of things spiritual and personal have diminished. In this modern scientific world how can the personalistic conception of the God of the Bible fit into our lives? An answer is needed, for a world without a deeper transcendent requirement for human existence is a world without meaning.

Hinson believes the answer begins with a better means of conceptualizing how God fits into the picture of our personal experience. How can our daily lives, which are dependent upon scientific understandings, and our religious lives, which are dependent upon the revelation of Scripture, be brought into harmony?

First Hinson points out two wrong but popular responses by believers to this question. One of these is "to rely wholly on the Scriptures for one's scientific as well as one's religious understanding and activity." This approach "compartmentalizes" life by requiring persons who generally accept scientific achievements in such areas as medicine and transportation to hypocritically deny the validity of the worldview that produced these achievements. God must be walled off from contact with everyday experience and so the believer lives in two worlds. A second wrong response is the total acceptance of the scientific rationale, leaving God out of the picture altogether. Christian thinkers who propose this answer suggest that the way to break down the false wall of separation between the secular and the sacred is to abandon the sacred. They argue that the present age seems to require persons to live independent of the concept of God and that since modern persons cannot think of God as God anymore, we should stop trying to explain things through the "God-hypothesis." The difficulty with this second approach, according to Hinson, is that the cure is worse than the disease. "To cure deafness, as it were, they recommended the cessation of speech."

According to Hinson, a better way to understand how God fits into the picture is to begin with the modern worldview and show how Christian revelation "addresses itself to man against that backdrop." He chooses process, or evolutionary, theology for this task. Using a modified form of the thought of Pierre Teilhard de Chardin, Hinson describes God as the personal force of love who is involved in the development or process of all things toward completion in himself. "He is all that will be, yet he is becoming. *Potentially* God has always been perfect love. What he adds to this potential, however, is the reality." Though somewhat philosophical, the strength of this approach is that it allows modern persons to perceive God as involved in every human activity as he draws them toward himself in future fulfillment.

God is not then, for Hinson, the clockmaker-god who created the world and left it to run by itself, allowing us to separate our daily activities from his unchanging and transcendent existence. Nor is he simply the processes of the world without existence apart from it. God is both immanent and transcendent. Hinson prefers the analogy of God as a chess master who responds to the multiple options created by the moves—free choices—that we make. He has an ultimate goal and is actively involved in bringing that goal to completion, but he allows us the freedom to take part in the process. This opens the door for evil and penultimate failure, but growth and freedom are a part of the essence of the personal and God is personal. God is also love and so the personal, loving God who guides our existence has willed human freedom while ensuring the ultimate triumph of good over evil.

The Christian's devotion is the life-style that allows fullest participation in those activities that cooperate with God's will in the creative process. Negatively, devotion is avoiding choices that would slow the working out of God's Life in our lives. Hinson condemns devotion that begins by dividing the world into spheres of sacred and secular. "The problem with the separation of sacred and secular is that it inevitably leads to the substitution of proximate for ultimate concerns." Any devotion that isolates the Christian from the world rather than identifying the Christian with the world where God is at work is a failure. Any devotion that considers all things to have the same significance for religion—that all things are sacred—is similarly far from the intention of God. "Surely the process of dehumanization is not to be seen as God's activity!"

Authentic devotional practices aim at "obtaining that surrender and acquiescence of will" through which all activities are gradually made sacred. All of life is sacred inasmuch as God is involved in it; devotional practices are important to the degree that they increase one's awareness of and participation with this involvement. Devotional practices alone are not this involvement, but they should lead to its reality. All activity can have meaning to the extent that it is brought under the rule of God.

The guiding principle in choosing meaningful activities is how well they increase love of God and of neighbor. Increasing love of God requires restoring the balance between the rational and the intuitive so that persons may experience transcendence and return love to the transcendent. Increasing love of neighbor means demonstrating *agape*-love, which is God's love in us flowing out to specific others without expectation of return.

The Christian is responsible for choosing purposeful, fruitful activities. The problem is how to relate our myriad of concerns to God's will in our lives and thus contribute to his ultimate purposes. "The place to begin, I believe, is with contemplation," writes Hinson. Through contemplation Christians gain a new perspective on life's activities and can then realign their lives with this perspective.

The contemplative style Hinson promotes is "the life of prayer." We pray not because of what we can get out of it. This "turns God into a accommodating heavenly bellhop." Nor do we pray because all that we do is prayer; this attitude "pays too little attention to the intention behind activities." We pray *"because we believe that God, as the heavenly Father, is a personal being."* God is father, *Abba,* and the personal seeks the personal.

Prayer is the process of communion in which we represent our ultimate concerns to a personal, loving God. It is the *"turning on"* to God that discerns his presence within the natural order and within humankind; it is the *"turning in"* by meditative methods to find God within the self; and it is the *"turning over"* of one's life in surrender to God.

Such prayer makes our lives transparent as our activities, purified by love, take on a new meaning. To describe what prayer does, Hinson returns to the model of the chess master. God directs events toward an ultimate conclusion, but he allows our input—prayer—to contribute toward his own decision making. Our prayers are not always answered as we wish. He will not disregard all the other moves or choices that come before and with our own, yet "is it too much to believe that sometimes our feeble outpouring of love in prayer, added to that of others and merged into God's boundless love may supply the extra something that will 'move mountains'?" Like the final snowflake which by its weight breaks a branch, prayer sometimes offers the deciding contribution to God's ongoing purpose.

The contemplative life-style of communion with God and participation in his continuing creation serves to "establish a different kind of rapport with the world and the society of men around us." This occurs, says Hinson, through the discovery of a Center around which our priorities and activities are rearranged.

This reordering of life through prayer in our society will mean a simplified life-style in which some activities and goods once counted as essential will be discarded. The simplified life-style will not be a rejection of the secular city nor a parasitic distancing from its dangers while enjoying its advantages. It will be a choosing informed by contemplation of the proper use of time and things. From the spiritual center Christians will scrutinize the whole calendar, asking, "Is this activity meaningful?" They will reject the fallacy that more is better, "learning what is sufficient, being content with enough, not requiring more and more." Hinson argues that such detachment will free us from ourselves to serve others. This simplification is not a matter of logical rule-making, but a transformation of perception brought about by a new relationship centered in communion with God through a contemplative life-style.

Hinson concludes with a chapter on aids to meaningful devotion. He recognizes the danger of letting the forms become mistaken for the goal of personal relationship with God, but believes the risk must be taken. He does not offer a "method" but points to the choices among the rich heritage of Christian tradition. His list includes: gathering with the community of believers, retreats, the Bible and other devotional literature (an annotated bibliography of selected devotional readings is given), audials, kinetic arts, asceticism, and journaling.

William Loyd Allen

RECOMMENDED READING

Edition used: Hinson, E. Glenn. *A Serious Call to a Contemplative Life-Style.* Philadelphia: Westminster Press, 1974.

―――. *A Reaffirmation of Prayer.* Nashville: Broadman Press, 1979. A book written to aid readers in the reevaluation of prayer in general and their own prayer lives in particular.

———. *Seekers After Mature Faith: A Historical Introduction to the Classics of Christian Devotion.* Waco, Tex.: Word Books, 1968. As the subtitle implies, this writing is a helpful and practical introduction to the great Christian devotional classics in an effort to deepen private devotion. It includes a psychological commentary by pastoral care authority Wayne E. Oates.

———, ed. *The Doubleday Devotional Classics.* 3 vols. Garden City, N.Y.: Doubleday, 1978. This three-volume set contains Protestant devotional classics from over three centuries. Hinson edits to focus on devotional concerns and adds a short biography and a textual introduction to each of the nine classics chosen.

REACHING OUT

Author: Henri J. M. Nouwen (1932-   )
Henri J. M. Nouwen was born in Holland, where he was educated and
ordained a priest. He has taught in Holland and Latin America and, in
the United States, at the University of Notre Dame and Yale Divinity
School. He is the author of several influential books, including *The
Wounded Healer* (1972), *Pray to Live* (1972), *Out of Solitude* (1974), and *The
Genesee Diary: Report from a Trappist Monastery* (1976).

Type and subject of work: An essay on Christian spirituality, concerned
with three movements of the spiritual life

First published: 1975

MAJOR THEMES

*The spiritual life is a reaching out to our innermost self, our fellow human
beings, and our God.*
   *Reaching out to our innermost self requires a movement from loneliness to
solitude.*
   *Reaching out to our fellow human beings requires a movement from hostility
to hospitality.*
   Reaching out to God consists in the movement from illusion to prayer.

   The plans for *Reaching Out* were first developed during a seminar on
Christian spirituality at the Yale Divinity School, Nouwen informs us in

his acknowledgments. He goes on to describe the book as an attempt to present his most personal thoughts and feelings about what it is to be a Christian. And he interprets the problem of articulating what it is to be a Christian as the problem of responding to the fundamental question, "What does it mean to live a life in the Spirit of Jesus Christ?"

Nouwen describes the spiritual life as involving constant movement between the poles of loneliness and solitude (here the polarity concerns our relationship to ourself), the poles of hostility and hospitality (here the polarity concerns our relationships to others), and the poles of illusion and prayer (the most important polarity, concerning our relationship to God).

The creative movement of the spiritual life, then, is a threefold movement *from* loneliness, hostility, and illusion and *to* solitude, hospitality, and prayer. The possibility of succeeding in the effort to accomplish this threefold task of the spirit requires a transformation in and through love. Love is a spiritual reaching out, a movement made known to us through Jesus Christ.

Nouwen begins his detailed account of the first movement (of the innermost self, from loneliness to solitude) by calling our attention to the universal fear of loneliness and to the suffering, sometimes leading to suicide, occasioned by profound loneliness. We fear loneliness and suffer from it, Nouwen suggests, because we suspect that no one cares unconditionally for us; accordingly, we fear that if we are with others we will be used, but we suffer from isolating ourselves because of this fear.

Often we attempt to resolve the problem of loneliness by denying it or by making the effort, sometimes frantic, to distract ourselves. Even worse, Nouwen suggests, is recourse to the "final solution": fleeing to others in the futile hope that togetherness will overcome loneliness. "As long as our loneliness brings us together with the hope that together we will no longer be alone, we castigate each other with our unfulfilled and unrealistic desires for oneness, inner tranquillity, and the uninterrupted experience of communion."

The resolution of the problem of loneliness requires the movement toward solitude, Nouwen contends. But the solitude is not to be achieved by isolating oneself spatially: the solitude that is needed is the "solitude of heart," an inner condition in which we are sensitive to our own deepest needs, in which we "become present to ourselves." By paying attention to oneself and appreciating the worth of oneself as a unique person, one is in a position to pay attention to others and to appreciate the worth of each one as a person. Solitude is a condition in which we can develop an inner sense of friendship and community.

Solitude makes possible a creative, loving response. Nouwen writes: "In the solitude of the heart we can truly listen to the pains of the world because there we can recognize them not as strange and unfamiliar pains, but as pains that are indeed our own." The solitude of the heart gives us the experience of what it is to be alone, what it is to be human, what it is to suffer, and what it is to enjoy life. Accordingly, we are ready to be compassionate and sympathetic even when we are powerless to do anything but respond in love. An inner solidarity with our fellow human beings stems from the willingness to face and to accept ourselves.

The second movement in the spiritual transformation of the self is one in which, having achieved solitude as a result of having "reached out" to oneself, one reaches out to one's fellow human beings by effecting the transition from hostility to hospitality. To make this transforming journey from pole to pole, one must be willing to create space for strangers: ". . . it is possible for men and women and obligatory for Christians to offer an open and hospitable space where strangers can cast off their strangeness and become our fellow human beings."

Nouwen urges that the term *hospitality* be understood in a sense made clear in biblical writings. To be hospitable is to offer the gifts of oneself to others and to be receptive and creatively responsive to their gifts, to "bring new life to each other."

We must recognize the fear and consequent hostility that we tend to feel and act on when we confront strangers. But hospitality, Nouwen argues, is a positive movement whereby one creates free space for others, thereby making it possible or even likely that the stranger will become a friend instead of an enemy. We are called upon, as Christians, not to change others but to provide them with the opportunity to be themselves and perhaps, in the process, to make new lives for themselves. We cannot force inner change, Nouwen reminds us, but "we can offer the space where such a change can take place."

Nouwen examines three forms that hospitality can take in three types of relationships: between parents and children, between teachers and students, and between healers and patients.

For parents to be "hospitable" to their children requires that they reach out to their children by providing the conditions within which the children can freely develop themselves as unique persons: "The difficult task of parenthood is to help children grow to the freedom that permits them to stand on their own feet, physically, mentally and spiritually and to allow them to move away in their own direction."

Nouwen argues against education when it is nothing more than a process involving requirements and obligations; education should be a liberating and creative enterprise. "One of the greatest problems of education," he writes, is that "solutions are offered without the existence of a question." The central questions of life are neglected in the student's pursuit of grades and credits, and all too often the teacher, also out of fear, encourages this debilitating pursuit. Teaching in a hospitable way requires that questions about "why we live or love, work and die" be raised and dealt with: ". . . teaching, from the point of view of a Christian spirituality, means the commitment to provide the fearless space where such questions can come to consciousness and can be responded to, not by prefabricated answers, but by an articulate encouragement to enter them seriously and personally." Consequently, Nouwen argues, the hospitable teacher *reveals* to the student the student's own gifts and *affirms* the values of those gifts.

When Nouwen turns to the relationship of "healers" to "patients," he states that he is concerned with the relationship between doctors, social workers, counselors, ministers, and others who belong to the "helping professions," and those they profess to help. He warns that because of the professionalization of the various forms of healing, the "healers" exhibit a growing tendency to exercise power instead of offering services. But Nouwen, although conceding that "technocratic streamlining" has resulted in professional depersonalization, argues that the healer has to keep striving for a spirituality by which healer and patient can "reach out to each other as fellow travelers sharing the same broken human condition."

Nouwen contends that the most important feature of the healing process is that of knowing the patient fully. Only when one knows the other can one reach out to the other. Furthermore, healing requires a hospitality that allows patients to become sensitive to their own stories so that they will be encouraged to find new and better ways of living.

Hospitality in whatever relationship requires both receptivity and confrontation, Nouwen argues. To reach out to others in a positive way requires being receptive to their ideas and values, to recognize what others present without attempting to manipulate them or impose our values upon them. At the same time, one must be honest and courageous in the presentation of one's own position: "No real dialogue is possible between somebody and a nobody."

To create free space for a stranger, to move form hostility to hospitality, there must be solitude in our lives. "The real host," writes Nouwen, "is the one who offers that space where we do not have to be afraid and where we can listen to our own inner voices and find our own personal way of being human. But to be such a host we have to first of all be at home in our own house."

"Poverty makes a good host," Nouwen asserts, and he goes on to explain that as long as one clings to private property, whether in the form of property, reputation, or ideas, and insists on flaunting these, one cannot open the door to others and offer them the free space to be themselves. The hospitable person exhibits a "poverty of mind," a spiritual willingness to admit the incomprehensibility of "the mystery of life." To be hospitable to others one must have achieved a "learned ignorance," which involves an openness to others and a willingness to learn and to allow others the freedom to instruct themselves.

Furthermore, Nouwen continues, a good host is "poor in heart." With poverty of heart we can receive the gifts of others; we can acknowledge the limitations of our experience; we can avoid the temptation to regard our way of knowing or believing as *the* way and, hence, as something to be imposed on others.

The third movement Nouwen discusses is the movement by which one reaches out to God; it is the movement from illusion to prayer. The greatest illusion, Nouwen claims, is the illusion of immortality, the illusion that we will live forever, that we are in control of our destiny, and that we are knowledgeable about our fundamental human condition. The symptoms of this illusion are sentimentality and violence: We treat others as though they were immortal, and we are angry and despairful when they leave us; again, by asking of others more than they can give, we prepare the way for violence when we are disappointed. "To reach a really nonviolent intimacy," Nouwen writes, "we have to unmask our illusion of immortality, fully accept death as our human destiny and reach out beyond the limits of our existence to our God out of whose intimacy we are born."

To pray is to reach out to God, but there is a paradox of prayer: ". . . we have to learn how to pray while we can only receive it as a gift." Learning to pray involves realizing the fragility of our mortal condition; prayer itself is a gift from God. Nouwen describes prayer as "God's breathing in us, by which we become part of the intimacy of God's inner life, and by which we are born anew."

Although God is beyond us, he is the center of all being; it is in the awareness of God's absence that we find he has been present and has filled our lives. Only when we come to the point of recognizing our illusions as illusions, Nouwen suggests, can we find that we have moved to prayer. The protest against what we take to be the absurdities of life can be converted to prayer; by prayer we are then lifted to God.

By what "rules" can one discover the prayer of one's heart, one's own way of coming into intimacy with God? Nouwen suggests three conditions: the reading of the Holy Scriptures, a listening during a quiet time for the voice of God, and a reliance upon a spiritual guide (someone who can be a spiritual director for us, helping us to avoid illusion and to find the way to the prayer of our heart).

Nouwen suggests that we turn to the wisdom of history through the notable spiritual figures who can serve as guides (persons such as Benedict, Francis, Teresa of Ávila, and including such recent figures as Dag Hammarskjöld, Martin Luther King, Jr., and Thomas Merton). He also calls attention to *The Way of a Pilgrim* as a spiritual guide to the way of the Hesychasts of the Eastern Orthodox church. (*The Way of a Pilgrim* is the

story of an anonymous Russian peasant whose spiritual search is satisfied by discovering that the Jesus Prayer—"Lord Jesus Christ, have mercy on me"—has become the prayer of his heart.)

The prayer of the heart, writes Nouwen, "requires first of all that we
make God our only thought." By emptying the mind of all distracting
thoughts, we prepare ourselves for God as our host: "And then we can
realize that it is not we who pray, but the Spirit of God who prays in us."

Nouwen concludes by stressing the claim that prayer, although personal, is to be shared with others in the community of faith. Prayer is the
language by which God's presence is realized in the midst of his people;
it is "the language of the Christian community," by which community is
created as well as expressed.

Ian P. McGreal

RECOMMENDED READING

Edition used: Nouwen, Henri J. M. *Reaching Out: The Three Movements of the
Spiritual Life.* Garden City, N.Y.: Doubleday, 1975. Nouwen refers us to
Saints Benedict, Francis, and Teresa of Ávila, and also to Dag Hammarskjöld, Martin Luther King, Jr., Thomas Merton, and *The Way of a Pilgrim.*
See the articles in this volume concerned with the works of these spiritual
writers (for Saint Francis, see Chesterton's *St. Francis of Assisi* and also the
anonymous *Little Flowers of St. Francis*) and on *The Way of a Pilgrim.*

THE OTHER SIDE OF SILENCE: A GUIDE TO CHRISTIAN MEDITATION

Author: Morton T. Kelsey (1917–   )
Morton T. Kelsey is an Episcopal priest, pastoral counselor, and former professor at Notre Dame.

Type and subject of work: A wide-ranging but practical manual on the rationale and methods of Christian meditation as a means for encountering God

First published: 1976

MAJOR THEMES

Ordinary persons can have a genuine encounter with God through the unique Christian methods of meditation.

The environment necessary for the growth and development of Christian meditation includes four elements: first, a worldview in which spiritual reality is taken seriously; second, a consciousness of personal human need; third, a realization that there is a spiritual reality with a loving will that has already conquered evil; and finally, an ongoing effort to form real human relationships.

Individual preparations necessary for entry into Christian meditation include setting aside time and purposely encouraging silence through certain means.

Prepared persons in the right environment who have an understanding of the nature and use of images plus techniques for developing imagination can have their inner and outer lives transformed by "doing" Christian meditation using biblical stories, dream images, and images from other sources.

In the introduction to *The Other Side of Silence* Morton T. Kelsey challenges the Western point of view that doubts "people's ability to reach out of the physical and material world and touch anything at all." To the contrary, Kelsey believes that encounter with God and the Risen Christ is a present possibility for every person, especially the simple and the beginner. "Our part is mostly to accept the hand already stretched out to us." Christian meditation is one means to such an encounter.

Kelsey distinguishes Christian meditation from Eastern meditation as follows: The first sees ultimate reality as "a Lover to whom one responds" whereas the second views reality as a "pool of cosmic consciousness in which one seeks to lose identity." Christian meditation is a response to the loving concern of God as known in Jesus of Nazareth; Eastern meditation emphasizes detachment from the world and individual consciousness.

The reality of an encounter with God can only be realized by opening oneself up to experiences beyond measurable, physical things, according to Kelsey. His basic perspective begins with the practice of meditation informed by devotional masters and the findings of depth psychology. Meditation is the setting up of conditions that will allow God to break through to us. This contact is made through the inner realm of dreams, intuitions, visions, and hunches.

Kelsey admits that this approach faces the problem of intimacy. Christian meditation is a difficult experience to share because it involves being confronted by God's love and then responding openly and totally with one's deepest self. This vulnerability requires the risk of change as does any love affair.

Personality types affect the avenue one takes after accepting this risk. Kelsey describes the basic distinctions through a discussion of Carl Jung's personality types, especially the extrovert and the introvert. Each type has its own best means for encounter but all can be open to God. Assimilation of this reality will always include something akin to poetry or art for it is the recognition of spiritual reality in earthly existence. Once the risk is accepted, the right spiritual environment must exist before the potential of meditation can be realized. Kelsey uses the analogy of a seed, which needs soil, moisture, and sunlight to grow.

"The flowering of the human soul" first requires planting the seed in the soil of "the reality of contact with a spiritual world," according to Kelsey. Drawing from Christian tradition and modern depth psychology he argues for the existence of two worlds: "the physical world of matter" and the "nonmaterial but even more real world-of-spirit." Humankind is a bridge linking these two realities and the human psyche or soul is the "instrument of communication between the two." Modern Western Christians have largely lost contact with the nonmaterial inner reality of spirit and therefore have lost the ability to affirm the whole of human reality, Kelsey believes. Meditation is the practice of entering into this inner realm where good and evil spiritual entities influence human existence. This is unlikely to happen unless the reality of the unseen spiritual world is affirmed. Such affirmation is a matter of practice and participation, not intellectual assent alone.

Next the soul "must be prodded from within by human need, the moisture that makes the seed . . . burst" and begin to grow. This bursting and growing is a painful process of death and rebirth. To begin it without a sense of a deep and actual need is unlikely and perhaps even dangerous. Kelsey explores the human experiences that "crack the husk" and point to the necessity of seeking God. He includes such crises as neurosis and depression, physical illnesses, and reflection on need and suffering in the modern world. Through contact with such evils the husk of unconcern may be broken and growth toward meaning begun.

The person who participates in spiritual reality and is "cracked open" by personal need to seek help from this experience will be warmed by the sunshine of God's "unbounded, overwhelming love." The unique Christian understanding that God is like the loving, caring Jesus of Nazareth is the light that draws forth growth and new life in the process of Christian meditation.

Kelsey adds one final condition for continued growth to spiritual maturity through meditation: the step of allowing our lives to become expressions in outer action of that love that draws us to itself. This keeps persons from becoming so involved in the unseen spiritual realities that they lose touch with the equally important outer realities. Meditation within an environment that includes the spiritual climate outlined above will be "as healthful and free of danger as possible."

Sharing liberally from his own journey, Kelsey then turns to the specific human preparations necessary to realize this meditation. The first step, he believes, is to set aside time to look within in meditation. He advocates "stopping times" daily of at least fifteen or twenty minutes at first. This halting of attention toward outward distractions is the key that unlocks the door to the inner life. Kelsey further suggests a couple of hours each week for "re-collecting time," to check life's activities against one's priorities.

In these times set aside, Kelsey points to silence as the way inward. Prayer as listening to God is his theme. This is done by intending to be silent, to be detached from whatever would interrupt this inner silence.

Solitude and a quiet place are required, not to make something happen but to allow it to happen. Using historical examples from Christian and non-Christian traditions along with his own personal account Kelsey describes the physical accompaniments, the silent but furious inner dialogue that continues when speech has stopped, the forceful emotions that arise when one has the courage to face oneself alone. This surrender of self to inactivity, solitude, and silence is a process of centering for the sake of *escaping to* the inner encounter with God.

Aids to this freedom in silence are listed by Kelsey. They include Eastern and scientific methods in the service of Christian meditation as well as Christian traditions such as the Jesus Prayer. The variety and comprehensiveness of these aids reveal that true meditative prayer is wholistic, including all aspects of the mind, body, and spirit.

Kelsey suggests that silence nurtured by a meditative environment opens the door "on a new dimension of reality." He compares silence to sitting in a theater waiting for one's eyes to become adjusted to the dim lights and for the play to begin. That which appears at this juncture in meditation is the kaleidoscope of images that arise from within.

He argues for the value and reality of these images, affirming them as one of the three main kinds of religious experience. The other two are the sacramental "in which the divine comes into focus directly through some element of the outer, physical world," and the contemplative, "an experience of union with the divine in which no outside elements are involved." The third, meditation in images, is the inner journey in which imagination is used to contact the reality of the spiritual world. All three are necessary for a balanced spiritual life, advises Kelsey, but the third is particularly valuable as a bridge between the inner and outer life of humanity. Its goal is love, its purpose looking for the Risen Christ and relationship with him. He supports his argument with a brief survey of the use of this method in Christian history.

Kelsey concludes his introduction of the nature and importance of images in the service of Christian meditation with a discussion of the ways in which these images can appear. They are four: numinous visions that seem unrelated to outside experiences; religious experiences from some event in the outside world; a sense of being one with the physical world; and "an experience of inner meaning by meditating on one's own inner experiences." The last is the way promoted in *The Other Side of Silence*. To understand these images one must look beyond rational and verbal representations just as art must be experienced beyond its verbal description to be really understood. The images point beyond themselves.

Having laid the groundwork for exploration of the inner world by Christian meditation, Kelsey proceeds to discuss dreams as the "best evidence of the existence of another level of reality and the best introduction to its nature." He outlines the use of dreams in Christian tradition, in modern psychology that probes different levels of reality, and ends by giving his own personal dream history.

Next, practical techniques for developing the imagination are offered. These are drawn primarily from depth psychologist Carl Jung and transpersonal psychologist Roberto Assagioli. In this stepping into symbolism the only rules "that come close to being inflexible" are the necessity of belief in the importance of images as reality and the requirement to set aside enough time for silence in order to break some attachment to the outer realm.

Kelsey believes the process he has described will introduce the Christian through images to a vast and substantial reality unknown to many modern persons. No individual alone can learn as much about this reality as is known about it through the combined insights of those who have traveled that way before. Therefore he offers a "check list of the venture inward." Travelers should stay in touch with the best understandings of psychology and science so as to avoid superstition and nonsense. They should also avail themselves of the ritual, sacred symbolism, tradition, and communion of the Christian Church in order to discern entities good from entities evil in the spiritual world. Thirdly, Kelsey suggests practical tips for keeping a spiritual journal, the best way to consider objectively meditative experience and to seek its meaning. Sharing one's inner life within a group of fellow travelers may also bring insights otherwise lost. Akin to this is the discipline of spiritual direction. The desirable qualities in spiritual directors, according to Kelsey, are unconditional acceptance, commitment, understanding of the human psyche, knowledge of the Christian way, and participation in the journey themselves.

Kelsey continues by giving examples of a "number of entrances to another world" to be used as stimulation for persons to branch out on their own. He suggests such means as Bible stories entered by imagination, listening in dreams for the Risen Christ, tongue speaking, and intercessory prayer. He also describes the use of moods in meditation and the technique of story and poetry as inner roadmaps. Kelsey describes such experiences in detail, giving specific examples. He closes the book with a series of meditations that he has found helpful through thirty years of experience, offering "some signs along the road to the universal language of prayer."

William Loyd Allen

RECOMMENDED READING

Edition used: Kelsey, Morton T. *The Other Side of Silence: A Guide to Christian Meditation.* New York: Paulist Press, 1976.

———. *Companions on the Inner Way: The Art of Spiritual Guidance.* New York: Crossroad, 1983. Drawing on forty years of personal experience as a guide and as one guided, Kelsey shares his insights on spiritual direction.

———. *Encounter with God: A Theology of Christian Experience.* Minneapolis: Bethany Fellowship, Inc., 1972. A manual intellectually demonstrating the possibility of encounter with spiritual reality and the implications that follow from this possibility.

———. *Tongue Speaking: The History and Meaning of Charismatic Experience.* New York: Crossroad, 1981. First published, 1964. By way of a discussion of speaking in tongues Kelsey gives a theological and psychological point of view by which this and other neglected aspects of New Testament experience can be understood.

CELEBRATION OF DISCIPLINE

Author: Richard J. Foster (1942–   )
Richard J. Foster is on the Theology faculty at Friends University in Wichita, Kansas, and is writer in residence there. He received his doctor of pastoral theology degree from Fuller Theological Seminary in Pasadena, California.

Type and subject of work: Exploration of key disciplines of the spiritual life in their relation to Scripture and the practical life of the believer within a Christian fellowship

First published: 1978

MAJOR THEMES

The classic spiritual disciplines are to be celebrated as guides that free people from slavery to ingrained habits, opening them to inner transformation, healing, and joy as they enter into deeper relationship to God.
The inward disciplines are meditation, prayer, fasting, and study.
The outward disciplines are simplicity, solitude, submission, and service.
The corporate disciplines are confession, worship, guidance, and celebration.

Celebration of Discipline is a clearly structured introduction to the spiritual disciplines, written with common sense and uncommon sensitivity. Though it builds carefully on Scripture and the recognized classics of spiritual devotion, it is a genuinely original and practical work, filled with profound insights and useful suggestions for the Christian life. Foster deals with an astonishing variety of material ranging across the inward, outward, and corporate disciplines that constitute a "pathway to spiritual growth."

"Superficiality is the curse of our age," writes Foster. The desperate need is not for more productive people, or more intelligent or gifted people, but for "deep people . . . genuinely changed people." The classic disciplines of the spiritual life are a call to move beyond the surface of life and into the depths of inner transformation. Following the disciplines does not require special talent or giftedness or vocation. They are, says Foster, for "ordinary human beings struggling with meaning and purpose in the midst of normal daily activities." Their intention is freedom from slavery to fear, pride, and self-interest. The primary requirement is a longing after God: "As the hart longs for flowing streams, so longs my soul for thee, O God."

Some cautions are in order: The disciplines can easily become mechanical outward forms that lead to death, for it is the inner attitude of the heart that is crucial for spiritual life. The changes needed within can come only through the grace of God. Both objective righteousness (justification) and subjective righteousness (sanctification) are gracious gifts from God that cannot be earned—only freely received. The disciplines are means of receiving this grace, a narrow pathway leading to "inner transformation and healing and joy immeasurable." The path does not produce the change. It only puts one in a place where the change can occur. Foster calls this the "way of disciplined grace," and challenges the reader to be among those who believe that inner transformation is a goal worthy of the best human effort.

The *Inward Disciplines* of meditation, prayer, fasting, and study especially fulfill the purpose of total transformation of the person. They aim at replacing old destructive habits of thought with new life-giving patterns and attitudes. They challenge men and women to move beyond superficial cultural attachments into the re-creating silences and unexplored inner regions of the Spirit, where exciting possibilities for new life and freedom exist.

Meditation, a central part of Christian devotion and a preparation for the work of prayer, is fundamentally a way of listening to God, of communing with the Creator and Lover of the world. It is inviting the Holy Spirit to come and work within. In contrast to Eastern meditation, which seeks, in detachment, to empty the mind and merge with cosmic consciousness, Christian meditation seeks detachment from cultural confusion in order to have a deeper attachment to God and other human beings. "Christian meditation leads us into the inner wholeness necessary to give ourselves to God freely, and to the spiritual perception necessary to attack social evils. In this sense it is the most practical of all the

Disciplines." Through meditation on Scripture—visualizing the gospel stories and entering into the first-century context—an actual encounter with the living Christ takes place where his voice is heard and his power felt. The written word becomes the living word through meditation.

While meditation introduces one to the inner life, it is the discipline of *prayer* itself that involves the deepest and highest work of the human spirit. "Prayer catapults us onto the frontier of the spiritual life. It is original research in unexplored territory." It is research in the school of the Spirit that is life-creating and life-changing. Prayer is the central avenue that God uses to transform human beings. The closer one comes to the heartbeat of God the more clearly is revealed the need and desire to be conformed to Christ. When real prayer happens, one begins to think God's thoughts, to desire the things God desires, to be taught from God's point of view. Prayer is both the simplest and the most sublime thing to which a Christian is called, from spontaneous prayers of praise and thanksgiving to the deep burden-sharing of intercession and the perseverance of soaking prayer.

The proper intention of *fasting* is to draw close to God and glorify God, but other blessings come as well. Things that control people are brought to the surface—anger, bitterness, jealousy, strife, fear, and especially pride—so that abstaining from food creates possibilities for change. Fasting helps in keeping perspective and in preventing cravings from overflowing their banks; it brings increased concentration and effectiveness in intercession, clearer guidance in decisions, and freedom from bondages and external control.

Informed by fasting and the other inner disciplines, *study* gives discernment about the self and the world. It is knowledge of the truth that brings freedom, and study is the process of absorbing something to make it one's own. Repetition channels the mind in specific directions; concentration centers the mind; comprehension brings full understanding and leads to insight and discernment; and reflection defines the significance of what is being studied. Through focused study, the desire to learn, and humility in asking questions and seeking answers, one's hunger for truth is satisfied and joy is gained.

Through the *Outward Disciplines* of simplicity, solitude, submission, and service, one gains integrity and compassion in relationships and learns to bless others without being manipulative or seeking control. In modern culture, people are fractured and fragmented, trapped in a maze of competing attachments. A need for security drives people into an insane attachment to things, into a lust for affluence that is psychotic because it has completely lost touch with reality. The discipline of *simplicity* strikes at the covetous heart of such greed and possessiveness, freeing one from the tyranny of self, the clamor for attention and self-recognition, and compulsive buying and unrealistic wish-dreams. Jesus saw the hold that wealth could have on people: "Where your treasure is, there will your heart be also!" He commanded his followers "not to lay up treasures for yourselves on earth." Simplicity makes it possible to be free and generous with one's time and possessions, to enjoy things without owning them, to reject what breeds the oppression of others. "Seek first God's kingdom and his righteousness," says Jesus, and the things of this world will take their proper place.

If through simplicity one learns to live with others in integrity, then *solitude* opens a way to be genuinely tuned into people when present with them. Solitude involves an act of listening. People are so accustomed to relying on words to manage and control others that to remain silent causes them to feel helpless and alone. In the silence, who will take control? God takes control but only as one trusts God to be at work. The fruit of solitude is increased sensitivity and compassion, a new freedom to be with others, and attentiveness and responsiveness to others' needs and hurts.

Submission is perhaps the most abused and misunderstood of the disciplines because it can lead to manipulation and a loss of freedom. But there is freedom in voluntary submission—the laying down of the terrible burden of always needing to get one's own way. Often, when expectations are not met, people are anxious and bitter for months and even years. In submission to God, in faith and trust in God to care for one's needs, there is freedom to let go of expectations, to give in more easily to others, to see more clearly the difference between stubborn self-will and genuine issues. Such self-denial is not groveling, or self-hatred, or rejection of individuality; rather it is the only true way to self-fulfillment. "He who would find his life, must lose it. . . ." In submission it becomes possible to love people unconditionally, to take joy in their success, to feel genuine sorrow at their failures, to discover that it is far better to serve the neighbor than to have one's own way. Power is discovered in submission.

Submission develops a heart for *service*. Jesus said, "Whoever would be great among you must be your servant." Authority for Jesus came not from position or title but from service, from washing one another's feet. True service, rooted in God, does not seek publicity, does not need to calculate results, is indifferent to status or worldly authority. Humility is worked into human lives through the discipline of service. To choose to be a servant is to be free from having to be in charge. The one who chooses to be taken advantage of cannot be manipulated. The one who chooses to be a servant becomes available and vulnerable. True service builds community. "It quietly and unpretentiously goes about caring for the needs of others. It puts no one under obligation to return the service. It draws, binds, heals, builds. The result is the unity of the community."

The *Corporate Disciplines*—confession, worship, guidance, and celebration—support and help maintain the well-being of the community. *Confession* is a corporate discipline because sin, in addition to offending God, tears and wounds the fellowship. The rhythm of confession, repentance, forgiveness, and new life in God's grace is essential for the health of the Church. This is not just a private matter between God and the individual, but a corporate reality of confessing sin to one another, praying for one another, and bearing one another's burdens. A healthy community is still a fellowship of sinners dependent on hearing the unconditional call of God's love and the demand for mutual confession and forgiveness to release the power that heals and transforms the fellowship. Through examination of conscience, true sorrow and repentance, and determination to avoid sin there comes an end to pretense and fear and an open door to the forgiving and empowering light and grace of Christ.

In the act of *worship*, the conscience is quickened by the holiness of God, the heart opened to the love of God, and the will devoted to the purposes of God. To worship is to experience the deepest reality, to touch Life and know and experience the resurrected Christ in the midst of the community. Worship is a human response to divine initiative. When the Spirit of God touches human hearts, igniting them by divine fire, then worship-service happens. It is human heartfelt response that pleases God and not the particular forms or structures of worship. Preparation for worship is to be filled with "holy expectancy" that God is present to teach and touch with living power. True worship causes one to let go of resentments, to have increased compassion, and to undertake holy obedience. If worship does not change the person, it has not been worship.

Guidance, too, has its communal side. Individual leading of the Holy Spirit can fall into self-absorbed subjectivism and must be balanced by God's guidance through the community. A knowledge of the direct, active, immediate leading of the Spirit comes out of community. It is an experience God gives as people gather together in expectancy seeking the life and power of the kingdom of God. Scripture itself is a form of corporate guidance that provides an outward authority to confirm the inward authority and leading of the Holy Spirit. God is seeking communities living under the immediate and total rulership of the Holy Spirit, determined to live out the demands of the gospel in a secular world. "In our day, heaven and earth are on tiptoe waiting for the emerging of a Spirit-led, Spirit-intoxicated, Spirit-empowered people."

Finally, all the disciplines, freely exercised, bring forth the doxology of *celebration*. The Westminster Catechism begins, "The chief end and duty of man is to love God and to enjoy him forever." Joy is at the heart of the Christian experience, and celebration is giving expression to that joy. The only reason one can begin in earnest to follow Jesus is the clear knowledge that joy is the end result, that nothing else will bring such happiness. This saves the other disciplines from becoming dull, self-serving tools in the hands of modern Pharisees. Joy produces energy, increases strength, and leads one on to deeper obedience. Blessed are those who have Jesus' commandments and keep them for their joy will be full. Without obedience, joy is hollow and superficial. Through obedience, the power in Jesus reaches into daily work and play and worship to bring freeing laughter and healing peace. "Rejoice in the Lord always."

The classic disciplines of the spiritual life provide a pathway through the superficiality, moral decay, and technological depersonalization of the closing decades of the twentieth century. Their purpose is freedom from slavery to fear and self-interest, their promise an "inner transformation and healing and joy immeasurable," their only requirement a longing to know the living God. Richard Foster has written a remarkable book, a classic in its own time, that offers great help to those seeking to deepen their spiritual lives. He points the way to a simpler yet richer way of being, a way of "disciplined grace," that challenges the reader, in the words of the apostle Paul, ". . . to press on toward the goal for the prize of the upward call of God in Christ Jesus."

Douglas H. Gregg

RECOMMENDED READING

Edition used: Foster, Richard. *Celebration of Discipline.* San Francisco: Harper & Row, 1978.

Boyer, Louis, et al. *A History of Christian Spirituality.* 3 vols. New York: Seabury Press, 1982. A fairly complete history and anthology, especially of the church fathers and Middle Ages, by a recognized Catholic scholar.

Foster, Richard. *Freedom of Simplicity.* San Francisco: Harper & Row, 1981. In the same engaging manner as in his *Celebration of Discipline,* Foster traces the roots of simplicity through the Bible and the history of the Church, showing the relevance of this discipline for modern times.

McNeill, Donald P., et al. *Compassion: A Reflection on the Christian Life.* Garden City, N.Y.: Doubleday, Image Books, 1983. Views the disciplines of service, community, displacement, prayer, patience, and action through the lens of compassion in a beautiful and moving way.

MYTH, FAITH AND HERMENEUTICS

Author: Raimundo Panikkar (1918–   )
The son of a Spanish Roman Catholic mother and a father who was an Indian Hindu, Panikkar was born in Spain. In 1946 he was ordained a Catholic priest and is attached to the diocese of Varanasi, India. He has three doctorates: one in chemistry, another in philosophy from the University of Madrid, and a third in theology from the Lateran University, Rome. He also studied at the University of Barcelona and the University of Bonn. Writing in six languages, he has published over thirty books and hundreds of articles. Panikkar taught at Harvard for four years, and since 1971 he has been professor of comparative philosophy and history of religions in the Department of Religious Studies of the University of California (Santa Barbara). Panikkar divides his year between the United States, Spain, and India.

Type and subject of work: Essay on the need for a faith that unites persons of various cultures

First published: 1979

MAJOR THEMES

Humanity is in crisis and must not shirk the facing of significant issues.
Myths form the context in which we live.
Faith is the characteristic that unites humanity.

True dialogue between persons of different cultures is a contemporary need.
Guidelines are required for the meeting of cultures.

Myth, Faith and Hermeneutics is the author's introductory statement
concerning his worldview. Panikkar sees himself as coming out of four
traditions: Christianity, Hinduism, Buddhism, and secularism. His
writings have discussed these traditions, and in this volume he provides an overview that is the basis for his own ecumenical thought and
life. His language is sometimes difficult because of two factors: First,
since he has written in six languages (and speaks several more), he can
draw nuances from French, German, Spanish, Sanskrit, Latin, Greek,
and English to particularize his meanings; second, where he finds the
expressions available to us to be inadequate, he formulates new words
to convey new concepts that he wishes to share.

Panikkar begins this work by stressing the urgency of what he is
about. He is convinced that humanity is in crisis and must face truly
significant issues squarely if we are to survive. The need to overcome
the subject-object dichotomy in our thinking, as well as the almost
schizophrenic split between *logos* and *mythos*, is extreme. He stresses
the necessity to bring back the unity of word and work—we must be
doers of the word.

The book has three basic parts, each dealing with a main word from
the title. "Myth" refers to that by which we live, "the ensemble of con-
texts you take for granted." One's myth is what makes one unique. This
differs from ideology, which is the demythicized portion of one's
worldview. Between myth and ideology is tolerance. It is important to
realize that true tolerance does not imply a relativization of truth. We
can tolerate only what we can understand with the *logos* or what we can
embrace in myth. We cannot reduce the truth of a myth to its conceptual truth; it must be understood. One might argue that Adam could not
have existed (as an individual—as if existence had to be limited to an
individually historical category), the apple could not have been real (as
if reality were limited by material dimensions), and the snake could
not have spoken (as if words were the only way to communicate), but
this does not obscure the notions of obedience, humility, responsibility, and other truths that the Eden myth represents.

The "primitive" does not question his myth. When he does, he attains the knowledge of good and evil. "We act morally as long as we do
not ask why." Reason, writes Panikkar, is unable to command what
ought to be. Conscience is killed in the attempt to reduce it to neat intellection. Questioning is a process of demythicizing, of destroying morals, yet we cannot *not* ask why. The way out of this apparent impasse is
to remythicize morals, but this cannot be conscious. But there is

Christ's observation: Blessed are the poor in Spirit. Panikkar identifies them as those who are unconscious of their value. What is necessary is the awareness of *faith*.

Next, the author takes up the problem of pain. Suffering appears to be the ultimate structure of the world, and myth tells us that it is somehow through affliction that the world is restored. But pain without myth is intolerable. It is in faith, that which stands as the basis of *all* religion, that we are able to go on. We can thus recognize God's creation as a sacrifice and that love gives the power to create.

One of the myths of the modern West is history. Panikkar warns that if we are not to lose our humanity, we must acquire a global awareness in the cosmotheandric (combined material, divine and human) dimensions of our destiny. One way to approach this is by understanding the sacrificial nature of reality. The author then discusses a Sanskrit myth that presents sacrifice as the primordial energy, prior to everything.

The final section of part one is on the myth of the human condition. Life takes primacy, Panikkar concludes, over any living individual; quality is more important than quantity. Life indeed is the bond that unites us, and this bond is placed in our hands. There is a transcendental desire which may be seen as the manifestation of each being's deepest dynamism, this desire being neither whim nor the result of a reasoning process but rather of an integral situation. "Each one desires that which engages his entire being." It is in the depths of this ontological desire that true freedom dwells.

Panikkar sees humankind as designated to function within the framework of faith and "whoever alienates himself from this sphere ends up destroying himself." Faith is the human characteristic that unites humanity. Furthermore, religious dialogue (which Panikkar sees as one of the most important problems of our time) must be held at the level of faith rather than of mere rationality, which divides instead of uniting. The writer is confident that faith can be recovered because it was never really lost.

Next comes a discussion of three instances of faith. One identifies faith with correct doctrine; a second identifies it with the moral deportment that leads us to our destiny; the third, which complements the other two which can be considered one-sided, is orthopraxis, linked to our very being as act. It is in this last that a person becomes totally whole, attaining fullness. Faith may thus be described as existential openness toward transcendence. This openness implies question which implies seeking, an endless search. The essence of faith lies not in the answer but in the question.

Western Church history is next summarized in five kairological moments: witness (until Arius), conversion (until the impact of Islam),

Crusade (until America's "discovery"), mission (until the end of colonialism), and dialogue (today). For the dialogue to be effective, it must contain a cultural dimension; rather than dialectical dialogue, rooted in reason, it must be dialogical, having an optimism of the heart. This new kind of dialogue integrates our testimonies within a larger horizon, a new myth.

Panikkar sees far-reaching consequences in the generalization that India opted for silence, the West for the Word. He then discusses the nature of love. The Eastern view tries to negate the ego element in human love: True love of another is for the other but not because that other is in some way "my" beloved (be it parent, friend, or the object of a romantic attachment).

A discussion of the quest for the supreme experience follows. Consciousness is something we share; experience is individual. The symbol is that which unites our three modes of consciousness: the experience, its manifestation, and its interpretation. Ultimately, being is nothing but symbol. The mystic runs the danger of emphasizing experience; the philosopher is tempted to focus on interpretation; the person of action mistakes the manifestation for the whole of reality. The balanced view does not reduce reality to any one symbol; it chooses neither subject nor object but mediates via the symbol.

Today we realize, as we look at the ways of East and West, that there is not a single cultural difference that can be specifically labeled Eastern or Western. Each is too variegated. We are reminded that most religions of the world were born in one area but flourished in another. In each human being there is an East *and* a West. This must be understood for *inter*religious dialogue to take place and must be preceded by an *intra*religious and intrahuman dialogue—an internal conversion by the person.

The author then considers four archetypes of the human being, and it is possible for all four to be found within the same religion. One is named transcendent transcendence: the experience of seeing the light face to face, where holiness may mean a lofty segregation. Another is immanent transcendence: stressing passivity, which is a negative path that denies individuality. A third is transcendent immanence: *nirvana* is the supreme experience here, being the realization that there is no supreme experience. Finally there is immanent immanence: there is no escape from the factual human condition; there is no world other than this one.

The section concludes with the following observations. Humanity's shift from an emphasis on objective values to experiential truth is a positive step toward a more complete understanding of the human situation. Orthodoxy itself cannot be a supreme value. But an important distinction must be made between relativism (a dogmatic attitude) and relativity (which says that nothing is absolute, that all depends on the relationship of everything to everything else). The conclusion then is that "human experience is not reducible to a single denominator." For Panikkar, the real theological and philosophical task of our time is not only to integrate the exigencies of the *logos* but also the realities of myth and the freedom of spirit. These ideas are taken up in "Hermeneutics," part three of this book.

The challenge to Christian faith today comes from within, from its own claim to universality. Any message directed toward humankind in general, but which ignores the variety of peoples, cultures, and religions, is suspect. If Christianity is to meet this challenge, it must renounce any allegiance to a single culture. The Spanish-born author of half Indian parentage says he is trying to reestablish the unity between theology and fundamental theology. He wants to liberate theology from dependence on anything outside itself (such as a particular philosophy or worldview).

This cannot be the work of Christians alone or exclusively of "religious" people. Dialogue is an important element here because it is more than merely a means of clarifying differing opinions. It brings us into contact in a way that is itself a religious category. True dialogue is full of faith, hope, and love. As Panikkar puts it, "The kingdom of God is *between* us."

The author next divides philosophy into four periods, not chronological or linear in tone but kairological moments that permeate one another. First is the religious epoch where philosophy was religion philosophically seen. The second era was metaphysical, wherein an objective distance was fostered (resulting in astonishment in the West, disillusion in the East, yet both indicating that things are not what we think they are). The third period is epistemological, which discovers unexpected dimensions of subjectivity, in which the individual is stressed. And the fourth dimension is the pragmatic or historical, where the emphasis is less on knowing the world than on controlling it.

The relationship between religion and philosophy may perhaps be seen in three ways: (1) One of these dominates the other (unacceptable); (2) each is completely independent and disconnected from the other (ignoring the fact that religion without philosophy is fanaticism and that without religion, philosophy examines a corpse, not a living organism); and (3) the two are intrinsically connected.

The first business of philosophy is to accept the *logos*, but without suppressing *mythos* (the second dimension of speech itself, the silence between the words) and *pneuma* (the unthinkable). The thought, the unthought, and the unthinkable—*logos, mythos, pneuma*—dwell within one another.

In early religions, God is not considered identical with Being, but three attitudes have contributed to such an understanding: anthropomorphism, human beings seeing God in their own image, without which there could be no prayer or human relationship with the divine; ontomorphism, the human demand that God not be whimsical, unpredictable—in other words that God be Being; and personalism, asserting that Being itself is personal and therefore capable of love, of a social context. Because some of this has been misunderstood it has led to a denial of God that is really only a part of a remythicization process. Several religious traditions assert that God is not only Being but corresponds to Non-Being as well. It is as inappropriate to affirm the one as it is the other. Human silence may be all that we can offer in describing God's nature.

We need guidelines for the meeting of cultures, urges the author. "The ideal is to discover the growing points in one culture that are sensitive to the problems of another culture." He follows this with a discussion of the Hindu concept of *karma*, which has three operative ideas: as the saving grace of sacrificial actions, as the path of action, and as the structure of temporal reality. *Karma* also expresses another truth for Panikkar, the interrelatedness of all things. Thus the human being is in no way a sole individual. The person may be seen as a cosmic artist, as one who can create or annihilate *karma*; in brief, the person is the center of freedom.

Next comes an analysis of the concept of infallibility, which can only be coherent in a closed system and leads to solipsism. The only correct expression of infallibility is through the "we" not the "I," and can have meaning only when it constitutes a unified whole. However, what truly constitutes religion is not doctrine but act. Infallibility entails a complete assumption of risk and is an awkward formulation of a grand awareness, that all humankind has the burden of this dignity.

Finally this leads to a discussion of freedom of religion and of religion as freedom. Religion can save us only if it puts us on the path to our ultimate goal which is liberation. Nonfree beings have no future, only a fate. The human being is the being that creates its own future. Human salvation, in fact, is not the liberation of humankind alone but of the whole cosmos. This denies that the world is to be vanquished, exploited. The message of Jesus is one of freedom. Christ, for Father Panikkar, is the principle of freedom illumining all who come into this world.

Harry James Cargas

RECOMMENDED READING

Edition used: Panikkar, Raimundo. *Myth, Faith and Hermeneutics.* New York: Paulist Press, 1979.

———. *Intrareligious Dialogue.* New York: Paulist Press, 1978. Christian, Hindu, and Buddhist traditions are all seen as responses to the human predicament.

———. *The Unknown Christ of Hinduism.* Maryknoll, N.Y.: Orbis Books, 1981. Updated version of a 1964 work discussing the relation between Christianity and Hinduism.

———. *The Vedic Experience.* Berkeley: University of California Press, 1977. The author's interpretation of crucial texts of the Indian Sacred Scriptures.

CENTERING PRAYER

Author: M. Basil Pennington, O.C.S.O. (1931–)
M. Basil Pennington is a Cistercian (Trappist) monk at Assumption Abbey, Ava, Missouri. Father Basil has written and lectured widely on Christian spirituality, particularly on centering prayer. He has led many workshops on prayer, and his lectures are available on audio and video cassettes. His published books include *Daily We Touch Him* (1977), *Centered Living* (1986), and *Thomas Merton, Brother Monk* (1987).

Type and subject of work: A practical guide to contemplative prayer

First published: 1980

MAJOR THEMES

Centering Prayer is a putting aside of all thoughts and images, a stilling of the senses and the mind, so that we can be one with God in the center of our being.

Centering Prayer comes out of an ancient tradition, both Eastern and Western.

To pray, one quietly moves in faith to God within us; a simple word of love is used to keep the Presence before us; if we are distracted, we use the word to return to the Presence; we pray the "Our Father" or some other prayer to come out of our contemplative state.

Centering Prayer is an affirmative response to God; it is an entering into the true relationship between ourselves and God; it is a total assent to be who we are.

In the experience of such prayer we sense our oneness with others; we are

filled with compassion; we know the love that henceforth will animate our activity outside of the time of prayer.

"Two things are new about Centering Prayer," Father Pennington writes: "the name and the packaging." In a workshop on contemplative prayer, in which the anonymous *Cloud of Unknowing*, a work from fourteenth-century England, was the principal written source, Father Pennington found himself often referring to Father Thomas Merton's idea that one attains to the experience of God by "going to one's center and passing through it into the center of God," as Pennington expresses it. The image of the center appealed to Pennington; the term Centering Prayer has certain advantages considered literally over the expression "Prayer of the Heart," an expression that has its origins in the Christian East.

But a method was needed to make clear what Centering Prayer is and how one can pray in that way. Father Pennington draws from the tradition built through the *Cloud of Unknowing* and the writings of such spiritual leaders as Evagrius Ponticus, John of the Cross, Brother Lawrence, Teresa of Ávila, and William of Saint Thierry, but he abstracts from the various writings a practical method consisting of certain steps to be taken in the course of contemplation; he writes not only for those charged with providing spiritual direction but also, and preeminently, for any person concerned to know the God within through being willing simply and quietly to be oneself before God.

Centering Prayer (which has as its subtitle, *Renewing an Ancient Christian Prayer Form*) was written, the author tells us, to provide practical help to those who want to pray but are uncertain of how to proceed. Prayer is a response to God, Father Pennington argues, and "the cry ['I want to pray'] comes from . . . some very deep part of our being, and we need to get in touch with that center and let our prayer arise from there." Pennington declares his intention to be that of sharing "this very simple form of prayer that has been a constant part of our Christian tradition" and to do so in a practical and concrete way so as to "facilitate and support the entrance into and regular practice of contemplative prayer."

At the outset of his book Father Pennington writes that he is attempting to share what Saint Paul called "the hidden wisdom of God," the Spirit to be found within us. Thus, he writes, "In Centering Prayer we go beyond thought and image, beyond the senses and the rational mind, to that center of our being where God is working a wonderful work." God has made us one with his Son, Pennington writes, and hence "where we are our truest selves, we are essentially prayer, total response to the Father in our oneness with the Son, in that love who is the Holy Spirit." Centering Prayer is a contemplative way of responding to God's presence, and it "is meant to open the way to living constantly out of the center, to living out of the fullness of who we are."

The "new packaging" of the traditional contemplative prayer takes the form of three rules:

> *Rule One:* At the beginning of the Prayer we take a minute or two to quiet down and then move in faith to God dwelling in our depths; and at the end of the Prayer we take several minutes to come out, mentally praying the "Our Father" or some other prayer.
>
> *Rule Two:* After resting a bit in the center in faith-full love, we take up a single, simple word that expresses this response and begin to let it repeat itself within.
>
> *Rule Three:* Whenever in the course of the Prayer we become *aware* of anything else, we simply gently return to the Presence by the use of the prayer word.

The Centering Prayer is an occasion of our simply being present to God, Father Pennington explains: "We settle down in our Father's arms, in his loving hands." The prayer word enables us to maintain the Presence and to restore it when we find ourselves diverted. The word is "not so much . . . a concept or an expression of the mind as a thing of the heart, of the will—an expression of love."

Father Pennington describes the act of Centering Prayer as "an affirmation," an assent to being who we are and to God's being who he is and to the relationship between us.

The consent to God's love is not an "extrinsic sharing in the life, the being, the beauty of God," Pennington writes; whoever has been baptized has been baptized into the life and love of the Son, and the Holy Spirit has been given to us as our spirit. Hence, In Centering Prayer, one assents to and delights in the Christ, the Spirit that is one with one's own life.

Father Pennington repeatedly warns against deliberately seeking certain results or benefits through Centering Prayer. The Prayer is not to be approached as a task such that, if properly performed, certain spectacular results will be achieved. The Prayer is not to be used instrumentally; it is to be lived as an end in itself: "We simply seek to be to God and let happen what may." To *be* to God is a matter of assenting to one's own being and hence to the Father, Son, and Spirit at the center of one's being. God is *not* to be found "in our thoughts and imaginings, our feelings and affections," Pennington writes, but "in the depths of our being, at the center, at the ground of our being, perceived by the searching light of faith or the knowing embrace of love."

One of the immediate effects of the Prayer, according to the author, is a painful sense of alienation. Having moved to the center, we experience alienation from ourselves, our Source, from others, and from an exploited creation. God created the world to share his goodness and beauty, Father Pennington writes, but we have misused our freedom and have chosen something less than God. In the experience afforded by Centering Prayer we realize in our being the kinds and degrees of alienation that the misuse of the will has generated. The true self, which is an image of God, is unfamiliar to the false self we have constructed.

But, Father Pennington reassures us, the painful sense of sin and alienation is "only the converse side of something very beautiful that is being experienced." In Centering Prayer we come to rejoice in our oneness with all; we become truly compassionate. "Out of such experience," the author writes, "necessarily flow kindness, patience, long-suffering, benignity." Hence, the fruits of Centering Prayer, by which its authenticity and worth are made known, are to be found not in the Prayer itself but outside the time of the Prayer, in a course of everyday life as "guided by the call of grace and the leading of the Holy Spirit."

But how is one to keep the light from fading? How is one to maintain oneself in the way of life that the experience of Centering Prayer inspires? Pennington suggests that we formulate a rule of life for ourselves, and he offers a method for doing so, a method originally described in the epilogue of his earlier work, *Daily We Touch Him.* Beginning with prayer and reflection by which we get in touch with our true selves and listen to the Spirit, we start the search for a personal rule of life with the honest and realistic effort to decide what our goals in life are to be if we are to make the best use of our gifts and talents and reach the ultimate goal of achieving "the fullest and deepest possible union with our God of love."

Having decided on one's goals in life, one then determines the means: what has to be done to achieve the goals. We need to be realistic, Pennington cautions us; we need to consider every level of ourselves. This is the second step in formulating a personal rule of life.

The third step is to review the past to discover what there has been within oneself that has prevented one from leading the kind of life that involves growth and the fullest expression of one's gifts as a person.

The most difficult step, the fourth step, is that of formulating a practical program for oneself, Pennington writes. Here one must decide on values and priorities and settle upon a life plan of action, a plan subject to modifications prayerfully arrived at.

Whatever course one decides on, Father Pennington counsels, one will need prayer: ". . . we need prayer more than we need food or sleep or anything else." The Lord wants our love, the prayer of love, and hence, the author continues, prayer should have a high priority in our lives. Father Pennington suggests that we devote twenty minutes twice a day to Centering Prayer. Some prayer is better than none, he concedes, but persons who claim to be so busy that they cannot give forty minutes a day to contemplative prayer probably have not been in touch with their true selves and are allowing circumstances and other people to direct their lives.

Father Pennington concludes his book with a series of five chapters in which he discusses spreading the word to others about Centering Prayer, taking part in workshops on prayer, the spiritual benefits of sacred reading, exercises by which one can attain to the state of relaxation that makes contemplative prayer possible, questions and answers about Centering Prayer (a very useful method for pulling everything together that he has explained at considerable length in the main body of his book), and Mary, the Mother of God, as our image of centering. In his epilogue, Father Pennington expresses his hope that the image of a world at peace, all living happily with all, is more vision than dream and that movement toward the realization of the vision can be facilitated through the practice of contemplative prayer.

Ian P. McGreal

RECOMMENDED READING

Edition used: Pennington, M. Basil. *Centering Prayer: Renewing an Ancient Christian Prayer Form.* Garden City, N.Y.: Doubleday, Image Books, 1982.

———. *Daily We Touch Him.* Garden City, N.Y.: Doubleday, 1977. This earlier statement of Father Pennington's faith and practical wisdom fills out his spiritual counsel and serves as an illuminating companion volume to *Centering Prayer.*

———., with Alan Jones and Mark Booth. *The Living Testament: The Essential Writings of Christianity Since the Bible.* San Francisco: Harper & Row, 1985. An indispensable anthology of religious writings, including most of the writers on Christian spirituality cited by Father Pennington in his book, as well as those discussed in this volume.

WE DRINK FROM OUR OWN WELLS

Author: Gustavo Gutiérrez (1928–   )

Of Amerindian ancestry, Gutiérrez experienced the pains of discrimination when he was quite young. As an undergraduate he became a political activist, then studied for a period at San Marcos University Medical School in Lima (the city of his birth) where he was attracted to psychiatry. He later entered the seminary and studied in France and Rome, preparatory to teaching in Lima's Catholic University. Ordained in 1959, Gutiérrez was assigned to the Department of Theology and Social Sciences at the Catholic Pontifical University in Lima where he currently works. He believes that Christian faith makes no sense if it fails to counter oppression of the poor, and he became an activist on this theme. His first book, *A Theology of Liberation* (1973), is one of the early documents on that subject.

Type and subject of work: Essay on spirituality as commitment to meeting the needs of the poor and the oppressed

First published: 1983

MAJOR THEMES

Now is a favorable period for a new spirituality.

The poor, the politically oppressed, are helping us to realize this new spirituality.

It is only in community that a proper framework for growth in faith can take place.

Theological reflection must lead to both contemplation and action.

Both the tone and the theme of *We Drink from Our Own Wells* are set early by Gutiérrez's insistence that no dimension of human life is untouched by the process of liberation. This is because liberation is an expression of God's saving action in history. The understanding of this is derived from a consideration of the poverty experienced in Latin America and elsewhere which can only be seen as destructive and death-dealing. The basic right to human existence is thus violated. Given the present upheaval, it is necessary to question the manner in which Christianity is being lived in Latin America, where there is clearly a need for political and spiritual discernment. Under a liberating God, a people crosses the desert to escape from exploitation to reach a promised land. Such is the thrust of Gutiérrez's Introduction.

Part one begins with the question of how God can be thanked for the gift of life by people on whom death is both prematurely and injustly inflicted. The poor and dispossessed are beginning to create a history rather than merely experience it. They are working toward their own liberation. In the Bible, children of God are promised a land of their own, yet many Latin Americans are as foreigners in the lands of their births. They are alienated from the status quo. This in spite of the fact that expressions of disagreement with things as they are oftentimes are treated with suspicion.

The theology generally accepted heretofore is being challenged. Christian spirituality has for too long been geared to minorities, select and closed groups. Everything was directed primarily for the quest for holiness in religious life. The movement of the "spirituality of the laity" early in this century was a reaction against such an attitude. The community quest for the Lord is not compatible with elitist models. The favored minorities were also privileged socially, culturally, and to a degree economically. Another aspect that is being challenged is the individualistic bent of spiritual emphasis. All of this distorts the teachings of Jesus.

As solidarity with the world's poor grows, old securities are collapsing. One of the results has been a lack of vital unity seen in the separation between prayer and action. Gutiérrez argues that this unity will not be recovered by elimination of one or the other but only through an effort to remain faithful to God in both prayer and concrete commitments.

While the poor are in a "foreign country," it is a land from which God is not absent, and seeds of a new spirituality are growing there. Wretchedness and oppression are not new, but the understanding of these injustices is, as is the seeking of the means of release. Now is an exceptional time in Latin America's history. A growing movement of solidarity is taking place in defense of human rights, particularly those of the poor. For Christians such action is based in love of neighbor and love of God in the underprivileged. This action is combined with an increase in prayer, and what we have, Gutiérrez writes, is a *time of martyrdom.* This fidelity unto death is a true wellspring of life and reflects the sacrifices made in the early Church in the face of Rome's imperial power.

Others like Saint Dominic, Francis of Assisi, Ignatius Loyola, and Teresa of Ávila worked for reform within the Catholic church by attempting to follow Jesus' teachings in their times. Now is another such period, a time for liberation. Nor is this movement restricted to within the Church but has a broader application.

Gutiérrez opens part two by noting that spirituality is "a walking in freedom according to the Spirit of love and life." Spirituality begins with an encounter with the Lord. This is supported by the Gospels, and today a distinctive way of being Christian is developing in Latin America: a commitment to the poor. One who follows Jesus is a witness to life, Gutiérrez insists, and he writes that this takes on a special meaning in Latin America where the forces of death have created a social system that harms the poor.

The way we follow Jesus will indicate whether our thoughts are those of God or merely our own. We will thus build either a solid Christology or something merely on sand. Those who lose their lives for God and his message will save their lives. The start of an encounter with God is initiated by the Lord, but we must be open to it. Nevertheless spiritual experience and reflection upon it are not the end of our responsibility. These are offered as a way of being Christian—though not, of course, the only way.

That initial encounter with God creates a discipleship in us, and we enter on a journey, a walking with the Spirit as Saint Paul stated it. In Romans 8 and Galatians 5 there is a significant synthesis of the following of Jesus as a life in the Spirit.

Flesh in Scripture refers initially to that of which people are made, and the whole person is thus signified. In the Semitic outlook flesh is a component in human solidarity. One who is of the same flesh is of the same ethnic group. But flesh also indicates aspects of mortality, Gutiérrez points out, of human weakness. Paul goes further and connects flesh with sin, with the law, with death. Thus to walk according to the flesh is to reject the Lord.

The word *spirit* first means natural phenomena, the wind and our breathing, and suggests something both unobtrusive as well as dynamic. For Paul, again, spirit refers to the whole person and also the attitude adopted by the person. So spirit stands in contrast to the passivity and weakness of flesh. Spirit further implies a life being lived in accord with the will of God. Love and fellowship are dimensions of a Spirit-centered life. Nor should we forget the concept that God is Spirit.

Another word used by Paul needs to be looked at if we are to understand the concept of life according to the spirit, and that is *body,* Gutiérrez writes. At times Paul has it mean something very akin to "flesh." But in certain passages the body is to be seen as the field on which the flesh (as death-dealing) operates. But the Spirit operates there also; therefore Saint Paul draws up his list of sins according to the flesh but not according to the body. The body, in fact, can live according to the Spirit, can indeed be the temple of the Spirit. The new life via liberation, the redemption of the body, is a transcending of death. And this is key: that the body freed from the forces of death will lead a life in the Spirit.

Pauline theology sees the possibility of incorporation into the body of Christ, this body being a factor in solidarity. This body of Christ must not be seen merely as a lovely metaphor but as an extension of Jesus' incarnation. The journey, through this body of Christ, from death to life, is one every Christian must make. The choice has to be made, between death and life, between death and spirit. To reject the power of the flesh is to choose Christian spirituality, to embrace the liberated body.

To encounter the Lord, then, is to be at the point of departure for a life in the Spirit. Father Gutiérrez is here writing not of individuals but of an entire people, with the Jewish exodus as a paradigm. The going out of Egypt was a breaking away from death, an ongoing process, a time of trial, a deepening in knowledge of God. On their way to the promised land the people were liberated from slavery and turned themselves into a nation. Life in the new land is to be lived in God's presence and in justice toward the needs of others. And again, this is on a community rather than an individualistic level.

The final part of this relatively brief book begins with a summation of the dimension of every journey in search of the Lord: encountering him, living a life according to the Spirit, and "a wayfaring that embraces all aspects of life and is done in community." This is what is happening in Latin America, according to Gutiérrez, where a new spirituality is germinating. The situation is characterized by great suffering out of which a new joy emerges which flows from the gift of life.

A requirement for solidarity is an ongoing, permanent conversion that indicates not only belief in God but an entering into communion with him and with our fellow human beings. Solidarity is the sign of Christian love today, yet it also requires a recognition of the presence of sin in the world. Sin works against the coming of God's kingdom, on both individual and communal levels. The acknowledgement of one's sins implies a will to return to virtue. The pardoning of sins, so important here, helps to forge community.

The author states flatly that "A concern for the material needs of the poor is an element in our spirituality." This he finds to be in keeping with the insights of Pope John XXIII's Second Vatican Council. What we do to the poor we do to Christ himself. Our acts must be inspired by love and true love can exist only between equals. We need to learn how to make love an effective force in history.

There is a necessity to be fully concerned about the needs of others rather than simply to act out of a sense of obligation to love. Many Latin Americans are trying to live the gratuitous love of God by committing themselves to liberating those who are enslaved. The notion of the gratuitousness of the Lord's love for us is fundamental to Christian life. We have to realize that God's is a love we do not merit but is that which he freely gives. "God first loved us" (John 4:19). Prayer can be an experience of gratuitousness that creates new methods of communications, sometimes regarded as a "useless activity" which, in a certain way, it is.

Joy is a victory over suffering, which is happening in Latin America, although the death-dealing conditions of that pain must never be forgotten. The faithful poor have always had a capacity for celebration beside harsh living conditions. This even though people who work to support the rights of the poor put themselves in danger. There is a great amount of witness, even unto physical death.

The hope of a resurrection helps to motivate these women and men, but this is to be seen not as an evasion of concrete history but as a genuine spiritual combat, Gutiérrez writes. A true awareness of the enormous poverty in which the huge majority of Latin Americans live has significantly changed the way the mission of the Latin American is seen. A change in the Christian commitment has also been brought about.

Commitment to the poor is a vital requirement for a proper detachment from material goods. Such a commitment is made necessarily in the face of the knowledge that "the situation of the poor will almost certainly overstrain the human capacity for solidarity." But the undertaking is not hopeless. It demands a large measure of humility, of a disposition of spiritual childhood the permanent model of which is Jesus' mother, Mary.

Even though the community aspect of the actions of Latin American Christians is prominent, there is also an experience of profound loneliness always lurking. Such a dark night possibility has always been a potentiality for those engaged with the spirit—here referred to by Gutiérrez as "The Dark Night of Injustice" in the social context. The situation of poverty and exploitation in which the poor live appears endless and can give rise to extreme solitude that is often accompanied by a fear not only of dying but of weakening as well. This leads to a new encounter with oneself and, above all, with God. Here trust in God and in the community is present, even though the period of darkness still persists.

Passage through solitude leads, Gutiérrez writes, to a profound involvement in community. Solitude is not to be equated with individualism (which is a withdrawal) because the loneliness in solitude gives rise to a hunger for communion. Nor should this be seen as a two-stage experience, first solitude, later community. "Rather it is within community that one experiences solitude." No one can cross the desert without the support of the community which is also the place where we join in the remembrance of the death and resurrection of Jesus.

In a very brief Conclusion, the Peruvian sees this as a favorable era in Latin America where authentic theological reflection is having its basis in both contemplation and act. This activity is a kind of walking on the road to holiness. The enterprise is a community exercise. "This spiritual experience is the well from which we must drink."

Harry James Cargas

RECOMMENDED READING

Edition used: Gutiérrez, Gustavo. *We Drink from Our Own Wells.* Maryknoll, N.Y.: Orbis Books, 1984.

Ferm, Deane William. *Third World Liberation Theologies.* Maryknoll, N.Y.: Orbis Books, 1986. A survey of the writings of major figures including Boff, Cardenal, Esquivel, and African and Asian writers as well.

———, ed. *Third World Liberation Theologies.* Maryknoll, N.Y.: Orbis Books, 1986. Titled the same as the previously listed book, this is a reader containing selections from writers representing many nations on several continents.

Gutiérrez, Gustavo. *A Theology of Liberation.* Maryknoll, N.Y.: Orbis Books, 1973. The first book by Gutiérrez, a pacesetter in liberation theology.

INDEX OF TITLES

Ascent of Mount Carmel (John of the Cross), 242–48

Beginning to Pray (Bloom), 627–31
Benjamin Minor (Richard of Saint Victor), 116–21

Celebration of Discipline (Foster), 655–60
Centering Prayer (Pennington), 668–72
Chapters on Prayer (Evagrius Ponticus), 34–38
Christian Nurture (Bushnell), 428–33
Christian Perfection (Fénelon), 346–52
Christian's Secret of a Happy Life, The (Smith), 438–41
Cloud of Unknowing, The (Unknown), 192–97
Commentary on the Song of Songs (Origen), 7–12
Conferences of John Cassian, The (Cassian), 51–56
Confessions of Saint Augustine, The (Augustine), 45–50
Cost of Discipleship, The (Bonhoeffer), 509–15

Dark Night of the Soul (John of the Cross), 242–48

Descent of the Dove, The (Williams), 524–29
Devotions Upon Emergent Occasions (Donne), 279–85
Dialogue of Comfort Against Tribulation, A (More), 226–31
Dialogue of Saint Catherine of Siena, The (Catherine of Siena), 171–75
Divine Milieu, The (Teilhard), 586–91
Divinity School Address, The (Emerson), 410–15
Double Search: Studies in Atonement and Prayer, The (Jones), 466–71
Dress of Virgins, The (Cyprian), 13–18

Enchiridion Militis Christiani (Desiderius Erasmus), 209–14
Essence of Spiritual Religion, The (Trueblood), 501–8

Fire of Love, The (Rolle), 149–52
Flowering Light of the Godhead, The (Mechthild of Magdeburg), 128–32
Four Books on True Christianity (Arndt), 261–66
Four Hundred Chapters on Love, The (Maximus), 76–81

Freedom of a Christian, The (Luther), 215–20

God Was in Christ (Baillie), 541–46
Grace Abounding to the Chief of Sinners (Bunyan), 326–31
Graces of Interior Prayer, The (Poulain), 452–58

Healing Gifts of the Spirit, The (Sanford), 622–26

If (Carmichael), 521–23
Imitation of Christ, The (Thomas à Kempis), 198–202
Instructor, The (Clement of Alexandria), 1–6
Interior Castle (Teresa of Ávila), 249–53
Introduction to the Devout Life (Francis of Sales), 267–72

Jesus and the Disinherited (Thurman), 551–55
Journal of George Fox, The (Fox), 340–45
Journal of John Woolman, The (Woolman), 385–90

Ladder of Divine Ascent, The (Climacus), 71–75
Ladder of Perfection, The (Hilton), 179–80
Lectures on Revivals of Religion (Finney), 405–9
Letters and Papers from Prison (Bonhoeffer), 509–15
Letters by a Modern Mystic (Laubach), 516–20
Letters of Saint Jerome, The (Jerome), 39–44
Letters to Malcolm: Chiefly on Prayer (Lewis), 615–21
Life of David Brainerd, The (Edwards), 372–77
Life of Moses, The (Gregory of Nyssa), 29–33
Life of Saint Anthony, The (Athanasius), 19–23

Little Book of Eternal Wisdom, The (Suso), 139–43
Little Flowers of St. Francis, The (Unknown), 144–48
Long Rules, The (Basil the Great), 24–28

Markings (Hammarskjöld), 603–8
Meaning of Holiness, The (Lavelle), 563–68
Meditations of William Saint Thierry, The (William of Saint Thierry), 100–104
Mind's Road to God, The (Bonaventura), 122–27
Mirror of Charity, The (Aelred of Rievaulx), 110–15
Miscellanies (Clement of Alexandria), 1–6
Mystical Element of Religion, The (von Hugel), 472–78
Mystical Theology (Dionysius), 57–59
Mysticism (Underhill), 479–83
Myth, Faith and Hermeneutics (Panikkar), 661–67

Names of Christ, The (de León), 238–41
New Seeds of Contemplation (Merton), 598–602
Nine Public Lectures (von Zinzendorf), 366–71
Noah's Ark (Hugh of Saint Victor), 93–99

On Listening to Another (Steere), 576–81
On Loving God (Bernard of Clairvaux), 105–9
On the Love of God (Francis of Sales), 267–72
Other Side of Silence: A Guide to Christian Meditation, The (Kelsey), 649–54
Out of My Life and Thought (Schweitzer), 496–500

Pastoral Care (Gregory the Great), 65–70
Pensées (Pascal), 315–19
Pia Desideria (Spener), 320–25

Pilgrim's Progress, The (Bunyan), 326–31
Plain Account of Christian Perfection, A (Wesley), 378–84
Poems of Gerard Manley Hopkins, The (Hopkins), 484–90
Practical and Theological Chapters, The (Symeon), 82–86
Practical Piety (More), 401–4
Practice of the Presence of God, The (Brother Lawrence), 336–39
Praktikos (Evagrius Ponticus), 34–38
Prayer and Modern Man (Ellul), 632–36
Prayers and Meditations of Saint Anselm, The (Anselm), 87–92
Prison Meditations of Father Alfred Delp, The (Delp), 582–85
Private Devotions (Andrewes), 297–302
Purity of Heart Is to Will One Thing (Kierkegaard), 421–27
Pursuit of God, The (Tozer), 547–50

Reaching Out (Nouwen), 643–48
Real Christianity (Wilberforce), 397–400
Religio Medici (Browne), 290–96
Revelations of Divine Love (Julian of Norwich), 181–85
Rule and Exercises of Holy Living and Dying, The (Taylor), 309–14
Rule of Perfection, The (Canfield), 254–60
Rules for Monasteries (Benedict of Nursia), 60–64

St. Francis of Assisi (Chesterton), 491–95
Saints' Everlasting Rest, The (Baxter), 303–8
School of Prayer, The (Wyon), 536–40
Self-Abandonment to Divine Providence (de Caussade), 434–47
Serious Call to a Contemplative Life-Style, A (Hinson), 637–42
Serious Call to a Devout and Holy Life, A (Law), 353–58
Sermons and Treatises of Meister Eckhardt, The (Johannes Eckhart), 133–38
Sermons of John Tauler, The (Tauler), 165–70
Shadow of the Almighty: The Life and Testament of Jim Elliot (Elliot), 592–97
Short and Very Easy Method of Prayer, A (Guyon), 332–35
Songs of Innocence and of Experience (Blake), 391–96
Sparkling Stone, The (Ruysbroeck), 153–58
Spiritual Exercises of St. Ignatius Loyola, The (Ignatius Loyola), 232–37
Story of a Soul, The (Thérèse of Lisieux), 446–51
Strength to Love (King), 609–14
Sun and the Umbrella, The (Ferré), 569–75

Temple, The (Herbert), 286–89
Testament of Devotion, A (Kelly), 530–35
Theologia Germanica (Unknown), 159–64
Third Spiritual Alphabet, The (Osuna), 221–25
Treatise Concerning Religious Affections, A (Edwards), 359–65

Varieties of Religious Experience, The (James), 459–65
Vision of God, The (Nicholas of Cusa), 203–8

Waiting for God (Weil), 556–62
Way of a Pilgrim, The (Unknown), 442–45
Way of Holiness, The (Palmer), 416–20
Way to Christ, The (Boehme), 273–78
We Drink from Our Own Wells (Gutiérrez), 673–78

INDEX OF CONTRIBUTORS

Allen, William Loyd: on *A Serious Call to a Contemplative Life-Style,* 637–42; on *The Other Side of Silence: A Guide to Christian Meditation,* 649–54; on *The Prison Meditations of Father Alfred Delp,* 582–85

Cargas, Harry James: on *Introduction to the Devout Life* 267–72; on *Myth, Faith and Hermeneutics,* 661–67; on *On the Love of God,* 267–72; on *The Confessions of Saint Augustine,* 45–50; on *The Dialogue of Saint Catherine of Siena,* 171–75; on *The Divine Milieu,* 586–91; on *The Imitation of Christ,* 192–97; on *The Poems of Gerard Manley Hopkins,* 484–90; on *The Story of a Soul,* 446–51; on *We Drink from Our Own Wells,* 673–78

Clarke Bowman L.: on *Letters and Papers from Prison,* 509–15; on *The Cost of Discipleship,* 509–15; on *The Descent of the Dove,* 524–29; on *The Varieties of Religious Experience,* 459–65

Dysinger, Luke E.: on *The Practical and Theological Chapters,* 82–86; on *The Praktikos and Chapters on Prayer,* 34–38

Faurot, Jean: on *A Dialogue of Comfort Against Tribulation,* 226–31; on *A Plain Account of Christian Perfection,* 378–84; on *Benjamin Minor* and *Benjamin Major,* 116–21; on *Christian Perfection,* 346–52; on *Commentary on the Song of Songs,* 7–12; on *Four Books on True Christianity,* 261–66; on *Noah's Ark,* 93–99; on *Pastoral Care,* 65–70; on *Private Devotions,* 297–302; on *Purity of Heart Is to Will One Thing,* 421–27; on *Religio Medici,* 290–96; on *The Dress of Virgins,* 13–18; on *The Letters of Saint Jerome,* 39–44; on *The Meaning of Holiness,* 563–68; on *The Mystical Element of Religion,* 472–78; *Theologia Germanica,* 159–64; on *The Rule and Exercises of Holy Living and Holy Dying,* 309–14; on *The Rule of Perfection,* 254–60; on *The Sermons of John Tauler,* 165–70; on *The Sparkling*

Stone, 153–58; on *The Vision of God*, 203–8; on *The Way to Christ*, 273–78

Ferré, Frederick P.: on *The Sun and the Umbrella*, 569–75

Ford, Paul F.: on *Letters to Malcolm: Chiefly on Prayer*, 615–21

Giles, Mary E.: on *Ascent of Mount Carmel*, 242–48; on *Dark Night of the Soul*, 242–48; on *Interior Castle*, 249–53; on *The Third Spiritual Alphabet*, 221–25

Gregg, Douglas H.: on *Celebration of Discipline*, 655–60; on *St. Francis of Assisi*, 491–95; on *The Freedom of a Christian*, 215–20; on *The Little Flowers of St. Francis*, 144–48

Hardesty, Nancy A.: on *Beginning to Pray*, 627–31; on *If*, 521–23; on *Lectures on Revivals of Religion*, 405–9; on *Mysticism*, 479–83; on *Revelations of Divine Love*, 181–85; on *The Book of Margery Kempe*, 198–202; on *The Christian's Secret of a Happy Life*, 438–41; on *The Flowing Light of the Godhead*, 128–32; on *The Healing Gifts of the Spirit*, 622–26; on *The Pursuit of God*, 547–50; on *The Way of a Pilgrim*, 442–45; on *The Way of Holiness*, 416–420

Helm, Thomas E.: on *Devotions upon Emergent Occasions*, 279–85; on *Enchiridion Militis Christiani*, 209–14

Hinson, E. Glenn: on *A Serious Call to a Devout and Holy Life*, 353–58; on *A Testament of Devotion*, 530–35; on *Grace Abounding to the Chief of Sinners*, 326–31; on *Listening to Another*, 576–81; on *The Instructor and Miscellanies*, 1–6; on *The Journal of George Fox*, 340–45; on *The Life of David Brainerd*, 372–77; on *The Life of Saint Anthony*, 19–23; on *The Pilgrim's Progress*, 326–31; on *The Saints' Everlasting Rest*, 303–8

Holley, David M.: on *God Was in Christ*, 541–46; on *The Essence of Spiritual Religion*, 501–8; on *The Journal of John Woolman*, 385–90

Houston, James M.: on *A Short and Very Easy Method of Prayer*, 332–35; on *Practical Piety*, 401–4; on *Real Christianity*, 397–400; on *Self-Abandonment to Divine Providence*, 434–37; on *The Names of Christ*, 238–41; on *The Temple*, 286–89

Leonard, William J.: on *Markings*, 603–8; on *Shadow of the Almighty: The Life and Testament of Jim Elliot*, 592–97; on *The Spiritual Exercises of St. Ignatius Loyola*, 232–37

McGreal, Ian P.: on *A Treatise Concerning Religious Affections*, 359–65; on *Centering Prayer*, 668–72; on *Out of My Life and Thought*, 496–500; on *Reaching Out*, 643–48; on *Songs of Innocence and of Experience*, 391–96; on *The Graces of Interior Prayer*, 452–58; on *The Mind's Road to God*, 122–27; on *The Prayers and Meditations of Saint Anselm*, 87–92; on *The School of Prayer*, 536–40; on *Waiting for God*, 556–62

Meindl, Robert J.: on *The Fire of Love*, 149–52

Pennington, M. Basil: on *Mystical Theology*, 57–59; on *New Seeds of Contemplation*, 598–602; on *On Loving God*, 105–9; on *Rules for Monasteries*, 60–64; on *The Cloud of Unknowing*, 186–91; on *The Conferences of John Cassian*, 51–56; on *The Ladder of Divine Ascent*, 71–75; on *The Ladder of Perfection*, 176–80; on *The Life of Moses*, 29–33; on *The Long Rules*, 24–28; on *The Meditations of William of Saint Thierry*, 100–104; on *The Mirror of Charity*, 110–15;

on *The Practice of the Presence of God*, 336–39

Porterfield, Amanda: on *The Double Search: Studies in Atonement and Prayer*, 466–71

Roth, John K.: on *Pensées*, 315–19; on *Strength to Love*, 609–14

Sattler, Gary R.: on *Nine Public Lectures*, 366–71; on *Pia Desideria*, 320–25; on *The Four Hundred Chapters on Love*, 76–81; on *The Little Book of Eternal Wisdom*, 139–43; on *The Sermons and Treatises of Meister Eckhart*, 133–38

Sherrill, Rowland A.: on *Christian Nurture*, 428–33; on *The Divinity School Address*, 410–15

Waters, Brent P.: on *Jesus and the Disinherited*, 551–55; on *Prayer and Modern Man*, 632–36

Willard, Dallas A.: on *Letters by a Modern Mystic*, 516–20

INDEX OF MAJOR THEMES

Acceptance, 576–81
Adam, the fall of, 274–78
Affections, religious, 359–65, 372–77
Agape, 570–75
Alienation, from God, 392–96
Apatheia, 2–5, 36–37
Asceticism, 134–38, 166–70
Atonement, 467–71
Attachment, and detachment, 586–91
Awakening, 479–83

Baptism, 510–15, 623–26; infant,
    429–33
Beatitudes, the, 510–15
Bible, the, 320–25, 327–31, 569–75;
    study of, 593–97
Bishop, requirements for the office of,
    65–70
Body: of Christ, 279–85, 510–15,
    586–91; and the soul, 76–81,
    279–85
Buddhism, 570–75

Calvinism, 428–33
Capitalism, 570–75
Cause, the universal, 585–89
Celebration, 655–60
Charity, 51–56, 110–15

Chastity, 198–202
Children, as sinful, 428–33
Christ, 467–71, 501–8; the Body of,
    279–85, 510–15, 586–91; as the
    bridge between heaven and earth,
    171–75; the call to, and holy obe-
    dience, 530–35; as our chief in-
    structor, 1–6; conformity to the
    life of, 593–97; the death of,
    20–23; dedication to, 402–4; the
    eternal, 570–75; the example of,
    192–97, 410–15, 603–8, 609–14; the
    forgiveness of, 87–92; God as re-
    vealed in, 510–15; gospel of,
    517–20; the historical, 541–46; hu-
    manity of, 154–58, 261–66, 541–46;
    human union with, 261–66; the
    imitation of, as the goal of Chris-
    tianity, 25–28; the immanence of
    God in, 510–15, 541–46; knowl-
    edge of, 238–41, 366–71; love of,
    and his Church, 7–12; as a media-
    tor, 122–27; obedience to, 144–48,
    166–70, 510–15; passion of, and
    patience, 60–64; the primacy of,
    33–35; and redemption, 101–4;
    resurrection of, 232–37; and salva-
    tion, 340–45; as our true Mother,

181–85; trust in, 438–41; and union with God, 160–64; the Universal, 586–91. *See also* Jesus, Prayer of

Christianity: conservative, 548–50; development of, through a process of spiritualization, 497–500; the goal of, 25–28, 35–38, 593–97; historical, 411–15; and the quest of the virtues, 35–38; as the religion of the heart, 402–4; true, spirit of, 397–400. *See also* Religion

Church, the, 569–75; call for renewal in, 320–25; history of the, 524–29; and the Holy Spirit, 524–29

Communion, 181–85

Communism, 570–75

Compassion, 386–90, 669–72; and discipline, 65–70

Confession, 655–60

Connectedness, 484–90

Conscience, 421–26

Constancy, 576–81

Contemplation, 116–21, 637–42, 598–602; and knowledge of God, 176–80; and love of God, 186–91; and the soul's relation with God, 149–52. *See also* Meditation; Prayer

Conversion, 405–9, 593–97

Creation, 181–85

Cross, the, 541–46

Death, 279–85, 310–14; fear of, 603–8; the soul at, 290–96

Deity, the, 57–59

Despair, 628–31

Detachment, and attachment, 586–91

Devil, the: and God, 181–85; and spiritual dryness, 52–56. *See also* Evil

Discipleship, the call to, 510–15

Discipline, and compassion, 65–70

Disciplines, classic spiritual, 655–60

Disobedience, 160–64

Divine, the, 603–8

Ecstasy, 166–21

Eternal Listener, the, 576–81

Eternal Now, the, 531–35

Ethics, as the essence of religion, 497–500

Eucharist, the, 192–97

Evangelization, 366–71, 570–75

Evil: as alienation from God, 392–96; and God, 20–23, 45–50; good and, 57–59, 274–78, 609–14. *See also* Devil, the

Expectancy, 576–81

Faith, 215–20, 336–39, 366–71; as the characteristic that unites humanity, 661–67; and community, 674–78; and the Dark Night of the Soul, 480–83; the element of risk in, 604–8; as the first step to contemplation, 599–602; and the intellect, 434–37; and knowledge of God, 203–8, 286–89; a living, and prayer, 536–40; unconditional, 347–52; as wisdom, 45–50

Fall, the, 274–78

Fasting, 655–60

Fear, 551–55; of God, 35–38, 78; as the starting point of love, 71–75

Forgiveness, 541–46

Freedom, 100–104, 610–14

Friendship, constancy of, 52–56

Gandhi, Mahatma, 610–14

Gnosticism, Christian, 1–6

God: alienation from, 392–96; ascent of the soul to, 243–48, 249–53; and Christ, as our chief instructor, 1–6; combat with, and prayer, 632–26; contact with, reestablishing, 582–85; the contemplation of, 35–38, 83–86, 599–602; and creation, 181–85; as the creator of beings, 77–81; dedication to, 13–18, 29–33, 353–58, 638–42; encounter with, through meditation, 649–54; and evil, 20–23, 45–50, 609–14; the existence of, 315–19; fear of, 35–38, 78; grace of. *See* Grace; and humankind, 524-29, 484-90; indwelling of, 83-86; inner conversation with, 517-20; kingdom of, 51-56, 261-66; knowledge of, and love, 76-81, 93-99, 139-43; human love of, 40-44, 94-99, 105-9, 336-39, 402-4; as love, 129-32, 139-43, 267-72; love of, 24-28, 105-9, 198-202, 521-23, 598-602; and Noah's Ark, 93-99; obedience to, 60-64, 144-48, 153-58, 385-90. *See also* Disobedience; oneness with, 668-72; perfectness of, 100-104; power of, 622-26; and prayer, 536-40, 616-21. *See also* Prayer; presence of, 530-35; reaching out to, 643-48; and redemption, 315-19; as revealed in Christ, 510-15, 541-46; and the self, 517-20; surrender to, 438-41; trust in, 192-97, 438-31; as the unchangeable Good, 159-64; understanding of, 203-8; union with, 153-58, 160-64, 176-80, 267-72; as unknowable, 30-33, 77-81, 290-96; vision of, and existence, 203-8; waiting for, 557-62; the will of, 254-60, 434-37, 517-20; as the will-to-love, 497-500; wisdom of, 210-14, 290-96; and the world, 76-81; worthiness before, 215-20

Good: and evil, 57-59, 274-78, 609-14; God as the only unchangeable, 159-64; and will, 421-26

Goodness, 100-104, 541-46

Gospels, the, 599-602

Grace, 327-31, 438-41, 446-51; and obedience to Christ, 510-15; and prayer, 452-58; and transformation of the soul, 452-58

Guidance, 655-60

Healing, spiritual, 622-26, 655-60

Heart, the: Christianity as the religion of, 402-4; and prayer, 332-35

Hermeneutics, 661-67

Hinduism, 570-75

Holiness, 378-84, 438-41; path to, and suffering, 446-51. *See also* Perfection; Sainthood

Holy Spirit, the, 524-29, 622-26

Hope, 101-4, 551-55

Humility, 60-64, 360, 363, 627-31; and holy obedience, 530-35; and perfection, 446-51

Illumination, 479-83

Imperialism, 570-75

Incarnation, the, 203-8

Innocence, 391-96

Jesus, Prayer of, 442-45. *See also* Christ

Judaism, 570-75

Justice, 309-14, 609-14

Knowledge, 209-14; egocentric, vs. God's love, 274-78; of God, and love, 76-81, 93-99; that exceeds understanding, 57-59

Listening, 576-81

Loneliness, 603-8

Love, 551-55; as the basis of all spirituality, 446-51; Calvary, 521-23; the Christian doctrine of, and nonviolent resistance, 610-14; divine, 233-37; fear as the starting point of, 71-75; God as, 129-32, 139-43, 267-72, 497; God's, 24-28, 105-9, 198-202, 521-23, 598-602; human, of God, 40-44, 94-99, 105-9, 336-39, 402-4; and knowledge of God, 76-81, 93-99; as the most durable power in the world, 609-14; obeyance out of, 24-28; as the paramount religious affection, 359-65; and perfection, 171-75; spiritual, 11, 35-38, 77-81; of virtue, 209-14

Marriage, renunciation of, 14-18, 40-44

Martyrdom, fruits of, 17

Meditation, 25-28, 649-54, 655-60.

See also Contemplation; Prayer
Memories, the "healing of," 623–26
Miracles, 410–15
Monastic life, 24–28, 35–38, 60–64,
    110–15; as a contemplative life,
    51–56; rewards of, 39–44; three
    forms of, Climacus on, 71–75
Monks, four kinds of, 60–64
Morality, 367–71, 405–9
Mysticism, 472–78, 479–83
Mystic Way, the, 604–8
Myths, the power of, 661–67

Nonviolent resistance, 610–14

Obedience, 60–64; to Christ, 144–48,
    166–70, 510–15; to God, 60–64,
    144–48, 153–58, 385–90; holy,
    530–35; to the Word, 171–75

Pastor, the role of the, 286–89
Perfection: achievement of, 336–39,
    379–84, 434–37, 438–41; and hu-
    mility, 446–51; and love of God,
    346–52. *See also* Holiness;
    Sainthood
Persecution, 226–31
Pilgrimage, 198–202
Poverty, 673–78
Prayer, 209–14, 233–37, 267–72,
    297–302; the ascent of the soul to
    God through, 249–53; and atone-
    ment, 467–71; Centering, 668–72;
    as the confession of sin, 87–92;
    and contact with God, 616–21;
    continual, attainment of, 52–56,
    442–45; and devotion to God,
    354–58; and faith, 536–40; and
    God's will, 536–40; and healing,
    623–26; and the heart's relation
    with God, 332–35; importance of,
    34–38; of Jesus, 442–45; listening
    as the ground of, 576–81; the
    meaning of, in modern society,
    632–26; mystic, 452–58; ordinary,
    four kinds of, 452–58; and the
    Presence of God, 336–39; pure,

and divine love, 77–81; recollec-
    tion as a process of, 222–25; and
    spiritual energy in the phenom-
    enal world, 460–65; three stages
    of, Climacus on, 71–75; vs. illu-
    sion, 643–48; vs. preaching,
    286–89; "with tears," 82–86. *See
    also* Contemplation; Meditation
Preaching, 286–89, 321–25
Priesthood, the, 40–44
Psychology, and religion, 459–65
Purgation, 479–83
Purity, as the foundation of theology,
    71–75

Racism, 570–75
Reason, 101–4, 116–21; and the exteri-
    or will of God, 254–60; Pascal on,
    315–19
Recollection, 222–25
Regeneration, of humankind, 524–29,
    583–85
Religion, 548–50; ethics as the essence
    of, 497–500; "family," 429–33;
    genuine, as an experience of the
    Divine, 603–8; of Jesus, 551–55;
    and mysticism, 472–78; spiritual,
    501–8. *See also* Christianity
Religious: beliefs, differences in,
    460–65; experience, James on,
    459–65. *See also* Christianity
Repentance, 274–78
Resignation, true, 274–78
Responsibility, 100–104
Revelation, 502–8
Reverence, for life, 497–500

Sainthood, 19–23, 303–8, 340–45,
    563–68, 491–95. *See also* Holiness;
    Perfection
Salvation, 309–14, 340–45, 367–71,
    405–9
Sanctification, 336–39, 416–20
Scriptures, the, 7–12, 209–14, 320–25
Self: -abandonment, and Christian
    perfection, 434–37; control of the,
    19–23; -examination, 233–37; in-

nermost, and the spiritual life, 643–48; -justification, and faith, 215–20; -knowledge, 116–21; -love, 346–52; -surrender, 604–8

Selfishness, 541–46

Service, 655–60, 491–95

Silence, and the listening process, 577–81

Simplicity, 386–90, 530–35, 655–60

Sin, original, 428–33

Sinners, the conversion of, 593–97

Sins, 187–91, 353–58; attitude towards, and conversion to Christianity, 379–84; the confession of, prayers as, 87–92; grief for one's, and love, 171–75; the remission of, 83–86

Social action, 531–35, 673–78

Solitude, 643–48, 655–60; and monastic life, 71–75; and sainthood, 20–23

Song of Songs, the, as a wedding poem, 7–12

Soul, the, 122–27, 128–32, 133–38, 149–52; ascent of the, to God, 243–48, 249–53; and the body, 76–81, 279–85; capacities of the, for holiness, 410–15; conditions of the, 171–75, 274–78; the Dark Night of the, 480–83; at death, 290–96; and the exercise of Christian virtues, 286–89; holiness as a state of the, 378–84; and monasticism, 25–28; preparation of, for spiritual experience, 233–37; and the process of prayer, 222–25, 333–35, 452–58; purification of the, 165–70; and salvation, 367–71; transformation of the, 452–58; the unification of the, 20–23; and the will of God, 254–60, 557–62

Stoicism, 2–5, 36–37

Submission, 655–60

Suffering, 346–52, 421–26, 434–37; God's, for humanity, 510–15; and holy obedience, 530–35; and the path to holiness, 446–51

Theology, 71–75, 674–78

Time, and temporal events, relation of, 45–50

Trinity, the, 181–85, 203–8, 434–37; and God's relation to humankind, 524–29

Trust, in God, 192–197, 438–41

Truth, 209–14, 315–19

Union, with God, 480–83

Uniqueness, individual, 484–90

Virginity, 14–18, 40–44

Virtue, 286–89; of Christ, 360–65; development of, 30–33, 52–56, 61–64; love of, 209–14

Vulnerability, 576–81

Wisdom, 238–41

Word, the divine, 8–12

INDEX OF AUTHORS

Aelred of Rievaulx, 110–15
Andrewes, Lancelot, 297–302
Anselm of Canterbury, 87–92
Arndt, Johann, 261–66
Athanasius, 19–23
Augustine, 45–50

Baillie, Donald M., 541–46
Basil the Great, 24–28
Baxter, Richard, 303–8
Benedict of Nursia, 60–64
Bernard of Clairvaux, 105–9
Blake, William, 391–96
Bloom, Anthony, 627–31
Boehme, Jacob, 273–78
Bonaventura, 122–27
Bonhoeffer, Dietrich, 509–15
Browne, Thomas, 290–96
Bunyan, John, 326–31
Bushnell, Horace, 428–33

Canfield, Benedict, 254–60
Carmichael, Amy Wilson, 521–23
Cassian, John, 51–56
Catherine of Siena, 171–75
Caussade, Jean-Pierre de, 434–47
Chesterton, G. K., 491–95
Clement of Alexandria, 1–6

Climacus, John, 71–75
Cyprian, 13–18

Delp, Alfred, 582–85
Dionysius, 57–59
Donne, John, 279–85

Eckhart, Johannes, 133–38
Edwards, Jonathan, 359–65, 372–77
Elliot, Elisabeth, 592–97
Ellul, Jacques, 632–36
Emerson, Ralph Waldo, 410–15
Erasmus, Desiderius, 209–14
Evagrius, Ponticus, 34–38

Fénelon, François, 346–52
Ferré, Nels F. S., 569–75
Finney, Charles Grandison, 405–9
Foster, Richard J., 655–60
Fox, George, 340–45
Francis of Sales, 267–72

Gregory of Nyssa, 29–33
Gregory the Great, 65–70
Gutiérrez, Gustavo, 673–78
Guyon, Madame, 332–35

Hammarskjöld, Dag, 603–8
Herbert, George, 286–89

Hilton, Walter, 176–80
Hinson, E. Glenn, 637–42
Hopkins, Gerard Manley, 484–90
Hugel, Baron Friedrich von, 472–78
Hugh of Saint Victor, 93–99

Ignatius of Loyola, 232–37

James, William, 459–65
Jerome, 39–44
John of the Cross, 242–48
Jones, Rufus, 466–71
Julian of Norwich, 181–85

Kelly, Thomas R., 530–35
Kelsey, Morton T., 649–54
Kempe, Margery, 198–202
King Jr., Martin Luther, 609–14
Kierkegaard, Søren, 421–27

Laubach, Frank C., 516–20
Lavelle, Louis, 563–68
Law, William, 353–58
Lawrence, Brother, 336–39
León, Fray Luis Ponce de, 238–41
Lewis, C. S., 615–21
Luther, Martin, 215–20

Maximus the Confessor, 76–81
Mechthild of Magdeburg, 128–32
Merton, Thomas, 598–602
More, Hannah, 401–4
More, Thomas, 226–31

Nicholas of Cusa, 203–8
Nouwen, Henri J. M., 643–48

Origen, 7–12
Osuna, Francisco de, 221–25

Palmer, Phoebe, 416–20
Panikkar, Raimundo, 661–67
Pascal, Blaise, 315–19
Pennington, M. Basil, 668–72
Poulain, R. P. Augustine, 452–58

Richard of Saint Victor, 116–21
Rolle, Richard, 149–52
Ruysbroeck, Jan van, 153–58
Sanford, Agnes White, 622–26
Schweitzer, Albert, 496–500
Smith, Hannah Whitall, 438–41
Spener, Philipp Jacob, 320–25
Steere, Douglas V., 576–81
Suso, Henry, 139–43
Symeon the New Theologian, 82–86

Tauler, John, 165–70
Taylor, Jeremy, 309–14
Teilhard de Chardin, Pierre, 586–91
Teresa of Ávila, 249–53
Thérèse of Lisieux, 446–51
Thomas à Kempis, 192–97
Thurman, Howard, 551–55
Tozer, A. W., 547–50
Trueblood, D. Elton, 501–8

Underhill, Evelyn, 479–83

Weil, Simone, 556–62
Wesley, John, 378–84
Wilberforce, William, 397–400
William of Saint Thierry, 100–104
Williams, Charles, 524–29
Woolman, John, 385–90
Wyon, Olive, 536–40

Zinzendorf, Nicholaus Ludwig von,
    366–71